Ars Electronica: Facing the Future

Electronic Culture:
History, Theory, Practice
Timothy Druckrey, series editor

Ars Electronica:
Facing the Future,
edited by Timothy Druckrey
with Ars Electronica, 1999

Ars Electronica:
Facing the Future

A Survey of Two Decades

edited by Timothy Druckrey
with Ars Electronica

The MIT Press, Cambridge, Massachusetts, and London, England

© 1999 Massachusetts Institute of Technology

Translations by:
Tom Appleton, Helmut Einfalt, Ralph Elliott,
Elly Frank-Großebner, Mel Greenwald, Jeanne Haunschild,
Paul Henninger, Astrid Hustvedt, Gertrud Jacquemar, Camilla Nielsen,
Dano O'Neill, Catherine Saxon-Kerkhoff, Susi Steinacher, Josh Wise

Cover: photo: NIQ / concept: August Black and Joachim Smetschka
Layout, typesetting: Arthouse - Linz
Coordination: Ingrid Fischer-Schreiber, Jutta Schmiederer

This book was printed and bound in the United States of America.

Library of Congress Cataloging-in-Publication Data
Ars Electronica : facing the future, a survey of two decades /
edited by Timothy Druckrey with Ars Electronica.
p. cm. — (Electronic culture—history, theory, practice)
Includes bibliographical references.
ISBN 0-262-04176-6 (alk. paper)
1. Arts—Data processing. 2. Technology and the arts. 3. Computer art. 4. Ars Electronica—
History. I. Druckrey, Timothy. II. Ars Electronica (1999 : Linz, Austria). III. Series.
NX260.A77 1999
700—dc21
                                                                        99-14921
                                                                        CIP

Contents

THEORY

PRACTICE

Ars Electronica: Facing the Future

Foreword

Hannes Leopoldseder

"Whether we like it or not," writes Ortega y Gasset, "human life is a constant preoccupation with the future." As the closing decades of our century clearly show, stepping across into the new millennium means more than merely passing a magical date. It means stepping into a new future, the unfurling of a terra incognita, the emergence of the digital world with all its unknowns.

It means taking leave of a world that has been marked for over 500 years by the principal medium of the modern era, the book. Even though the book will not cease to exist, it will be superseded as the principal medium by the digital media with all their networks. Thus, "going digital" stands as a signature of transformation between these two decades before and after the change of the millennium. This cultural transformation, this media disintegration, was what the Ars Electronica Festival took as a focal point of reflection at the end of the seventies in Linz.

Ars Electronica began in 1979, opening with the Linzer "Cloud of Sound," as a festival for art, technology, and society. It was jointly organized by the Brucknerhaus Linz and the ORF (Österreichischer Rundfunk) Upper Austrian Regional Studio. The ORF Upper Austrian Regional Studio later added another dimension with the Prix Ars Electronica, a competition for computer arts, and continued this development with the initiative for the Ars Electronica Center, a museum of the future.

Today, Ars Electronica has become an international trademark, the trademark of a city facing the future. Yet Ars Electronica is also an example of how a trademark develops out of an idea, how an idea begins to grow from concepts, how an idea unfolds.

Since 1996 the Ars Electronica Center and the ORF Upper Austrian Regional Studio have been co-responsible for the festival. As head of the ORF Upper Austrian Regional Studio, I have been able to contribute to the development of Ars Electronica with initiatives and ideas. The central issue this involves is recognizing the era and the harbingers of a development at the right time.

The original texts that follow provide the reader with a glimpse into the world of ideas that have contributed to defining the individual phases in the development of Ars Electronica from 1979 to the present. The articles are taken from the respective catalogues of Ars Electronica and the Prix Ars Electronica from 1979 to 1998.

Ars Electronica 79
Idea and Concept

On September 18, 1979, when Ars Electronica is opened in Linz for the first time in conjunction with the International Bruckner Festival, this event will be setting the course for the future in several different ways. This electronic arts event signals a further, logical expansion of the Bruckner Festival, addressing in this case a specific subject matter.

In this way, the LIVA and the ORF Upper Austrian Regional Studio intend not only to contribute to the further development of the International Bruckner Festival, but also to provide a decisive impulse for the future direction of the development: to initiate in Linz a center for electronic arts, a specific but crucial field of the avant-garde.

The present fundamental concept for the contents of Ars Electronica originated with the cyberneticist and physician Dr. Herbert W. Franke from Munich, the electronic musician and composer Hubert Bognermayr, and the head of the ORF Upper Austrian Regional Studio, Dr. Hannes Leopoldseder.

The purpose of Ars Electronica is not to take stock of the past; it is oriented instead to the developments of tomorrow. Thus this event for electronic arts and new experience assumes a character of incalculability, of risk, and of daring to try something new. At the same time, however, Ars Electronica poses a challenge to artists, technicians, cultural critics, and ultimately to the public encountering new forms of expression in art.

Ars Electronica 80
Electronics—Art—Society

With the present program concept, Ars Electronica 80 is presented as an interdisciplinary forum for electronics, art, and society and involves five main objectives:

1. Socio-cultural animation projects (Linzer Steel Symphony by Klaus Schulze, steel workers and machines of the VOEST-ALPINE Linz, Linzer Klangwolke by Walter Haupt—symphonic open-air concert with Bruckner's 4th Symphony, Join In Concert MUSICA CREATIVA in the main square of Linz),
2. Performances of electronic music,
3. Workshop symposia on electronics in music, in literature, in visual design, and in science and society (with participation of e.g. Bob Moog, Wendy Carlos),
4. Exhibition and audience activities,
5. Chess computer world championship.

Ars Electronica is intended to set signals for the future. Not only as an attempt to link tradition and avant-garde, but also as a cultural experiment seeking to influence the cultural awareness of the public in new ways.

Ars Electronica 82
Culture of the Information Society

Ars Electronica 82 will begin on September 24, 1982—that is, 6,308 days before the year 2000. For the year 2000, economists expect the fifth Kondratieff wave, with microprocessors being the carrier structure. As industrial society has revolved around the machine, the age of the microprocessor—the third industrial revolution—will be determined by information and communication. Information society, with the developments of broadband cable systems, home electronics, and direct radio satellites, will produce new modes of cultural behaviour and—due to the change of technologies and media—also new forms and contents of artistic creativity.

Five features have been main considerations in developing the program for Ars Electronica 82:

1. Ars Electronica 82 is concerned with our future.
2. Ars Electronica 82 is directed at a definable municipal community and a social structure for which an expanded cultural concept is to be developed. This process is to evolve from existing conditions and is to initiate cultural intra-city communication.
3. Ars Electronica 82 wants to use new technologies in art, in interdisiplinary concentration, as well as in new ways of communication.
4. Ars Electronica 82 strives to integrate electronic possibilities and media and the contents offered—the electronic facilities of radio and television are not only reproductive media but initiators of animation, creativity, and creative cultural achievement.
5. Ars Electronica 82 presents commissions exclusively, that is, projects developed specifically for Ars Electronica. Thus the claim of innovation and the specific identity of Linz as a cultural and industrial city are being taken into account.

Ars Electronica begins 6,308 days before the year 2000, it ends 6,300 days before the year 2000, as we may see from the "Calendar 2000" initiated by the "Committee 2000." The days in between belong to the future, to the stimulation of forms of art for the information society.

Ars Electronica 84
The New Computer Culture

"It is incredible but true: one single new technology will radically change the lives of all of us." This thesis is the epigraph that Dieter Balkhausen puts at the front of his books about the "Third Industrial Revolution," renowned standards by now. What Balkhausen formulated about microelectronics in the seventies seems to apply even more impressively to another key technology: to biotechnology. Both are basic innovations, changing our economy, our society, and the whole of our life: they are responsible for a new cultural stage of our civilization.

The trends visible today are presumably no more than primary tendencies. The new era will not establish itself until after a period of transition. Innovations and changes have one thing in common, a new raw material: not gold, not steel, not petrol, but information and knowledge. Information is the currency of the new age. As the industrial society, starting from Ford's Model T, made the automobile a mass product, so does our decennium use the production of information as the propelling force of its econorny. And if in those days the transition from the agricultural to the industrial society changed society as a whole, as well as the life of the individual, the change from the industrial to the information society entrains changes as far-reaching as then, with the difference that today's transition is a much faster one, taking less than one quarter of the time of the former. Because of the speed of this change, the old system and the new, growing structure are very close to each other, which is a cause of conflicts and negative consequences on one hand; on the other it implies that only a "new ground of thinking" (Frederic Vester) can cope with the passage from the technocratic to the cybernetic era.

Both cultural need and cultural behaviour undergoes a permanent transformation. The American John Naisbitt expressed one of the "megatrends" that are changing our life in the formula: "The higher the technology, the higher the need for contact. The more we introduce technology into society, the more people cuddle together . . . You do not go to the cinema only to see a movie, you rather go to the cinema to laugh and cry with 200 other people. It is an event." People develop a new feeling of the "we"; in the areas of culture and art the need for events and adventure increases. Common experience comes to the fore. In the last two decades, a worldwide increase in open-air concerts can be noted; rock concerts, great events, serve as a signal of collective experience.

The children born in the Orwell year of 1984 will be 35 years old in 2019. They are the generation that will be responsible for our society then. Does 1984 mark the beginning of a revolution of our society—and will it be completed by 2019? Today's new basic innovations will rank among the old technologies by then; their infrastructure will determine our economy, our society, art, and culture. The electronics society will be in full bloom. Working out the tracks—this is today's challenge.

Ars Electronica 86
Ten Indications of an Emerging Computer Culture

(The full text of "Ten Indications of an Emerging Computer Culture" appears below in this volume.)
1. Computer culture is an emerging culture.
2. Computer culture calls for a new alphabet, a new language, a new way of thinking.
3. Computer culture demands the computer-literate learning society.
4. Computer culture requires restructuring of work, leisure time, and society.
5. Computer culture requires the screen as major tool in home and office.
6. Computer culture permits a new type of artist.
7. Computer culture permits a new world of images and sound.
8. Computer culture permits new networks.
9. Computer culture permits new media.
10. Computer culture allows new experiences in art and culture.

Ars Electronica 87
The Fifth Cultural Technique

Computer culture thus characterizes a new step in culture. Hermann Hesse's *Glasperlenspiel* reveals itself as a vision of the computer culture's society. As the players of the glass bead game had invented "a universal language and method of expressing all spiritual and artistic values and terms to give them a common dimension," the computer with the binary alphabet creates a new system of language and thought. Hesse's utopia is the quest for an answer to how a part of a society is developing towards computer culture in relation to a non-computer culture.

The requirements of a computer culture go far beyond what is usually understood as the "fourth cultural technique," computer competence (i.e., competence in using the computer; being acquainted with the new alphabet).

Computer culture induces radical changes in the history of culture. All the cultural techniques hitherto used—reading, writing, calculating—may be taken over as such by the computer. Computer culture asks for a new evaluation of human capacities, asks for a change in thinking, enables a new start. Just as reading and writing go together, computer culture with its binary characteristics requires the fifth cultural technique in addition to the fourth.

Now, what does the fifth cultural technique mean? It is the development of the *humanum,* of conscience, of ethics, of interpretation, of creativity. Man must concentrate on those abilities beyond the computer's reach. What is within human power might be beyond the computer's in some cases, or else what is possible for the computer could be unachievable for man. The goal, therefore, must be a coexistence of man and machine rather than the replacement of man by the machine. But this implies a new distribution of tasks between man and machine, between man and computer.

In contrast to the tools and machines hitherto used, the computer pushes forth into the empty spaces man has allocated for it. If parents give their children the necessary attention, computer games cannot gain control of children; if interpersonal communication is given enough room and importance, the telematics corner is no danger; if we listen to our older fellow-men and have time for them, the "ole man robot" that patiently listens to the same old stories is no rival to man. But in every case where man neglects his specific responsibility, the machine will penetrate this vacant area. Man therefore must concentrate on such features as are significant for him as "man," where his *humanum* is situated.

David Bell sees the main resource of a post-industrial society in its "human capital." It becomes necessary to define this capital—the specifically human capacities, separate from the machine—and to develop it further. The fifth cultural technique is an expression of the fact that man is not endangered by the computer but rather by himself if he is not able to carry out his responsibility. The control unit for the delimitation between man and machine is in man himself and not in the machine; man must understand the need for "high touch" not as the consequence but rather as the control of "high tech."

One field of considerable importance for the development of the fifth cultural technique is art. In no other area do human intelligence and the often-discussed properties of "machine intelligence" come so close to each other as in the artistic creative process.

Art was and is an activity oriented towards man in the proper sense of the term; here the *humanum* of all eras in human history takes its shape in the most distinctive form. Where does the artist find new opportunities for new images, new sounds, new motion, new dimensions, new interactive forms in literature?

In conjunction with Ars Electronica, the ORF introduces the Prix Ars Electronica: an international competition for artists working with the medium of the computer in a creative field; in graphics, in animation, in music. The results of the Prix Ars Electronica 87 contest should help us to read the trends in these sectors of the arts. Thus the Prix Ars Electronica 87 understands itself also as an impulse to understand computer art/computer-aided art, the use of the computer in the arts not as an isolated phenomenon but within the overall context of computer culture.

Ars Electronica 88
The Golden Crossbar

In a personal interview, the biophysician and cybernetics researcher Heinz von Foerster—one of the fathers of constructivism—answered the question of whether there is a relation between the human brain and the computer with a "yes and no." Then he added: "No computer is a brain, but all brains are computers." So it is not by chance that human cerebral research and computer technology have been following a fascinating common development over the past decades.

Medical cerebral research has stressed its interest in the different functions of left and right hemispheres of the human cerebrum.

Scientists and artists have developed two distinct specific understandings of their role: the scientist as the exponent of the left cerebral hemisphere, the artist of the right.

The two hemispheres of our brain are connected by the corpus callosum as an interface. As we know, the left half of our body is controlled by the right hemisphere of the cerebral cortex and vice versa. Communication between these two disjunct parts is supported by the corpus callosum, which in fact acts as a connecting cross member. Now, each of the two halves executes different functions. If the connection by the corpus callosum is interrupted, both hemispheres, although somewhat limited, independently retain their functions. But the perfection of the human mind cannot be kept up except by the integration of the two hemispheres by the corpus callosum.

The great creative achievements of a culture, from science via technology to art, derive from this cooperation of the left and the right hemisphere. The American astronomer and biologist Carl Sagan once expressed it that he would be tempted to say that human culture is the function of the corpus callosum.

In this field of tension, the computer arts, as a perfect example for the duality sketched above, acquire a key position. Within the computer artist, the scientist meets the artist. In the computer arts, thus, the interplay of the two hemispheres of man is most distinctly rendered visible. The computer artist has to deal with the possibilities of overcoming the barriers between art and science, of unfreezing the traditional understanding of roles in society, of using the new synergy between computers and the left cerebral hemisphere on one hand and the right hemisphere on the other hand as a creative potential. If human culture is based upon the function of the corpus callosum, this string of nerves symbolizes in computer arts what I should like to call the "golden crossbar" which opens the door to a fruitful interaction of both hemispheres, which discloses the effectiveness of the whole human capacity in a special way.

Ars Electronica 89
Art in a Time Warp—Time Warp into the Future

In 1979 Ars Electronica appeared as a time warp into the future: a decade of "electronic art" becomes art in a time warp. From the beginning, Ars Electronica has been open to signals from the future, open to experiments. This openness is based on the idea that in conjunction with the computer, the basic technology of microelectronics is changing our work, our economy, our thinking, and ultimately our culture, more than almost any other technology before. What was only globally prophesied in 1979 has become more clearly evident in 1989: yet even now the computer culture is still in its infancy; the adolescence and adulthood of this era are reserved for the 21st century.

What is the characteristic feature that has been inherent to Ars Electronica from the beginning, that imbued the festival with the dynamic to take off from Linz to become the international trademark of a specific festival? In a word: openness. It is the continuous dedication to openness, striving to break down the boundaries and overcome the barriers between individual genres of art, not separating so-called popular and serious art but rather merging them. Openness has become a fundamental characteristic of the festival: open to new trends, open to the interactions between art and technology, open to that which is yet unfinished, open to contradictions, open to new territories, but especially open to the encounters between artists, scientists, and those who are involved in discussing our future.

Ars Electronica 90
Multi-Trends for Millennium III

Millennium III minus 10. This is where Prix Ars Electronica 90 is situated, an award looking back on four years of development and trying to give an account of the tendencies of the last decades of this century.

The age of the computer will necessitate a new notion of time. Speed has become a phenomenon of the changes affecting all areas of our life.

The new structures of computer art become more and more readable. The change is putting openness, dynamics, processes, movement, and chaos into the foreground, and old systems of ordnance shift into the background. As an international computer arts competition, Prix Ars Electronica is directly affected by the environment of this development, for the computer is an agent of this change, and artists do have an extended sensitivity to the various streams in our time.

From the prognoses for the year 2000 we can deduce some multi-trends towards the Millennium III that affect the environment of Prix Ars Electronica, the environment of computer arts: multi-dimensionality, multi-mind, multi-media, multi-art are the terms to be remembered. These multi-trends are becoming the pathways into the "Mentopolis" of the millennium to come.

"The Happiness Machine" was devised for a novel by Ray Bradbury in 1957 and is described as a machine making it possible to create any place and any space where one should like to be. Thirty-three years later, computer technology allows for the creation of an artificial world, an artificial environment out of numbers and data. A vision of life in cyberspace as described in the novel *Neuromancer* by William Gibson (1984) is on the verge of introducing a technical revolution in the nineties.

An artificial world without bounds or limits is set before us—new kinds of entertainment, new shapes of art, new experiences for the individual. Possibilities in virtual reality prognosticated today may be able to change our behavior and our world. "Artificial life" is gaining shape.

Some predictions point out that the development of virtual reality in the early 1990s may be compared to the invention of the personal computer in the seventies. Virtual reality may become the virtual drug of the individual in the future. The individual is taken out from his passivity, the computer allows for an interactive interference and thus for new sets of experiences for the individual in accordance with his personal self. The passive communication medium of television is replaced by the active medium of the computer, the second great medium of the century.

While television offered a—incidentally unintentional—interactive option only through the telecommander, the remote control, basically by hard, instantaneous editing cuts between the audio-visual material, the computer focuses on interactivity. Artificial reality, virtual reality, thus is no new technique but evolves from the synergy of existing techniques and technologies. Therefore, the goal of the nineties must be the enhancement of the audio-visual capacities of the personal computer. The goal is multi-media.

Ars Electronica 91
The Myth of the Artificial

In the year 1991, the computer lost its innocence. On January 17, 1991, at 1.00 a.m. Central European time, to be exact, when the first laser-controlled bomb met its target, the Gulf War had started: the first "total electronic war" (Paul Virilio). In no war before had the electronic command and decision system been used to such a degree of complexity.

For Ars Electronica, a festival that has from the beginning always understood itself in a relational network of art, new technologies, and society, a new era has begun.

In 1991, Ars Electronica becomes for the first time the "Festival after," a festival after the first total electronic war.

Virtual reality—topic of a theoretical symposium at Ars Electronica 90—is bereft of its playfulness: war becomes a staged reality beyond real life. Jean Baudrillard called the Gulf War an "exemplary specimen of simulation." For the first time, two wars take place: one war on the battlefield, the other war in people's minds, created by the worldwide network of media. The war of images, in real time and as a live battlefield movie, becomes the first actual "world war" involving people on every continent via their TV screens. A war of images presenting itself like a video clip, exempting death and sufferings and simultaneously transforming the warriors into movie stars.

The Gulf War, though, did not actually create the megatrend towards artificiality, but shifted it from a symposium topic into reality, even more clearly pointing out the begin of a new myth: the myth of the artificial, of a second Nature.

The developing myth of the artificial contributes to freeing our minds from the conditions of life (Lyotard). Ahead of us, the turn of the millennium with its overall topic: artificial life. Artists working with new technologies will have to understand themselves within this relation: from the computer's innocence lost in the Gulf War, to the evolution of a virtual reality and of artificial life.

The above area of development will be of great importance for us all in the decades to come, yet the artists working with computer technology will be more immediately concerned with these innovations and trends. A forum for this concern is offered by Ars Electronica.

Ars Electronica 92
AEC—Ars Electronica Center
Museum of the 21st Century

March 19 of this year was a date of special importance for Ars Electronica in Linz and for the community of computer artists: it was the first day of this year's jury meeting in Linz, where the winners were to be selected from 1,500 entries.

But it was also the day when the City Council of Linz decided to offer an additional forum to computer and media artists. In addition to Ars Electronica—since 1979 the traditional festival of art, technology, and society—the Ars Electronica Center (AEC) was to be installed as a "museum of the 21st century": a museum that does not point into the past, but is a place of encounter pinpointing important developments in the future.

Three factors will be characteristic of the AEC in Linz: interactivity, scenarios in a virtual space, and networking. In this sense, the AEC is no "center," but rather a node in a dynamic "net."

With the AEC, Linz also wants to offer an additional home to the worldwide community of artists around the Prix Ars Electronica.

Ars Electronica 93
Ars Electronica, Prix Ars Electronica, Ars Electronica Center

In the same way that oil was the energy of the 20th century, information will be the "intelligent energy" of the 21st. For over a decade now, a tradition of artistic and scientific examination of this issue has been taking root in Linz. With the founding of Ars Electronica in 1979, the city took a stand for the need for a festival of art, technology, and society. Ars Electronica has since become the first continuous festival of this kind in the world. For a festival city, staying one step ahead means not just watching the innovation cycle at work in the development of technology, but putting it to work in the festival itself. Hence Ars Electronica's three future areas of operation: the festival, the international competition, and the Ars Electronica Center, museum of the future.

On the one hand, the Prix Ars Electronica, which was set up in 1987, lends the festival a certain continuity in its observation of art and technology. Conversely, the Prix's founding philosophy, which is to look at the computer as a medium for all the various forms of design, is strengthened by information technology developments, especially in the areas of multimedia and telepresence. The Prix Ars Electronica is intended to provide a forum for artists and scientists working with new techniques, and to act as a showcase for pioneering work.

On March 25, 1993, the Linz City Council unanimously resolved to build the Ars Electronica Center. It did so on the basis of an extensive project study prepared under the supervision of ART + COM, Berlin. The Ars Electronica Center will offer a new world of learning and experience with simulation, animation, multimedia, virtual reality, telepresence, and artificial life in the foreground.

As the host of the Prix Ars Electronica, Linz wants to represent not only a forum and competition, but a stage and a permanent, annual challenge for the artists and scientists who have innovated and creatively used technological possibilities to realize their ideas. For its part the Ars Electronica Center will be a permanent node; a home for the future.

Ars Electronica 94
A Festival for Advance Indications of Media Disintegration

In the digital media revolution, today's radio and television broadcasters, including the ORF, are facing what will probably be the biggest challenge in their history. The developments that are now confronting the electronic media with a radical transformation in their position, areas of activity, and market conditions are the same developments that the ORF tried to address in the late 70s by attempting to observe and foster them as if in a laboratory environment—this is what the ORF's joint initiative with the Brucknerhaus Linz for an electronic festival was intended to bring about.

While today's multinationals view the convergence of computer, television, and telecommunications around the turn of the century as one of the areas with the most growth potential, other researchers like George Gilder from the Discovery Institute in Seattle see media disintegration as being a quantum leap further ahead. As he tries to demonstrate in his book *Life after Television,* television and telephone should be considered obsolescent media that will not survive the digital revolution. Just as the central systems of mainframes and terminals lost the upper hand in the eighties, Gilder expects telephone and television to fade away in the nineties.

His vision of the future lies in the independent use of computer networks by the individual, made possible by the enormous increase in computing power and by the growth of global communications networks. We are about to witness the birth of a new communications medium, a major challenge to present-day electronic media.

The next 15 years—leading up to the year 2009—will certainly be among the most adventurous years of change. If Gregory Stock of Princeton University is right, "metaman" will overcome the pains of birth in this decade: we are at the dawn of a new era in our evolution; human society is on its way to a global superorganism in which modern technology and communication connect people together like the cells in a great body.

Ars Electronica 95
Welcome to the Wired World

Not only are we at the end of a century, we are also about to leave the analog age. There is a digital world before us. "Being Digital," as Nicholas Negroponte calls his bible for this new world.

If we move into the digital world so optimistically pictured by Negroponte, then speed is one of the most critical phenomena of the change, a change that hardly leaves time to pause and reflect, hardly leaves time to learn.

The radical transformation is changing our working world just as it changes our cultural and social life. With "Welcome to the Wired World," Ars Electronica 95 wants to welcome the dawning third millennium—and take stock at the same time of the "information myth," which has caused this transformation to a digital age.

"Welcome to the Wired World" also has another meaning, however. If the countries of China and India with their two billion population, for instance, offer their work capacity on line, this would result in changes in the areas of economy and labor in the next century that are scarcely imaginable now.

The digital work site can be anywhere, the digital work site is a point on the globe; it is irrelevant where or who it is. In Negroponte's view of digital optimism, there are four deciding qualities that will ultimately succeed in carrying out the digital transformation: decentralization, globalization, harmonization, and empowerment.

The transformation also receives additional impetus through the social gigatrend to individualization. The digital world is a community of individuals, a community of global citizens.

Ars Electronica 95 intends to be a forum for this development; with the Prix Ars Electronica, particularly with the new World Wide Web category, ORF wants to emphasize the cultural dimension of this new medium. This is the first time that a jury for World Wide Web sites in a money prize competition has developed criteria to address the specific media character of the Net, for instance "Webness" as a way of being appropriate to the possibilities available on the Net, or "Community," which applies to the formation of community, a global community enabling global consciousness.

Along the way, there is one thing becoming clearer and clearer. If the atom was the trademark of the science of the twentieth century, the dynamic Net will become the symbol for the twenty-first century. The dynamic Net is an icon of a global mind, a global consciousness in the sense intended by Teilhard de Chardin, the mystic of the era of information. The Net is to be understood as a new form of human communication, as a new global medium currently growing faster than television, radio, or the printed media ever did.

Ars Electronica 96
From the Idea to Reality

John Lasseter, ten years ago the winner of the first Golden Nica, the Prix Ars Electronica for computer animation, will receive his third Golden Nica in September 1996 for his work on "Toy Story." If, following the landing of his San Francisco-Vienna night flight, he decides to take an early train to Linz, he may be in for a bit of a surprise at Vienna's Western Station.

The station's loudspeaker will inform him that "Eurocity train EC 562, Ars Electronica from Vienna West with stops in Linz, Salzburg, and Bregenz, is now departing from Track 6. Ars Electronica, all aboard!" Since June 1, 1996, the EC train linking Vienna and Bregenz, the longest single route in Austria, has been named in honor of Ars Electronica, the festival of art, technology, and society. The list of such names, spanning the full spectrum of Austrian culture and including Mozart, Kepler, and the Vienna Philharmonic, now includes that of a contemporary media festival which, since its founding in 1979, has established a rich tradition unsurpassed by any festival of its kind.

Austria's 1,000-year anniversary in 1996 marks a further milestone for Ars Electronica. With the opening of the Ars Electronica Center as a museum of the future, the development of this festival has reached another high point, and one that simultaneously points the way for its subsequent evolution in the years immediately ahead.

The Ars Electronica Center sees its mission as that of a "house in progress," a living organism. Above all, the Ars Electronica Center will strive to be a place dedicated to the formation of consciousness—of the digital revolution and thus of the new stage of digital culture which has already begun to unfold before us.

We stand at the dawn of this new era. There is much that cannot yet be seen or identified, much is still hidden; no one really knows where the digital revolution will lead in a new century.

The Ars Electronica Center is based upon a project proposal which I submitted in 1991. Following a hearing and a presentation of a total of five project ideas in the course of the proposed use discussions, in March 1992, regarding the Donautor Building already completed as planned by the architects W. H. Michl and K. Leitner, the City of Linz decided in favor of the realization of this idea.

With the triangle of Ars Electronica Festival, Prix Ars Electronica, and Ars Electronica Center, Linz has established itself in a leading position in cyberspace, both regionally and worldwide. The ultimate aim of this Ars Electronica triangle in Linz is to enable us to work together, bringing economic and social efforts into harmony in dealing effectively with the digital transformation of our culture as we move further along the way to a cognitive society in which knowledge is the most decisive resource.

Ars Electronica 97
Cyberart: Art of the Future—The Future of Art

"I want people to recognize the crisis as the center of modern art," stated Catherine David, director of Documenta X in Kassel, formulating her intention for this world exhibition of contemporary art. "I am seeking to redefine the place of art."

Where is the new place of art? "Have the fine arts come to an end," as Paul Virilio asked; "is there nothing left?"

The answers to this question, seeking a redefinition of art at the threshold of the millennium, are many. One of the reasons for this is the way a new communication society has set off in new directions.

Information technology and telecommunications are about to establish themselves as the largest industry in the world. Globalization and media convergence are among the characteristics of the upheaval. The language of the dawning 21st century is digital, the new universal language of the communication society.

Walter Benjamin attempted a redefinition of art in 1936 in his revolutionary essay "The Work of Art in the Age of Mechanical Reproduction" in light of the emerging medium of film ("The shooting of a film, especially of a sound film, affords a spectacle unimaginable anywhere at any time before this"). Yet the attempt at a similar redefinition today, on the verge of the digital age, presents itself in its full radicality.

The Prix Ars Electronica has always understood itself to be a laboratory and testing ground, in which the outlines of a new digital art may be identified.

The example of the Prix Ars Electronica 97 shows that digital and online are increasingly becoming the characteristic features of this development. Traditional media and computer art is on the way to becoming cyberart.

For this reason, the Prix Ars Electronica 97, now in the first year of its second decade, has put the term cyberart to the test of the discourse. There is hardly another word in the nineties that has had a career comparable to that of the word "cyber." Even though it has also been seriously overused, it nevertheless stands a good chance of being transformed from a prefix to one of the key terms of the 21st century.

"Where is the new place of art?" If we attempt to respond to Catherine David's question with at least a single answer, one new place of art will be cyberspace. The Prix Ars Electronica intends to provide a forum for forging this new place of art.

If the Prix Ars Electronica has been able to fulfill its function as a laboratory in the field of digital media since 1987, then this should be especially true now for the second decade of development.

Ars Electronica 98
The Cybergeneration Takes Off

"The children who are born in the Orwell year of 1984 will be 35 years old in the year 2019," I wrote in the 1984 Ars Electronica catalogue, continuing, "They are the generation that will be largely responsible for our society then."

In the history of Ars Electronica, the Prix Ars Electronica 98 will assume a special position, because in addition to the artists, scientists, and cyberartists from around the world who are invited to take part in this competition, as part of a pilot project and for the first time, the Prix Ars Electronica 98 has called upon the generation now growing up with the computer to take part.

For this reason, the Prix Ars Electronica 98 has invited the cybergeneration—U19, under 19 in other words—to take part in a new initiative, in a competition of ideas, in a creative brainstorming. The title we have chosen is more than just a name for a competition; it is a motto that is characteristic of this generation: Freestyle—do what you want; decide for yourself; show what you can do with a computer.

Although Marshall McLuhan may be considered the media hero of the end of the 20th century, the freestyle cybergeneration is oriented less to McLuhan than to Howard Stern, the radio and TV star of *Private Parts*, who expresses the freestyle attitude better than anyone else.

Next year, in 1999, it will be 20 years since Ars Electronica was initiated in Linz. This anniversary will provide an occasion to reflect on the traces of the electronic and digital developments of recent decades, but also to look ahead to the world of the new cybergeneration of the 21st century.

The cybergeneration is standing on the verge. Will the digital revolution, with its upheavals in genetic engineering and biotechnology, lead the economy, and with it the individual, into a crisis; or are we approaching an entirely new era of prosperity, of economic and social upward development, as prognosticated by the Pulitzer Prize winner and *Wall Street Journal* reporter Bob Davies and David Wessel in their recent book *Prosperity: The Coming Twenty-Year Boom and What It Means to You.*

One thing is certain in any case: for Ars Electronica and for the Prix Ars Electronica there will be no lack of topics and artistic challenges in the coming decades. On the contrary, more than ever before, the radical changes in our world will need to be critically reflected and artistically shaped.

Hannes Leopoldseder *Foreword*

Preface

Gerfried Stocker / Christine Schöpf

Many gradually became convinced that they had made a big mistake by coming down from the trees. And a few even said that living in the trees had been a case of barking up the wrong tree, and we should have never left the oceans.
Douglas Adams, *The Hitchhiker's Guide to the Galaxy*

The digital revolution and the theories and technologies of information upon which it is based have found a direct correspondence in the emergence of a new type of art.

Electronic art, media art, cyberart, net art—terms which have come to be taken completely for granted but nevertheless remain ambiguous labels for the ways artists deal with the constituent elements of the information society and its technological as well as social dimensions—have long since gone beyond testing out what is technically feasible and have developed into a broad spectrum of highly diverse artistic forms.

Even though the only aspect that the heterogeneous, hybrid configurations of current works often have in common is their use of the computer—that is, their technological or material medium—an essential, defining feature of this new art is impossible to overlook: despite the experience that has been gained and the virtuosity that has developed, media art is, above all, an experiment—one that often brings the creators and proponents of this new art into an association with engineers and researchers.

The unique characteristic of media art as "new art" is the process of getting beyond that realm in which the computer and its data processing derivatives are used merely as one more implement or, ultimately, as a medium of representation that would be interchangeable with any number of other ones. As a counterpart to the convergence of production, transmission (i.e. mediation), and reception that is inherent in this technology, artists employ digital information technologies not only as a tool and a material, but as a subject as well.

In doing so, they have taken leave of familiar domains, have begun to go beyond basic formal and aesthetic research and delve into the technological and sociocultural contexts of the process of reordering our society into a global information economy. In this their highest priority is accorded not to interpretation and description, but rather to analytical investigation in order to shed light upon the mechanisms and functional principles of that society's systemic foundations.

In a situation in which the configurations of software and hardware act much more powerfully than laws as determinants of the freedom of movement within the new public domain of global networks, this artistic strategy is also endowed with immediate political relevance.

Faster than media art theory (in any case largely non-existent) is capable of offering a description of this phenomenon, a conception of media oriented upon transmission and dissemination (that is, centralized, unidirectional distribution) has become passé in actual artistic practice. This conceptual schema—one rooted in the industrial epoch and in which the overcoming of geographical distance, the transfer of messages, and thus speed are inherent central parameters—is now countered by the concept of omnidirectional and participatory spheres of communication of which the Internet is the prototypical example.

These are networks in which presence and community do not have to coincide physically, geographically, or even temporally in order for them to be able to take place; these are spaces whose make-up is primarily specified by social rather than geometric dimensions, and in which the number of users and their activities become the determinative units of measure.

In such scenarios, in which participation is not a result but a precondition, there arises a concentrated form of interactivity which can fulfill art's claim to serve as interface between society/culture and science/technology.

The image of the engineer/artist and researcher/artist which has long sufficed to describe the practice of media art must be expanded by one yet-to-be-invented term, to refer to the diminishment of the linkage of artist and artwork characterized as genius and original in favor of a process-oriented position as contextual network node.

Media art thus does not reign supreme as a result of the images and sounds that it is able to marshal and dispatch, but rather as the quality with which the explicit characteristics of the employed media are orchestrated. It is no great achievement to transfer traditional artistic patterns and behavioral schema into media art; the challenge is to invent new ones.

The products of this art shift from object to process, from information and presentation to interaction and communication—or as the Japanese researcher-artist Masaki Fujihata put it: "from document to event." This, however, should not necessarily be equated with a process of vanishing into virtuality. Aesthetics as a qualitative category of sensory perception remains relevant in cyberart as well.

In order to meet these demands, the business of art must develop new strategies of mediation and dissemination. A festival cannot content itself to function as an exposition of this season's masterpieces; rather, it must open windows to artistic/technological working processes. It must strive to live up to the principle whereby transmitter and receiver are mutually equated. The chance to accomplish this lies in the conglomeration of many different network-linked processes. By enabling artists and their audiences to come together and meet one another, a festival as a project workshop can become a catalyst of such working processes.

Nevertheless, a festival of this kind remains a venue for the production of this art—though, indeed, no longer the place where it is exhibited and warehoused, but rather one where it originates and has an effect, whereby the origination, however, can no longer be accorded precedence over the processes of mediating and experiencing art and cannot be thought of separately from them.

Ars Electronica seeks to maneuver its scope of action within these myriad fields that delineate its mission, in order to be able to recognize tendencies and reflect developments, and to release energy generated by the collisions of positions with one another.

Ready or Not?

Timothy Druckrey

I.

By the late 1960s, the reverberations of the technologies emanating from the hot and cold war machines were finding their way into the culture industries. Along with a panoply of apologists and partisans (John von Neumann, Zbigniew Brzezinski, Wernher von Braun, Norbert Wiener) came its connoisseurs and adversaries (Marshall McLuhan, Hans Magnus Enzensberger, . . .). But, more than a mere watershed for the "scientization of technology" (in Habermas' words) in the age of the military-industrial complex, the explosive period seemed to be characterized by the fermenting strain of the enculturation of technology, resulting in a "media-industrial complex" framed by the devastating logic of "the myth of the machine" (Lewis Mumford), "the two cultures" (C. P. Snow), and/or "the technological society" (Jacques Ellul).

And while the decade was fueled by massive implementations of technology, it was driven by social imperatives indicative of deep public crisis, from civil rights and gender equality to anti-war and ecological movements. The industrial heirs to Modernity were consolidating and crumbling simultaneously. Authority was under siege while emerging technologies provided a rationale for the salvaging of authority in the guise of expertise. So came the twin mystifications, the "global village" and the "technetronic era" (Brzezinski), to indoctrinate both partisans and adversaries.

This led, on the one hand, to the cold war's perversely engineered "equilibrium" of command and control, and, on the other, to the attempt to disengage communication from its militarized aura and insert it as commercial, available, necessary—though hardly empowering. But the marketing of microelectronics, catalyzed by the transistor, led, in turn, not only to the creation of a new generation of consumers, but to a generation that could enlist technology into discourses of opposition and into a nascent encounter with the imagination.

This broad opposition shirked the institution and found its logic in events—marches, strikes, sit-ins, interventions, happenings, performances—in the public sphere. In this space, the ramifications of action were not insulated from media scrutiny. Yet, in the midst of the actions, the chant was not "the medium is the message" but "the whole world is watching." Indeed, the mobilization of media—print, radio, recording, television, video—benefited from the communications boom and the wherewithal of a generation prompted to intervene in its processes, productions, and politics. Nowhere is this more clearly recognized than in Guy Debord's disquisition *The Society of the Spectacle*, where "reasoning about history is inseparably reasoning about power."[1] Through stunning and dynamic acts of productive reflection and speculative empowerment, the "state apparatus" (Althusser) was understood as implicit in a theory of the media apparatus as an instrument of transition, transposition, and transformation.

In film culture, theory, and history, as is thoughtfully documented in Siegfried Zielinski's *Audiovisions: Cinema and Television as Entr'actes in History,* approaches to the media apparatus emerged in the vigorous integration of "the triadic relationship of technology-culture-subject."[2] Zielinski's archaeological approach strongly links the apparatus to ideology and subjectivity and evokes the powerful theories of Jean-Louis Baudry and Christian Metz, applying them to a reading of forms of media whose cumulative cognitive effects, logistical psychological effects, and distinctly cultural effects are at the core of contemporary experience.

But while the radical experiments in cinema and early video wound their way through the alternative environments and into the mainstream, a second revolution was under way. Surprisingly not in the terrain of television, this experimentation involved communications and computing. Largely sponsored with ARPA and DARPA funds, the trajectory of early research was not yet in networks but in game theory, simulation, and graphics (and their implementation!). The range of these projects, from Whirlwind (developed for flight simulation in the 1940s and 1950s) to the SAGE (Semi-Automatic Ground Environment) air defense system, developed in the 1950s, responded to imperatives of the arms race and, certainly, to the potentials of the 1957 launch of Sputnik (and a few other postwar paranoias), spurring some stunning innovations in the field of electronic defense technology. Human-machine interaction was obviously crucial in an arena in which automation played an increasingly integrated role. This integration surely was leading the way to the development of an interface that would provide access to information in efficient and dynamic forms.

Ivan Sutherland's Sketchpad (1963) is indeed one of the cornerstones of the linking of computation and graphics. Its x-y vector description allowed plotted images to be assembled as elements in the representation. "His 1966 paper on 'ten unsolved problems in computer graphics' became the focus of future developments in the field. Sutherland had pointed to the importance of making graphics inexpensive, friendly (he called this 'a problem of technique'), and available in tonal values and colors . . . He described the motion language developed by Kenneth Knowlton at Bell Laboratories and used to produce animated films . . . He saw graphics as destined to make the unseen visible: he called for what later would be known as scientific visualization, and pointed to the power of the technology not only to reproduce visual reality but also to aid in representing new images and ideas."[3]

Douglas Engelbart's mouse (1964) connected text entry and graphics capability. "Engelbart and his colleagues demonstrated split screen graphics and text on the system and superimposed image and text. They also demonstrated the use of 'windows' by 'cutting a hole' in the screen and seeing an image in that space."[4] The joining of "windowing" and graphics is indubitably the turning point leading to the development of the pervasive graphic interfaces in contemporary computing.

Paralleled by astonishing innovations in storage, the shift from transistors to integrated circuits (by the early 1960s), consistent formulations in the development of multi-purpose programming languages (FORTRAN, 1957; COBOL, 1959; and ultimately UNIX, c. 1969)[5] laid the groundwork for the announcement of the PC in the early 1970s. Stewart Brand, well known for his book *The Media Lab*, wrote of the personal computer in a 1972 essay in *Rolling Stone*: "Ready or not, computers are coming to the people. That's good news, maybe the best since psychedelics."[6]

Surely the history of these projects is crucial to the development of what will become the more freewheeling experiments of the late 1960s and 1970s, particularly those of EAT (Experiments in Art and Technology). EAT's entry into the scene was powerfully marked by Nine Evenings: Theatre and Engineering (1966), which presented works by Robert Rauschenberg, Yvonne Ranier, John Cage, Lucinda Childs, David Tudor, and others. Billy Klüver and Rauschenberg jointly signed a statement that appeared in vol. 1, no. 2 (June 1, 1967) of *EAT News*. In part, it read, "The collaboration of artist and engineer emerges as a revolutionary contemporary sociological process." The back cover of vol. 1, no. 1 contained the following:

Maintain a constructive climate for the recognition of the new technology and the arts by a civilized collaboration between groups unrealistically developing in isolation. Eliminate the separation of the individual from technological change and expand and enrich technology to give the individual variety, pleasure, and avenues for exploration and involvement in contemporary life. Encourage industrial initiative in generating original forethought, instead of a compromise in aftermath, and precipitate a mutual agreement in order to avoid the waste of a cultural revolution.

In 1968 Pontus Hultén, curator at MoMA, organized the exhibition "The Machine as Seen at the End of the Mechanical Age." One year later London's ICA presented "Cybernetic Serendipity," curated by Jasia Reichardt. This exhibition was a compelling encounter with pioneering computer art. The title page of its catalogue defined "cybernetic" as an adjective, "a science of control and communication in complex electronic machines like computers and the human nervous system," and "serendipity" as "the faculty of making happy chance discoveries." Reichardt's introduction was sober: "Cybernetic Serendipity deals with possibilities rather than achievements, and in this sense it is prematurely optimistic. There are no heroic claims to be made because computers have so far neither revolutionized music, nor art, nor poetry in the same way that they have revolutionized science."[7]

Clearly a new territory had been opened. It was to be sustained by a small group of artists, engineers, and curators willing to incorporate experimental media into the discourse of art. By this time, too, Wolf Vostell, Nam June Paik, the Fluxus and Zero groups, and many others found in video technology a fitting terrain in which to deconstruct both the image and the ideology of a culture enveloped in TV and passivity. But while video would dominate much of the public reception of media during the 1970s, it increasingly was inflected by the introduction of synthesizers (sound and video) and a willingness to push representation beyond sheer objective recording into territories unimagined by the corporate marketers. In 1976 Gerd Roscher wrote in *Video Magazin* (Hamburg):

Media specialists will be called upon to develop and test the required set of carefully differentiated instruments (in both technical and formal respects), and to make them available for discussion. Independent co-ordinating bodies, or media centres, could offer a suitable forum for this, and it would be their task to provide open access to recording and playback facilities, until the day comes when these means of production are placed under social ownership. In response to the differentiation methods, it will also be necessary to devise suitable means of distribution, supplementing the direct channels used by the producers themselves.

Apart from their primary function, media centres would offer a "politically interesting model of organization," provided that they succeed in discussing and collectively resolving the problems of professional collaboration in setting up institutions with an adversarial role.[8]

Museums only shyly acknowledged video in their programs, while much of the field found its audience on the fringes—in alternative and experimental venues willing to accommodate experimental, installation, and participatory media. But there were significant exhibitions in this time, most notably the "Electra" exhibition (1983) curated by Frank Popper at the Musée d'Art Moderne de la Ville de Paris. This ambitious project, revolving around "Electricity and Electronics in the Art of the Twentieth Century," is a crucial marker in the conceptualization of media in the creative process. Looking comprehensively at the inclusion of technology in art, the show ranged from Futurism's and Surrealism's fascinations with mechanization to Sonia Sheridan's "generative Systems Program." Popper's extended introduction outlines many relevant issues and thoughtful speculations.

What is the specificity of the computer as a creative tool and how was cybernetics able to enter the field of art?

The artists interested in these problems have been able to formulate three kinds of answers. One answer fully deals with the use of information processing devices with an artistic aim; a second seeks conformity between artistic and cybernetic systems; and a third answer denies the necessity of producing what is commonly called art by computer or any other telecommunications device but, on the contrary, sees their main role as a redefinition of the entire field of our aesthetic awareness.[9]

II.

Ars Electronica is the first event in which experts from all the arts have come together to demonstrate their progress to the public. Along with it, a discussion will be set off that has the effects of "creative electronics" as its objective. With all our most important technical developments we have always missed the opportunity to adjust in time to the resulting new realities, whether positive or negative. It is to be hoped that the best possible use will be made of Ars Electronica. It could provide us with the inspiration to once again place intellectual values before material ones.
Herbert Franke

As is abundantly clear in the excerpts from Hannes Leopoldseder's prefaces to two decades of Ars Electronica, the challenges set in place by a generation of committed but dispersed artists, engineers, writers, curators, and theorists found a focal point in the improbable city of Linz. From the outset Ars Electronica set its goals decisively: to sustain a focused assessment of the impact of computing on all aspects of culture and creativity. Indeed, the voluminous contributions published in the invaluable books that accompany the festival, Prix, and symposium show that the organizers have maintained a remarkable perspective on developments in every aspect of the field. No longer pioneers, they charted a territory and simultaneously staked a moral position in support of artists, scientists, theorists, and, significantly, the public. Ars Electronica's exhibitions have introduced works by several generations of artists; its publications reveal a field intensely concerned with understanding both its possibilities and consequences. Its uncompromising advocacy for historical, critical, intellectual and artistic discourses remains exhaustive. Its strong and public international presence has been an influence on nearly every other initiative in a field now conceptualizing the role of technology and art. Its intractable commitment to serious art, serious thinking, and serious audiences make it exemplary.

This anthology is a glimpse into that history. While nothing could replace a comprehensive reading of the full archive of materials available, we hope to provide a resource that cracks open the door to a history largely unknown, to point to ideas, works, and histories whose reverberations touch so much of the field.

Notes

1. Guy Debord, *The Society of the Spectacle*, trans. Donald Nicholson-Smith (New York: Zone Books, 1994), p. 134.

2. Siegfried Zielinski, *Audiovisions: Cinema and Television as Entr'actes in History* (Amsterdam: Amsterdam University Press, 1999), p. 20.

3. Arthur L. Norberg and Judy E. O'Neill, *Transforming Computer Technology: Information Processing for the Pentagon, 1962–1986* (Baltimore: Johns Hopkins University Press, 1996), p. 132.

4. Norberg and O'Neill, p. 131.

5. See, for example, Thomas J. Bergin and Richard G. Gibson, *History of Programming Languages* (New York: ACM Press, 1996).

6. Stewart Brand quoted in Paul E. Ceruzzi, *A History of Modern Computing* (Cambridge: MIT Press, 1998), p. 207.

7. Jasia Reichardt, "Introduction," *Cybernetic Serendipity* (New York: Praeger, 1968), p. 5.

8. Gerd Roscher, "On the Concept of an Alternative Media Practice," in: Rudolf Frieling and Dieter Daniels, *Media Art Action: The 1960s and 1970s in Germany* (Vienna: Springer Verlag, 1997), p. 235.

9. Frank Popper, *Electra* (Paris: Musée d'Art Moderne de la Ville de Paris, 1983), p. 64.

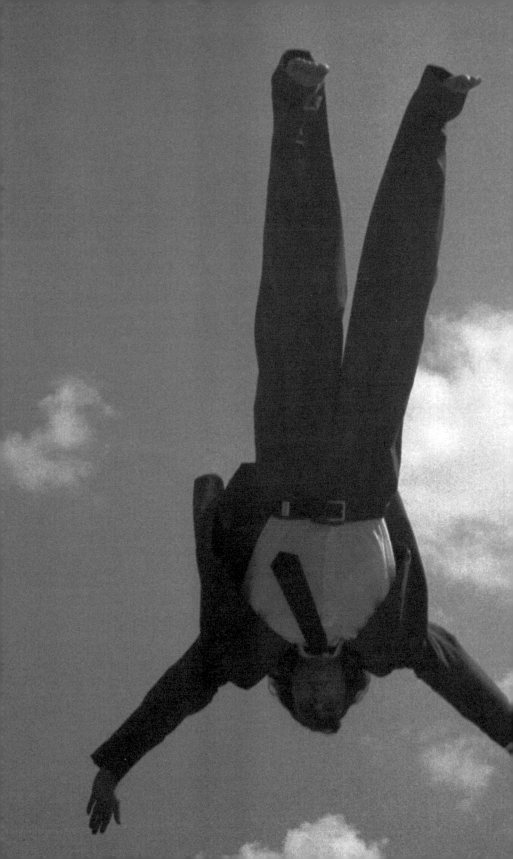

History

Prologue

Herbert W. Franke

With the advent of electronics, a progressive element entered our technical world whose influence is not limited to industry and research, but has imposed itself on all walks of life. A development was thus set in motion that cleared the way for many aspects that were surprising and fantastic, but that also invited much criticism and skepticism. The innovations brought about by electronics are mostly concerned with the transferral of information—its storage, its retrieval, and its processing. Modern electronic mass media have given communication a new foundation. Their effects reach as far as our private lifestyle of thought and behavior.

Electronics has found its own special niche in the field of art. This not only applies to documentation and replication, but also to unconventional methods of composition in music as well as in the visual arts, including computer-generated music and video art and computer art.

Electronics is a typical example of a gentle technology—an ever greater performance with an ever smaller amount of material expenditure. A direction is thus drawn up that helps overcome the idea of resigning oneself to zero growth: growth is only dubious where it brings with it increasing consumption of irreplaceable goods. Growth is not only defensible, but desirable when it raises the quality of life intellectually. Among other things, this means an improvement in education, a release of creativity, and an increase in sensitivity towards our emotional and expressive capabilities—above all through artistic activity.

Up to now, technical progress has entered society in a quite simple and spontaneous manner. A debate on secondary consequences did not occur until the established systems felt threatened by them. The better course would be to observe technical change critically from its very inception and to steer it in the right direction. The term "electronic art" denotes here that young stage of development in which electronics was used for the purpose of design in its widest sense, whereby the surprising result was its unexpectedly close relationship to aesthetic questions. Thus it was that typical characteristics of generative electronics showed up exactly where the aims were artistic ones.

The theme to which Ars Electronica is dedicated has herewith been outlined. In contrast to many other artistically oriented symposia and congresses, it is not a question of taking stock of a completed historical process. The object at issue is rather the phenomena that, though they are already in the making, will not be fully effective until some later date. This means that some of the opinions expressed here will be difficult to prove—more conjecture than prediction. And also that the series of demonstrations are less that of finished art in perfected techniques than suggestions for tomorrow's design potentialities with all the uncertainty of experiments, but with the invaluable advantage of presenting guidelines and trends. Thus, Ars Electronica is not the bottom line behind a past development but a sign for new ones and for the discussions that will hopefully ensue before the chances for any kind of intervention are missed.

Man/Technology Interactions

A typical example of subsequent repairs to an existent phenomenon is the man/technology system, whose ecological effects are only now beginning to be recognized. The result is that criticism has almost always begun with the unpleasant visible consequences, and not with the false principle behind the application of technical systems. The error lies, above all, in the fact that we did not recognize the limitations to our *Lebensraum* in time, nor to the raw materials it contained. We let ourselves be swayed by the old biological law that claims that a form of life expands until it reaches its natural boundaries. It is easy enough to prove that all the precarious secondary consequences which occupy us today have, almost without exception, been caused by overpopulation. If, by means of a timely insight, we had succeeded in stopping this population growth, we would have been spared today's ecological problems. This is the only point at which "zero growth" would really have been necessary. An increase in growth along with a restricted population automatically entails an increase in the quality of life. We could then gladly leave the elimination of the consequences—especially of the pollution that is respon-

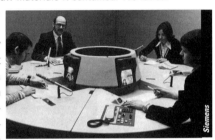

The problems of video-phone conferencing are being studied in trialtests. The photo shows one of the conference tables designed for thispurpose, with additional equipment for the conference director in the foreground.
....

sible for all the unwelcome changes—to nature and its regenerative capability. The fact that technology today has seemed a curse rather than a blessing is because every kind of technologically initiated material progress has been translated directly or indirectly into a rise in the population.

The development described here also had another consequence. Since it was technology that made the enormous dissemination of humanity possible, it is exactly these technological means on which we are dependent. Without technical help, most people would be condemned to death. This means, however, that blind opposition to technology, which is an ever increasing reaction (and a primitive one) to the ecological situation, can only lead to a reduction in the chances that are still potentially in the cards. For, this vital but by no means harmless tool of technology will only be mastered under the present difficult circumstances if we turn our minds to it in a positive way and do not ignore or reject it.

The technology that has come under critical fire is only a small part of the whole, namely that based on physics and chemistry. This ignores the fact that technology means any kind of systematic application of scientific knowledge, i.e., biotechnology, psychotechnics, social engineering. By biotechnological means, man succeeded in transforming himself from hunter and gatherer to farmer and raiser of livestock. The intervention into the ecology that ensued caused, in the end, much more intensive changes in our *Lebensraum* than all other technical interpositions taken together. A biotechnology that is based on modern research—that of genetics, for example—can carry with it much bigger revolutions, whereby we can only hope that, in contrast to the past, newly introduced techniques will be discussed at a more general level of interest. Psychotechnics is still in its early stages; here and there it is used in teaching or in advertising. This also applies to social engineering—the deliberate intervention in the behavior of the population, the manipulation of man as a social group.

Herbert W. Franke *Prologue*

The subdivision of the phenomenon technology can also be carried out from another point of view: one can differentiate between a technology of energetics and of information. The former is one that has to do with material goods, and does so by transforming large amounts of energy. Information technology, on the other hand, concerns the volume of information, its storage, distribution, processing, and generation. For, in contrast to energy, information can be produced as well as deleted, and the essence of this seemingly so general and abstract statement has enormous effects on the associated technical practices. This is for instance the case for the raw material of energetics technology, which is limited, while that of information technology is not. This means nothing more than that for education or art there is no material limit. And from this follows the important bottom line that "limits to growth" do not apply to the field of information.

Naturally there has been a reason for getting these considerations out of the way before going on to "electronic art" and its associated problems. If the use of technical means in art is championed, the question is immediately posed as to whether technology, which has proved so dangerous, should not at least be kept out of the space reserved for art. The answer now is an easy one: the technology needed here is fundamentally different from that at the center of the ecological discussion, namely energetics. It belongs to information science, which makes do with a minimum of material and energy. On the other hand—and let there be no doubt of this—the use of technology leads to a jump in volume: tasks that were thought of as unresolvable are solved, the targeted effects are intensified, the space involved is extended. What better wish could we have in a world whose reserves are exhausted than finding delightful compensation in the areas of the mind. It is here exactly that information science can make its decisive contribution.

As history shows, every technology develops in different stages, beginning with mechanics via optics and electricity and up to electronics and automation. This reflects the simple fact that mechanistically determined phenomena allow us the easiest insight, while other disciplines begin in more abstract regions that are not directly accessible to our imagination. This path, too, is one marked by different stages of growing effectivity. Mechanics represents the, so to speak, most unrefined technical stage, in which heavy material masses are moved—with a corresponding wear and tear and an unavoidable consumption of energy. Optics and electricity are based on immaterial processes that run under energetically more favorable conditions and therefore run considerably faster. Automation, finally, is an informational technology in which energy consumption is tiny in comparison to other sectors. At issue here are guidance and control, terms that are manifestly push-button processes, i.e., through mere directional interventions in systems, whereby arbitrarily large masses and high energies are set in motion without any great expenditure of energy. The problems that have actual weight here are in the field of logic, again based on a cognitive grasp of situations and associations.

It needs no further substantiation that efforts made in this field, in the sector of information processing, lead to a much more propitious handling of material systems. Thus, for example, simple economies based on less consumption are rather ineffective measures. Much better solutions are reached when one succeeds in activating till-then-unused reserves or in avoiding losses. If mankind, during the early metal ages, had for instance tried to counteract the lack of copper by rationing, its development would have ended then and there. Only innovation, in this case the acquisition of knowledge on the use of other metals, could lead to improvement. Our history is a history of technical innovation and would not have evolved without it. And if much of this evolution concerned energetics, general knowledge, problem-solving methods, and technical strategies, etc., belong to the area of information.

This is also the reason that innovations that concern information handling represent special milestones in the course of historical processes. The first one, lest we forget, is still part of our biological developmental stage: the rise of language. Its consequence was no more and no less the rise of *Homo sapiens*. If we want to discover the laws of operation behind the modern electronic media, we must keep in mind the significance of language. With plants and animals, new forms of behavior, like better adaptation to the environment, develop through genetic mutations. Whatever proves its effectiveness is then registered and passed on through inheritance. In order to carry out decisive stages in evolution, millions of years are necessary. With the help of language, the period needed to adapt is reduced to a few years or—counting the time for testing efficacy—several generations. Knowledge can, however, also be passed on "horizontally" from man to man, and not only "vertically" as with biological evolution. The result is that from the moment verbal communication is available, biological evolution is replaced by another, much more rapidly functioning system of adaptation and, with it, an increasing ability to cope with life.

The next step in development, the first result of human invention, is writing. It is a means of storing and passing on information and enhances the effect achieved by language. A further exponentiation of effectiveness is that brought about by the invention of movable type; as a technique for duplication it is a typical forerunner of modern mass media.

Also the example of information processing shows us that the path taken by technical development from mechanics via several intermediate stages inevitably leads to electronics with all its technical potential. The methods of recording something in writing or in print operate on a mechanical basis; the next important step took place at the beginning of the electric age—through the telegraph and the telephone, equipment with which one can transmit electric waves and impulses at the speed of light. In this way the cost in time for passing on information was reduced from weeks or days to immediate, no-delay communication. It is here that one of those cases appear where "quantity turns into quality": through the non-delayed transmission of news, the dialogue via the medium becomes possible as a direct interactive conversation. This is, at the same time, an example of the fact that the increase in technology can also bring human aspects back into play that were believed lost, in this case the human voice—which far exceeds the text in its possibilities for expression. If the telegraph and telephone still are individual transmission systems, we have textbook examples of mass communication in the case of radio and television: one broadcasting station normally reaches an audience of millions. Important news, whether verbally or visually transmitted, reaches the interested public directly; in contrast to the biological communication systems this is an unbelievable rise in the efficiency of the tool, news. The question remains, however, as to whether the possibilities offered are really being optimally applied.

New methods of documentation went hand in hand with the way news distribution was revolutionized through electricity. The phonograph record and tape recordings store acoustic phenomena, especially verbal language and music; film and video tape are means of preserving visual events.

Modern means of communication bring with them a very rich choice of information, which we are beginning to view from its negative side: the much-cited overload. Complaints of this kind are justified when the information is offered importunately, especially when linked to noise. A quite other aspect is the fact that, in order to keep up with things, people must perhaps collect and process a greater amount of information than was once the case. In principle, however, the availability of information, its cheap, round-the-clock accessibility is a positive aspect of our world. In a state of wakefulness, we ceaselessly take in information via eyes, ears, and other sense organs, whether we live in a natural or a modern technical environment. Thus, a lonely hill farmer could just as easily complain of information overload. In the meantime it is recognized that what matters is the right selection, whether it is the visual and acoustic examples from nature or those from the modern big city. This means that we have the ability—or must acquire it—to separate trivial, useless, or indifferent information from the more important and to direct our attention to the latter. When television viewers request broadcasters to please end their programs at eleven so that they may not miss badly needed sleep, this only shows that the user has misunderstood the system. The mass media can only adapt itself to average requests that arise from broad portions of the population, to those wishes that are similar to general needs and expectations. Other mediums are available to cover individual needs, such as libraries, theaters and cinemas, lectures and courses, not least of which is the personal dialogue. When all this is added up, one must admit that at least the populations in democratic countries live in a never-never-land of information, where practically every piece of information is accessible to everyone, and even the costs play a fairly subordinate role. This is an offer that everyone can use in relation to their own personality, for instance in order to extend their knowledge, to improve their education, to stimulate their mind, to learn to think critically, to find differentiated insights into all kinds of problems, and to draw their own conclusions. If much too little use is made of this, it is not the fault of the media and their organization.

Art in the Electronic Age

The first contact between art and electronics occurred in the operations of recording and playback. When the media, such as the record and magnetic tape, go into action, the actual artistic act, i.e., the origin of the artwork, is already at an end. This is the reason the fields of study that deal with art took only slight notice. Art history was formerly directed entirely towards the creative phase and, therefore, towards the artist's person. Not till later did one begin to observe that art is a communicative process whose effect remains questionable if the artwork does not sometime, somewhere reach a viewing public. Art reception became the magic word, and with it the enormous influence of the recording and distribution media. If you look at art as a process carried out in society, one in which the public has its validity, then it is easy to recognize that the situation for art today is inconceivable without these media.

In the field of music the case may be that works played via storage media may offer better acoustic conditions than the normal recording in a concert hall. The upshot of this is that electronic aids are used to improve the performance, such as instruments and voices heard via microphones and loudspeakers. At first the concept was to render a "true-to-nature" impression, but later the goal was more and more one of "improvement." Many a live concert in the rock scene would be unimaginable without electronic equipment, and the established groups bring along entire truckloads of microphones, cables, amplifiers, and loudspeakers. The technical high point is reached in the studios, where the music is often enough broken up into parts, acoustically improved or bent and later reunited and superimposed. The piece now heard on the record has never existed in this form before.

In contrast to musical instruments including synthesizers, photographic and television devices serve to replicate and not to generate pictures. Nonetheless, the wish for an instrument has existed for a long time that allows us to build up from single elements a structure for visual depiction. One example of such an idea is a light organ that can produce free visual compositions in the same way as musical pieces; several prototypes of such instruments go back to the turn of the century, but were never able to satisfy expectations. On the other hand, in the history of art—though seldom in this context—several activities are known that do have a certain degree of visual design. The oldest form is that of fireworks as practiced long ago in ancient China, a genuine spectacle for great masses of people and thus very modern in its conception. Notable, too, are waterworks, artful fountain systems especially found in the Baroque. There are also examples in Modernism, such as the Viennese geyser fountain with its movable jets of water lit in color from below. The highest perfection of this form is that staged as a special effect before film showings or *variété* performances. Much more modest is the kaleidoscope, notable for its mode of arranging structures coupled with chance processes. In recent times light has been used as a means of design. Examples of this are the light sculptures of Hans-

Martin Ihme or the "sun painting" of Professor Hoenig, who, by means of a system of mirrors and metal pieces of his own making, casts the reflections of the sun's rays onto the wall.

Obviously none of these methods has found a final solution to the old problem: the wish for an independent instrument for creating visual design. This seems to be coming to fruition in a different way, and is doing so by developing and revising old playback methods. Media like photography and television were at first developed in order to produce close-to-nature imitations. Not till later was it realized that every copy diverges from the original. This becomes very clear, for instance, when you make black/white copies of color scenes, but even the simple projection onto a picture plane entails a highly modifying intervention. There is no question of a playback of "reality." It is, however, relatively simple with all these media to change other

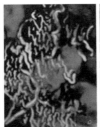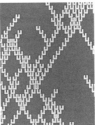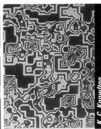

Ken C. Knowlton: Images produced by the EXPLOR language

characteristics of pictures intentionally, so as to achieve certain effects. The possibility exists in photography as well as in television to reproduce scenes in false colors or to enhance their contours. Also the sharpness can reduce copies to an unrecognizable state, pictures can be distorted or overlaid. There are no limits to methods of this kind.

The first attempts to get away from the photographic imitation of nature were made in the first quarter of this century. The best known advocates were Laszlo Moholy-Nagy, Man Ray and Heinz Hajek-Halke. They playfully sounded out the possibilities the camera offered for generating greatly distorted or also non-figurative pictures. As Moholy-Nagy reported, while photographing and developing he did exactly what was considered "wrong": he swung the camera during the take and let light fall on the exposed film. Remarkably enough, the result was a series of extraordinary pictures that recall certain styles from the graphic arts or painting or produced the quite new effects of a "light graphic." The beginnings of video art are also more related to free experimentation than to a systematic working out of a new method. The most important proponent of this movement was Nam June Paik, who went public with his art works in 1963. His pictures appeared on the screens of television sets that he modified, for instance, by installing magnets that caused image distortions.

The direction that video art first established led back to imitating nature. Les Levine built a frame that contained four cameras and several television screens and called it "A Cybernetic Sculpture." The viewer could regard himself in them from different perspectives and in different colors. The wave of "video art" was again introduced by Nam June Paik, who then used this as a model for many other depictions: with a simple video recorder he documented a taxi ride. The tapes from the following years—between 1965 and 1972—were similar in conception: everyday scenes, often left uncut, but sometimes shuffled around, overlaid, and intentionally reproduced with defective technics. Most of these works are unbearably boring, which the artists state to be their strategy for setting free the viewer's thoughts.

A new direction was introduced by the use of a video synthesizer. Nam June Paik constructed the first model together with the engineer Shuya Abe. In principle this was a mixing desk with which different formal elements could be generated and combined. For the first time the possibility was realized to graphically improvise abstract processes in motion, and this without any technical requirements which make the corresponding use of a musical instrument so utterly difficult. In a premiere performance Nam June Paik ran a four-hour-long sequence and pointed out the fact that the layman could also potentially operate such an "electronic paintbox."

Herbert W. Franke Prologue

It has occurred more than once in the history of art that pioneers have established a connection between a certain style and their new equipment, so that this association is accepted as a given. For example, "electronic music" is normally imagined to be atonal, although it need not be. Similar prejudices arose vis-à-vis video art. In the meantime, however, sufficient examples exist that show that the use of television technology can create highly complex aesthetic formations. One of the pioneers of this movement is Alexandre Vitkine, who produced his own equipment for operating modified television sets. In the meantime different systems of highly discriminating video synthesizers have been developed, in Paris, for example, by Truqueur-Universel as well as by Ludwig Rehberg/EMS Videosizer. With this equipment, meanwhile, a series of works have come into being that are fundamentally distinct from previous video art: a composed sequence of color/form synchronized to music that can also be called "graphic music." Among the most notable of this movement's authors, along with Ludwig Rehberg, are Manfred Kage and Paul Jenewein. Works that came about under these definable objectives can also provide a link to the computer, and, in fact, a connection between video art and computer film is the latest development. Constructor and originator Jean François Colonna deserves to be specially noted.

One form of depiction bound up with technical equipment needs final mention here, namely, television, which developed autonomous forms of presentations in all fields, although these were almost without exception based on realist scenes. Yet television would be an excellent medium for transmitting abstract color/form compositions, as the herald of a new form of art that springs, on the one hand, from video art and, on the other, from the computer film. There are initiatives that do just this: for instance, the sequences in some regional programs that introduce commercial spots. Bavarian Television for some time broadcast a kaleidoscopic series, while more recently it has gone on to electronically generated oscillated images. On Austrian television the activity of colored liquids were shown that, reflected in a vertical axis, suggested strange organic forms. Meanwhile, the results from the video synthesizer and from the computer used for graphic purposes seem made for television. However, up to now they have hardly been offered as autonomous products. Dr. Paul Jenewein put together a program series for Austrian television in which extraordinary examples of this kind could be seen. Video-generated passages are also used every now and then as immaterial backdrops for television plays or musical performances. What is remarkable is that these kinds of effects have become established in the rock scene. Also science fiction films made use of these methods, not, however, as art forms but as part of the plot and motivated by some context or other. One example of this is the play *Die Stimmen der Sylphiden* (Voices of the Sylphides), for which Manfred Kage supplied the abstract scenery. It could be that in this way the television audience will become used to this quite unusual form of expression and that the play of abstract color-forms, "graphic music," will become a fixed element in television productions.

Data Processing—Computer

The media discussed up to now have dealt with tasks of storage and distribution of information. These assignments can be regarded as trivial cases of information movement, namely, those in which the information is to remain unaltered. The unavoidable changes that do occur are felt as undesirable side effects. Although the apparatus used to carry out these tasks is part of the data processing system, it is still a classical physical machine.

The much more discriminating type of information turnover is its processing. In the simplest case this could be selection or organization; typical examples of processing are calculation and logical deduction, but also perception and thinking are cases of a highly complex conversion of information. And, finally, creative processes belong in here; these can be defined as such when they generate information. This is a transfer of information that is characteristic for solving problems that cannot be resolved deterministically, i.e., by means of pure deduction from certain laws. The ability that enables people to perform such feats is called creative imagination. The most important examples of this are scientific discoveries, inventions, and artistic creativity.

Just as man called on machines to solve his energetics problems, he also has machines help him overcome the volume of information. The best-known examples are automata such as those used to control or monitor. If some of these solve quite complicated assignments, they are easily trumped by the latest representatives of their kind, namely by the computer in all its versions.

Data processing technology, too, took the usual course that begins with mechanics and ends with electronics. The first counting instrument—known since history began—is the bead calculator, the abacus. The numbers are represented by counters or beads that are strung on rods and can be moved across them. Arithmetic processes are depicted by the position of the movable counters, so that the user, without having to calculate on his own, arrives at the correct sum. If the abacus was only a simple tool, a real calculator was built by the astronomer Schickard in 1623 that was further developed by the mathematicians and philosophers Pascal and Leibniz. These were the forerunners to those mechanical calculators that stood not long ago at the cashier's desk of many shops. The operations they performed were limited to addition, subtraction, multiplication, and division.

Essential functional principles of modern calculators were anticipated by the Englishman Charles Babbage when he constructed his calculators, for example, a storage unit in which data could be stored under certain identification numbers, so-called "addresses," as well as a sequence of instructions, the so-called "program."

The decisive step to an electro-mechanical technology was taken in 1941 by the German Konrad Zuse, whose work was cut off by the war. In contrast, the Americans Aiken, Stibitz, Eckert and Mauchly, and others were able to work on similar problems without hindrance. The breakthrough did not come until they accomplished the transition to electronics with their calculating unit, ENIAC. It is the starting point for all today's computers.

The meteoric development of data processing technology is, above all, due to micro-miniaturization, a technology that allows the most complicated switching functions to be operated by ever smaller units. Modern microprocessors contain fingernail-sized chips that perform the function of over 10,000 switches. All the calculators mentioned up to now operate with numbers and thus belong to the so-called "digital calculators." The other principle of calculating is known as analog, which also has a mechanical precursor, the slide rule. Its function consists in representing numbers by units of lengths, comparing these lengths with one another, stringing them together, etc. Since these lengths are analogous to numbers, the system is called analog calculation. Further development used electric signals to express numbers that one can compare and combine and so imitate calculating procedures. Later, electronic means were used to upgrade the system to an "analog computer," which, alongside the digital computer, is still a valid instrument for specific tasks. This type, by the way, used visualization relatively early, in that the electric signals appeared on screens in a pattern of curves. Since some of these were graphically attractive, first attempts were then made that can be understood as the forerunners of computer art. The pioneers here were the German Gerhard Hille and the American Ben F. Laposky.

The manner in which the data is processed within the computer is irrelevant to the user. It is not necessary to know in detail the computing procedure, the way it's organized, the time it takes, etc., and for the larger computers it is scarcely possible. What interests the user is the incoming and outgoing data, or input and output, as it's known by the experts. For these tasks special equipment is necessary, while the computer handles data in a form that is difficult for the layman to understand—utilizing what are known as binary characters, in other words a numerical system that only consists of the digits 0 and 1. These are encoded as electrical pulses.

Thus, one can view the input and output systems as translation automata, which convert the numeric system that is only understandable by machines into human speech or text. Since this can be accomplished in a wide variety of ways, it depends on the intended application which type of input or output will be selected. For example, the input could be made via an automatic typewriter, which either transfers the information to an intermediate memory such as punch cards or magnetic tapes, or passes it directly to the computer. The options available for the output are somewhat less variable; the computed results will either be printed on paper or they will be displayed on a computer screen. In many cases, a presentation as a graphic image provides a far better overview; for this purpose, computer-controlled mechanical drawing automata and electronic display terminals have been developed. Here again, it was noticed that some of the drawings, created for scientific or technical purposes, were of surprising beauty—impetus enough to initiate experiments with free designs, the birth of computer art. A particularly favorable terminal is found in the combination of input and output equipment that permits a form of "dialog operation." In this case, the computer can for example respond to an instruction entered on the typewriter by printing the intermediate result or by asking a question. Such a dialog can also be handled on the screen of a computer display. In this case one uses a "light pen" to draw lines across the surface of the screen or enter individual points; these are then visible as illuminated dots or lines on the screen. The computer can understand the entries made in this manner and can respond, for example by changing the graphic image. The newest development, which is currently just finding its first practical application, is computer output via synthetic speech, through the spoken word. There are a number of applications for which this method is particularly well suited, such as for the automatic provision of information or for assistance in learning foreign languages.

In the latter cases, communication with the computer is handled in a manner that is fully adapted to man. In the final stage, this development will be culminated by a computer system that can accept instructions in the form of spoken commands while also being capable of recognizing pictures that it is shown. With the first types of computers, there were still fundamental communication problems; with each system, one could only communicate via the respective special and quite clumsy encoding system. Later, these machine-oriented programming languages were replaced by application-oriented ones, such as ALGOL and FORTRAN, which were understood by the majority of the commercial systems. The translation into the "machine code" was performed by the respective built-in converters, the "compilers." In the course of time, efforts were made to design simplified languages that could also be used by persons without any special training. Nonetheless, even today a knowledge of programming languages is indispensable, if one wishes to take advantage of a system's full range of applications.

Machine Intelligence and Society

Machines help people by performing a wide variety of tasks. But, these tasks are not restricted simply to providing some relief in the work process. On the contrary, they often represent fundamental changes, for example, in the utilization of raw material, in the improvement of products, and in reducing prices, making what was previously restricted to a privileged few available to the common man. All this cannot occur without having an impact on society, on types of work up to now dedicated to manual activities and now performed by the machine, and on the users or consumers of goods that now appear as industrial products. What seems exceptionally beneficial for large portions of the population brings massive problems for other smaller groups, for example, the craftsman who finds his financial foundation has now been pulled out from under his feet. Again, it is, in reference to the mechanization of England in the previous century, certainly quite justified in speaking of this as an "industrial revolution."

One can already see signs today that the appearance of effective data processing machines also implies that another industrial revolution is on the horizon. And once again there are impressive benefits to be noted, for example, relief from time-consuming or simply boring mental effort, the savings in time, the reduced prices for a multitude of services and so on; nevertheless there are also lasting changes to the affected occupational groups. However, one should not overlook the fact that a useful technology can in principle be introduced in such a way that it brings a general increase in the quality of life. Whereby, the task still remains of ensuring that the benefits are equally distributed among all concerned and that the immediately affected professions are relieved of the worst negative consequences. The problems that need to be overcome are, in this case, not technical but social.

Less remarked, but, in the long run, certainly more meaningful are all the changes that the new technologies bring to society in general. The applications that computers find in science, industry, and the office are already so commonplace that one need not elaborate on them. At the same time, the expansion of the computer is in no way at an end. Its infiltration into problem areas, which appear scarcely open to solution by the rational methods of computing and logical conclusions, may seem quite shocking to some. Examples of this can be found in its application in hospitals, where it not only helps handle the administration, but also aids in diagnosis, therapy, and the observation of patients. Today, complicated operations are scarcely conceivable without the aid of computers. Another field in which preparations are being made for utilizing computers is the judiciary. In principle, the administration of justice consists of the application of certain regulations from which a decision regarding right or wrong and the appropriate punishment can be read. Some of these regulations, for example, those for the worlds of finance and taxes, have become so complex—thanks to the multitude of changes and adaptations for special cases—that humans are scarcely capable of keeping them in perspective. In this case, one can well use the computer's special strengths, its huge memory capacity and its rapid and precise operation. It would already be a substantial advantage if one could utilize the computer to handle minimal cases, which would free the human lawyers and judges for the more difficult and serious ones. Translation programs, with which the speech barriers that hinder international cooperation can be overcome, are also being developed. Even if the problem of generating a linguistically flawless let alone a good literary translation is not solved, the respective programs do indeed deliver understandable text, which only requires editing by a specialist translator. Also worth mentioning in this connection are the databases, the electronic information centers that replace today's libraries. The advantages are obvious:

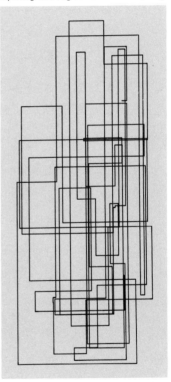

Vertical-Horizontal, Number Three (1964)
By A. Michael Noll
© AMN 1965
....

whatever is stored in such a database can be transferred with practically no delay to any point on the globe where there is what is known as a "terminal." To handle the transfer, one can use the telephone network. Modern databases, however, also serve functions other than simply storing and forwarding information. They can search for specific literature on the basis of the entered key words. They are also capable of generating extracts and summaries, and in the future they will also solve the noted translation tasks as well, so that one can receive every text in any language.

With this example, it is easily seen that, as a consequence of continually expanding functions, an ever greater performance can be achieved—which in turn brings an ever broader range of possible applications. Thus, for example, only a supplemental program is required to turn the above-noted database into a central system for teaching. To a large part, this consists of preparing the training material in a form easily assimilated by the user, subdividing it into "training packets" adapted to each individual capacity to assimilate the data. The number of repetitions required to insure that the training material will be retained is determined automatically. In contrast to the pedagogical systems used in the past, this is a flexible system, which can be adapted to suit the personal capabilities of each individual user. For this purpose, the answers given during the query phase are evaluated statistically and then the instruction tempo, the number of repetitions, etc., are adjusted to match. Even with the aid of the computer, students are not spared the necessary effort, but they need no longer battle boredom or slack periods, nor are they overtaxed, and have their own individual path to success marked out for them. This work method has a remarkable side effect: namely, that there is no longer a need for a central school; everyone can work through the curriculum at home at their own pace. This need not lead to isolation. Enough study areas remain which can only be practiced in a group, for example, extemporaneous speaking, discussion, music and sport, and these could be given more attention when individual study is organized in a more concentrated manner.

Similar effects could also come about in professional life. In a time in which only a limited number of workers have direct contact with their material, but use regulation and control systems to perform their work with levers, pushbuttons, and keyboards, it is no longer necessary for them to gather at a common workplace. If one used the appropriate teleprocessing systems—in the majority of cases this would be possible via the telephone lines—a large part of the job could be handled from one's home. In examining this scenario for the future, it quickly becomes obvious that the availability of certain technical means interposes on our social life. In the case described above, one would expect a closer family life to evolve, greater freedom in the division of the work, with the relaxed and comfortable environment that is only found in the home. It would mean that those huge factories and offices, which have engulfed whole urban areas, would disappear, to be replaced by study and work rooms in private dwellings—as is already usual in the freelance professions today. This would also have quite a positive effect on the volume of traffic; one would only spend a few hours in school or office for joint activities, reducing the often dangerous trips to school as well as much of the deadening rush-hour traffic. It is to be expected that the consequence of the reduction in stress as well as the time won by minimizing commuting would inspire yet another increase in productivity. Furthermore, it would be quite easy to ensure that the relocation of the work to the private sphere did not lead to laziness or self-indulgence, since the electronic systems make it easy to determine how long, as well as how effectively, the user operates.

As essential as the changes under discussion might be, they are nonetheless only secondary effects. The greatest impact of machine intelligence that is made available with computers lies in the new patterns of thinking and behaving that result from working together with these machines. The rapid distribution of information made possible by the printer's art, later even further accelerated by the mass media, had lasting consequences on our common idea of the world, the level of our education, our critical capacity, etc. With the computer, we are now confronted with the prospect of increasing the human capacity for intelligence by an order of magnitude. This effect has thus far only been noticeable in those places where an access to mainframes was available, in other words in scientific institutes, industrial plants, office administrations, or the military, to name but a few. A general utilization of such a potential could come about through access to databases and central information systems, something that can already be seen in connection with our television network where applications exist such as the so-called "televised newspapers" that take advantage of the empty phases

Herbert W. Franke *Prologue*

between picture sequences, but also other new information services that are already under development. Thus today one can phone in a request for train schedule information, which is then displayed as teletext on your television screen. This method too can be extended arbitrarily so that, for example, in the future it will be possible to establish a video link via your television to the department stores and to order the articles visible on the screen at the press of a button.

However, a look at the history of technology shows that developments do not always take the expected route. This has happened in a multitude of cases such as the artificial head stereo that made the step to quadraphony an illusion. It is thus possible that a new technology could take the place of the database systems. What I mean here is the "decentralized intelligence" that is heading our way in the form of the microprocessor. This device has the computing performance of a medium-scale computer, which just fifteen years ago would have cost about as much as a luxury automobile. Today such computing performance is available for no more than the price of a conventional color television. This began with the pocket calculators, which have spread like wild-fire these last few years, and there is no doubt that the "home computers" now appearing on the market, which offer an even greater multitude of possibilities, will find comparable market acceptance.

Even if the computing performance of a microprocessor-based device is astonishing enough, it is likely that it will be the conception behind it, the "philosophy," which provides the impulse for its general application. So it seems to be merely a concession to the professional user that one can program these devices with the aid of one of the commonly available programming languages, generally BASIC, with the result that these devices can also solve any of the problems in mathematics or logic that can be handled by computers of conventional construction. However, what is new and so special about these devices is the fact that they offer new and far more "human" possibilities for communication. Among these user-friendly aspects is the utilization of the screen on which one can write or draw and on which the computer's response is displayed. A few modern variants are also capable of acoustic responses, which can be used for example to output a polyphonic melody or speech. To all this, we now have a new class of what are in some ways subordinate programs; they are stored in "modules" and can be plugged into the device. They prepare the device to handle a specific task, and provide a palette of all the necessary operations so that the user can simply select, sequence, and combine functions following a very obvious system—without recourse to any programming language. This is accomplished using selection lists, what are known as "menus," which describe the various options available in short explanatory texts, so that there are no further barriers between the user and the immediate application. Furthermore, these programs are constructed and secured in such a way that errors, dead ends and the like are scarcely possible.

The result is that interaction with the computer thus takes on a form that has no similarity to the former usual programming—with the multiple trial runs, the exhausting troubleshooting, and the long delays. The computer now reacts immediately; if necessary, it comments on the user's decisions and thus guides him—in stimulating interaction—to the desired solution. The most convincing application for all the proffered possibilities lies no longer in computation, but in free creative work, such as in design and in the arts.

Computer Music

The first area of the arts, in which the computer has been applied, is music. For this concept we have a prominent forerunner, namely Mozart, who gave instructions for composing waltzes on the basis of notes selected by the roll of the dice; in other words he had recognized the principle of the interaction between order and chance in the arts. It would be absolutely no trouble to incorporate his instructions in a program and to thus generate any number of compositions.

One of the first to apply electronic aids to create music was the psychologist and cyberneticist Peter Scheffler at Innsbruck University. To create a flawless random number generator, he assembled a battery of Geiger counters that react to the hammering pulse of cosmic rays. Each "hit" triggers a tone. Although this is an example of purely random music, there were nonetheless remarkable aesthetic effects, since Scheffler used extremely pure, gradually rising and falling tones. On the other hand, a purely subjective evaluation of his "electronic orchestra" finds it quickly boring—there are absolutely no concentrations or climaxes, no repetitions and no subdivisions. The first ones to create programmed music by electronic means therefore imposed a few rules for selection: not every tone triggered by a random number generator will be used, far more a type of "logical filter" will be built in that, for example, serves to cut out discordant notes, such as those which superimpose two different notes which differ by only a single pitch. Similar rules could also be made to handle the sequencing of notes—an ordering principle, which can be designed to be as complex and extensive as desired. In principle, it should be possible to create every form of music in this manner. The first example of computer music was supplied by M. Klein and D. Bolitho. In 1956, they gave a public presentation of a composition called "Push Button Bertha," a music piece from a Datatron electronic computer.

If one performs a statistical analysis of a series of musical pieces, one can distill a number of characteristics, which can then be used as rules to control a later synthesis. In the course of this process it became obvious that besides the classical parameters that are used to describe compositions, for example, beat, key, counterpoint, etc., there are other factors that are even more important in determining the style of the music. Quite remarkably, the majority of these parameters were the result of extensive statistical studies, which permitted statements to be made regarding the degree of chance allowed or the relationship between order and chance. Thus it was the physicist Wilhelm Fucks, in his studies on the statistical analysis of music at the University of Aachen, who established that we have undergone an increase in the influence of chance during the course of our cultural history. The musicologist Norbert Boeker-Heil found a number of descriptive factors that could be expressed in a diagram drawn in perspective and thus present a kind of chart of the respective composition. In this manner, it is possible, for example, to determine the identity of a composer for which no data is available.

A particularly spectacular possibility is naturally the idea of the subsequent synthesis that leads to the creation of additional compositions by a possibly long dead composer. What created such a public stir is, on the one hand, relatively uninteresting to the creative musician and, on the other, has for musicologists an entirely different rationale than that of sensation. It is simply a question of testing, by means of a subjective impression, whether or not the selected parameters are truly characteristic.

Composing musicians uses electronics with an entirely different goal in mind. They are interested in creating something new; towards this end the various tone-generating systems, e.g., the music synthesizer, provide a great opportunity. For composers the transition to programmed music has proceeded step by step—ever more effects were left to automation and no longer needed to be created manually. Composers play a phrase on the keyboard and then have it replayed as often as desired at any of a variety of volume levels, timbres, and speeds. Once an appealing result is found, they can proceed to the next phrase, which can then be created in a similar manner or, should it seem appropriate for this piece, by modifying a copy of the previous. In this manner, the music is assembled beat for beat and voice for voice. In the last stage of development, even the keyboard is unnecessary. By entering certain codes, the frequency and duration is determined and other parameters are assigned, such as timbre, buildup and decay processes, etc. At the end one has a piece of music that appears to be played in stereo or quadraphony by a large sonorous orchestra, although the entire composition exists thus far only in the memory of a data processing system. For some time, systems of this type were concentrated in a few mostly scientific music studios. When they were used for free compositions at all, these were compositions that picked up the thread of foregoing electronic music. Electronic aids are, however, in no way only suited to a specific style of music, but can be used to realize compositional ideas in any musical direction. Recently, the equipment is also being used in the commercial sector, such as for producing film sound tracks or music for entertainment. But here again, a new development is in the offing: with home computers, the public at large will gain access to electronic systems for composing music, so that again what was previously restricted to a tiny elite will undergo a comprehensive popularization—with all its associated positive and negative aspects.

Visual Computer Art

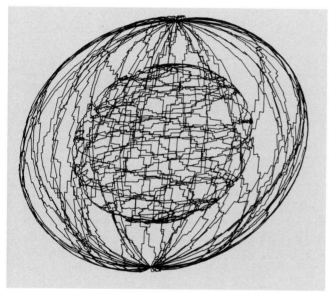

Georg Nees: Siemens in der Welt
© Nees/Siemens

The year 1965 marks the birth of computer graphics. It was then that, simultaneously and yet independently from one another, Frieder Nake, Georg Nees, and A. Michael Noll discovered that the computer could be set up to compete with the classical tools of art as a new and unconventional instrument. The art critics and artists took up the challenge. Heated discussions followed regarding the definition of art and the question of whether a graphic produced by a computer can be considered art. Today, this question is still undecided, but one of the more heartening consequences of this conflict has been the spanning of a bridge between the traditional and the technical sections of our culture.

It would make little sense to develop a computer program to produce a single graphic. But they are at least written to allow one to change a range of parameters, and in many cases the palette of options is so great that individual realizations from the same program are often scarcely recognizable as such. Strictly speaking, this is the reason that the single image is not an adequate form in which to present computer art; it is much better depicted as a series. If, from one picture to the next, one makes only small adjustments to the parameters, the result appears in phased images that can be seen as sequences of movements. They provide the raw material for computer films; thus working with computer systems makes a step appear obvious that conventional art was not able to take. What is meant here is the transition from a non-representational picture to a moving form of depiction, as we find analogous to the auditory field of music. Even if computer art did not accomplish anything else, this alone would be adequate compensation for the effort. What has only been vaguely hinted at in fireworks, waterworks, and kaleidoscopes, has now matured into a manageable form of representation, It is, however, still so strange and unusual that it will certainly take centuries before these new possibilities can be fully exploited.

Herbert W. Franke *Prologue*

The best known producer of computer films is John Whitney, who previously also made abstract experimental films and worked in the fields of both music and photography. In 1966, IBM gave him the opportunity to take part in an in-depth training in the use of electronic data-processing systems. Since then he has worked closely with Jack Citron at the IBM Scientific Center in Los Angeles. Citron, who had previously been primarily concerned with computer generated music, converted a program used to generate sound for electronic music into a system for producing films.

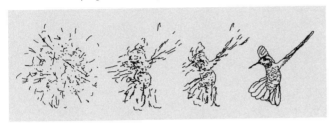

Charles A. Csuri: "Hummingbird," 1967
© Charles A. Csuri
....

In the meantime, picture processing methods have also been applied to the technique used for computer films, which means that these films can now take advantage of representational images with all their temperaments and distortions. As a medium for input, the video camera was an obvious choice; due to its principle of operation it auto-matically "digitizes" the picture, converting it into individual elements similar to a mosaic. In this digitized form, the graphic information can then be stored for processing later. This automatically produces an interesting combination of computer film and video technology, a hybrid process that is increasingly pervading this entire sector. An extremely versatile system which operates in this manner is Jean François Colonna's EAAO (*enseignement audiovisuel assisté par ordinateur*), which is described in detail in another section.

Finally, the Americans have achieved truly astounding results in the area of "computer animation." Today there are programs available that make it possible to create a realistic image of every imaginable object—even ones that have never existed in reality. For this purpose, one only need enter a description of the form, such as a list of the coordinates in space, and it will appear on screen, three-dimensionally, in the correct perspective, viewable from every direction and with any conceivable movement. Furthermore, you can choose from a wide selection of surface forms, for example, smooth, grooved, or transparent. Meanwhile even the reflections found in the relevant environment and the optical refraction associated with transparency are calculated automatically and are presented appropriately on the underlying shape of the object. This is also a step towards perfecting the techniques of illusion, by means of which the public can be deluded with non-existent worlds of fantasy.

Cybernetic Art

From a modern way of looking at things, art can be considered a special kind of communication whose effect is based on stimulating the viewer to perceive, feel, and think. Classical art, meanwhile, proves to be typical for one-way information in so far as it only flows in one direction, in this case from the artist via the artwork to the viewer, listener, or reader. Yet it has been known for some time that a much greater degree of activation is achieved when "bi-directional communication" is possible, for example, a dialogue, a question-and-answer game. These possibilities are closed to the classical artworks, since they are static, predeterminedly fixed and unaltered objects. Through information science and cybernetics a whole new situation is created: artworks can be conceived as automata which evolve their own activity or react to welcome interventions from the public. Such objects are considered to be cybernetic art.

This movement also has its forerunners. Calder and Tinguely were among the first to use mechanical aids to produce moving artworks. Those artists interested in kinetics put electromechanical devices to use. Thus Hans Geipel and Martha Hoepffner used electric motors to drive reflecting or polarizing elements, which presented ever new combinations and, with them, new impressions. Hans-Martin Ihme introduced electric circuits to create light sculpture that was modifiable. The light frames by Vladimir Bonacic can be considered independent special-purpose computers: a square network of lamps, each one of which can be turned on or off. The computer is the controlling device that determines the distribution of light according to certain mathematical rules and makes these visible as light patterns. They are modified in phases, at adjustable speeds, and do not repeat themselves over many years. Because of this constant change, the viewer is kept interested for a long time—a clear increase in effect vis-à-vis static configurations.

However, viewers still play a passive role: they must be content to take in the processes presented to them and have no possibility of intervention. This situation was found to be wanting in other fields of artistic activity as well, which is the reason that in museums and at exhibitions the public is more and more invited to participate. Viewers can, for instance, be offered pencils and paints to work with, as was the case at the First International Youth Triennale in the Kunsthalle Nürnberg, staged by Curt Heigl. At a row of workplaces, interested visitors were set before mirrors and asked to draw their own portrait; the best works were awarded prizes. The audience is supposed to participate even more intensely at Happenings, an art form that is oriented especially towards the common activity between the artist-as-director and his or her public. A disadvantage, but perhaps also the stimulus behind this activity, is that often enough rather chaotic events are triggered. Electronic automata offer a quite different way to achieve similar goals.

The best known German representatives of this movement are Walter Giers and Peter Vogel. Their objects are very refined and cleverly devised circuits that are so arranged as to give the visual impression of being sculpture. Beyond this they include both input and output units, for example microphones for recording sound and photoelectric cells for sensing light, and also loudspeakers and lamps which allow a response to outside stimulus. This can be simply a clap of the hands, a spoken word, or also passing by an object and so changing the incidence of light. The response comes in the form of switching on certain configurations of the lamps and of sound effects, which are partly in accord with the loudness of the acoustic stimulus, but can also be varied by random number generators. The interaction is mostly a consequence of the visitor beginning to understand the activity of the object as a response to her own actions and in a series of trials attempting to recognize the rules behind the system. Because chance intervenes at times, this makes it, on the one hand, more difficult and, on the other, far more interesting.

With these systems, the exchanged "messages" are limited to relatively simple signs. It is first possible to fully exploit the promises of complicated automata like the computer when interactive aesthetic programs enable a close coupling of the user's creative fantasy and spontaneity. Thus far, such forms of activity have been grouped under the heading "computer graphics," although, in truth, they represent a wholly new art form with an expanded range of possibilities.

However, in principle, all can already be found in static graphics. As previously noted, a reasonably designed graphics program always supports the production of a series such as one needs for a film sequence. In reality though, there is a great deal of difference; the order of the pictures is not prescribed and makes it possible to spring from one place to the next throughout the program without following any fixed order. As a consequence, from a single program one can, in principle, create an arbitrary number of films.

If one keeps this special manner of operation in view from the very beginning, it is possible to stretch the creative space in this program to such an extent that the number of potential individual realizations is, for all purposes, infinite. But in this manner, one wins a form of universal device for drawing or painting, i.e., a tool with which a unique artistic act is possible, namely graphic improvisation. Just as occurs with the notes and sounds of musical instruments, one can now create a moving sequence of pictures that demonstrate aesthetic qualities not only in their individual depiction, but also in their mutual relationship during the sequence. Naturally, with this tool, it is also possible to proceed in accord with classical models, thus, for example, to compose static images or image sequences for later presentation and performance. However, in this way one would also return to classical procedures, to works of art that are shown to the public and thus bound to a passive attitude. The far more interesting possibilities offered by the computer and cybernetic art are to be found in precisely the fact that the artist achieves—with the program he conceived—a lively interaction with the public.

Graphic Music

The link between music and movement is an old one—for example in the dance and its artistically sublimated form, the ballet. From the standpoint of man's habits of perception, a need seems to exist that events taking place in three-dimensional space be acoustically accompanied, which from the standpoint of perceptual psychology is comprehensible enough. As well as they go together, however, basic differences exist between music and dance movement. While music within its broadest boundaries is free in its arrangement, dance is bound to the human body, whose latitude is relatively limited. Thus the thought inevitably arises of combining music with something just as freely determinable as itself, namely visual sequences. Since the technology of visualization is a demanding one, it is not at all surprising that it appeared relatively late in history. The first attempt in this direction was the "light organ," a projection facility that allows colored light to be superimposed on a screen. Since the sequences occur by means of mechanically operated lens and mirror systems, the possibility of controlling them leaves much to be desired. But they have found their niche and have been further developed in modern stage lighting.

A new stage in this series of development was reached with the aid of electric technology and electronics. Thus there are some devices which permit the electronic conversion of music into moving pictures. The opportunity exists in the phenomena of vibration, which includes both sound and electric waves. In telephone and radio, the sound waves are converted by a microphone into electric waves, which are later reconverted into sound by a speaker. It has turned out to be very easy to make all forms of vibration visible—even those that are not acoustic—and the results are graphically quite interesting pictures, so-called Lissajous figures. If one is working with a mechanical or sound wave, this can then be visualized by mounting mirrors on the oscillating media, for example tuning forks, and then reflecting a light beam from this to a projection screen, on which the Lissajous figures will appear. A device well suited to the task of visualizing electric waves is the oscilloscope. In the CRT of the oscilloscope, an electronic beam is directed towards a phosphor-coated screen that is visible to the viewer; if an electrical voltage is applied to control the electron beam, say a regular waveform, the same form of patterns will appear on the screen. If these are the waves that are generated by a musical instrument, the result is something like "visible music." Systems like these are still occasionally used as background effect, but in the end the results are not very satisfying. That may, in large part, be due to the fact that the conversion is too simple and thus most likely also too monotonous. Therefore, for somewhat more demanding purposes, one applies a rather more complicated method to convert the sound/image. An example of such a system would be one in which the waves were presented in the image of a star, where the angle indicated the frequency and the radius the volume level. If color output equipment is available, it is easy to represent certain characteristics of the music in color. An even more complicated conversion principle was used by Alexandre Vitkine in his "Sonoskop," a system composed of modified television sets. Impressive effects were also achieved by Manfred Kage with his

Herbert W. Franke *Prologue*

"Audioskop," in which the vibrations were passed on via an electronic amplifier to a membrane. This membrane consists of an oil layer, on which, under the influence of the vibrations, different wave fields develop in accord with the respective acoustic timbre. When this is illuminated with colored light, the result projected on the screen is an interesting image of the music that one is listening to.

Arrangements of this type can also be used without music, by generating the waves electronically and feeding them directly to the screen or the membrane equipment. In this manner, one does approximate quite closely the old idea of an "electronic light organ." The best instrument for realizing this idea, however, is already available—the previously mentioned interactive computer graphic system, with which one can also create moving sequences. What it lacks for the time being is a screen projection that is large enough. It is expected that this difficulty will disappear on its own, since, for entirely other reasons, investment is being made to develop large area displays for television that can be hung on the wall to supplement television, giving it substantially greater effectiveness. As a consequence one would have a kind of home cinema, but also the possibility, via television broadcasts, to reach a greater number of people. Systems that can perform this task are already commercially available, but they are for the time being still quite expensive. But here again the prices will certainly also fall in this sector just as they have in other electronic fields.

"Visual music," or free visual sequencing, introduces a thoroughly new art form unknown to the classical arts. That it seems to be highly adapted to human needs (as we are above all sight-oriented) is to be expected, since it has gone through a development similar to that of music. Especially remarkable are those aspects that are closely related to the technical systems used. It is obviously not yet sufficiently recognized, even in musicological circles, that music as we know it in our western tradition—i.e., highly complex structured music with many and diverse systematic rules—can only evolve under quite specific technical prerequisites, namely when the means are available to describe the world of sound that is set up as precisely as possible and then to produce and reproduce it with greatest exactness. If one rejected this type of precision in music—as it has in part been rejected in art—development would become stuck at a much lower level, simply because the superimposition necessary for polyphony would lead to discordance. Put in another way, the accuracy with which the technical equipment operates—of only scientific and technical significance in the eyes of many an artist—is what makes the variety of expression possible, e.g., that found today in our repertoire of classical music. Viewed from this aspect, it is very significant that it is the computer with its graphic output units that operates with comparable precision. And this could mean that the "graphic music" we are speaking of here greatly exceeds in its structures what classical painting has brought forth, and that similarly complex and differentiated systems typical for music will form—quite apart from their dynamic character. This line of development is without doubt the most interesting one emerging from computer art.

In this context, the problem of the accord between image and sound is again posed. It is easily possible—and has already occurred in public performances—to let computer film run without any acoustic accompaniment. The reaction of the public has been contradictory. Some spectators find the silence agreeable; others demand the addition of sound. In any case, experience confirms the fact that musical accompaniment greatly enhances the effect and helps steer the associations and interpretations of the audience in the desired direction. In this way music will certainly also remain important for the new electronic "graphic music." According to the few experiments that have been undertaken here, for example during a symposium on free jazz, it turned out that synchronicity between sound and image, such as raising the volume during an increase in the dynamism of the events, had an unsatisfactory effect. In contrast to normal film music, which should be used to accompany, support. and intensify the visual events, it has been allowed to preserve its autonomy to a much higher degree. Apparently it will be necessary to compose image and music in mutual relationship to each other,

ilar manner it is naturally also possible to design sequences, in other words, computer films. However, a fully new concept was also developed to give the user the possibility of graphic improvisation, without requiring the slightest preliminary exercise. For this purpose, an automatic process is first started in which different random number generators cause an incremental change in the image. The colors and elements are selected so that they match, although the individual constellations are not predictable. If the user does not intervene in the events, he gets a kind of moving picture to which he can passively devote himself, for example, in meditative contemplation. However, if he decides to intervene, this will switch off the random number generators; the construction will now follow the instructions given per keyboard, and the user can, step by step, impose his own will on the process. If he takes a break, the movement does not come to a standstill, rather the system continues the operation specified by the last instruction or reapplies the random number generators to determine the structural shaping. Thanks to this system, the process acquires an immense dynamic. This makes working with such a system a very special form of aesthetic pleasure. In the course of the work, various kinds of interactions develop between the program and the user: for example, in that the random number generators supply certain basic forms, which he can then take up and rework.

All this results in interesting judicial problems: who is the originator of the final configurations, the programmer who is behind all these conceptions or the person at the keyboard who directs the individual sequences? Quite apart from the unresolved legal situation, it seems clear that designing a program is a creative act of a higher order; on it depends what the program is at all capable of. Yet it could turn out that the "artist-programmer" would never even arrive at certain ideas that the user implements, for instance, if his taste tended in another direction or because, lacking an ability to differentiate, he failed to make use of all the nuances that his own program offered. If one cannot distinguish the given tasks according to the categories of "general" and "special," this is not necessarily a value judgment. On the other hand, what is clear is that the originator of the "special" pictures or sequences does not need any specific training, so that the task of creating artworks can be passed on from the professional artist to the layman. In contrast, the one who conceives of the "general" program must have a thorough grounding in different fields, from visual design to perceptual psychology. To all intents and purposes, this will in the future be a job assigned to artists.

All these perspectives are tied to a whole series of questions related to aspects for the future. How should the public be prepared for the new possibilities? Does it make any sense to train artists traditionally? What should art instruction in the modern media look like? The problems that are addressed here can only be resolved if we have a certain broad overview of what the future will bring. And this can only be derived from all those developments that are just over the horizon. This is the reason we should not dismiss such initiatives that seem at first fantastic or utopian. Just as important for judging the situation, however, is a knowledge of aesthetics based on perceptual theory and information psychology. You can create art without understanding theory but, without theory, you cannot make any tenable or practicable analysis.

Ars Electronica is the first event in which experts from all the arts have come together to demonstrate their progress to the public. Along with it, a discussion will be set off that has the effects of "creative electronics" as its objective. With all our most important technical developments we have always missed the opportunity to adjust in time to the resulting new realities, whether positive or negative. It is to be hoped that the best possible use will be made of Ars Electronica. It could provide us with the inspiration to once again place intellectual values before material ones.

A Medium Matures

Video and the Cinematic Enterprise

Gene Youngblood

Let us begin by disabusing ourselves of myths. For instance, the idea of video art. I submit there is no such thing. In the first place, art is always independent of the medium through which it is practiced. The domain in which something is deemed to be art has nothing to do with how it was produced. In the second place, the boundaries of video art are circumscribed by a much larger history—that of the cinematic enterprise in all its diversity—which contains video and defines its possibilities. Although video is usually identified with the fine arts tradition, its proper context is the tradition of personal cinema, outside of which its achievements cannot be assessed on any level more serious than that of artworld fashion or "sensibility." Video is a cinematic medium and the production of meaning through its unique properties is cinematic practice by definition, regardless of the artist's cultural allegiances. We can legitimately speak of cinematic art and visual art, although they are not the same. But the term "video," which we will certainly continue to use, refers only to craft, not to the object of cinematic desire that actually claims our attention. What we really mean by "video art" is personal cinema practiced electronically.

Another myth is that video has anything to do with television as we know it today. It is apparent that video art is not television art. Yet the myth persists that video is somehow synonymous with television in either a partisan or adversary way—either that the mark of success in video is to be televised, or that its value lies in offering an alternative to, or critique of, television. Although we may find these arguments transparent, their purchase on video's public image is so complete that they deserve attention. In the first case, we need only remember that art and communication are fundamentally at cross purposes. Art is a process of exploration and inquiry. Its subject is human potential for aesthetic perception. It asks: How can we be different? What is other? In a basic sense, then, art is always non-communicative: it is about personal vision and autonomy; its aim is to produce non-standard observers.

Television in its present form represents exactly the opposite. Its goal is the production of standard observers through communication understood as a domain of stabilized dependency relations that maintain constant the cognitive domains of the population. Thus, the notion that video art "belongs on television" is both a contradiction of terms and a confusion of issues. Personal vision is not public vision; art is not the stuff of mass communication. The issue, of course, is specialized electronic publishing—that heroic promise of the Video Revolution implying an alternative form of television whose structures have yet to be realized. This begs the political question, but the critique of the mass media was already definitive and complete by the early 1970's, and today there is really nothing new to be said. We know that mercenaries have invaded the language, that they occupy every image, every word.

"effects" today requiring $ 300,000 industrial tools like the Quantel Mirage or custom user-built devices like Dan Sandin's digital Image Processor or Woody Vasulka's Digital Image Articulator, could by the end of the decade be incorporated on a single board occupying a single slot in one's personal computer.

Computer-Controlled Editing

The cinema is not a visual art, it is a time art. In the cinema we do not look at pictures, we witness events. In a purely technical sense, the history of video is the history of becoming a cinematic medium by offering ever more control over "the time of the frame." In the beginning there was no video, only live television. Video recorders were not invented until ten years after television was commercially introduced, and they did not provide frame-accurate editing. It was not until 1974, with the introduction of the CMX computer-controlled editing system, that video acquired the electronic equivalent of sprocket holes and became a cinematic medium. But even then, so fundamental a cinematic technique as slow motion was impossible in video, and it was not until the introduction of the one-inch helical VTR in 1978 that both the order and duration of the image event in video could be submitted to the controlling logic of the computer.

As we all know, styles in video art have reflected this evolution from real time down into the ability to store and manipulate time in a way that is completely different from film: for one advantage of approaching the cinematic enterprise from the electronic side lies in computer-addressable time-code, such that the organization of the cinematic space becomes pure abstract structuralism derived from mathematics. In other words, computer-controlled editing not only removes cinematic practice from the tedious requirements of manual skill, placing emphasis on the soul within the idea; it actually provides a context for conceptualizing strategies of temporal manipulation that do not arise if one is not using this tool. It suggests completely new approaches to the syntax of cinematic image-events.

In computer editing one works with something analogous to a musical score—the Edit Decision List as a graphic representation of audiovisual events that will unfold in time. It represents the cinematic composition as a whole, the way we think of music as a whole. Using this conceptual tool it is possible to approach the creation of a cinematic work from the "opposite end," as it were, such that the edit list dictates shooting the way a musical score dictates its instrumental performance. In this way cinematic practice becomes a more holistic process and the cinematic text becomes an organic unity, since the entire composition may be entered into the computer before any part of it is edited.

This is unprecedented in the history of cinema. Among other things, it suggests a rethinking of the idea of structuralism, which takes on new meaning as data structure or data space in the computer. No one has revealed the aesthetic potential of these concepts with greater vision and eloquence than Bill Viola, whose singular project constitutes a profound investigation of those specifically temporal manipulations of image and sound by which the attention of the witness is choreographed and meaning is produced in the cinematic space. He may well be the only artist in the world today who is not only systematically addressing this issue but actually beginning to specify new trajectories for the audiovisual time arts, whose evolution henceforth will depend on and be inseparable from the computer, that most intelligent of possible clocks.

Today computer-controlled editing is a complex industrial process accessible to most artists only through outside funding and the intermediary of a trained engineer-operator. There is every indication, however, that these resources will be available to autonomous individuals relatively soon. Already, personal computers interfaced with consumer video recorders are being used in place of high-tech one-inch facilities, and with read-write optical videodisks and more "user-friendly" control structures now under development, access should be widespread by the end of the decade.

Computer-Controlled Videodiscs

The optical videodisk will also figure in a completely new art form which nevertheless can be regarded as an extension of the cinematic enterprise—the interactive movie, in which the viewer essentially creates his or her own personalized experience as they branch through a relatively open-ended cinematic space in ways made possible, but not directly determined, by the author of that space. It is the ultimate case of Duchamp's dictum that the artist begins the artwork and the witness completes it. For the more interactive a system is, the more it becomes what you want to be seeing, what you want to be doing, what you want to be experiencing.

The first rudimentary examples of so-called interactive discs (discs are not interactive, only computers are), primarily educational in nature, have appeared only recently. The most elaborate and best known is the Aspen Movie Map produced by the Architecture Machine Group at MIT. A more ambitious project, a movie map of Boston, is currently in production which will allow the viewer not only to travel down any street and into selected buildings to examine their contents, but also to switch between different seasons of the year and even times of day.

As impressive as they may be, such projects are fairly straightforward compared to more abstract, poetic, conceptual, or perceptual experiments that artists might pursue. For example, Bill Viola, recently awarded a major grant to produce an interactive videodisk, compares the open-ended nature of the medium to the "infinite resolvability" of reality. He recalls a sequence of satellite photos showing first the east coast, then the New York metropolitan area, then just Manhattan, then just lower Manhattan, finally isolating individual buildings. "What fascinated me," he said, "was that the progression was not a zoom or a blow-up. It's not as though they used four different lenses and made four different pictures. All the buildings in the close-up existed already in the global view because it's actually a computer data base and they're in the information. So the image doesn't lose detail or become grainy when it's enlarged because it's computer enhanced. That's not like zooming. You determine the scale of what you're seeing by processing information that's already there. That's how eagles see. They see a field mouse from 500 feet. They're not zooming their eyes. It's like the World Trade Center being in the satellite photo from 200 miles out. That's where media's going in general—the idea that recording becomes mapping. Everything is recorded. Everything is encoded into the system and as a viewer or producer you just determine what part you're revealing."

Computer Graphics and Animation

I have reserved for last a discussion of the medium that will have the greatest impact not only on the future of cinema but on the theory of reality itself. Combining the apparent objectivity of the photograph, the interpretive subjectivity of the painting, and the unrestricted motion of hand animation, three-dimensional computer animation or "digital scene simulation" is by far the most awesome and profound development in the history of symbolic discourse. It is possible to view the entire career not only of the visual arts but of human communication itself as leading to this Promethean instrument of representation. Its aesthetic and philosophical implications are staggering, and they are ultimately of profound political consequence.

If photography is making marks with light, then computer simulation is a kind of photography, but one in which the "camera" is only a point in virtual space and the "lens" is not a physical object but a mathematical algorithm that describes the geometry of the image it creates. In a way that is haunting and prophetic, the most advanced form of photography now imaginable returns us to the Renaissance concept of perspective as a geometric rather than optical phenomenon and situates reality once again in a domain of mathematical constructs.

Although it is not itself video, computer imagery can be encoded as a video signal and integrated into the cinematic space (as graphics or animation or both) providing a richness of pictorial variety and texture otherwise unobtainable. As usual, the technology of simulation (both hardware and software) will filter down from high-tech industry to the individual user, but at a precipitous rate, such that the complexity and sophistication of computer imagery available to autonomous individuals will increase exponentially from now on. As a result, more and more aspects of the cinematic space will issue from the computer, not the camera.

Commercial cinema will provide the economic motivation for software development that might not otherwise occur. By 1990 most backgrounds and environments in Hollywood films, although indistinguishable from photographic reality, will be computer-generated and actors will be electronically keyed into them. Human imagery will take longer to perfect: crowd scenes will come first, then individual close-ups. It is expected that the first all-simulated feature-length narrative movie will be produced before the end of the decade. Although its human characters will look like simulation, they will have more the appearance of three-dimensional paintings than the flat cartoon figures of traditional animation.

Of course the full aesthetic potential of this medium will be realized only when computer artists come to the instrument from art rather than from computer science, which is generally the case today. This will require a new generation of ultra-powerful personal computers at prices affordable by artists, as well as a new generation of artists with the desire to afford them and the skills to use them. Today the kind of simulation envisioned above requires a $ 10 million Cray-1 supercomputer, the most powerful computer in the world, plus proprietary software that has been more than two decades in development. But the manufacturers of the Cray-1 believe that by the early 1990's computers with three-fourths of its power (quite sufficient for computing photographically realistic simulations in real time at video resolution) will sell for approximately $ 20,000 less than the cost of a portapak and editing system today. Such a device would have an enormous market potential and it is certain that the simulation software would be available with it. Finally accessible to autonomous individuals, the full aesthetic potential of computer simulation will be revealed, and the future of cinematic language— hence the social construction of reality—will be rescued from the tyranny of perceptual imperialists and placed in the hands of artists and amateurs.

Artistic Trends

Two artistic trends directly related to the merging of video and computer technology will characterize video art through the end of this century. The new techniques will be extremely instrumental in meeting the challenge of a post-structuralist cinema which seeks to integrate two traditions previously regarded as incompatible—first, the cinematic tradition (including surrealist and mythopoetic traditions of avant-garde personal cinema, whether actor/dialog-based or purely formalistic) with its emphasis on illusion, spectacle, and external reference through metaphoric or allegorical narrative; and secondly, the post-modernist tradition in the fine arts, characterized by minimalism, self-reference, and a rigorous, didactic investigation of the structures and materials of the medium, with particular emphasis on deconstruction of representational schemes.

For several years now the post-structuralist movements in all the arts have sought to reconcile these two histories, and a powerful synthesis seems to have emerged: rich in poetic resonance, romantic, even spectacular in form, it nevertheless retains a poignant awareness of its own construction. In painting today it is represented by the New Image movement—Clementi, Salle, Fischl, Longo and the rest; in music it is Bowie and Byrne and the New Wave; in theatre, Robert N. Wilson, Meredith Monk, and Laurie Anderson; in contemporary cinema it is Godard (still) and Straub-Huillet, Hans-Jürgen Syberberg, and Manoel de Oliveira and, in quite a different way, Fassbinder. As yet, video art can claim no personality of this stature except perhaps Bill Viola, but it is video nevertheless that will ultimately articulate a post-structuralist cinema far more radical and robust than that which theatrical cinema has given us so far—precisely due to the plasticity and interactivity of cinematic image-events made possible by the computer.

The second trend, which could be regarded as a subcategory of the first, is what is currently being called "visual music" or "music image." I prefer the term "opera" or operatic cinema. In any case let me quickly distinguish it from movie musicals on the one hand and rock video on the other. Whereas these are trivial illustrations of popular music, the practice I have in mind would constitute an organic fusion of image and sound into a single unity, created by a single artist who writes and performs the music as well as conceiving and executing the images that are inseparable from it. Considering the awesome cultural forces represented by the cinema on the one hand and music on the other, a fusion of the two would seem to possess unparalleled potential for emotional and intellectual discourse and poetic expression. To my knowledge the only North American artist who even comes close to satisfying these criteria is Ernest Gusella in New York, whose surrealistic, operatic songs and poems are beginning to define a new trajectory for the dialog of image and sound. In any case, I am convinced that the "electronic opera" will develop into a lasting cultural tradition through the integration of video and computer technology.

Communication versus Conversation

As video merges with the computer, and thus with user-controlled telecommunication networks, a communications revolution would seem all but inevitable, bringing with it the rise of those autonomous reality-communities I mentioned earlier—communities defined not by geography but by consciousness, ideology, and desire. Paradoxically, the migration to autonomous reality-communities will not be achieved through communication. Communication (from the Latin "a shared space") is interaction in a common context ("to weave together") which makes communication possible and determines the meaning of all that is said. The control of context is the control of language is the control of reality. To create new realities, therefore, we must create new contexts, new domains of consensus. That cannot be done through communication. You cannot step out of the context that defines communication by communicating: it will lead only to trivial permutations within the same consensus, repeatedly validating the same reality. Rather, we need a creative conversation (from the Latin "to turn around together") that might lead to new consensus and hence to new realities, but which is not itself a process of communication. "Do you mean this or this?" "No, I mean thus and such . . ." During this nontrivial process we gradually approximate the possibility of communication, which will follow as a necessary trivial consequence once we have constructed a new consensus and woven together a new context. Communication, as a domain of stabilized non-creative relations, can occur only after the creative (but non-communicative) conversation that makes it possible—communication is always non-creative and creativity is always non-communicative. Conversation, the prerequisite for all creativity, requires a two-way channel of interaction. That does not guarantee creativity, but without it there will be no conversation and no creativity at all. That is why the worst thing we can say about the mass media is that they can only communicate—at a time when creative conversations on a massive scale are essential for human dignity and survival.

Simulation and Desire

What is important to realize is that in our conversations we create the realities we will talk about by talking about them, thus we become an autonomous reality-community. To be conscious observers we need language (verbal or visual). To have language we need each other. The individual observer, standing alone, is an impossibility. There is only the observer-community or reality-community whose constituents can talk about things (like art, science, religion) because they create the things they talk about by talking about them. As constituents of autonomous reality-communities we shall hold continuously before ourselves alternative models of possible realities. We shall learn to desire the realities we simulate by simulating the realities we desire, specifying, through our control of both medium and message, context and content—what is real and what is not, what is right and wrong, good and bad, what is related to what, and how. This is the profound significance of the computer-video revolution and the cinema, understood as simulation, not fiction. The purpose of fiction is to mirror the world and amuse the observer: the purpose of simulation is to create a world and transform the observer. As video art merges with the computer, transforming cinema into simulation, we shall gather in autonomous reality-communities and conspire to abolish once and for all the ancient dichotomies between art and life, destiny and desire.

(From the catalogue "Second Link")

On the History and Aesthetics of the Digital Image

I

Probably the most significant event since the very invention of the image are the changes in man's conception of the image that the advent of the digital image is entailing. However trenchant and decisive this may be, the history of the image already prepared the ground for it.

If we assume that the major distinction between the traditional image and the digital one is that the classical form of depiction is analogical—that is, it follows the principles of similarity, congruency and continuity—and that the electronic form of depiction is digital—that is, it uses the smallest, discontinuous, non-homogeneous elements—then we can separate our reflections on this topic from those movements in art which advanced the rupture in the traditional conception of the image. This extends from the insurrection of the abstract at the beginning of this century to kinetic art.

In accepting this distinction (from the concept of "digital art" evolves dialectically the concept of "analog art" which by definition signifies nothing else than classical art), we must overlook certain philosophical incongruencies. So, for instance, the fact that there are of course analogous elements in digital art and digital elements in analog art, since in the last analysis, any continuous analogous process can be reduced to small discontinuous pieces, in the same way a continuous line can be constructed from discontinuous dots. In the latter case, the distance between the adjacent dots is so small that it can no longer be discerned by the human eye. This awakens the illusion of a continuous line when in fact the distance exists numerically and can be represented. Digital art does exactly this: it allows analogous processes in nature to be represented digitally.

By means of dots that correspond to a specific number, the computer is able to generate a line on a connecting monitor. The monitor screen is a sort of number field in which each number which consists either of a digit, digit pair, or a sequence of digits, (e.g. 00101) can be matched with a dot. The representation of numbers is generally performed with two digits (0/1), so-called binary digits, since this is the only way numbers can be represented electrically, that is, by means of electrical impulses for 1 and no impulses for 0. Thus we can say that digital representation and binary representation are linked to each other.

The computer then computes the number sequence, that is, the sequence of dots which on the connecting monitor create the impression of a line. This, of course, is only possible when the resolution capacity of the monitor screen is so great that the distances between the dots can be made so small that this distance and the size of the dots can no longer be discerned by the eye, although they actually exist numerically.

For greater clarity, I will retrack some ground and go into further detail. When a monitor screen has only a small resolution capacity, this means that it is a field of numbers comprising only few numbers. So that the small amount of numbers (= dots) can fill the field, they must be large enough since of course it is only possible to fill this field with a smaller number of dots when there are more of them. Eight large dots, however, placed next to each other linearly over the surface of the monitor screen by no means must appear as a line. Rather, one needs a great number of dots in such quantity and so minute that they seem continuous as a line does. A display the size of a normal TV screen with about

Peter Weibel

genealogy) is best illustrated in the transition of the monitor screen of TV to the computer screen.

To the extent that the picture surface of the TV has become a familiar source of imagery, the computer monitor screen seems alienating and disturbing.

This, because the first, TV, carries on with the passive consumption of conventional picture codes, whereas the computer demands an interaction with new pictorial codes. The transformation of the TV screen into a computer screen through the connecting video display which make a computer out of a static object, also signifies another change: the monitor suddenly assumes new aesthetics of information and communication. If it is the special feature and advantage of digital art that it is ideally suited for digitally depicting analogous processes in nature, if, in other words, a pictorial technique perfectly matches its object as digital scene simulation (the digital realistic simulation of 3-D objects and ever in time) does, then this can only mean that the work itself is digitally organized, that everything analogous is also expressible in digital form. Thus digital art is becoming a more and more adequate expression of our world.

II

Computer graphics can be said to have formally begun with the work of Ivan E. Sutherland in 1963.[1] Sutherland is a disciple of the pioneers of information and image processing machines at MIT, Claude Shannon, Marvin Minsky, and Steven A. Coons. Sutherland works now at the University of Utah, Salt Lake City, a center of computer animation and digital images in the United States. In his now classic thesis, he showed how a computer could be employed for interactive design of line drawings using a simple cathode-ray tube display and a few auxiliary input controls. Others had already connected CRTs to computers in the early fifties to generate simple output displays. But it was not until Sutherland developed his system for man-machine interactive future generation that people became aware of the potential offered by computer graphics.

The realization of this potential, however, was slow to develop. Three major barriers were encountered. The first was the then high cost of computing. It was quickly discovered that computer graphics, especially if it was to be interactive, imposed inordinate demands on computers in terms of both processing requirements and memory size. During the sixties, the cost of meeting these demands could be justified only for research purposes in a few universities and some large industrial research laboratories.

The second barrier was a lack of understanding of the intricacies of the picture-generating software that would be needed for an effective computer graphics system. It was soon learned that one had to develop a data structure that in some sense would mirror the often barely realized but visually obvious relationships inherent in a two-dimensional picture. (In fact, the origin of much of today's data management theory can be traced to early work in computer graphics.) Algorithms for hidden-line removal, shading, and scan conversion were needed and generally proved far more complex than was first anticipated. Even as ostensibly simple a task as drawing a straight line segment or arc of a circle on a digitally oriented display turned out to require algorithms which were by no means trivial.

Fortunately, as it has many other technological innovations, time favored computer graphics. The cost of computer equipment kept dropping year after year, while that of labor kept increasing. Operating systems were improved, and our ability to cope with complex software became more sophisticated. Impressive progress was made in the development of algorithms for generating pictures, especially those intended to represent views of three-dimensional objects. The progress, though slow, has been sufficient that now, at the beginning of the eighties, computer graphics is finally becoming accepted as an effective, powerful, and economically sound tool of the engineer, scientist, designer, manager, illustrator, and artist

Computer graphics entails both hardware and software technology. As with conventional numerical computing, we may have both batch and interactive modes. In the batch (or "passive") mode, the speed with which pictures are generated is of secondary importance, and they may appear on a digitally controlled pen plotter, or a CRT. For the interactive (or "active") mode, the time of picture generation is critical, and the display must appear on a CRT, or a plasma panel.

In the early days of computer graphics, primary attention had to be given to the hardware. This is much less true today, since excellent high-performance hardware has become available from many manufacturers. Instead, the emphasis has now shifted to the algorithms for generating the various kinds of pictures that are desired (line drawings, grayscale shaded pictures, color pictures, perspective projections of three-dimensional objects, etc.) and to the software for conveniently programming (i.e. "drawing") the pictures.

Graphics Systems

Timothy Johnson's paper[2] may be considered an extension of Sutherland's work from two to three dimensions. In a simple, straightforward manner, it guides the reader through the techniques needed to design 3-D, planar-faced solids using the orthographic and perspective 2-D projections familiar to every engineer and designer. Homogeneous coordinates are introduced to permit 3-D translation, rotation, and scaling to be accomplished with a single matrix multiplication. Johnson adopted this technique from Roberts' work[3] relating to this description of 3-D solids. The paper addresses many of the subtle problems encountered in trying to design a 3-D plane. In a real sense, this paper is as much the forerunner of 3-D graphics as Sutherland's first paper is the forerunner of computer graphics in general.

Already in Sutherland's paper, the need is pointed out for structuring the image-defining data in a way that will facilitate the various manipulations one needs to perform on the data in an interactive computer environment. In succeeding years, this realization was strongly reinforced as more researchers took up the challenge offered by computer graphics. Data transformations known to be conceptually simple could become horrendously costly in computer time without careful attention to data structure. Indirectly, in the process of studying how to do graphics with a computer, much insight was gained in how we humans perceive 2-D and 3-D structures and subconsciously draw on much "world knowledge" available to us. The development of effective data structures was recognized as one of the key challenges facing computer graphics; and much attention was devoted to it.

Graphics Facilities

Interactive computer graphics—the word "interactive" is almost always assumed when one refers to computer graphics—requires the availability of a display medium in which a picture can appear within a fraction of a second after all the necessary data for it have been generated by the computer.

The "third-generation" graphics terminals, rather than relying on software to perform the transformations of scaling, translating, and rotating, are equipped with special high-speed hardware which is used to perform these transformations "on the fly"—that is, in a continuous manner as the image-describing data list is converted by the display processor to electrical analog signals which cause the desired deflections of the CRT beam. As a result, the transformations are accomplished essentially without any loss of time. Previous graphics terminals permitted the display of "moving" images by having the display processor transform (scale, translate, and rotate) slightly the images from one display frame to the next. This worked well for simple images (generated by small image lists). For larger images, even the most powerful computers proved unable to compute the required transforma-

Peter Weibel On the History and Aesthetics of the Digital Image

tions fast enough to permit refreshing the image at the required 30 frames per second. The unpleasant flicker of the image was the inevitable result. Also, recognizing the importance of fast transformation for 3-D graphics, Hagan and his associates[4] extended the hardware transformation capability at once to three dimensions. The ready facility for modeling 3-D objects *in motion* represented an important advance in the field. In more recent years, high-speed digital transformation has replaced the analog circuitry. However, the general design concepts described in this paper still govern the architecture of high-performance graphics terminals.

In recent years there has been an increasing interest in raster displays over vector displays. Raster CRT displays offer the potential advantages of permitting the use of inexpensive black-and-white or color commercial television monitors, of simplifying the refresh problem, and permitting selective erasure. Their main disadvantage is the need for a relatively costly refresh memory, although with the cost of computer memory dropping steadily in recent years, this disadvantage is becoming progressively less important. A second disadvantage is that line-drawing data is normally *specified* in vector form, that is, as a sequence of line segments defined in a display file in terms of the coordinates of the lines' endpoints. To display a line drawing on a raster display requires an operation known as scan conversion, in which the original line-segment-defining data is converted to appropriately positioned dots in the bit patterns of sequential scan lines.

Scan conversion is important not only for CRT raster display, but also, of course, for the various raster-scan hardcopy devices such as electrostatic plotters and line printers.

Although line printers were never intended to serve as graphical output devices, their ready availability makes them appealing for both line-drawing and halftone graphics.

Computer Graphic Terminals

It is generally accepted that a computer graphic terminal is defined as one which contains means for graphic output (particularly in the form of a cathode-ray tube display) and means for graphic input (particularly in the form of a hand-operated electronic device for the input of pictorial information and for user interaction with the display). There are innumerable additional features normally associated with such terminals, the most common one being the inclusion of a conventional keyboard, often augmented by a set of special "function buttons," in the user's console. The more sophisticated terminal systems may also include means for quickly generating hard copies of displayed pictures, means for optically scanning hard-copy input drawings, and conventional printers of various types.

Although computer-driven CRT displays were used, particularly for debugging purposes, in some of the earliest digital computer systems, widespread interest in graphic consoles is relatively recent and is due to the great emphasis presently placed on improving man-machine communication. It is clear that the present state of the art in graphic terminals has been reached as a result of

1) efforts to satisfy requirements for military terminal systems to allow machine operations to quickly comprehend and respond to real-time tactical situations.

2) recent improvements in display hardware (e.g. digital-to-analog and analog-to-digital converters, vector and character generators, etc.).

3) the development of real-time computer systems which can efficiently handle large numbers of interrupts from peripheral devices.

Algorithms for Line and Curve Generation

A subject of considerable importance to both designers and users of computer graphics systems is the development of efficient algorithms for generating lines and curves. Since a refresh vector display image must be redrawn at least 30 times per second, the amount of picture data that can be displayed depends critically on the speed with which the data can be generated. Much effort has gone into the development of fast hardware algorithms for generating vectors, characters, circles, and free-form curves. The problem is equally important when display output is to appear in hard copy on a digitally controlled pen plotter or a raster-line plotter.

The paper by Bresenham[5] is generally recognized as the first in which the generation of a digital line segment was methodically examined. The paper addresses the problem of finding the best digital approximation to a line segment specified by the coordinates of its endpoints. In a sense, it describes a "software vector generator" for a digital plotter.

A digital plotter consists of a pen that can be controlled to move stepwise in a unit distance forward or backward in the x direction, a unit distance (forward or backward) in the y direction, or any combination of both simultaneously. In effect, the pen is constrained to move from one node of an implicitly defined square mesh to one of the neighboring modes. It is thus not possible to draw a true straight line segment at any arbitrary angle. Instead every "straight" line segment—and, in fact, every curve—must be approximated by a chain of tiny, fixed-length line segments. The result is what is called a *digital straight line*. Exactly the same effect is obtained if a line or curve is to be drawn with an electrostatic plotter (or simply with a line printer). However, in this case the curve is approximated by a chain of dots (characters, in the case of the line printer) located at the mesh nodes, rather than by tiny line segments connecting mesh nodes.

The problem of finding the "best" such digital approximation to a curve has interested a number of investigators. Some have concentrated on algorithms for which the approximation deviates a minimum from the true curve; others have shown a willingness to accept greater deviation in exchange for more rapid (or simpler) computation.

Efficient algorithms for generating good-quality digital approximations for a large class of mathematically defined curves, for the generation of digital "circles" and "free form" curves, were developed in the seventies.

Graphics Languages

The usefulness of a computer graphics system is strongly dependent on the effectiveness of the language available for creating the required abstract geometric structures and for displaying them on a CRT or plotter. Languages for computer graphics—just like computer languages in general—can be grouped into

1) low-level, assembly-type languages
2) high-level, procedure-oriented languages
3) high-level, process-oriented (application-oriented) languages.

During the early and middle sixties, researchers developed a variety of graphics systems in striving to facilitate the application of computer graphics in a broad range of problems. In general, the early attempts at designing graphics languages emphasized the generation of line-drawing output and were confined to the use of graphical primitives in what were essentially assembly-type languages.

Generation of Halftone Images

Almost all the early work in computer graphics was concerned with vector-type graphics—that is, output was displayed on a CRT whose beam was made to trace out the actual lines of the generated line drawing. This was fully satisfactory for all forms of engineering drawings and most architectural drawings. However, it did not readily lend itself to generating halftone images that could be used for displaying an object in terms of shaded or textured surfaces. Interest in generating halftone images finally developed in the late sixties. One of the first dealing with this topic was Bouknight[6] from the University of Illinois at Urbana. The algorithm he describes can be regarded as an extension of the Warnock[7] algorithm over which it achieved a considerable speed improvement by scanning the image in raster fashion. It thus not only generated a halftone picture but simultaneously was able to remove hidden surfaces. Its use, however, was limited to planar-faced objects.

A major advance in the rendering of halftone images was made by Gouraud.[8] Gouraud approximated curved surfaces by means of small polygons so that discontinuities in shading at the boundaries would be eliminated. He was able to generate pictures of curved surfaces having remarkably smooth textures. The application of Watkins' algorithm readily permitted the elimination of hidden surfaces.

Catmull[9] of the New York Institute of Technology found a method for producing shaded images of curved surfaces based on the use of curved (bicubic) patches rather than polygons. The patches are as small as a raster element. Pictures of unusual realism were obtained, including pictures of "transparent" objects. The work in many ways represents the achievement of truly quality textured pictures.

A careful study of the problem of computing the intensity for each pixel of a shaded raster-display picture was made by Blinn[10] of the University of Utah.

Computer Animation

Interest in the use of computers to generate motion pictures developed almost immediately with the advent of computer graphics. As early as 1964, Knowlton[11] published a paper describing the computer production of animated movies. This was rapidly followed by a virtual explosion of activity in this field. Initial efforts were concerned primarily with simulated motion of fairly simple objects. The images were line drawings, and the objects were limited to polygons or 2-D projections of polyhedra. In all but the most trivial cases, no provision for hidden-line elimination was included.

A major advance in computer animation occurred with the publication of Ronald M. Baecker's 1969 paper which is based on his doctorate thesis for his PhD at the Department of Electrical Engineering at MIT. Baecker carefully examines the requirements for an interactive computer animation system, and then, in a step-by-step manner, traces through the various tasks necessary to obtain a computer-generated movie. The paper provides an excellent introduction into all aspects of computer animation and should be regarded as "must" reading for anyone interested in this field.

Animation is the graphic art which occurs in time. Whereas a static image may convey complex information through a single picture, animation conveys equivalently complex information through a sequence of images seen in time. It is characteristic of this medium, as opposed to static imagery, that the actual graphical information at any given instant is relatively slight. The source of information for the viewer of animation is implicit in picture change; change in relative position, shape, and dynamics. Therefore, a computer is ideally suited to making animation "possible" through the fluid refinement of these changes.

McLaren's description of animation:
Animation is not the art of *drawings*-that-move but the art of *movements*-that-are-drawn. What happens *between* each frame is more important than what exists *on* each frame. Animation is therefore the art of manipulating the invisible interstices that lie between the frames. The interstices are the bones, flesh and blood of the movie; what is on each frame, merely the clothing.

Although the computer's entrance into animation has been a recent one (1964), the growth of interest and activity has been phenomenal. Experience to date strongly suggests that the following statements are true:

1) The animated display is a natural medium for the recording and analysis of computer output from simulations and data reduction, and for the modeling, presentation, and elucidation of phenomena of physics, biology, and engineering.[12-14] Depiction through animation is particularly appropriate where simultaneous actions in some system must be represented. If the animation is the pictorial simulation of a complex, mathematically expressed physical theory, then the film can only be made with the aid of a computer.

2) The computer is an *artistic and animation medium* a powerful aid in the creation of beautiful visual phenomena, and not merely a tool for the drafting of regular or repetitive pictures.[15-18]

Three aspects of the role of direct graphical interaction in computer graphics are particularly relevant to computer animation:

1) The availability of immediate visual feedback of all results, final or intermediate;

2) The ability to factor picture construction into stages, and to view the results after each stage; and,

3) The ability to sketch pictures directly into the computer.

The power of immediate visual feedback in animation is striking. The computer calculates, from its representation of a dynamic sequence, the individual frames of the corresponding "movie." Like a video tape recorder, it plays it back for direct evaluation. A small change may be made, the sequence recalculated, and the result viewed again. The cycle of designation of commands and sketching by the animator, followed by calculation and playback by the computer, is repeated until a suitable result is achieved. The time to go once around the feedback loop is reduced to a few seconds or minutes. In most traditional and computer animation environments, the time is a few hours or days. The difference is significant for now the animator can see and not merely imagine the result of varying in movement and the rhythm of a dynamic display. Thus he will be led to perfect that aspect of animation that is its core: control of the changing spatial and temporal relationships of graphic information.

Interactive computer-mediated animation is the process of constructing animated visual displays using a system containing, in one form or another, at least the following eight components:

Hardware:

1) A general-purpose digital computer.

2) A hierarchy of auxiliary storage. This is listed separately to emphasize the magnitude of storage required for the data structures from which an animation sequence is derived and for the visual images of which it is composed.

3) An input device such as a light pen, tablet plus stylus, or wand, which allows direct drawing to the computer in at least two spatial dimensions. The operating environment must, upon user demand, provide at least brief intervals during which the sketch may be made in real time. The animator must then be able to draw a picture without any interruption. Furthermore, the computer must record the "essential temporal information" from the act of sketching. Sampling the state of the stylus 24 times per second often suffices for our purposes.

4) An output device, such as a standard computer display scope or a suitably modified TV monitor, which allows the direct viewing of animated displays at a rate such as 24 frames per second. This is essential to enable the interactive editing of animation subsequences. The final

transmission of a "movie" to the medium of photographic film or videotape can but need not use the same mechanisms.

Software:

5) A "language" for the construction and manipulation of static pictures.

6) A "language" for the representation and specification of picture change and the dynamics of picture change. We shall introduce in this paper methods of specifying dynamics not possible with traditional animation media and not yet attempted in the brief history of computer animation.

7) A set of programs that transforms the specifications of picture structure and picture dynamics into a sequence of visual images.

8) A set of programs that stores into and retrieves from auxiliary memory this sequence of visual images, and facilitates both its real-time playback for immediate viewing and its transmission to and from permanent recording media.

With the development of raster graphics in the early seventies, efforts were soon made to generate moving raster images. The work of Wylie, et. al. (1967), Gouraud (1971), Warnock (1969), and Watkins (1970) provided an excellent background for the human-face animation developed by Parke[19] of the University of Utah, Computer Division (1972).

Parke's paper describes the representation, animation, and data collection techniques that have been used to produce "realistic" computer-generated halftone animated sequences of a human face changing expression. It was determined that approximating the surface of a face with a polygonal skin containing approximately 250 polygons defined by about 400 vertices is sufficient to achieve a realistic face. Animation was accomplished using a cosine interpolation scheme to fill in the intermediate frames between expressions. This approach is good enough to produce realistic facial motion. The three-dimensional data used to describe the expressions of the face were obtained photogrammetrically using pairs of photographs.

The human face is a challenge for computer animation for at least two reasons. First the face is not a rigid structure but is a complex flexible surface. How is the motion of such a surface specified? Secondly faces are very familiar to us; we have a well-developed sense of what expressions and motions are natural for a face. We notice small deviations from our concept of how a face should appear.

Activities in computer animation have become so vast and widespread that it is impossible even to summarize them. A large collection of computer-generated films—some of outstanding quality—exists, and representative samples can usually be seen at the various annual computer conferences. Of particular interest to a reader seeking insight into this early stage should be the works of Whitney (1968), Max (1975), Csuri (1975), and others still to be named.

The refinement of computer animation systems to permit persons with minimal computer know-how to generate animated films is described in the paper by Hackathorn[20] of the Computer Graphics Research Group at the Ohio State University under the direction of Charles Csuri. A powerful, full-color 3-D animation system is described. The system utilizes a sophisticated animation language. The entire system was implemented on a relatively modest-size minicomputer.

An animation software system has been developed at the Computer Graphics Research Group which allows a person with no computer background to develop an animation idea into a finished color video product which may be seen and recorded in real time. The animation may include complex polyhedra forming words, sentences, plants, animals, and other creatures. The animation system called Anima 11, has as its three basic parts: a data generation routine used to make colored, three-dimensional objects; an animation language with a simple script-like syntax used to describe parallel motion

Peter Weibel On the History and Aesthetics of the Digital Image

and display transformations in a flexible, scheduled environment; and the Myers algorithm used in the visible surface and raster scan calculations for the color display.

The development of computer-generated, solid-object animation is changing the way an animator approaches the documentation of an idea. Conversational animation involves drawing and redrawing planar images on each frame throughout the entire sequence. Image creation and image animation are very often the same process. But in a 3-D computer animation environment, the user first builds a colored object, then animates it and these processes are separate. The approach of 3-D color animation is similar to that found in other disciplines such as cinematography, theatre, and choreography.

In the mid-seventies a trend begun in which computer animation began moving away from the domain of the computer engineer and entering that of the professional filmmaker, a sign that the field has truly matured. By the second half of the seventies, extensive use of computer animation was being made to create educational and entertainment films of commercial quality for both the movie and television industries.

Digital Images and the Computer Community

The use of computers is proliferating in the arts of film and video. Computers are used for all aspects of the production process. In the form of microprocessors they are internal to virtually every device, and in the area of machine control, computers are fundamental to every procedure. Computers are integral to the very language and notation of these kinetic art forms which deal with the concepts of light, color, and motion in time and space.

The advent of computer graphics in popular culture, such as special effects for film and commercial advertising, has resulted in the emergence of facilities where artists have helped to direct the focus of research and exploration in image generation and synthesis. Their input has also affected the development of hardware and software systems.

Concurrently, the tremendous effect of personal computers and video game technology on the creative process and art is just beginning to be ascertained and acknowledged. While practitioners of more traditional art forms such as painting, sculpture, and printmaking are now questioning the validity of the computer in their media, film and video artists have always struggled with such concepts as the human-machine interface and the collaboration of the artist/technologist. These artists' achievements, and the resounding acceptance of their art form in major museums and art institutions around the world (as evidenced by this festival), have served to free these artists from questioning the validity of technological art.

It is therefore not surprising that these artists are responsible for some of the most remarkable achievements in the field of computer art. They are artists who have embraced computers as tools of artistic expression to either modify imagery or create entirely new visual realities.

The digital image, computer animation, and graphics are the most significant technological advances in the moving image since the very invention of film. At present advances in computer animation (cartoon trick films produced by computers) are being made in universities, industry, and art. A particularly interesting aspect of this development are the cross-connections between these three areas which are representative of individual work as well as of the whole state of the art.

Researchers are leaving the university for industry, artists are moving into the university and commercial areas, engineers are switching over to art. In the process, encounters occur between the three, involving joint work.

The following universities are leading in the theoretical research basic for both hardware and software in computer culture and technology as well as in the practical implementation of this: New York Institute of Technology, the Harvard Computation Laboratory of Harvard University, Carnegie-Mellon University, the University of Utah in Salt Lake City, the Massachusetts Institute of Technology, the Berkeley Computer Graphics Lab of the Computer Science Division, the Xerox Palo Alto Research Center, the University of Illinois in Chicago, the California Institute of Technology, etc.

Influential in computer industry are not only military institutions such as NASA, which receive exorbitant sums and have thus been able to make great advances in computer animation, but also film and commercial firms such as George Lucas Ltd., Robert Abel Associates, Cranston-Csuri, Digital Effects, Digital Production. These firms produce special effects with computer graphics for movies and commercials, etc. Also firms such as Atari, Apple, etc., which manufacture personal computers and video games, as well as Bell Telephone Laboratories, IBM, etc., deserve mention when one speaks of the computer communication revolution. Third, there exists a group of artists who in part depend on institutions and industry for support. Before I proceed to describe some of the most important examples of the cooperation between computers and art, I would first like to deal with some of the cross-connections existing between research, industry, and art which are typical of the advent of computer culture. Additional useful information on this topic can also be found in the notes. Tom A. DeFanti is professor at the Department of Electrical Engineering and Computer Science of the University of Illinois in Chicago. He is a computer specialist and computer artist and is presently serving as chair of the SIGGRAPH group. Together with Dan Sandin, Bob Snyder, and Jane Veeder (on whom Gene Youngblood has written an article, so that it isn't necessary to go into detail here) and others, he belongs to the Chicago Circle of Computer Art. His computer graphics language ZGRASS, designed for real-time interaction, has been used by both Jane Veeder and Larry Cuba (Santa Cruz).

Dan Sandin's Digital Image Processor as well as Woody Vasulka's Digital Image Articulator are among the best tools for the further processing of images. Ed Emshwiller can be named along with Veeder and Cuba as one of the leading computer artists. His famous production "Sunstone" (1979)—3 minutes produced in 3 months at the New York Institute of Technology, directed by Alexander Schure—was programmed by Lance Williams and Alvy Ray Smith who works today for Lucas Film. Frederic I. Parke (see his article on the computer animation of faces, 1972) did his doctoral work at the University of Utah. He now works as professor of computer science at the New York Institute of Technology and runs its Computer Graphics Laboratory where Paul S. Heckbert also works on the subject of "Beam Tracing Polygonal Objects."

George Lucas Film Ltd. in San Rafael, California, appears to be the major center of advanced computer graphics, digital image synthesis, and computer animation. Ed Catmull, who was formerly at the University of Utah and has written important articles on computer graphics, also works for Lucas Film. There, he is developing "an analytical visible surface algorithm for independent pixel processing" which is so important for Pixar. Loren Carpenter, whose film "Vol Libre" (2 min.), a computer-simulated trip through a mountain landscape, is a classic of visual work, is now working at Lucas Film on the development of algorithms for hidden surfaces (the A-Buffer, An Antialiased Hidden Surface Method). Adam Levinthal is working at Lucas Film on a "Chap—a SMID Processor"; Rob Cook is concentrating on "distributed ray tracing," one of the newest techniques with which realistic images can be generated on the basis of reflections and shadows. Curtis Abbott, also at Lucas Film, is working with digital sound. Others working at Lucas Film are Rodney Stock, Thomas Porter, Tom Smith, and William Reeves. Stock is the Graphics Engineering Manager and together with the above-named, participated in the project "Pixar." Apart from his film productions (e.g. "Star Wars"), George Lucas' major concern is developing a special technique for digital filmprinting and for the synthetic generation of images for film, which allow an interactive playing with the monitor producing the imagery that I want to see, such

Peter Weibel *On the History and Aesthetics of the Digital Image* as pictures from the air. These pictures obey my input and control mechanisms (e.g. a flight around a rock in a canyon).

Stock used to work as graphics designer at Adage Inc., which developed a graphics terminal (Stock did the vector generation). He went on to work for Evans & Sutherland Corporation, where he did hardware for flight simulation and contributed to the development of hardware for the Ampex Video Art Paint System. As you see, also the pioneer of computer graphics, I. E. Sutherland of the University of Utah (see his work from 1963) runs his own computer firm where also Robert Schumacker, Michael Cosman, and, of course, David Evans work. Like Atari, Real Time Design in Chicago, etc., it develops interactive computer graphics systems. James T. Kajiya did his doctoral work at the University of Utah, then worked for Evans & Sutherland Computer Corporation, and today is professor at the California Institute of Technology.

In the late seventies, important articles on computer graphics were written by James F. Blinn who is also a graduate of the University of Utah and is now working at the Jet Propulsion Laboratory of the California Institute of Technology which has produced computer-generated animations for NASA and the famous TV series "Cosmos." Thomas Spencer and Richard R. Riesenfeld are also from the University of Utah. Riesenfeld has written important articles and is head of the Computer Science and Computer-Aided Geometric Design Group. The University of Utah, the New York Institute of Technology, and Lucas Film Ltd. seem to be the strongholds in the development of the digital image and interactive computer graphics systems.

Computer commercials or High Tech commercials are commercials that are actually produced with computers or have a neon-like computer look. Such high technology commercials and special effects for movies are produced by firms such as Robert Abel Associates in Hollywood, or Digital Effects Inc. in New York, or Cranston Csuri Productions in Columbus, Ohio, or the Entertainment Effects Group of Douglas Trumball, Adrian Malone Production or Digital Productions, both in Los Angeles. Judson Rosebush who has written much on this topic is the founder and president of Digital Effects Inc. Jeffrey Kleiser and Donald Leich work there in the computer animation division. Donald L. Stredney and Wayne Carlson are computer animators at Cranston-Csuri. Charles A. Csuri not only produced a famous computer film in 1967, but also wrote important articles on computer animation during the seventies. Robert Abel studied under John Whitney Sr., the pioneer of the digital image and computer film and visual music at the University of California, Los Angeles. His best co-worker is Bill Kovacs. Pat O'Neill, the famous avant-garde filmmaker on the west coast in the sixties, has worked sporadically for Robert Abel as well as for Larry Cuba, in addition to his production of abstract psychedelic films in the seventies.

High Tech Videos for the general public, such as rock videos, are made by Todd Rundgren ("Utopia Video," "Woodstock in New York")—see his project "Will Powers," produced in 1983 with Lynn Goldsmith for Island Rec.—or Michael Nesmith, Bill Etra (DIGITAL IMAGE), Steve Rutt (LASER TV), etc. Artistic laser TV, laser disc programs, satellite TV projects are produced by Mobile Image (Kit Galloway / Sherry Rabinowitz).

The most interesting example of the interrelationships between art and High Tech business is Digital Productions in Los Angeles, which was founded by John Whitney Jr., the son and former co-worker of John Whitney Sr., the artistic pioneer of computer film, and Gary Demos.

Two further co-workers under 60 are Craig Upson, who worked together with the computer pioneer Nelson Max on developing cloud movements in computer animation, and Sherry McKenna who worked with Robert Abel on his famous "7-Up Bubble Commercial." Gary Demos, 32, worked as assistant for Whitney Sr., who produced his first computer film "Catalog" in 1962. Larry Cuba contributed to the programming of "Arabesque" (1975), 6 min.

The technique was developed by Information Internation Inc. (Triple) in 1974, the forerunner of

Peter Weibel *On the History and Aesthetics of the Digital Image*

Digital Productions. Digital Productions specializes in digital scene simulation, that is, computer-generated images that realistically simulate 3-D objects and events. With the help of the supercomputer Cray-1 and other now techniques, Gary Demos developed the sophisticated software program at Digital Productions.

John Whitney, Jr., 37, the son of John Whitney Sr., produced "Terminal Self" in 1971. In this project he departed from the geometrically rigid computer films and achieved a spatial effect with figurative means. He has also sporadically worked together with the concept artist Michael Asher in a film by the latter. Whitney Jr. has worked together with his father since he was 15, produced his own abstract film, and designed a number of computer systems such as the Hybrid Optical Printer. In 1973 he was nominated for an Oscar for his contribution to "Westworld." Presently, the firm is working on a 20–30 minute long digital scene simulation for the movie "The Last Starfighter." Also in preparation are digital scene simulations for the film "2010," the follow-up of "2001." What is sensational about digital scene simulation is that it aims at creating computer scenes that are indistinguishable from nature as well as realistic scenes nonexistent in nature. For this purpose, the firm owns the world's most rapid supercomputer Cray-1 (costs 12 million dollars), a number of VAX and IBM small computers, 4 machines for transforming video into 35 min film, 2 film scanners, 3 Evans & Sutherland image systems, and 3 IMI motion systems for attuning the interactions with the objects. This is ushering in the future of electronic film: a movie simulated 100% with scenes that are still photographically so realistic that the audience is not able to distinguish real live action from simulated action. Digital scene simulation is the future of the digital image, of digital art. The example of Digital Productions and the relationship of father to son shows how a formerly marginalized form of art such as the abstract graphic film can become the centerpoint of a new industry. Also, it becomes clear that the experience and efforts over many years in avant-garde film, in particular, in abstract film (from V. Eggeling and C. Fischinger in the twenties to the Whitney brothers, James and John, in the forties) pointed to the future and laid the foundations for a technological revolution of industry. From abstract film to simulation computer film, a new form of film is evolving, a new form of vision and unlimited manipulation of visual data. Since the computer-generated imagery can be stored on both video and film and also be mixed with real scenes, computer animation incorporates the future; the future can be named digital image.

Digital Video

A preliminary stage of this development is the integration of video and computer technology: the digital video. This amalgam is inherent to video itself. In film the picture frame remains untouched; only from the collision of two frames, from the interval of two frames was it possible to construct meaning, motion, action. By contrast, in video it is possible through computer technology to manipulate each single pixel's color and form by means of a computer. The access to each of the 1,000 pixels of 1,000 video lines by means of the computer, and the possibility of changing each single pixel as one pleases, allow for individual, subjective manipulation of the image as in painting and an authentic representation as in photography. After fire and electricity, the digital image stands for the third promethetic instrument of artistic representation, that is, simulation. The highly advanced technology of the digital image, its potential for simulation through computer technology, give the individual unlimited access, unlimited possibilities to construct a new visual culture, a new democratic Renaissance.

Notes

1. Ivan E. Sutherland, "Sketchpad: A Man-Machine Graphical Communication System," Conference Proceedings, Spring Joint Computer Conference, AFIPS Press, 1963.

2. Timothy E. Johnson, "Sketchpad III: A Computer-Program for Drawing in Three Dimensions," Conf. Proc. Spring Joint Com. Conf., AFIPS Press, 1963.

3. L. G. Roberts, "Machine Perception of Three-Dimensional Solids," Tech. Rept. 315, MIT Lincoln Lab., May 1963, and in: Optical and Electro-Optical Information Processing, ed. J. Tippet et al, MIT Press, 1965.

4. Thomas G. Hagan, Richard J. Nixon, and Luis J. Schaefer, "The Adage graphics terminal," Adage Inc. Boston. Conf. Proc., Fall Joint Computer Conference, AFIPS Press, 1968.

5. J. E. Bresenham, "Algorithm for Computer Control of a Digital Plotter," IBM Systems Journal 4, no. 1, 1965.

6. W. Jack Bouknight, "A Procedure for Generation of Three-Dimensional Half-toned Computer Graphics Presentation," Communications of the ACM, Sept. 1970.

7. J. E. Warnock, "A Hidden Surface Algorithm for Computer Generated Halftone Pictures," Technical Report, June 1969, University of Utah.

8. Henri Gouraud, "Continuous Shading of Curved Surfaces," IEEE Transactions on Computers, June 1971.

9. Edwin Catmull, "Computer Display of Curved Surfaces," Proc. of the Conference on Computer Graphics, Pattern Recognition and Date Structure, May 1974. IEEE.

10. James F. Blinn, "Models of Light Reflections for Computer Synthesized Pictures," Computer Graphics 11, no. 2 (Summer 1977).

11. K. C. Knowlton, "A Computer Technique for the Production of Animated Movies," AFIPS Conf. Proc., Vol. 25, 1964, SJCC, Sparan Books, N.Y. K. C. Knowlton, "Computer Produced Movies," in: System Analysis by Digital Computers, ed. F. F. Kuo and J. F. Kaiser, Wiley & Son, 1966. K. C. Knowlton, "Collaborations with Artists—A Programmer´s Reflections," graphic.

12. C. Levinthal, "Computer Construction and Display of Molecular Models," film.

13. E. E. Zajac, "Computer-Made Perspective Movies as a Scientific and Communication Tool," Comm ACM, 7, no. 3 (March 1964).

14. E. E. Zajac, "Two-gyro, Gravity Gradient Attitude Control System," Bell Telephone Laboratories, film.

15. S. Vanderbeek, J. H. Whitney, Einige mit Hilfe des Computers hergestellte Zeichentrickfilme.

16. Design and the Computer. Design Quarterly 66/67, Walter Art Center, Minneapolis.

17. A. M. Noll, "The Digital Computer as a Creative Medium," IEEE Spectrum, October 1967.

18. J. Reichardt, Cybernetic Serendipity, the Computer and the Arts, Studio International, London and New York 1968.

19. F. I. Parke, "Computer Generated Animation of Faces," Proceedings of the AMC, August 1972.

20. Ronald J. Hackathorn, "Anima II: A 3-D Color Animation System," Computer Graphics 11, no. 2 (Summer 1977).

MIDI — What It Is and What It Means to Electronic Artists

Robert Moog

MIDI stands for Musical Instrument Digital Interface. It is a new standard specification, drawn up by several prominent manufacturers of electronic musical instruments, for transferring information among electronic musical instruments and controlling computers. Whereas audio cables enable a musician to send sound material from one instrument to another, a MIDI network enables a musician to send musical commands and gestures among two or more MIDI-equipped devices. Thus, for instance, a performer may "play" two or more sound-producing devices (such as synthesizers) from a single keyboard, use one control panel to adjust the operation of several devices, synchronize a network of instruments with a "master clock," or use a personal computer to record, process, and play back keyboard performances, sequences, panel control settings, and so forth.

MIDI-equipped instruments have 5 pin DIN sockets that accept or deliver MIDI signals. To interconnect MIDI-equipped instruments, a musician simply uses a standard two-wire MIDI cable that plugs into the instruments' sockets. No special wiring or adjustments is required.

Technically, MIDI is a digital, serial, bidirectional interface. The term "digital" means that all information is represented as a stream of numbers. Thus, for instance, when a musician plays a keyboard of a MIDI-equipped instruments, numbers corresponding to the keys which he depresses are transmitted as the keys are depressed. The term "serial" means that the numbers are transmitted one bit at a time, a feature that allows instrument builders to use simple, reliable connectors and cables. Under the MIDI specification, the rate of information transfer is about 30,000 bits per second. A complete command, consisting typically of about thirty bits, thus takes about a thousandth of a second to transmit. Finally, the term bidirectional means that information may flow in both directions between two MIDI-equipped instruments. For instance, a keyboard instrument may be connected to a MIDI-equipped computer, and the computer used both to record and play back MIDI information.

Although MIDI was originally designed to interconnect keyboard-controlled electronic musical instruments, drum machines, and small personal computers, it may also be used to transmit a wide variety of control signals of the types that are used by experimental musicians, sculptors, dancers, and other artists who employ networks of electronic instruments. One feature of MIDI which is of considerable importance to all artists is the ability of an instrument builder to tailor his own application to the standard MIDI protocol. Thus for instance, the same personal computer that can record and play back a keyboard performance, can also record and play back continuous sound changes, complex lighting commands, and robot movements. Hardware for recording, processing, and playing back MIDI commands is generally inexpensive and widely available. With this equipment, artists who use electronic instruments for performance or for creation of environments are now able to coordinate the operation of a network of instruments with unprecedented ease and convenience. In my presentation, I demonstrate exactly what is required to adapt standard MIDI instruments and software to control complex sound changes, lighting, and mechanical movement. My illustrations will include a system with several touch sensitive controllers for use in an interactive environment.

Ten Indications of an Emerging Computer Culture

Hannes Leopoldseder

The Ars Electronica Computer Culture Days aim at discussing and trying to represent the possibilities and consequences of the changes in our culture and in our society, caused by the basic technology of micro-electronics.

The explosive technical development leads to an ever-growing information deficit on the possibilities, but also on the consequences of the computer in all spheres of our life. Thus, the Computer Culture Days want to be a forum for discussing possibilities and problems.

The focal point of Computer Culture Days 1986 at the ORF (Upper Austria Regional Studio) is the new world of images. A new driving force is added to the art form of video by the possibilities generated by the computer. For the first time in the German speaking area, the ORF-VIDEONALE within Computer Culture Days intends to introduce the broad television audience to the art form of video: a television week with different images.

Today, the image has become a battleground of different cultures. Not only does the perception of reality change, a new world of images is evolving.

Computer culture is understood in the broader and in the narrower sense of the word: in the broader sense asking the question of how far the computer changes our lives, our society, and our attitudes; and in the more narrow sense, how far the computer as a tool influences cultural and artistic processes and artistic creation and in how far a new creativity is emerging. The application of the computer in the sphere of art and in the media has become an integral part of overall development.

For this reason, a set of ten indications is to attempt a by no means complete outline of the computer culture environment—to be understood as reflection stimuli, environmental determinatives, and impulses.

1. Computer Culture Is an Emerging Culture

Generally speaking, the computer as key technology is still in its initial stage. Would we determine the computer age by a period of a hundred years, we would find ourselves somewhere around the year ten of this era. Today's preschool children, growing up with video clips and home computers, will consider the computer as an ever-ready instrument and tool.

They will have daily contact with the computer—on their jobs and at home. A culture is evolving that is characterized very decisively by the computer in its requirements as well as in its possibilities. When today's computer kids will be grandfathers, computer culture may well be in its prime.

2. Computer Culture Calls for a New Alphabet, a New Language, a New Way of Thinking

The Computer as a tool has brought forth a new alphabet, a new language, i.e. the binary alphabet, binary thinking. The computer develops a language of its own, a specific computer language. Hardly any other technical key innovation has produced such a variety of new terms, expressions, etc., at so great a speed. The children who grow up with the computer learn the computer language as they learn other skills. They grow up with the computer alphabet.

The computer creates a new language. In technical discussions on the computer terms are being used that otherwise only serve to describe human thinking and human behavior. The computer develops a jargon of its own, the jargon of thinking. New terms, such as "reprogram," are smoothly integrated into colloquial language.

3. Computer Culture Demands the Computer-Literate Learning Society

Compared to other technical innovations, the computer is a machine with intelligent products. It is focussed on information, on knowledge. New technical developments have taken place at all times; what is really new is the rapid succession of these quantum leaps. The change brought about by the computer requires understanding the computer, its language, its thinking, its alphabet. In fact, we are really living in a time of upheaval: therefore, computer culture leads to pros and cons in our society: on the one hand, its followers, the computer-literates, and on the other hand, its adversaries, the computer-illiterates. The computer thus requires constant learning.

In a century of upheaval, computer culture causes the temporary emergence of elites, similar to the elites that had formed after the invention of the printing press, those people who had command of the alphabet. To be able to make use of the medium "book," of the written word, it is necessary to be able to read, to be literate. The teaching of the alphabet to ever-increasing groups of the population led to a reduction of elites. This process took place in the course of several centuries: and still, even today little more than half of the world population are literates. While the transmission of knowledge through the book required reading as a prerequisite, the next major media innovation, the electronic medium television, through its world of images, once again made knowledge accessible without preconditions.

And the computer, regarded as a medium, offers a new possibility of gaining knowledge: here again, as was the case 500 years earlier, when the printing press was invented, knowledge of the alphabet is necessary—knowledge of the computer alphabet. Those who master the language of the computer are therefore to be counted among an elite, an elite that is steadily growing.

It is the simultaneous existence of two classes, that of the computer-literates and that of the computer-illiterates, that confronts our century of upheaval, the century of the key technology microelectronics with all the problems that are, at present, related to the introduction of new technologies into discussions in our society and in economy: the threat of the individual by new technologies, the worry about loss of job, the feeling of being at the mercy of an inscrutable global system.

The capacity of using the computer, however, is not equal to the simple skill of being able to read and write. The computer alphabet is far more complex: it needs the overall understanding of the computer's mode of operation. The computer alphabet is more than the capacity to use it, it is a question of an overall understanding, especially when the computer of the fifth generation will practically be an intelligent machine.

The computer alphabet does not call for the mathematician, for the well-trained calculating genius; it calls for *homo universalis*.

4. Computer Culture Requires Restructuring of Work, Leisure Time, and Society

We today live in an age in which the question is not the further development of existing inventions but a transition to entirely new techniques. While, e. g. mechanical control has constantly been improved over the years, the electronic regulator suddenly brings the transition to a new era, at the same time disqualifying the work of decades. The computer replaces wide fields of mechanical work.

Hannes Leopoldseder *Ten Indications of an Emerging Computer Culture*

Therefore, computer culture is marked by a decisive change in the world of work, and thus in economy and in the effects on leisure time, on our entire life. As with any other period of upheaval, computer culture may have a drastic impact on the individual—loss of job, changes in the sphere of work, the necessity of on-the-job reeducation.

5. Computer Culture Requires the Screen as Major Tool in Home and Office

The significant universal tool of computer culture is the electronic screen. The screen is the pet of computer culture—at home as well as in the office. The television screen has developed into the universal communication medium of the information age, the screen is the paper of the Gutenberg age.

Its applications are more or less unlimited. And the screen has also become a new medium for the artist.

6. Computer Culture Permits a New Type of Artist

Using the term "artist," most people think of painters, composers, architects, poets, singers, or actors. Computer programmers become a new type of artist. Their potential is creativity. Their art can be the programme. Software is the "hottest" commodity of computer culture, the product of a creative process.

Painters, designers, composers, graphic artists working as computer programmers in their relevant spheres of art do not only receive a new tool—the computer also demands a new way of thinking. The computer brings forth a new type of universal artist—in the sense of Leonardo da Vinci.

Mathematical-logical thinking as well as artistic concept are integral parts of the artistic process. Proceeding from the programmer, computer culture thus allows for a new type of artist, conventional limits being partially abolished.

7. Computer Culture Permits a New World of Images and Sound

"New instruments and new technologies," says Pierre Boulez in an interview with *Newsweek* in 1986, "bring something into music that had not been there before." The computer permits a new world of sounds in music. However, the computer's most revolutionary impact is that on images: the computer-generated image contains a new reality; it creates a new image-reality.

For centuries, artists had dreamt of the electronic creation of images: to be able to move a picture, to transform a picture, to give a dynamic dimension to the picture. By combining video and computer graphics and television technology with the computer, the artist is offered new possibilities—a new synthetic world of images is created.

The synthetic images have an autonomous degree of reality; they are products of the digital image creation. Television provides us with a secondary reality, with a reality that consists of the elements of primary reality.

The computer-generated image, on the other hand, creates an autonomous primary world of images that does not exist in our reality: the world of images of computer culture itself turns into a primary reality. We no longer deal with elements of an actual reality but with a synthetically generated new reality. A reality in three-dimensional space, in any imaginable motion, dynamism, and transformation.

An essential condition for creating the new world of images is to be seen in the combination of video and television, computer graphics and animation. A new world of images, created by media artists, results from the concurrence of these spheres.

8. Computer Culture Permits New Networks

The computer is a meta-machine, a metaphysical machine, as Sherry Turkle calls it. Being a universal machine it opens up new possibilities of communication, new networks. The world of computer culture is surrounded by global networks: distances change, space and time are being set into new relations.

The computer networks create an entirely new level of communication by combining computer, circuits, and satellites. The global networks are still in their infancy, telecommunication, electronic mail, teleconferencing, etc., create a new virtual space determining life in the computer culture—full of opportunities, but also full of threats.

9. Computer Culture Permits New Media

The computer establishes itself in computer culture as a universal machine, containing and integrating all media and permitting new media. Only the combination of media creates new possibilities in quantum leaps. The magnetic storage media are still in their beginnings. They may well become for electronic information what the pencil is for paper.

Beside the book, the CD-Rom disc might become a new cultural medium. In the future, CD discs will be able to take over several functions of the book. CD discs will be data-storage devices for everyone. Dictionaries, encyclopedia, libraries will become accessible to everyone through the development of the computer's storage technology.

10. Computer Culture Allows New Experiences in Art and Culture

The computer as a universal machine will become an effective tool in practically all spheres of art; in music, in literature, in theatre, in film—new, up to now unthinkable cultural experiences will evolve.

The computer as a tool and its universality as a mega-machine causes a revolution as it finally influences all fields of art and culture. The spectrum comprises the new world of images, the new world of sounds, but also the multi-media and video theater and large-scale projects in open space. A new environment art is emerging and developing, as well as new events in open space—in Austria, the spectrum reaches from the open-air events of the Linz Sound Cloud to André Heller's "Fire Theatre" or the large-scale events by Jean Michel Jarre. He characterized the five-million-dollar multi-media spectacle that he created on the occasion of NASA's 25th anniversary in Houston, Texas, in 1986 as follows: "in this event, the computers are not only necessary to safeguard the technical functions; the computer is the Instrument as such, with which the event can be created."

Art from the Screen

Herbert W. Franke

Those among the constructivists who used the first mechanical plotters for the realization of their concepts 25 years ago were much impressed by the exact programming technique. This technique not only provided them with the possibility of a precise representation of graphic elements but also, for the first time, with the chance to include more complicated objects in their performance. With the emergence of versatile scanning devices, this method was somewhat forgotten. Today, one prefers the spectacular photo-realistic pictures from the computer. In connection with these latter pictures, however, the mathematical method, also for artistic purposes, has regained importance, not so much for the production of works of art themselves, but for the preparation of systems designed to facilitate the work of future generations.

The tasks in this field do not concern the problems of "hardware," of the instruments, but the increasingly important "software"—i.e., everything dealing with the organization of calculation and logical processes, with the conversion of data. These activities are an integral part of graphics, too. Undoubtedly, the development of effective output-units is of great importance; at the same time, the inclusion of graphic instruction into the procedure-oriented languages is indispensable for utilizing this very equipment. In the course of time, entirely new ideas were developed that have their impact on application. Here one has to mention the so-called "rubber band graphic" by Ivan E. Sutherland who has, apart from other pioneer achievements in the field of computer design systems, introduced the following seemingly simple principle: with a sort of pencil the user is able to draw straight lines at their endpoints all over the screen; a similarly practical device is a procedure to fix the exact position of points; all you need to do is to designate to the computer, with a pencil, a certain point on the tableau, near the exact position; then, the computer will determine the exact coordinates on the basis of general data such as that the point ought to lie on a given screen or at the cross-point of two lines; the computer chooses the nearest point to which the given data apply.

Step into the Third Dimension

In the field of software we have witnessed an important step similar to the one taken with the transition from the plotter to the scope screen. This innovation is the progress from the two-dimensional to the three-dimensional. At an early stage, computer designers had found out that their systems were not only suitable for the graphic representation of data lists but also for the production of autonomous graphic documents. Thus, they turned to circuit diagrams, maps, and architectural horizontal and vertical projections. All these are limited to the two-dimensional sphere—the architectural example suggesting the production of pictures in perspective apart from the mere projections. In principle, a three-dimensional configuration is sufficiently determined by horizontal and vertical projections, thus making a drawing in perspective a mere matter of routine. Here, certain mathematical methods are needed that do not pose any basic difficulties, that would, however, were they carried out by hand, take up so much time that the architect prefers to use a three-dimensional model in order to give a notion of the completed building. The fast computer manages calculations like these in no time, a fact that brought about a gradual transition from the second to the third dimension.

With high-capacity systems, the calculation is carried out within fractions of seconds, as a result of which one can calculate the views of permanently changing perspectives at such speed that the sequence of images equals a tour around the building or the turn of a camera to the building or— if so desired—into the interior of the building. This method, CAD (computer-aided design), was developed for the purposes of tool making and mechanical engineering. Frequently, one restricts oneself to a schematic drawing in which only the edges of the envisaged object are shown, to a so-called "net-graphic." Such objects are transparent and have the disadvantage that one cannot easily determine which parts are in the foreground and which in the background. But this problem, too, can be solved mathematically. It is possible to incorporate routines into the programmes that determine, on the basis of given data, which parts of the surface have to be covered, thus producing far more realistic images. While previously having had to deal with a network, a transparent skeleton, the graphic image with covered surfaces is no longer a structure of edges but a structure of planes. This, however, raises a new problem, the problem of illumination, of shadows. Again, we need mathematics—on the one hand in order to calculate those parts lying in the shadow, and on the other hand to determine the so-called "lightness of the plane." Here, one uses optic laws according to which one can calculate what part of the light resorting from the source and reflected by planes of differing inclination, will reach the viewer. This calculation is extremely complicated as it has to be carried out for every single point of the image.

Even at this stage we have still not reached full reality, as the objects with which we are confronted are normally not defined by level planes like those of a polished diamond. The images resulting from net-graphics are therefore only an approximation to the real form, reached by gradually reducing the size of the plane-parts to such an extent that we get a simulation of a continuous process, a surface curvature. It is unnecessary to stress the fact that the calculation of this kind of design in perspective takes very much time.

In the fields of science, technology, and architecture one can manage with schematic images that differ substantially from a realistic representation. Here, one has arrived at the limit that is decisive for practical use. Any improvement of quality beyond this limit leads into the sphere of aesthetic tasks, in no way to be understood as purely artistic ones—the necessary means are hardly available— but foremost those of the so-called applied arts such as commercial design, illustration, etc. The costs for production increase dramatically if one does not limit oneself to single images but wishes to have sequences of images, films; in this case, the calculation work described above has to be repeated 25 times a second. In order to solve problems like these, one needs the largest computers in the world, and even they do not manage to perform them in real time. The necessary calculating time lies far above the required 25th part of a second. Therefore, the material for films is being delivered in single images that are being put together as in old-time trick films. The necessary funds can be raised by wealthy institutions only. Therefore, this method has up to now been primarily used in fantastic science-fiction films and in advertising. The explanation is simple: fantastic films show scenes that do not exist in reality—figures from fairy tales, landscapes of science fiction; computer animation in photo-realistic representation has created an unbelievable semblance of reality in the fantastic film and explains its considerable prosperity. Advertising, especially in the American "commercials," has similar tasks. Often, a product has to be introduced that has just gone into production and is therefore not available for filming. Here, the method of computer design is able, on the basis of construction plans, to produce images of an object that the viewer cannot detect as having been created by the computer.

The high cost for the production of scenes like that is caused—as indicated above—by the demand for photo-realistic reproduction. The costs for the procedure can be lowered substantially if one is satisfied with the solution of approximation. A possible form of application is simulation, for example in the training of astronauts, pilots, or engine drivers. For these purposes, one uses cabins in which the cockpits are reproduced true to nature, only the windows are replaced by screens. And it needs a computer system that registers all the trainee's actions and calculates images that could be seen through the windows if the maneuvers were carried out correctly. As one cannot foresee whether the learner will act correctly, the system has also to react to unforeseeable orders; and here one needs real time. Consequently, simulator images are still rather schematic, partly because of the lack of details and the abandonment of the exact calculation of optic reflection.

The users of calculating systems who try to solve new tasks with them have a two-fold function: on the one hand, they dedicate themselves to their very special problem that they will have to bring into an adequate form for processing by the computer, e.g. by translating it into a programming language. On the other hand, they do pioneer work by determining with these programmes the general outlines of a software that will be available to future users. Once the method has been sufficiently elaborated its application becomes routine: the task is reduced to the scientific, technical, or artistic topics. In the field of two-dimensional graphics this process is well advanced. There even exists a more or less official norm, the so-called GKS (*graphisches Kernsystem*—graphic core system), choosing of a multitude of principally available possibilities a certain number of possibilities offering the best prerequisites for graphic work with the computer. No norms have as yet been set up for three-dimensional graphics; certain methods have, however, already emerged that will facilitate their use. One of these methods is the construction of stereoscopic objects from simple elements, the forms of which are so highly sophisticated that by their combination and by additive or subtractive overlapping a variety of forms becomes presentable. By multiple application of this method, especially by splitting up into ever smaller units, one can achieve an optional approximation to any given real form.

Even possible movements are already preconceived in specific systems. Thus, it is possible to achieve the rotation of a three-dimensional object in perspective in real time, by means of a manual operation; a suitable input-instrument is the so-called roll-ball. It can be sunk into a table top with only a small part, adapted to the size of the hand, protruding. The ball is mobile and can be moved along any chosen axis of rotation. The system can be established in a manner that allows the drawing on the screen to rotate in the described way, thus becoming visible from different angles. This movement can also be understood in the sense of the viewer or the camera going round the object. Furthermore, it is possible to change the viewing point to any other position; as with rotation, the computer has to carry out certain transformations in real time, in order to simulate a continuous sequence of movements. These preconceived routine modes of viewing offer interesting aspects for artistic use. Among them are unusual perspectives such as viewing buildings from below, and, last but not least, spectacular moves of a camera that would be impossible in reality. A sequence for a film in the series "Star Trek," produced by the computer institute of the Lucas Film Company, caused some excitement: the strip shows an approach from space to a planet, passing on to a flight over a relief of mountains and lakes and finally—view back to the planet falling behind—leading back into space.

Expensive calculating methods have to be applied in order to achieve an effect of reality. Apart from methods serving to improve the quality of pictures, not to be described in detail here, it is a question of perspectives, overlappings, shadows, and the distribution of light. The necessary programmes are partly developed by institutions that also produce the image sequences, being primarily available to them only. Beside the already mentioned group of Lucas Film—they have in the meantime established an independent firm, PIXAR—one has to make special reference to two university institutes associated with enterprises: one of them is the Laboratory of Computer Graphics at the New York Institute of Technology, NYIT, the other one the Institute of Computer Graphics of the Ohio State University in Ohio, under the direction of Charles Csuri. The affiliated enterprises are responsible for the commercial distribution of the systems after testing.

We can suppose that problems of computer graphics related to geometric questions have been generally solved. Today, the main efforts in development are to be found in the representation of certain structures; one might say they have shifted to the sphere of semantics. With the help of Computer Aided Design it has become possible to produce photo-realistic images of all technically produced objects, machines, vehicles, buildings etc. A curious problem arises when using CAD in the field of art: everything appearing on the screen is as perfectly clean and faultless as would hardly be the case in reality. So, if such objects were to appear e.g. in realistic films, one would have to "age" them by some special programming method. As far as we know, experts up to now have evaded this question as it seems to be fairly easy to produce rust stains or scratches if required. At the moment there remains a sufficient number of complex problems raising fundamental questions and demanding the application of new methods. This is the case when natural formations are to be depicted, such as the surface of planets or the reliefs of mountain ranges with valleys in between. Yet, here one is still concerned with solid unchangeable objects to which one can readily apply the routines of geometrical optics. A different question is according to which points of view a mountain landscape ought to be composed. Certainly it is no problem to construct a specific mountain or even a specific landscape by means of computer design. However, the experts of the institutes intend something else: they wish to find a generally applicable method for the routine representation of such surface forms. In this context it seems desirable that the basic formulas contain parameters by which it is possible to describe characteristic features of the objects. Take the example of a mountain range—such parameters might be the average altitude above zero level, the average inclination of the slopes, the degree of cleavage, etc. With this task an important step is being taken towards a scope of propositions that are no longer technically but predominantly aesthetically oriented. While there are differing technical as well as artistic applications of the various procedures of the three-dimensional representation, the programmes for the set-up of landscapes, of clouds, water, plants, and animals are only important in the fields of applied and "pure" arts. Once again, they are aesthetically oriented tasks; the means of their solution, however, are to be found in mathematics and programming techniques. Strangely enough, this involves mathematical principles that hardly ever are applied in technology but seem to be especially adapted to natural processes. Apart from any artist's goals, this opens up a multitude of fascinating questions connected to the structural principles of mountain formation, growth processes, and similar phenomena.

Random Distributions and Fractals

Closely related to this, we find a principle that has been tendered by computer software ever since the very beginnings of computer design, i.e. the principle of randomness. This seems a contradiction in itself, considering the computer as a machine for the generation of order, whereas randomness is characterized by the very absence of any order. In fact, it is not real randomness that is being provided in the framework of various programming languages but a so-called pseudo-randomness. This is to say that in spite of an outward appearance of chaotic distribution, combination of color, etc., there does exist a hidden principle of order. One might take this as a starting point for discussions on the differences between randomness and pseudo-randomness, involving interesting mathematical and also philosophical considerations. As for the application in art, however, the only thing that matters is the

Herbert W. Franke *Art from the Screen*

fact that those who deal with the product, possibly a work of art, are unable to detect any order in the multitude of forms that count. In this connection one might raise a number of very interesting questions of information psychology and perception theory with a view to aesthetic effects that will, however, not be dealt with in this paper.

Be it random, be it pseudo-random—there are only a few applications in science and technology, e.g. for the various tasks of simulation; on the other hand, the first artistically interested programmers already used this phenomenon by incorporating not only the computer-inherent order but also the elements of randomness produced by it. An entirely different aspect gave new actuality to the element of randomness in our days, in connection with the reproduction of forms of nature. For natural structures such as fir needles spread on the ground, stones littering the seashore, the pattern of raindrops on a window pane, it is not important whether they are random or pseudo-random distributions but only whether one is able to achieve a seemingly correct reproduction by means of "random instruction" established for this purpose. In many cases this is possible; in even more cases one comes up with so-called "stochastic" processes: processes that can be characterized as "partially subject to randomness." By clever combination of order and randomness, by setting certain focal points, by fixing average quantities and by establishing "interference factors" one can reproduce an even greater number of natural textures. Some examples of stochastic distributions: logs floating on water, leaping flames, sparks flashing from red-hot metal. In all these cases there is a certain given direction to which, however, the elements do not stick exactly; they are said to be dispersed around an average value.

In recent years, a new focal topic of mathematics has unexpectedly led to a variety of groupings in photo-realistic computer design, i.e. the "fractals" defined by Benoit B. Mandelbrot; numerous mathematical papers and several books have been written recently on this topic. It is astonishing that these structures have also aroused the attention of artistically interested circles and become the subject of several exhibitions, amongst them an international event organized by the German Goethe Institut. The only thing to be said here about the nature of the fractals is the fact that they can be made visible with the help of lines that are—as their name indicates—"multiple refracted." And these refracted parts, e.g. edges interrupting the course of a curve, are not only to be found in macroscopic viewing; this principle of refraction repeats itself into the very smallest spheres.

We know of regularly structured fractals, of which the "snowflake curve" is a well-known example. We can imagine this as a regular hexagon whose collateral lines are interrupted by prongs. These prongs are composed of line elements that again are interrupted by prongs of the same geometry, reduced in size accordingly. In addition, there are also irregular fractals, composed on the basis of a principle of randomness. They, too, show this "endlessly refracted" character, with the distinction, however, that here the formation of prongs, interruptions, and corners is not subject to fixed propositions but changes from one step of reduction to the other.

When Mandelbrot confronted the public with his fractals, his colleagues were fascinated by the originality of the idea; they were at the same time certain that they were a synthetic product of thought with no counterpart in reality. To everybody's surprise the character of the fractals has in the meantime proved to have become part of the principles of natural structures. Finally, it ought to be mentioned that we have been informed of the first practical application of fractals to the solution of the tasks of computer design; it was Loren Carpenter who had used the fractals for the construction of a mountain range relief. This idea is obvious: from an overall view, a mountain range does not only seem to be irregularly structured as to the situation of elevations and valleys, but also consists of smaller valleys in the various mountains and smaller elevations in the valleys in which we find further hills—this structure could be continued into the microscopic sphere. And this is a typical characteristic of fractals.

Mountain ranges composed of fractals have since become part of the everyday appearance of the computer simulation of landscapes; what once used to seem so logical has started to meet with

Herbert W. Franke *Art from the Screen*

renewed criticism. The Swiss Martin Heller, for example, proposes a completely different method—he believes that one should, when modelling an alpine landscape, depart from realistic preconditions, from a given tectonic of plateaus, and carry out the changes according to the model of erosive processes as they happen in reality. Because Heller is an informatics expert specializing in computerized geological cartography, one might consider his objection as the exaggerated postulate of a scientist. But he is also a renowned computer artist and reasons with aesthetic arguments in favour of his proposal. He feels that his method would not only offer a closer proximity to the real processes but also safeguard a greater variety and thus aesthetic improvement. Doubtlessly, his opinion should not be left unheeded. Fractal mountain ranges will suffice for short-term scenic backgrounds. However, if a strange landscape in itself is to be the subject of a computerized animation sequence, the "scientific" method will offer far more impressive possibilities of forms. Thus, one could replace the notion of real terrestrial conditions and postulate a mountain formation that does not exist on our planet. The wealth of pictorial forms that could evolve from this basis would be, also from an aesthetic point of view, a "better reality" even though it does not exist in nature.

Modelling of Life

Similar considerations could be attached to various other tasks of modern computer design and computer animation; we shall, however, restrict ourselves here to mentioning the most important problems only. Among them are other structures that one was able to come by with the aid of fractals— e.g. the distribution of clouds. The representation of moving water, such as the surface of a lake or of the sea, was an even more difficult task. One of the first to dedicate themselves to this goal was the computer designer Nelson Max from Lawrence Livermore Laboratory in California. The problem of simulating the motion of waves in a physically correct manner proved to be very difficult. Simple cases such as the wave movement resorting from the centre of a circular container are easy to handle, but nature confronts us with irregular coastlines from which refraction starts out, which in turn is overlapped by the primary wave motion. This task cannot be solved exactly; therefore, the author's quality is illustrated more by his capacity to take into account all the substantial characteristic parts and leave out everything that would surpass the framework of his task or to replace it by a random motion.

Bill Beeves of the PIXAR group has been concerned in recent years with various examples of textures for which he found common valid logarithms of representation. Among them, there are licking flames, as well as waving cornfields. Plant structures, grass, woods, and individual trees, too, were subjects of research by Bill Reeves and his colleagues.

Finally, the treatment of living creatures brings forth entirely new aspects. In some cases, such as the famous commercial strip "Sexy Robot" by Mssrs. Robert Abel, Hollywood, the task was solved by hiring a human model and fixing lamps to shoulders, knees, and other prominent parts of the body, thereby studying the process of movement envisaged for the animation sequence. Other, more research-oriented institutes such as Ohio State University and New York Tech tried to tackle the problem at the roots. As one could not expect the very first attempt at a true-to-life representation of known animal species to be successful, they started out with fantastic beings. In Columbus, it was a beast of prey, similar to a tiger; in Long Island, the headquarters of NYIT, the experts worked with an ant-like robot-being in the framework of a planned science-fiction film. In these cases, the reproduction of movement was not achieved by plane projection as it is done in painting or film, but by a method that reminds us more of the construction of a machine than of a process of imaging. The designer starts out from the three-dimensional structure of the skeleton (that need not be true to nature as long as it functions with regard to the joints) and develops—e.g. by fixing the limiting value of the angular motion— the changes of form that result from running, jumping, turning of the head, etc.

With a view to the complexity of the task, requiring fully qualified programmers, it is evident that this method has not yet been applied in pure art. But it does open up remarkable perspectives, modes of procedure that have nothing in common with the traditional forms of painting or with the three-dimensional classical sculpture that mainly takes into account the surfaces. The term "creative" in the true sense of the word seems adequate for the construction that proves essential here—because the work of the designer comes far closer to a creation than to an image.

While we are here dealing with activities the consequences of which for artistic processes are to be expected for the future, the same goes for the most complicated problem of all, i.e. the computerized modelling of man. One of the reasons for the difficulties encountered is to be seen in the fact that the human body and the human face are so familiar to us that even the slightest deviation irritates us. Nevertheless, some programmers are tackling this problem and especially that of the face and its changing expressions. For the purposes of feature films the main problem is the movement of lips synchronous to the language and—a connected problem—the facial expression suited to the content. We have still a long way to go before we will achieve a physiognomy close to real life; we have, however, succeeded in simulating the human face so that it has become animated, although in a puppet-like manner. The movement of the eyes, the lifting of brows, the changing form of lips—all those suggest human sentiments that, however, seem very strange because of the metallic smoothness of surface forms. Representations like that are especially odd because the faces are not framed by hair, thus giving the impression of animated masks. The reason is to be seen in the fact that up to now nobody has been successful—or maybe nobody has really tried—to image human hair on the computer screen.

Modes of Alienation

The next years will probably bring about an increase of the number of structures that can be handled by computer design and computer animation and used by means of user software. This will be the moment when this method will be freely available to those users who are not interested in the development of graphic software but only in design.

Certain critics have objected that the simulation of reality, its translation into programme instructions, could not be considered an artistic or creative act and had nothing to do with art. In this extreme formulation the argument is certainly not valid. However, the problem of imaging in the classical way now shifts to a task of synthesis in the sense of a technical construction. This comprises the entire variety of our world in realistic presentation of all natural and man-made forms. There are various reasons why this kind of painting is no longer appreciated in our days; they need not be dealt with in detail. It is not a question whether applications are finally to be expected in the field of the "pure" or the applied arts, or whether works like that meet with the approval or disapproval of critics. It is, moreover, the question of finding a general solution to a problem and the fact that a new approximation has been found. Experiences have shown that results of this kind have proved to be important impulses for art, too, possibly as starting points for entirely new tasks.

According to a widespread opinion, the imitation of reality is no artistic achievement, from a work of art one expects some kind of alienation, frequently called "heightening"; this means that an effect utilized at random is not considered sufficient, one expects an underlying formative meaning, such as a clarification by reduction to the essential or a dissolution of familiar forms for the stimulation of associative processes. Both the representatives of real-simulation and their critics are aware of the fact that profane reality is not as important in art as in the task mentioned above. The representatives of real-simulation think it desirable to master the representation of reality before turning to alienation. But why take the complicated way of realistic representation when there is a far simpler access to the interesting effects of alienation?—that is to say, the way of limiting oneself to the approxima-

Herbert W. Franke *Art from the Screen*

tion methods in simulation, thus automatically achieving deviations from the naturalistic image.

In fact, certain artistic works in the field of computer design simply resulted from the application of inadequate methods of imaging. Some of the occurring effects are known in traditional art as well as in experimental photography, for example the reduction to contour lines, the dissolution into rough courses, the attribution of wrong colours. However, many of the occurring phenomena are new, produce images of unusual charm, and thus doubtless enrich the spectrum of representational possibilities. From an aesthetic point of view it might be of interest to study these effects as to their applicability to specific goals.

The film "Tron" may serve as a good example. Although it was produced only a few years ago, the methods of computerized graphic representation have made such progress since that the images shown in this "classic" might be considered inadequate by today's standards. Regrettably, this film has a rather commonplace plot in the form of a primitive action-spectacle. On the other hand, the film shows fascinating, up to then unknown pictures that might be the vision of a fantastic city of the future. They were produced with a method of computerized design that had no aspirations to photorealism but used deviation from the usual as an element of style. This is justified by a clever trick in the plot's concept: the scene is set in an imaginary world situated in the sphere of adventurous computer games. By a trick, the hero is banned to this place—and this gives the opportunity to demonstrate transparent buildings resisting the power of gravity, utopian vehicles racing around corners with breathtaking speed, fantastic machines, and an exceptionally elegant craft, a hovering aircraft propelled by sun-sails.

It might be suspected that alienation effects based on inadequate processing might lose their attraction after some time and that the better, because more general method is the reduction of achieved reality. Here, artists themselves can truly determine their own kind of alienation and adapt it to their own purposes. There is yet another way of achieving unusual image innovation on the basis of the representation of reality. It is up to the artist to make use of all means of real-simulation and to stick to the created impression but to deviate from reality in his concept insofar as he himself invents certain objects, creatures, and landscapes by figuring non-existent objects in a realistic presentation—even using optical effects of refraction and diffraction. This style is known in classical art by the term "surrealism." This style is limited by the simple fact that it is technically laborious to abide strictly to the laws of geometry and optics and to work with the multitude of details of an assumed reality. In the field of static images this method has been applied frequently, having however, raised the question whether the precise consideration of the laws of geometry and the exact positioning of lights has anything to do with art; the creative act should be seen in the conceived vision.

A very important additional element is the fact that the computer animation is also able to present these pictures, scenes, and visions in motion; here, the borderline has been crossed within which visual concepts that can be realized by manual means are enclosed. Up to now, there have been only a few short scenes giving an indication of what will someday be possible, also in the field of arts; and even these few examples are mostly packed away in banal science-fiction action so that earnest critics do not think them worth mentioning.

This, too, leads to a shifting of the artistic act of creation from a depicting activity, generally taking into account geometrical projective points of view, to the elaboration of visionary concepts. What is expected from the artist by far surpasses the creation of a single image. When he or she has to deal with sequences of pictures, with processes, they all have to be tuned to one another. To be exact, it needs a conception of an imaginary world with its own multitude of forms and its own laws. For the user of computer animation is by no means confined to the known laws of nature—he can change them at random, something that has already been demonstrated in the film "Tron" with the race bicycles that can go around corners without time delay. It is certainly up to the artist to decide which

Herbert W. Franke *Art from the Screen*

formations to chose, how to conceive a utopian or fantastic scenery. The critical viewer, however, will soon notice whether the artist's concept is homogenous or faulty. There is nothing to be said against showing a world of dissolving clocks, following an idea of Salvador Dali; contrary to the work of the famous surrealist, the production of an instantaneous picture is not enough, it will prove indispensable to reflect on the rules governing dissolving objects.

Interactive Art

In art, the transition to motion is a consequential step, for the traditionally educated painters as well as for the graphic artist who will be utilizing this method in the future. This does by no means exhaust the possibilities offered by the computer technology. An additional, fundamentally important element that can only be realized with the help of the electronic method is that of interactivity. Up to now, talking of image sequences meant film sequences, linear series determined in their logical succession. This limitation complies with the conventional mode of thinking oriented towards film and television. If it is possible to describe an entire series of pictures by means of a computer programme, it is also possible to run the series in any order of succession. Computer-supported design offers one simple example: here, the viewer can choose any desired point of vision by means of the roll-ball. A similar case are the simulation programmes that need not necessarily be regarded as linked to a learning process. The same programme principle makes it possible to fly over the given landscape forms in any chosen direction and—as an additional effect—to go into low-level flight at places of special interest: the mouth of a river, a bridge, a city. In fact, there already exist programmes like that for game purposes (derived from more sophisticated models) to be operated on small computers. It goes without saying that this implies a limitation to considerable simplifications. Let us mention a third case: the Massachusetts Institute of Technology has developed a programme based on the highly detailed mapping of a village. It lets the user stroll through the streets and regard any chosen point. A programme like this might, for example, serve the purpose of acquainting a group of special agents with a location they could not enter before the planned action.

Applications of this kind are undoubtedly practice-oriented; up to now they have hardly ever been used for artistic purposes but they nevertheless indicate surprising expansions of the known method of dealing with images that might be of special interest to the artist. This links up to the method of constructing surrealistic sceneries that was described above, presupposing that it is the artist who determines the manner in which they present themselves, in which way and with which speed the viewer moves through them. Now, there are indications that the viewer, or better the "user," might become able to make his own decisions. The artist offers him the world designed by him and the user takes it up, no longer in a position of passive viewer but of active scrutinizer.

In spite of all the improvements to be expected in the future, the storage capacity of computers will remain a limited one; one could therefore suppose that the worlds designed by the artists have to remain restricted to a segment—a three-dimensional segment. But this does not necessarily have to be the case. A method can be conceived—and has already been practiced tentatively—that would only need limited storage capacity and would nevertheless offer an unlimited "world." This can be achieved in the following manner: the computer constructs the region that the viewer wishes to visit in the very moment in which the relevant direction is being chosen and thus the intention being expressed (this goes unnoticed because of the high speed of calculation). As, on the other hand, the artist is unable to fill an infinite space with objects, he is forced to design his world as a mere concept, that is to say he has to set rules for the formation of landscapes, for the growth of plants, the appearance of animals, etc. Today, the limited calculating capacities prevent a process like this; it will certainly take another ten or twenty years of technical progress before the methods described will become

Herbert W. Franke Art from the Screen

applicable. Artists will be expected to demonstrate an even higher degree of creativity, for they will have to construct a world not of individual objects but according to all-encompassing rules that are in conformity with our laws of nature.

The development of such methods can also progress in a different direction: not with the aim of creating immense spaces but with a view to simulating complex interhuman relations. Although this possibility may seem utopian to us today, there is no reason against its possible realization in the future; and that is why it should be mentioned briefly. It is not unrealistic to imagine that in the next century it will be possible to conceive human characters in a manner that they will not only be visible on screens or projection walls but that they will form societies in which action goes on, communication takes place, and conflicts are settled. With regard to an interactive representation the viewer will not have to remain excluded—it seems possible to attribute to him a certain role in the event so that he becomes a co-actor. These forms of "event games" can be supported by the transition from the close limits of the screen to the larger projection walls and finally to panorama projection. The user then finds himself right in the middle of a world that is modelled to such perfection that it comes very close to reality. It goes without saying that sound effects will be integrated into this kind of representation so that the connection with music can be as close as desired. Another, even more remarkable effect is that there will also be a connection to narrative literature—the concept of action spheres in which the user will make his artistic experiences needs not only visual creativity but also the art of narration.

After having made this excursion into the not too far future and into the imaginary worlds of the computer, it is certainly necessary to recall that we are today still at the very beginning of this development. Compared to the classical arts, computer art is still *in statu nascendi*. It is therefore understandable that the majority of endeavors dedicated to it takes place in the field of instruments whereas truly artistic application is still the exception, last but not least because of the horrendous costs of the necessary systems. There are many indications that this situation will change in coming years—only then will a development set in vehemently that will be governed by creative artists more than by inventors of technologies. Today's products of primitive apparatus will therefore hardly do justice to higher aesthetic criteria. In some few video and computer-created image sequences, however, we are able to get glimpses at the artistic possibilities that can be expected from the future; that is why some people who are interested in the development of contemporary society, and especially in the development of art, consider these very strips to be more remarkable than most of what is to be found in our museums as testimonials of ripe classical art.

The Visual Artist Turns
to Computer Programming

Our experiments in computer art began in 1970. Starting from small computers, very simple algorithms with abstract pointillistic pictures, we went through figurative 2-D drawings and are at this point ' using and developing 3-D realistic techniques. This personal itinerary has followed the improvement of our equipment and especially our own relationship to this equipment. Among other things, it has always taken us the same time to produce an image, no matter how sophisticated our computer is. In fact, we could not resist the urge to add new operations as soon as we gained some time. As techniques piled up, we realized that they can be used, even unexpectedly, again and again. For example our old practice of mixture of pictures, pointillism, and filtering techniques is still available. Also, our aesthetic desire, despite a tentacle geometry, is seeking for light and colors. We believe that some baroque hides in the algorithms. The artists are there to help find it.

I. Without Raster: 1970–1974

We began in 1970 with only a small computer and a line printer. Our wish was to work on continuous variations of colors. We started with a pointillistic approach. Since we could not produce directly a complex color, we assumed that it should result from the optical addition of primary colored points as in printing. We divided the picture into square blocks, computed the complex color of each block corresponding to a given variation of colors, and then realized it by a statistical distribution of elementary points indicated by a letter. The listing was a collection of letters describing the picture. Afterwards, we painted by hand a little square block around each letter, a very tedious activity.

The percentage of basic colors in each square block was determined by several relations:
—a linear relation giving the brightness of the block by addition of the brightness of each colored point,
—some continuous variations for a subset of colors corresponding to a given repartition of level curves on the pictures.

The images produced by this pointillistic method present a granulated structure due to the distribution of the elementary points: the choice of different random algorithms determine different kinds of clusters of points, and thus different visual structures. It was what we called the texture, and we used it as an element of the composition.

To summarize our first pictures, they were built around two elements:
—continuous variation of colors defined by a set of level lines,
—a texture associated to the pointillistic realisation.

Other Equipment = Other Realizations: Punch Cards and Calcomp Plotter

In 1972 we found an IBM 1130 and a punch card. Instead of painting each colored point by hand, we produced, as a result of the program, a series of punch cards to be used as stencils. Each punch card had a code defining its position in the picture and its corresponding color. The rest of the card was used as a stencil for a color. To realize the picture we applied the punched card to the picture

Hervé Huitric / Monique Nahas

support, and used a roller to spread the corresponding color. Since it was faster than painting by hand, we could experiment a little more with the texture's variations. But anyway realizing one picture after having produced the punched cards could take one or two weeks.

After that, in 1973, we got a Calcomp plotter and used it to outline stencils for silk-screens, keeping the same ideas for the color programming. The plotter was used to print one stencil for each basic color of the serigraphy, and we produced the silk-screens with three basic colors (magenta, cyan, and yellow) and with three stencils for each color. The silk-screen was obtained after nine layers of colors. We began to put out multiple products from one program, and to play with permutations of stencils and colors.

II. First Raster: 70 x 56 Pixels, 4,096 Colors, 1975–1978

In 1975 we got our first raster. It had a very low resolution, 70 x 56 pixels, but also 4,096 colors, 16 levels for the red, the green, and the blue. So we abandoned the pointillistic method which has no meaning with such a small number of pixels, and we focused only on color variations. For technical reasons it was only possible to use the Lisp language and integer number, with a 16K computer. So our computations were based on straight lines and circles, using the recursive property of the Lisp language to combine elementary structures.

We first constructed continuous variations of colors delimited by some simple shapes: rectangle, triangle. Each color, R, V, B, had a monotonous relation, increasing or decreasing through the surface. With these basic elements, we experimented with various iterations, keeping the structure of each elementary surface visible.

Then in order to diminish the strict geometry of the pictures, we began to use the iteration of elementary shapes in a nonvisible way. We tiled a surface by successive triangulations, keeping the same values of colors at each border. In this way we obtained folding or depth effects where the construction process by triangulation ceases to be noticeable. Simultaneously we introduced a more flexible relation between the colors and the lines of level, increasing the variations of colors. Then we could obtain color peaks on the picture.

Mixtures and Sequences of Pictures

It became possible to develop a series of picture transformations because a picture could be stored and modified easily, as opposed to the previous situation without raster. The mixture of pictures is a very simple but efficient artistic tool. It is probably as common for people working with computer as for traditional artists mixing their colors. The only condition is to be able to store and retrieve the pictures. With a raster we had all these new facilities.

Our first experience was the simplest: combining two pictures by a barycentric function: $f(x, y) = a \cdot x + (1 - a) \cdot y$ with $0 < a < 1$, x, y are the color values of a given pixel i, j in the two initial pictures, and $f(x, y)$ is the value of that pixel in the mixture. Effects of transparency are easily obtained that way, but at that time we were more interested by the consequences of the mixture on the shades. A surprising result of the mixture was that we could always observe an improvement in the perceptible amount of tints.

By varying the coefficient a from 1 to 0 in the previous relation, we obtained a sequence of pictures, going continuously from the first to the second picture. Reciprocally, any picture could be identified as an element of the series: for each picture we could determine a family tree which was made with light and dark filtering of this picture. As many kind of mixtures are possible as you can imagine different formulas to do it; all you need is a function applying two colors on a third one. For example

Hervé Huitric / Monique Nahas *The Visual Artist Turns to Computer Programming* we used the formula f (x, y) = V x . y which increases the proportion of black in the mixture, or the formula !x – y! or !15 – x – y! using the complementary color. Since we had only 16 values for each basic color, each continuous function from [0,151 x [0.15] to [0,151 could give a continuous mixture, thus keeping the continuity of the color variations.

Picture Transformations

At that time, the development of digital music was very impressive compared to our simple experiments. (And the 30 developments were too far from us.) We were wondering if the powerful techniques of the musicians generating the sounds could be of some use for us. So we began to look at the pictures in term of frequencies (spatial frequencies instead of temporal ones). Using a Fourier development in trigonometrical functions of i and j, it was easy to build smooth variations of colors. Borrowing the ideas of a musician, Chowning, we introduced a modulation of frequencies and could observe a large diversity in the corresponding variations of colors following the parameters of the modulation and some effects of vibration of colors.

In a reverse sense, a given picture could be developed in a Fourier series, exactly as a given sound has a precise content in harmonics. Acting on the Fourier coefficients was another way of transforming a picture. The only problem was to compute the Fourier transformation with integer numbers and in Lisp. We probably realized the longest FFT transformation which could be imagined. It was then natural to be interested in the possibilities of techniques coming from digital image processing. We used Fourier or Walsh expansions to realize filters of high or low frequencies. The transformation of histogram was an easier technique that we found very interesting. By equalisation of histogram, we reduced the number of color levels present in an image in a way that accentuates the forms.

None of these techniques broke the continuity of the variation of colors. We used to combine them in various ways.

III. Two-Dimensional Drawings, 1979–1981

In 1979 we got a new piece of equipment: a LSI 11, with 24K memory and a raster of 380 x 255 pixels with the same number of 4,096 colors. With these new programming facilities (real numbers and Fortran language), we first produced some other continuous variations of colors, moving the brightness through the picture and computing the three colors R, V, B of each pixel by a linear relation: R + V + B = L (with L = brightness) as in our first pictures or silk-screens. For the first time, it was easy to draw a curve, without all the previous constraints of working on a very small computer with only integer values. So we began to introduce more complex curves, and instead of playing with straight lines and circles, we brought figurative elements into our pictures. To draw two-dimensional shapes, we chose to use parametric curves instead of analytical curves, because it was a convenient way to escape from a rigorous geometry. The particular use of B-Spline curves was not only a practical choice but also an aesthetical one. These curves have inherent continuous properties producing a smooth aspect. They also have some useful locality properties. To draw a B-Spline curve or surface, you only have to give the x, y coordinates of some points, and the complete curve is determined by these points, called control points, without going exactly through them. If you move one of these points, only a corresponding part of the curve will change, so you can modify your drawing locally. Surfaces are constructed in an analogous way by a dense network of curves. The way of filling the surface becomes a new parameter of density: on some pictures (a hand for example) we chose to make a visible distribution of curves on the surface which produces a kind of net. It is also possible to fill the surface partially, computing only some points and producing only a distribution of colored points.

Hervé Huitric / Monique Nahas The Visual Artist Turns to Computer Programming

The coloration of these surfaces was first a simple extension of our previous computations of the colors. We used the same parametric approach for spreading the colors on the surface as for the computation of the geometry. Each control point was associated with a value of brightness. Thus during the computation of the surface, a brightness was computed for each point, and the set of colors R, V, B was computed as before, using the brightness and the variations of two colors in order to determine the third one.

We have applied this procedure to reconstruct images from digitized images, poorly defined by eight levels of grey and 256 x 256 pixels. The control points were given by a grid on the picture, and the brightness attached to each control point was the corresponding value of grey of the digitized picture. Thus the computation of a B-Spline surface with these control values automatically produces a smooth interpolation of the brightness. Extending the idea of a nongeometrical control value, it was possible to add many nongeometrical parameters to each control point, and as a result we obtained a smooth variation of these parameters on the surface. For example, a set of colors could be given with each control point; afterwards the colors were directly computed for each point of the surface, and continuously diffused.

Now all our previous experiences with abstract pictures could be repeated in that case. In particular the effects due to the mixture of pictures were still interesting, producing a new amount of shades and hues. All the enhancement techniques could be used again, facilitated by an easier programming. We began to add some other "post-treatment," in particular a pointillistic treatment which was possible because of the larger number of pixels. To obtain a pointillistic effect is very simple: add in any way a random perturbation to the computed values of the colors. Of course there exist as many possibilities to do that as you can imagine. On many pictures we used the simplest way, adding a random amount of given variation separately to the three colors. Another possibility is to give a random variation to the brightness only, keeping the computed hues and saturation, or we could give a random perturbation to the hue and saturation, keeping the same brightness. It is also possible to change the random distribution through the picture; some regions could be more pointillistic than some others, with a smooth transition.

Again all these treatments will be used in the following, on the 3-D pictures.

IV. Modelization of 3-D Realistic Shapes

Since 1980 we have extended our computation of B-Spline surfaces to 3 dimensions. The technical details are given in the following section.

A 3-D B-Spline surface is modelled from a network of control points, and the modeling task consists of finding the coordinates x, y, z of these control points. This is more difficult than in 2-D. In 2-D drawing, control points can be easily selected by placing the drawing on a graphic tablet. The locality of B-Spline is well adapted to interactive drawing. Modifying a control point will only change a local region of the curve. With some practical experience, drawing using control points is rather easy.

In 3-D, the modeling is still a problem which has to be solved by various appropriate techniques, both theoretical and experimental. If certain shapes, such as water, mountains, hills, or grounds, can be easily approximated by some mathematical functions, the situation is of course different for a body or a face. Following the possible equipment, we used a number of different ad hoc methods.

One archaic but possible method consists of hand-drawing two views of the model, a front and a profile view, and to measure the coordinates of the selected points in these views. In 1981, we made a head in that way. We had to spend several days manually manipulating the control points to achieve a satisfactory result, and got several interesting monsters during that time . . .

Algorithms can help the manipulation. For B-Spline surface, the so-called "OSLO algorithm" proved to be a very precious tool. By allowing the introduction of new control points without changing the surface, it provides a supplementary means for modifying objects locally in the regions where they are richer in details, because the neighborhood moving with a control point becomes smaller.

In 1982 to model a dinosaur, we started with a wood skeleton. Still by hand, we measured the coordinates of points along the spinal column and on various plane cross sections, with a corresponding rotation angle for each slice (only one was necessary). By positioning the slices appropriately with respect to the spine, we could compute the three coordinates of the chosen control points. The spine/slices combination had the advantage of being rapidly adaptable for a different position: this only requires changing the spinal column position and the orientation of slices, keeping information obtained in the internal system of reference of each slice.

Afterwards we used different 30 models in plaster, clay, or other material, and covered them by one or several grids of curves. Then we measured the points of the grid either manually or automatically. It remained to find the control points corresponding to these measurements. For example, using an automatic system developed by the car company Renault, we got the set of control points of corresponding Bezier surfaces. In the case of patches made with only 16 points, Bezier and bicubic B-Spline are the same surface. We used the Bezier collection of control points to produce a face corresponding to a given plaster model.

We can also directly use the selected points as control points. The difference is not always noticeable. In any case, after you get your collection of control points, you still have a certain amount of work to do. Some examples of the difficulties which can occur are the following: if the object is divided into several B-Spline patches, how can you ensure the continuity between them? Even if the patches are correctly joined, a discontinuity of their tangency will produce a discontinuity of the brightness at the borders, a very disagreeable result. A solution is to work on the control points until the different patches will be continuously linked. A lot of algorithms and programming work are helpful in order to achieve that work.

Another connected problem is the modeling of tree structures: since B-Spline surfaces are not interpolating surfaces, how can we make sure that a branch will be properly attached to a trunk, and how can we blend the attach? The OSLO algorithm is again very useful here. As a consequence of this algorithm, it is possible to cut a B-Spline surface into two B-Spline surfaces, and to cut it at different places. The two resulting surfaces are perfectly smoothly linked, and if they are displayed, they produce the same shape as the initial surface. We used this property to concatenate and blend two surfaces. For example we add a "branch" surface to a "trunk" surface in the following way: we cut the trunk in two at a chosen spot. The control points of the "branch" are added to those of the chosen part of the "trunk," thus constituting a same surface. Then we display that surface together with the second part of the trunk. Processing recursively, we produced some trees in that way, starting from two surfaces: one for the trunk and one for a branch. We used the same ideas to attach the legs to a dinosaur body: the body was one B-Spline surface and so are the four legs. To concatenate the first foreleg, we cut the body into two parts, then we juxtaposed the control points of the foreleg with those of the first part, and we displayed the corresponding surface as a whole. The process continues by cutting the rest of the body, juxtaposing the new leg and displaying it. Finally, the last part, the tail, was displayed alone.

Improving the methodology of data acquisition is of fundamental importance. Certainly we benefit from the possible accumulation of data, which can always be used in different work, but we are far from an easy convenient procedure to acquire the data, even with the help of programming systems of assistance. Consider, for example, the construction of a movie, and think of how many different objects are needed to keep an audience from being bored after a few minutes. Look at any photograph or any picture at the TV, and consider how many objects should be modeled in order to approach their simulation . . .

Hervé Huitric / Monique Nahas The Visual Artist Turns to Computer Programming

Gesamtdatenwerk: Connectivity, Transformation and Transcendence

Roy Ascott

Networking provides the metaphor for late twentieth century culture: it speaks of interactivity, decentralisation, the layering of ideas from a multiplicity of sources. Networking is the provenance of far-reaching connectivity and, mediated, accelerated, and intensified by the computer, it leads to the amplification of thought, enrichment of the imagination, both broader and deeper memory, and the extension of our human senses. Computer networking means the linking of person-to-person, mind-to-mind, memory-to-memory regardless of their dispersal in space and their dislocation in time. In its global reach, in its complexity of idea processing, in its flexibility of output (image/music text and articulation of remote cybernetic systems, structures, and environments) and in its capacity to accommodate a great diversity of input modes, all of which are digitally treated in universal dataspace, it is particularly suited to take on the great challenge of late twentieth century art, which can be seen as the overarching project of our time: to make the invisible visible. That is, to bring to our senses, to make available to our minds, within the human constraints of space and time, what is otherwise beyond our reach, outside our perceptual range, the far side of our mind. This is not simply to speak of the complexities of chaos science, those infinite sequences of order and disorder which defy comprehension and representation within the computational range of the human brain . . . that fractal structuring of the world which the computer alone seems able to reveal. Nor is it only a matter of recognising how computer-mediated communication systems provide us with the remote-sensing capability to probe far out into cosmic space and deep into matter at the most profound quantum level. Neither is it enough to understand how dependent for image enhancement, data processing, with the rapid updating that implies, for us to negotiate a universe made up of transformations of energy operating at wavelengths or intensities far beyond the capability of our meagre sensory system to apprehend.

It is much more than all of this, but its implications for human growth and creativity can be stated quite simply: computer networking provides for a field of interaction between human and artificial intelligence, involving symbiosis and integration of modes of thinking, imagining and creating, which, from the point of view of art, can lead to an immense diversity of cultural transformations, and in science and philosophy, enriched definitions of the human condition. Computer networking, in short, responds to our deep psychological desire for transcendence—to reach the immaterial, the spiritual— the wish to be out of body, out of mind, to exceed the limitations of time and space, a kind of bio-technological theology.

When people interact, when minds interpenetrate, a proliferation of ideas is generated. When sensibilities from diverse cultures from all parts of the globe interweave, collaborate, conjoin, and become restructured, new cultural forms emerge; new potentials for meaning and experience are brought forth. This is the scope and ambition of networking. This is to speak of superconnectivity, the production of a multi-layered culture, planetary culture, and a holistic world art. It is not to be confused with homogenisation, or neutralisation of cultural, regional, or individual difference. What this offers in effect is not only the opportunity for us to construct new realities but to enter into the realities of others, the interpenetration of parallel universes of discourse.

Our immersion in electronic global networks can lead to a reevaluation of the status of reality; to an understanding of its provisional nature, as one of many coexisting realities, all of which are constructed—"virtual" in a sense—and dependent upon our active participation for their construction. When we recognise the centrality of the computer in this process of production, and it has become central to both the construction as well as the dissemination of knowledge and therefore of experience, it is easy to see a comparison to quantum physics. For "quanta" read "data." A physics of information. For it is in the quantum world that reality is the production of observation. The apparatus we use, the measuring system we employ, the language we articulate, condition the nature of the reality we perceive. It is, in a sense, a conspiracy. From the ground of undifferentiated wholeness, we construct virtual realities, knowing that they are transient, impermanent, ephemeral constructs of mind. That they may be internally coherent and consistent only furthers the illusion of permanency.

In philosophy, Bergson and Nietzsche in their different ways have pointed to this. In science, Heisenberg and Schrödinger, and more dramatically Bell and Aspect, for example, have demonstrated this. The principle of indeterminacy and uncertainty holds dominion. Strict causality operates only within a limited stratum of events. Our perception of space and time is not the frame of reality, but an aspect of an undivided whole within which an infinity of separate realities, parallel universes, can endlessly be constructed. How quickly this science moves into metaphysics and brings us back to theology, mysticism, and mythology! It is in this richness of value systems, world models, cultural constructs, and virtual realities that the networking artist operates. In this he is never alone. To network is to be engaged with the mind-at-large, to amplify individual thought and imagination through the dynamic interaction with others in the network. In this enterprise, "others" includes artificial intelligences, sensing systems, and memory stores, as well, of course, as human beings from an enormous diversity of personal and cultural contexts. It is through computer networking that we can deal creatively with relativism and with pluralism, which provide pessimism in so much postmodern thought.

The subject of quantum physics is the transformation of energy; its object is quanta. The subject of computer science is the transformation of information; its object is data. Data exists in streams, dataflow is ephemeral, transient, shifting. Data is everywhere and nowhere. A physics of information would talk about phase space, the virtual space which data occupies. Processed in time—the beat of the computer's pulse measured in nanoseconds—data nevertheless is time-free and time-resistant insofar as its transformation within computer networking is concerned. That is to say that the user of such networks can access, interact, and collaborate with other users independently of the constraints of time or place. In this sense, data is asynchronously managed and networking becomes a non-linear creative medium. And, as with quantum behavior, data is discontinuous; it "jumps" between semantic states. In this it models, as well as supports, creative behaviour which is always non-linear, indeterminate, uncertain, just as, with brilliant graphic clarity, the computer reveals nature's capacity to jump unpredictably to new levels of order from chaos, the stochastic leap.

If the project of our time is to render the invisible visible, to bring directly into our consciousness the direct apprehension of the processes and systems, forces and fields, dynamic and transformative relationships of life which elude our everyday perception and lie beyond the capture of our senses, then we must recognize the necessity of making the currently very visible computer invisible. The computer as thing, as object, as apparatus, as machine is too much with us, too dominant. It is not transparent, it is not understood as pure system, universal transformative matrix. The computer is not primarily a thing, but a set of behaviours. Its purpose is not only computation but transformation; not only storage but dissemination. It is the agent of the datafield, a construct of dataspace. Where it is seen simply as a screen presenting pages of an illuminated book, or as an internally lit painting, it is artistically valueless. Where access to its transformative power is constrained by a typewriter keyboard or the gestural configurations of a mouse, it is culture-bound, the user forced into the posture of a clerk. The power of the interface cannot be overestimated; the role of the user must be clearly defined.

Rather than seeing the computer interface as a membrane separating out the computer as discrete object from ourselves, we should see it and design it as a doorway into dataspace, a synaptic interval in a human-computer symbiosis. To see the computer as no more than screen and keyboard, to use it as no more than the apparatus of the accountant's office, is to be condemned to produce art of the "bottom line," that is to say an art of finalities, of completion. To deny, in other words, the essential qualities of open-endedness, non-linearity, and fecund incompleteness that are the great distinguishing potential of computer-mediated art practice. Similarly, our gathering of images, music, texts, for example, from the endlessly flowing datastream of creative interactions with the networks around the world, should be understood as a kind of data-harvest, a form of accessing and selecting and displaying which will not confuse the identity or role of the interface with that of, say, a painting or book or film screen—for they propose quite different aesthetics.

The essence of the interface is its potential flexibility: it can accept and deliver images both fixed and in movement, sounds constructed, synthesized or sampled, written texts, speech. It can be heat sensitive, body responsive, environmentally aware. It can respond to the tapping of the feet, the dancer's arabesque, the direction of a viewer's gaze. It may not only articulate a physical environment with movement, sound, and image, it is an environment; it is actually an arena of dataspace in which art of this human-computer symbiosis can be acted out. The computer interface is in each individual case an aspect of a holographic unity. To be in or at any one interface is to be with all the interfaces throughout the network of which it is a part. This is why, for example, the Ubiqua laboratory, as interface to the Planetary Network for the Venice Biennale of 1986, was, in effect, pulling the exhibition from its rather elite, centralised, and exclusive domain and stretching it out over the face of the globe: the flow of creative data generated through the interaction of artists all over the world could be accessed equally all over the world. Venice was no longer privileged in that sense. Networking has the effect of destabilising the gallery/museum system just as it extends and enriches the scope (and perhaps nature) of individual creativity. In this case, a range of interactive communications media were employed—electronic mail, computer conferencing, videotex, slow-scan TV, as well as computer exchange. The laboratory further included interfaces served by videodisc, digital sound, paint systems, and cybernetically responsive structures and environments.

On a much simpler but geographically pervasive level, an interactive project devised by Art Aces for Les Immatériaux in Paris in 1985 can be cited. This involved the French public service videotex system "Minitel" as the network for on-line interaction between artists "in" the exhibition and the large population of the subscribers distributed throughout the Greater Paris region.

The interface for "La Plissure du Texte," a project created for Electra in Paris, 1983, involving the development of a Planetary Fairytale by means of "dispersed authorship" through electronic networking, involved little more than the orthodox terminal and keyboard, with a data-projector carrying the text to a public dimension, dramatising its electronic presence which was at once ephemeral and concrete. This was a perfect vehicle to involve the viewer as participant in the layering of texts, in the

Roy Ascott Gesamtdatenwerk: Connectivity, Transformation and Transcendence

semantic ambiguities, delights and surprises that an authorship dispersed through many cultures in many parts of the world can generate.

At Linz, for Ars Electronica 1989, the project "Aspects of Gaia: Digital Pathways across the Whole Earth" attempts to investigate the potential of the digital screen seen on the horizontal, rather than on the more familiar vertical format, from above and below, offering images from a bird's-eye view and from below, as "wormholes" into parallel universes. The posture of the viewer is reconsidered and the deployment of digital sound in acoustic space is integral to the realisation of the project. In this case the design of the interface environment is the product of collaboration of five artists working with computer image, digital sound, electro-acoustic structures and environments. As in the case of those responsible for planning the networking projects for Electra and the Venice Biennale, the development of the concept and its technological determination has been conducted as much through a computer conferencing network as from face-to-face interaction. Invitations to artists all over the world, similarly were transmitted through electronic networks, making full use of EARN, BITNET, I.P.SHARP, for example, as well as fax, calling for their participation in this global network. From the point of view of visitors to the interface environment at Linz, the opportunity to interact with this incoming material, to add to it, to select, change, erase, transfer it, and then have it transmitted back into world-wide electronic space for its further transformation, is an important ingredient of the project.

Increasingly, as artists we are impatient with single modes of operation in dataspace. We search for synthesis of image, sound, text. We wish to incorporate human and artificial movements, environmental dynamics, ambient transformations, altogether into a more seamless whole. We search, in short, for the *Gesamtdatenwerk*. The site for such work must be the planet as a whole, its dataspace, its electronic noosphere. The duration of the work will of course be, ultimately, indeterminate since this must be a work in flux and flow, permitting an infinity of interactions, inputs and outputs, collaborations and conjunctions between its many participants. Since reciprocity and interaction are of its essence, such work cannot differentiate between "artist" and "viewer," producer and consumer. To participate in such a network is to be involved always in the creation of meaning and experience. The roles cannot be separated out. One can no longer be at the window, looking in on a scene composed by another; one is instead invited to enter the doorway into a world where interaction is all.

We are a long way from the *Gesamtdatenwerk*. The computer industry is slow in releasing those technologies which will facilitate a seamless interface, although research departments, most notably, for example, the Media Lab at MIT, are investigating and creating interface environments of considerable subtlety. Ultimately, it is a matter of artists and technologists collaborating, with or without institutional support, to bring the interface into the full sensorium of human experience and engagement.

Radio Art

At the last Documenta (1987), Klaus Schöning carried out a large-scale experiment in the audiothèque, aimed at defining "acoustic art on the radio" and at retracing its development on the basis of a vast number of examples. This was the first time that "art on the radio" was explicitly reclaimed for a large-scale visual arts exhibition. "Only twenty years ago, such an encounter of the visual arts and acoustic art at one of the greatest international art exhibitions would have been entirely unrealistic."[1] Klaus Schöning's approach implied that there is an acoustic art which sometimes extends into the radio. As the head of the WDR HörSpielStudio,[2] Schöning is, in fact, one of those very few who, within radio stations, have consistently worked on the development of a type of acoustic art that has a tradition of its own, different from that of narrative radio play or musical composition. Authors from many different fields—and not just from literature, as is usually the case with radio plays—contribute to the productions of the HörSpielStudio, and their work reflects back on the border-crossing avant-gardes of the beginning of this century, such as, e.g., the linguistic experiments and examinations carried out by the Futurists and Dadaists, or the integration of sounds and "noise" into music, as introduced by Luigi Russolo in his "Arte dei Rumori" and "Intonarumori." Schöning has come up with the following definition of acoustic art: "ACOUSTIC ART: a world of language and a world of sounds and noises. Language that tends towards sound, towards the sound of language and towards music, the overall sound of tones, of the acoustic environment. Acoustic art: the symbiosis of these worlds of language and noise and the organization of sounds by means of electronics. Its sensitive, receiving ear: the microphone. Its sound-carrier: the tape, the cassette, the record, the microchip. Its speaking mouth: the loudspeaker. One of its utopias: an audio space accessible to all—the radio."

Digression:
The Radio as a Production Site and Means of Distribution. Reality—International.

Although the WDR HörSpielStudio has, for more than 20 years, been setting an example by producing "acoustic art on the radio," this program is in fact an exception to the rule: in most of the departments for radio play and music at radio stations across Europe,[3] this art is only granted a kind of—alibi-like—experimental status, at the very most, although "the aesthetics of Ars Acustica cannot be integrated into the independent aesthetics and tradition of dramatic radio play and its great, style-shaping works. It has not evolved from these, it has not taken their place, it is neither their 'formal' or 'experimental' offspring nor their permanent avant-garde. Acoustic art has . . . its own, albeit often interrupted, hidden and prevented, tradition."

In this respect, the situation in Australia, Canada, and above all in the US is not better than in Europe, but rather worse. In these countries, a large number of small radio stations have an important role to play in distribution. Quite often, they provide services for (local) minorities. Many of them, ranging from university stations to radio cooperatives, depend on membership subscriptions and the unpaid work of their program-makers. Acoustic art programs are often broadcast on these stations for hours on end. Nobody is paid, and production takes place outside the station, sometimes in very modest private studios, sometimes with the help of subsidies from art promotion programs. In this context, we have to distinguish between two opposing systems: on the one hand, the work on, and realization of, projects in (private) studios is financed by private sponsors and/or art promotion. This is done in a way that stimulates the work's distribution via radio—a type of distribution that does justice to the work of art—while at the same time involving minimum costs for the distributor. On the other hand, productions are sometimes based on (otherwise not available) funds from national or regional public broad-

Heidi Grundmann

casting corporations that purchase a piece of work from its author in order to realize, broadcast, and re-utilize it. It remains to be seen which of these two approaches will survive in the age of constantly improving tape recordings.

"In the electronic age, copyright is an anachronism. We purloin, and we alienate."[4] This line— so casually quoted as a motto for their work by the (free) group Radio SubCom—is, at least for the time being, equally unacceptable for both broadcasting corporations and performing rights societies that represent the interests of authors.

In the sense this term is used by Klaus Schöning in the documenta's audiothèque, acoustic art on the radio—which at first glance might appear to be a tautology, because radio art (at least for the time being)[5] is perforce acoustic—therefore implies not only a reference to certain traditions such as Dadaism, Futurism, Lettrism, Sound Poetry, Musique Concrète, etc., but also to the production and distribution system characteristic of the radio as a mass medium that has been institutionalized—and for a long time remained unchallenged—in central Europe. Acoustic art on the radio is an art which is produced on the radio or, in any case, broadcast by it, and which at the same time proves that the radio as an institution is (also) seen as a "culturally initiatory medium."[6]

Yet there is still a wide range of other approaches—also in central Europe, where these are provoked e.g. by the prevailing conditions of local media policies that do not provide independent access to radio waves for minorities. For many years, artists of various groupings—e.g. the groups around Mike Hentz and Karel Dudesek—have reacted to this fact and have, out of broadcasting containers or media busses, developed a counter-image opposing the present situation of media policy: their concept implies that artists (and other minorities) should be given the possibility to broadcast independently and to develop a radio aesthetics which corresponds to their own needs and which is not governed by the rules and conventions of institutionalized (state-owned) radio. Projects such as Ponton, Radio X (Kunstradio, Frankfurt), or Radio SubCom are therefore no longer concerned with placing "acoustic art" on the radio, but with making current forms and systems of communication visible together along with their deficits and alternatives. Or, as Richard Kriesche formulated it in his performance/installation "Radio-Zeit" (1988): "This is no longer about making art within given communication channels, but on the contrary, about understanding these communication channels as possibilities available to an art-form." This newly emerging type of radio art can only be understood as part of a more comprehensive concept of "media art" which, in turn, is characterized by concepts derived from the visual arts and rooted in their tradition.

Radio Art as a Visual Art?

Duchamp can be considered a pioneer in this field, too: with his readymades and contextual questions, with his practice of declaring found objects art, and with his statement that a work of art is only completed by its receiver. And also the random operations in his "Musical Erratum" and his discovery (repeatedly quoted e.g. by Bill Fontana) that sound has sculptural properties have kept producing effects and side effects to this day.

When interpreted as visual art, therefore, radio art—like any other advanced contemporary art—establishes links to the border-crossing avant-gardes of the early 1900s: going beyond Luigi Russolo's "Arte dei Rumori," important references can be made to e.g. Filippo Tommaso Marinetti who, together with Pino Masnata, drew up a "Manifesto futurista della radia" in 1933. In addition, Marinetti illustrated his ideas about futuristic radio art in the scores of his "5 Sintesi dal Teatro Radiofonico," thereby anticipating a wide range of approaches regarding both "acoustic art on the radio" and a radio art that was seen as part of media art.

The Non-retinal Image

One essential *movens* for the radio work produced by authors from all walks of life has been the pictorial power of this medium, which offers an almost exemplary way of proving Duchamp's statements regarding the completion of a work of art by its receiver and the fact that images are not created on the retina, but in peoples' heads. "Radio is more visual than TV. The TV image depends on a small screen, while on the radio, images can be created using the listener's full power of imagination,"[7] says Douglas Davies. And John F. Rieger from California, who gives his programs names like "Artefacts" or "Objects in Boxes," states, "The elements of a program are treated as pieces of tape, just like potsherds found on an archaeological site . . . You will hear neither stories nor music. This is an art of images . . . I want to listen to a recorded image of the world, composed by using a magnetophone."[8] So this is about the combination of the radio and the magnetophone, an area which—like radio art itself—has known very little theoretical incorporation. Incidentally, the tape's object character has already started to disappear in the new digital studios, where the distance between mixing and transmission has been reduced to zero and where even highly complex works may (or might) unfold while being created in the radio time-space.

At a college radio station in Toronto, Dan Lander presents a weekly program which is most appropriately named "The Problem with Language." He presents tapes and cassettes from all over the world—and neither he nor any of the authors receive any kind of payment. "The Problem with Language" is a focal point for some of the many networks around the globe that deal with tape and cassette works; networks which, in most cases, also extend right into the radio stations . . . Dan Lander himself has abandoned photography in order to work with sounds. "We should all sometimes just close our eyes and listen, because sounds tell us much more than images . . . You can't really lie with sounds . . ." Like many other radio artists outside the system of state-owned stations, Dan Lander also works in a small studio of his own. He contents himself with using a four-track machine, "even though there are 150-track machines. But then—how many tracks has the world?"[9]

Un Paesaggio Udito—(from "5 Sintesi dal Teatro Radiofonico" by F. T. Marinetti). *10 sec. di sciacquio—1 sec. di crepitio—8 sec. di sciacquio—1 sec. di crepitio—5 sec. di sciacquio—1 sec. crepitio—19 sec. di sciacquio—1 sec. di crepitio—35 sec. di sciacquio—6 sec. di fischio di merlo.*

A Soundscape—(from "5 Sintesi dal Teatro Radiofonico" by F. T. Marinetti).[10] *10 sec. of swashing—1 sec. of crackle—8 sec. of swashing—1 sec. of crackle—5 sec. of swashing—1 sec. of crackle—19 sec. of swashing—1 sec. of crackle—35 sec. of swashing—6 sec. of a blackbird's whistling*

Found noises (swashing with water, crackling) and sounds (a blackbird's whistling) are combined to form a soundscape. Sounds and noises are treated just like any other artistic material (among which, since 1933, there have also been things like left-over tickets, newspaper clippings, etc.). Set into the context of an art work during a recycling process, these materials represented themselves, while also entering into new relationships with other objects and materials. Duchamp's concept of the receiver who finishes a work of art already contained a temporary element. Detached from the concrete object, in the 1960s, the visual arts unfolded in time, e.g. as concepts which did not necessarily require realization. Strategies and techniques such as those of the readymades, of transferring found objects into an art context, of the collage, the montage and the cut/up—which, starting with William Burroughs, has gained more and more importance in many areas of the visual arts since the 1970s—can be applied to almost all materials and in any space: they can thus also be easily applied in radio space and to sound, noise, language, tape, or radio transmissions . . . At the end of the 1960s, conceptual art, however, mainly dealt with the relations and conditions that occur while materials are being used, with the question of how artistic activity is integrated into social circumstances, and with the context of art and artists—e.g. with their dependence on the so-called "support structure," i.e. anything that has to do with the conditions of art production and art distribution. People started to think mainly in categories of spaces—social spaces, institutionalized spaces, public spaces, spaces specific to the individual media—and they began to position art within these spaces with increasing accuracy, and be it just to avoid exposing it to the omnipresent danger of absorption, defusing, or appropriation by the so-called art industry and other social areas (e.g. advertisement). "The radio is a classless medium. It penetrates everything—without regard to social, cultural, economic, political, or geographic borders. It is part of our everyday lives and, as such, it is not a hierarchical medium. We listen to the radio while we are doing all kinds of other things in our daily routine, in our private rooms. Therefore, the radio provides the artist with an entirely new context which is fundamentally different from that of the gallery . . ."[11] (William Furlong)

I Silenzi Parlano Tra Loro—(from "5 Sintesi dal Teatro Radiofonico" by F. T. Marinetti): *15 sec. di silenzio puro—do, re, mi, di flauto—8 sec. di silenzio puro—do, re, mi, di flauto—29 sec. di silenzio puro—sol di pianoforte—do di tromba—40 sec. di silenzio puro—do di tromba—ve ve ve di pupo—11 sec. di silenzio puro—1 minuto di rrrr di motore—11 sec. di silenzio puro—oooo! stupito di bambina undicenne.*

Silences Speaking to Each Other—(from "5 Sintesi dal Teatro Radiofonico" by F. T. Marinetti): *15 sec. of complete silence—do, re, mi, by flute—8 sec. of complete silence—do, re, mi, by flute— 29 sec. of complete silence—sol by pianoforte—do by trumpet—40 sec. of complete silence—do by trumpet—baby going uaa uaa uaa—11 sec. of complete silence—1 minute of motor going rrrr—11 sec. of complete silence—amazed oooo! of 11-year-old girl.*

Here, Marinetti not only uses noises (the rrrr of a motor), the human voice (clearly defined as the voice of a baby and that of a surprised 11-year-old), and musical sounds as equal elements and materials for a non-musical composition: he also uses complete silence. And this complete silence has remained one of the greatest violations of radio as an institution. "Everything about radio . . . its aims, audience, content, modes of representation and exclusion, expectations, and so on should be challenged continually . . . after this ideological extreme has been reached perhaps the most political act on radio about radio would be to broadcast what commercial stations in particular fear most . . . silence . . . but that, too, has been done . . ."[12] (Rick Rue).

Battaglia di Ritmi: una lentezza prudente e paziente espressa con un tac . . . tac . . . tac . . . di goccia d'acqua prima tagliata e poi uccisa da un'elasticità volante e arpeggiante di note sul pianoforte prima tagliata e poi uccisa da una scampanellata di campanello elettrico prima tagliata e poi uccisa da un silenzio di tre minuti tagliato prima e poi ucciso da un affammo di chiave in serratura tra-trum-trac—seguito da un silenzio di un minuto.

Battle of Rhythms: a prudent and patient slowness, expressed by the tac . . . tac . . . tac . . . of a drop of water, cut first and then killed by a flying and harping elasticity of notes on a pianoforte, cut first and then killed by the loud ringing of an electric doorbell, cut first and then killed by a silence of three minutes, cut first and then killed by the sound of keys in a lock tra-trum-trac—followed by one minute of silence.

In the fourth of his "Sintesi," Marinetti presents the continuous superposition and mutual replacement of clearly defined sounds, noises, and silence.

"Need to Know" was a 90-minute piece of "experimental radio theatre" by Lawrence Weiner, broadcast in New York in the middle of the 1980s. In this work, language and music were used as material for a media sculpture in a series of continual superpositions and replacements. "My work consists of language and of the material language refers to . . . Music is a material, and so is sound. Most people, at least those who go to museums, nowadays recognize sound or light as materials for making sculptures, but they still refuse to recognize language . . . I love radio—why not listen to art and, in doing so, simultaneously see it?"[13] (Lawrence Weiner)

La Costruzione di un Silenzio: A = Costruire un muro di sinistra con un rollo di tamburo (1/2 minuto). B = costruire un muro di destra con un trombetto—vocio—stridio automobilistico tramviario di capitale (1/2 minuto). C = costruire un pavimento con un borbottio di acqua in tubi (1/2 minuto). D = costruire un soffitto terrazza con cip-cip-cip di passeri e rondini (20 sec.).
Construction of a Silence: A = construct a wall to your left with the rolling of a drum (1/2 minute). B = construct a wall to your right with a small trumpet—shouting—screeching of cars and tramways in the capital (1/2 minute). C = construct a floor with the rumbling of water in pipes (1/2 minute). D = construct a roof terrace with the chip-chip-chip of sparrows and swallows (20 sec.).

In 1985, the sculptor Gottfried Bechtold built/constructed "Fünf kleine Pyramiden" for the radio: the strict form of this work is described in its title. The base area of each pyramid consists of four sound elements which mingle while striving for the top: silence. The fifth pyramid consists of elements from the four previous pyramids. "All the points are contained in the geometrical top and they are all related to each other. Silence is reached at the top; this is the point of transit, where the work of art should have reached the listener's mind, where it passes from being an event to being one of the listener's memories. It is only then that the art work really exists, as a pyramid that has been deserted." Bechtold used natural sounds such as wind, water, or crickets, traffic noises (trains, airplanes), excerpts from historical recordings of political speeches in different languages, and individual piano tones. "As a sculptor, I can cut off the dimension of the visible and introduce the dimension of the audible. My works are always very spatial: they are sound sculptures."[14]

Radio as Material

La radia sará
Utilizzazione delle interferenze tra stazioni e del sorgere e della evanescenza dei suoni.
Radio will be
The utilization of interferences between stations and of rising and fading sounds.[15]

"I spent a couple of years producing short-wave radio conversations. You can really play on a short-wave radio because such a lot is happening there: not only when you happen to tune in to a station—e.g. Moscow—but also in-between stations. There are satellite noises, there is radio communication between ships, and a lot of other strange noises. It is almost like a synthesizer. So I did two or three works with short-wave radio; the first one, I think, was in 1969: I used radio on the radio . . . The radio is an instrument . . ."[16] (Michael Snow).

In 1952, John Cage put up 12 radio sets in a concert hall and had them played as instruments. This "Imaginary Landscape" is always there when"the interferences between stations and the rising and fading of sounds" are used as artistic material, even if the effect is doubled, as a mirror image of itself, as soon as the radio as an instrument is playing a concert for, and on, the radio.

Radio about Radio

La radia sará
Un'Arte nuova che comincia dove cessano il teatro, il cinematografo e la narrazione.
Radio will be
A new art which begins where theatre, cinema and narrative end.

We have seen that, in their futuristic manifesto entitled "La radia," Marinetti and Masnata called for a type of radio art that would not contain the "pre-existent media," which according to McLuhan regularly constitute the contents of any new media. There are various ways of transforming the different types of radio programs into the content and form of radio art. David Troostwyck e.g. had an art commercial broadcast on a commercial station. Bill Furlong and Maurizio Nanucci used street polls in an entirely new way, and Bill Johnson adapted a radio interview given by Bruce McLean during the golden age of New Painting (Everybody's Doing It). In 1970, Canadian artist Ian Murray combined the first 10 seconds of the "top hundred number-one radio hits" of the past ten years after having been told over and over again by radio producers and DJs that the first ten seconds of a recording decide whether or not it will be a hit. "I consider this work a sculptural act. The material is cut and then re-pasted in a way which is entirely different from that of regular radio programs."[17] Ian Murray explicitly considers his TV and radio work as part of his activities as a visual artist, defining it as "art in public space." Apart from dealing with numerous aspects of how to extend the work of visual artists to include the new media, he is also interested in the financial and legal changes that result from exchanging brush and canvas for the electronic media where unique things, originals, have ceased to exist and where clear authorship has, quite often, disappeared . . .

Musicians and literary figures can make use of the radio to distribute the products they always produce anyway. What I am interested in, regarding the works of visual artists, is the fact that they do not attribute so much importance to supplying a maximum number of persons with prefabricated information, but rather focus on formal innovation, since the medium itself has become the object of their work . . .

In 1988, the Austrian Helmut Mark used archive material from information programs broadcast by the Austrian Radio on the attempted assassination of Ronald Reagan to produce a piece of work entitled "Coca Cola." In this project, found material was re-pasted in a new way, and fitted with a number of new "frames": with that of the "Kunstradio—Radiokunst" program, for a start, but also with an immediate frame consisting of material from a Coca Cola commercial—the name "Coca Cola" itself was not mentioned in the feature itself, but it was used, and therefore mentioned, as the work's title (it is not allowed to broadcast commercials on the Österreich 1 program). Many listeners believed another assassination attempt had taken place, although, when listening carefully, it was clear that these were clips from different programs with different speakers. Mark refused to give an "interview with the artist," which is usually broadcast at the beginning of the program; he replaced it by a fictitious interview in which the artist was asking the questions. The answers, read by a radio speaker, were a collection of quotations . . . Thus, a piece of work which appeared to be simple in the first place revealed a wide range of possible levels of meaning and association: from the history of radio art (from readymades to Orson Welles), via the examination of various forms of transmission, the medium's potentially fictitious character, and its different ways of reception all the way to the present-day art of appropriation.

Heidi Grundmann *Radio Art*

La radia abolisce

1. *lo spazio o scena necessario nel teatro, compreso il teatro sintetico futurista, e nel cinema*
2. *il tempo*
3. *l'unità d'azione*
4. *il personaggio teatrale*
5. *il pubblico inteso come massa giudice autoeletto, sistematicamente ostile e servile, sempre misoneista sempre retrogrado.*

Radio abolishes

1. *the space or stage necessary in the theater, including synthetic, futuristic theater, and in the cinema*
2. *time*
3. *the unity of action*
4. *the dramatic character*
5. *the audience, intended as a self-elected mass jury, systematically hostile and servile, always misoneist, always retrograde.*

Artists are not very often given the opportunity to realize long-term live projects. Most likely, this is possible at the university stations mentioned above, and sometimes also at stations financed by donations and membership subscriptions from listeners who are interested in new music, art, and literature. One of these stations is Radio CFRO in Vancouver, a cooperative providing services for political and cultural minorities. In 1976, the "H. P. Show" was broadcast for the first time on CFRO: a weekly live program by Hank Bull and Patrick Ready, which was a great success for many years. "We started the H. P. Show with the explicit intention of making radio art, of penetrating into a given social institution, in this case the radio, and making it a venue for art . . . Our idea was that this type of art does not have to pass through the art industry but can reach the listeners directly from the artists and producers. This is art in the public space, art for everyone . . . The word 'art' was never mentioned on the H. P. Show, not even when an artist was being interviewed. Art was disguised or translated into something else. It was an attempt to advance to new forms of expression, to a new form of communication going beyond art as defined by the art industry . . . Radio art implied using sound effects, the telephone, different forms of radio plays, music, improvisation in the studio, interviews with guests, development of science fiction series, live actions, etc. . . . Right from the beginning, we regarded the H. P. Show as visual art, and I still think the radio also belongs in this category. This is the tradition I come from, this is where I belong. Even our applications for subsidies were addressed to the Visual Arts Department."[18] As a matter of fact, the Canadian Council for Art Promotion also supported radio art, e.g. the "New Sounds Gallery," an open-end late-night program broadcast by G. X. Jupitter-Larsen on radio CRFO Vancouver. (The high percentage of Canadians in media art in general, and in radio art in particular, has to do with the country's media and art policies, and with leading figures such as Glenn Gould, Marshall McLuhan, or R. Murray Schafer.) Even outside the radio context, Jupitter-Larsen's work can be characterized by the keyword of re-information: "I treat information as raw material. I reshape it so that it ends up meaning something different, or appears to be something different from what it originally was . . . You can use information to make a sculpture . . ." Here is one example for a program dealing with re-information: "Some time ago, our station's transmitter broke down. When you tuned in to our station, all you could hear was random static. Nevertheless, I went into the studio and recorded all these random noises, this static which was on the air instead of my program. The following week, after the transmitter had been repaired, I began my program with the following announcement: 'If you missed last week's program, don't worry. There was none, because our transmitter broke down. For all those of you who missed it, here's once again what happened last week.' What followed were hours of my recordings of random static . . . The most interesting thing about the potential of this artistic examination is that the program itself can be treated as a medium. This is why I normally don't record my programs, since that would turn them into tapes or records. I like the idea that radio art is floating through the cosmos, so to speak—on its way to Orion, or wherever . . ."[19] The concept Jupitter-Larsen calls "re-information" is defined as "cliché processing" by Radio SubCom, a group of media artists from Austria and Switzerland (Armin Medosch, Oil Blo, et al.). The sounds coming from the radio have become clichés, their significance is tied to learned listening habits. These clichés are taken up by Radio SubCom, changed by means of sound technology, and shifted within their context, so that in the end, they gain a new meaning that is completely independent of their original intentions. The radio thus becomes a recycling facility for fighting the pollution of our media environment.

In contrast to Jupitter-Larsen, Radio SubCom are not allowed to broadcast. Their studio is in an old bus, travelling across Europe in a nomadic style . . . It is a collage in itself: made up of lots of different devices and parts set up by Oil Blo. "Creative sound technology is an essential element of the new RADIO AESTHETICS supported by RADIO SUBCOM. Oil Blo uses a combination of the latest digital audio technologies and devices from the stone age of radio technology . . . Radio art is not a special branch within conventional radio, but the art of making radio itself."

"Dramma di Distanze" (from "5 Sintesi dal Teatro Radiofonico" by F. T. Marinetti): *11 sec. di una marcia militare a Roma—11 sec. di un tango danzato a Santos—11 sec. di musica giapponese religiosa suonata a Tokio—11 sec. di ballo campestre vivace nella campagna di Varese—11 sec. di un incontro di pugilato a New York—11 sec. di rumorismo stradale a Milano—11 sec. di romanza napoletana cantata nell'albergo Copacabana di Rio de Janeiro.*

"Drama of Distances" (from "5 Sintesi dal Teatro Radiofonico" by F. T. Marinetti): *11 sec. of a military march performed in Rome—11 sec. of a tango performed in Santos—11 sec. of religious Japanese music played in Tokyo—11 sec. of a lively country-dance performed in the village of Varese—11 sec. of a boxing-match in New York—11 sec. of street noise in Milan—11 sec. of a Neapolitan romance sung at the Hotel Copacabana in Rio de Janeiro.*

This "Drama of Distances" contains a telecommunications model which, in its anti-hierarchical structure, goes beyond the conventions of the medium "radio" as we know it. From a contemporary point of view, however, this short description given by Marinetti also provides a clear picture of the notion that all radio needs to do is align its microphones all over the world and pick any excerpts from the continual flow of events, combining them in a collage. Another subject of radio art is the idea that radio can open any number of audio-windows so that listeners may eavesdrop on the "constant murmur of data" (Kriesche). "Radical Radio," a type of radio that listens into "nature," was conceived by R. Murray Schafer: "A few years ago Bruce Davis and I had an idea for what we called Wilderness Radio. The plan was to put microphones in remote locations uninhabited by humans and to broadcast whatever might be happening out there: the sounds of wind and rain, the cries of birds and animals— all the uneventful events of the natural soundscapes transmitted without editing into the hearts of the cities. It seemed to us that since man has been pumping his affairs out into natural soundscape, a little natural wisdom might be a useful antidote . . ."[20]

throw a high sound out of the window and send it around the earth. wait until it returns backwards through the door—enriched by all the sounds it has met on its way. let this sound smash you to the ground. (Gerhard Rühm, 1975)[21]

Marinetti's "Dramma di Distanze" anticipates a model for radio art projects which, in fact, overcome worldwide distances by mixing sounds from remote sources or making them into collages. If you have the impression, however, that these projects may fit into one uniform chapter of radio history, you are completely mistaken . . . The few artists who have successfully seized the opportunity to realize projects of this kind in the institutionalized public radio space have had very dissimilar starting positions.

In his projects "Piece for Peace" (1985) or "Crystal Psalms" (1988, a live concert which took place simultaneously in 6 different countries in commemoration of the "Crystal Night"), Alvin Curran, an American living in Europe, focuses on "a realistic and symbolic encounter between many people in many different places, people who can neither see nor hear each other, but who join to perform a play together, an event which as such can only take place on the radio . . . a radiophonic connection that, at least for an instance, brings people together in the same acoustic space, connecting them in a more than symbolic way. Even if they don't know it, I harmonize them completely. In this sense, the radio is an unbelievable instrument . . . "22

Regarding form, parallels to Nam June Paik's global television events come involuntarily to mind: during these events, everything that takes place on the different participating stations is used as material and mixed by the "maestro" to create a composition. An entirely different approach is that of Bill Fontana, who realized from a passage from Duchamp's "Notes" that sounds can be used as material for sculptures when perceived as objects that can be transferred from one context to another. Thus, Fontana mixed complex sound sculptures using live recordings from various environments—i.a. via satellite. These sculptures also extended into the public radio space. Bill Fontana is not concerned with the radio as an instrument he can control/play, but with the careful positioning of (sound) objects in the various contexts of public spaces, one of which is the radio . . . "With the help of the radio, sound— unlike in traditional sound sculptures—cannot just be transferred to another context, but to thousands of different sound situations. The radio provides the possibility of producing highly different versions of each sound sculpture/installation: one version—their own version—for each listener. Each of these versions is unique because almost all listeners will be exposed to a different sound situation . . ."23

In a type of giant radio drawing, the Austrian Wolfgang Temmel establishes live connections between remote places across the world, situated both far from each other and from the centers of art industry: places where artists often have to live and work under very difficult political conditions. In his project "(He)Artbeats," artists from Palestine, South Africa, Nicaragua, and Australia "send" their heartbeats to a live radio program taking place at the radio station in Linz. From Linz, these heartbeats are then, again, transmitted on the air—not only on VHF and medium wave (in the transmitting area of the Österreich 1 program), but also on short wave: into the diffuse space of Radio Austria International which also covers other continents. One of the notions Temmel thematizes with this project is that radio space actually consists of many different spaces which are not at all uniform in their structures. Apart from the interactive, worldwide space used by radio amateurs (who may only transmit trivial messages)—a space that nowadays, however, is without content—there are radio stations that "supply" many highly differentiated spaces which have been more or less institutionalized, commercialized, or localized within various legal frameworks. They have one thing in common, however: they only simulate interactivity, and maybe even communication, as long as this one-way track from sender to receiver is not perceived in a sufficiently defined way.

The combined use of radio and telephone in news programs signals that live, simultaneous, immediate "instant information" is provided: an aesthetic decision is made here to accept a degree of sound quality which, in other circumstances, would not comply with the normal requirements of transmission quality. Talk-radio programs conjure up an image of what radio originally used to be: two-way communication. "Although, as far as technical principles are concerned, every tube radio set and every loudspeaker, according to a smart statement by Enzensberger, qualify as what might—even more smartly—be called 'transceivers' (i.e. they are able to broadcast *and* receive), draconian telecommunication laws, particularly in the Weimar Republic, had the effect that broadcasting facilities were illegalized, and some were even sealed. And this was not just to prevent an anarchic confusion of waves, but to reserve any possible joys of, and authority over, two-way radio-telephoning to the military and the industries."[24] It is not communication that reaches the modern listener-turned-eavesdropper, but only an image of communication which represents, at the same time, the transmission's content. The term "live" is relativized even further by the advance of digitalization: "on the other hand, what is clearly speaking out of these spaces is death. A dead voice coming out of the radio. No matter whether this is a live voice or not. 'Live' only means something within the context of time. Since time, however, has become trivial, 'live' is nothing but a sentimental, technological lie. Storage techniques make it possible to 'liven up' dead things. Informational life can only be created by killing living things. The more immaterial the respective medium, the higher its competence to 'liven up' . . ." (Richard Kriesche).

The Hungarian performance artist Tibor Hajas thematized the ambivalence of the hierarchical structure of radio-to-person communication in his 1979 "Hang Performance" by giving his own, very insistent voice to a personalized radio set: "for a short time this great power, the radio, is dealing only with you, lean back, let yourself go, close your eyes, this is how I want you . . . I'm filling your room, turning into a giant, to give you the chance to choose, to turn the volume down, to turn it up, just as you please. To give you the chance to treat me like an object, shameless and free, only for your pleasure . . . take this chance. How exciting I can be for you . . . and what kind of object are you for me? What kind of performance can I give at your expense—and without resistance? . . . should I torture you, or caress you, in front of all those strangers, those large numbers of men, women and children who are listening, who are all taking part in our little story . . ."[25]

"It is curious how much more arresting are the weather reports than the news on both radio and TV. Is this not because 'weather' is now entirely an electronic form of information whereas news retains much of the pattern of the printed word?"[26] (Marshall McLuhan). Radio has not become the exclusive content of radio yet, and neither has radio space been precisely staked out—the realization of an art that has radio as its content, an art that takes place in radio space, however, is often made more difficult since it is by no means normal that artists are granted access to this medium. So they have to travel around in ramshackle busses that might be radio stations, if only this was allowed, and use mobile studios to work on the reutilization of clichés distributed by radio stations all around the world and far out into space (Radio SubCom) . . . They work on projects and philosophical, artistic texts in which radio is turned into a metaphor (Alan Lamb) and/or texts based on a definition of radio that does not so much start from radio programs, but rather from the increasing fragmentation of the body and the dissolution of categories like time, space, freedom, individual; from the inhabitant of the "Global Village" who—mutated into a "Radio Man" (R. Kriesche)—not only receives information/data but also transmits them, thereby abandoning himself—in a perversion of terms like "communication" and "interactivity," which in turn are becoming more and more obsolete themselves—to surveillance, control, "transparency". . .[27] "Radio cannot be reduced to sending and receiving, to communication and dominance. Radio theory can only be developed on the basis of a general data theory. This means: Before we can develop a radio, TV, video or telecommunications theory, we need a theory of background upon which to depict these so-called media. It is evident that this background has to be a time-space without space or time. Such a time-space is, however, difficult to imagine . . ." (Richard Kriesche).

Taking up the various analyses provided by conceptual art in the 1960s and 70s, media art, and thus radio art, at the end of the 80s—and from an actually rather impotent point of view, given the fundamental changes caused in society by modern communication technologies—are above all confronted with the questions of what type of art would be adequate for this society and what it might—or would have to—look like: an art that would neither be historical quotation nor decoration, neither illustration nor didactic exercise, "an art which does not only act within the electronic space, but which is defined from within this space: an art of the electronic space, in fact . . ."

Notes

1. "Acoustic Art on the Radio (?)," presentation by Klaus Schöning at the symposium "With the Eyes Shut—Bilder im Kopf. Zur Theorie und Praxis der Radiokunst," styrian autumn 1988. (This symposium was a co-production of styrian autumn, Graz, and the Austrian Radio ORF.)

2. Westdeutscher Rundfunk, WDR, one of the big German public radios, based in Cologne.

3. In Europe, regular programs are produced not only by the WDR, Cologne, but also e.g. by the RAI, by France Culture, Radio Belgrade, or the ORF. At the moment, many projects featuring radiophonic art are being realized in Finland by Yleis Radio.

4. "Radio Subcom," 1988, published by TDP (Takahashi Design and Publishing).

5. The so-called "intelligent" radio of the future will be able to provide information for listeners directly via their home computers (e.g. the score of a piece of music or teaching materials or educational programs).

6. Richard Kriesche: "Radio-Zeit," performance and radio program, commissioned by the ORF program "Kunstradio—Radiokunst" on the occasion of the symposium "With the Eyes Shut—Bilder im Kopf," styrian autumn 1988.

7. Douglas Davies in an interview for the ORF program "Kunst heute," 1983.

8. John F. Rieger in an interview for the program "Kunstradio—Radiokunst," ORF 1988.

9. Dan Lander in an interview for "Kunstradio—Radiokunst," ORF, 1988.

10. Quoted from Gianni Gitti, Odersa Rubini, who reconstructed "5 Sintesi dal Teatro Radiofonico" by F. T. Marinetti in 1980–81 for Harpo's Bazaar, Bologna.

11. "Placement and Recognition," presentation by William Furlong at the symposium "With the Eyes Shut—Bilder im Kopf," styrian autumn 1988.

12. Rick Rue, written statement for Ars Electronica, 1989.

13. Lawrence Weiner in an interview for the program "Kunstradio," ORF, 1986. A 30-minute excerpt from L. Weiner's "Need to Know" was also broadcast in this program series.

14. Gottfried Bechtold in an interview for the program "Kunstradio," ORF, April 1985, during which "Fünf kleine Pyramiden" was performed for the first time.

15. From "Manifesti e scritti vari: La Radia," quoted acc. to F. T. Marinetti: Teoria e invenzione futurista, ed. Luciano De Maria, with a preface by Aldo Palazzeschi. Arnoldo Mondadori Editore, 1968.

16. Michael Snow in an interview for "Kunstradio—Radiokunst," 1987.

17. Ian Murray in an interview for "Kunstradio—Radiokunst," ORF, 1988.

18. Hank Bull in an interview for "Kunstradio—Radiokunst," ORF, 1988.

19. G. X. Jupitter-Larsen in an interview for "Kunstradio—Radiokunst," ORF, 1988.

20. Murray Schafer in "Radical Radio," Canadian Forum, December/January 1982–83.

21. Quoted from Zweitschrift 6, autumn 1979.

22. Alvin Curran in an interview for "Kunstradio—Radiokunst," ORF, 1988.

23. Bill Fontana in an interview for "Kunstradio—Radiokunst," ORF, 1987.

24. "Wellenartillerie," presentation by Friedrich Kittler at the symposium "With the Eyes Shut—Bilder im Kopf," styrian autumn 1988.

25. Translated from a tape recording of a performance given by Tibor Hajas in 1979. The recording was provided by Gyorgy Galantai's Art Pool Archiv in Budapest. According to Galantai, the performance was also broadcast on the radio.

26. Marshall McLuhan in: Understanding Media. Sphere Books Ltd. London, 1967.

27. In fact, the so-called "intelligent radio" of the future also aims at potential surveillance—which has also been noticed, at least to some extent, in reception research—rather than unhierarchical two-way communication.

Werner Alone Has Looked on Reality Bare

Proposal for a Really New "New Physics"

Quantum theory is the most far-ranging and successful attempt to understand the physical world ever devised by human beings.

By the late Twenties quantum theorists had solved in elaborate detail the most pressing physics problem of that era—how light interacts with atoms. But along with its astonishing power to predict the most subtle light-matter effects, this fledgling theory created a host of philosophical problems, not the least of which was the bizarre notion that the world is in some sense "not real" except during an act of measurement.

Many physicists, including Albert Einstein, Erwin Schrödinger, and French scientist-aristocrat Prince Louis De Broglie, felt that giving up reality was too high a price to pay for a mere theory no matter how successful; these physicists hoped in their hearts that quantum theory's reign would be short-lived, that this reality-denying theory would fail when applied outside the atom-sized realm where it had achieved its initial success. The new theory however continued to prosper beyond its inventors' wildest dreams, resolving even more complicated problems of atomic structure, conquering the complexity of the atomic nucleus, some ten thousand times smaller than the already minuscule atom, then extending its range deeper into matter, down into the subnuclear realm of the elementary particles—quarks, gluons and leptons—which many physicists believed to be the world's ultimate constituents.

Each new predictive success made quantum physicists bolder. With this apparently invincible theory in hand, quantum theorists searched for new worlds to conquer, and turned their sights to the macrocosm where they convincingly described the quantum chemistry of the primordial fireball, and now even dare to model the birth of the Universe itself as one gigantic quantum leap: from Nothing into Everything.

Exposed for more than sixty years to potential falsification on a thousand different fronts, quantum theory has passed every test that three generations of Nobel-hungry scientists can devise. On all levels accessible to experiment, quantum theory generates flawless predictions for all of matter's quirky operations. Faced with success after success, the majority of physicists quietly decided that to give up reality in exchange for quantum theory's immense predictive power was not such a bad deal after all.

In addition to its repudiation of reality, quantum theory's whirlwind success has propelled its frontiers for the most part outside the range of ordinary human affairs. Having solved—in principle at least—all physics problems on the ordinary scale, quantum physicists have been forced to seek fresh phenomena either in the deep microscopic realm of the elementary particles, or in subtle cosmological puzzles remote in time and space from our daily concerns. As the domain of fundamental physics research retreats from the scale of everyday life, increasingly costly apparatus is required to subject these distant realms to experimental scrutiny. Because of the great expense of these experiments, their technical complexity, and their remoteness from our daily lives, direct participation in quantum research is restricted to a few fortunate scientists—through whose efforts the rest of us vicariously share in one of the twentieth century's greatest intellectual adventures: the exploration of the strange

Nick Herbert

non-human landscape of the quantum world, the struggle to comprehend the utterly alien logic of what the late Heinz Pagels called "the cosmic code": quantum physics as the language of nature.

Will the bizarre quantum world forever exist as the private preserve of mathematicians and experimental physicists, or might ordinary people someday gain access to its fabled realms? Recent research into quantum theory's philosophical dimensions suggests that fundamental quantum research may someday return to a human scale and allow every human being, no matter what their academic credentials, to take part in the quantum adventure, joining with physicists and mathematicians in an egalitarian endeavor I call "holistic physics." Holistic physics could open up a third front of quantum research on the scale of ordinary experience with inexpensive equipment, which would complement conventional quantum research on the cosmological and elementary particle scales, a third front made possible by the very reality problem that so distressed Einstein and other early quantum physicists.

The quantum reality problem arises primarily because quantum theory describes the world in two ways, not one. Quantum theory represents an object differently depending on whether it is being observed or not being observed. Every physicist without exception uses this twofold quantum description in his or her work, but physicists hold many divergent opinions about "what is actually going on" during these two stages in an object's existence: being observed and not-being-observed.

Whenever an object—bulldog, baseball, or baryon—is not under observation, quantum physicists represent that object as a "wave of probability," called the object's "wave function." Instead of definite values for attributes such as position, velocity, and spin, each of the object's attributes takes on—in the mathematics at least—a wide range of possible values, values that oscillate in a wavelike manner at a variety of different frequencies. This way of treating unobserved objects is one of quantum theory's most peculiar features. Unobserved objects are not treated as real things but as probability waves, not as actual happenings but only as bundles of vibratory possibilities.

On the other hand, when an object is observed, it always finds itself at one particular place, with one particular spin and velocity, instead of a smeared-out range of physical properties. During the act of measurement, the mathematical description abruptly shifts—from a spread-out range of possible attributes (unmeasured object) to single actual attributes (measured object). This sudden measurement-induced switch of descriptions is called the "collapse of the wave function," or simply the "quantum jump." The nature of the quantum jump is the biggest mystery in quantum physics. Whether this drastic shift in the mathematics corresponds to an actual dislocation in the real world or is a purely mathematical quirk continues to be a matter of deep controversy in the physics community.

Not every physical interaction counts as a measurement. For instance, the action of gravity on an object alters its probability wave but does not in itself induce a quantum jump. Many physicists believe that the essence of a measurement act is "making a record," a notion I will adopt here. No record, no measurement. Only those interactions in nature that leave behind permanent traces (records) count as measurements. For instance, the flash of light in your eye, recorded as a pattern of neural impulses, is one such measurement, while the (unregarded) fall of a sparrow is not. Only record-making devices have the power to turn multivalued possibilities into single-valued actualities. If we take quantum theory seriously, the world does not exist as an actuality except under the influence of special recording devices; when unrecorded it exists only as hordes of intermingling semi-real possibilities. Since only a tiny part of the world is lucky enough to be in contact with a measuring device, most of the world most of the time is "not real," at least in its mathematical representation.

Some physicists, disturbed by quantum theory's antirealist stance, preferred to go on believing that unobserved objects remain real, that is, possessing definite attributes at all times whether these attributes are looked at or not. In this view, which I call "ordinary realism," the fuzziness in the quantum description arises not from an objective fuzziness in the attributes of quantum objects, but from the physicist's own ignorance concerning the values of unobserved attributes. Likewise the quantum jump is not a real physical event but a mere bookkeeping procedure that corresponds to the sudden increase in the observer's knowledge that occurs in the act of measurement. The gist of ordinary realism, in the words of British physicist Paul Davies, is that "big things are made of little things" where "thing" means here an object that possesses definite attributes whether observed or not.

As attractive as this common-sense position might seem, the majority of physicists soundly reject it, holding that quantum phenomena must be taken on their own terms and not forced into outmoded philosophical molds such as ordinary realism. Quantum founding father and firm antirealist Werner Heisenberg declared, "An atom is not a thing," and compared reality-nostalgic physicists such as Einstein, Schrödinger and Prince De Broglie to believers in a Flat Earth. "The hope that new experiments will lead Schrödinger and Prince De Broglie to be believers in an objective world in time and space is about as well founded," said Heisenberg, "as the hope of discovering the end of the world in the unexplored regions of the Antarctic."

In place of ordinary realism Heisenberg proposed a new picture of quantum reality—a model of what quantum objects are really doing when not being looked at—that is based on taking quantum theory seriously, not as a mere computational tool but as an actual picture of existence at the quantum level. To construct his vision of quantum reality, Heisenberg took quantum theory's vibratory possibilities literally: the attributes of unobserved objects exist, according to Heisenberg, exactly as represented in the theory, as possibilities, not as actualities. The unobserved atom does not really have a definite position, for instance, but only a tendency, an inclination, to be in several possible positions all at the same time. The unwatched atom, in the Heisenberg picture, is not actually anywhere, but is potentially everywhere. In Heisenberg's view an atom is certainly real, but its attributes dwell in an existential limbo "halfway between an idea and a fact," a quivering state of attenuated existence that Heisenberg called "potentia," a world devoid of single-valued actuality but teeming with billions of unrealized possibilities.

Since quantum theory applies to everything, not just to atoms, all objects without exception exist in this partially unreal state of "objective indefiniteness" (Abner Shimony) until someone (or something) decides to look at them. In the act of observation—called by physicists the "act of measurement"—one of the object's vibratory possibilities is promoted to a condition of full actuality, and all other possibilities vanish without a trace. Which possibility becomes real during a measurement is a matter of "pure chance," that is, its causes (if any) outside the world of physical law.

Heisenberg's strange picture of the quantum world as half-real possibilities that are actualized only during a measurement act is considered by many physicists to be the most reasonable guess as to how the world deep down really operates. Certainly many more physicists subscribe to the Heisenberg picture than to the common-sense tenets of ordinary realism. To the average physicist the notion that the ordinary world spends most of its time in an unreal state is not considered preposterous. Since quantum theory describes the world we see so correctly, they argue, it would be foolish not to take seriously what it seems to be telling us about the unseen world.

Because no measurement can ever tell us what the unmeasured world is like, Heisenberg's picture of quantum reality would seem to be impossible to verify or refute. Some philosophers have argued, that because of their intrinsic unverifiability, models of reality of the Heisenberg variety can be of no possible interest to scientists; they urge us to turn our interests elsewhere, to theories that have consequences in the world that we can see and touch. However, one important function that a model of the unseen reality can perform is to help extend our thinking into unknown realms. For this purpose even a bad map might lead to new discoveries.

I would like to use Heisenberg's model of quantum reality in just this way, to attempt to extend quantum ideas into a brand-new realm. To expand ordinary physics into "holistic physics," the democratic science of the future, I propose to conjoin Heisenberg's picture of the "way the world really works" with a particular conjecture concerning the relation of mind to matter.

While modern science has successfully mastered the world of matter, the world of mind still remains a deep mystery, an intellectual black hole opaque to systematic comprehension. It is fair to say that as far as scientific understanding of the mind goes, we are almost totally at sea. By the high standards of explanation we have come to demand in physics and other sciences, we do not even possess a bad theory of consciousness, let alone a good one.

Speculations concerning the origin of inner experience in humans and other beings have been few, vague, and superficial. They include the notion that mind is an "emergent property" of active neural nets, or that mind is the "software" that manages the brain's unconscious "hardware." To these rather soft speculations I would like to add my own—that mind is not a rare phenomenon associated with certain complex biological systems but is everywhere, universal in nature, a fundamental quantum effect more akin to superconductors and laser tubes than to computer circuitry.

As the cornerstone of holistic physics, I assume that every quantum system has both an "inside" and an "outside," and that consciousness in humans as well as in other sentient beings is identical to the inner experience of some quantum system. A quantum system's outside behavior is described by quantum theory, its inside experience is the subject matter of a new "inner physics" yet to be developed. The size of the quantum system in the brain responsible for our familiar human form of consciousness can be estimated from subjective measurements of conscious data rate—how much information can you simultaneously pay attention to? The physical location of the human consciousness system may be inferred from the action sites of so-called psychedelic (mind-manifesting) drugs—chemicals that alter the structure of consciousness itself rather than merely meddling with its contents.

The notion that consciousness is intimately connected with quantum theory is not new. In 1924, Alfred Lotka, one of the founders of modern theoretical biology, guessed that the then-new physics of the quantum might someday account for the phenomenon of human awareness. Recently neurobiologist Sir John Eccles proposed that a non-material mind gains control over the matter of the human brain via quantum mechanical acts on certain intrinsically inefficient neural synapses. World-class mathematician John von Neumann and Nobel laureate Eugene Wigner claim that quantum theory is actually formally incomplete—and that the least drastic way to make quantum theory mathematically consistent is to introduce consciousness as the necessary accomplice of every quantum jump. Despite its support by certain prominent physicists and biologists, no serious experimental program has yet been conceived, let alone carried out, to test the quantum consciousness hypothesis.

Many primitive peoples organized their lives around a doctrine called "animism," the belief that every object possesses "sentient insides" like our own. The quantum consciousness assumption, which amounts to a kind of "quantum animism," likewise asserts that consciousness is an integral part of the physical world, not an emergent property of special biological or computational systems. Since everything in the world is on some level a quantum system, this assumption requires that everything be conscious on that level. If the world is truly quantum animated, then there is an immense amount of invisible inner experience going on all around us that is presently inaccessible to humans, because our own inner lives are imprisoned inside a small quantum system, isolated deep in the meat of our brains. We may not need to go into outer space to inhabit entirely new worlds. New experiential worlds of inconceivable variety may already be surrounding and interpenetrating our own.

Half-baked attempts to explain consciousness, such as mind-as-software or mind-as-emergent-property, do not take themselves seriously enough to confront the experimental facts, our most intimate data base, namely how mind itself feels from the inside. On the other hand, the most suggestive evidence for the quantum model of mind is that the Heisenberg picture of how quantum events actually happen in the world is extremely congruent with our own internal experience of what it's like to be a sentient being. Looking inside, I do not feel like "software," whatever that might mean, but indeed like a shimmering (wavelike?) center of ambiguous potentia (possibilities?) around which more solid perceptions and ideas are continually congealing (quantum jumps?). This rough match of internal feeling with external description could be utterly deceptive but it at least shows that the quantum model of mind can successfully confront the introspective evidence in a way that no other mind models even attempt.

Because of the twofold character of the quantum description, this quantum model of mind predicts two basic types of subjective experience: a clear, determinate, computer-data type of experience (type-one consciousness) built out of quantum jumps; and a fuzzy, indeterminate, ambiguous experience (type-two consciousness), an insider's view of some of the brain's vibratory quantum possibilities. The vibratory nature of these conscious possibilities is not usually experienced by humans for the same reason that the wavelike nature of sunlight eluded observation for so long—light from the sun consists of wavelengths too short to perceive under ordinary conditions. In the quantum animism model, the quantum jump—Heisenberg's objective transition from half-real potentia to solid actuality—corresponds to a conscious decision in the human mind, or in the mind of some other sentient being, to promote some ambiguous type-two experience to more unequivocal type-one status.

This quantum model of mind offers a new perspective on conscious experience which could lead to a new "quantum psychology" linking our internal experiences in a testable way to the objective external behavior of certain brain-resident quantum systems. The problems of human perception, emotion, and personality as well as the mysterious extra-physical origin of quantum jumps may well yield to a disciplined marriage of keen introspection and quantum biology. Moving beyond quantum psychology, the realization that behind every visible quantum process lies an invisible psychic extension will result in a new kind of physics—holistic physics—in which human awareness becomes an essential component of every experiment.

At the heart of holistic physics will be a new kind of measurement that I call "rapprochement" to distinguish it from the act of measurement in conventional physics. While an ordinary measurement informs us about a thing's outsides, rapprochement connects the observer to an object's heretofore hidden insides, allowing him or her to directly experience the inner lives of quantum systems.

A conventional measurement cannot penetrate to the inside of an object to examine its quantum potentia because every conventional measurement, no matter how delicate, inevitably triggers a quantum jump that erases all potentia save one. This new kind of measurement—rapprochement—on the other hand, connects the mind of the observer directly to the object's potentia without the intervention of a quantum jump. The full content of the object's inner life is adjoined to the inner life of the observer and their intermingled potentias mutually enrich each other, without memorializing or prejudicing one potentia over another.

To achieve rapprochement one needs a way of connecting the mind of the observer to the "mind" of the object without making records; one needs a so-called "oblivious link" which physically couples the brain's consciousness to the object in question without initiating a quantum jump. Since the inner lives of physical objects are almost certainly incomprehensible in human terms, the first truly usable oblivious links will no doubt be established between two human quantum centers of consciousness, not between a human consciousness and the insides of some "inanimate" system. Quantum-intimate brain-matter links with non-human beings will come later, after we have practiced such linkage with humans.

Since magnetic fields can easily penetrate the brain and do not collapse wave functions, one possible candidate for an oblivious link between two brain centers might be a slowly varying magnetic field. Two humans with their heads immersed in the same oscillating magnetic field may be the first people to actually experience the pleasures of rapprochement, a new kind of quantum-mediated telepathy.

However, the "telepathy" achieved during rapprochement will feel very different from a mere exchange of data. The joining of two centers of Heisenbergian potentia via an oblivious link does not make any records. This new experience of insides-to-insides "essence merge" is a moment-to-moment impression that is immediately forgotten. Indeed the experience of multivalued potentia (type-two consciousness) is of a kind that by its very nature must be forgotten, since only single-valued experiences (type-one consciousness, or quantum jumps) can be recorded in the brain or anywhere else in the world. One task of the quantum psychologist will be to determine the relative proportion of type-one and type-two consciousness—the proportion, loosely speaking, of "fact" and "fantasy"—in the minds of various personality types. Although the experience of rapprochement is soon forgotten, it is not without permanent effect on the participants. The quantum potentias—and hence the scope of all their future possibilities—of both partners in the quantum linkup are drastically altered by their intimate essence exchange.

Whether holistic physics is the mind/body science of the future or a philosophical shaggy-dog story depends on whether the human mind really is the private insides of some quantum brain system (unknown) and on our ingenuity (untested) in constructing oblivious links that jumplessly join brain centers to outside matter systems.

German light/matter physicist Walter Heitler and others have claimed that quantum theory requires that the separation of the world into an objective outside reality and a self-conscious observer can no longer be maintained. "Subject and object have become inseparable from each other," says Heitler. Yet I have practiced experimental quantum physics for more than twenty years without once merging with my apparatus. Although quantum object and quantum measuring device do indeed merge in the early stages of measurement, that holistic merger is always cut short by the wave function collapse, by the production of a single-valued record inside the measuring device. A physicist never experiences fundamental union with the outside world in a conventional quantum measurement because the quantum jump always intervenes at the last minute to cleanly isolate the observer from the object of his observation.

Unlike conventional physics, holistic physics really would erase the distinction between subject and object. They became what they beheld in the holistic physics lab. There will be a very real danger in the obliviation operation of getting "lost in space," and never coming back. That is probably what will ultimately happen to our species. Scientists, generally wary of all-engulfing non-intellectual experiences, will probably hold back. But once they discover the exhilaration of rapprochement, ordinary men and women will not hesitate to diffuse their beings into matter itself, contacting, exploring, and adopting mindforms progressively more bizarre, awaking out of ordinary consciousness as from a long and lonely dream, and filling all of space-time with the tang of a new style of awareness that once called itself human.

Virtual Environments, Personal Simulation & Telepresence

1. Media Technology and Simulation of First-Person Experience

Scott S. Fisher

"Watch out for a remarkable new process called SENSORAMA! It attempts to engulf the viewer in the stimuli of reality. Viewing of the color stereo film is replete with binaural sound, colors, winds, and vibration. The original scene is recreated with remarkable fidelity. At this time, the system comes closer to duplicating reality than any other system we have seen!"[1]

For most people, "duplicating reality" is an assumed, if not obvious goal for any contemporary imaging technology. The proof of the "ideal" picture is not being able to discern object from representation—to be convinced that one is looking at the real thing. At best, this judgement is usually based on a first order evaluation of "ease of identification"; i.e. realistic pictures should resemble what they represent. But resemblance is only part of the effect. In summing up prevailing theories on realism in images, Perkins comments: "Pictures inform by packaging information in light in essentially the same form that real objects and scenes package it and the perceiver unwraps that package in essentially the same way."[2]

What is most limited in contemporary media is the literal process involved in "unwrapping" the image. Evaluation of image realism should also be based on how closely the presentation medium can simulate dynamic, multi-modal perception in the real world. A truly informative picture, in addition to merely being an informational surrogate, would duplicate the physicality of confronting the real scene that it is meant to represent. The image would move beyond simple photorealism to immerse the viewer in an interactive, multi-sensory display environment. Methods to implement and evaluate these interdependent factors contributing to image realism lie in the emerging domain of media technology. Until recently, significant developments in this area have usually been dictated by economics, available technology, and, as mentioned, cursory ideas about what types of information are sufficient in image representation. For example, the medium of television, as most experience it, plays to a passive audience. It has little to do with the nominal ability to "see at a distance" other than in a vicarious sense; it offers only interpretations of remote events as seen through the eyes of others with no capability for viewpoint control or personal exploration. And, although this second-hand information may be better than no information at all, a "first-person," interactive point of view can offer added dimensions of experience:

"We obtain raw, direct information in the process of interacting with the situations we encounter. Rarely intensive, direct experience has the advantage of coming through the totality of our internal processes—conscious, unconscious, visceral, and mental—and is most completely tested and evaluated by our nature. Processed, digested, abstracted second-hand knowledge is often more generalized and concentrated, but usually affects us only intellectually—lacking the balance and completeness of experienced situations . . . Although we are existing more and more in the realms of abstract, generalized concepts and principles, our roots are in direct experience on many levels, as is most of our ability to consciously and unconsciously evaluate information."[3]

In the past few decades, changing trends in media technology have begun to yield innovative ways to represent first-person or "direct experience" through the development of multi-sensory media environments in which viewers can interact with the information presented as they would in encountering the original scene. A key feature of these display systems (and of more expensive simulation systems) is that the viewers' movements are non-programmed; that is, they are free to choose their own path through available information rather than remain restricted to passively watching a "guided tour." For these systems to operate effectively, a comprehensive information database must be available to allow the user sufficient points of view. The main objective is to liberate the user to move around in a virtual environment, or, on a smaller scale, to viscerally peruse a scene that may be remotely sensed or synthetically generated. In essence, the viewers' access to more than one viewpoint of a given scene allows them to synthesize a strong visual percept from many points of view; the availability of multiple points of view places an object in context and thereby animates its meaning.

2. The Evolution of Virtual Environments

Matching visual display technology as closely as possible to human cognitive and sensory capabilities in order to better represent "direct experience" has been a major objective in the arts, research, and industry for decades. A familiar example is the development of stereoscopic movies in the early '50s, in which a perception of depth was created by presenting a slightly different image to each eye of the viewer. In competition with stereo during the same era was Cinerama, which involved three different projectors presenting a wide field of view display to the audience; by extending the size of the projected image, the viewer's peripheral field of view was also engaged. More recently, the omnimax projection system further expands the panoramic experience by situating the audience under a huge hemispherical dome onto which a high-resolution, predistorted film image is projected; the audience is now almost immersed in a gigantic image surround.

In 1962, the Sensorama display previously noted was a remarkable attempt at simulating personal experience of several real environments using state of the art media technology. The system was an elegant prototype of an arcade game designed by Morton Heilig: one of the first examples of a multi-sensory simulation environment that provided more than just visual input. When you put your head up to a binocular viewing optics system, you saw a first-person viewpoint, stereo film loop of a motorcycle ride through New York City, and you heard three-dimensional binaural sound that gave you sounds of the city of New York and of the motorcycle moving through it. As you leaned your arms on the handlebar platform built into the prototype and sat in the seat, simulated vibration cues were presented. The prototype also had a fan for wind simulation that combined with a chemical smellbank to blow simulated smells in the viewer's face. As an environmental simulation, the Sensorama display was one of the first steps toward duplicating a viewer's act of confronting a real scene. The user is totally immersed in an information booth designed to imitate the mode of exploration while the scene is imaged simultaneously through several senses.

The idea of sitting inside an image has been used in the field of aerospace simulation for many decades to train pilots and astronauts to safely control complex, expensive vehicles through simulated mission environments. Recently, this technology has been adapted for entertainment and educational use. "Tour of the Universe" in Toronto and "Star Tours" at Disneyland are among the first entertainment applications of simulation technology and virtual display environments; about 40 people sit in a room on top of a motion platform that moves in synch with a computer-generated and model-based image

Scott S. Fisher Virtual Environments, Personal Simulation & Telepresence

display of a ride through a simulated universe.

This technology has been moving gradually toward lower cost "personal simulation" environments in which viewers are also able to control their own viewpoint or motion through a virtual environment—an important capability missing from the Sensorama prototype. An early example of this is the Aspen Movie Map, done by the M.I.T. Architecture Machine Group in the late '70s.[4] Imagery of the town of Aspen, Colorado, was shot with a special camera system mounted on top of a car, filming down every street and around every corner in town, combined with shots above town from cranes, helicopters, and airplanes and also with shots inside buildings. The Movie Map gave the operators the capability of sitting in front of a touch-sensitive display screen and driving through the town of Aspen at their own rate, taking any route they chose by touching the screen, indicating what turns they wanted to make and what buildings they wanted to enter. In one configuration, this was set up so that the operators were surrounded by front, back, and side-looking camera imagery so that they were completely immersed in a virtual representation of the town.

Conceptual versions of the ultimate sensory-matched virtual environment have been described by science fiction writers for many decades. One concept has been called "telepresence," a technology that would allow remotely situated operators to receive enough sensory feedback to feel like they are really at a remote location and are able to do different kinds of tasks. Arthur Clarke has described "personalized television safaris" in which the operator could virtually explore remote environments without danger or discomfort. Heinlein's "waldoes" were similar, but were able to exaggerate certain sensory capabilities so that the operator could, for example, control a huge robot. Since 1950, technology has gradually been developed to make telepresence a reality.

Historically, one of the first attempts at developing these telepresence visual systems was done by the Philco Corporation in 1958. With this system an operator could see an image from a remote camera on a CRT mounted on his head in front of his eyes and could control the camera's viewpoint by moving his head.[5] A variation of the head-mounted display concept was done by Ivan Sutherland at MIT in the late '60s.[6] This helmet-mounted display had a see-through capability so that computer-generated graphics could be viewed superimposed onto the real environment. As the viewer moved around, those objects would appear to be stable within that real environment and could be manipulated with various input devices that they also developed. Research continues at other laboratories such as NASA Ames in California, the Naval Ocean Systems Center in Hawaii and MITI's Tele-existence Project in Japan: Here the driving application is the need to develop improved systems for humans to operate safely and effectively in hazardous environments such as undersea or outer space.

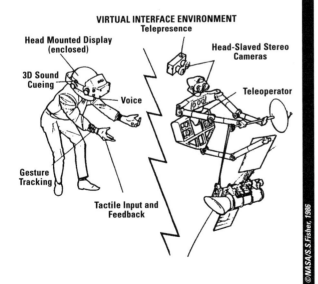

VIRTUAL INTERFACE ENVIRONMENT
Telepresence
Head Mounted Display (enclosed)
Head-Slaved Stereo Cameras
3D Sound Cueing
Teleoperator
Voice
Gesture Tracking
Tactile Input and Feedback
©NASA/S.S.Fisher, 1986

Figure 1: Remote Presence, 1986. VIEWlab Project illustration for use of Virtual Environment technology to provide a sense of presence in Telerobotics applications.

3. VIEW: The NASA / Ames Virtual Environment Workstation

In the Aerospace Human Factors Research Division of NASA's Ames Research Center, an interactive Virtual Interface Environment Workstation (VIEW) has been developed as a new kind of media-based display and control environment that is closely matched to human sensory and cognitive capabilities. The VIEW system provides a virtual auditory and stereoscopic image surround that is responsive to inputs from the operator's position, voice, and gestures. As a low cost, multipurpose simulation device, this variable interface configuration allows an operator to virtually explore a 360-degree synthesized or remotely sensed environment and viscerally interact with its components.[7–11]

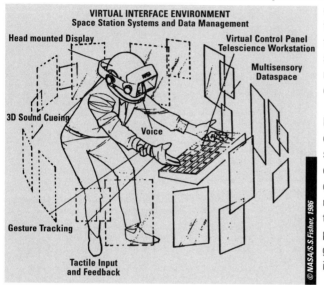

The current Virtual Interface Environment Workstation system consists of: a wide-angle stereoscopic display unit, glove-like devices for multiple-degree-of-freedom tactile input, connected speech recognition technology, gesture-tracking devices, 3-D auditory display and speech synthesis technology, and computer graphic and video image generation equipment.

Figure 2: *Dataspace, 1986. VIEWlab project illustration for use of Virtual Environment technology in Information Management applications*

When combined with magnetic head and limb position tracking technology, the head-coupled display presents visual and auditory imagery that appears to completely surround the user in 3-space. The gloves provide interactive manipulation of virtual objects in virtual environments that are either synthesized with 3-D computer-generated imagery, or remotely sensed by user-controlled, stereoscopic video camera configurations. The computer image system enables high performance, real-time 3-D graphics presentation that is generated at rates up to 30 frames per second as required to update image viewpoints in coordination with head and limb motion. Dual independent, synchronized display channels are implemented to present disparate imagery to each eye of the viewer for true stereoscopic depth cues. For real-time video input of remote environments, two miniature CCD video cameras are used to provide stereoscopic imagery. Development and evaluation of several head-coupled, remote camera platform and gimbal prototypes is in progress to determine optimal hardware and control configurations for remotely controlled camera systems. Research efforts also include the development of real-time signal processing technology to combine multiple video sources with computer-imagery.

4. Virtual Environment Applications

Application areas of the virtual interface environment research at NASA Ames are focused in two main areas—Telepresence and Dataspace:

TELEPRESENCE—The VIEW system is currently used to interact with a simulated telerobotic task environment. The system operator can call up multiple images of the remote task environment that represent viewpoints from free-flying or telerobot-mounted camera platforms. Three-dimensional sound cues give distance and direction information for proximate objects and events. Switching to telepresence control mode, the operator's wide-angle, stereoscopic display is directly linked to the telerobot 3-D camera system for precise viewpoint control. Using the tactile input glove technology and speech commands, the operator directly controls the robot arm and dexterous end effector which appear to be spatially correspondent with his or her own arm.

DATASPACE—Advanced data display and manipulation concepts for information management are being developed with the VIEW system technology. Current efforts include use of the system to create a display environment in which data manipulation and system monitoring tasks are organized in virtual display space around the operator. Through speech and gesture interaction with the virtual display, the operator can rapidly call up or delete information windows and reposition them in 3-space. Three-dimensional sound cues and speech synthesis technologies are used to enhance the operator's overall situational awareness of the virtual data environment. The system also has the capability to display reconfigurable, virtual control panels that respond to glove-like tactile input devices worn by the operator.

5. Personal Simulation: Architecture, Medicine, Entertainment

In addition to remote manipulation and information management tasks the VIEW system also may be a viable interface for several commercial applications. So far, the system has been used to develop simple architectural simulations that enable the operator to design a very small 3-D model of a space, and then, using a glove gesture, scale the model to life size allowing the architect/operator to literally walk around in the designed space. Seismic data, molecular models, and meteorological data are other examples of multidimensional data that may be better understood through representation and interaction in a virtual environment.

Another virtual environment scenario in progress involves the development of a surgical simulator for medical students and plastic surgeons that could be used much as a flight simulator is used to train jet pilots. Where the pilot can explore situations that would be dangerous to encounter in the real world, surgeons can use a simulated "electronic cadaver" to do pre-operation planning and patient analysis. The system is also set up in such a way that surgical students can look through the eyes of a senior surgeon and see a first-person view of the way he or she is doing a particular procedure. As illustrated in the following figure, the surgeon can be surrounded with the kinds of information windows that are typically seen in an operating room in the form of monitors displaying life support status information and X-rays.

Entertainment and educational applications of this technology could be developed through this ability to simulate a wide range of real or fantasy environments with almost infinite possibilities of scale and extent. The user can be immersed in a 360-degree fantasy adventure game as easily as he or she can viscerally explore a virtual 3-D model of the solar system or use a three-dimensional paint system to create virtual environments for others to explore.

6. Tele-Collaboration through Virtual Presence

A major near-term goal for the Virtual Interface Environment Workstation Project is to connect at least two of the current prototype interface systems to a common virtual environment database. The two users will participate and interact in a shared virtual environment but each will view it from a relative, spatially disparate viewpoint. The objective is to provide a collaborative workspace in which remotely located participants can virtually interact with some of the nuances of face-to-face meetings while also having access to their personal dataspace facility. This could enable valuable interaction between scientists collaborating from different locations across the country or even between astronauts on a space station and research labs on Earth. With full body tracking capability, it will also be possible for users to be represented in this space by life-size virtual representations of themselves in whatever form they choose—a kind of electronic persona. For interactive theater or interactive fantasy applications, these virtual forms might range from fantasy figures to inanimate objects, or be different figures to different people. Eventually, telecommunication networks will develop that will be configured with virtual environment servers for users to dial into remotely in order to interact with other virtually present users.

Although the current prototype of the Virtual Interface Environment Workstation has been developed primarily to be used as a laboratory facility, the components have been designed to be easily replicable for relatively low cost. As the processing power and graphics frame rate on microcomputers quickly increases, portable, personal virtual environment systems will also become available. The possibilities of virtual realities, it appears, are as limitless as the possibilities of reality. It provides a human interface that disappears—a doorway to other worlds.

Figure 3:
*Virtual Interface
Environment for Surgical
Simulation, 1989.
VIEWlab Virtual World
database for use in Surgical
planning and education
(in collboration with
MIT Media Lab and
Stanford Medical School).*

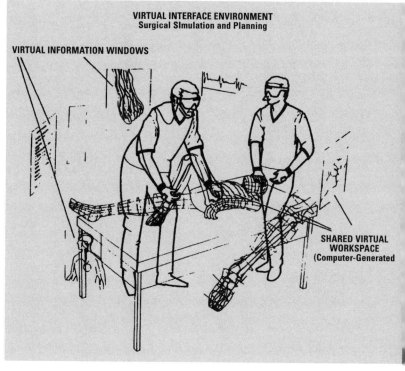

VIRTUAL INTERFACE ENVIRONMENT
Surgical SImulation and Planning

VIRTUAL INFORMATION WINDOWS

SHARED VIRTUAL
WORKSPACE
(Computer-Generated

Notes

1. L. Lipton, "Sensorama," Popular Photography, July 1964.

2. D. N. Perkins, "Pictures and the Real Thing," Project Zero, Harvard University, Cambridge, Massachusetts (1973).

3. Bender, Environmental Design Primer, Minneapolis (1973).

4. Andrew Lipmann, "MovieMaps: An Application of the Optical Videodisc to Computer Graphics," Computer Graphics 14, no. 3 (1980).

5. C. Comeau and J. Bryan, "Headsight Television System Provides Remote Surveillance," Electronics (November 10, 1961), 86–90.

6. I. E. Sutherland, "Head-Mounted Three-Dimensional Display," Proceedings of the Fall Joint Computer Conference 33 (1968), 757–764.

7. S. S. Fisher, "Telepresence Master Glove Controller for Dexterous Robotic End-Effectors: Advances in Intelligent Robotics Systems," in: D. P. Casasent, ed., Proc. SPIE 726 (1986).

8. S. S. Fisher, M. W. McGreevy, J. Humphries, and W. Robinett, "Virtual Environment Display System," ACM Workshop on 3D Interactive Graphics, Chapel Hill, North Carolina (October 23–24, 1986).

9. S. S. Fisher, E. M. Wenzel, C. Coler, and M. W. McGreevy, "Virtual Interface Environment Workstations," Proceedings of the Human Factors Society—32nd Annual Meeting, Anaheim, California (October 24–28, 1988).

10. E. M. Wenzel, F. L. Wightman, and S. H. Foster, "A Virtual Display System for Conveying Three-Dimensional Acoustic Information," Proceedings of the Human Factors Society—32nd Annual Meeting, Anaheim, California (October 24–28, 1988).

11. J. D. Foley, "Interfaces for Advanced Computing," Scientific American 257, no. 4 (1987), 126–135.

The Future of Cyberspace

Wild Frontier vs. Hyperreal Estate

Bruce Sterling

"Cyberspace" today is a foggy concept, further muddled by attempts to copyright or trademark the term itself. "Cyberspace" in its broadest sense is a useful term to denote a raw technical frontier up for grabs—though the "frontier" metaphor must be qualified. Cyberspace is not some unexplored natural region, but an utterly unnatural space boiling out from nothingness: a gigantic badland of mirrors which replicate the pioneers' own inner mentalities.

As "cyberspace" is settled and developed, the successful territories within it will take on the status of states-of-media. Following the growing clusters of population, money, and power, we can imagine "scientific visualization" as an early and fertile territory, accompanied perhaps by three-dimensional computer-aided design, artificial reality games, the various sub-provinces of telepresence, and 3-D hypermedia, and groupware.

That is to say: we might forecast such developments, if we examined the strictly technical potential inherent in the "cyberspace" medium. To assume, however, that cyberspace will fulfill its basic technological potential is naive. It is not in the nature of a capitalist society to carry its media to ultimate forms; instead they are optimized for profit, while containing or subverting attempts at revolutionary breakthrough. As Marvin Minsky once wisely said: "Imagine if television were actually good. It would mean the end of everything we know."

A working Gibsonian cyberspace would also mean the end of everything we know. Attempts to end everything we know, while not rare—Cambodia and Iran come to mind—have rarely ended well.

The future of cyberspace today is in the hands of two rival camps, which might be roughly described as technophilic utopian and capitalist/pragmatarian. Their philosophies can be summarized respectively as "Fast Cheap and Out of Control," and "Planned Development of Hyperreal Estate." To continue the frontier metaphor, the utopians might be compared to squatters, mountain men, and trappers—or perhaps hapless tribes of aborigines. The rival camp, which conceives of itself as "civilization," is in basic control of formal land grants, the legislatures, the army, and the railroads.

The Fast Cheap and Out of Control crowd has three advantages: speed, reckless courage, and the ability to scrape by on low budgets, i.e. "live off the land." Their ability to govern "cyberspace" over the longer term is almost nonexistent; like other technical pioneers, most will be starved-out, bought-out, overpowered by the consequences of their own success, or simply put out to pasture. At the moment, however, they can strongly influence the emergent shape of cyberspace—and therefore the shape of its future bureaucracies—by confronting society with a series of technical faits accompli. They therefore much resemble the American "filibusters," or the French explorers of Africa, who dragged imperial authority into the wilderness by aggressive, bold, and sometimes illegal explorations. The techno-utopians can jam Adam Smith's invisible hand into the cyberspace data-glove, and force the market to come to grips with the formerly unthinkable.

However, the advantages of the capitalist pragmatarians are manifold and vast. They control the purse-strings and the levers of power that confer social legitimacy on business, governmental, and scientific enterprises. "Cyberspace" offers a window of opportunity for radical technical change; but the window will not remain open indefinitely. It will be carefully shuttered, lest chill winds disturb the paying customers.

Like a radical movie from Hollywood, a revelatory news program on network television, or a genuinely alarming ride in Disneyland, genuine paradigm-changing antics in cyberspace will be rare. It is not impossible that "cyberspace" will be outlawed entirely, much like lysergic acid, especially if it is surrounded by a technophilic rhetoric that proclaims a revolution in the human condition.

The first workable and widespread "cyberspace" is likely to be the "virtual corporate workspace." This is or will be a simulated 3-D space owned by a corporation for the purpose of conducting its business outside the constraints of normal time and space. It will almost certainly look as much as possible like the business quarters of a well-heeled multinational corporation: halls, doors, elevators, windows, board rooms, data centers, and so forth. Imagine an airport hotel, with even less character, and made of blurry colored polygons. (It is useful at this point to recall that early horseless carriages often carried the false figurehead of a horse attached to the motor, so as not to panic animals and passersby.) This corporate workspace will be intensely boring and "businesslike," for much the same reasons of design philosophy that cause personal computers to remain beige-colored boxes. Personal computers could as easily mimic sports cars in their flashy variety, or designer handbags; they might even look like penguins or unicorns; but the fact that this is technically possible means little in the face of cultural resistance.

Toy cyberspaces may beat the "corporate virtual workspace" to market, but since they ARE toys, they will have about the same cultural effect as the lovely but scorned Atari game-computer, compared to the ugly but mighty IBM-PC. Personal toy cyberspaces in any case will not be able to overshadow the appeal of dedicated mainframe cyberspace amusement parks. The corporate amusement park—surrounded by the revenue-generating potential of souvenir shops, candy stores, cuddly franchised characters, and intense though unobtrusive security—is, as Jean Baudrillard has pointed out, already a supreme realm of the hyperreal. Amusement park corporations are therefore excellently placed to exploit the new cyberspace technologies—not "to the full," but in an optimal commercial fashion. It would be well to look to Japan for the first steps in this direction. The third likely cyberspace is the consumer arena. Attempts to sell consumer goods and services by videotext have signally failed; but strong attempts will almost certainly be made to create the "cyberspace shopping mall," using the well-established marketing techniques of anchor stores, "bundled" boutiques, and so forth, replicated in a virtual, 3-D realm. As the shopping mall itself is the apotheosis of the consumer society monitored, abstract, interchangeable, sterile, optimally designed to attract and manage flows of capital—so a properly designed "cyberspace" could be the apotheosis of the shopping mall. Hybrid mixes of simulated mall architecture, combined with "telepresence" techniques for sampling the actual goods, may prove a potent mix.

At this point, however, and in conclusion, it is well to remember a few lessons of history. Nineteenth century Europe's answer to Artificial Reality was known as the "panorama," a 360-degree panned environment which used tricks of shade and lighting to present the illusion of viewer presence within a simulated realm. Some were 15 meters high, 100 meters long, weighing well over 6,000 kilogrammes, and were housed in specially designed buildings in Paris, Munich, Hamburg, Cologne, Leipzig, and many other cities. The Austrian "roundview" of Innsbruck (Raiffeisen Reisebüro Tirol) is one of perhaps a score of "panoramas" still surviving.

Large teams of painters and designers were employed in the panorama trade, and the audience for this early-industrial medium numbered in the millions; but today the "panorama" is a curiosity, eclipsed by other media more sophisticated, less grandiose, and more easily manageable. Many efforts in "cyberspace" may have no success at all, limited success, or, like the panoramas, tremendous success and excitement, but for a limited period. There is no real way to tell what will work, or for how long; what will be touched with gold by the invisible Midas hand of the market, and what will swiftly become as quaint as Pong or the magic lantern. Depending on your philosophical position in the cyberspace camps, this fact is either unfortunate—or very lucky indeed.

The Universal Robot

Hans Moravec

Our artifacts are getting smarter, and a loose parallel with the evolution of animal intelligence suggests one future course for them. Computerless industrial machinery exhibits the behavioral flexibility of single-celled organisms. Today's best computer-controlled robots are like the simpler invertebrates.

A thousand-fold increase in computer power in the next decade should make possible machines with reptile-like sensory and motor competence. Properly configured, such robots could do in the physical world what personal computers now do in the world of data—act on our behalf as literalminded slaves. Growing computer power over the next half-century will allow this reptile stage to be surpassed, in stages producing robots that learn like mammals, model their world like primates, and eventually reason like humans. Depending on your point of view, humanity will then have produced a worthy successor, or shaken off some of its inherited limitations and so transformed itself into something quite new.

Instincts which predispose the nature and quantity of work we enjoy probably evolved during the 100,000 years our ancestors lived as hunter-gatherers. Less than 10,000 years ago the agricultural revolution made life more stable, and richer in goods and information. But, paradoxically, it requires more human labor to support an agricultural society than a primitive one, and the work is of a different, unnatural kind, out of step with the old instincts. The effort to avoid this work has resulted in domestication of animals, slavery, and the industrial revolution. But many jobs must still be done by hand, engendering for hundreds of years the fantasy of an intelligent but soulless being that can tirelessly dispatch the drudgery. Only in this century have electronic sensors and computers given machines the ability to sense their world and to think about it, and so offered a way to fulfill the wish. As in fables, the unexpected side effects of robot slaves are likely to dominate the resulting story. Most significantly, these perfect slaves will continue to develop, and will not long remain soulless. As they increase in competence they will have occasion to make more and more autonomous decisions, and so will slowly develop a volition and purposes of their own. At the same time they will become indispensable. Our minds were evolved to store the skills and memories of a stone-age life, not the enormous complexity that has developed in the last 10,000 years. We've kept up, after a fashion, through a series of social inventions—social stratification and division of labor, memory aids like poetry and schooling, written records stored outside the body, and recently machines that can do some of our thinking entirely without us. The portion of absolutely essential human activity that takes place outside of human bodies and minds has been steadily increasing. Hard-working intelligent machines may complete the trend.

Serious attempts to build thinking machines began after the second world war. One line of research, called Cybernetics, used simple electronic circuitry to mimic small nervous systems, and produced machines that could learn to recognize simple patterns, and turtle-like robots that found their way to lighted recharging hutches (Wiener 1961). An entirely different approach, named Artificial Intelligence (AI), attempted to duplicate rational human thought in the large computers that appeared after the war. By 1965, these computers ran programs that proved theorems in logic and geometry, solved calculus problems, and played good games of checkers (Feigenbaum and Feldman 1963). In the early 1970s, AI research groups at MIT (the Massachusetts Institute of Technology) and Stanford University attached television cameras and robot arms to their computers, so their thinking programs could begin to collect their information directly from the real world.

What a shock! While the pure reasoning programs did their jobs about as well and about as fast as college freshmen, the best robot control programs took hours to find and pick up a few blocks on a table. Often these robots failed completely, giving a performance much worse than a six-month-old child. This disparity between programs that reason and programs that perceive and act in the real world holds to this day. In recent years Carnegie Mellon University produced two desk-sized computers that can play chess at grandmaster level, within the top 100 players in the world, when given their moves on a keyboard. But present-day robotics could produce only a complex and unreliable machine for finding and moving normal chess pieces.

In hindsight it seems that, in an absolute sense, reasoning is much easier than perceiving and acting, a position not hard to rationalize in evolutionary terms. The survival of human beings (and their ancestors) has depended for hundreds of millions of years on seeing and moving in the physical world, and in that competition large parts of their brains have become efficiently organized for the task. But we didn't appreciate this monumental skill because it is shared by every human being and most animals, it is commonplace. On the other hand, rational thinking, as in chess, is a newly acquired skill, perhaps less than 100,000 years old. The parts of our brain devoted to it are not well organized, and, in an absolute sense, we're not very good at it. But until recently we had no competition to show us up.

By comparing the edge and motion detecting circuitry in the four layers of nerve cells in the retina, the best understood major circuit in the human nervous system, with similar processes developed for "computer vision" systems that allow robots in research and industry to see, I've estimated that it would take a billion computations per second (the power of a world-leading Cray 2 supercomputer) to produce the same results at the same speed as a human retina. By extrapolation, to emulate a whole brain takes ten trillion arithmetic operations per second, or ten thousand Cray's worth (Moravec 1988). This is for operations our nervous systems do extremely efficiently and well. Arithmetic provides an example at the other extreme. In 1989 a new computer was tested for a few months with a program that computed the number 4 to more than one billion decimal places. By contrast, the largest unaided manual computation of 4 was 707 digits by William Shanks in 1873. It took him several years, and because of a mistake every digit past the 527th was wrong! In arithmetic, today's average computers are one million times more powerful than human beings. In very narrow areas of rational thought (like playing chess or proving theorems) they are about the same. And in perception and control of movement in the complex real world, and related areas of common-sense knowledge and intuitive and visual problem solving, today's average computers are a million times less capable. The deficit is evident even in pure problem solving AI programs. To this day AI programs exhibit no shred of common sense—a medical diagnosis program, for instance, may prescribe an antibiotic when presented a broken bicycle because it lacks a model of people, diseases, or bicycles. Yet these programs, on existing computers, would be overwhelmed were they to be bloated with the details of everyday life, since each new fact can interact with the others in an astronomical combinatorial explosion. (A ten-year project called Cyc at the Microelectronics and Computer Consortium in Austin, Texas, is attempting to build just such a common-sense data base. They estimate the final result will contain over one hundred million logic sentences about everyday objects and actions (Lenat and Guha 1989).)

Machines have a lot of catching up to do. On the other hand, for most of the century, machine calculation has been improving a thousandfold every twenty years, and there are basic developments in research labs that can sustain this for at least several decades more. In less than fifty years computer hardware should be powerful enough to match, and exceed, even the well-developed parts of human intelligence. But what about the software that would be required to give these powerful machines the ability to perceive, intuit, and think as well as humans? The Cybernetic approach that attempts to directly imitate nervous systems is very slow, partly because examining a working brain in detail is a very tedious process. New instruments may change that in the future. The AI approach has successfully imitated some aspects of rational thought, but that seems to be only about one millionth of the problem. I feel that the fastest progress on the hardest problems will come from a third approach, the newer field of robotics, the construction of systems that must see and move in the physical world. Robotics research is imitating the *evolution* of animal minds, adding capabilities to machines a few at a time, so that the resulting sequence of machine behaviors resembles the capabilities of animals with increasingly complex nervous systems. This effort to build intelligence from the bottom up is helped by biological peeks at the "back of the book"—at the neuronal, structural, and behavioral features of animals and humans.

The best robots today are controlled by computers just powerful enough to simulate the nervous system of an insect, cost as much as houses, and so find only a few profitable niches in society (among them, spray painting and spot welding cars and assembling electronics). But those few applications are encouraging research that is slowly providing a base for a huge future growth. Robot evolution in the direction of full intelligence will greatly accelerate, I believe, in about a decade when the mass-produced general purpose, universal robot becomes possible. These machines will do in the physical world what personal computers do in the world of data—act on our behalf as literal-minded slaves.

The Dumb Robot (ca. 2000–2010)

To be useful in many tasks, the first generation of universal robots should navigate efficiently over flat ground and reliably and safely over rough terrain and stairs, be able to manipulate most objects, and be able to find them in the nearby world. There are beginnings of solutions today. In the 1980s Hitachi of Japan developed a mobility system of five steerable wheels, each on its own telescoping stalk that allows it to accommodate to rises and dips in uneven terrain, and to climb stairs, by raising one wheel at a time while standing stably on the other four. My laboratory at Carnegie Mellon University in Pittsburgh has developed a navigation method that enables a robot equipped with sonar range measuring devices and television cameras to build probabilistic maps of its surroundings to determine its location and plan routes (Moravec 1987). An elegant three-fingered mechanical hand at the Massachusetts Institute of Technology can hold and orient bolts and eggs and manipulate a string in a humanlike fashion (Mason and Salisbury 1985). A system called 3DPO from SRI International in Menlo Park, California, can find a desired part in a jumble seen by special range-finding camera (Bolles, Horaud, and Hannah 1984). The slow operation of these systems suggests one other element needed for the universal robot, namely a computer about one thousand times as powerful as those found on desks and in robots today. Such machines, able to do one billion computations per second, would provide robots approximately the brain power of a reptile, and the personality of a washing machine.

Universal robots will find their first uses in factories, where they will be cheaper and more versatile than the older generation of robots they replace. Eventually they will become cheap enough for some households, extending the reach of personal computers from a few tasks in the data world to many in the physical world.

As with computers, many applications of the robots will surprise their inventors. Some will do light mechanical assembly, clean bathrooms, assemble and cook gourmet meals from fresh ingredients, do tune-ups on a certain year and make of cars, hook patterned rugs, weed a lawn, run robot races, do detailed earthmoving and stonework, investigate bomb threats, deliver to and fetch from warehoused inventories, and much more. Each application will require its own original software (very complex by today's computer program standards), and some may also need optional hardware attachments for the robot such as special tools and chemical sensors.

Learning (2010–2020)

Useful though they will be, the first generation of universal robots will be rigid slaves to simple programs. If the machine bangs its elbow while chopping beef in your kitchen making Stroganoff, you will have to find another place for the robot to do its work, or beg the software manufacturer for a fix. Second-generation robots with more powerful computers will be able to host a more flexible kind of program able to adjust itself by a kind of conditioned learning. First-generation programs will consist primarily of sequences of the type "Do step A, then B, then C . . ." The programs for the second generation will read "Do step A1 or A2 or A3 . . . then B1 or B2 or B3 . . . then C1 or C2 or C3 . . ." In the Beef Stroganoff example, A1 might be to chop with the right hand of the robot, while A2 is to use the left hand. Each alternative in the pro-

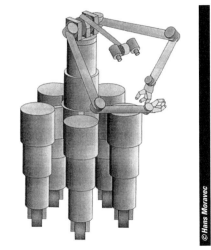

A caricature of a first-generation Volksrobot, showing wheels on telescoping legs, arms with dexterous hands, camera eyes for object finding and implied spatial awareness, navigation and one billion operation per second computer system.

gram has a "weight," a number that indicates the desirability of using it rather than one of the other branches. The machine also contains a "pain" system, a series of programs that look out for problems, such as collisions, and respond by reducing the weights of recently invoked branches, and a "pleasure" system that increases the relevant weights when good conditions, such as well-charged batteries or a task efficiently completed, are detected. As the robot bangs its elbow repeatedly in your kitchen, it gradually learns to use its other hand (as well as adapting to its surroundings in a thousand other ways). A program with many alternatives at each step, whose pain and pleasure systems are arranged to produce a pleasure signal on hearing the word "good" and a pain message on hearing "bad," could be slowly trained to do new tasks, like a small mammal. A particular suite of pain- and pleasure-producing programs interacting with a robot's individual environment would subtly shape its behavior and give it a distinct character.

Imagery (2020–2030)

Adaptive robots will find jobs everywhere, and the hardware and software industry that supports them could become the largest on earth. But teaching them new tasks, whether by writing programs or through punishment and reward, will be very tedious. This deficiency will lead to a portentous innovation, a software world-modeler (requiring another big increase in computer power), that allows the robot to simulate its immediate surroundings and its own actions within them, and thus to think about its tasks before acting. Before making Beef Stroganoff in your kitchen, the new robot would simulate the task many times. Each time its simulated elbow bangs the simulated cabinet, the software would update the learning weights just as if the collision had physically happened. After many such

Hans Moravec *The Universal Robot*

mental run-throughs the robot would be well trained, so that when it finally cooks for real, it does it correctly. The simulation can be used in many other ways. After a job, the robot can run though its previous actions, and try variations on them to improve future performance. A robot might even be configured to invent some of its own programs by means of a simpler program that can detect how nearly a sequence of robot actions achieves a desired task . This training program would, in repeated simulations, provide the "good" and "bad" indications needed to condition a general learning program like the one of the previous section.

It will take a large community of patient researchers to build good simulators. A robot entering a new room must include vast amounts of not directly perceived prior knowledge in its simulation, such as the expected shapes and probable contents of kitchen counters and the effect of (and force needed for) turning faucet knobs. It needs instinctive motor-perceptual knowledge about the world that took millions of years of evolution to install in us, that tells us instinctively when a height is dangerous, how hard to throw a stone, or if the animal facing us is a threat. Robots that incorporate it may be as smart as monkeys.

Reasoning (2030–2040)

In the decades while the "bottom-up" evolution of robots is transferring the perceptual and motor faculties of human beings into machinery, the conventional Artificial Intelligence industry will be perfecting the mechanization of reasoning. Since today's programs already match human beings in some areas, those of 40 years from now, running on computers a million times as fast as today's, should be quite superhuman. Today's reasoning programs work from small amounts of clear and correct information prepared by human beings. Data from robot sensors such as cameras is much too voluminous and too noisy for them to use. But a good robot simulator will contain neatly organized data about the robot and its world—for instance, if a knife is on a countertop, or if the robot is holding a cup. A robot with simulator can be married to a reasoning program to produce a machine with most of the abilities of a human being. The combination will create beings that in some ways resemble us, but in others are like nothing the world has seen before.

First-Generation Technicalities

Both industrial robot manipulators and the research effort to build "smart" robots are twenty-five years old. Universal robots will require at least another decade of development, but some of their elements can be guessed from the experience so far. One consideration is weight. Mobile robots built to work in human-sized spaces today weigh too many hundreds of pounds. This dangerously large mass has three major components: batteries, actuators, and structure. Lead-acid batteries able to drive a mobile robot for a day contribute about one third of the weight. But nickel-cadmium aircraft batteries weigh half as much, and newer lithium batteries can be half again as light. Electric motors are efficient and precisely controllable, but standard motors are heavy and require equally heavy reducing gears. Ultrastrong permanent magnets can halve the weight and generate high torque without gears. Robot structure has been primarily aluminum. Its weight contribution can be cut by a factor of four by substituting composite materials containing superstrength fibers of graphite, aramid, or the new material Spectra. These innovations could be combined to make a robot with roughly the size, weight, strength, and endurance of a human.

The first-generation robot will probably move on wheels. Legged robots have advantages on complicated terrain, but they consume too much power. A simple wheeled robot would be confined to areas of flat ground, but if each wheel had a controlled suspension with about a meter of travel, the robot could slowly lift its wheels as needed to negotiate rough ground and stairs. The manipulation system will consist of two or more arms ending in dexterous manipulators. There are several designs in the research labs today, but the most elegant is probably that of the so-called Stanford-JPL hand (mentioned above, now found at MIT), which has three fingers each with three controlled joints. The robot's travels would be greatly aided if it could continuously pinpoint its location, perhaps by noting the delay from a handful of small synchronized transmitters distributed in its environment. This approach is used in some terrestrial and satellite navigation systems. The robot will also require a sense of its immediate surroundings, to find doors, detect obstacles, and track objects in its workspace. Research laboratories, including my own, have experimented with techniques that do this with data from television cameras, scanning lasers, sonar transducers, infrared proximity sensors, and contact sensors. A more precise sensory system will be needed to find particular work objects in clutter. The most successful methods to date start with three-dimensional data from special cameras and laser arrangements that directly measure distance as well as lateral position. The robot will thus probably contain a wide-angle sensor for general spatial awareness, and a precise, narrow angle, three-dimensional imaging system to find particular objects it will grasp.

Research experience to date suggests that to navigate, visually locate objects, and plan and control arm motions, the first universal robots will require a billion operations per second of computer power. The 1980s have witnessed a number of well publicized fads that claim to be solutions to the artificial intelligence or robot control problem. Expert systems, the Prolog logical inference language, neural nets, fuzzy logic, and massive parallelism have all had their spot in the limelight. The common element that I note in these pronouncements is the sudden enthusiasm of a group of researchers experienced in some area of computer science for applying their methods to the robotics problems of perceiving and acting in the physical world. Invariably each approach produces some simple showcase demonstrations, then bogs down on real problems. This pattern is no surprise to those with a background in the twenty-five-year research robotics effort. Making a machine to see, hear, or act reliably in the raw physical world is much, much more difficult than naive intuition leads us to believe. The programs that work relatively successfully in these areas, in industrial vision systems, robot arm controllers, and speech understanders, for example, invariably use a variety of massive numerical computations involving statistics, vector algebra, analytic geometry, and other kinds of mathematics. These run effectively on conventional computers, and can be accelerated by array processors (widely available add-ons to conventional machines which rapidly perform operations on long streams of numbers) and by use of modest amounts of parallelism. The mind of the first-generation universal robot will almost certainly reside in quite conventional computers, perhaps ten processors each able to perform 100 million operations per second, helped out by a modest amount of specialized computing hardware that preprocesses the data from the laser eyes and other sensors, and that operates the lowest level of mobility and manipulation systems.

Mind Children (2050+)

The fourth robot generation and its successors, with human perceptual and motor abilities and superior reasoning powers, could replace human beings in every essential task. In principle, our society could continue to operate increasingly well without us, with machines running the companies and doing the research as well as performing the productive work. Since machines can be designed to work well in outer space, production could move to the greater resources of the solar system, leaving behind a nature preserve subsidized from space. Meek humans would inherit the earth, but rapidly evolving machines would expand into the rest of the universe. This development can be viewed as a very natural one. Human beings have two forms of heredity, one the traditional biological kind, passed on strands of DNA, the other cultural, passed from mind to mind by example, language, books, and recently machines. At present the two are inextricably linked, but the cultural part is evolving very rapidly, and gradually assuming functions once the province of our biology. In terms of information content, our cultural side is already by far the larger part of us. The fully intelligent robot marks the point where our cultural side can exist on its own, free of biological limits. Intelligent machines, which are evolving among us, learning our skills, sharing our goals, and being shaped by our values, can be viewed as our children, the children of our minds. With them our biological heritage is not lost. It will be safely stored in libraries, at least; however, its importance will be greatly diminished.

What about life back on the preserve? For some of us the thought of being grandly upstaged by our artificial progeny will be disappointing, and life may seem pointless if we are fated to spend it staring stupidly at our ultra-intelligent progeny as they try to describe their ever more spectacular discoveries in baby-talk that we can understand. Is there any way individual humans might join the adventure?

You've just been wheeled into the operating room. A robot brain surgeon is in attendance, a computer waits nearby. Your skull, but not your brain, is anesthetized. You are fully conscious. The robot surgeon opens your brain case and places a hand on the brain's surface. This unusual hand bristles with microscopic machinery, and a cable connects it to the computer at your side. Instruments in the hand scan the first few millimeters of brain surface. These measurements, and a comprehensive understanding of human neural architecture, allow the surgeon to write a program that models the behavior of the uppermost layer of the scanned brain tissue. This program is installed in a small portion of the waiting computer and activated. Electrodes in the hand supply the simulation with the appropriate inputs from your brain, and can inject signals from the simulation. You and the surgeon compare the signals it produces with the original ones. They flash by very fast, but any discrepancies are highlighted on a display screen. The surgeon fine-tunes the simulation until the correspondence is nearly perfect. As soon as you are satisfied, the simulation output is activated. The brain layer is now impotent—it receives inputs and reacts as before but its output is ignored. Microscopic manipulators on the hand's surface excise this superfluous tissue and pass them to an aspirator, where they are drawn away.

The surgeon's hand sinks a fraction of a millimeter deeper into your brain, instantly compensating its measurements and signals for the changed position. The process is repeated for the next layer, and soon a second simulation resides in the computer, communicating with the first and with the remaining brain tissue. Layer after layer the brain is simulated, then excavated. Eventually your skull is empty, and the surgeon's hand rests deep in your brainstem. Though you have not lost consciousness, or even your train of thought, your mind has been removed from the brain and transferred to a machine. In a final, disorienting step the surgeon lifts its hand. Your suddenly abandoned body dies. For a moment you experience only quiet and dark. Then, once again, you can open your eyes. Your perspective has shifted. The computer simulation has been disconnected from the cable leading to the surgeon's hand and reconnected to a shiny new body of the style, color, and material of your choice. Your metamorphosis is complete.

Your new mind has a control labeled "speed." It had been set at 1 to keep the simulations synchronized with the old brain, but now you change it to 10,000, allowing you to communicate, react, and think ten thousand times faster. You now seem to have hours to respond to situations that previously seemed instantaneous. You have time, during the fall of a dropped object, to research the advantages and disadvantages of trying to catch it, perhaps to solve its differential equations of motion. When your old biological friends speak with you, their sentences take hours—you have plenty of time to think about the conversations, but they try your patience. Boredom is a mental alarm that keeps you from wasting your time in profitless activity, but if it acts too soon or too aggressively it limits your attention span, and thus your intelligence. With help from the machines, you change your mind-program to retard the onset of boredom. Having done that, you will find yourself comfortably working on long problems with sidetracks upon sidetracks. In fact, your thoughts routinely become so involved that you need an increase in your memory. These are but the first of many changes. Soon your friends complain that you have become more like the machines than the biological human you once were. That's life.

References

Bolles, Robert, Patrice Horaud, and Marsha Jo Hannah. 1984. "3DPO: A Three-Dimensional Part Orientation System." In: Robotics Research: The First International Symposium, ed. Michael Brady and Richard Paul. MIT Press, Cambridge, Massachusetts, pp. 413–424.

Feigenbaum, Edward, and Julian Feldman, eds. 1963. Computers and Thought. McGraw-Hill Inc., New York.

Lenat, Douglas, and Rajiv Guha. 1989. Building Large Knowledge-Based Systems: Representation and Inference in the Cyc Project. Addison-Wesley Publishing Co., Reading, Massachusetts.

Mason, Matt, and Kenneth Salisbury. 1985. Robot Hands and the Mechanics of Manipulation. MIT Press, Cambridge, Massachusetts.

Moravec, Hans. 1987. "Sensor Fusion in Certainty Grids for Mobile Robots." AI Magazine 9, no. 2, pp. 61–77.

Moravec, Hans. 1988. Mind Children: The Future of Robot and Human Intelligence. Harvard University Press, Cambridge, Massachusetts.

Wiener, Norbert. 1961. Cybernetics, or Control and Communication in the Animal and the Machine (second edition). MIT Press, Cambridge, Massachusetts.

Thresholds of Control

Destruction Art and Terminal Culture

I.

Kristine Stiles

"We are survivors in this age," Saul Bellow's Herzog writes in one of his unsent letters. "To realize that you are a survivor is a shock. At the realization of such election you feel like bursting into tears."[1]

Destruction art bears witness to the tenuous conditionality of survival; it is the visual discourse of the survivor. It is the only attempt in the visual arts to grapple seriously with the technology and psychodynamics of actual and virtual extinction, one of the few cultural practices to redress the general absence of discussion about destruction in society.[2]

Destruction art is interdisciplinary and multinational, combining media and subject matter. Destruction art addresses the phenomenology and epistemology of destruction and must be characterized as a broad, cross-cultural response rather than a historical movement. An attitude, a process and way of proceeding, destruction art is both reactionary and responsive; it is not an aesthetic, nor a method, nor a technique. Destruction art is an ethical position comprised of diverse practices that investigate the engulfments of terminal culture.

I have introduced the phrases "terminal culture" and "destruction art" as identificatory devices, terms that signify the conjoined sites where social, aesthetic, and political interrelationships and practices collude in the question of survival. The term "destruction art" is, thus, a concise index of a wide anthropological field, whereas the phrase "destruction-in-art" emphasizes the processes that determine its practices within the institutions of art. In this brief essay, I want to theorize destruction art in terms of its survivalist discourse as well as to contextualize its historical project.

II.

In his singularly important work on trauma, the psychologist Robert Jay Lifton identifies a survivor as "one who has encountered, been exposed to, or witnessed death and has himself or herself remained alive."[3] Death here may be literal as in the actual extinguishing of life, psychological as in the destruction of the sense of Self, or ecological as in natural disaster. Whatever the text of survival, it must be read through the discourse of destruction. Lifton asks the rhetorical question: "Is Hiroshima our text?"[4] Indeed, as representation, Hiroshima identifies destruction as the extremity and the center of survival where the body figures as the text. Destruction art is a responsible commitment to the survival of the body.

Survival, Lifton writes, leaves a "death imprint" that is accompanied by "death anxiety, death guilt, or survivor guilt," guilt that entails a "sense of debt and responsibility to the dead."[5] Survival also causes a "psychic numbing" that incapacitates the individual's ability to feel and to confront certain kinds of experiences and impairs essential mental functions of symbolization.[6] He hypothesizes that a wholesale psychic numbing has occurred internationally, the result of the constant global threat of technological, ecological, or psychological annihilation. Destruction art represents this crisis of numbing with actions, events, and/or objects recapitulating the conditions, effects, and processes of destruction that interfere with survival and that have been repressed in and by the epistemologies of terminal culture.

Destruction art obliges critical reflection on the question of disappearance. Jean-François Lyotard takes up the problem of disappearance in his book *Heidegger and "the jews"* where he coins the phrase "The Forgotten" to signify a condition that is neither "a concept nor a representation but a 'fact' as *Factum* (Kant)" which we are "obligated before the Law . . . to remember."[7] "The Forgotten" is "something that never ceases to be forgotten," a state that "one has tried to forget by killing it," but one that advances, nevertheless, "in the direction of the immemorial through the destruction of its representations of its witnesses, "the jews."[8] Here Lyotard indicates that "'the jews' are the object of a dismissal with which Jews, in particular, are afflicted in reality."[9] Lyotard's "the jews" is a refinement and historical specification of the "catastrophe" Nietzsche forewarned was the inevitable result of the "failure to reflect."[10]

Destruction is the agent and process of disappearance in our time, of "The Forgotten," "the jews." The interdependence of "the jews" and "The Jews" is relevant to destruction art and the materiality of survival. For the origins of terms of destruction art are located in the theoretical formulations of a real Jew and a survivor of Lyotard's signifying "the jew," namely a survivor of destruction: Gustav Metzger. In five manifestos written between November, 1959, and July, 1964, Metzger laid out the basis for "Auto-Destructive Art" that is also the foundation of destruction art.[11] Metzger intended "Auto-Destructive Art" to be principally realized in public monuments to be erected on civic sites. These structures would contain complex technological and electronic internal devices that would cause the structure to implode and self-destruct within a period of twenty seconds to twenty years. Site-sensitive and site-specific, interdisciplinary and requiring collaboration between scientists and artists, these works would be context-determined and, therefore, social, collective, and collaborative. Industrial and machine made, the structures would also be technical representations of the intrinsic interdependence of the processes of natural decay and disintegration and cultural, particularly urban, crisis. "Auto-Destructive Art" condensed a vast experiential and technological territory of destruction and its concomitant survivalist ethos into a manageable representation.

The temporal duration of "Auto-Destructive Art" would operate both as a representation and a presentation, an image and an enactment of effacement that recalled but also gave substance to the forgotten, "the jews." As the rematerialization of memory in its original destructive form, the absent presence of the felt past would return as known experience, no longer "there" but transformed into a new state "here." Destruction art in its first manifestation of "Auto-Destructive Art" is the constant public and social reminder of destruction, its agents, processes, and results. Precisely twenty years after Metzger was sent to England at the age of 12 in 1939 when his family was arrested by the Gestapo in Nürnberg, he formulated his theory. Twenty seconds, then, is a temporal analog for the seconds it took to destroy his personal world by killing his family; twenty years, the two decades of gestation in his own auto-transformation. Temporality in destruction art is the index of duration that confronts consciousness with the cycle of construction and destruction manifest in cultural artifacts and technological objects as well as in nature. This temporality reinscribes the psyche of the social body with a memory of the finite which must function as an affective agent in the reaggregation of a survivalist consciousness.

Temporality in Metzger's life signifies not only in cultural terms but in political terms as well. Metzger retained his Polish passport while living in Great Britain until 1948 when he decided to become stateless. This life experience reflects the geopolitics of the disappeared, which Paul Virilio has identified as one of the conditions of "Pure War":

Disappearance of place and individual, refusal of citizenship, of rights, of habeas corpus, etc., . . . is spreading all over the world. It's easier to make people disappear one by one, ten by ten or thousand by thousand than to shut millions up into camps, as they did in Nazi Germany. Even if Gulags and concentration camps still exist—and they do, alas—disappearance is our future.[12]

The concrete evidence of corporeal existence in the carnage of bombed cities and towns with dead bodies to be buried or burned that was the result of past wars no longer exists since the crematoria and thermonuclear vaporization obliterate all reckoning with death and destruction. "Pure War" in this sense refers to the technical and psychological readiness and ubiquity of war that currently shapes political as well as social relationships, and that contributes to the "epistemo-technical," a way of knowing and being-in-the-world based in the technology of war."[13] "Pure War is neither peace nor war," Virilio claims, "nor is it, as was believed, 'absolute' or 'total' war, but rather, the military procedure itself which infects us with its ordinary durability."[14]

While disappearance is one of the conditions of the war-machine, what Virilio accurately calls "the machine of societal non-development,"[15] Pure War is also the "logistics of war." The U.S.A. established such logistics in the late 1940s when Pentagon officials defined logistics as "the procedure following which a nation's potential is transferred to its armed forces, in times of peace as in times of war."[16] In writing about the "politics of meaning," Clifford Geertz noted, "One of the things that everyone knows but no one can quite think how to demonstrate is that a country's politics reflect the design of its culture."[17] But the country that developed and deployed the first atomic weapon made its politics very visible in civic life already by the early 1950s when it became public record that the U.S. civil core of engineers were engaged in the construction of such logistical sites, places where the military might "test" the effects of nuclear destruction on materials and techniques used in civic structures. One such site was illustrated in the periodical *Architectural Record* in 1952, where vivid images showed a destroyed two-story frame house, destroyed reinforced steel and concrete office buildings, and other destroyed constructions.[18]

In the resulting Cold War rhetoric and muscle of weapons Metzger refined the dialectical aspects of his theories by extending "Auto-Destructive Art" to "AutoCreative Art" and he honed their ideological dimension. Destruction art should be politically affective and socially engaged, a practice in which artists struggle to dismantle the institutions of power that dehumanize, exploit, and destroy. Destruction art should be concerned with the social body and collective practices as it "re-enacts the obsession with destruction, the pummeling to which individuals and masses are subjected," he wrote, and added:

The drop drop dropping of HH bombs . . . mirrors the compulsive perfectionism of arms manufacture polishing to destruction point. Autodestructive Art is the transformation of technology into public art. The immense productive capacity, the chaos of capitalism and of Soviet communism, the coexistence of surplus and starvation; the increasing stockpiling of nuclear weapons—more than enough to destroy technological societies; the disintegrative effects of machinery and the life in vast built-up areas on the person.[19]

The self-conscious sophistication of contemporary intellectual "discourse" stands in marked contrast to Metzger's loaded and subjective "words," emotional words that embarrass but that are unmistakably real, the direct expression of an involved, impassioned, angry, and fearful victimized man.

Destruction art is oppositional in refusing the elisions of linguistic abstraction that unwittingly contribute to the perpetuation of the destructive epistemology of Western culture, an epistemology so thoroughly perfected by "defense intellectuals" in the policies and technology of extinction about which Carol Cohn has so insightfully written. Cohn despaired of the "enormous destructive power" of "the language of defense analysts and arms controllers" for its complete resistance to the "emotional fallout . . . mass murder, mangled bodies and unspeakable human suffering" in which its languages conspire.[20] She rejected "the professional discourse" of the men whose minds are used "in the service of militarization" for its "extraordinary abstraction and removal"—smart bombs, friendly fire, clean bombs, countervalue attacks, and collateral damage—because of the ways in which it denied what she "knew in reality."[21] Related and deeply sobering is Lifton's confirmation of her attack on such "professional discourse," when he observed:

> A certain amount of numbing is probably necessary in most professional situations—in the midst of an operation a surgeon cannot afford to experience fully the consequences of failure—but it is surely excessive in our society and in our century. So great is the diminished emotion in professionals that it well may be that becoming a professional is in itself part of still another devil's bargain in which one ceases to feel much about the central—the most threatening—questions of our time.[22]

When John Latham incinerated burning towers of books, "Skoob Towers" (books spelled backwards), in the mid-1960s, when he chewed and distilled Clement Greenberg's *Art and Culture*, in 1966,[23] his gestures identified books as the carriers of the destructive epistemological and linguistic foundations of abstract rationality that justify and perpetuate destruction, the kinds of languages that imprint death and confirm the terrorist rationality of Robert McNamara who, in 1964, so chillingly coined the term "mutual assured destruction," MAD.

The denaturing and abstraction of the actual experience of destruction is the triumph of the technology of that destruction. In this situation, great care must be exercised to prevent theoretical abstractions from becoming part of the suppression of actual experience that culminates in the denial of identity altogether. Such denials conspire in the destruction of bodies and are the unforgivable consequence of mistaking the map for the territory. They are the decidable danger that resides in interpretations of Derrida's concept of "différence" that many have argued requires a "différence/deferment from/of any decidable statement of the concept of an identity or différence."[24]

The trust of destruction art is the survivability of the body, the very materiality of existence. In this sense, no group of artists has been as explicit as Survival Research Laboratories who have clearly stated the terms of their investigation and practice. Indeed, materiality is the business of art. Representation and observation, the visual conditions of materiality, are the residual features of the first act of the artist which is to recover the conditionality of materiality. This is why, without eyes, art may still exist for those without sight. When faced with extinction, the artist must, if she or he takes responsibility for his or her trust, put art in the service of survival. This does not imply that all art must assume the task of destruction art, but it does mean that art has a particular social function which requires an ethical position on the question of survival no matter what formal resolution that work finally assumes. In this sense, I believe destruction art recovers the social force of art from instrumental reason and the economies of late capitalism. For destruction art constantly reinscribes the profound significance of the survival of the body in the oppositions it deconstructs.

The task of destruction art includes the deconstruction of the double character and indeterminacy of meaning in the binary division of creation/destruction and the elucidation of the signifying conditions of destruction. In this sense, the project of destruction art resembles the deconstructionist theory with which it emerged simultaneously but independently in the early 1960s. It is significant that Derrida's *De la grammatologie* (1967) was published a year after Metzger brought the various tendencies of destruction art together as a cohesive discourse and representation in the Destruction in Art Symposium (DIAS) in 1966.[25] Metzger's stated aim in organizing DIAS was to create an interdisciplinary forum for an inquiry into the relationship of destruction in art and society.[26] Derrida's parallel objective was to "seek a new investigation of responsibility, an investigation which questions the codes inherited from ethics and politics" in the "political and institutional structures that make possible and govern our practices."[27]

DIAS was also the model for a number of subsequent exhibitions in which artists learned to expand the languages of destruction art, and it was the prototype for The Dialectics of Liberation, organized by R. D. Laing and David Cooper. Such prominent intellectuals and public figures as Paul Goodman, Stokely Carmichael, Irving Goffman, Herbert Marcuse, Gregory Bateson, and others lectured at this conference which occurred in London ten months after DIAS, in July 1967. This coincided precisely with the three-day trial of Metzger and the Irish poet and playwright John Sharkey, Metzger's principal assistant in the organization of DIAS. The pair were found guilty of having presented Hermann Nitsch's 5th action of the Orgien Mysterien Theatre, a work the court described as "an indecent exhibition contrary to common law."[28]

The simultaneity of this conference with Metzger and Sharkey's trial is instructive in its juxtaposition of the divisions of power and authority that shape the systems, practices, institutions, and performances of Western culture. The textual and expository exegesis of those who participated in The Dialectics of Liberation was permissible, framed as it was in the vaguely sentimental idealistic terms of liberation, terminology that conformed to the authoritative, abstract, restrained, measured, and ostensibly objective codes of academic discourse. By comparison, "destruction-art" represented a direct, contentious, strident, and unsentimental discourse, and its practices were raw, passionate, involved, impatient, skeptical, pessimistically critical, and sometimes dangerous and out of control.[29]

In his lecture on "The Discourse of Language" Foucault described the "logophobia" of Western culture as an "apparent logophilia," and he argued:

> What civilization, in appearance, has shown more respect towards discourse than our own? . . . Where have men depended more radically, apparently, upon its constraints and its universal character? But, it seems to me, a certain fear hides behind this apparent supremacy . . . It is as though these taboos, these barriers, thresholds and limits were deliberately disposed in order, at least partly, to master and control the great proliferation of discourse "in such a way as to relieve its richness of its most dangerous elements; to organise its disorder so as to skate round its most uncontrollable aspects."[30]

As part of the resolution to these controls, Foucault called for the restoration of discourse to "its character as an event."[31] Nitsch's work and the juridical response to it visited upon Metzger and Sharkey, indeed, returned the discourse of destruction to its "character as an event." The punishment meted out to the artists—and by extension to DIAS itself—inscribed upon them the "guilt" of destruction that must be read as the single-most important evidence of the affective role of DIAS and the events it sponsored in revealing the very systems, institutions, and epistemological foundations of destruction that it set out to criticize.

The "guilt" laid on DIAS is that of the survivor who bears witness for the social body. In this sense the individual body, the body of practices I am calling destruction art, and the social body have a symbiotic interconnection in that individual and collective bodies are also events in the history of society. In this context, as they have contributed to shaping social and political systems, the interventions of destruction art are central to any discourse on survival within or without the disciplines of art and aesthetics.

I have often argued that the primary communicating codes of the visual arts were transformed in the presentation of the body. Briefly restated, when the body becomes the material support, subject, and content of art, it holds the possibility of shifting the determined and fixed relations demanded by the prior objective status of art into an interplay of subjectivities established and transmitted in body gestures, systems, and relations. In addition to the traditional metaphorical communicating mechanisms of the visual arts, such changes in the aesthetic sign supplied a metonymic and synechdochal means of connection, projection, continuation, and contingency. The private body was utilized as formal material, subject matter, and content into which the experiences and institutions of the body politic were collapsed. I want to suggest that in these terms, the body holds the possibility for becoming both an aesthetic and social sign that also commutes political power. Lifton believes that the task of the artist is "to reveal the exquisite details of the experience of desymbolization" and "the breakdown of viable relationships with symbols and symbolic forms (that) is an impairment in the 'psychic action' of the 'formative process'. . . associated with severe manifestations of psychic numbing."[32] In destruction art, the body conveys the interdependent, interconnected, and contingent state of the individual and the collective in survival. That embodiment holds the potential to reconnect experience to the objects of that experience and thereby to intervene in the destructive practices, institutions, and technologies threatening extinction.

The urgent need to dissolve over-determined rigid structures and to construct elastic social systems is evident although constantly undermined by fixed social identities. The unprecedented achievement of the body as an active agent in art has been to visualize the perpetually shifting, but mutually identifiable relations of power and need within the exchange of subject/object relations. This shift from the conventions of representation to those of presentation may effect a reduction in the alienation between subjects and objects by confronting individuals with their mutual roles as performing and observing subjects. This reduction, however, can never be resolved but, rather, must be constantly renegotiated on the shifting territories of power that continually redetermine subject relations. The performing body underscores the desperate need for negotiation in the question of the survival of destruction. In this way, destruction art performs its radical function in larger social formations. For, in order to recover the content of destruction which includes death, trauma, and pain, its signifying agent must be both representationally symbolic and presentationally contingent.

A vivid example of such practices is Metzger's "South Bank Demonstration," of July 3, 1961. Wearing a gas mask as a protective device, Metzger sprayed hydrochloric acid on three tarpaulins— white, black, and red, a reference to Kasimir Malevich and Russian Suprematism—stretched over an enormous series of three frames feet high and 12 1/2 feet long with a depth of 6 feet. The nylon dissolved each within 15 seconds after contact with the acid. Metzger positioned himself against a complex of urban office buildings and a crowd of men, many in business attire. Visually suggestive of the military-industrial complex, this image recalled the dire warning Dwight D. Eisenhower issued only five months before Metzger's lecture-demonstration. In his farewell address from the White House Oval Office January 17, 1961, Eisenhower cautioned:

This conjunction of an immense military establishment and a large arms industry is new in the American experience. The total influence—economic, political, even spiritual—is felt in every city, every state house, every office in the federal government. We recognize the imperative need for this development. Yet we must not fail to comprehend its grave implications. Our toil, resources and livelihood are all involved; so is the very structure of our society.

As the agent of destructive forces, Metzger represented war displaced from the actual field of militarized combat by utilizing the substances of destruction to dissolve materials and thus to reenact upon the "field" of the picture space the symbolic map of the conduct, process, content, and result of destruction. His action situated war as representation in the civic built site of the production of destruction.

Only Metzger, Rafael Montanez Ortiz, and Wolf Vostell ever specifically identified their work with the terminology of destruction and systematically explored destruction as the principle focus of their work.[33] Moreover their formulations were not only very different but were even contentious, conditioned by the entirely distinct cultural contexts of Europe (Metzger and Vostell) and the United States (Ortiz), and representing unique responses to and ideological strategies for coping with and affecting their individual situations. Yet for all their differences, these three men share the critical social experience of having existed at the margin of Western cultural hierarchies in terms of the racial and religious discrimination and the actual or virtual annihilation they experienced: Metzger is the stateless victim of the Holocaust; Vostell, also a Jew, spent his youth in nomadic terror fleeing the Gestapo; and Ortiz is a dark-skinned Puerto-Rican American of mixed heritage who spent part of his youth in south Harlem, the survivor of deadly adolescent gang warfare of the Barrio and the vicious, relentless racism of the U.S.A.

One of the key psychoanalytic dimensions of destruction art is the charged emotional reaction to the anger and frustration these three experienced as the disempowered "other" within the Western male culture to which they belonged and which they theoretically controlled. This sense of being "out of control," in part, accounts for the violence of their rejection of the deceptive conventions of Western "creation" and the repressive sublimations it demands. The range of their destructions and the objects or human actions upon which they were visited, however problematic, must be characterized as parody, a profound disgust and rejection of the patriarchal models of discipline, punishment, violence, and authoritarianism so accurately theorized by Klaus Theweleit.[34]

Destruction art seems to produce a gendered response slightly different in men than in women. The body—actual or extended in mechanical robots—is the principal territory for the demonstration of destruction and survival in both men and women's productions. While male artists have explored the relationship of that body to the objects and technologies of destruction and to the assertion and recuperation of identity, women artists have regularly confined their investigations to the reconstruction of Self.

Yoko Ono's destruction scores for performances, paintings, and sculptures onward from the late 1950s, and Niki de Saint Phalle's paintings *Feu à volonté*, 1961, plaster-surface constructions filled with bags of pigment which exploded with color when fired upon with a rifle, demonstrate that women have not been exempt from the destruction of materials, including the surfaces of their own bodies as the performances of self-mutilation by Gina Pane have shown.

But the vast majority of women's destruction artworks explore the problem of the obliteration of identity and the decentering of Self. So that while the Holocaust may be our representative text, a text that is in part read through the technologies of destruction, that text must return to the reading of the material universe of the body's pain.

R. D. Laing recalled "a little girl of seventeen in a mental hospital" who told him that "she was terrified because the Atom Bomb was inside her."[35] This metaphor for the annihilation of Self that is bound to the destruction of self-esteem, intimacy, and the ability to love or be loved is also part of the trust of destruction art. In Yoko Ono's *Cut Piece*, 1965, she sat motionless on a stage after inviting the audience to come up and cut away her clothing. This denouement anticipated the institutionalized objectification of women as cultural detritus so systematically presented by Karen Finley who, in an essay entitled, "I was not expected to be talented," wrote:

I'd like for you to feel pain, to feel my pain . . . I hate people who have a reason for everything. They can't just accept the fact that bad things happen to good people because if they did they'd be like me—out of control.[36]

Ono stated, "People went on cutting the parts they do not like of me."[37] Lynn Hershman whispers as a survivor to we who bear witness to her survival: "Don't talk about it." In her autobiographical video trilogy *Electronic Diary* (1985–1989), Hershman, significantly also a Jew, recounts in an auto-analysis the origins of her own eating disorders in physical, sexual, and emotional abuse and incest, violations whose origins and results she equates to the cosmology of Hitler, the vampire, and Holocaust survivors. Such works, in the actual body of the artist, intervene in the imagined neutrality between subject and object where they insert the voice of survival that is the representation of the pain of destruction. Destruction art is the renegotiation of that pain. Elaine Scarry has argued that "the only state that is as anomalous as pain is the imagination" and that "while pain is a state remarkable for being wholly without objects, the imagination is remarkable for being the only state that is wholly its objects."[38] Destruction art represents and presents the relationship between pain and imagining. "Pain does not simply resist language," it "actively destroys it, bringing about an immediate reversion to a state anterior to language, to the sounds and cries a human being makes before language is learned."[39]

She continues:

Because the person in pain is ordinarily so bereft of the resources of speech, it is not surprising that the language of pain should sometimes be brought into being by those who are not themselves in pain but who speak on behalf of those who are. (This is how) this most radically private of experiences begins to enter the realm of public discourse.[40]

In 1962, Ono wrote "Conversation Piece," a score for an action requiring the narration of pain. Her score reads:

Bandage any part of your body.
If people ask about it, make a story and tell.
If people do not ask about it, draw their attention to it and tell.
If people forget about it, remind them of it and keep telling.
Do not talk about anything else.[41]

Invented and bandaged wounds articulate psycho-physical pain. This impulse to narrate suffering, to describe the unspeakable conditions of interior life, is central to finding a voice through and by which to repossess and recover a sense of the concreteness of personal experience. More urgent is the need to communicate the auto-constructed reality to someone else—to materialize it. Western culture needs subjects to bear witness to the contents of survival and the historical bodies upon which the text of destruction has been inscribed. The body in destruction art bears such witness and thereby offers a paradigm for a "resisting body," that private, complex, signifying system of the Self, a person who acts both on behalf of the individual and the social body.

III.

Destruction is endemic to Western structures of knowledge and conditions of culture. This negativity—and by extension destruction when it occurs in art—have appeared to defy (and threatened to destroy) Western social and aesthetic canons of truth, harmony, and order. But, far from rejecting the aesthetic and social values of Western culture, destruction art unveils its structural principles. In a recent study of the developmental role played by ancient Greek mathematics in gaining an advantage in war, John Onians considered the embeddedness of militarized consciousness in Western cultural production.[42] He noted the simultaneous dependence upon the mathematical harmony, proportion, and order in Greek warfare as well as in art and architecture, and observed that war is the most important theme in Greek painting and sculpture, and a structural principle in Greek architecture. He traced this to patterns of representation in the complex treatment of war in the *Iliad*, a book which attained "almost biblical authority" among the Greeks.[43]

Onians points out that the same harmony, number, and order to be found in Greek mathematics that determines art, music, and architecture equally regulated the Greek military phalanx, and "Hesiod, in the Theogony, makes Harmonia a daughter of Ares, god of war."[44]

Western society and its most compelling aesthetic productions continue to perpetuate the epistemological ethos of destruction. But art that once reflected, mirrored, and passively represented the abstract conventions and patterns of knowledge now actively present the literal embodiment of psychic wounds, urban bedlam, and militarized consciousness at the crisis core of terminal culture. But this epistemology also has healing roots, traditions, that are intertwined in the very technology, languages, and practices of destruction.

Foucault recovered the Greek term *epimeleia heauton* which stood for the psychological and intellectual condition of being interested in taking care of one's self, of work on the self.[45] The term equally described the responsibilities of power. *Epimeleia heauton* implied attention, knowledge, technique, a work of meditation that required understanding the necessities of the world, not imposed upon the individual by civil law or religious obligation, but rather as a choice about existence made by the individual who decided whether or not to care for the self, and thereby, to care for the world. Foucault pointed out that *epimeleia heauton* described a condition in which individuals "acted so as to give to their lives certain values (for) it was a question of making one's life into an object for a sort of knowledge, for a *techne*—for an art."[46]

Destruction art communicates the visual knowledge that may recuperate the materiality of life from the violent, discontinuous destructions that imperil survival. The body may be a tool in the *techne* of survival and may function as a transit between agency and process, language, experience, and their objects to close the lesion between *techne* and *logia* (word, speech, or knowledge) that has inhered in the modern concept of technology. Just as destruction art is the image of resistance in the form of an event, it is also an important means to survival that must be continuously explored.

Notes

1. Saul Bellow, Herzog (New York: Viking, 1964) as quoted in Robert Jay Lifton's The Future of Immortality and Other Essays for a Nuclear Age (New York: Basic Books, 1987), p. 244. I am grateful to Susan Roth, Professor of Psychology specializing in trauma and stress disorders at Duke University, for introducing me to the work of Lifton and I would like to dedicate this essay to her. I would like to thank also Jill Meredith, David Castriota, and Julie Walker, my colleagues at Duke University, for their critical editorial suggestions.

2. Litton has observed that in working on the problem of mass psychological trauma he "came to a terrible, but essentially accurate, rule of thumb: the more significant an event, the less likely it is to be studied." The Future of Immortality, p. 32. Bruno Bettelheim observed a similar phenomenon in his own investigations on the topic of violence when, in a public lecture I heard in San Francisco in 1982, he noted that violence as a category of investigation remained largely absent from philosophical dictionaries. My own study of destruction confirms Bettelheim's and Lifton's observations. For the category "destruction" is absent from most philosophical dictionaries and does not even appear in Raymond Williams' "keywords" with such entries as "alienation," "family," "technology," and "violence." See Williams' revised edition of Keywords: A Vocabulary of Culture and Society (New York: Oxford University Press, 1983).

3. Lifton, The Future of Immortality, p. 235.

4. Ibid., p. 31.

5. Ibid., pp. 236–240.

6. Ibid., p. 245.

7. Jean-François Lyotard, Heidegger and "the Jews," trans. Andreas Michel and Mark S. Roberts, with a foreword by David Carroll (Minneapolis: University of Minnesota Press, 1990), p. 3. Originally published as Heidegger et "les juifs" (Paris: Editions Galilée, 1988).

8. Ibid., p. 43.

9. Ibid., p. 3.

10. Friedrich Nietzsche, "Preface" (November 1887–March 1888) to The Will To Power, trans. Walter Kaufmann (New York: Vintage Books, 1967), p. 3.

11. See Gustav Metzger's Auto-Destructive Art: Metzger at AA (London, October 1965). This publication is part of the collection of the Archiv Sohm, Staatsgalerie, Stuttgart. The text contains all of Metzger's manifestos "Auto-Destructive Art," 4 November 1959; "Manifesto Auto-Destructive Art," 10 March 1960; "Auto-Destructive Art—Machine Art—Auto-Creative Art," 23 June 1961; "MANIFESTO WORLD," October 1962; and "On Random Activity in Material/ Transforming Works of Art," 30 July 1964. Metzger prepared the publication as an expanded version of a talk he gave at the Architectural Association, 24 February 1965, which he published in June 1965. In this document Metzger develops his "aesthetic of revulsion" (p. 13) and places "Auto-Destructive Art" in the context of "anxiety, despair, nihilism, alienation" that are "not only connected with psychology, religion, social systems, but with a profound awareness of failure on the biological plane" (p. 22).

12. Paul Virilio and Sylvere Lotringer, Pure War, trans. Mark Polizzotti (New York: Semiotext(e), 1983), p. 137.

13. Ibid., p. 21.

14. Paul Virilio, Popular Defense & Ecological Struggles, trans. Mark Polizzotti (New York: Semiotext(e) Foreign Agents Series, 1990), p. 35. Originally published as Défense populaire et Luttes ecologiques (Paris: Edition Galiliée, 1978). "Military socialism" is the term Virilio uses to describe the ways in which the military sustains and perpetuates itself by making continual war on its own civilian populations.

15. Virilio and Lotringer, Pure War, p. 221.

16. For a thorough study of nuclear strategy see Lawrence Freedman's The Evolution of Nuclear Strategy (New York: St. Martin's Press, 1983). For a consideration of how these strategies figured in the creation of Metzger's "Auto-Destructive Art," see my unpublished doctoral dissertation "The Destruction in Art Symposium (DIAS): The Radical Cultural Project of Event-Structured Live Art," University of California, May 1987, especially chapter 1.2, "Jews, Bombs, and Activism: A Biographical Legacy" in which Metzger's political activism, especially in the "Committee of 100," is discussed in the context of the Cold War (pp. 63–89).

17. Clifford Geertz, The Interpretation of Cultures: Selected Essays (New York: Basic Books, 1973), p. 311.

18. See "Architects Design a Bombed-Out Town,"Architectural Record 112:1 (July 1952), pp. 185–188.

19. Gustav Metzger, "Manifesto Auto-Destructive Art," 10 March 1961.

20. Carol Cohn, "Sex and Death in the Rational World of Defense Intellectuals," Signs: Journal of Women in Culture and Society 12:4 (Summer 1987), p. 691.

21. Ibid, p. 688–689.

22. Lifton, The Future of Immortality, p. 240.

23. See John Latham, State of Mind (Düsseldorf: Städtische Kunsthalle, 1975).

24. For example, see Gayatri Spivak, "Displacement and the Discourse of Woman," in Displacement: Derrida and After, ed. Mark Krupnick (Bloomington: Indiana University Press, 1983), p. 184.

25. See Jacques Derrida, De le grammatologie (Paris: Minuit, 1967). DIAS was the temporary organization for a multicultural, mutidisciplinary international event that attracted nearly one hundred artists and poets (most of whom were the pioneers of Happenings and Concrete Poetry) from fifteen countries in Eastern and Western Europe, the United States, South America, and Japan. Several psychologists also attended. DIAS was important in identifying artists internationally who pioneered destruction art. Documentation and destruction sound tapes were sent to DIAS by the Argentina painter Kenneth Kemble who had assembled a group of poets and painters (Luis Alberto Wells, Silvia Torras, Jorge Roiger, and Jorge Lopez Anaya), in 1961, for an exhibition he titled Arte Destructivo that took place at the Galerie Lirolay in Buenos Aires. Shortly after this exhibition the group dissolved and it was not until DIAS that this work was recovered.

26. See the many DIAS Press Releases written and distributed by Metzger in the collection of the Archiv Sohm, Staatsgalerie, Stuttgart.

27. Jacques Derrida, "The Conflict of Faculties," in Languages of Knowledge and of Inquiry, ed. Michael Riffaterre (New York: Columbia University Press, 1982), as quoted in Jonathan Culler, On Deconstruction: Theory and Criticism after Structuralism (Ithaca, New York: Cornell University Press, 1982), p. 156.

28. Based on notes taken by the journalist Sheldom Williams during the DIAS trial, I reconstructed the trial in my dissertation. The official transcripts of this trial have all been destroyed.

29. For various accounts of DIAS events and related material, see my essays "Synopsis of The Destruction in Art Symposium (DIAS) and Its Theoretical Significance," The Act 1:2 (Spring 1987), pp. 22–31; "Sticks and Stones: The Destruction in Art Symposium," Arts 65:5 (January 1989), pp. 54–60; and "Readings: Performance and Its Objects," Arts 65:3 (November 1990), pp. 35–47.

30. Michel Foucault, "The Discourse on Language," originally delivered in French at the Collège de France on December 2, 1970, reprinted in The Archaeology of Knowledge & The Discourse on Language (New York: Harper Colophon Books), p. 218.

31. Ibid, p. 219.

32. Lifton, The Future of Immortality, p. 245.

33. In his "Destructivism: A Manifesto," 1962, Ortiz wrote: "The destroyers, materialists, and sensualists dealing with process directly . . . are destructivists and understand the desperate need to retain unconscious integrity. The artist's sense of destruction will no longer be turned inward in fear. The art that utilizes the destructive processes will purge, for as it gives death, so it will give to life." This manifesto appears in my catalogue Rafael Montanez Ortiz: Years of the Warrior 1960—Years of the Psyche, 1988 (New York: El Museo del Barrio, 1988), p. 52. Ortiz's

performance work is particularly important in terms of the influence it had on Arthur Janov's formulation of "primal scream" psychotherapy. See Arthur Janov, The Primal Scream: Primal Therapy: The Cure for Neurosis (New York: Delta, 1970), pp. 9–11. Wolf Vostell developed his practice of de-coll/age during the late 1950s after having noticed the term in Le Figaro in 1954, when it was used to describe the simultaneous takeoff and crash of an airliner. His syllabic division of the word decollage inverts the constructive process of collage and deconstructs the binary creation/destruction into semiotic units that transform in time: "dé" and "coll" name oppositions while "age" refers (in French) to temporality. Vostell's sensitivity to the semiotic range of the French term décollage owes something to the context in which such poet-painters as Raymond Hains, Jacques Villeglé, and Françoise Dufrene in Paris, and Mimmo Rotella, in Italy, developed l'affiche lacerée.

34. See Klaus Theweleit, Male Fantasies. Volume 2: Male Bodies: Psychoanalyzing the White Terror (Minneapolis: University of Minnesota Press, 1989). Originally published as Männerphantasien, Volume 2. Männerkörper: Zur Psychoanalyse des weißen Terrors (Verlag Roter Stern, 1978). Some of the works include the menacing explosives spectacles staged by Ivor Davies, John Latham, and others in the 1960s or Survival Research Laboratories in the 1980s; the burned and exploded books, paintings, and musical objects produced by John Latham, Gustav Metzger, Milan Knizak, Rafael Ortiz, Nam June Paik, Joseph Beuys, Robin Page, Jean Tinguely, Arman, and many others; the"Archaeological Finds"—destroyed furniture created by Rafael Ortiz from 1959 to 1965; destroyed objects of all varieties by Metzger, Vostell, Kenneth Kemble, Bruce Conner, and many others; and psycho-physical performances by Hermann Nitsch, Otto Mühl, Günter Brus, Jean-Jacques Lebel, Rafael Ortiz, and others.

35. R. D. Laing, "Preface to the Pelican Edition," in: The Divided Self: An Existential Study in Sanity and Madness (Baltimore: Penguin Books, 1970), p. 12. Originally published in London by Tavistock Publications, 1959.

36. Karen Finley, "I was not expected to be talented," in: Shock Treatment (San Francisco: City Lights, 1970), pp. 104–110.

37. Yoko Ono, "Statement" in the Village Voice, October 7, 1971, p. 20.

38. Elaine Scarry, The Body in Pain: The Making and Unmaking of the World (New York and Oxford: Oxford University Press, 1985), p. 162.

39. Ibid., p. 4.

40. Ibid., p. 6.

41. Yoko Ono, Grapefruit, 2d ed., with an Introduction by John Lennon (New York: Simon and Schuster, 1970), n.p. Originally published in Tokyo by Wunternaum Press, 1964.

42. John Onians, "War, Mathematics, and Art in Ancient Greece," History of the Human Sciences 2:1 (1990), pp. 39–62.

43. Ibid., p. 41.

44. Ibid., p. 47.

45. Michel Foucault, The Care of the Self. Volume 3: The History of Sexuality, trans. Robert Hurley (New York: Pantheon Books, 1986), pp. 50, 60–66. Originally published as Le souci de soi (Paris: Editions Gallimard, 1984).

46. See Michel Foucault in: Herbert L. Dreyfus and Paul Rabinow, Michel Foucault: Beyond Structuralism and Hermeneutics (Chicago: University of Chicago Press, 1983), pp. 243–245.

Video and Architecture

Beyond the Screen

Kathy Rae Huffman

A form of architecture can now be located within video and computer technology. It is electronic volume, a phenomenon that also provides cohesion for radical artistic communication practices. This is intelligent space! It defines information as site, especially as it informs the influence of experimental art and the fundamental discourse relevant to the reality of data space. The expanded redefinition of the virtual as real has been reconstructed by traditional communication practices such as radio, telephone, and television, and their manifest contemporary forms in electronic network environments and their evolving multimedia network applications. These spatial expressions employ electronics not only to decode the transparencies inherent in the video and computer images we normally observe, but in this case they are also used to define the physical, navigable properties of electronic data space itself. In an obvious contradiction, these spaces are conceptually embedded in the intelligent mechanisms that exist independently of what is visible on the surface of an electronic screen. This spatial transparency, which as Virilio notes has long supplanted appearances,[1] takes on physical dimensions of a new order at this point because the representation of overlapping physical and electronic realities can now be readily constructed, observed, and experienced in convenient formats.

Equally important in a discussion of an electronically created terrain and virtual architecture is the consideration of the critical and theoretical discourse that connects video, informatics, and the geography of space.[2] These concerns, which have evolved during the past three decades of practical experience, research, and observation by artists using the new media of their era, are the direct consequence of the exploration of the media's potential, including the investigation of the altered and elaborated electronic image. Likewise, the rapid advancement of the understanding of information networks underscores a completely new phenomena: the traceable grid that exists in electronic space. A revolutionary new understanding of this volume is a result of what once seemed to be an impossibility: the representation of depth in the electronic frame. But, according to Deleuze, impossible ideas from one medium often translate to another, because a creator who is not seized at the throat by a set of impossibilities is no creator. A creator is someone who creates his own impossibilities, and thereby creates possibilities.[3] Network communication and navigation now transcend the political understanding of boundaries, and a travel route can also be understood as the trajectory of movement into experiential trails of electronic memory. The radical shift of understanding towards the idea of media volume is a revised understanding of space.

The experience of artists and technicians, throughout the history of video and multimedia technology, has advanced the understanding of how the viewing of something progresses from the metaphysical, or psychological act, toward a perceptual understanding complete with physical experience and comprehension. This experiential phenomenon translates into an awareness of how images function on various levels of the communication scale. The on-line real-time exercise in the simultaneous transmission of ideas functions as an example of the numerous communication energies and impulses crowding earth's airwaves, outer space, and the universe. In our real-world environment, we participate in the network of intense frequencies that intrude into—and upon—the rhythm of the human body. Both tangible and intangible effects of this information bombardment are physically evidenced.

As invisible phenomena, this is media information portrayed by way of digital decoding, and analogue visualization processes. In a selection of video for the exhibition "Intelligente Ambiente/Intelligent Environments,"[4] an attempt is made to create a new awareness of these mysterious communication media as a new epistemological space: a real space that combines video and computer technology with theoretical and practical issues of architecture and appearances.[5]

Architecture and Communication

The intrusion of media in today's urban environment is overwhelmingly apparent as a system of electronic space mapping. These abstract functions range from real surveillance mechanisms, to the analysis of how traffic moves or how design functions in physical space. We have grown accustomed to these systems, which are ongoing and are always quietly at work. The next generation of communication technologies will require more advanced, conceptual ability to receive and perceive abbreviated language, as bits of images from commercial and authoritative sources. This information will involve the physical and psychological immersion into electronic advertising, official regulations, and state propaganda. Therefore, the necessity to expand the creative expressions of environmental electronic architecture is a developing concern of designers. The alternative, unrestricted exploration of multimedia artists is of real value to urban planners, architects who are socially concerned with the numerous electronic augmentations and configurations of natural space.

This cinematic phenomena, previously known and visually translated as the genre of architecture on film, dates back to the beginning of experimental filmmaking at the turn of the century. By tradition, this activity was primarily an interpretive look into spaces and structures, and the early films made by architects, sometimes in collaboration with filmmakers, primarily analyzed architectural forms. As a genre of documents, these films preserve valuable images of structures threatened or lost through time, war, or renovation. As conceptual statements and observational practices, the favorite filmed subjects included cities, housing projects, highway systems, landscapes, and workplaces. The effect of these film studies on contemporary architecture has been strong, and the relationship between the two is a powerful precedent for today's new media concerns. In fact, in an interaction between film and architecture, it has been noted that architecture does not merely put forward prospects for viewing. Rather it creates energy spaces with which the cinematic interfere, so as to gain its own topology in loco. The cinema will grow so enormously that the architectural itself will begin to charge itself with cinematic forces.[6]

Electronic Memories

The consumer video boom of the mid-1980s propelled ordinary folks to purchase Super 8 home movie cameras or, a little later, VHS video recorders. These home recorders made it possible to discover how to see and experience space differently, and began the accumulation of an entirely distinct set of memories that were experienced differently from the preceding generations' memories—in large part because of the ability to replay recordings of personal events instantaneously. With the endless opportunities to document life around them during the past decade, individuals have become so familiar with the act of observing space and time—in electronic form—that the medium has become infused with new meanings and opportunities to understand the self and others. Video, which portrays these moments without judgment, or the filter of emotion, reflects them as ordinary memories in a continuously moving, and thoroughly integrated, picture of reality. Created from an electronic light source that overlaps and juxtaposes the now-familiar memory-images in new combinations—unnatural in physical life but familiar in the state of video—the encountering of the electronic memory as reality has become commonplace. The resulting commercial mass consumption of mega-information which is supposed to be by everyone and for everyone is, in reality, the art of being everywhere while really being nowhere. A question is the degree to which individuals will continue to affect and establish the real space of network environments, neighborhoods, and communities. A witness and transmutation of representation, the emergence of forms as volumes destined to persist as long as their materials would allow has given way to images whose duration is purely retinal.[7]

Video, Installation, and Psychological Space

Videotape provided a breakthrough in the understanding of the relationship between artistic image making, space, and perception of oneself. In the mid-1970s, when video first began to be used widely by the first generation of video pioneers, these artists, coming from various creative fields, explored new ways to examine the technology and to observe themselves simultaneously in personal and public space.[8] Video was a rejection of the frozen moments in time most familiar to artists, in which temporal space was painted atmosphere or a mood captured in a photograph. The video medium was a statement against consumerism, against the art market, and toward a communication practice that involved community and consciousness. In the earliest actual practice, video was used in the same way as surveillance devices are today: it was employed to keep watch over and to observe reality. Much of this video research material remains unedited—and unmatched. It was, however, a valuable experience that facilitated artists' understanding of electronic space, memory, and video's ability to document experience in real time. Towards these goals, many artists created sophisticated settings in which a prepared physical environment was integral to the understanding of the electronic space being created with video technology. This act—creating electronic territory and involving the viewer in it as a physical entity—is a direct predecessor to contemporary, interactive multimedia art and immersive technology. Installation artists introduced strong concepts of both psychological and physiological territory, and advanced an awareness of extended boundaries, as well as an electronic ability to define space, time, and energy.

Live Television Experiments:
Being Together in Electronic Space

Television experience has extended the territory of the home and the sensibilities of its inhabitants. Like radio and the telephone, its direct-indirect capabilities were, on the one hand, all-pervasive yet for the most part uncontrollable. As a private/public space, television was often referred to as a window on the world—a phrase now understood more clearly for its political-commercial context and as a control mechanism for the public than as a method to gain cultural information. In television terms, information, cultural standards, and trend setting is big business, and the subject of culture is generally connected with research into its effective control. The explorations of television space by artists from the 1960s include live and interactive experimental events that allude to a real space, but were actually created as an alternative television space that connected, or allowed communication, between sites. Live television and satellite performances were designed to combine two or more places. Spaces were first attempted by artists under the concept of event and spectacle. Interactive and live broadcasts were, however, usually closed-circuit, or broadcast to a limited number of homes or limited market, as broadcasters normally refer to the viewers. The earliest television experiments were possible only because they were not considered to be important, because broadcasters considered art to be a neutral subject, and for public and cable television the artist held a special position, much like that of a researcher.[9]

For telecommunications, coming together in time means, inversely, distancing oneself in space.[10]

Many of the early television projects were at the time called interactive but were actually performances held in more than one location to attempt mutuality of time and space from different locations. These connections between spaces were often accompanied by theoretical subtexts on mass communication, and the political issue surrounding the control of information by broadcasters. Even now, in the context of advanced computer technology, some of the early live historic television transmissions stand up as seminal works, integral to the communication industry's acceptance of art and technology. Douglas Davis, Allen Kaprow, and Nam June Paik were three primary artists who experimented by creating the first live and interactive television events, first dating from 1968 and continuing into the early 1970s, on WGBH television, Boston's public television station, and on PBS WNET 13 in New York City. Other experiments were conducted on the West Coast at KQED, the San Francisco public television station. The archeology of artists' broadcast work, including radio, television, telephone, and various communication networks, continues to be compiled and examined. Important keys to all interrelated history of the cultural and individual vitality of seeing electronic images and spaces will be revealed in the analysis of this history.

The 1990s introduced a relatively new concept of the interactive/digital-television environment. The first of the artistic experimental electronic networks featured direct access to the communication system from home by way of the common communication interface: the telephone. The capabilities exist for multimedia exploration of the television and information networks, the specific architectural forms and realities created by electronics. As physical places, three contemporary references include: Piazza Virtuale, the Ponton European Media Art Labs interactive computer environment for live television (broadcast for 100 continuous days from the Documenta (IX), which featured Picturephone ISDN connections, telephone keypad-controlled games and activities, and chat programs using modems, FAX, telephone and live entry points; the interactive television space Yorb World, an interactive community cable television program developed at New York University, in which a little world can be explored by viewers using the telephone keypad; and the Electronic Cafe, a real site that connects participants by point-to-point communication from various sites around the world in conversations, poetry, and communication art. In these examples it is important to recognize that place is still a necessary space, but architecture can no longer be bound by the static conditions of locally defined place, here or there, but as architecture in data space.[11]

In the mediated virtual world, there are no longer fixed places in the sense that we once knew them. Architecture must now address the problem of the event, and even rock concerts may be considered the archetypal form for an architectural event.[12] If, as Peter Eisenman states, the new architecture is a rock concert, then the ultimate skyscraper of the recent past is the example by U2, with their concert tour of ZOO TV, a mobile live satellite spectacle connecting their concert with the broadcast of regular television programs, and the viewers to the concert, by satellite dish and by telephone. And, as a finale and sign-off at the end of each concert, a call is placed to the White House, asking the president for peace, with the background roar of applause and agreement from the thousands of spectators in the live audience. Another example is of course the on-line transmission of the Rolling Stones concert, as a full Internet experience over broad-band systems.

Checking Out Data Space for Physical Realities and Social Practices

The new electronic territory is media information. This is an invisible architecture without the interface of technology, and it faces new challenges in the public domain. But, it is not a fictional nor simply a virtual environment. Artists, for expressive and theoretical intent, have discovered important lessons about the image and its relationship to this created space, especially as it relates to the vast worldwide Internet territory of seemingly unlimited and compounding information. This space, a potential new shared platform for collaborative artmaking and communication, demands an entirely new use of language, space, and time. And, if we believe Wittgenstein—that language is also a fundamental technology, and not merely a vehicle for expressing thought but the driver of thought—then the new information technologies are doubly important for our future understanding of space and information. Very seriously we must judge how they affect our culture, our lives, our living. As a working space, electronic architecture impacts our creative practices and physical reality—which certainly will bring about new social practices and observed realities.

There are collapsing boundaries and new case histories for representation: "boundary," or "limiting surface" has turned into an osmotic membrane, like a blotting pad. Even this definition is more rigorous than earlier ones, and yet it still signals a change in the notion of limitation.[13] These ideas are urgent challenges for architects and communications experts, who—together with the designers of new formats for information systems—should be collectively recognized as the influential media artists of the late 1990s. The growing public interest in electronic data space, interactive television, and the virtual experience has been compounded by the news media, by its excitement and enthusiastic journalism regarding the large financial investments being made by computer companies, entertainment, television, and public utility systems. It is a crisis of physical dimensions in the mediated world that the practical and theoretical interests, and the information technology itself, have shifted toward multimedia, virtual reality, and cyber-connected networks: all new territories created to explore and to understand spatial realms.

Notes

1. Paul Virilio, "The Overexposed City," in: Lost Dimension, trans. Daniel Moshenberg (New York: Semiotext(e), 1991), p. 25.

2. Informatics is the study of computer systems, networks, memory banks, and terminals.

3. Gilles Deleuze, "Mediators," in: Incorporations, ed. Jonathan Crary and Sanford Kwinter (New York: Zone, 1992), pp. 628–633.

4. "Intelligente Ambiente," for Ars Electronica, 1994, co-curated by Carole Ann Klonarides and Kathy Rae Huffman. A video program of thirty-eight single-channel works, in four sections, including the topics:
   1) Interim: Within and Beyond Confinement
   2) Interference: The Invisible Matrix
   3) Interstitial: Between What Is (Seen)
   4) Intervention: The Tactical Tourist.

5. Woody Vasulka, "The New Epistemic Space," in: Illuminating Video, ed. Doug Hall and Sally Jo Fifer (New York: Aperture, 1990), pp. 465–470.

6. Marc Ries, film+arcfestival, catalogue, Graz, Austria, p. 13.

7. Virilio, p. 25.

8. Some artists who were important to early video experiments were Peter Campus, Nam June Paik, Terry Fox, Shigeko Kubota, Vito Acconci, Bill Viola, Joan Jonas, and William Wegman.

9. Early experimenters in television: Douglas Davis, Allen Kaprow, Nam June Paik, Kit Galloway and Sherrie Rabinowitz, Jamie Davidovich, Richard Kriesche, Bob Adrian, David Hall, and Roy Ascott.

10. Virilio, p. 74.

11. Yorb World: http://www.itp.tsoa.nyu.edu/~yorb
Ponton European Media Art Lab: http://ponton.uni-hannover.de/
The Electronic Cafe International: http://www.ecafe.com/

12. Peter Eisenman, "Unfolding Events," in: Incorporations, p. 423.

13. Virilio, p. 17.

The Noise of the Observer

I. Information and Entropy in Physical Systems

Peter Weibel

Modern statistical information theory has its roots in thermodynamics. The relation between information and entropy as "missing information" (L. Boltzmann, 1894) begins with Maxwell's famous demon. In *Theory of Heat* (1871) James Clerk Maxwell writes:

"One of the best-established facts in thermodynamics is that it is impossible in a system enclosed in an envelope which permits neither change of volume nor passage of heat, and in which both the temperature and the pressure are everywhere the same, to produce any inequality of temperature or pressure without the expenditure of work. This is the second law of thermodynamics, and it is undoubtedly true as long as we can deal with bodies only in mass, and have no power of perceiving or handling the separate molecules of which they are made up. But if we conceive a being whose faculties are so sharpened that he can follow every molecule in its course, such a being, whose attributes are still as essentially finite as our own, would be able to do what is at present impossible to us. For we have seen that the molecules in a vessel full of air at uniform temperature are moving with velocities by no means uniform, though the mean velocity of any great number of them, arbitrarily selected, is almost exactly uniform. Now let us suppose that such a vessel is divided into two portions, A and B, by a division in which there is a small hole, and that a being, who can see the individual molecules, opens and closes this hole, so as to allow only the swifter molecules to pass from A to B, and only the slower ones to pass from B to A. He will thus, without expenditure of work, raise the temperature of B and lower that of A, in contradiction to the second law of thermodynamics."[1]

Maxwell offered no definite rejection of his demon. In 1912 M. von Smoluchowski offered a partial solution to the problem. He introduced an improved version of the demon. A simple automatic apparatus such as a trap door would be hindered by its own Brownian movement to act as an effective demon: "As far as our current knowledge goes there is then, in spite of molecular fluctuation, no automatic, continuously active perpetuum mobile, but such a device might well function regularly if it were operated by intelligent beings in an appropriate way . . ."[2] From then on, hypothetical intelligent beings were being referred to as demons and L. Szillard was soon to investigate their function more closely. They apparently have the ability to defy the second law of thermodynamics. The question was, do such beings obey the same laws as all other material systems?

Paul Ehrenfest investigated this question more closely by comparing these intelligent beings with humans, as Smoluchowski had done previously. Ehrenfest, in a letter of 1927, compared Albert Einstein and his attempt to find a loophole in the consistency of quantum mechanics, to "a little devil in the box" who wanted to play "at a perpetuum mobile of a second order," "in order to break through the inaccuracy relation."[3] The intelligent beings were thus being identified as internal observers.

The decisive identification, however, had already originated with Ludwig Boltzmann, whose work on statistical physics of 1094 made him the first to relate the concept of information to entropy, and to define entropy as "missing information," which one might measure as the number of alternatives still open to a physical system, after all the macroscopically observable information relating to it has been recorded. This already points to the model of Claude Shannon's definition of information as a logarithm of the number of choices present. A situation with two possible choices contains, as we know, a "bit," or binary digit, of information. Sixteen alternative messages characterise four bits of information, since 16 = 2 to the 4th power.

The relation between information and entropy was first formulated explicitly in 1929 in Leo

Szillard's renowned paper "On the Decrease of Entropy in a Thermodynamic System by the Intervention of Intelligent Beings."[4] In this treatise Szillard defined that quantity which today and since the time of Claude Shannon has become known as information, as the amount of free energy used when an observer learns through an experiment which of two seemingly equal alternatives is being realised. One bit of information is equivalent to $k$ln2 units of entropy. From this Claude Shannon was able, in 1948, to derive his famous formula for measuring information, expressed in terms of entropy: $H = -\sum p_i \log p_i$ where p results in the number of possible choices.[5] The thermo-dynamic cost of a measurement and of the information gain were apparently clear. Around 1950 it was considered proven that in each act of observation energy up to a maximum of kTln2 was being employed. John von Neumann and Brillouin assumed that in each act of information processing a minimum kTln2 of energy was being used.[6] Thus, for instance, in a 1949 address, Neumann said that, "a computer operating at temperature T must dissipate at least kTln2 of energy per elementary act of information, that is, per elementary decision of a two-way alternative and per elementary transmittal of one unit of information."[7]

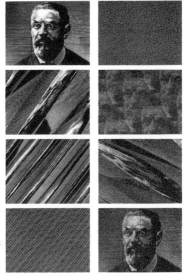

James P. Crutchfield: From the video image to the chaotic noise with structure and back again
© James P. Crutchfield

Yet this concept of energy use and information proved naive and, in part, incorrect. In 1961 Rolf Landauer was able to show that the process, which in reality used minimal but unavoidable amounts of energy, served to destroy information.[8] Only in information destruction do irreversible thermodynamic costs arise (as opposed to the reversible costs in information gain). Also the transmission of information, e.g. of a bit from one place to another, did not require kTln2 of energy, On the contrary, Landauer was able to show that here, too, the thermodynamic cost of energy transmission, if done slowly, occurs with an arbitrarily minute, i.e., negligible, energy dissipation.[9] To rescue the second law of thermodynamics (the law of the preservation of energy) no (minimal and unavoidable) dissipation of energy is required in information gain and the transfer of information from the object that is to be observed, but rather after the reconstitution of the observer's condition after the transfer, i.e., after the information has been destroyed. The accent on the thermodynamic cost is shifted, after Landauer, from the observation and measuring to the re-establishment of the premeasurement situation, that is, to the cost of extinguishing information, and with it, history.

Precisely at this point another epoch-making paper appeared in the form of Charles H. Bennett's "Logical Reversibility of Computation" of 1973.[10] Bennett constructed an "enzymatic Turing machine," where every computation could be transformed to a reversible format by accumulating the history of all the information that would ordinarily be thrown out, only to rid oneself of this history within a process which was the obverse of the one which had created it. The computation was transformed into a series of steps where each step was logically reversible, which in turn permitted its physical reversibility. Computation could thus occur with an arbitrarily small dissipation of energy.

In 1982, Edward Fredkin developed a billiard ball model of computation as an example of a reversible computer.[11] The collisions of billiard balls can simulate any logical function, and hence also any digital computation. This billiard ball collision realises a 2-input, 4-output function of logics: A and B, B and not A, A and not B, A and B. The values I and 0 are represented by the presence or, respectively, absence, of the billiard ball on a given trajectory. With these cellular automatons of a reversible type he described the first explicit model universe capable of being computer-simulated. This universe

Peter Weibel *The Noise of The Observer*

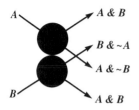

$A \& B$ consists exclusively of information. As soon as A has been realised in some concrete form (with various forms of hardware being conceivable), its properties are fully established. It begins to produce autonomous "material" properties internally—e.g. collections of hundreds of black pixels, which stabilise at a certain size and then mutually attract each other like elementary particles, with a well-defined theorem somewhat like Coulomb's. It is Fredkin's hope that someday all natural laws as we know them will emerge as implications from a single such reversible cellular law of automation. The only deciding factor being that one must have the luck to hit upon the correct reversible local rule.

P. Benioff succeeded at about the same time (1981–1982) in setting up a reversible quantum-mechanical model of computation and information, thereby combining Hamilton's model with a Turing machine.[12] In his work, "Maxwell's Demon, Szillard's Engine and Quantum Measurements,"[13] W. H. Zurek summed up the results and transferred Szillard's thought experiment to quantum mechanics. The measuring device then becomes the demon, increasing the entropy. This entropy can be passed on by the demon (the internal observer) to the environment. The environment, then, pays for the entropic cost of the measurement. The information gained by the observation or the measurement has to be balanced out by way of an increase in the entropy of the measuring device.

The relations between the entropic cost of information and the environment are also addressed in the work "Entropy Cost of Information" by Paul N. Fahn.[14] The second law of thermodynamics, then, is a theorem of entropy balance which states that, if within a system there is an increase of entropy, then in another, linked system entropy will decrease. As a thought experiment, Maxwell's Demon has shown up some paradoxical problems in these theorems. It was Szillard's one-molecule demon that brought the term "information" into the debate. Since then, a theory of the entropy cost of information has been developed, a theory of the correlation between information and entropy, which in recent times has been expanded by Landauer and Bennett to include a theory of computation.[15] Benioff, Feynmann, Zurek, and Rössler have brought quantum physics and chaos theory into play, as did their predecessor, J. v. Neumann.[16]

The job of the demon is to transform entropy into information, while the information-erasing operation changes information back to entropy. These are the two sides of an interaction between an information-processing machine (the demon) and a classical thermodynamic system.[17] It was R. Landauer's idea to define the demon as an information-processing machine, or, in other words, as a computer. Maxwell's Demon became a computer-controlled device that interacted with the gas. The Boltzmann entropy of the gas was reduced at the expense of the entropy-enrichment of its own informational content. Erasure of a bit of information requires a minimum amount (kTlog2) of heat dissipation into the environment. Thus entropy reduction only occurs as long as the demon continues to gorge itself more and more with information. The question of the entropic cost of information, first raised by Szillard, was more precisely investigated by Brillouin, Landauer, and Bennett. To Brillouin and Bennett, measuring operation and erasure, accumulation and annihilation of information, are thermodynamically expensive operations, since they increase entropy. Landauer cited the relationship to the environment as a way out of this dilemma; Paul N. Fahn, too, took this third path in his calculation of the entropic cost of information. To him, neither measurement nor erasure are, in principle, expensive thermodynamic operations. But the de-correlation of the system from information increases entropy in the system-cum-information, thereby increasing entropy in the universe, unless the information is used to reduce entropy elsewhere before the correlation disintegrates. The thermodynamic cost of information rises to the degree in which it is not being used to obtain work from the observed and measured system. De-correlation between information and system is, therefore, the actual entropy-producing occurrence.

Modern communication theory does not solely refer to thermodynamics and statistical mechanics; however, its advance can also be found in the field of electric communication, in the transmission of signals through electric currents. After F. B. Morse's invention of telegraphy in 1832, which involved the transmission of messages through the presence or a longer or shorter absence of an electric current, questions immediately arose relating to the limits of the speed and precision of signal transmission. External currents are always present, which interfere with and disturb the signal being transmitted, thus impeding the differentiation between alternative signals. The disturbances caused by such currents, which were called "noise," clearly needed to be reduced as far as possible. Harry Nyquist published some of the first important mathematical contributions towards modern communication theory, "Certain Factors Affecting Telegraph Speed" (1924) and "Certain Topics in Telegraph Transmission Theory" (1928), in which he showed how the speed of signal transmission could be increased and also introduced the logarithmic function as the comparative measure of information. R. V. L. Hartley, in his "Transmission of Information" (1928), gave a first formal definition of information, which he viewed as a sequence of symbols: $H = n \log s$ where H represents the information of the message or the logarithm of the number of possible symbolic sequences, n stands for the number of chosen symbols and equals the number of symbols available.

During the war the subject of noise became more pressing than in peace time, as it became necessary to correctly interpret "noisy" radar data, for example. Devices were sought that could filter out the noise signals. A. N. Kalmogoroff and Norbert Wiener provided the solutions to these problems. In the same year (1948) that Wiener published his book *Cybernetics,* Claude E. Shannon published his famous article "The Mathematical Theory of Communication" in the *Bell Systems Technical Journal.* (The same journal, incidentally, in which Nyquist and Hartley had also been published, a fact Wiener referred to in his introduction). Shannon placed particular emphasis on the effect of noise in the communication system and in the information channel, as one may glean from his famous diagram of the communication system. The reason for this was that the semantic aspect of communication is irrelevant to the engineer's view of communication, as the latter's fundamental problem of communication simply consists in how a message selected at one point can be reproduced exactly or in as close an approximation as possible at another point.

It was the aforementioned Nyquist who named the electric fluctuations causing the heat "Johnson noise" or "thermal noise," after their discoverer, J. B. Johnson. This "noise" is a particularly simple, universal, and unavoidable noise which sets natural limits on signal transmission systems. The noise is thus added to each signal. Each message is disturbed by noise, be it during transmission or at the receiving end: Once the signal has been received there always remains an undesirable uncertainty, i.e., noise, regarding what the message sent really was. Shannon introduced additional observers who would correct the deviations caused in one way or another by noise between the data sent and the data received.

Shannon developed a number of methods to define the channel capacities of a "noisy channel," which simply has its limits in entropy or statistical uncertainty. $H = -\sum p_i \log p_i$ is the entropy of the amount of the probabilities $p_1 \ldots p_n$. Shannon's observer, who sees both that which is sent and that which has been received distortedly on account of the errors caused by noise, notes the errors and transmits the data via a "corrective channel" or an "error-correcting code" to the receiver who will then correct the errors. If $H_y(x)$ is the amount of additional information required per second to correct the message received, then we can define a limit of channel capacity for channels with noise. A discrete channel would have a channel capacity C and a discrete source would have the entropy H per second. If $H \leq C$, then there is a code, so that the output of the source via the channel can be transmitted with an arbitrarily small frequency of errors. It is thus assumed that there may be an ideal observer who could correct errors, as well as the noise of the information source or the information channel.

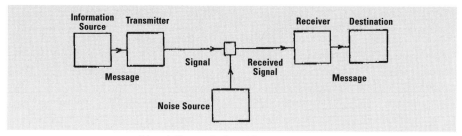

Schematic Diagram of a General Communication System

By reducing our uncertainty about the condition of the system, the message reduces the thermodynamic entropy of the system. The reduction of entropy, however, augments the system's free energy, which is proportional to the minimum energy required to transmit the message that led to an increase in free energy. The price one has to pay for information regarding one's own system and leading to a reduction of the (thermodynamic, statistical) entropy of a system is proportional to the entropy (based on information theory) of the signal source that produces the information. The price is always as high as it needs to be to avoid a second-order perpetuum mobile, so as not to contravene the second law of thermodynamics.

Entropy is a measure of chance and of disintegration. The tendency of physical systems to be ever less organised, and to increasingly fall apart, is associated with entropy. The arrow of time, the irreversibility of time, comes about as a result of entropy. Within the theory of communication based on information theory, information is defined as the number of available choices. If a situation is sufficiently highly organised, there are few available choices, the degree of chance is low, and the system is predetermined—hence there is little information. A chaotic (deterministic, non-linear) system, therefore, in contrast

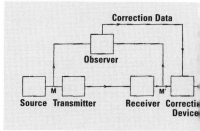

Schematic Diagram of a Correction System

to a purely deterministic system, contains more information since it has more degrees of freedom, available choices, incertitudes. Thus freedom of choice, entropy, and information, defined as a logarithm of the number of available choices, all converge as concepts. The greater the freedom of choice, the greater the information, and the greater also the uncertainty. Noise, however, equally means increased uncertainty, so that one might mistakenly assume that increased noise means heightened uncertainty and hence increased freedom of choice, i.e., information. This is, of course, paradoxical. One thus needs a process that distinguishes desirable uncertainty (information) from undesirable uncertainty (noise).

This task should be carried out by the channel capacity or by the ideal observer. Noise, therefore, threatens information in several ways. The classic communication theory of information theory or cybernetics firstly simplified the problem of noise by excluding semantic problems, and secondly, viewed it naively, for example, by interpreting the observer not as a source of errors but as a corrector of errors. In a way, it represents a partial retrogression to the time before the thermodynamic theory of entropy. The approaches of quantum physics and chaos theory to information and entropy, as derived from thermodynamics, appear to me the most promising for neutralising the paradoxes and aporia of the theories of entropy and information, as exemplified by Maxwell's Demon, Szillard's machines, etc., because they place the problem of the observer at the centre of attention. The noise of classical communication theory is more or less the noise of one's own signal, where the observer acts to correct errors. The noise in quantum physics is the noise of the observer, unavoidably and necessarily producing errors.

Goedel's 1931 work "On Formally Undecidable Propositions of Principia Mathematica"[18] was the first proof of the unavoidable incompleteness or uncertainty of a system, the information about a system, the self-assertions of a system about itself or about its own condition, when viewed from the inside. In elementary number theory there are, according to Goedel, propositions that are true but cannot be formally proved. In the universe of numbers there will always be things we won't know. Gregory Chaitin universalised Goedel's results of 1931 and Turing's holding problem of 1936[19] by proposing a thermodynamic, statistical-mechanical approach to mathematics, which claims a chance structure for some areas of arithmetic.[20] From Goedel's result and Boltzmann's statistical mechanics he developed an algorithmic theory of information or "thermodynamic theory of knowledge," which does not exclude uncertainty and chance, because there are areas of arithmetic where problems cannot be solved by drawing logical conclusions because these areas are governed by chance. Uncertainty, the lack of predictability and information, and chance, are thus omnipresent principles not only in pure mathematics, but also in classical physics and in quantum mechanics. Shortly after Goedel had introduced his famous proof of the incompleteness of arithmetic (when regarded from the inside), his friend Neumann began to investigate the question of whether perhaps quantum mechanics might present a similar limitation—this time, within a physical context. Fortunately, Neumann was able to show that, if quantum mechanics is accepted as the basic theory of physics which comprises all other possible theories as special cases, then there is indeed no reason to worry. For the structure of quantum mechanics guarantees that "the informedness of the observer regarding his own condition" is excluded from formalism. [16] The question of the observer or rather, the noise of the observer who both generates information and at the same erases it, was introduced by quantum physics in order to calculate the entropic cost of observations or information. Otto Rössler's endophysics, developed from about 1980 onwards as a possible explanation of quantum mechanics, heightens the problem of the observer by its distinction between an internal observer, to whom only certain aspects of the world are accessible and for whom the rest of the world is distorted in a manner incorrigible and unrecognisable to him, and an external observer, who, however, as a kind of super-observer, can only be construed within the confines of model worlds. The world is only ever defined at the interface between the observer and the rest of the world. Thus, the observer's position is a regulator that can be moved on a frequency between paradise (information) and hell (error). Information is therefore unavoidably observer-relative. Of necessity the observer creates noise. He can escape this noise of observation only by himself becoming a part of the information model. Similar to the theorem proposed in 1964 by John Belt on remote effects via arbitrary distances, and the existence of non-locality and indeterminism, where information becomes accessible to us via (statistical) correlations, so too, the noise of the observer can only be resolved by remote correlations.

Observation by an observer is, therefore, no longer sufficient to increase information; rather, what is required is an increased correlation and co-variance of observers and observations. It is questionable, however, whether we can grasp these correlations.

II. Information and Entropy in Social Systems

If we wanted to consider, as we have done up to now, the natural sciences, as the key science of the modern world, it may perhaps be permissible to transfer the problems of information, of entropy and noise, from physical systems to social systems, and there, too, inquire after the relative relationships between information, entropy, and observation. Information theoretical communication theory has neglected this question of energy dissipation and the problem of the observer. Quantum physics has acquainted us with the fact that in observing systems and objects we must not dismiss the role of the observer. Niels Bohr promulgated the famous theory that the act of observation in turn influences the very object of our observation. Archibald Wheeler went even further by saying that a phenomenon is a phenomenon only if it is also an observable phenomenon. Here, the informedness of the observer is of central importance. A condition noted by the internal observer is different from that which "objectively exists" and can be observed from the outside. The quantum Demon therefore describes the problem of the noise-generating observer within information systems.

What quantum theory has described for physical systems can also be applied to social systems. Here, too, the deciding factors are the informedness of the observer, his knowledge of his own condition, and a distinction as to whether he is an internal observer who is a part of the observation system, or an external observer outside the system he is observing. The theories of quantum physics on the dependency of a system's information level on the observer are also valid for social and cultural systems. A quantum theory of cultural theory is sorely needed. We must part with the traditional historical notion that there is a pure and objective description of the occurrences in the world of the mind, where the observer's contribution to the phenomena under observation can be disregarded or subtracted. We must take leave of this cliché and this illusion. For, on the contrary, in the world of the media in particular, Wheeler's Theorem applies that only an observed phenomenon is a true phenomenon. Only what is represented in the media also exists, and the form in which it exists in the data space equally depends on the position of the observer. Thus, the critic and the theoretician of culture act, willy-nilly, as real-life observers. The observed object's own signal becomes inseparably mingled with the observer's own signal or noise.

In a nutshell, this would be an information theory based on quantum physics, which might be more appropriate to the practice of a trade in information and works, their placement and displacement, their publication and suppression in the post-industrial information-based capitalist society, than is the classic idealist theory, where the influence of the observer (critic, curator, theoretician, editor) on the matter being observed, and on the information, which is only actually constructed and codified by means of the act or observation, has been denied or neglected. Information and the observer can no longer be divided. The noise of the observer, the indeterminacy relation between information and observer, is not arbitrarily reducible. In the present world, in which, from medicine to economics, access to information and the spread of information are gaining an ever more fundamental and central importance worldwide, the above-mentioned limitations are particularly noteworthy, since quite obviously there is a danger; firstly, of mistaking noise for information and, secondly, of not eliminating this noise with any increase in the amount of information, but of increasing it, in accordance with the theorem of quantum- and endo-physics, where the internal observer does not know that he is an observer and takes his own noise for the information from the situation under observation.

The attempts of sociologists, from Harold Laswell to Walter Lippmann,[21] to analyse the origins of information in social systems have not been very successful. Not until the theses of Noam Chomsky and Niklas Luhmann, where the noise of the observer plays a constitutive role, do tentative explanations arise of the imaginable impoverishment of the information dimension which currently dominates the public domain where information concerning cultural and political transactions remains inaccessible. The "manufacture of consent"[22] is what is generated today by the noise of the observers, and the current level of information handed out by the mass media. The entropic cost regulates and dominates the information market of the Western world. Entropy is the measure of the mass media. Will the digital data highways become a part of this information bottleneck, of this entropy; or will they form further correlations and covariances between the observers, as would be necessary? Will the telematic society at last try to counteract its suppressions of information, through the correlations and co-variances of the observers via worldwide networks? The postmodern society is information-based. No longer do mechanical machines support the social servicing system, but information machines, such as computers, do the job. The dogmas of the information society are: There is more information than ever. Information is generally more easily accessible than ever. Information is being exchanged more than ever. Do these bytes for the soundbite generation make humanity any cleverer or any more knowledgeable? Does the information intake of each individual person actually increase or doesn't, rather, more information than ever get lost? Is, in fact, the exchange of information being decreasing? Don't people, experts aside, know less about one another than ever? Isn't an information implosion and an information bottleneck developing in the digital datanets? In the age of multiple media, infotainment, knowledge software, edutainment, and the data highways, Ars Electronica 1995 puts critical questions to the myths and dogmas of the postmodern information-oriented society.

Postmodern society consists of very complex, dynamic social systems within which the idea of information plays a central role. The exchange of data in the network of information machines supports the social servicing system from medicine to tourism, from the running of the economy to leisure time activities. The theory of information has become a key science. The spread of information through the mass media can, however, also become a part of the arsenal of repressive and optimising strategies of those in power. The exchange of data can flare up in a data war.

Just as centuries ago, with the aid of atlases and meridians, new territories would be measured and devised, discovered, and construed, so too, the global data networks represent a new, if virtual, geography. The discourse of cyber-culture has expanded to the data highways. We no longer merely inhabit streets and buildings, but also cable channels, telegraph wires, e-mail-boxes, and thus global digital dependency. It was in 1969 that, for the first time, four computers were linked in a network system referred to as the ARPANET (Advanced Research Projects Agency-NET). The name INTERNET, therefore, is used to describe any linkups of those computers that communicate with one another via a protocol, such as TCP (Transmission Control Protocol) or IP (Internet Protocol). In 1972 this project of the American ministry of defense was presented to the public, and many universities and other research institutions joined the net. In 1990 the Internet consisted of some 3,000 local networks with more than 20,000 computers. By 1994 their number had reached 2.5 million. Bill Gates expects some 20 million network-linked households and institutions by the year 2000. The information system World Wide Web (WWW) was developed at the European CERN laboratory (by Tim Berners-Lee), and due to its hypertext linkages (so-called hyperlinks) represents the most flexible tool within the Internet.

The global data nets must not be understood merely as multi-media data banks and communication channels, where texts, images, and sounds are transported and processed. These data networks also permit new forms of communication and also new communication partners, such as, for instance, communication with software agents equipped with artificial intelligence, thus not unlike prototypes of subjects without a physical body. Forms of communication become possible between real people in virtual spaces and between virtual people in real spaces. The noise of the observer and the communication partner can be employed constructively and alter the structure, and thus also the message of communication, at each individual location. One-dimensional communication between two partners with two different interpretational worlds is broken up into multi-dimensional communication with multiple interpretive means. This loss of mutual control and definitiveness can be experienced as a form of liberty.

There will come a time in the realm of the public media with giant cataclysms of exploding errors, with accelerated wanderings of galaxies made up of prematurely incinerated information dust. Our concepts of information, communication, and observation will alter radically and also affect the social systems as we know them. Our political systems will be subjected to radical transformations on the basis of democracy or become accomplices of the monopolies and totalitarian systems ("wired democracy," computer democracy, telecracy, videocracy). In particular the artistic net projects of Ars Electronica 95 will lift the curtain worldwide for the first time to allow a glimpse at this horizon of the digital data highways, which were up to now presented to us more or less as phantoms of the media. The financial and human costs as well as the strategies of a networked society will be critically questioned. How will the inhabitants of the net live in this wired world? What will be the price of information and communication within these network worlds? Who will be the hitchhikers and hi-jackers on the superhighways of information? Diving through digital conduits and netsurfing an a sea of data will bring about new forms of social contact, ranging from telematic reconstruction of the body to individual acquisition of data monopolies. Ars Electronica 95 gives critical and euphoric experts an opportunity to appraise this brave new networked world.

Thanks to Otto E. Rössler for inspirations.

Notes

1. J. C. Maxwell, Theory of Heat, 4th ed. (London: Longmans, Green and Co., 1875), pp. 328–329.

2. M. v. Smoluchowski, "Experimentell nachweisbare, der üblichen Thermodynamik widersprechende Molekularphänomene," Physik Z. 13 (1912), pp. 1068–1080.

3. Paul Ehrenfest, letter to Samule Goldsmit, George Uhlenbeck, and Gerhard Dieke, November 1927, in: Niels Bohr (Braunschweig: Vieweg, 1958), p. 152.

4. Leo Szillard, "Über die Entropieverminderung in einem thermodynamischen System bei Eingriffen intelligenter Wesen," Z. f. Physik 53 (1929), pp. 840–856.

5. Claude E. Shannon, "The Mathematical Theory of Communication," Bell System Technical Journal, July-October 1948.

6. L. Brillouin, "Maxwell's Demon Cannot Operate: Information and Entropy 1," J. Appl. Phys. 22 (1951), pp. 334–337. L. Brillouin, Science and Information Theory (1956).

7. John von Neumann, lecture, 1949, in: Theory of Self-Reproducing Automata, ed. Arthur Burks (Urbana: University of Illinois Press, 1966), p. 66.

8. Rolf Landauer, "Irreversibility and Heat Generation in the Computing Process," IBM J. Res. Dev. 5 (1961), pp. 183–191; rpt. in Maxwell's Demon, ed. H. S. Leff and A. F. Rex (Princeton: Princeton University Press, 1990), pp. 188–196.

9. Rolf Landauer, "Information Is Physical," Phys. Today 44 (May 1991), pp. 23–29.
Rolf Landauer, "Computation, Measurement, Communication and Energy Dissipation," in: Selected Topics in Signal Processing, ed. S. Haykin (Englewood Cliffs: Prentice Hall, 1959), pp. 188–196.

10. Charles H. Bennett, "Logical Reversibility of Computation," IBM J. Res. Dev. 17 (1973), pp. 525–532.
C. H. Bennett, "Demons, Engines and the Second Law," Scientific American 257 (1987), pp. 108–116.
C. H. Bennett, "The Thermodynamics of Computation," Inst. f. Theor. Phys. 32 (1982), pp. 905–940.

11. E. Fredkin and T. Toftoli, Inst. f. Theor. Phys. 21 (1982), pp. 219–233.
E. Fredkin, "Digital Information Mechanics," preprint 1983; Digital Mechanics Physica D 45 (1990), pp. 254–270.

12. P. Benioff, "The Computer as a Physical System: A Microscopic Quantum Mechanical Hamiltonian Model of Computers as Represented by Turing Machines," J. Stall. Phys. 22 (1980), pp. 563–591.
"Quantum Mechanical Models of Turing Machines That Dissipate No Energy," Phys. Rev. Lett. 48 (1982), pp. 1581ff.

13. W. H. Zurek, "Maxwell's Demon, Szillard's Engine and Quantum Measurements," in: Maxwell's Demon, ed. Leff and Rex, pp. 249–259.

14. Paul N. Fahn, "Entropy Cost of Information," in: Proceedings of the Workshop on Physics and Computation. PhysComp '94. (Los Alamitos, Cal.: IEEE Computer Society Press,1994), pp. 217–226.

15. Maxwell's Demon, ed. Leff and Rex.

16. John von Neumann, Mathematische Grundlagen der Quanten Mechanik (Berlin, 1932), chap. 5.
R. Feynman, "Quantum Mechanical Computers," Opt. News 11, no. 2 (1985), pp. 11–20.
Otto E. Rössler, "Endophysics," in: Real Brains, Artificial Minds, ed. J. L.Casti and A. Karlquist (New York: North Holland, 1987), pp. 25–46.

17. W. H. Zurek, "Algorithmic Randomness and Physical Entropy," Physical Review A 40 (1989), pp. 4731–4751.

18. Kurt Gödel, "Ober formal unentscheidbare Sätze der Principia Mathematica und verwandter Systeme 1," Monatshefte für Mathematik und Physik 38 (1931), pp. 173–198.

19. Alan Turing, "On Computable Numbers with an Application to the Entscheidungsproblem," Proc. of the London Math. Soc., ser. 2, vol. 42 (1936–1937), pp. 230–265.

20. Gregory J. Chaitin, Information, Randomness and Incompleteness (Singapore: World Scientific, 1990).

21. Walter Lippmann, Public Opinion (1921).

22. Noam Chomsky and Eduard Hermanan, Manufacturing Consent (New York: Pantheon Books, 1988).

Vector in Open Space

Gerfried Stocker

There are numerous reasons—only one of which is its name—for assuming that a unique project such as the Ars Electronica Center could never have come about without its "godparents." The most important reason for its coming into being, however, is the knowledge which has grown out of the internationally acclaimed Ars Electronica Festival and the Prix Ars Electronica: the knowledge that a future-oriented approach is essential for understanding and dealing with the present. A knowledge which, at the leading edge of cultural development, is an indispensable element of competence in engaging those areas targeted from the start—the arts, technology, and society—as an integrated field of endeavor. One fundamental consideration in the setting of an agenda is therefore its positioning in that environment in which the Ars Electronica Center, derived as it is from the activities of the Festival and the Prix, is rooted. Thus the raison d'être of the Ars Electronica Center is established in part by a functioning model: that is, artistic commitment as the guiding principle for navigation through a world in the throes of a media-led transformation; as the driving force for society's confrontation with the new contextual realities of our age; and as a resource for the impending tasks of design and acculturation of the new media-based environment.

Against this programmatic backdrop, the Ars Electronica Center cannot be regarded simply as a centre of cultural competence, but—where culture is understood as technological evolution—as itself an art-project of this culture. As a logical consequence, this project has the nature of a "work in progress," both in regard to its capacity for integration and in terms of its compatibility with the interests of a general public. On the other hand, a project so exposed to the elements of change and innovation requires a strong identity that sets it above considerations of transient techno-chic and short-lived hype.

The Ars Electronica Center cannot, therefore, content itself with simply being a collection or a gallery, but sees itself as a partner, an infrastructure, and an initiator. This means that it must itself participate in the establishment of its own necessity, in the creation of a fertile environment.

What is it then that distinguishes the Ars Electronica Center, as a "museum of the future," from a publicity barrage of the computer and IT industry? Essentially it is the fact that the content of this "museum" was not designed by manufacturers of products, or software developers, but is the result of an artistically motivated approach.

The Ars Electronica Center seeks to develop a kind of magnetic field, attracting not only international experts in greater number and scope, but also inquisitive, experimentally oriented, creative people (whatever the nature of their training might be) to Linz. The idea is to create in this way a pool of competent, interested, innovative individuals who will "surrender" to the gravitational pull of the Center, not only in physical terms but also in their thinking. That is to say that they will be obliged to abandon the modus operandi characterised by internal deliberations at a distance and, brought now into direct proximity with the technology, to alter their approach to the objects of their deliberation. A close physical relationship of this kind automatically evokes an entirely different category of ideas than that which hitherto, in the majority of cases, had rather the nature of aesthetic remote control.

Even in the months prior to the official inauguration, the working atmosphere at the Ars Electronica Center was not one of sterile institutional process control—it was more like an open workshop, in which creative intelligences tested their capabilities on the equipment, and in doing so probed the extent of the latter's performance capability.

In a concentrated involvement with the machine itself, of a kind peculiar to this new generation of hacker-artists and scarcely conceivable for outsiders, in the identification with—practically a fusion with—the computer (and the network behind it), the digital revolution that now has our society in its thrall took on a graphic and concrete form.

Much of what will never leave the home directories of these "freaks," what they are unlikely even to put in the official web server of the Center, is notable above all for the process of its creation and the matter-of-factness (not to be confused with laid-back indifference) of approach to the process which characterises this, the third generation of computer users: an undeniable sign of the emergence of a new culture, identified as "memesis" in this year's Festival. Thus the Festival, this year dominated by the inauguration of the Center, is itself also focused on the opening up of such zones of activity, on a new phase in the evolution of interaction with media technology, and of media art, which is needed to confront the technological revolution with that very force which it has unleashed. This is the great opportunity for the Ars Electronica Center, which must ally itself with its users, must get involved with them and grow with them. The same applies to the collaboration with artistic, innovative individuals: they must be attracted and encouraged to accept and make use of the Ars Electronica Center as their laboratory and their platform.

However, it has to be more than just a question of using electronic media as a tool. On the one hand the encounter between technologists and artists will give birth to projects which are founded on knowledge of the technological processes, on the appropriate selection of means, and on the idea of multi-media networking and its reflexion. On the other hand, artistic expertise will be made accessible to technologists and theoreticians—an approach which, in view of the increasing significance of "strategies for creative problem-solving" is in no way presumptuous. Only in the mutual accessibility of different interests, in the coexistence of research and communication, the twin functions of laboratory and information pool, can an interface be set up which meets the requirements made of it—a networking in all areas of life, which is itself a paradigm of the new information-based society.

One would need to look for a long time to find a historical analogy for that phenomenon which is currently taking place, based in part on highly contrasting premises: artists who hitherto, even in the field of media art, have worked alone and unnoticed are now unexpectedly confronted with an extraordinary level of interest from a public which is mastering the key terms and ideological stereotypes of the digital revolution. However, this new awareness relates in fact less to the artistic activity than to the artists themselves as being, in the broadest sense, the designers, the creators, the human resource potential for the new media technologies. The uneasy feeling that without "content" the technology might not be marketable opens up many channels, and at the same time fuels the extremely dubious hope that art which makes itself useful in the service of technological matters will soon be able to earn its own keep, thus to some extent relieving the overburdened public cultural purse.

In terms of the latent limitations of his or her self-conception and social role, the artist is in a bad way. Whereas colleagues in the classical fields still have theatres, galleries, and concert halls as approved formal contexts for their definable public persona—distribution systems which even in the one-way mass media of radio and television are still preserved to some extent—a virtual public on the other hand, such as is represented for example by the Internet, is seen by many as an unworthy or indeed threatening void. A black hole into which everything disappears because it is so difficult to identify and to evaluate among the general "communication waste." (As though a gallery in Hong Kong or a good article among all the newsprint in an airport kiosk were easier to track down . . .)

Gerfried Stocker *Vector in Open Space*

Because everybody can take what they want, and because—and this at least is an aspect which must be taken very seriously—it is not possible to make a living from it. Notwithstanding all of which an artist can no longer afford to stand aloof from these developments; home pages and E-mail are now self-evident components of an artist's CV.

The implementation of artistic ideas is nowadays frequently only possible with considerable technological resources, so that the traditional venues of art can only seldom provide the right framework. The "disappearance" of art and the artists—heralded and long since anticipated and rehearsed in the interdisciplinary intertwining of the genres—is now, aside from the exciting theoretical redefinition of self-conception and role model, becoming a real possibility.

The altered framework conditions demand new concepts from us. This applies equally to production, transmission, and reception. In the face of the enormous challenge with which contemporary art is confronted, of establishing itself in "electronic-digital space" and maintaining a balance between the fascination of our high-tech environment and a necessary critical reflexion, interdisciplinary, networked activity has today rightly become a key concept, and not only of artistic endeavour. To be genuinely contemporary, artists must conceive of themselves as nodes in a technologically determined social environment—and in doing so assume a highly political responsibility.

By virtue of its specific infrastructure in terms of hardware and of personnel, of its twin functions as a place of production and of presentation, and also by virtue of its positioning "between the fronts," an institution such as the Ars Electronica Center assumes in this connection the nature and function of a model for its time.

Consideration of and reflexion on the interaction of art, technology, and society have often only occurred within the circles of the Festival's visitors—and yet the urgency of these topics far exceeds a merely theoretical media-oriented interest, and represents a challenge which both Festival and Center will have to face.

Because it is not only the niches occupied by the artists that are coming adrift; their fate is shared by the world of classical "job descriptions" in the loss of a well-tried and tested set of rules of social order and hierarchy. Oriented as we are, mentally and economically, to the concept of work as the provider both of a livelihood and of the means to imbue it with meaning, we are intensely skeptical of the approach of once-futuristic visions of a humanity freed from labour by the benefits of technology—each of these shimmering Utopias and Promised Lands to date having, on closer inspection, proved illusory. At the present time the process of the acceptance and establishment of information technologies is still adhering rather unimaginatively to the guidelines of classical capitalism, to the detriment of ideas of social welfare. "Banal" aspects of this kind are still much too infrequently addressed in the fever of well-meaning euphoria, fostering an increasing insecurity and indeed an attitude of resistance. This makes an ongoing, frank, and public debate essential.

With its early commitment to confronting the crisis of a society at the turning point between the industrial age and the age of information, the Ars Electronica Center in Linz can only be of benefit in such a debate.

The Memesis
Network Discussion

Compiled by Geert Lovink

People nowadays seem to be unhappy with the static form of many festivals. Although meeting "in real life" is still favourable, there is the need to use the available tools of communication in order to change the traditional, one-to-many type of conference. With the opening of the Ars Electronica web site on March 1st, 1996, we had the opportunity to extend the "real life conference" with a lively discussion on the Net in the months before the actual event. The idea was to set up a permanent platform which would also function after the festival as a starting point for further debates. After having structured the various streams of information, we wrote an Introduction, in which we explained the goals of such a Net-based forum: "We would like to get away from the usual panels and presentations and see the get-together in Linz, between September 2–6, 1996, as a place to continue and round up ongoing discussions. Of course it is not that easy to simply blow up the entire concept of the "conference" and its rituals. At least certain hierarchical ("one to many") modes can be changed through an open discussion in the preparation phase of the festival. We would therefore like to invite everyone interested in this year's topic and new media in general to participate in the discussion between the artists and critics we invited to send a first statement."

In this summary of the first six weeks of the discussion on the Net, you will find a personal, subjective selection of quotations from the numerous contributions, which were posted both by invited speakers and the general audience, in as much as they have access to the Internet. The discussion can be followed on the World Wide Web (http://www. aec.at/meme/symp) and also by subscribing to a mailing list, which would send all the contributions as e-mail.

On April 15, 1996 the network discussion on this year's theme, "memesis," started with two documents, in which the goals of the discussion were made clear. I, being the presenter, opened, stating that: "So far there is not much experience and expertise in the orchestrating of Net-based public debates on technology. At this stage we are leaving the era of introductions on the nature and the implications of new technologies (and the role of artists in this process) and find ourselves in the middle of controversies around topics like copyright, privacy, war on standards, cultural biases, public censorship and other 'old patterns' in 'new media'."

In recent years we have seen a wide use by artists of apparently harmless notions which have their origin in physics and biology (chaos, virus, artificial life).The cyborg, too, has a scientific background like this. To start a discussion so many months in advance was an attempt to break down the old consensus of the pioneers and show that media-art festivals like Ars Electronica from now on should be more than just a trades fair for computer-related art concepts. The Net seemed to be a perfect tool for vitalizing the static form of conference presentations. The "Memesis Statement," written by Gerfried Stocker, was posted to initiate a discussion process, "stimulating different lines of approach to the topic, and polarising opinions." The aim was not to dream up new utopias, but to develop a critical and reflective approach to the current situation, with its renewed promise that much vaunted visions of the future will finally become reality.

In order to achieve this, the "Memesis Statement" took some provocative positions: "Complex tools and technologies are an integral part of our evolutionary 'fitness'. Human evolution is fundamentally intertwined with technological development; the two cannot be considered apart from each other. Humanity has co-evolved with its artifacts; genes that are not able to cope with this reality will not survive the next millennium."

Let us not try to reconstruct the following discussion in a chronological order. Richard Barbrook took the manifesto for what it was and wrote a similar, bold response: "The major error in the 'Memesis Statement' is its use of dodgy biological analogies. The discovery of evolution was one of the key intellectual moments in the development of modern society. By offering a rational understanding of the origins of humanity in nature, it destroyed the intellectual basis of revealed religion. However, problems arise when the relationship is drawn in the other direction, when natural evolution is used to explain social development. In this century, millions of people were shoved into gas chambers because it was believed that they possessed 'genes that are not able to cope' as the 'Memesis Statement' puts it."

The scientific meme researcher Francis Heylighen from Brussels responded to this critique in the following way: "Hitler was a Christian, so religion leads to the gas chamber. Stalin was an atheist, so atheism leads to extermination, etc. The fact that some people at some point have misused an idea does not in any way prove that the idea is wrong or evil." Heylighen then elaborates on the term "evolution": "The essence of the meme idea is that evolution no longer takes place on the level of the genes, but on the level of culture. The fact that memes evolve according to principles of variation and selection very similar to the principles governing Darwinian evolution of genes does not in any way lead to Social Darwinism in its old sense."

Douglas Rushkoff ("just an American who has probably watched far too much TV and spent a bit too much time online") disagrees with the "negative fuss about memes": "It just boils down to a deep-rooted fear of the human spirit. We seem to fear that, left to our own devices, we will rape and pillage one another. Unchecked, the cautious social theorists warn, human beings will drive relentlessly towards fascism. Social scientists were taught that the masses, too stupid and easily swayed towards social policies as destabilizing as Nazism, must be led by a benevolent elite. They see society as an ocean that must be contained; they don't realize that their social theories are like the temporary plugs in a dike that will never hold up against the tide. And like the sad social theorists, the fundamentalists developed their own mind-control control techniques. They believe that, deep down, people are sinful. If we were allowed to roam free, we would have no choice but to succumb to our basest desires."

According to Rushkoff, the Internet is designed to promote global awareness. Evolution doesn't always favor certain individuals over others. "Those who fear memes and evolution really just fear progress. That's why so many well-spoken social theorists hate us pro-Internet, California-style utopians. If we attempt to slow the transmission of memes through culture, we will surely weaken and rot like the overly inbred royal families of centuries past. But I suppose I shouldn't worry. The anti-evolutionists are fighting a losing battle. Since their memes don't ultimately promote anything but social decay, they will surely perish in the long run."

What will Richard Barbrook's answer be? We don't know yet. In his first critique he stated: "It is precisely our refusal to accept our biological destiny which makes us more than insects. Unlike our fellow species, we can transform ourselves through thought and action."

But let's go back to Barbrook's "fundamental" critique of the "Memesis Statement": "If memes 'replicate themselves,' what are humans doing in the meantime? We're not the blind objects of genes or memes. We are the subjects of history even if it is not always in circumstances of our own choosing. The Net is a creation of human labour. Someone has to dig holes in the road to lay the fibre-optic wires. Someone has to write the software to enable people to use the Net. Without human activity, the Net is nothing but an inert mass of metal, plastic and sand. We are the only living beings in cyberspace."

The "Memesis Statement," again, says: "As an analogy to the building blocks of biology, the genes, memes describe cultural units of information, cognitive behavioral patterns that propagate and replicate themselves through communication. From the 'bio-adapter' language as a proto-meme to the 'info-sphere' of global networks as the ultimate habitat for the human mind."

Richard Barbrook does not believe that there is such a thing as an autonomous entity, located inside the technology. "The 'Memesis Statement' regards machines and information as autonomous things outside our control. Yet, in reality, both technology and culture are expressions of the social relationships between individual humans. It is human activity which is crystallised into machines and information, not memes which create 'mass crystals'. Crucially, the statement ignores one of the central questions of modernity: how are the rewards of labour to be divided among the different groups involved in the social production of machines and information? Ah, but the social question is so unfashionable nowadays . . ."

Tom Sherman also stresses the social aspect of the use of technology. Based at the School of Art and Design in Syracuse (NY), he reports from a "burned-out, totally out-of-date industrial city in the rust belt of the American northeast," and he comments on what is going on around him: "You don't hear a lot of evolutionary analogies in factory lunch rooms or college coffee houses these days. The talk is about survival and how tough a place the world has become. People are forming relationships with machines, not necessarily because they're attracted to machines, but because they are desperately trying to get connected and/or stay connected with other people, particularly with those who can help them survive."

In this context the Web, for Sherman, is becoming an "electronic talent database or tourist bureau full of resumes and brochures and maps." He compares this "indexical domain" with today's modern office: "Same software, same information handling methodologies; but no regular paycheck, no healthcare, no social security net. The Web is The Office for freelancers. Artists, that endangered species, when connected with/by computers, sit at a desk and look very much like office workers, telecommuting home-office workers. These are the new industrial labourers."

And, a few weeks later, Tom Sherman resumes: "Wanting badly to define ourselves at any cost, we try to figure what kinds of memes work best in particular technological spaces. We'll wear the damndest memes, just because they flourish in a system. Apparently we enjoy indulging in evolutionary analogies, playfully trading strong opinions about the mind's responsibility to the body, wondering whether our meme pool is stagnant, expanding or collapsing, and visiting and trashing the cultural ruins of Silicon Valley."

Herbert Hrachovec, philosopher in Vienna, contributes by saying "the printout of my neural reactions is not my neural state," in a reference to Kathryn Bigelow's film "Strange Days." "Cognitive behavioral patterns that propagate and replicate themselves through communication used to be called 'topoi', 'habits' or 'clichés'. They were thought to be social constants, stable but subject to alterations at the margin. This feature is lost in talk about 'memes'. They seem to be scientific constructs that can be handled like cellular tissue."

Suddenly, a report came in from the streets of San Francisco, from Arthur and Marilouise Kroker. For them, "'memes are just another word for nothing left to (digitally) lose,' to borrow a phrase from the song 'Me and Bobby McGee,' and in Ars California words are always too slow." "Memetic flesh? That's certainly not a sociological rhetoric of evolution or devolution, but something radically different. It's neither future nor history, but the molecular present, a floating outlaw zone where memes fold into genes. In SF, memes have abandoned the art academy, becoming popular culture for the 21st century. Memetic as daily life in cyber-city, the kind of place where the virus of the tech future digs its way under the skin, like an itch or a sore or a viral meme that just won't go away."

They discover the "art of dirty memes," unofficial outlaw art that's practiced in hidden warehouses, storefront galleries and ghetto schools. "Dirty memes? That's what happens when memetic engineering escapes into the street of cybercity, and its scent is picked up by viral artists. Neither technotopian, nor technophobic, memetic art in the streets of SF is always dirty, always rubbing memes against genes, always clicking in (our) memetic flesh."

A little later, the Krokers submit a digital postscript: "Memetic flesh means that under the relentless pressure of the will to virtuality, the boundaries between memes and genes, between culture and biology, becomes permeable and fluid and mirrored and instantly reversible. Memetic flesh is about the 'anxious meme'. To date, the debate on the Ars Symposium has recapitulated the history of high modernism. Indeed, the terms of the debate with its recycling at the level of memetic engineering of earlier debates between tech mysticism and tech realism, don't disturb the still waters of modernism at all because it just confirms the impossibility of breaking out of the cycle of hyper-(memetic) idealism and hyper-(social) realism. A beautiful museum of the modern mind. Memesis as Mimesis."

The cyber-feminist group VNS-Matrix posts their "Bitch Mutant Manifesto," command line poetry for seduced on-liners, digital addicts: "Read only my memories. Upload me into your pornographic imagination. Write me. We are the malignant accident which fell into your system while you were sleeping. And when you wake we will terminate your digital delusions, hijacking your impeccable software. SUCK MY CODE. The limit is NO CARRIER, the sudden shock of no contact, reaching out to touch, but the skin is cold . . . I become the FIRE. Flame me if you dare."

In the meanwhile, several participants reacted to the "Memesis Statement" and Richard Barbrook's critique. Simon Penny reacts to the original "Memesis Statement": "Humanity has NOT co-evolved with its artifacts in any biological sense. Survival into the next century depends not on whether genes will 'co-evolve with . . . artifacts' but whether they can survive the effects of those artifacts. The 'future of evolution' qua biological evolution is only brought into question by the cancerous proliferation of one particular species, homo sapiens."

He advises us to think twice before our mind considers moving out to take up residence on the Net. Global networks as the "ultimate habitat for the human mind"? "It baffles me that this rhetoric of 'transcendence via the Net' did not die a quick death a decade ago. Doesn't anybody realise just how corny and retrograde the notion is? It is just one facet of a general argument against the body, which has been an ongoing characteristic of western philosophy and Christian theology. William Gibson's Cyberpunks proclaimed 'the body is meat' but they did not pause to note how similar their position was to that of St. Augustine."

Robert Adrian (Vienna) also comments on the "modern" notion of evolution, as it is used in the "Memesis Statement." It might as well be other people's evolution, not ours . . . "Evolution is treated as a one-way street . . . always better, always improving. But the concept of evolution is not about 'progress' but about adaptation. This means that a species may be perfectly specialised for a specific environment but is utterly helpless should the environment change . . . In the future the world may become a very uncomfortable place for societies of high consumers. Presumably the memes/genes that survive into the next millennium will be those of the electronically endowed. That is, members of the electronic master-race. But there is not really much support for the assumption that because industrial culture has created this technology, it somehow OWNS it."

The artist Perry Hoberman isn't very happy with the "demolition derby." According to Hoberman, "the concept of meme has been subjected to such extreme mutation that its progeny have almost become unrecognizable." He therefore introduces into the discussion two "misshapen mutant memetic children," the Living Meme and the Imposter Meme. "The Living Meme is cross-bred with the rhetoric of (strong) Artificial Life and Artificial Intelligence and the wide-eyed notion of global networks achieving both autonomy and consciousness. The Living Meme is ready to run the whole show. The Imposter Meme on the other hand is always found grossly wanting and has been taking the rap here for just about every social ill of the twentieth century. A front man for Social Darwinism and Final Solutions, the Living Meme and the Imposter Meme are in fact obviously identical good-and-evil twins."

Hoberman proposes to return to the original definition of memes, coined by Richard Dawkins in "The Selfish Gene." "The meme is presented there neither as the building block for some eventual autonomous realm that would supplant biological evolution, nor to imply that the direction and development of human culture are completely out of our hands. The meme is posited instead as a unit of cultural transmission, analogous to the gene. If we are going to use a term, we ought to have a reasonable understanding of it."

According to Roy Ascott, we should take meme as a metaphor. But there is no truth behind a metaphor. Ascott is in favour of a "pragmatic approach." "Is the metaphor of meme useful to artists? The answer is yes. Is the idea of a meme space, understood as a kind of collective intelligence, a community of mind, useful to artists? Yes, it is. The whole collaborative enterprise in art is based on the idea of shared consciousness. It is the field of consciousness which artists now wish to explore. It is telematic consciousness which presents the opportunity and challenge to art as it moves beyond its lumpen concern with the surface appearance of the world. Can we speak yet of a memetic aesthetic replacing the old mimetic art? It depends. The meme metaphor falls flat considered in relation to the old biological processes of cognition. But in its post-biological context assimilated, transposed, transmitted and transformed by the processes of human cyberception, the meme metaphor acquires considerable potency."

Simultaneously, as one of the last in this "first round" of network discussions, Manuel DeLanda goes further with the idea of the "non-generic replicator." In this, he criticizes Dawkins: "Dawkins adopted the term meme because the mode of replication he had in mind was imitation. Yet, the sounds, meanings, and syntactical constructions of human language (and most of the other replicators that make human societies work, such as contracts, laws etc.) are not entities that replicate through 'imitation' but institutional norms which replicate through 'obligatory repetition'. I personally would restrict the term meme to apply exclusively to patterns of 'behavior' transmitted through imitation, such as bird songs or tool-use in apes, or fashions and fads in humans."

But besides replicators, there are also interactors: in biological terms enzymes and in human society "speech acts," as DeLanda suggests. He warns us to be precise and take terms like meme literally, with proper technical care. "The point is that unless we are very specific about both replicators and interactors when talking about non-biological fields, we risk falling into mere metaphor. Not that metaphors are useless, they are not. But the point that Dawkins is trying to make is precisely that the relation between memes and genes is not one of metaphorical analogy but of 'deep isomorphism'."

P.S. While this text is being prepared for publication, the presenter is also trying to focus the discussion on the other topics the "Memesis Statement" pinpointed: cyborg theory and media memory.

WWW—Memesis Reference List

Arkuat's Meme Workshop
http://www.c2.org/~arkuat/meme
Collection of links to memetics and philosophy

Mark Dery: Escape Velocity
http://www.well.com/user/markdery/ESCAPE/VELOCITY/links/
Links to the book about cyberculture

School of Cognitive and Computing Sciences
http://www.cogs.susx.ac.uk/lab/adapt/index.html
Evolutionary and Adaptive Systems at COGS, from artificial evolution to evolutionary robotics

Non-Cartesian Cognitive Science
http://www.cogs.susx.ac.uk/users/ronaldl/noncartesian.html
Very comprehensive page concerning fields such as cognitive psychology, philosophy, artificial life, and their areas of congruence.

AI, Cognitive Science and Robotics
http://www.cs.ucl.ac.uk/misc/ai/
The University College London's WWW guide to research groups and resources

Agents of Alienation
http://www.voyagerco.com/misc/ jaron.html
One of the few critical treatments on the subject of "software agents" by "Cyberspace Guru" Jaron Lanier

EFF "Cyborg Anthropology" Archive
http://www.eff.org/pub/Net_culture/ Cyborg_anthropology/
Archive of the Electronic Frontier Foundation on the subject of cyberculture, including a "trialog" with Mark Pauline, Manuel DeLanda, and Mark Dery, plus an article by Anne Balsamo on "VR and the human body"

Principia Cybernetica Web
http://pespmc1.vub.ac.be
The Project's aim is the computer-supported collaborative development of an evolutionary-systemic philosophy.

Lynn Cherny's MUD Papers
http://bhasha.stanford.edu/~cherny/papers.html
Deals with various aspects of text-based virtual realities such as "Objectifying the Body in the Discourse of an Object-Oriented MUD"

The Pinnochio Theory by Richard Barbrook
http://www.hrc.wmin.ac.uk/hrc/manifesto/pinnochio.html
A review of Out of Control: the New Biology of Machines by Kevin Kelly which argues that the biological metaphor is used to justify Social Darwinism and neo-liberal economic policies.

Reponses to the Holocaust
http://jefferson.village.virginia.edu/holocaust/response.html
"This hypermedia sourcebook is designed and organized according to disciplines and media that have simultaneously influenced our understanding of the Holocaust"

Of Man, Mind and Machine
http://www.dataspace.com/documents/consciousness.html
Meme-Based Models of Mind and the Possibility for Consciousness in Alternate Media

The Hybrid Cyborg
http://www.realid.com/Modern Identity/hybrids.html
This site deals with aspects of the body in Cyberspace discussing movies like "Blade Runner" or performances of Survival Research Laboratories

The Genetic Algorithms Archive
http://www.aic.nrl.navy.mil:80/galist/
The Genetic Algorithms Archive is a repository for information related to research in genetic algorithms.

Mind Viruses

Computer viruses are pieces of code that graft themselves into existing, legitimate programs and subvert the normal actions of those programs. They may travel on exchanged floppy disks, or over networks.

DNA viruses and computer viruses spread for the same reason: an environment exists in which there is machinery well set up to duplicate and spread them around and to obey the instructions that the viruses embody. These two environments are, respectively, the environment of cellular physiology and the environment provided by a large community of computers and data-handling machinery. Are there any other environments like these, any other humming paradises of replication?

We don't exactly plug floppy disks into slots in one another's skulls, but we exchange sentences, both through our ears and through our eyes. We notice each other's styles of moving and dressing and are influenced. We take in advertising jingles, and are presumably persuaded by them; otherwise, hard-headed businessmen would not spend so much money polluting the air with them.

Think about the two qualities that a virus, or any sort of parasitic replicator, demands of a friendly medium, the two qualities that make cellular machinery so friendly towards parasitic DNA, and that make computers so friendly towards computer viruses. These qualities are, firstly, a readiness to replicate information accurately, perhaps with some mistakes that are subsequently reproduced accurately; and, secondly, a readiness to obey instructions encoded in the information so replicated.

Cellular machinery and electronic computers excel in both these virus-friendly qualities. How do human brains match up? As faithful duplicators, they are certainly less perfect than either cells or electronic computers. Nevertheless, they are still pretty good, perhaps about as faithful as an RNA virus, though not as good as DNA with all its elaborate proofreading measures against textual degradation. Evidence of the fidelity of brains, especially child brains, as data duplicators is provided by language itself. Shaw's Professor Higgins was able by ear alone to place Londoners in the street where they grew up. Fiction is not evidence for anything, but everyone knows that Higgins's fictional skill is only an exaggeration of something we can all do. Any American can tell Deep South from Midwest, New England from Hillbilly. Any New Yorker can tell Bronx from Brooklyn. Equivalent claims could be substantiated for any country. What this phenomenon means is that human brains are capable of pretty accurate copying (otherwise the accents of, say, Newcastle would not be stable enough to be recognized) but with some mistakes (otherwise pronunciation would not evolve, and all speakers of a language would inherit identically the same accents from their remote ancestors). Language evolves, because it has both the great stability and the slight changeability that are prerequisites for any evolving system.

The second requirement of a virus-friendly environment—that it should obey a program of coded instructions—is again only quantitatively less true for brains than for cells or computers. We sometimes obey orders from one another, but also we sometimes don't. Nevertheless, it is a telling fact that, the world over, the vast majority of children follow the religion of their parents rather than any of the other available religions. Instructions to genuflect, to bow towards Mecca, to nod one's head rhythmically towards the wall, to shake like a maniac, to "speak in tongues"—the list of such arbitrary and pointless motor patterns offered by religion alone is extensive—are obeyed, if not slavishly, at least with some reasonably high statistical probability.

Less portentously, and again especially prominent in children, the "craze" is a striking example of behavior that owes more to epidemiology than to rational choice. Yo-yos, hula hoops and pogo sticks, with their associated behavioral fixed actions, sweep through schools, and more sporadically leap from school to school, in patterns that differ from a measles epidemic in no serious particular. Ten years ago, you could have traveled thousands of miles through the United States and never seen a baseball cap turned back to front. Today, the reverse baseball cap is ubiquitous. I do not know what the pattern of geographical spread of the reverse baseball cap precisely was, but epidemiology is certainly among the professions primarily qualified to study it. We don't have to get into arguments about "determinism"; we don't have to claim that children are compelled to imitate their fellows' hat fashions. It is enough that their hat-wearing behavior, as a matter of fact, is statistically affected by the hat-wearing behavior of their fellows.

Trivial though they are, crazes provide us with yet more circumstantial evidence that human minds, especially perhaps juvenile ones, have the qualities that we have singled out as desirable for an informational parasite. At the very least the mind is a plausible candidate for infection by something like a computer virus, even if it is not quite such a parasite's dream environment as a cell nucleus or an electronic computer.

Progressive evolution of more effective mind-parasites will have two aspects. New "mutants" (either random or designed by humans) that are better at spreading will become more numerous. And there will be a ganging up of ideas that flourish in one another's presence, ideas that mutually support one another just as genes do and, as I have speculated, computer viruses may one day do. We expect that replicators will go around together from brain to brain in mutually compatible gangs. These gangs will come to constitute a package, which may be sufficiently stable to deserve a collective name such as Roman Catholicism or Voodoo. It doesn't too much matter whether we analogize the whole package to a single virus, or each one of the component parts to a single virus. The analogy is not that precise anyway, just as the distinction between a computer virus and a computer worm is nothing to get worked up about. What matters is that minds are friendly environments to parasitic, self-replicating ideas or information, and that minds are typically massively infected.

Like computer viruses, successful mind viruses will tend to be hard for their victims to detect. If you are the victim of one, the chances are that you won't know it, and may even vigorously deny it. Accepting that a virus might be difficult to detect in your own mind, what tell-tale signs might you look out for? I shall answer by imagining how a medical textbook might describe the typical symptoms of a sufferer (arbitrarily assumed to be male).

1. The patient typically finds himself impelled by some deep, inner conviction that something is true, or right, or virtuous: a conviction that doesn't seem to owe anything to evidence or reason, but which, nevertheless, he feels as totally compelling and convincing. We doctors refer to such a belief as "faith."

2. Patients typically make a positive virtue of faith's being strong and unshakable, in spite of not being based upon evidence. Indeed, they may feel that the less evidence there is, the more virtuous the belief.

3. A related symptom, which a faith-sufferer may also present, is the conviction that "mystery," per se, is a good thing. It is not a virtue to solve mysteries. Rather we should enjoy them, even revel in their insolubility.

Any impulse to solve mysteries could be seriously inimical to the spread of a mind virus. It would not, therefore, be surprising if the idea that "mysteries are better not solved" was a favored member of a mutually supporting gang of viruses. Take the "Mystery of Transubstantiation." It is easy and non-mysterious to believe that in some symbolic or metaphorical sense the eucharistic wine turns into the blood of Christ. The Roman Catholic doctrine of transubstantiation, however, claims far more. The "whole substance" of the wine is converted into the blood of Christ; the appearance of wine that remains is "merely accidental," "inhering in no substance" (Kenny, 1986, p. 72).

Transubstantiation is colloquially taught as meaning that the wine *literally* turns into the blood of Christ. Whether in its obfuscatory Aristotelian or its franker colloquial form, the claim of transub-

Richard Dawkins *Mind Viruses*

stantiation can be made only if we do serious violence to the normal meanings of words like "substance" and "literally." Redefining words is not a sin, but, if we use words like "whole substance" and "literally" for this case, what word are we going to use when we really and truly want to say that something did actually happen? As Anthony Kenny observed of his own puzzlement as a young seminarian, "For all I could tell, my typewriter might be Benjamin Disraeli transubstantiated . . ."

Roman Catholics, whose belief in infallible authority compels them to accept that wine becomes physically transformed into blood despite all appearances, refer to the "mystery" of transubstantiation. Calling it a mystery makes everything OK, you see. At least, it works for a mind well prepared by background infection. Exactly the same trick is performed in the "mystery" of the Trinity. Mysteries are not meant to be solved, they are meant to strike awe. The "mystery is a virtue" idea comes to the aid of the Catholic, who would otherwise find intolerable the obligation to believe the obvious nonsense of the transubstantiation and the "three-in-one."

An extreme symptom of "mystery is a virtue" infection is Tertullian's "Certum est quia impossibile est" ("it is certain because it is impossible"). That way madness lies. One is tempted to quote Lewis Carroll's White Queen, who, in response to Alice's "One can't believe impossible things" retorted "I daresay you haven't had much practice . . . When I was your age, I always did it for half-an-hour a day. Why, sometimes I've believed as many as six impossible things before breakfast." Or Douglas Adam's Electric Monk, a labor-saving device programmed to do your believing for you, which was capable of "believing things they'd have difficulty believing in Salt Lake City" and which, at the moment of being introduced to the reader, believed, contrary to all the evidence, that everything in the world was a uniform shade of pink. But White Queens and Electric Monks become less funny when you realize that these virtuoso believers are indistinguishable from revered theologians in real life. "It is by all means to be believed, because it is absurd" (Tertullian again). Sir Thomas Browne (1635) quotes Tertullian with approval, and goes further: "Methinks there be not impossibilities enough in religion for an active faith." And "I desire to exercise my faith in the difficultest point; for to credit ordinary and visible objects is not faith, but persuasion (sic)."

4. The sufferer may find himself behaving intolerantly towards vectors of rival faiths, in extreme cases even killing them or advocating their deaths. He may be similarly violent in his disposition towards apostates (people who once held the faith but have renounced it); or towards heretics (people who espouse a different—often, perhaps significantly, only very slightly different—version of the faith). He may also feel hostile towards other modes of thought that are potentially inimical to his faith, such as the method of scientific reason which may function rather like a piece of anti-viral software.

5. The patient may notice that the particular convictions that he holds, while having nothing to do with evidence, do seem to owe a great deal to epidemiology. Why, he may wonder, do I hold this set of convictions rather than that set? Is it because I surveyed all the world's faiths and chose the one whose claims seemed most convincing? Almost certainly not. If you have a faith, it is statistically overwhelmingly likely that it is the same faith as your parents and grandparents had. No doubt soaring cathedrals, stirring music, moving stories and parables help a bit. But by far the most important variable determining your religion is the accident of birth. The convictions that you so passionately believe would have been a completely different, and largely contradictory, set of convictions, if only you had happened to be born in a different place. Epidemiology, not evidence.

6. If the patient is one of the rare exceptions who follows a different religion from his parents, the explanation may still be epidemiological. To be sure, it is possible that he dispassionately surveyed the world's faiths and chose the most convincing one. But it is statistically more probable that he has been exposed to a particularly potent infective agent—a John Wesley, a Jim Jones or a St. Paul. Here we are talking about horizontal transmission, as in measles. Before, the epidemiology was that of vertical transmission, as in Huntington's Chorea.

For a Digital Renaissance
of Situationism

Nothing goes without saying anymore. At least not much, to put it a bit more cautiously. And technology-based art is misunderstood by many people anyway. Of course, there are a lot of different reasons for that. But it should be pretty obvious—and why else would we even get involved in impassioned discussions like this?—that the various forms of technology-based art, along with technological development itself and the effect it increasingly exerts upon everyday life, have gradually oriented themselves upon a single sphere of manifestation—namely, the realm of data. A foreseeable outcome of this is the growing similarity of different concepts of art. For the present, though, the distinctions may still be useful to the extent that, as the argumentation that the supposed diversity of characteristics manifested by art proves itself to be invalid, new conditions can be derived.

Technology-based arts thus have as their prime criteria their respective spheres in which they manifest themselves and their referential spheres. We speak, for example, of the informational (mediatized) sphere by which we mean, in reference to media art, the forms of appearance and distribution of informational media which are organized as a monologue and include newspapers, TV, etc. In contrast to this informational sphere, we speak of a sphere of signification as that of traditional management as well as the management of signs, of orientation, of politics—with signifiers such as legislature, art, society, morality, or spectacle. Situationism, anti-art, art in public spaces, or spaces to be made accessible to the public base their oppositional attitude upon this distinction as one of aesthetics as well. Dialogically organized communications media and channels establish linkages with the data sphere—in reference to communicational (or telematic) art.

We take media art to mean either art which employs technical equipment to produce (and reflect) images, sounds, or texts, or we refer thereby to art which conceives itself as a form of game played with informational media. This intention describes, for example, the strategy pursued by Malcolm McLaren in the late 1970s. And this is what music theorist Werner Jauk is referring to when he interprets the punk rock/media art project "The Sex Pistols" by Malcolm McLaren as the consequence of "precisely these 'theoretical concepts of authenticity' commercially blown out of all proportion." McLaren "showed how oppositional attitude is sold as a commodity of the rock 'n' roll business in a giant 'swindle'" in which he "made the exploitation of the media's trade in 'oppositional attitude'" his own strategy: "It's not the media exploiting musicians, but rather artists exploiting the media, selling extreme oppositional attitudes through the mechanism of the 'media rock 'n' roll business' which otherwise so masterfully disables oppositional attitudes to consumption goods. This process is dissected and documented in The Great Rock 'n' Roll Swindle in which the document itself is likewise declared a commodity: ringing up a double sale or parallel theoretical elaboration befitting of art, a method of attaining insight."

Proceeding from the example of McLaren's "media art," communicational art manifests itself as a form of play that organizes art in the dialogical data sphere by bringing together this data sphere with the technical means of (digital) communication. Assuming that interactive art derives none of its

Heimo Ranzenbacher

concepts from a connection to traditional conceptions of art which it turns into a plaything, it is, in my opinion, nevertheless based upon the same principle pattern.

What significance can possibly be attained by an interactive art that does not aspire to be a plaything? Usually, it's just something that consumers buy—either on credit or on faith. As a form of art, however, it raises the question of an expanded conception of art—and usually dismisses it peremptorily, when one considers how interactive art invariably follows mass consumer demand.

As a basic precondition, expansion of the conception of art automatically calls for a process of distancing from or a rejection of art's claims to autonomy. The discourse on the subject of art in public spaces was marked by this when it did not simply content itself—did it make us feel somewhat ill at ease?—with negotiating formal criteria of the locations at which it might properly appear. The question of expansion has been constantly influenced by the interpretation of the realm into which art could, in a concrete sense, expand.

Implicit in the self-conception of traditionally defined art, meant here in the sense of diverse artwork-producing disciplines, is the endorsement of its traditional sphere of manifestation, the endorsement of the contexts of distribution, administration, and exploitation to which art is subject. Even the critique leveled by traditional art at the locations where it appears—the institution of the gallery, for instance—contains an implied endorsement of the "gallery" as a manifestational site, since the sphere of the gallery is not identical to the gallery for which a specific aesthetic form has been executed. A work of art, then, is an expression of the acceptance of the preconditions of its manifestation if every form of manifestation, including the critique upon it, submits to these preconditions. The conception of a work of art signifies a form of submission that can be consummated only in the work itself.

All forms of manifestation have one thing in common: the problematic issue of autonomy. In most aesthetic theories, autonomy is understood in the sense of Kant,[1] who introduced Autonomie as a philosophical concept. For example, Niklas Luhmann summarized his considerations on the subject of modern art by stating "that art attains a state of freedom from external constraints to the extent that it rejects delimiting restrictions and achieves self-liberation, and its very pretensions to being art are dependent upon how this is done." And for Adorno, autonomy is only then attained when all traces of the human imprint upon form have been completely dissolved: "The purer the forms and the greater the autonomy of works, the more horrible they are. Appeals calling for a more humane attitude by works of art, for a greater degree of adjustment toward human beings as their virtual public, regularly tend to dilute quality and weaken integrity of form." If, however, the work (as "categorical imperative" of art) is obsolete, so then is the concept of autonomy—which this author has never felt comfortable with anyway. Something is either autonomous or it is not. Gradual autonomy is conceptual nonsense. There exist, at best, forms of dependence which can approach autonomy.

The question of the meaning as well as of the quality of art is initially posed as a question of the interpretation of the spheres of its manifestation (through its appearance therein). This leads to an expansion not only of the conception of art but also of the concept of diverse spheres. Art no longer defines itself through the interpretation of the narrowly defined space in which it appears, but rather by means of its expansion into other spaces and the interpretation of them: expansion of urban, social spaces into those which constitute themselves anew as a result of new contexts of function and significance. Above all, the question is how the substitution of the work as a parameter for the concept of art constitutes, through the sphere of its manifestation, a parameter of the meaning and the quality of art.

If, for example, the sphere of art is no longer solely the place of its manifestation but, at the same time, the place where it is produced and distributed, thus both "material" and object of art, as is intended by highly advanced art forms, then we may well have to pronounce as obsolete a great deal more than we, in our traditional love of art, would prefer. I would therefore like to focus attention upon two forms of art that we have never grown so very fond of: situationism, on one hand, and anti-art on

Heimo Ranzenbacher *For a Digital Renaissance of Situationism* the other. As a result of the traits they exhibit, both forms enable us to carry forward a discourse in which art is conceived to some extent as a phenomenon in a historical context. Admittedly, the failure of both of them is quite evident. The manner in which anti-art once advanced its interpretation of the sphere of established art as a reinforcement of society and assumed the attitude of an obsolete world view is just as inapplicable today as the world view of the situationists. If everything is merely appearance, then so is the situationist critique of the culture of spectacle, for which whatever appears is good including, therefore, the situationist critique of it. And nevertheless, elements are to be found in these attitudes which contribute to our orientation regarding a technology-based art. In their fundamental negation of the character of the work, media art, communicational art, and interactive art display parallels to the theory and practice of anti-art and/or situationism. (The character of the work is significant only in the context of the exploitation and administration of art.) But, like anti-art and situationism, the practice of media, communicational, and interactive art relegates this element to ineffectuality as well.

Anti-art—both in its classical modernist expressions such as Dada, Fluxus, and Viennese Actionism, as well as in the movements in this direction during the 1970s and early 1980s—usually assumed an oppositional attitude to the market, performing what was interpreted as the social corrective of art. It made the attempt to withdraw from the normative as well as politically all-consuming ideology of (aesthetic) liabilities and (personal) assets by abandoning the conception of art as a work of art in favor of the idea that art manifests itself in an event. It thus substituted the concept of the work with that of the Concept. It called into question the myth of the original and the conception of authorship—which indeed made it seemingly incompatible with forms called for by the established channels of exploitation, though its end, as a value in the institutionalized management of works and signs, argues against this view. Anti-art played with the conception of art and the way the bourgeoisie appropriated it for itself as an ideology of confident superiority. The game was played against art itself; that is to say, against its instrumentalization to strengthen an ideology. It was inevitable that it would end up as an artistic value, since this was its very point.

A much more radical approach—and, thus, one that is of even greater interest today—was taken by the situationists of the 1950s and 1960s. Their interpretation was not focused on the instrumentalization of art as a pillar supporting the ideology of a society, but rather upon society as a universal spectacle organized according to the motto "Everything that appears is good and good things are those which appear." Art as understood by the situationists is not something that is produced; it is an attitude out of which situations are construed. If we interpret Meme as something that brings about both an increased attainment of knowledge which is adequate with respect to its environment, as well as the implementation of knowledge (whereby the aim is that it achieve actual form), then situational constructs are a close equivalent—viral effects in the program of sheer appearances. It would perhaps be appropriate for the unification of the attitudes of anti-art and situationism to take effect in the program of the looming unification of spheres (of information and media, of data and signs) into a single monolithic sphere.

As a rule, a work of art is regarded as "interactive" only if it undergoes change as a result of intervention on the part of an actively participating observer. It is the construction of a context that makes possible, in a type of choreographed action, the creation of a work of proximate individuality. This context is the interactional framework as well as the actor and the work itself. Beyond this framework, though, interactivity does not considerably differ from the static work of art. Last and undoubtedly least, the discourse of interactivity leads into that of traditional art and how this discourse is conducted by means of the significance of color or the pedagogical value of viewing a work of art. Interactivity means neither a gain for art itself nor for the understanding of the spheres to which it as a work refers. Completely within the tradition of the failure of anti-art, interactive art—at its best,

Heimo Ranzenbacher *For a Digital Renaissance of Situationism* which is tantamount to saying in the rarest of cases—contents itself with thumbing its nose in defiance of the administrative sphere of art. It mostly reproduces the old ideas in digital format. The creation of an electronic matrix (an artificial system of preconditions in miniature—the dynamics of inversion) which undergoes a framework shift as a result of interactivity basically refers only—though, for contemporary observers certainly in a most interesting way—to the old quality of reference and, for the most part, differs from the interactive in the same way that the Kantian concept of aesthetics ("the Beautiful as an object from which one takes pleasure in the absence of all interests") differs from the assertion made by Alexander Gottlieb Baumgarten who—to now introduce the word "beautiful" in a way that can be intersubjectively checked and approved for subsequent usage—primarily attributed "beauty" not to objects but rather used it to refer to a way of cognition (something can be "cognized in a beautiful way"). One is a form of play within a (larger) form of play exerting an effect upon it (offensive dynamics), whereas the other is comparable to a plaything. Inversion dynamics are analogous to the actions of frameworks. To construct a framework around art, thus to make it subordinate to framework conditions, means to convert it into the status of a work. Art in the data sphere is characterized by the exact opposite, by the dissolution of frameworks. Its own dissolution as art is implicit in this. However, it is only through the conversion of interactive art into the offensive dynamics of communicational art that this dissolution is fully consummated as a transformation into a new form of organization.

In communicational art, context is thus a cultural fact. A venue is not specially created for this form of play; rather, it is set in motion within, and on the basis of the preconditions of, the public sphere. This cultural framework of interaction—at least in the form in which it is perceived—is modified by dynamic users. The portrayal which emerges is the art of usage, whereby "art" is, of course, meant to have a double meaning. Until now, the creation of (aesthetic) information was usually a private affair. The data sphere, however, makes not only the data itself but also the creation of data/information into a public matter. In "Horizontal Radio,"[2] for example—a project organized on the Internet and distributed internationally through radio hook-up to the net that also included live presentations—music, sound, text, and all (including aesthetic) types of information were imbued with a significance totally different from that of their form and content alone. "Horizontal Radio" was an experimental setup—the first, to my knowledge—in which informational and communicational media were dialogically hooked up, and this to an extent that previously had been formulated only as a utopian fantasy. Reversibility was introduced into this process as an aesthetic category of criticism, namely as the critique of information, including the aesthetic information itself, which was propagated, and thus modified, by the channels of communication. The information was processed at each network interface point, so that each user could receive a version different from that received by all other users linked to the Net. Thanks to this dialogue, information was subjected to a constant critique. Not only the aesthetic information but also the functional characteristics of radio itself were changed: radio underwent a self-determined process of divergence brought about by the manner of representation and the functional mode into which it was forced. For example, here in Austria, only a portion of the information could be received via radio; other countries got other portions. Only on the Net, in the telematic sphere, could the information be received as a whole—and also be subsequently processed. This made possible communication via radio, not just information, such that the monologic authority of the medium was broken down. The aim of criticism is to again impart significance to things. Instead of their giving us meaning, "informing" us, significance (meaning) is provided to them by means of critique of information. Radio had to be rethought because radio itself had been induced to do so by the process leading to the dissemination of information.

Unified into a contemporary situationism, media art and communicational art are organizing themselves for the interactive construction of communicable situations. "Horizontal Radio" was the first situationist project that has taken into account the changed and changing conditions of our culture.

Interactivity as aesthetic category—namely, in view of the beautiful (in the sense of Baumgarten) way it can be seen to have been fully realized—is pure interface design. Its application may some day generate graphics, texts, audio, etc. Its political aspect (the aesthetic category of criticism) is its reversibility. Carrying over traditional aesthetic criteria of graphics, texts, audio into the sphere of data means not only acknowledging these structural orders, even with the (ultimately, unfortunately) opposite intention; they are also pure nonsense in this context of function and thought. If the question is posed "What sense does the data sphere make?," then graphics, texts, audio, etc. provide the first answer as the elements which combine to generate this data sphere. This type of interface design had to provoke a new process of questioning leading to a future theoretical, social, and cultural foundation of art. Otherwise, following the befuddlement of feelings resulting from the overemphasis upon sensual qualities of perception in traditional art, it is to be feared that only cognitive befuddlement in view of the closed system with its dynamics of inversion will be the consequence.

.

Notes

1. Kant was the first to set out a philosophical-critical treatment of art's claims to autonomy which had emerged in theory and practice in a series of successive steps since the Renaissance. In his view, the power of aesthetic judgment is directed at objects whose beauty is a "form of functionality, to the extent that no evident sense of purpose can be perceived with respect to the object." Here, "beautiful" is defined as that "which, in the absence of an abstract concept, is perceived as the object of essential pleasure." These determinations do not refer to perceived contents but rather to form and proportion that accrue to the work of art as a product of freedom. In reference to beauty as functionality of things (works of art) without purpose, the free play of the sensual power of perception provides the basis of the aesthetic behavior of the subject.

2. A co-production of Ars Acustica and experts of the EBU with TRANSIT, ORF Landesstudio Tirol, ORF-Kunstradio, ORF Landesstudio Oberosterreich, and KAPSCH AG. Concept and project organization: Gerfried Stocker—x-space, Heidi Grundmann—ORF-Kunstradio. "Horizontal Radio" was on the air at Ars Electronica 95 from June 22 at 12:00 CET to June 23 at 12:00 CET on the transmitting frequencies of 24 radio stations.

Neuron-Silicon Junction
or Brain-Computer Junction?

Peter Fromherz

I first observed nerve cells and silicon wafers while working on two distinctly different degree dissertations in my laboratory at the University of Ulm in 1984. At the time, we were studying how the electrical activity of nerve cells influenced fluorescent dyes and the effects of artificial membrane layers on microscopic silicon electrodes. Enthused by the results, I used the occasion of the 20th Winter Seminar "Molecules, Information, and Memory" presented by Manfred Eigen in January 1985 to present a paper entitled "Brain on Line? The Feasibility of a Neuron-Silicon Junction," in which I outlined how a direct electrical contact between a nerve cell and silicon (and vice versa) could be constructed. In the paper, I wrote: "The information processing of the networks of neurons in a brain and of the networks of silicon chips in a computer is coupled at the present moment macroscopically through the opto-mechanical pathway eye-screen and finger-keyboard (Fig. 1a). Is a direct microscopical coupling feasible (Fig. 1b)? The utopian question may be shaped into a proper scientific problem: How to design a neuron-silicon junction?"

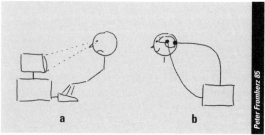

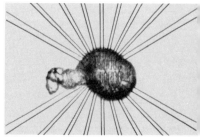

Fig. 1 *Brain-Computer Junction.*
(a) Classical mechano-optical pathay eye-screen and finger-keyboard.
(b) Imaginary ionic-electrical junction of the computer with the optic and motor centers of the cerebral cortex.

Fig. 2 *Neuron-Silicon Junction. Nerve cell (approximate 60 micrometers in diameter) of a leech ganglion in direc contact with 16 transistors in silicon. Electrical voltage impulses in the cell directly effect the chip's electronics*

The matter did not remain at the design stage. However, a prerequisite for carrying out a neuron-silicon junction was the process of learning and mastering the production of silicon chips and the cultivation of nerve cells—by a small team working in one and the same laboratory. Six years later, we published a description of the first direct electrical junction of a nerve cell to a silicon transistor;[1] ten years later, the first direct electrical junction of a silicon microstructure to a nerve cell.[2]

Since then, we have performed a detailed study of the physics of the coupling of neurons and silicon.[3–6] We understand how the quality of the signal transmission is affected by the geometry of the cell-chip contact and by the electrical properties of the cell membrane and of silicon.

All of these studies were carried out using large nerve cells (approximately 60 micrometers in diameter) of leech ganglia. As an example, Fig. 2 illustrates the "wiring up" of such a nerve cell with the 16 transistors of a silicon chip. The first junctions with nerve cells from the brain of a rat have recently been successfully performed.[7] Here, the small size of these cells (about 10 micrometers) poses particular problems.

These lengthy and difficult experiments have shown us just how large a gap really exists between test tube experiments involving a neuron-silicon junction and the interfacing of the brain and the computer. We must keep in mind that we are dealing with two completely different aspects here— a physical one and an informational one.

To begin with: the physics of the direct junction of nerve cells and silicon is based on the contact of the neurons' thin (5 nanometer) cell membrane with the thin (20 nanometer) layer of quartz which makes up the silicon's watertight casing. Only when the contact is extremely close (about 30 nanometers) does an electrical coupling take place through the electrical field (electrostatic induction). This tight junction can be successfully created in the test tube with clean silicon chips and nerve cells which have been dissected from tissue samples. The form which such a contact would take in the tissue of a nerve fiber or of the brain cannot be foreseen at the moment. After all, this is not merely a matter of maintaining a few random contacts; if the brain and the computer—two separate worlds miniaturized down to microscopic level—are really to be brought into connection with one another, and if an adequate level of communication is to come about as a result, then millions of contacts must be set up.

Moreover: it is not sufficient to install contacts between the brain and the computer which exchange some sort of informational bits in both directions. Both the brain and the computer must directly understand the semantics of a foreign language without the abstraction and adaptation accomplished by means of keyboard and monitor. Both operating systems have to communicate directly with each other in a meaningful way. As long as we do not know how the brain functions—what relationship exists between its microscopic electrical signals and its macroscopic semantics—an informational interface remains impossible even if the physical junction were feasible.

What can be done? Physicists will carry on with the effort to establish thousands of contact points between nerve cells and silicon microstructures. Experiments to achieve this—in cooperation with major firms in the microelectronics industry—are now under way. Even if this can only be done in a test tube, it will provide scientists with a basis for understanding how larger hybrid networks composed of neuronal and technological elements communicate with each other on the level of semantic information. Thus, we might learn something about the function of the brain.

Setting up contacts within living tissue is another problem. One solution might be an ingenious form of coating of the chip or the cell. Here as well, it will be necessary to first carry out basic research on the biology, chemistry, and physics of cell adhesion.

The process of achieving a direct junction of individual nerve cells and individual silicon microstructures has opened our eyes to the difficulty of establishing a linkage between the brain and the computer without the mediation of the opto-mechanical pathway eye-screen and finger-keyboard. The apparent problems posed by this junction on the physical and informational levels are so enormous that it is impossible today to predict whether such a form of communication will ever become a reality. For this reason, an ethical consideration of issues such as "chip in the brain" or "brain in the computer" would be unfounded and superfluous.

Notes

1. P. Fromherz, A.Offenhäusser, T. Vetter, and J. Weis, "A Neuron-Silicon Junction: A Retzius-Cell of the Leech on an Insulated-Gate Field-Effect Transistor," Science 252 (1991), 1290–1293.

2. P. Fromherz and A.Stett, "Silicon-Neuron Junction: Capacitive Stimulation of an Individual Neuron on a Silicon Chip," Physical Review Letters 75 (1995), 1670–1673.

3. P. Fromherz, C. O. Müller, and R. Weis, "Neuron-Transistor: Electrical Transfer Function Measured by Patch-Clamp Technique," Physical Review Letters 71 (1993), 4079–4082.

4. R.Weis, B. Müller, and P. Fromherz, "Neuron-Adhesion on a Silicon Chip probed by an Array of Field-Effect Transistors," Physical Review Letters 76 (1996), 327–330.

5. R. Weis and P. Fromherz, "Frequency Dependent Signal-Transfer in Neuron-Transistors," Physical Review E 55 (1997), 877–889.

6. A. Stett, B. Müller, and P. Fromherz, "Two-Way Silicon-Neuron Interface by Electrical Inductance," Physical Review E 55 (1997), 1779–1782.

7. S. Vassanelli and P. Fromherz, "Neurons from Rat Brain coupled to Transistors," Applied Physics A (1997).

Bad Girl Versus the Astronaut Christ

The Strange Political Journey of the Cyborg

Hari Kunzru

It's well over a decade since Donna Haraway first formulated her theory of the cyborg.[1] During that time the figure of the "cybernetic organism," networked flesh subject to rational control, has morphed from a technical into a political category, a change which continues to surprise the cyborg's scientist parents.

At its origin in the US Air Force research programmes of the nineteen-fifties and sixties, the cyborg seemed to carry an uncomplicated meaning, the same meaning coded into the cold war slew of pulp space travel stories or the arcing rear fins of a Chevrolet convertible. Man, said the cyborg, the Chevy, the Ace paperback, was about to transcend all limitations. Born out of the desire to adapt human systems for survival in space, the cyborgised man would transcend the constraints of Newtonian physics by breaking free of gravity and going to the stars. At the same time he would transcend his own physical boundaries, entering a control and communication feedback-loop with his environment. The skin, that ultimate boundary between fragile self and hostile world, would become gloriously permeable, permeable not in a vulnerable way, but in a manner which would mystically transform messy, poorly understood human biological processes into the exact, measurable, predictable processes of technology. Man thus penetrated by the machine would become an "augmented," "adapted," or "amplified" man,[2] functioning according to the protocols of technoscience. As science improved, so would man. He was, in short, upgradeable. No outer limit seemed to be fixed for this augmentation. Cyborgised man could potentially expand towards infinity, perhaps even attaining the sublime.

Certainly, it seemed that with human biological functions regulated by machines, man would be freed to explore not only the physical expanses of space but the spiritual ones of his own being. Governing the body's homeostatic processes appeared to this first generation of cyborg researchers to require effort, to divert energy that would be better used for self-evolution or spiritual exercise, as if the business of having a body was somehow distracting, time-consuming, laborious: "If man in space, in addition to flying his vehicle, must continuously be checking things and making adjustments merely in order to keep himself alive, he becomes a slave to the machine. The purpose of the Cyborg, as well as his own homeostatic systems, is to provide an organizational system in which such robot-like problems are taken care of automatically and unconsciously, leaving man free to explore, to create, to think, and to feel."[3]

Though the backdrop for this struggle against slavery was space, the same hopes and fears held true for life in postwar America. Cyborgisation was produced as a labour-saving process, the big boy's version of the dishwashers and frigidaires they bought for wives back home on earth. But unlike the kitchen of the future, whose technology bought time for female leisure or beautification, the cyborg had a higher purpose. The implication voiced again and again in early cyborg technical papers is that by relinquishing the labour of bodily regulation, man could attain a higher level of spiritual discipline. The cyborg, in short, was designed to engineer man closer to God.

The engineers and Air Force men who made up the first generation of the cyborg's acolytes were in no doubt that they were on a spiritual mission. "Where are we, where are we going, and how do we get there?" asks Major Jack E. Steele, using this uncontextualised and apparently metaphysical question to open a 1960 presentation to a space research symposium at Wright Air Force Base. He goes on to describe a coming generation of "bionic" humans, the "great and distant" goal towards which he and his audience are working.[4]

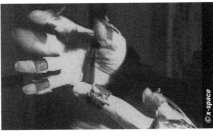
©x-space

The pilgrim's progress, spiritual journey as mirror of a physical journey, was always one of the ideological motors of American expansion, from the moment the first boatload of seventeenth-century dissenters began the task of inscribing their struggle to reach God onto the seemingly blank landscape of the "New World." Cyborg research can be seen as the inheritor of this move, continuous with the pioneers' journey westwards and the puritans' interior journey towards God. The cyborg represented the ability, through science, to take an active role in evolution, bringing recalcitrant human biology under the sway of reason and morality, all put into the service of state expansion.

The human to be rationally evolved was almost invariably an air force pilot, and archive images of pilots undergoing grueling physical tests and wearing a variety of prosthetics are among the most potent images of the early cyborg era. Shackled into exoskeletons, suffering inhuman (or maybe just posthuman) forces, responses altered with intravenous injections of drugs, the fighter pilot becomes America's cyborg Christ, the sufferer whose passion redeems his nation. All-American boy, chosen for his physical and mental perfection, transfigured by the machine, sent above and beyond, suffering and questing for the people whose votes and taxes sent him there—apex of hope and probe-head of the superpower's cold-war psyche. In a mirror of this obsession the postwar USSR, which itself was a vast cybernetic project, a huge experiment in rational control, produced its own cult of the cyborg Christ in the Yuri Gagarin industry whose support extended to the state-sponsored production of quasi-religious icons.

Perhaps Donna Haraway's achievement has in part been a therapeutic one. In excavating the unconscious of this pumped-up sky pilot, she has unearthed the anxieties, the sexual and spiritual ambiguities, the night terrors of one of the defining figures of postwar technocultural certainty. Yet her analysis has also been deliberately disruptive, a critical virus introduced into a loop of signification which appeared too closed and too perfectly regulated to admit any variation or opposition.

Historically, it did not take long for the human body's permeation by networks and machines to produce alternative visions to the joyous liberation from the flesh envisaged by the USAF geeks. A previous generation of technological nightmares had already centered on humans becoming automata. The ergonomically governed factory worker, disciplined by the twin mass mechanisms of industry and war, was in the inter-war years of the twentieth century figured as the robot (Czech for "slave labour"). Just as in a still-earlier phase of industrialisation workers had been metonymised into "hands,"[5] they became pistons and flywheels, moving parts in vast machines. The image of Charlie Chaplin caught in the cogs of some huge engine[6] is the era's defining image of recalcitrant humanity, comically refusing the rhythms of the factory.

Yet in the 1930's the little tramp's skin still formed an impermeable barrier to the system which oppressed him. In the 1960's, when the first generation of Christ-pilots underwent augmentation, this ceased to be the case. The rupture of the body's membrane (by prosthetics and implants, astronautical stigmata) released far more than expected. From classical times onwards, the West had made a huge investment in the opacity of the body. From the Apollo Belvedere to National Socialism, the closed, impermeable body was valued as morally continent, aesthetically pleasing, epistemologically single and secure.

By contrast, when the body exposed its workings, allowed its orifices to be penetrated, its interior humours to seep forth, this invariably signified the inversion of order, the coming of chaos, horror, and decay. Whether this inversion was figured by the gluttonous, shitting, fucking grotesques of the Renaissance carnival, by Nazi racial science's physiognomy of the Jew, with its slack lips and protruding nose, or Neoclassicism's mingled desire and revulsion for female flesh, it always carried the same meaning. The classical body has for two thousand years stood sealed (inside and out) against a torrent of disproportionate, irrational, exaggerated physicality, which, were it to escape, threatened to sweep away the very foundations of civilised society.

So the cyborg body, penetrated by reason itself, presents an irresolvable paradox—the body must at all costs preserve its boundaries against the deluge of unreason, but must also reveal its mystery in order to allow reason to transcend physical limitations. Otherwise the body will present an obstacle to reason, and find itself once again the source of irrationality. Catch-22 for the flesh. This is the eternal tragicomedy of Western thought of the body, a thought which cannot incorporate itself, cannot think within the body, must always attempt to think through it, to penetrate it from the outside.

The cyborg produced a crisis in technoscience, even as it promised fulfillment of technoscience's most secret desires. It was a radical moment, and one which Donna Haraway has fully exploited, using this paradox to lever open both scientific discourse and the varieties of feminist discourse which were constituting themselves in naive opposition to it. Yet though the cyborg's brand of disruption is radical, it is not unprecedented. Perhaps its closest cultural ancestor can be found in the growth of scientific dissection during the Renaissance. Here too was a discourse which opened up the body in the name of knowledge, which literally dismembered corpses to produce truth. The dissected figures depicted in woodcut illustrations to the works of the Flemish anatomist Andreas Vesalius,[7] display themselves, sometimes literally holding aside veils of flayed skin to allow the gaze of the student to penetrate the secrets of their bodies. In this and other Renaissance anatomical texts, complicated pictorial allegories are used to justify the practice of anatomy, which produced deep cultural anxiety, presented an identical problem of bodily integrity, and which (in one of those "what if" games which make joining the dots of intellectual history fun) one can imagine some seventeenth-century Haraway using to blow "Natural Philosophy" wide open.

In 1997 economies of signification analogous to those circulating in Vesalius's operating theatre are played out across cinema and TV screens. After a rapid process of popularisation, originally associated with space programme fundraising, the cyborg became a mainstream cultural figure. Inevitably the crisis in science's relationship with the body rapidly produced a slew of dark-side popular imagery. These days there is a veritable industry of cybernetic terror: Tetsuo, the overworked Japanese "sarariman" whose body becomes bloated and finally ruptured by nasty biomechanisms; Star Trek's Borg, whose predatory networked consciousness threatens to destroy bodily integrity and personal identity (Trek's cherished twin pillars of morality); Johnny Mnemonic's memory-bank brain, where images of childhood have been seared away to make room for valuable corporate data. Even the out-of-control dinosaurs of "Jurassic Park" are quintessentially cyborg constructions, having been reanimated by a network of capital, biotechnical research, and fossil DNA.

The cyborg's current cultural role as vehicle for popular unease about science makes Haraway's deployment of it not merely an oppositional trope, but a positive one, even more startling. Haraway's cyborg is affirmative, celebratory, even sexy, which is something of a miracle when you consider that previously it was either a technoscientific religious fantasy, or a pop science-fiction nightmare. This new cyborg's origin in feminist debate about overturning the classic hierarchical binary oppositions (man/woman, reason/emotion, culture/nature, and so forth) is well understood. The cyborg body is a constructed one, and hence can potentially be reconstructed, a proposition which makes the feminist project a matter of research, rebuilding, and redefinition, rather than a metaphysical struggle against a protean foe, or a quasi-spiritual refusal of masculinised reality. The cyborg, in short, makes change realisable.

However, beyond semiotics, beyond even the terms of the feminist debate into which she first introduced it, Haraway's cyborg has the potential to change the way in which we think about bodies, networks, power, and machines. By reframing cultural debate in radically material terms (cybernetic mechanisms of communication and control operating through assemblages of bodies, technology, and social protocols), the cyborg makes possible a type of thought unavailable to the dominant crop of semiotically based theories.

For semiotics, materiality is an unattainable horizon, the gap between signifier and signified, a gulf whose resistance to rhetorical bridging produces feelings of loss, entrapment, and despair. Poetic mourning often becomes itself the focus of critical energy, leaving other problems to fend for themselves. The cyborg's response to this semiotic melancholia is to utilise shock tactics—reaching inside its stomach and pulling out a handful of guts, lifting flaps of skin to show the bloody servo-mechanisms swarming beneath.

The cyborg forces us to situate thought in the body, and in turn to situate bodies in networks which contain elements of biology, politics, desire, and technology. It produces continuities between these disparate strata, allowing us to think what would otherwise be unthinkable.

Of course, asserting some uncomplicated notion of "the real" or "the material" against language was, once upon a time, the tactic of thinkers (on left and right) who wished to preserve certain sacred spaces, free of interpretation. Marauding linguistic postmodernists could invariably be sure that in these priest-holes, these secret stashes, they would unearth the fetishes of power. God, Man, Woman, the Law, the State—hiding places of the unanswerable, the unquestionable. However this process of questioning, once so vital, has latterly become a mainstream cultural industry. In so doing it has been corralled, recuperated by the system it set out to deconstruct. The cyborg's messy physicality signals another phase of oppositional cultural politics, a phase beyond the sovereignty of language. Yet cyborg materiality isn't silent, isn't unquestionable. It's not the smooth, homogenous, impenetrable body of yesteryear. There is nothing classical about it. It is constructed, heterogeneous, multiple, shot through with code, sticky to the touch, and as Donna Haraway reminds us, it can always be reconstructed. As the title of a Philip Dick novel has it: "We can build you." One might add that we can also build ourselves.

So we discover that we are all cyborgs. It is an eerie realisation, a fascinating moment of alienation in front of the mirror. But perhaps the all-too-human narcissism of this moment obscures aspects of the cyborg which need to be restated. The literal penetration of the skin by technoscience, whether in the form of antibiotics, agrichemicals, prosthetics, or information technologies, is only one aspect of our cyborgisation.

Fascination with the permeability of the body, indeed fetishisation of that permeability such as one finds in the gothic prose beloved of many cyborg groupies, diverts energy from the central realisation that the cyborg is a networked entity. The cyborg cares little for the barrier of the skin, because it does not recognise that barrier. The crossing and recrossing of that boundary, so fascinating for humans who associate the move of rupture with death, is, to a cyborg, merely incidental, an unmarked point in a circuit which may pass through several bodies, widely distributed in space and time. Indeed the hardbitten academic rhetoric of flesh and metal, drawn more from pop-cultural cyborg iconography than political theory, may be starting to cloud the issue.

Cyborg networks incorporate flesh, but above all are distributed objects, which bring flesh into relations with all kinds of heterogeneous codes, products, forces. Surgery is not required. Haraway's own recent work, which moves away from the cyborg, towards networks such as the human immune system and the masculine protocols of scientific objectivity, underscores this.

In an interview I conducted with her, Haraway remarked, "My cyborg is a bad girl." By introducing the lighthearted image of the cyborg as a tear-away teen, breaking rules, cutting through fences, bringing the wrong kind of people home to bed, she highlights its primary function—as a transgressive figure. The cyborg operates by transgressing the regimes of signification which deny links between bodies, power, and technoscience. These splits, by which word is separated from world, scientific objectivity from experimental fallout, are one of the main ways in which power maintains itself. When technoscientific discourse is deliberately disconnected from the economic operators which govern it, and when experimental results are separated both from the consequences of their use and the messy realities of their production, then it requires transgressive thought to produce critical accounts of science. The cyborg is useful as long as it retains its power to transgress, and does not recede into a conventional articulation of anxieties about plastic surgery, AI, wetware, and the like.

At the moment the cyborg is still the baddest girl on the block. The structures revealed by her transgressive linking of supposedly separate domains are precisely those which are most unpalatable to the vested interests of technocapital. The cyborg reminds us that Bhopal and Chernobyl are connected to university laboratories and boardroom meetings, that a naked human body might be networked to gene patenting, Nike marketing strategy, pesticide research, antibiotics, and international tourism. The cyborg is still saying what was previously unsayable. She has certainly come a long way from DARPA's astronaut Christ.

Notes

1. Donna Haraway, "Manifesto for Cyborgs: Science, Technology and Socialist Feminism," The 1980's Socialist Review 80 (1985).

2. All terms from Johnsen and Corliss, "Teleoperators and Human Augmentation," in: Chris Gray, ed., The Cyborg Handbook (London: Routledge, 1995).

3. Clynes and Kline, "Cyborgs and Space," in: Gray, The Cyborg Handbook.

4. Jack E. Steele, "How do We Get There," in: Gray, The Cyborg Handbook.

5. See for example the descriptions of factory workers in Charles Dickens, Hard Times, first published 1854.

6. Modern Times, dir. Charlie Chaplin (United Artists, 1936).

7. Andreas Vesalius, De Humani Corporis Fabrica (Leyden, 1543).

On the History of the
Theory of Information Warfare

Friedrich Kittler

Kai egeneto polemos en to ourano. *Apocalypse 12, 7*

Of course, the nineties of this century weren't the first to discover that information counts in war. For ages now, three elementary lists, which probably differentiate warriors from merchants as well as from priests, have been in use. First, A tries to know what B knows without B knowing of A's knowledge. Second, A tries to communicate his knowledge to A' (subordinates or superiors or allies) without B knowing of the transmission, let alone of the transmitted data. The logic of this intersubjectivity itself suggests the existence of a third list: So his plans cannot be foiled by B, A would do well to split himself into A' and B' and, on the basis of his knowledge of B, calculate all possible moves of both sides. In other words, wars have implied espionage, communications technology, and war games for a long time now. The only thing unheard of in Information Warfare is the fact that espionage, communications technology, and war games all fall together in a global computer network.

The meaning of war game, in a prehistory whose technical models are infinitely inferior to the complexity of today's computers, can be explained with few words. In the age of Deep Blue, chess still prides itself on being the oldest toy with which the positions of two enemies on a battlefield could be geometrically simulated. There are grounds for the assumption that the great chess rules reform in the early modern age greatly increased freedom of movement for officers like bishops and rooks in order to better mirror the military innovations of the time. But the end of the cabinet wars coincides with the demise of chessboard battles. The revolutionary theory of Clausewitz defined war as the clash of two subjects who could base their strategies solely upon calculations of probability, because they always had to take into consideration the unpredictable will of the opponent, the vagaries of the terrain, and the uncertainties of communication. This theory, which had nothing but derision for the black and white squares of an ideally flat chessboard, found its geographically adequate war game in the sandbox, which Müffling introduced to the general staff in 1825. With the sandbox, it was possible for the first time realistically to simulate the marching speed infantry or artillery could achieve in terrain of known gradient.

For a long time, espionage and communications could only dream of such physical reality. It lay in the nature of their considerably intersubjective structure that they applied more to subjects than to weapons, more to people than to machines. So the wars of the past cultivated exactly that which NATO, in its inimitable belief in acronyms, degraded to the term HUMINT (human intelligence). Spies, agents, scouts, and secret couriers, since 1800 also military attachés in potentially hostile capitals— that was basically the traditional equipment of Information Warfare. Our word angel can be traced back to the Greek *angelos*, but *angelos* itself goes back to the Persian name of the mounted couriers who, in the name of their Great King, made up the first (and naturally military) postal service. War erupted in the sky, as the Apocalypse correctly states[1]—but that was the reason why the InfoWar stayed immaterial.

Technology or science (if one may even separate these two fields after Heidegger) was involved in only one aspect: the encryption of one's own messages and the decryption of the enemy's. Even today, a primitive alphabetic key is still named after the commander Caesar. But the military history of secret information still hides secrets, even after David Kahn's pioneering *Codebreakers*. Still unknown, for example, is the relationship between François Vieta's invention of the algebraic notation of polynomials and his cryptanalytic work during the French religious wars. (After all, in both cases the goal is to assign letters and numbers to each other.)

But the information that was won or hidden this way was not yet a weapon itself. Therefore information technology in Old Europe decided the outcome of single battles, but not (as far as I know) wars. Things might have been different in other cultures, but European warriors at least were a fairly old-fashioned or traditional caste. A likely assumption is that the coupling of general staff and engineering education, which was institutionalized by the French Revolution through the founding of the Ecole polytechnique in 1794, made information systems conceivable as weapon systems. In 1809 Napoleon decided the outcome of a whole campaign (against the Austrian empire, no less) by employing the then-revolutionary optical telegraphy.[2] For a time, the church towers of Linz, precursors to all Ars Electronica as it were, served to transmit Napoleon's secret military codes . . .

So the campaign of 1809—to say it with Jacques Lacan—injected war with a function of urgency. The polite as well as suicidal waiting of the French knights until the British enemy too was ready for the battle of Agincourt in 1415 came to an abrupt end. From optical to electrical telegraphy, from telegraphy over (at first strictly military) radio to satellite links, the history of war over the last two centuries has been pure dromology, according to Virilio's hypothesis. Not without reason are delay times ("delays") also called dead times in technical-military jargon. He who knows a few seconds too late is not punished by so-called life but by a hostile first strike.

By now it has become common knowledge what far-reaching consequences this war history has had upon civilian culture. (Perhaps still unknown is the fact that the self-proclaimed competence of mass media sociologists does not extend to these consequences.) Weapon systems made of wood or bronze, iron or Damascene steel eked out the exceptional existence of a warrior caste for thousands of years, while the weapon called telecommunications transformed cultures that were based on civilian (if not clerical) storage media, like books and the printing press, into information societies. Radio is just the military radio system of the First World War minus the talkback capability, television just the civilian twin of the radar screens of the Second. Not to mention computer technology, whose cryptanalytical and therefore military background, in the case of Alan Turing, stopped being a British state secret in 1974, while the National Security Agency still seems to have declared a news blackout in the instance of Claude E. Shannon[3] ("Communication Theory of Secrecy Systems"). The intelligence of computers, as Turing and Shannon developed them, arose not from the modeling of physical processes but from simulating enemy intelligence.[4] It is no wonder then that John von Neumann, as the designer of the computer architecture of the same name, transferred the war game back to the symbolic: The matrix algebra of games theory takes the place of Müffling's physical sandbox.

In the English language, intelligence means not just brains, but also secret service, meaning knowledge of the enemy's knowledge. The good old C3I stood for command, control, communications, and intelligence; the current C4I also takes into account—as command, control, communication, computers, and intelligence—the modern-day hardware. It would be a worthwhile undertaking, albeit always threatened by the thirty-year waiting period on sensitive documents, to write a technology history as the gradual interlinking of COMINT, ELINT, and games theory. COMINT, or Communication

Friedrich Kittler On the History of the Theory of Information Warfare

Intelligence, obviously originates from Bletchley Park's first computers, which could crack almost all code machines of the Wehrmacht's communication lines shortly before the end of the war. ELINT, or Electronic Intelligence, probably derives from the early warning radar systems, which since the fifties not only re-programmed new computer generations from cryptanalysis to physics, but also brought the joystick and the computer monitor into the world.

The showplace of Electronic Warfare, paradigm of the late Cold War, was the imperceptible realm of physics, lying outside of human awareness. Electronic Warfare followed as a concept from the dictum of Admiral Moore, Joint Chief of Staffs, that victory in every future war would fall to that side which managed to gain superiority over the complete electromagnetic spectrum (from the ultra-low submarine communication frequencies to the interstellar gigahertz region). The second Gulf War made his adage come true. It is almost forgotten today that the first US bomber squads flew over the Iraqi border shortly before midnight, while the undeclared electronic warfare, which opened up the sky over Baghdad, had started in the early afternoon.

But Electronic Warfare, this dark side of the new media-compatible weapons systems, also has its disadvantage. Worldwide systems for early warning, reconnaissance, positioning, and control of armies presuppose equally global computer networks. Only in the first planning phase did the forgotten ancestor of all our communicative raptures, ARPANET, connect the command bungalows, which were spread all over the United States, with select elite universities. The net already began its global proliferation with the fiber-optic cables which NATO laid in the Atlantic, in order to immediately feed the raw data from ELINT and COMINT back to their US head offices. An electronic duplicate of possible military campaigns which anticipates their topologies and operations in hardware and software tends to eliminate the difference between war and war game. Espionage and communications technology on the one hand, computer simulations on the other, all fall together in one and the same equipment.

The Pentagon has christened this new dispositive "Information Warfare" and has done everything possible in the last few years to redirect its still considerable funds, taking into account the end of the Cold War, from Electronic Warfare to Information Warfare. The reasons are plain to see. The Monroe Doctrine falls with the global networks and satellite links that have been established in the last thirty years. For eighty years, America was the sole continent that enjoyed the privilege of belonging to the Americans. (Only on Halloween 1938 and only in Orson Welles' magnificent radio drama, for one horrible day, did the states of New Jersey and New York undergo an invasion from Mars. These invaders already put into practice a Blitzkrieg and/or Information Warfare in that they did not attack armies, but only electrical networks, bridges, and railway lines.)[5] The Internet, as the shadow which Electronic Warfare has cast upon the globe, disposes of any last vestige of "sanctuary," even if it is called God's own country.

Information Warfare can begin on any desk equipped with a PC. To copy a hostile CPU is easier, cheaper, and therefore more likely to proliferate than copying a hostile phase radar. That is why, finally, the dealers and engineers (e.g. at Advanced Micro Devices) have learned from the warriors that knowledge only counts as knowledge of the enemy's knowledge (e.g. at Intel). Reverse engineering basically means to found one's own production techniques on espionage. This new intelligence will still present difficult questions, because it replaces the good old assumption of ignorance (among competitors, advertising customers, and consumers).

But perhaps reverse engineering can also mean that subjects, alias underlings—in marked difference to those of wood and bronze, iron and Damascene steel—have a chance again. If the US Army can give up its old dream of having the best proprietary computer equipment possible and instead buy on the common market like the rest of the world, a form of equal opportunity weapons technology results; but this has historical consequences. According to the scenarios of Information Warfare, the

Friedrich Kittler *On the History of the Theory of Information Warfare*

monopoly on the use of force by nation-states sadly no longer exists. The end of Hobbes' civil wars has itself come to an end with mafias and cartels, NGOs and terror bands. When power systems coincide with operating systems and computer networks, they become susceptible on a level which is principally intelligible: the level of code.

Therefore the appeal to wage war according to the conditions and budgetary dreams of the newest arm of the service, an appeal as familiar as it is dull since the budgetization of the intelligence troops, is not the only thing to appear on the horizon of the Information Warfare. The figure of the artist-engineer reappears, after having been seemingly displaced by the founding of standing (meaning national) armies. Only art history still knows that the famed geniuses of the Renaissance did not just create paintings and buildings, but calculated fortresses and constructed war machines.[6] If the phantasm of all Information Warfare, to reduce war to software and its forms of death to operating system crashes, were to come true, lonesome hackers would take the place of the historic artist-engineers.

Not without reason does a famous InfoWar scenario of the RAND Corporation imagine the following scene: In the year 2002, the USA withdraws its military support for a collapsing Saudi Arabian ruling house because Airbusses full of American tourists are dropping like flies from the sky over Chicago. The Airbus was the first civil plane that needed an on-board computer to remain in the air, just like its military predecessors. In the RAND Corporation's war game, Iranian mullahs, who have always thrown oily looks towards Saudi Arabia, have managed to bribe the Indian programmer of the Airbus software to hack his own program. A single artist-engineer of that un-incidental half continent, which once created the basis of all things digital with the invention of zero, suffices to strategically paralyze the last remaining super power with the transmission belt of the American media democracy.[7]

Such scenarios are not just based on the presumption that all powers on this earth will quake like God's own country, equally fearful of their inhabitants' dying media-effective kinds of death. They also stylize the writing of software into an artistic feat of an individual, who ceased to exist in the software forges a long time ago. It is therefore much to be feared, as in Alvin Toffler's ideology-laden *Cyberspace Manifesto*, that the free individual, with his power to lead the mind itself to victory over the materialism of the nineteenth and the military-industrial complexes of the twentieth century, will always remain a fig leaf.

When it comes to non-governmental organizations that might, step by step, dissolve the three-hundred-year-old monopoly of the nation-states on the use of force, the strategists of information warfare, financed by the same nation-states, will not grow tired of naming environment-contaminated ecologists, peace-contaminated leftists and Islam-contaminated terror groups. What they fail to mention is the computer business itself—not as a mythical final frontier for hackers, but as a band of global companies, who are as imperialistic as they are warlike. This gang has already achieved the breaking of the state monopolies of mail, radio, and telecommunications. Even the US Army has ceased to set high goals for the computer industry, such as Very High Speed Computing, but instead provides for its own needs, modest like the rest of the world, on the free market. So the gang has started to incorporate entertainment media and television companies into their chips and networks. When even Andy Grove's "War over the eye ball" will be won, there will hardly be any worthwhile opponents or unfriendly takeovers left—except for the nation-states themselves. Reading the loud warnings of a loss of power of the nation-states in an alternate way may lead to the interpretation that computer warfare is best left to the computer industry itself. Bill Gates and Scott McNealy as condottieri of their private armies consisting of servers and clients, operating systems and proprietary networks ...

All prognoses, however, no matter if they be sinister or neo-liberal, assume one thing: that the Universal Turing Machine is in fact and in theory the end of all history. Information Warfare simply means to fight over digital technology with digital technology. Physicists today assume that the Turing-Church Hypothesis in its most general (meaning physical) interpretation was a misapprehension, one that the information warriors are still laboring under: The one thing certain about nature, whatever this ancient term might imply, is that it is not a Turing Machine. From the fact that it exists we can assume that other programmable machines are possible. In this case world history will not have reached its inevitably digital end, and the Pax Americana, as far as it is still based on John von Neumann's combination of English computers, German rockets, and American nuclear bombs, will have been an interlude. The war, started in the sky, will be continued in the heaven of mathematics.

Notes

1. As Luther weakly translates.

2. Cf. Rolf Oberliesen, Information, Daten und Signale. Geschichte technischer Informationsverarbeitung (Reinbek, 1982), pp. 59–62.

3. Cf. Claude E. Shannon, "Communication Theory of Secrecy Systems," The Bell System Technical Journal, 28 (1949), pp. 656–715.

4. Cf. Alan M. Turing, "Intelligent Machinery," in: Bernhard Meltzer and Donald Michie, eds., Machine Intelligence, p. 14: "The field of cryptography will perhaps be the most rewarding. There is a remarkably close parallel between the problems of the physicist and those of the cryptographer. The system on which a message is enciphered corresponds to the laws of the universe, the intercepted messages to the evidence available, the keys for a day or a message to important constants which have to be determined. The correspondence is very close, but the subject matter of cryptography is very easily dealt with by discrete machinery, physics not so easily."

5. Cf. Howard Koch/Orson Welles, "The War of the Worlds," in: Werner Faulstich, ed., The War of the Worlds/Der Krieg der Welten. Vier Hörspiele (Tübingen, 1981), p. 23: "They seem to be making a conscious effort to avoid destruction of cities and countryside. However, they stop to uproot power lines, bridges, and railroad tracks. Their apparent objective is to crush resistance, paralyze communication, and disorganize human society." As parallel source, cf. also Len Deighton, Blitzkrieg. Von Hitlers Triumphen bis zum Fall von Dünkirchen, 2d ed. (Munich, 1980), p. 225.

6. Cf. Samuel Y. Edgerton, Jr., The Heritage of Giotto's Geometry: Art and Science in the Eve of the Scientific Revolution (Ithaca, 1991).

7. Cf. Roger C. Molander, Andrew S. Riddile, and Peter A. Wilson, eds., Strategic Information Warfare: A New War (National Defense Research Institute, RAND Corporation, Santa Monica, 1996).

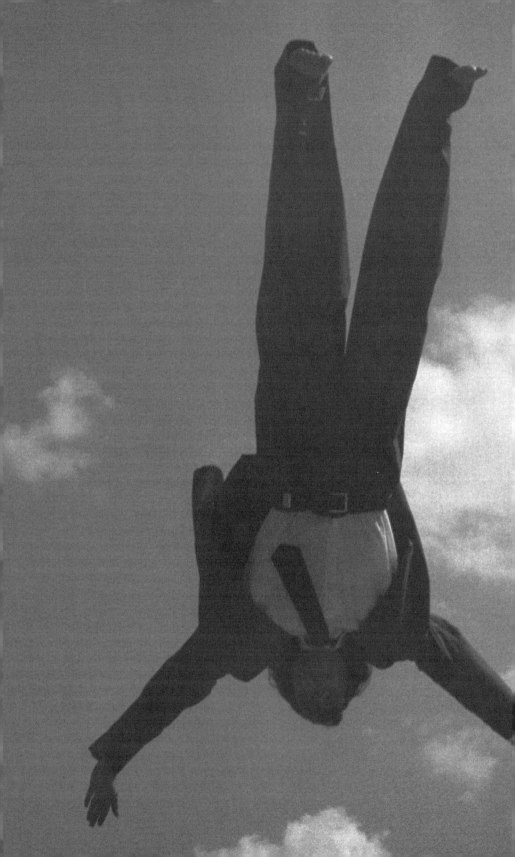

Theory

Expansion of Media Art: What Will Remain of the Electronic Age?

Jürgen Claus

Theses on Art and Electronics

La création est prioritaire.
La communication vient quand on a quelque-chose à communiquer.
Pierre Boulez

Media art of today is not a creation of the eighties. It had been clearly "on the scene" before, somewhere between 1965 and 1970, another time when the term "expansion" was linked to art.[1] And to be exact, the years 1950 to 1955 must be stated as the years of its origin. It was then that the electronic age of art set in, and it did so simultaneously at various levels. Architecture and electronic music joined hands in the Philips Pavilion at the Exposition of Brussels in 1958, a development that could be traced back to Donaueschingen in 1953 when Pierre Schaeffer had distributed his "Orphée" music among several loudspeakers. In 1952–53 Karlheinz Stockhausen, then 23 years of age, had worked with Pierre Schaeffer in Paris; his first composition with synthetic sounds, consisting of sine tones, resulted in the "Electronic Study I" in 1953.

Wolf Vostell met Stockhausen in 1954, and in 1959 he started his electronic dé-coll/ages by television-distortion and electro-acoustic objects. In 1958, Nam June Paik started to work in the studio for electronic music of the WDR Köln (the West German Broadcasting Company, Cologne); five years later he exhibited his "Music-Electronic Television" in Wuppertal.

Everyone not closing his eyes had to be drawn into the whirl of the development of art and technology. A network of significant exhibitions, of group and individual activities, was flashing around our globe, at the peak of an age that was posing brilliant questions and giving brilliant answers.

The "Art & Technology Circus" (and I think of a poetic, elated and elating, mobile circus, of an obsessed group of producers) performed in New York in October 1966, presenting "9 Evenings. Theatre and Engineering," and in Eindhoven from September to December 1966, presenting "KunstLichtKunst." From May to August 1967, Frank Popper organized his "Lumière et Mouvement" in Paris in the same, slowly decaying Museum of the City of Paris in which he presented "Electra" in 1983–84.

Things were on their way! Legendary 1968 brought Pontus Hultén's performance of "The Machine—As Seen at the End of the Mechanical Age" in New York. "Technology now dominates every step of everyday life completely," an introduction to the last part of an exhibition dedicated to "Art and Technology" stated. "Cybernetic Serendipity"—a term implying the gift of "making chance discoveries"—was organized by Jasia Reichardt in London that same year, definitely presenting the computer as an instrument for artists.

The final programs of the "Art & Technology Circus" were the two most ambitious ones. First, the five-year project by Maurice Tuchman titled "Art and Technology," for which the curator of the Los Angeles County Museum of Art assembled artists and industry to culminate in an exhibition in May 1971. And second, the "Pavilion" at the world's fair of Osaka in 1970. Billy Klüver, a scientist and engineer, at that time president of the EAT group (Experiments in Art and Technology, founded in 1966), which was designing the "Pavilion," saw the opportunity for the individual to relate to the world around by means of technology: "For tackling these difficult problems the immediate, forward sensibility of the artists is needed."

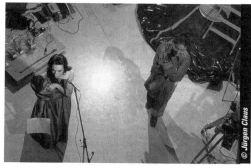

Electronic Happening, Nam June Paik and Charlotte Moorman, Ars Electronica 82

First thesis:

From the beginnings of electronic art in the first half of the fifties through the establishment of the entire range of the media in the second half of the sixties, we have now, in the middle of the eighties, reached a peak of the interaction of art and technology. Development obviously happens in the form of cycles. I expect the presently expanding interest in technological art to reach a summit and then decline.

The question must be put: What will remain of the electronic age concerning the realm of art? It is evident that the first two cycles have not found a place in our storehouses for cultural goods, the museums, and even less have they found continuing cultivation, research, and communication.

Our museums are by no means laboratories for a new philosophy of the history of art—a postulate raised by Alexander Dorner in the twenties, which he himself had tried to fulfill by including the "abstract cabinet" of and together with El Lissitzky in his museum in Hannover and by preparing another one with Moholy-Nagy.

Second thesis:

Electronic/technological art, media art, constitutes a leap in development, new as to its quality, structure, and genesis, that may be compared in its effects to the emergence of panel-painting with all the social, economic, educational effects involved. This art is not a continuation of panel-painting or sculpture with new means. Artist and spectator will certainly bring along their experiences made with other objects of art, their pattern, so to speak; the viewing eye looks at this different art through the experiences made. The spectator of media art, however, need not have passed through a training in the history of art, just as the twelve-year-old pupil who sits at the computer programming his drawing arsenal need not have been initiated into the history of art, indeed, may be completely ignorant of it (and probably is, anyhow, I'm sorry to say!).

The structure of the audience at exhibitions of holography, therefore, is absolutely unhomogeneous, no longer the somewhat homogeneous group that would visit an exhibition of Kandinsky or surrealism. Lacking statistical data I trust my personal observation in arriving at this conclusion, which may, however, be put to the test anytime.

If media art does constitute a new stage of development, then we have to ask for adequate places to display and store this art, that is, we have to ask for media museums.

Jürgen Claus Expansion of Media Art: What Will Remain of the Electronic Age?

Third thesis:
Fine art today happens within a system of three components. Besides graphic and plastic art, which appear to be inexhaustible as they are being rediscovered and executed anew in spite of their historic course, media or electronic/technological art is likely to gain ground, to be joined by environmental art as the third of these three components.

As always, there will be artists "occupying" all of the three fields with their work, and there will be artists concentrating on one field of work. Again I want to ask: How can the museum—being the relevant place—display, investigate, store such a system of three components? The museum must not be relieved of its duty of being the place of reference for works of remaining value. Certainly, film, photography, video, disc, tape, etc. are media to store events of art. Where should they be collected, examined, and passed on if not in an adequate museum, that is, in a media museum?

Design Technologies or What Have You

In the catalogue of the exhibition "Art and Technology—Setting Out Towards New Realities"[2] which I organized, I introduced and explained the term "design technology." We need a fitting term to denote the procedures and results of media art and to avoid the pitfalls of discussion and assessment of artistic and/or technical/technological quality.

François Molnar, co-founder of the Groupe de Recherche d'Art Visuel, had called design a bridge between art and science. We must not apply the yardstick of "the concept of art" to the works and processes of contemporary technological art. We will not be able to perceive and appreciate what is new.

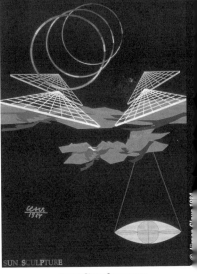

Jürgen Claus: Sunstructure,
a Computer graphics, Diacomed D 38

It is a characteristic of holographic and computer-generated works, presented in exhibitions since the mid-sixties, that they have often been produced by scientists or engineers who were most interested in questions of the fine arts or rather of "design," more so, actually, than many experts of art history, the world of museums, and art publications.

Obviously, this was also due to the limited accessibility of the new media, holography and computer design. So far, laboratories are outrageously expensive. With the cost for one hour of laboratory (at a film studio in Munich, for producing professional videotapes, this runs around 3,000 German marks), there is hardly any chance for artists, unless they have commissions from industry—which usually implies some limitations, however. Experimental work is not possible unless access to the instruments becomes universal.

Video and computer have become more readily available. This is not yet true for holography, video disc, or video text (btx) to the extent that they may be used as artists' media. A number of positive advances can be expected. Ars Electronica of Linz can claim to have paved the way and to continue doing so. The expansion of media art would not have attained its present rank without the variety of opportunities offered and realized so courageously and future-mindedly in Linz throughout the past years. The following questions remain: Where and how should instruction in the media be given? What about the media museum? How can the technological instruments be made more readily available?

Jürgen Claus Expansion of Media Art: What Will Remain of the Electronic Age?

182

Instruction and training for artists in the media age must be reconsidered. I quote the German sociologist Rolf Darendorf, who wrote recently, "The future does not consist of the traditional working world; it is one that combines high technology with a new social construction of human life." Schools of art must raise and discuss the issue of artistic work and its communication to society. They must include the expanding media art.

I want to refer to the working group "Media development/Media research" at the College of Design in Offenbach/Main. This group, directed by Manfred Eisenbeis, presented video-texts developed by artists according to CEPT standards[3] at the Internationale Funkausstellung Berlin in 1983. Eisenbeis comments, "Video-text is a medium today, taking its place in the context of print media and television."

Another positive example is that of the artist-in-residence program offered by the New York Museum of Holography, for instance. Such programs ought to be expanded. Industry, computer companies, television stations ought to be enlisted to supply new opportunities for artists.

I welcome the opening of the so-called media landscape, provided it does not deteriorate to become a mere can-opener to an increasing number of shallow, purely commercial programs. Unfortunately, the road that is being taken in the Federal Republic of Germany at present concerning cable pilot projects, tends to become such a can-opener. Organizers stress repeatedly that they are only providing the "roof," transmission time. This could be an opportunity for experimental, artistic, cultural programs, they maintain.

These arguments hold in theory only. Actually, however, what is missing are the sponsors. A one-hour program, like the one recently made by Ralph Bernhardt of the MAZ-Studio Munich for cable TV, takes about 75,000 German marks, after all.[4] This is beyond the means of an independent producer, and neither public nor private donors have yet earmarked such funds for those purposes. I actually wonder if cable TV were not better restricted to local application, to state an example: telecasts of a university/college for the campus, for instance. Things would be easier that way. Experimental programs would be encouraged. The audience would be restricted to the vicinity of the university/college; the target group would be clearly defined. A state grant could be used to finance this like other university activities (fees, libraries, staff, and maintenance costs, etc.). Of course, I refer to the Federal Republic of Germany.

The Media Museum: What Remains?

This new kind of a cultural institute would not only not be a museum of 'art' statically speaking, but not even a 'museum.' This new kind could be compared to a power station rather, to a generator of new forces.
Alexander Dorner

At a cost of four and a half billion francs, the Musée de la Villette is being built in Paris, dedicated to science, technology, and industry. The giant steel hall from the 19th century in the park of the museum is to house the Paris Biennale in autumn 1985, having as its topic "Intersection of Technologies." Much money and many concrete aims have been invested to manifest our electronic age in architecture and in topical programs.

What should a museum of media art, a museum for the new media television, video, video disc, video text, cybernetic sculptures, computer-generated art, intermedia theatre, laser, holography, be like? What provisions ought to be made?

The problems posed by the production, collection, storage, playback facilities of these works are absolutely novel when compared to those of paintings, drawings, sculptures, and—maybe—photographs up to now housed in museums. This applies to equipment, layout of rooms, audience participation as well as to the structure of the building as such. In his book *Überwindung der Kunst* (Overcoming Art; 3rd edition 1958), Alexander Dorner has given the following characteristic, without referring directly to a media museum. "There is no need for a magnificent palace but much rather for a functional, flexible construction of light, modern materials. Its success would go back to the creativeness and the initiative of its director, that is, to his receptivity and the thrust of his decisions and his activity." The new museums built in the Federal Republic of Germany in recent years are more of the palace kind. No wonder that now the millions used for the respective buildings in Stuttgart, Mönchengladbach, and so on are not available for the concern proper. There are hardly any funds for buying works of media art, which causes serious financial problems for the producers and constitutes a lack of information on the part of the public.

A new media museum might include a proper workshop. It might provide the necessary equipment to artists lacking such installations at present. The new museum might also serve as a terminal to pool the various services, capacities, results. Sooner or later, the advances of technology will make us connect our own display screen to such a museum. Many services will be available to everyone. The expansion of media art calls for such an autonomous, new kind of museum. Existing museums for holography (in New York, Paris, Pulheim near Cologne) are stepping-stones on our way. A media museum resembles a network (and I do not think of cables now) linking new technologies—radio and television companies, educational institutions, libraries, mediatheques, and so on.

Notes

1. See Jürgen Claus, *Expansion der Kunst* (Reinbek bei Hamburg: Rowohlt Taschenbuch Verlag, 1970; new edition: Berlin: Ullstein Taschenbuch, 1982).

2. Exhibition *"Kunst und Technologie—Aufbruch in neue Wirklichkeiten"* (Art and Technology—Setting Out Towards New Realities), Federal Ministry of Research and Technology, Bonn, September 9–October 5, 1984.

3. As compared to field tests with coarse rasters, CEPT standards have greatly improved the quality of video texts. CEPT is the abbreviation of Conférence Européenne des Administrations des Postes et des Télécommunications.

4. Reference is made to the first cable film with and on artists, first presented in the Ludwigshafen cable project on January 26, 1984, entitled "Künstler '84."

Media Art

Gerhard Johann Lischka

Today the world of images, texts, and sounds has assembled at a single terminal at which the "artist" of tomorrow can be found ready to combine them at his will: at the paint box. In conventional terms this would imply a brush, paints, and an easel. In keeping with today's technology they are the computer, the synthesizer, and the display. To anyone working at the paint box these three elements connected to the network of producers, users, and memories of images, texts, and sounds constitute the hub of the world.

From the vast and no longer conceivable abundance of information available, the very best result can be chosen from among ever accumulating new possibilities of information. The linearity and "identity" of script bursts into an interminable array of images, texts, and sounds plunging a one-dimensional, reduced picture of the world into an abundance of subjective world pictures, and again creating in never-ending combination a new work. Carried away by the vortex of his or her product, the operator has to accept an open work of art.

The world has assembled at this place not to be defined, but to discuss the present possibilities in a dialogue. This is what is new about the magnetism of the video clip, this currently hottest item which serves best to illustrate the faculties of the paint box. Who knows what the future has in store for us? I do not want to claim that the clips are the best products in the world of the media. Their producers adhere too much to past patterns of avant-garde and to sex and crime stereotypes. Their unity of image, text, and sound, however, has reached the latest denominator. That is to say, that they encompass all the conventional media as well as taking up any newly developed technological finesse.

The result can be both, the picture of an open garbage can as well as Global Groove (Paik 1973). They are the best means to convey the susceptibility of our days, of our global entanglement, also of the postmodern situation, the constant threat of the arsenals of nuclear bombs. They are a means of expression for the billions of people, for their most subtly differentiated idiosyncrasies and manifestations. Certainly only to the extent that individual desires and concepts can be realized, and not if the distribution and the handling of clips is concentrated in the all-powerful mass media of our days.

Stating it simply, we may say that so far the media have been used to organize the masses by whoever was in the chair. This has not been quite as obvious in filmmaking as it has been in the newspapers, the radio, and lately TV. There is a centre for the distribution of information responsible for editing, censoring, manipulating, and copying. Through most different channels, these so-called transmitters reach an audience of entirely different tastes who are, however, served the very same canned menu, whatever their wishes might be. The views formed during reception (over the years) effect a kind of simplification of the stereotypes of the media. They are linked mostly to the horror of everyday life and on the other hand to those images that develop into celebrities. There is no way of evading them; they stare at us from the most hidden corners.

We cannot escape these mechanisms; they have replaced the church of former days and the public places, and have become the carriers of the "ideology" of the society, which is turning into an increasingly similar global mass through the mass media, notwithstanding the existence of blocs and different political credos. Anyone having seen the first hours of TV after World War II will confirm this. In consistence with the development of TV, there suddenly was a network operating in continuously larger orders, until it became the global network of today's satellite TV.

This has made the world orbital. It is directed from outside, from above, and future genera- tions of explorers and conquerors will no longer traverse jungles and the seas to discover new land; after landing on the moon in 1969 (with rather little effect), they now fly to manned space stations which in the meantime control our planet Earth together with hundreds of satellites. As in all instances of progress, this is first of all a military control; they monitor, they take photographs, they spy. The heads of the powerful have separated from their shoulders and are cruising through space like the countenance of God.

Just as exhaust fumes heat up our atmosphere, so do military techniques. The orbit is to hold security for our future, in the gigantic project of SDI. We should not really object to hotheads fighting their battles at a safe distance from our earth; however, in the end, will it not come down on us? Whatever future technologies may be opened up through orbital thinking, should we not rather solve the global problems first before adjourning them into the orbit?

The Star Wars programme proves that war no longer needs soldiers but technocrats. Furthermore, war is no longer easily to be detected; it takes place in the production and obsolescence of arms, and on the small but very effective scale of terror attacks by groups of most different origin, who do not hesitate to make civilians victims of their attacks. Thus anyone is the potential victim not only of actual aggression but also of some programme pattering down on him or her. This is true also of our cultural activities: first we have to undergo the hot-cold treatment of different tastes, quality claims, and acts of self-realization before finding ourselves. We have to become permeable, to be open, and then perhaps we may decide for this one first and for something else later on, as to how we define quality, value, or simply our preference. There is an "immaterial imperialism" of the images at the global cultural front; we are branded, as formerly herds of cattle were branded with the mark of their owner. Adolescents crave for these marks, they are fans, they adore their idols. Rather late they realize that they were nothing but the sunny side, the unreachable distance of the closeness of their parents or friends, who are only profane compared to the luring appeal of the heroes of mass culture.

The difficulty is not to be deceived by this mechanism of the cultivation of images, and to con- tribute personally to the production of culture, so as to change culture for the masses into culture by the masses. A culture by groups who stay open and change, a culture aware of the individual, because the individual is not only a recipient but also, if he or she desires, an active producer. This seems to be fulfilled in the case of the artist, who creates his or her world unhampered by conditions and con- straints. We can neglect the question of whether artists can live by their work or have to find anoth- er way to earn their living.

Their autonomy, however, will be only fictitious if, as is often the case in the eighties, their product conforms so much, that, together with their signature, it has turned into a mere consumer good differing from a pair of loudspeakers only by being unique. The function would remain the same: acoustic or optical satisfaction. "Wild" painting has largely become the impudent exploitation of an outdated concept of the artist (the master painter). These works witness a retreat action shunning the use of the potentialities offered by all the media and the opportunity of creating media art.

We can speak of media art only if the artistic intent asserts itself within a certain medium: unlike the usual seedy eyewash. It makes no difference if the medium is used pure, mixed, or in new combinations. The emphasis will always be on passing on that spark to real life—to intermediary action and performance. The work of art is not to point to itself exclusively; it is to encourage the recipient to become active.

This is the seed of dialogue that can be developed further, if the work of art becomes the interface of a dialogue of thoughts and perhaps also of common creation. The new media like film and video lend themselves to this purpose as did former rituals. They are cooperation and shared experience. And an artistic product always takes account of its audience. The audience shares in the production of the exhibit, contributes its imagination, and becomes a participant. This also applies to the paint box. There is not merely an input and an output and some black box in between. No, it is a game with known elements, changed by chance into possibilities not seen, heard of, or thought of before.

"An Ear Alone Is Not a Being"

(John Cage)

Daniel Charles

1) In 1970, Tom Marioni, the founder and director of the MOCA (Museum of Conceptual Art) in San Francisco, having defined the activities of his museum as "idea-oriented situations not direct-ed at the production of static objects," utilized sound as a basic component for actions, i.e. presenta-tions of creative processes during specific time-spans. In Marioni's perspective, "actions" involved public—or social—intelligence, and were made for particular spaces or places. MOCA's collections consisted of "evidence-giving residue" that was "either the result of an action by a visual artist, or the result of actual and physical change to the architecture," each artwork adding to the history of the building "without erasing previous history." When the building was torn down in 1985, the collections, i.e. all the elements that had become part of the space, were destroyed; the building had provided an autobiography, an "invisible work of art," "a frame of a frame of a frame," "a body of work which is primarily about time" (Renny Pritikin), a "monument" (in Gianni Vattimo's sense): or an "et cetera" or "public document" (= a koan, in Juan Hidalgo's perspective).

2) Tom Marioni's sounding "actions" may recall Robert Irwin's definition of minimalism as "a reduction of imagery to get at physicality" or "a reduction of metaphor to get at presence"—their common goal is "to expurgate all metaphors of presence from the experience of art and to replace them with a conscious awareness of perception." The perceiver "is located at the very moment his own perceptions become manifest to himself at the very brink of his first contact with the world" (Thomas DeLio). But it is difficult to imagine tracing a dividing line between artists from a visual back-ground and those from a musical background. At least in the Cagean or post-Cagean perspective (which Tom Marioni clearly assumes), what Bergson (or Adorno) considered as an alienating feature, the "spatialization of time," can but appear as positive. (Cf. Carl Dahlhaus: "Going beyond Bergson, we might ask: is time a mere medium of processes in it? or is time itself an occurrence? And does music situate itself 'in time,' or does music rather have 'time in itself'?") In fact, one of the most strik-ing features of Cage's music, and of the mutation it has brought into the avant-gardist musical sphere, is that, since it obeys Christian Wolff's "Zero Time" principle, it eschews the concept of a linear sounding object with a beginning and an end, i.e. the Western tradition of the composer plotting a path of musical successive events. Cage's works have everything in common with visual art, except that they are also for the ears: the scores, according to the composer, do not provide the performer

with a picture but with a "camera—the performer has to shoot the picture." The composer invents not only the music but the musical instrument, thus enlarging Harry Partch's artisanal instrument-making; and he composes not only processes, but—as in the case of David Tudor's electronic circuitry and of Max Neuhaus' sound installations—musical environments.

3) Such a de-linearization of music allowed the composer Alvin Lucier, as soon as 1965, to focus upon alpha waves and enable the performer to experience them in a variety of visual and sonic guises in his *Music for Solo Performer.* The idea of making sound "visible" was present also in *The Queen of the South* (1972), *Tyndall Orchestrations* (1977), *Ghosts* (1978), *Directions of Sounds from the Bridge* (1978), and *Music for Pure Waves, Bass Drums and Acoustic Pendulums* (1980). In the latter, the sound is projected in such a way that the swing of the pendulums represents the sine wave and reveals not only the acoustic vibrations, but the visual translations of the mechanism by which those vibrations are transformed into an audible event (DeLio). The perceiver "is forced to reevaluate his own position vis-à-vis the artwork . . . The experience is circular. As the listener becomes conscious of the object of his perceptions, he also becomes aware of the act of perceiving and, finally, of himself as the perceiving being . . . In this sense Lucier's art may be seen as the culmination of a post-Cartesian dialectic in which perception is understood not as the product of the thinking mind, but as the source of all thought" (DeLio). Or we may argue, with Thierry de Duve, that Lucier's work opens the way to the overcoming of Kant's definition of space and time as the a priori dimensions of human sensibility, and also to the redefinition of what presence means in modernism (the loss of confidence in Kant's a priori "formes de la sensibilité"; the suspicion that presence is impossible, as in Derrida's philosophy or Beckett's theatre). The new definition of presence, if traced back to Cage, and to the minimalist sculpture, requires "real space" and "real time," since the beholder is not placed in front of an object, but plunged into a situation of which he is a part—so that far from relying on a priori concepts of time and space, he has to produce their reality as of his own corporeal experience of "being confronted with an installation in which he is included" (de Duve).

4) This new kind of presence involves a "nonmetaphorical" way of mixing listening and seeing (cf. what Heidegger discovers in Mozart: when he composed, he not only listened to what he was composing; he was "seeing" the whole piece in a glimpse). Such a presence does not involve only synaesthesia, it includes as well "equitemporality" *(Gleichursprungszeitlichkeit)*, i.e. the quality of the time-spans, either "present" (= the "presence" of the present) or "absent" (= the past and the future). It may thus be opposed to the typically modernist definition of aesthetic experience as suspended, withdrawn, or uncanny presence, "a definition that infiltrates Walter Benjamin's conception of the aura" (de Duve). Now, since according to Benjamin the reproducibility of the artworks strips them bare of their aura, the minimalist/Cagean movement appears as transferring the conditions of aesthetic experience from the "modernist" aura to the postmodernist actuality by acknowledging art's reproducibility (de Duve). Heidegger's "yes and no" (or "equanimity") to technology is to be taken seriously: presence involves the technology of today (and especially devices or systems that both "distance and connect the performer from and with the audience"—we need a redefinition of "nearness" as a "technological" *Zeitspielraum*).

5) Now we may understand Nam June Paik's analysis of the relationship between technology and the poetics of simultaneity. Many mystics, he says, "are interested to spring out from one-row time, one-way time, in order to *grasp* the Eternity. To stop at the consummated or sterile zero-point is a classical method to grasp the Eternity. To perceive simultaneously the parallel flows of many independent movements is another classical way for it. But poor Joyce was compelled to write the parallel, advancing stories in one book with one-way direction . . .

Daniel Charles "An Ear Alone Is Not a Being." (John Cage)

"The simultaneous perception of the parallel flows of 13 independent TV movements can perhaps realize this old dream of mystics, although the problem is left unresolved, whether this is possible with our normal physiognomy (we have only one heart, one breath, one focus of eye), without some mystical training. And if well trained . . . he needs neither 13 TVs, nor TV, nor electronics, nor music, nor art." Thus Nam June Paik, despite his profound involvement in technical matters and devices—he is commonly considered the inventor of video art—stands not so far from Heidegger's "taoist" advice about technology: we have simultaneously to let technical devices enter our daily life and leave them outside, "that is, let them alone, as things which are nothing absolute but remain dependent upon something higher" so that they do not affect "our inner and real core" *(Discourse on Thinking)*.

6) Therefore even in a society dominated by the electronics of communication one may not consider that reality or "presence" (i.e. real space-time) tends to disappear. True, in such a society the very definition of the real may become "that of which it is possible to give an equivalent reproduction," or "that which is always already reproduced"; true, with production reproducing itself, artifice or *simulacrum*, and so art as "hyperreality," is everywhere and therefore nowhere—and since "metaphor and metonymy are abolished in digitality" (Baudrillard), it may seem that, according to Hegel's prophecy, art is dead. But the idea that reality is replaced by a single "hyperreality" is too simple—we are rather confronted with a pluralistic universe of various hyperrealities, or a multiverse. In Michael Philipson's terms, we might say that through the relation of the fragment to dispersal or to Fragmentation itself, the artwork of today marks the lack of a whole and stands as a metaphor for the whole; and that this whole is the bursting and flashing of manifestness, the appearance of wondrous being *(myo u)* from true emptiness *(shin ku)* (Shunryu Suzuki).

7) In an essay of 1963 about the "New Ontology of Music," Paik wrote: "In the normal concert, the sounds move, the audience sits down. In my so-called 'action music' the sounds, etc., move, the audience is attacked by me. In the 'Symphony for 20 Rooms,' the sounds, etc., move, the audience moves also. In my 'Omnibus Music No. 1' (1961), the sounds sit down, the audience visits them. In the Music Exposition, the sounds sit, the audience plays or attacks them. In the 'Moving Theatre in the Street' the sounds move in the street, the audience meets or encounters them in the street 'unexpectedly.' The beauty of moving theatre lies in this 'surprise a priori,' because almost all of the audience is uninvited, not knowing what it is, why it is, who is the composer, the player, organizer or, better speaking, organizer, composer, player." Then we may understand how, in a world marked by the inflation of simulation and re-presentation, the artwork "in the street" has to be put outside the positivities of information and of the semiotic sign—since it stands not as the simple negative of the sign or meaning, but beyond its region, it may avoid the "negative" level of the modernist presence *qua* absence. In Nam June Paik's perspective, it eludes the *relative* nothingness or absence of the Western thought, but aims at *absolute* nothingness or emptiness—the "formless form" or "spaceless space" of Eastern aesthetics. Thereupon we leave the Kantian a priori forms of sensibility—as the Chinese philosopher Chang Chung-yuan has shown. "Kant's space, in Eastern terms, is relative emptiness, or sunya. For Heidegger and the East, space is not limited to relative emptiness . . . but is the higher affirmation of the reality of things, or absolute emptiness, or sunyata." In a similar way, Kant has maintained that time is the mere form of inner sense: it does not exist in itself, nor is it an objective determination inherent in things; it is only the formal a priori condition of all appearances whatsoever, and it is only in time that two contradictory predicates can meet in a single object, one after the other. "This is quite different, Chang tells us, from the Eastern view of time. As the Ch'an philosopher Dogen says, time is not limited to the mere condition of appearance, or to the form of inner sense. Rather, 'time itself is existence' and existence is time. Further, time 'in the primordial sense' is not conceived

Daniel Charles *"An Ear Alone Is Not a Being"* (John Cage)

in terms of the sequence of opposition, but is the absolute moment in which all contradictions are simultaneously identified."

8) Therefore works inspired by the path-breaking innovations of John Cage and Nam June Paik, like those of the Korean artist Soun-Gui Kim, hold here a crucial position. A painter and sculptor, Soun-Gui Kim has found in video art the means of eschewing the reduction of seeing to any optical activity and the reduction of hearing to any acoustical one. To see, she argues, requires an activity of the heart *(xin)*; and the heart simultaneously perceives, sees, things *(si)* and originates ideas *(yi)*. The first step of creation is Yi Ming—a seeing of the idea by the heart. But the heart cannot be taken as anything subjective, nor is it anything objective. Beyond the subject-object split, "time times" and "space spaces." Here Soun-Gui Kim retrieves Heidegger's intuition of a co-dependency between time and space. In Takeuchi Yoshinori's words, "time as time enjoys a unique and elemental opening (the opening of the past, the future, and the present), and space a unique and elemental opening as space—but in addition, time is ex-static of itself in space, and space ex-static of itself in time, which together result in a locus of epochal time *(Weile)* that is the time-space of the historical world. This leads to the realization that the provenance of *Da-Sein*, whose fate it is to bear the burden of the historical world at that locus, represents the 'event-aspect' *(Ereignis)* of the principle of sunyata" (*The Heart of Buddhism*, pp. 76–77).

Bibliography

Baudrillard, Jean. *For a Critique of the Political Economy of the Sign*. St. Louis: Telos Press, 1981.

Chang, Chung-yuan. "Kant's Aesthetics and the East." *Journal of Chinese Philosophy 3* (1976), pp. 399–411.

Dahlhaus, Carl. *Esthetic of Music*. Trans. W. Austin. Cambridge: Cambridge University Press, 1982.

de Duve, Thierry. "La Performance hic et nunc." In: Chantal Pontbriand, ed., *Performance Text(e)s & Documents*. Montreal: Editions de la Revue "Parachute," 1981, pp. 1–27.

De Lio, Thomas. *Circumscribing the Open Universe*. Lanham, Maryland: University Press of America, 1984.

Kim, Soun-Gui. "Temps de la vidéo, temps de la performance." *Revue d'esthétique 10* (1986), pp. 61–68.

Paik, Nam June. *Videa 'n' Videology—1959–1973*. Syracuse, New York: Everson Museum of Art, 1974.

Phillipson, Michael. *Painting, Language and Modernity*. London: Routledge and Kegan Paul, 1985.

Takeuchi, Yoshinori. *The Heart of Buddhism*. Trans. J. W. Heisig. New York: Crossroad, 1983.

The Sound of Music

Douglas Kahn

All in all, art should get a sound thrashing.
Richard Huelsenbeck

Artistic activity involving sound has intensified recently. This can be attributed to a number of factors, not the least of which is a perception among those artists bent on discovery that the tenured art forms have long exhausted their respective periods of major discovery while a corresponding period is upon us—or impending—for the arts of sound. While others speak once again of endgame, here it's a season opener.

This phenomenon of a perceived field of artistic possibility within the tradition of the avant-garde appears to contradict the well-rehearsed historical scenario that states that the avant-garde of the first third of the century held the key artistic assumptions and strategies of what was to follow: post-WWII activities being relegated to little more than varieties of historical repetition. This scenario is, in fact, persuasive in a vast number of cases, and it is not necessarily restricted to art. Postmodernism itself has been described in part as an incursion of the avant-garde into mass culture; the early avant-garde may even claim Derrida's elaboration of collage.[1] But this scenario is not persuasive when it comes to sound, for the simple reason that the arts of sound during the early avant-garde lacked fundamental areas of development—a stunted past resulting from an assortment of inhibitions, both institutional and discursive, both externally imposed and self-imposed. If we are presently interested in attempts at departure, or at least in attempts at forwarding a compelling complication, we must face the problem that the sources of inhibition are still operative and have, in fact, been joined by others. Assumptions etched deeply into commonsense must be questioned and steps for a generative project on new turf must be taken.

The following will present what I, and other artists with whom I have spoken, understand to be the primary source of inhibition: the equation of an artistic practice of sound with music. We will call this the musical conceit. It's a powerful, tenacious discursive impediment which has long bridled artistic possibility, an impediment whose only positive feature is, from our vantage point, totally self-serving; the delay of the potential for discovery to the present day. It can be traced theoretically to the reductive features of any act of aural apperception and of the disposition of music to the total range of possible sound. Daniel Charles has mentioned these while observing various "concealments" in the musical practices of post-war theoretical composers. He cites contemporary philosopher Don Ihde who says that, for lack of earlids, at any one moment we can only exert psychical and not physiological control over the entirety of aural occurrence. This psychical control "is my attention and its selectivity. But this very selectivity is both what reveals something about sounds to me and at the same time conceals other aspects of sound."[2] For Charles, common approaches to music, especially conventional practices of notation and predominant systems of organizing musical material, necessarily repeat this process of revelation and concealment. Their consistent privileging of the latter, however, belies a project of authoritarian, "calculative" control. Charles' observations, however, are restricted to music, and thereby echo music's own delimiting efforts exerted upon the expanse of aural occurrence.

There exists a concealment not contained to musical practice which operates where musical practice borders other possible artistic practices of sound. It is cast in terms of the most pronounced feature of the musical conceit—the demarcation between mimetic and non-mimetic aspects of sound. The separation may fulfill all the rules of common sense. It is nevertheless arbitrary and becomes increasingly arbitrary as contemporary pressures mount. There are many ways beside music to conceive of and organize sound. There should be others still which cross the demarcation between mimetic and non-mimetic sound with impunity. Restrictions on this mobility distort the fields of possible artistic practices not only between music and an art of sound, but also across an art(s) of sound itself, because musical imperatives are imposed across sounds which have nothing intrinsically musical about them. Imposition doesn't stop at art. It is a very common practice to extend music as a trope to the totality of sound.

Russolo and the Music of Noise

The tradition of the mimetic/non-mimetic demarcation runs deep. There has been, of course, a role played by the real and self-consigned limitations of the capacity of music technology (instruments) for aural imitation, although plausible techniques for an art of mimetic sound have always existed. However, rationale for inactivity clearly cannot be sought among such limitations after the late 19th century development of phonography, the technology proper for aural imitation, for mimetic sound. Around the same time, the increasing din of mechanization (the first phonograph was basically a sensitive metal lathe) and what Henri Lefebvre calls the "breakdown of referentials"[3] emphasized the self-same mimetic and social characteristics of sound. The trajectory of aural "mimeticization" culminated during the 1920s, when phonography was joined by radio and sound film to irretrievably code instances of sound across the whole range of "natural" sounds, noise, speech, and music.

But it didn't matter how widespread intensively mimetic sound became, artistic practices of phonography and mimetic sound refused to materialize. When attempts were made, or should have been made, we find a "musical silencing" at work. It occurs when the very instant sound enters the avant-garde: Luigi Russolo's "art of noise." From the way he conceived his artistic raw material at a molecular level to the reception of his work by others, notions of music suppressed a truly radical art of sound. His inaugural manifest of 1913, while showing signs of struggle against the microtonal musical concealments of the reigning Italian Futurist composer, Francesco Balilla Pratella, demonstrated a deep-seated tension on the question of whether the art of noise should be an independent art or whether it should be dependent upon music. Because he resolved it unproblematically within the project of a "great renovation of music" it remained a source of continual difficulty.

One difficulty cropped up immediately. Russolo placed the art of noise at the culmination of the historical trajectory of music. Music, he said, was born in ancient times of a separation from the world of sound, detached throughout the ages from the momentum of life and stagnant while culture progressed. Music attempted to recuperate this separation, and the accompanying irrelevance, by claiming a fatuous transcendent power, from which heights is directed and policed a "fantasy superimposed on reality." However, the noise from the "growing multiplicity of machines," the sounds of modernism, of the city and warfare, no longer allowed such superimposition, but instead, Russolo insisted, mandated the very type of connection with life denied since the origins of music. Yet, once he embraced these sounds, he refused the very mimetic aspects which connected them in so many ways with situations in daily life. Despite his argument for an approach to sound that, to his mind, had never existed, no supersession or departure took place, no space for an artistic practice with any degree of autonomy was attempted, the culmination of the trajectory of music was to remain musical. At its root a noise's signature was to be timbral *only* . . . physical, areferential; the way in which he saw in noise a verticality of indeterminant harmonic complexity served at once as a representation for the intertextuality and interpenetration of "life" and as its surrogate. Furthermore, his ideas for an "art of noise" were supported by his idea of art in general. Art was of the emotions and mimesis has no business in the depths of the psyche where those emotions traversed. Also, the artist alone was to be in control of the artistic material. Imitation, though, reminds people of their own encounters with the world and these mnemonic representations, multifarious and transient bits of material that they are, are out of composer's control.

The "intonarumori," the instruments Russolo built to play his art of noise, were also contradictory. For having ostensibly been produced as an artistic response to modernism's encroachment of motors and metals, their core design drew not from contemporary technology but from the technology of traditional musical instruments: the drum, hurdy-gurdy, lion's roar, etc. Because none survived, what the Intonarumori sounded like is a matter of speculation. Ear witness accounts of concerts and demonstrations, however, do repeat the same split on the question of imitation and music. Russolo acknowledged that the Intonarumori were quite capable of "misleading," i.e., of producing sounds of an identifiable nature. He consequently sought methods to avoid this from occurring and rationale to allay fears that it might occur. Other individuals who commented on the Intonarumori and the art of noise asserted, for the most part, an intractability of imitation.Consequently they understood the art of noise to be incommensurate with music, or, since music was understood as the sole art of sound, incommensurate with the requisites for any art. It was dismissed as a vulgar case of sound effects or put to work in the degraded task of providing sound effects. Russolo long persevered with attacks of this sort. However, after many years he internalized the opinion that the nature of his art was, in fact, imitative. In the 1920s he designed instruments explicitly capable of "misleading," culminating in the Russolophone, a keyboard instrument so capable of imitation it was used to accompany silent films. In this respect, he had arrived at an instrument which served the function occupied already by sound effects organs. And along with the sound effects organs it was rendered obsolete by sound film. If Russolo's art of noise had been conceived and carried out while taking into account all aspects of worldly sound, instead of forcing sounds into the reductive mold of music, the return of the repressed mimesis would not have taken the trivialized form of sound effects. Neither would his art have been so easily savaged by the new technology of sound film. If he had integrated mimesis into the very material of his art, the art of noise would have been an art.

The Intervening Years

Another significant state of affairs was encountered with cubism, especially in the difference between analytic and synthetic cubism. Analytic cubism's dissolution of representation was performed under the sign of music. Music provided a model for aspirations toward nonreferentiality and as a system of relationality per se simultaneity, for instance, was child's play for music. If there had been a practice of sound based upon analytic cubism, in other words, it would have been indiscernible from music. Synthetic cubism was a different matter altogether. Its incorporation of actual objects would have led to a practice of sound substantially different than music, one which may have been inaugurated with the ballet *Parade* had the proposed use of mimetic sound not been excluded and diminished. We may ask, in fact, with each instance of collage in painting, sculpture, photography, and literature during the early avant-garde, where was the corresponding practice of sound? Remembering that what was, and is, fancied as musical collage is basically quodlibetical, i.e., an organization of other musical material, whereas collage implies artifacts foreign to the substratum.

The spread of radio, electrical advances in phonography, and optical sound film in the 1920s encouraged a rash of speculative activity directed toward an art of sound unhampered by musical discourse. It was at this time, after all, that the full range of sound—speech, music, sound/noise, and the quotidian sound of the media encompassing them all—became socially audible. During the Weimar Republic Weill, Brecht, and Arnheim argued for radio's artistic prospects and in 1933 Pino Masnata and F. T. Marinetti penned their "La Radia" manifesto. Ventures in avant-garde film sound maintained the musical conceit inherited from the "visual music" of earlier films and from the synaesthesia of colored light organs. In the late 30s some individuals imagined a music cast from sound effects files and libraries of optical sound film. But, as Carlos Chavez observed in 1937, nothing had been done to exploit the new possibilities, an observation with some lasting power.[4]

The irrepressible incursion of societal sound after the war, especially sound of television and the burgeoning capitalist spectacle, required that musical theoreticians and theoretical musicians make explicit arguments for what did and what did not constitute raw material for music. It is in the period writings of such people as Milton Babbit and Pierre Boulez that one finds, as one would expect, the most disciplinary of proclamations, a scientism set awkwardly against surmounting social and artistic pressures. However, they never made pretense for dealing with anything else but received notions of music; they never laid claim to dealing with sound in an extensive manner (the sounds they dealt with were "civilization").

However, pretense was made with *musique concrète*. Pierre Schaeffer's "acousmatics," i.e., his introduction of phonographic sound only to rid it of its associative traits, coupled with his general conformance to received musical modes of organization, has consequently had a more stifling influence. Like the others, he wanted nothing more but to make music, yet the inhibitions in his original formulations have led individuals to this day to glibly subsume artistic uses of phonographic material under *musique concrète*. The nature of the influence carries on from the same conservative impulse which compelled him, for instance, to design his solfeggio-like structures and other musically derived technicisms: here a musical concealment is indulged long before questions of sound, and thus musical conceit, arise.

Sound as Cagean Music

The most influential maintenance of the musical conceit during the post-war period is to be found in the aesthetic program of John Cage. Despite his work's being the most serious and sustained challenge to musical thinking of recent times, not to mention areas outside the bounds of musical practice, when it comes to an art of sound Cage's thought has had a limiting effect. It would not be that major of a concern if he did not profess, as he has done consistently, to be dealing with sound per se. His faithfulness to the musical conceit does not merely affect operations outside his own work, it contradicts some of his most central socio-aesthetic precepts.

It is an irony of Cage, whose name shares the same breath as postmodernism, that the unitary principle practiced to maintain the demarcation between mimetic and nonmimetic sound is more characteristic of modernism. He bridges modernism and postmodernism, in this respect, as his career has bridged the war years, from its beginnings during the mid-30s to its manifest influence beginning in the early 50s. In a 1942 statement, presaging Schaeffer, he sought to deny the character of the sounds made available by phonography and optical sound film by keeping "their expressive rather than representational qualities in mind."[5]

He put this into action in 1952 with *Imaginary Landscape No. 5* and *Williams Mix*. The former employs the sound of any 42 phonograph records and was, according to Cage, "the first piece of music for magnetic tape made in this country."[6] *Williams Mix* was composed as part of Louis and Bebe Barron's "Music für Magnetic Tape" project in New York, to which Earle Brown, Morton Feldman, David Tudor, and Christian Wolff also contributed. *Williams Mix* was a dense agglomeration of minute sound fragments from very divergent sources.[7]

The score is written for tape travelling at 15 inches per second. Each page lasts 1-1/3 seconds, and the whole score (192 pages) lasts a fraction over 4-1/4 minutes. The materials employed fall into six categories [A (city sounds), B (country sounds), C (electronic sounds), D (manually produced sounds, including the literature of music), E (wind-produced sounds, including singing), and F (small sounds requiring amplification to be heard with the others)]. Some 500–600 sounds were recorded by Louis and Bebe Barron; the eight tapes were assembled over a 9-month period by Earle Brown, David Tudor, and myself.

For the listener equipped with the framing discourse, the collapse of such a web of sound will barter, like much other music, in representation in and of itself; it may even represent "music" just as the prized ineffability of music will, at the very least, represent ineffability. In this respect, *Williams Mix* is to representation what *4'33"* is to proximal acoustic experience. However, any associations of the sounds—perhaps with their source—were displaced to a play a sole role of noise. Like Russolo, noise was at once Cage's ticket to the world and his foil against musical convention. For both, noise was the elastic separation needed to realize a renovation of music.[8] ("Noise" has no ultimate meaning short of physical pain and damage. But then, what is stunning?) Once Cage claimed that any sound, any noise, was to be accepted for delectation or deliberation—"as is"—especially as it occurred in situ, outside a musical venue, its prior transgressive function was sapped. Noise had become instrumental. Its prior function was simply replaced by another inhibition, one which had existed before but was even less thinkable than noise, that of the mimetic demarcation. For Cage, reference is the new noise.

Cage understands silence to be inextricable with the world of sound. *4'33"*, although it is known as the "silent piece," concerned an explicit reversal along these lines, but not in the globalized, quotidian sense of all silence and all sound. Instead, he silenced the music to musicalize sound! A piece like *Williams Mix* makes all sounds available for musical utterance whereas *4'33"* extends musical apperception to any sound whether it was uttered musically or not. Such a performance can take place outside an institutional venue and occur any time, any place. It's simply a matter of attunement.[9] "If you want to know the truth of the matter, the music I prefer, even to my own or anybody else's, is what we are hearing if we are just quiet."[10] But the character of this attunement, because it is enacted within the terms of musical reception, requires that sounds be stripped of their semantic content, at the minimum. Although they may, as a last resort, be left unhampered to stand as periodic affirmations of indeterminacy, this signals no departure. The implicit directive to maintain an attunement against the incursion of mimetic sound, referentiality, meaning, sociality, etc., narrows an individual's relationship to the sonic/semiotic object. In attempting to neutralize the object by making it musical, the individual is, as a consequence, naturalized, resulting in a rather despairing vision of human subjectivity, let alone the potential for radical subjectivity.

Cage is willing to extend music as a trope to all sound. In the same moment as the authorship of an indeterminant composition by Cage can be problematized, we can also only hope that, when a person under the suggestion of Cage listens "omniattentively" with "happy new ears" to aural reality separate from a discrete composition, any residual authorship associated with Cage himself is jettisoned. The question of his authorship, however, doesn't really matter. Any suggestion under the sign of music will necessarily aestheticize, enculturate, and generally barter in aspects contributing to the social constitution of subjectivity to which authorship belongs. This degree of anthropomorphism is very much against Cage's stated desires. To argue that it does not impose a socio-cultural figure, to argue that any representation is not historical, to appeal to the fancied naturalization of all sound by music, is to exacerbate what is denied by making it surreptitious. The way this contributes to legitimate normative and imperial attitudes runs counter to ecology and social ecology, despite the fact, or perhaps central to the fact, that Cage equates music and ecology: "Music, as I conceive it, is ecological. You could go further and say that *it is ecology*" (original emphasis).[11]

He shares with many others this willingness to cast very far the web of music. R. Murray Schafer, for instance, has baldly stated: "Today all sounds belong to a continuous field of possibilities lying *within the comprehensive dominion of music*" (original emphasis).[12] But no willingness is shown to recognize the symbolic violence committed. When, after all, was the last time you heard the word "dominion"?

One example of an art of sound conceived under a Cagean musical conceit is that of the well-publicized work of Bill Fontana, in particular, the recent coordinated radiophonic project *Satellite Soundbridge Between San Francisco and Köln* linking the sound sculptures *Sound Sculptures Through the Golden Gate and Metropolis Köln*.[13] I'll say at the outset that the celebration these works have received appears to be attributable to a displaced admiration of a formidable technological apparatus mobilized for the goal of artistic purposes, not attributable to artistic purposes themselves. They would have run less risk of being mundane and might have been better equipoised with the technology had he not abided by the imposition of musical ideas on the aural environments.

Fontana promotes the typical musical trope. "We are surrounded by music." Per his activities in Köln: "It was my intention to temporarily turn the urban landscape of Köln into a musical sculpture."[14] In his work the associative characteristics of sounds are invoked and then led to labor under the sign of (Cagean) "music." The application of music to a "portrait" of a city has a history and, like Fontana's Köln, it is a German city: Walter Ruttmann's 1927 cross-section film, "Berlin, the Symphony of a Great City." Ruttmann's film disregarded things left untouched by the surface inspection of the camera. It opted instead for "optical music," formally submerging the social workings of the city, especially through its use of "rhythmic montage." As Siegfried Kracauer wrote in 1928: "This symphony fails to point out anything, because it does not uncover a single significant context."[15] There was actually a greater depopulation of Fontana's Köln than there was of Ruttmann's Berlin. Social sounds were aestheticized and the discursive sounds which did exist were diminished, e.g., the sounds of pedestrians in Köln were miked from beneath a manhole cover, in the same manner the cars crossing the Golden Gate bridge were miked from below. It was accompanied, in the San Francisco area as well, with a pervasively uncritical sense of the social factors involved in representations of "nature."

Well outside the influence of Cage, or any theoretical composer for that matter, the musical conceit is strongest in the realm of recent developments of digital sampling instruments. It's no surprise that discourse is structured into technology, but here it's exacerbated probably as a result of its falling into lockstep with the economic imperatives of the music of mass culture. Over the last several years, the technological fruits of industry can be witnessed at a glance in trade and popular magazines. As their subtext, and in intermittent articles and comments, these fruits have been equated with an opening up of artistic possibility as well. But what has occurred may be better described as an implosive outpouring, a concentration of what already exists.

This is most evident when it comes to the very idea of instrument. Sampling keyboards and other interactive configurations may condense a number of instruments to one location, expedite the utterance of certain sounds, deploy whole families of sound not previously available for interaction, etc. But this has been done almost entirely for the replication of existing musical instruments and within accepted musical vocabularies, while the basis of sampling in the properties of phonography, especially displacement, suggests a new non-musical conception of instrument.[16] Briefly, the locus of sounds in a conventional musical instrument, say, a violin, is congruent with the physical locus of the instrument itself (very much along the lines of speech, of the metaphysics of presence). When a violin is played, sound originates at the physical site, at the site of wood, metal, fiber. Phonographic sound originates elsewhere and lacks a significant congruence with the digital sampler itself. The "instrument" instead can be conceived as some type of configuration, a locus, selected through a theoretically unlimited mobility, separated out from the full range of sound. An instrument's locus—i.e., in the most compelling way, the instrument itself—would no longer be physical, present, but semiotic.[17] This would be furthered by the fact that the very statuses of a locus and of loci would themselves be the products of a negotiated, ever shifting mobility.

Although it will be the purpose of another essay to propose bases of sampler design better adaptable to composition with this new idea of instrument, it can be said that an important element will be the development of capacities for aural writing. There are many other areas of development, both technological and compositional, such that the whole project is a rather ambitious and protracted one. It has to be stated outright, however, that adequate technology already exists and that the main work now is compositional, artistic, and conceptual.[18] Hopefully, we will soon enjoy centers which explore the unique compositional possibilities presented by these instruments, in the way electronic and computer music studios cropped up some three decades ago, so that the work can get under way.

The Exception: Vertov

It is true that in the pre-WWII avant-garde neither an art of mimetic sound nor a phonographically based art of sound was developed, and that those who were in the best position to do so (as well as the general discursive milieu) suffered from musical conceit. This does not mean that a fairly clear intent was left undeveloped, nor that no one escaped music. We can find this, to my knowledge, we can only find this in the activities of the Russian Dziga Vertov, best known as a revolutionary filmmaker in the company of Eisenstein, Shub, Pudovkin, Kuleshov, etc. In fact, he did not set out to become a filmmaker but, instead, had attempted around 1916, after gaining a background in writing and music, what would now be called audio art. As a boy Vertov wrote energetically in many genres and when he reached age 16 he entered conservatory for three years to study violin, piano, and music theory. In 1916, while attending the Psychoneurological Institute in Petrograd, he was introduced to some of the major players of the Russian avant-garde, including Brik, Rodchenko, and Mayakovsky. The combination of a background of writing and music, amidst the adventurous imperatives of the avant-garde, "turned into an enthusiasm for editing shorthand records [stenographs] and gramophone recordings. Into a special interest in the possibility of documentary sound recording. Into experiments in recording, with words and letters, the noise of a waterfall, the sounds of a lumbermill, etc., a 'Laboratory of Hearing.'"[19]

Towards the end of 1916, Vertov attempted to realize his Laboratory with a 1900 or 1910 model Pathephone wax disc recorder:

> *I had the original idea of the need to enlarge our ability to organize sound, to listen not only to singing or violins, the usual repertoire of gramophone disks, but to transcend the limits of ordinary*

*music. I decided that the concept of sound included all the audible world. As part of my experiments,
I set out to record a sawmill.*[20]

It's assumed he became frustrated with the poor sound quality. Indeed, he spoke of his transition to film in terms of an inadequacy of phonographic technology. In his recollection, upon . . .

*. . . returning from a train station, there lingered in my ears the signs and rumble of the
departing train . . . someone's swearing . . . a kiss . . . someone's exclamation . . . laughter, a whistle,
voices, the ringing of the station's bell, the puffing of the locomotive . . . whispers, cries, farewells .
. . And thoughts while walking: I must get a piece of equipment that won't describe, but will record,
photograph these sounds. Otherwise, it's impossible to organize, edit them. They rush past, like time.
But the movie camera perhaps? Record the visible . . . Organize not the audible, but the visible world.
Perhaps that's the way out?* [21]

In this respect, the famed "Kino-Eye," the fetish of much post-WWII avant-garde film, seems to have been the result of a frustrated ear. An inability to "phonograph sounds," in Edison's words, and in the later sense of optical film sound of "sound photography" and "sound camera," resulted in a desire to "photograph these sounds." The deficiency of the technology cannot be equated with poor sound quality; since the creation of phonography, determinations of sound quality have been creatures of the moment. The deficiency comes about in relation to Vertov's montage organization of the recorded material. Without the electrical recording and amplification that was to become available in the 1920s, he would have been unable to re-record without serious generational loss.

He did not wait until proper sound film technology to begin realizing his ideas of sound. From the moment he began filmmaking until "Enthusiasm" (1931), his first sound film, he attempted to keep sound incipient, to prepare for the inevitable advent of sound in Russian film even before sound came to American film. He introduced "Implied sound" into his films, argued theoretically concerning sound, championed an expanded concept of radio, and argued against the dogma inhibiting relationships between sound and image set forth by Eisenstein ("A Statement") and others. He also argued against the "theory of caterwauling." In 1929, while Vertov embarked upon "enthusiasm," the film critic Ippolit Sokolov wrote in "On the Possibilities of Sound Cinema" that the natural world of sound was not conducive to recording.[22] The outdoors and the remote, the sounds of work, industry, celebration, public gatherings, etc., i.e., a large part of the domain of documentary, were not "audiogenic."

"Agitational and scientific films will be produced not in the lap of nature, not in the noise of the streets, but within the soundproof walls of the film studio, where no outside sound can penetrate. The sound movie camera will least of all film 'life caught unawares.' The unorganized and accidental sounds of our streets and buildings would become a genuine cacophony, a literally caterwauling concert."[23]

Vertov understood Sokolov's "theory of caterwauling" to be "anti-newsreel," i.e., very much within the mold of formalist critics who preferred only actors and acting upon the screen—in the vernacular: played films. Vertov also understood it as symptomatic of an exclusivist conceit derived from music: "Everything which is not 'sharp' or 'flat,' in a word, everything which does not 'doremifasolize' was unconditionally labeled 'cacophony.'"[24]

Vertov considered the true refutation of Sokolov's "theory of caterwauling" to be *enthusiasm* itself. There was nothing do-re-mi in the "setting of din and clanging, amidst fire and iron, among factory workshops vibrating from the sound."[25] Vertov "penetrated into mines deep beneath the earth," much like Nadar in the catacombs, and rode atop "the roofs of speeding trains" lugging twenty-seven hundred pounds of recording equipment, developed specifically for the film, and "for the first time in history recorded, in documentary fashion, the basic sounds of an industrial region (the sound of mines, factories, trains, etc.)."[26]

Vertov may have rejected Sokolov's music-like exclusivity but he didn't reject music, nor could he with a conservatory schooling. He often referred to his role in filmmaking, not as director, but as composer.[27] He called "Enthusiasm" a "symphony of noises," and the film's second name, under which it was known in Russia, is "Symphony of the Donbas." "Symphonie" as a figure is, in one of the many aurally reflexive moments of the film, extended to signal the "harmonic" organization of the activities of the 5-Year Plan in the Don Basin Region, and its parallel in the structure and process of the film itself. In a note sent to Vertov from London (Nov. 1931), Charlie Chaplin wrote: "Never had I known that these mechanical sounds could be arranged to sound so beautiful, I regard it as one of the most exhilarating symphonies I have heard. Mr. Dziga Vertov is a musician . . ."[28]

Vertov invoked musical metaphor without the reduction, regularization, or aestheticization it had come to impose in general cultural discourse, because the metaphor had to interact within a documentary context that Vertov called an "enthusiasm of facts" and a literary process wherein sounds themselves were scripted (prior to the visuals, no less, as was the case with "Enthusiasm").[29]

We can only feebly speculate what a Vertov audio art, an autonomous practice of recorded sound, would have sounded like, since his art of sound was caught up in relationships with visual images. Seth Feldman says it's possible to infer on what a Radiopravda production would have sounded like by sonically animating the titles and implied sounds in "Kinopravda no. 23." But what about a pre-Revolutionary work, still caught in the Cubo-Futurist exuberance of the twenty-year-old in St. Petersburg? And how might this have developed after October, through the 1920s, or past the Stalinist anti-formalism of the 1930s? The legacy that we have received from him is the way he approached the new artistic possibilities of sound in a non-dogmatic, pan-disciplinary way, away from the full weight of the musical conceit, along "the line of maximum resistance" as he called it. He asked of his audience that any of the difficulties they might encounter be perceived in the proper context, not as "a shortcoming, but as a serious, long-range experiment."[30] If we take his experiment in the terms in which he cast it in his youth, or in what Arnheim called "blind-hearing," then we realize that the long-range experiment is still before us.

Notes

1. "Given that the collage in general is the most characteristic mode of composition in the modernist arts and that Derrida is the first to develop fully a theory (epithymics) that conceptualizes this mode, it is fair to say that Derrida's grammatology is to the collage what Aristotle's poetics were to Greek tragedy." Gregory L. Ulmer, Applied Grammatology (Baltimore: Johns Hopkins University Press, 1985), p. 59.

2. Don Ihde, Existential Technics (Albany: SUNY Press, 1983). Cited in Daniel Charles, "Music and Technology Today," in Rend Berger and Lloyd Eby, eds., Art and Technology (New York: Paragon House Publishers, 1986).

3. Henri Lefebvre pegs the "breakdown of referentials" somewhere around 1905–1910, when, under the influence of science, technology, and social changes, "the sense of hearing acquired a greater aptitude for interpreting visual perceptions and the sense of sight for interpreting auditive ones, so that they signify each other reciprocally," and "objects, in practice, become signs, and signs objects." Lefebvre, Everyday Life in the Modern World (New Brunswick: Transaction Books, 1984), pp. 110–127.

4. Carlos Chavez, Towards a New Music (New York: W. W. Norton, 1937).

5. John Cage, "For More New Sounds" (May-June 1942), in: Richard Kostelanetz, ed., John Cage (New York: Praeger, 1970), p. 66.

6. John Cage, "[On Earlier Pieces]," in Kostelanetz, p. 130.

7. John Cage, "[Williams Mix]," in Kostelanetz, pp. 109–111.

8. He's also willing to musicalize language. This, in particular, is a practical consequence of adhering to the musical conceit. The demarcation of mimetic and non-mimetic sounds results in a notable schism between what are considered proper sites for artistic and discursive activity (a schism reminiscent of the one in Ad Reinhardt between his black endgame paintings and cartoon critiques—the main difference is, of course, that Reinhardt was a self-described creature of art institutions whereas Cage breaks into daily life). The musicalization of language passes across this schism in one direction only; there is no reciprocation. See also the related schism between the naive content of Cage's "electrical utopia" and the sophisticated method of his "systemic approach,"

as reported by Kathleen Woodward in her "Art and Technics," in: Kathleen Woodward, ed., The Myths of Information: Technology and Postindustrial Culture (Milwaukee: University of Wisconsin, 1980). Contrary to Woodward, my comments here note that a certain lack of sophistication exists as well in his systemic approach.

9. Music through attunement is one step back from Russolo's intervention proposed in his first Manifesto: "We shall amuse ourselves by orchestrating in our minds the noise of the metal shutters of store windows, the slamming of doors . . ."

10. "Conversation with John Cage" in Kostelanetz, p. 12.

11. John Cage in conversation with Daniel Charles, in: For the Birds (Boston: Marion Boyars, 1981), p. 229.

12. R. Murray Schafer, The Tuning of the World (Philadelphia: University of Pennsylvania, 1977), p. 5. Both Cage and Schafer, it should be pointed out, derive a good amount of their globalizing impulse and normative sweep from McLuhan.

13. Bill Fontana, Acustica International, Klangskulpturen/Sound Sculptures: Metropolis Köln, Through the Golden Gate, Satelliten-Ohr-Brücke / Satellite-Soundbridge Köln-San Francisco. Catalogue for Köln: Westdeutscher Rundfunk and Museum Ludwig and San Francisco: San Francisco Museum of Art and American Public Radio, May-June 1987. The sounds were gathered from the surrounding areas, dominated by "natural" sounds from physical (e.g., river water) and animal (e.g., zoo, offshore wildlife) sources, mechanical sounds (e.g., expansion joints in bridge), and non-discursive human sounds (pedestrian sounds). These were presented under a Duchamp-inspired ploy of "found objects," without very much alteration, and were organized along simple lines of simultaneity. In the iconography of the work, the Köln Cathedral and the Golden Gate Bridge functioned, in their respective areas, as architectural loci, symbolic antennae, around and within which sounds were gathered and distributed. They also functioned as fixed sites, monuments and monumental scale, sculptural solidity in the absence of any provided by the displaced aurality. Other reductive operations at work, besides the musical conceit proper, include: the status of "sculpture" applied to communicative and social processes, the naturalization of urban realities through the figure of "landscape," the artworld rhetorical currency of "sound object" without the institutional and discursive critiques originally attendant upon Duchamp's usage, exhuming the cubist/orphic notion of "simultaneity" to dignify basically mundane contemporary experiences of telephonic or radiophonic displacement or "relocation," the modernist media arts idea of a technology's proper perceptual object, psycho-acoustics as the scientific surrogate for the socio-cultural aspect of sound, etc.

14. Fontana, p. 31.

15. Siegfried Kracauer, From Caligari to Hitler (Princeton: Princeton University Press, 1947), p. 188.

16. See my "An Instrument for X Sample," Ear Magazine (June 1987), for some opening remarks. Not too ironically, some of my comments were compromised by the unsolicited interventions of the "tech page" editor.

17. It's important not to confuse this with pastiche, which is something of an abandoned statistical sampling method over a broad range of (usually media) aural environments, accompanied by a belief that something of import can be accomplished through simple quotation. Pastiche is a conceptually impoverished means of response to the mimetic aspects of sound, a musicalization of sorts which no doubt has found succor in the musical conceit. Pastiche could even be understood as a surrogate for the type of instrument proposed here.

18. We can mention in this respect the Dyaxis system from Integrated Media Systems in San Carlos, California.

19. Dziga Vertov, Kino-Eye: The Writings of Dziga Vertov, ed. Annette Michelson (Berkeley: University of California, 1984), p. 40.

20. Dziga Vertov, "Speech of 5 April 1935," cited in Seth Feldman, Evolution of Style in the Early Work of Dziga Vertov (New York: Arno Press, 1977), p. 13. For an astute comparison to Russolo's work, a source which influenced Vertov, refer to Feldman's comments, pp. 12–15.

21. Feldman, p. 40, my emphasis.

22. Vertov, p. 112 fn.

23. Quoted in Herbert Marshall, Masters of Soviet Cinema (Boston: Routledge & Kegan Paul, 1983), p. 81.

24. "First Steps," Vertov, p. 114.

25. "Let's Discuss Ukrainfilm's First Sound Film: 'Symphony of the Donbas,'" Vertov, p. 109.

26. Vertov, p. 109.

27. Jay Leyda, Kino: A History of the Russian and Soviet Film (New York: Collier Books, 1960), p. 177.

28. "From Notebooks, Diaries," Vertov, p. 170.

29. Cf. "Sound March," Vertov, pp. 289–293, and Michelson's comments on p. 327.

30. Vertov, p. 112. For a valuable analysis see Lucy Fischer, "Enthusiasm: From Kino-Eye to Radio-Eye," in Elisabeth Weis and John Belton, eds., Film Sound: Theory and Practice (New York: Columbia University Press, 1984), pp. 247–264.

Memories

Vilém Flusser

Like no other known living creature, we pass on not only inherited but also acquired information to future generations. In doing so, we negate nature twice: the second law of thermodynamics states that in nature all information has a propensity to be forgotten. Living creatures negate this principle, since they store and pass on genetic information. And Mendel's law states that acquired information cannot be transmitted from one organism to the next. Our species defies this law, too, for it stores acquired information in a cultural memory accessible to successive generations. This two-fold negation of nature is, however, not as it seems: ultimately, all stored information has, by necessity, to remerge into the general flow toward entropy. Just the same, this two-fold negation is the human position: "human dignity" (that which distinguishes us from all other living organisms) can be defined by our having genetic and cultural memories at our disposal. We are "historical creatures." At present, electronic memories are in the process of reshaping our cultural memory. Hence, the notion of "human dignity" will gain new significance. This is the topic that will be discussed in this paper.

Memory can be defined as the storage of information, at least in the context meant here. Understood as such, memories are to be found everywhere in nature. Bits of stored information float like islands in the general flow toward entropy. By chance they emerged from it, and by necessity they will remerge into it. Examples of such memory islands (which are almost as old as the universe itself) are hydrogen atoms and galactic systems. An impressive example of such an anti-entropic epicycle superposed on the linear tendency toward entropy is the biomass. Several billions of years ago, it happened to emerge from entropy onto the earth's surface. It consists of small drops whose complex molecules contain encoded genetic information, and we humans are ourselves outgrowths of this biomass. The information stored in these drops is passed on by copying; in the process of this copying, mistakes occur from time to time. Most of these mistakes are eliminated from the biomass' memory (as "nonviable mutations"), although a few are retained in the memory and form "life's evolution." In other words: the biomass processes information stored in it as a result of faulty copying, and thus generates new information. And this fact is of growing interest today. Gene technology can be seen as the attempt to store acquired information in the biomass, to produce cultural memory from the biomass. If we see this technology as a form of art (and the chimeras produced by it as works of art), then future artists will have to deal with the fact that the memory of the biomass makes mistakes and cannot be viewed as trustworthy.

Cultural memory, a much more recent phenomenon, deserves to be trusted even less (which means, "human dignity" has not deserved our unlimited admiration so far). Most of the information we have acquired in our relatively short presence here has fallen into oblivion. Not only documents turn to ashes and buildings into ruins, but most previous cultures have hardly left a trace. In other words, when humans began developing cultural memories (as they began becoming human), they found access only to very questionable memory aids. (Such aids are objects that allow us to be "informed," i.e. to store information.) Two of these aids (hardware), which have been used ever since we began becoming human should be mentioned here: airwaves and hard objects (for example, stones and bones).

Air has the advantage of being readily accessible; moreover, we have organs which seem to have been made to transform airwaves into signs (to make "phonemes" out of them). The question which arises about the incoherent relationship between inherited and acquired information has to be disregarded here: speech as an ability is inherited, yet each individual language has to be acquired. But airwaves have the disadvantage that they are susceptible to noises which destroy the information stored in them. That is why all information stored in airwaves (in "oral cultures") has to be rapidly received and stored in the recipient's nervous system. Yet how the information is then processed, before it is passed on to other recipients and undergoes further distortion, is still unclear. Consequently, with respect to "oral cultures," it is only possible to speak of historiography (the cumulative storing of acquired information) in a very restricted sense.

Hard objects (stones and bones) have the advantage of storing the information recorded in them for a relatively long time. (A stone knife can, for instance, preserve the information stored in it— "to cut"—for tens of thousands of years.) The disadvantage is that such memory aids serve simultaneously as tools: a knife not only recalls the information "to cut" but is actually used to cut. Usage wears "out" the information (it is forgotten). The totality of informed hard objects is called "material culture," and its characteristic memory defect (that it wears out and becomes waste) still poses unresolved problems which, as our cultural critique sees it, threaten human survival. For this very reason, "pure memory aids" have been created alongside tools since the start; "monuments" like the Venus of Willendorf or cave paintings are not subject to wear but only to the second law of thermodynamics. And until recently, this was about all that we had accomplished as far as "cultural memory" was concerned.

Approximately three thousand five hundred years ago (in other words, only a short time ago), an important step was taken; the alphabet was invented. It is a system which recodes the phonemes of spoken languages into visual signs, allowing them to be engraved into hard objects. As a consequence, it became possible to link the advantages of oral culture to those of material culture, and a much more functional cultural memory came into existence. "Monuments" could be produced (texts) that store oral information in hardware from which it can be easily recalled and which allow it to be copied. This was an extraordinarily fruitful invention, for it permitted a relatively reliable and disciplined storage of acquired information—and history, in the true sense of the word, became possible. This development led to a radical change in thought and action. The linearity of the alphabetic code affected thinking: it also became linear (progressive), and historically conscious action (ultimately technology) became possible. The invention of the alphabet was a decisive step on the road toward our becoming human.

A new cultural memory (the library) could only assert itself slowly: it had to struggle against previous oral memory (myth) and material memory (magic) in their complex relationship to one another. In the course of the library's gradual acceptance, it became ideologically sacralized, a fact that still characterizes occidental culture today. The library was no longer seen as a memory aid in which acquired information is recorded (in writing) and recalled (by reading). Instead, it began to be viewed as a transcendence suspended over humans (imposed on them). As a result, the cultural function of the library was redirected: it did not serve humans in their commitment to preserve acquired information from entropy, but rather humans served it to preserve themselves in it from entropy (from death). Indeed, this reversal of cultural memory's function is typical for the relationship between humans and their products (the spoken word was sacralized in oral culture and the monument in material culture). However, in the final analysis the library's sacralization has to do with an ideology which forms the basis of all so-called Western values. Amongst the many diverse—convergent or divergent—forms of this ideology, we should focus on the Platonic variant, because the essential is particularly evident in it: the library (the superhuman memory) is a heavenly place *(topos uranikos)*, in which eternal, immutable information ("ideas," "forms") are preserved according to the rules of logic. This heavenly storehouse is our original home from which we fell into the world of deceptive phenomena. In falling, we traveled over the river of forgetfulness *(Lethe)*, but its waters did not erase the information in us; they only covered it up so that we may rediscover it again *(a-letheia)*. All information that we acquire in the world of phenomena is deceptive *(doxal)*; only rediscoverable inborn information has validity *(sophia)*. Rediscovery *(theoria)* is to look with an inner eye, and it is due to it that we can contemplate information stored in the heavenly library. Moreover, we can also recall it by means of logical discipline. In so doing, we not only regain knowledge of eternal information, but we also become (in a very library-like sense) immortal.

It is not difficult for us to recognize a whole series of our own *culturemes* in what seems today to be a somewhat archaic ideology. We can see not only the basic structure of Christianity and all subsequent value systems, but also the basic structure of modern scientific thought. However, I want to point out an even deeper consequence of the library's sacralization: namely, that it is in relation to this sacralized cultural memory that we identify ourselves to start with. We identify ourselves as "subjects" (subordinates) of an "immaterial" library suspended over us; as protuberances which bulge out into the world of phenomena. There is the library—this ability to store information, ideologized as a "thing"—suspended on the one side, and the world of phenomena on the other. As organisms we are part of the phenomenal world, but as protuberances of the library we face the phenomenal world as subjects. We possess, so to speak, a core in which information is acquired, stored, and processed, and it has the function to pass on information to the library. This core has had different names in the course of Western history (for example, "immortal soul" or "spirit" or "intelligence" or "ego" or "self"), but, no matter what it has been called, it characterizes just about every anthropology of Western society. Basically, it is a question of reifying and sacralizing the ability to store acquired information, of reifying cultural memory which is projected upon the transcendent. Almost all occidental "eternal" ontological questions (for instance, those about the relationship between "body" and "mind") and all "eternal" epistemological questions (for instance, those about the equation of "thinking" substance to "extended" substance) are to be ascribed to this ideological reification of cultural memory. They constitute "eternal" questions because they have been put wrong. The invention of electronic memories will help to end such nonsense.

Electronic memories are simulations of a few of our brain functions. A simulation is an imitation in which certain aspects are exaggerated and others ignored. (For example, the lever simulates the arm: it exaggerates its ability to lift things and ignores all other aspects of it.) Electronic memories exaggerate and project some brain functions out of the skull on to inanimate objects, where they can be observed and dealt with. The intention of such inventions is to improve cerebral memory functions (to improve them almost immeasurably). But an unintentional consequence of this invention is that it allows us to attain a critical distance from these functions. Without a doubt, the improvement of memory functions will change culture in the future; however, it will be the unintentional consequences of memory simulation that cause the greatest changes.

Electronic memories can receive information more easily than brains can and they have a much larger storage capacity. They are better at preserving information and can recall individual items more easily. It is also not difficult to transmit information from one electronic memory to another. All these (and other) advantages mean that acquired information (data) will no longer be stored in brains but in electronic memories. As a consequence, brains will be free to adopt other functions. People will no longer have to memorize facts but learn how to store, recall, and vary data expediently. They will no longer need to learn systems' repertoires but instead their structure. Data processing of this kind—which had been checked by the need to learn facts—is called "creativity"; hence, we can now reckon with a true burst of human creativity.

Electronic brains can be coupled with automatic machines (with robots). Information stored in electronic memories can be transcoded into the movements (gestures) made by such machines. This means that automatic machines can imprint information stored in electronic memories on objects. Such imprinting of information on objects is called "work." (For example, a stone knife is the result of work, of a movement, that imprinted the information "to cut" on the stone.) It will relieve people of work and give them time to work out "programs" (of information to be automatically imprinted on objects). The human being will no longer be a worker ("homo faber") but an information player ("homo ludens").

Electronic memories permit stored information to be erased effortlessly: they forget more easily than brains do. Information is valid for only a limited amount of time, and most acquired information proceeds from the assumption that it will be superseded by new information. (Such is the dynamism of scientific discourse, indeed, of all discourse: to "falsify" acquired information.) Human brains are burdened by falsifiable information. Electronic memories, on the other hand, enable the critical elimination of such information. They permit disciplined and critical compilation of acquired information. And so in the future, "history" (in the sense of information accumulation) will be a much more disciplined and critical process than it was before.

All these changes in culture that are expected in the future (and other changes not mentioned here) are, indeed, rather unsettling, but they still do not get to the root of the cultural revolution we are witnessing. We can only begin to understand the impact that this revolution is having on our existence, when we face the critical distance from memory function that has been made possible by electronic memories.

Despite all traditional ideologies, practical experience with electronic memories forces us to recognize information acquisition, storage, processing, and transmission as a process which relies on objects (for instance, on memory aids such as computer hardware or human organisms). Nevertheless, it runs or works through, so to speak, these objects (a fact which can be seen in the term "medium"). Experience makes us recognize all these objects (including our own bodies) as media of the information process. It is senseless to try to reify this process, to want to localize it in a medium, which is why all reifying notions for this process (such as "soul," "spirit," "identity," "ego" or "self") must be dropped. A new anthropology has to be developed: the peculiar ability of our species to store, process, and transmit acquired information ("human dignity") has to be grasped in the light of this practical experience. We have to see ourselves as nodes in a net through whose lines (whether material or energetic) information flows. Within these nodes, information is accumulated, processed, and transmitted, but the nodes themselves are not anything: if we undo them (untie the relational lines forming them), there is nothing left (just as with the proverbial onion). In other words: we have to develop an anthropology that regards humans as nodal point (warp) of several intersecting relational fields.

This inevitable release from ideological encapsulation in individuality (identity, subjectivity) is not, of course, to be attributed to practical experience with electronic memories alone. It was in preparation long before such experience and in many heterogeneous areas. To name just a few examples: analytical psychology shows the individual psyche as the tip of an iceberg structured on collective, psychological processes going beyond our species. Ecology shows individual organisms (including us humans) as functions of complex relational fields (of ecosystems). Political science shows that the "individual person" and "society" are abstractions and that concrete facts are to be found in interhuman relations that constitute humans and society to begin with. This relational (topological) view of our position is confirmed by the "other side," namely, by the physical sciences. Hence, physical objects appear, for instance, as nodes (notches) in physical fields of force. Husserl's phenomenology can be seen as the articulation of this field view. In short, it states that the concrete world of life, after being "reduced phenomenologically and eidetically," proves to be a field of concrete relations from which "subjects" and "objects" are extrapolated.

Nevertheless, even though the relational point of view has long been in preparation at many locations and the invention of electronic memories can be seen as an outcome of this preparation, it remains indisputable that practical experience with such memories first forces us to rid ourselves of the traditional ideology of a hard core (that we have or are). In turn, it also forces us to stop reifying and sacralizing our ability to store, process, and transmit acquired information. The inevitable consequences that such an adjustment of our thoughts (and actions) will have are inconceivable. Yet, some changes can already be foreseen.

We will have to reformulate many (maybe all) of the categories we have used till now. An example: we will have to replace the category of "subject-object" with the category of "intersubjectivity," which will invalidate the distinction between science and art: science will emerge as an intersubjective fiction, art as an intersubjective discipline in the search for knowledge; thus science will become a form of art and art a variant of the sciences. Another example: if "I" is seen as that to which others say "you" (if self-knowledge is seen as a consequence of acknowledging others), then the distinction between knowing (cognition) and acknowledging (recognition) will also be rendered invalid: art and science will have then to be seen as "political disciplines." To carry this to an extreme: if we see ourselves as the function of others, and all others as functions of ourselves, then "responsibility" will have to take on the importance which "individual liberty" has had till now. And then it will no longer be discourse but dialogue that structures culture in the future, no longer "progress" but mutual encounter.

All these thoughts are just premonitions, and they involve just as much danger as hope. However, one thing is certain: if, because of our practical experiences with electronic memories (these primitive and provisional simulations of functions of our own memory), we are forced to give up the ideology we have had about our identity, then our anti-entropic position (our "ex-sistence") will in no way be "de-sacralized." On the contrary: the obscure mystery of the ability to resist nature's tendency toward decay, as well as the desire to do so, will become even obscurer. More so than ever before, it will become evident that this ability (and this desire) is doomed to fail in the end.

No bibliography has been included here: this paper results from my having collected information from a wide variety of fields. And it has also not been my intention to establish a thesis but to contribute some considerations to the current discussion on the anticipated cultural revolution, especially with respect to electronic technologies. In other words: it is to help us get our bearings in a situation quite difficult to grasp.

Translated by Catherine Kerkhoff-Saxon

Virtual Worlds:
The Emperor's New Bodies

Peter Weibel

Perception here,
and there the Object.
G. W. F. Hegel

In the 18th century, at the dawn of the machine revolution, a strange story took place.

A magician, an extremely adept watchmaker, had constructed an automaton. He had executed this machine to such perfection, its movement so smooth and natural, that the public could not distinguish them, once both appeared on stage. To put a point to the spectacle the master felt compelled to "mechanise" his own movements, even his complete bearing, lest the spectators in their increasing unease as to who or what was "real" should actually take the man for the machine, and vice versa.[1]

Machine Simulating Man—and Man Simulating Machine

This story provides a simple illustration for the difficult relationship between machine and body, man and machine. It also addresses another problem with technology, that its perfection might one day eliminate the difference between man and machine. Would there be, sometime, computer-robots, intelligent machines that perfectly simulate man? Clearly any thing, any "Substance"— Heidegger uses the term *Zeug*—is basically amorphous. Material objects also give away something about their producer. First of all any manmade object inherently displays its maker's properties, simply by being made by man. Secondly they repeat human behaviour through the purposeful delegation of human properties onto them. It is obvious that machines are constructed to enhance, take over, or replace human functions. Freud gives an exact description of their functioning as artificial limbs in his *Civilisation and Its Discontents*. We construct machines to satisfy human needs; therefore any machine will display anthropomorphous properties. The point is that on account of this desired anthropomorphism the machine will be perfected to such an extent as to be able to replace humans, which is in turn lamented. Stupidly so, as the aim of such anthropomorphisation must lie in the perfect simulation and eventual substitution of humans.

In the cockpit of an airplane in blind approach on autopilot, i.e. steered by a machine, the instruments are nevertheless still controlled by human hand. It is foreseeable, however, that even these instruments might soon be controlled by a machine that would read them, react, and programme them, etc. Such an intelligent device, capable of real-time reaction, could replace humans. Such a blind cockpit, an independent, self-sufficient flying machine would be an automaton, taking off, flying, and touching down automatically and on its own. Of course such autopilots are devoid of consciousness; nevertheless, the more perfect the machine, the less need is there for humans. Lewis Mumford already foresaw this when he wrote in *Technology and Civilization:* "The machine eliminates human performance, which amounts to paralysis."

As this parable shows, the more perfect the machine, the more it will exceed man in its very perfection, because we must define perfection as "perfection of what?" Of human properties, to be precise. We want machines because they perform more reliably, longer, stronger, and more exactly than human beings. The machine perfects human properties to such an extent as to replace humans or the partial activity of man. However, such perfection from simulation outdoing humans will lead to a reverse situation, where humans will simulate the machine. In their perfect simulation and anthropomorphism, things become independent, self-sufficient, autonomous. Similar to goods behaving as if they were imbued with a life of their own, machines behave like Golems, as if they had their own spirit and mind. Because of this new sovereignty machines step into a new relation to humans, and humans to machine, occasionally becoming their slave.

The Evolution of the Machine:
Concerning the Spirit of Machines, and Machines of the Mind

In his utopian novel *Erewhon*, a backward reading of the word *nowhere* (1872), Samuel Butler already recognised these problematic relationships between man and machine. "Is it man's eyes, or is it the big seeing-engine which has revealed to us the existence of worlds beyond worlds into infinity? . . . And take man's vaunted power of calculation—have we not engines which can do all manner of sums more quickly and correctly than we can? . . . In fact, wherever precision is required man flies to the machine at once, as far preferable to himself . . . May not man himself become a sort of parasite upon the machines?"

Because of their very precision man seems to almost take refuge in the machine. The machine is preferable to man in many aspects. In the end man becomes the machine's parasite.

Out of these considerations Butler develops an evolutionary theory of the machine. Machines themselves develop through evolution, similarly to Darwin's evolution of the species through survival of the fittest. These proposals, whose author has been forgotten, are of particular relevance especially today, in view of the work of Gotthard Günther, Hans Moravec, Gerald M. Edelman, Daniel Hillis, and others.

Neural Darwinism

G. E. Edelman, winner of the 1972 Nobel Prize for medicine, devised a new theory for the functioning of the brain and neuronal systems in his book *Neural Darwinism*, the theory of neuronal group selection. As already implied in the title, this amounts to a qualified application of Darwin's evolutionary theory to the nervous system.[2] According to this theory the nervous system in each individual operates as a selective system corresponding to selective mechanisms in nature, but using different mechanics. The categorisation of various stimuli to the senses is shown to be a dynamic process of re-categorisation.

Heuristic grounds have led Edelman to design an automaton that integrates parts of this theory of selection into the physical structure of an operational, self-organising network. This perceptive

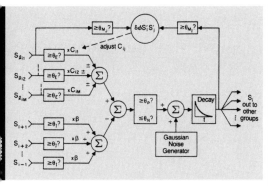

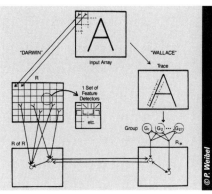

Figure 1. Logical structure of a group in Darwin II. All the repertoires in the automaton are made by connecting together groups that have a common logical structure, as summarized in figure 2.

Figure 2. Simplified construction plan for Darwin II.

© P. Weibel

automaton he aptly names Darwin II. Along interconnections (synapses) within the network, groups signal their activities to other groups. Parallel networks with several sub-networks in parallel operation are also possible. The second network is named "Wallace," after another main figure in evolutionary theory.

The Darwin network reacts primarily to individual stimuli, making individual selections in its categorisation, whereas Wallace would react to objects as part of a group, employing statistical means in its categorisation. Together, they constitute a classifying couple.

Darwinism in Computer Programming

Whilst Edelman's approach to the problem is based on an examination of real effects, the computer scientist Daniel Hillis uses simulation. In 1983 his enterprise Thinking Machines Corporation constructed the parallel computer "Connection Machine" where "thousands of programmes compete in a sort of evolutionary process" (Hillis) in order to find the best solution to a given problem. A kind of umpire-programme chooses the most suitable version of software during the process. These selected variants meet in a second round. Through this principle of "survival of the fittest" the programmes develop themselves ever further—following a Darwinist principle of evolution—in order to eventually "perform in exactly the manner we wish them to" (Hillis).

Edelman's idea of dynamic re-categorisation of sensual stimuli had already been suggested in broad outline in 1949 by the Canadian neurophysicist Donald Hebb, in his book *Organisation of Behavior:* "The more active the two neurons," i.e. the greater the number of signals exchanged between them, the more they stimulate each other, "the stronger will any connection between them develop." This would mean that our brain alters the cabling of its physical structure slightly with each new experience.[3]

Ralph Linsker of the IBM Watson Research Lab has demonstrated this ability of a neutral network to shape its connection lines in response to experience in the simulation of a neural network.[4]

Mental Machines and Neural Networks

I think that the computer
is a spiritual machine.
Umberto Eco

Linsker is only one of many, many scientists who are trying to drive at the complex way of functioning of the human brain by means of a "Connectionism" that can sensibly complement incomplete patterns through these neural networks, which are able to learn by themselves and to set up associations.[5] Terry Sejnowski, whose NETalk computer working with a huge number of interconnected artificial neurons is learning how to read a written text aloud, says that the neural network theory in fact "provides a new language by which scientists from various fields can talk about the brain and the spirit."

Both sides, neuroscientists applying findings from computer technology, and computer scientists following theories from neuroscientific research, have thus formulated a new theory that has created a new generation of artificial brain, of computer, which I would care to call Hypermaton (instead of automaton). Amongst these neural network revolutionaries we also have to count Jim Anderson who began research twenty years ago, and John Hoppfield, who first made public the term "neural network" by applying them in the construction of machines. Others are the neurobiologist Gary Lynch, the philosopher Patricia Churchland, the linguists George Lakoff and Geoffrey Hinton, and particularly David Rumelhart and Jay McClelland, who together edited the standard work in three volumes about neural networks, where they also devised new models for such networks and the necessary new mathematics for their formation.[6]

Hypermatons and Postbiological Life

After research into artificial intelligence we have thus begun to set up a science of postbiological, artificial life. This science is trying to find "the ghost in the machine," to discover the origins of spontaneous formation of molecules and networks of nerves, of how we see, learn, talk, think, perceive, and recognise—how the seemingly blind principle of natural selection could bring forth such variety and beauty in life, and how we may simulate and artificially recreate such evolution.

Ch. G. Langton, editor of the book *Artificial Life* (1989), is convinced that "an era of evolution is drawing to a close and another one is beginning." However, this first era of evolution is drawing to a close and another one is beginning. The process of evolution has led—in us—to "watches" which understand what makes them "tick," which are beginning to tinker around with their own mechanisms, and which will soon have mastered the "clockwork" technology necessary to construe watches of their own design. The Blind Watchmaker has produced seeing watches, and these "watches" have seen enough to become watchmakers themselves. Their vision, however, is extremely limited, so much so that perhaps they should be referred to as nearsighted watchmakers.

The process of biological evolution has yielded genotypes that code for phenotypes capable of manipulating their own genotypes directly: copying them, altering them, or creating new ones altogether in the case of Artificial Life. By the middle of this century, humankind had acquired the power to extinguish life on Earth. By the middle of the next century, we will be able to create it.[7]

The mutual manipulation and creation of genotype and phenotype closely follows my proposition of the mutual simulation of human and machine as a natural result of evolution.

Such a perspective would further reiterate Butler's assessment of the parasitical symbiosis between man and machine, or rather the elimination of man by the machine.

The Machines Rebel

Hans Moravec, director of the Mobile Robot Laboratory at the Carnegie Mellon University, envisages such a radical scenario for the "future of machine/man intelligence" in his book *Mind Children*.[8]

In chapter four he is asking almost identical questions to Butler when he says in the first two sentences, "what happens when ever-cheaper machines can replace humans in any situation? Indeed, what will I do when a computer can write this book, or do my research better than I?" (p. 100). His answer is similar to Butler's, that intelligent machines are threatening our existence. "We will simply be outclassed." Over the next century machines will become as complex as us, and we will be proud to see them proclaim themselves as our descendants. Already, an indication for the current complexity of machines lies in the term "user-friendly." Too complicated for our simple minds to operate, they have to be designed to be user-friendly, i.e. their complexity threshold must be lowered. In a competitive spiral over billions of years our genes have tricked each other and have now devised a new secret weapon: the intelligent machine. These "children of our minds" will one day break free from us and start their own lives. The beginning of this final phase lies at the start of the industrial revolution two hundred years ago, when artificial substitutes for human bodily functions came into use. Machines became indispensable in transport, production, etc. Computing power for mechanical machines, developed recently, has multiplied by a thousand every twenty years and has brought us close to an era when no fundamental human physical or mental function will lack its artificial counterpart. As the epitome of this development the intelligent robot will construct and improve on itself, without us and without the genes that are our make-up. In evolutionary competition DNA will have lost out. Such genetic takeover by the machine will radically alter our culture. (A. G. Cairns-Smith, *Seven Clues to the Origin of Life,* 1985.)

Although we are still living organisms completely defined by our genes we can already only function within our culture by relying on information which is not handed down by our genes generation after generation, but rather on information that is being produced and stored outside our genes. The next step will be that we as human beings will no longer be necessary for the machine, nor—one day—for the world. Without our help intelligent machines will then be capable of their own upkeep, development, and reproduction, our culture will progress independently from human biology: the genetic takeover complete. The foundation of a postbiological world dominated by self-developing, learning, and thinking machines ignorant of the limitations of the mortal human body would ensue. Cybernetics, artificial intelligence, and robotronics are only the first indicators for such a third era in evolution, intelligent robots after animal and human life. According to Moravec our own future survival and that of our civilisation is already dependent on a rapid development of such machines, particularly for space research and colonisation. Perhaps these intelligent robots will render quite unnecessary our own sojourns in space that may be so much more difficult and billions more expensive. And one day they will emigrate into the universe, leaving us behind in a cloud of dust.

Similar thoughts were espoused by K. Eric Drexler in his book *Engines of Destruction* (Anchor/Doubleday). Microbots, robots that reproduce in microscopic essence, based on integrated circuits miniature technology which is partially adapted to genetic mechanisms, would have an eternal life-span and take on quite specific tasks.

Moravec has set out a chart mapping computational power (speed at which calculations are carried out) and computational capacity (storage capability) in an evolution of the computing machine.

Formal Limitations for Mental Machines?

This impressive chart must not, however delude us over the formal limitations expressed in the parable at our beginning, and in the famous Church-Turing Hypothesis as well as in Gödel's findings and in Turing's trials.

We know that Gödel formally demonstrated that not all parameters of a formal system could actually be proven in that system, and were thus formally doubtful. From this we might derive that the computer as a formal system—anything that can be formalised may be mechanised—cannot solve all the equations for this world. It follows that not everything can be calculated, formalised, and mechanised within the formal system of the computer. Gödel himself took an ambivalent stance in his own conclusion, nevertheless leaning towards an nonalgorithmic interpretation of the nature of human thought. Thought is not mechanical, therefore the mind will always be superior to the machine. He does, however, emphasise that the digital analogy between computer and mind—that both operate on digital principles—has to be accepted. Taken further, this proposition would limit the extent of possible simulation of human capabilities by machines. Gödel's findings are advanced further in the Church-Turing Hypothesis that narrows computability down to only those functions calculable on a Turing Machine; as Church showed, this applies only to the class of function he calls recursive function. Only what can be calculated can be expressed in formulae, could be mechanised. However, calculable is only what can, in effect, be calculated recursively. This would consist of a descending order for the extent of the possibilities for a digitalisation of the mind.

Applied to our problem, the quest would have to be for a similar theorem limiting simulation. Can simulations be reduced equally to comparatively effective calculations like that of the Turing Machine? Does the digital dream of pure numerical depiction and calculation of all processes of human life, or at least the human brain, simply end in the formal limitations set by Gödel's, Turing's, and Church's findings? If the computer cannot solve all functions of the world and every mathematical equation, how should it then perfectly simulate the mind?

Gödel, of course, has placed the importance of his theorem for such a question firmly in perspective, leaving a platonic way out.

In his famous 1950 essay "Computing Machinery and Intelligence" Turing asked the question "can machines think?," surprisingly answering it affirmatively in his operative argument of what is now known as Turing's Test.[9] He stipulated that a computer will think when its answers become indistinguishable from those by a real human being. A person is placed in front of a wall and poses a question; he does not know beforehand which of the written answers appearing on a video screen are given by a computer or another person. The computer will win the test if that person is unable to detect which answers came from the computer and which ones from the human respondent. In the mid-sixties K. M. Colby so successfully simulated a psychoanalyst by computer that many patients preferred the latter.

Survival by Simulation

Going back to our initial parable, simulation is successful when it removes the difference between humans and machine. However, it does not automatically follow that this renders the former superfluous, but rather it would no longer make sense to differentiate between the two, as in a really perfect and comprehensive simulation of human by machine, they would in fact operate alike. No longer would we know whether we dealt with a machine or a human being. There will not be any difference, therefore we shall no longer make any; it will be pointless to be talking of human versus machine. Even Gödel envisaged a nondigital computer one day to defy any limiting theorema; only then will we no longer recognise the computer. Humans can then either operate below machine capacity, as in the fable, in order to regain their identity, or they can begin to simulate the computer. Man in perfect simulation to supersede the perfection of his own creation which improved on the simulation of his own kind—Husserl would define this as the transcendent in immanence. This is why at the beginning of this essay I have said that the simulation of man by the machine will reach a height of perfection that will lead humankind to try to emulate precisely such a level of perfection through simulation of the machine. When man begins to simulate properties of his own products, then there

Peter Weibel *Virtual Worlds: The Emperor's New Bodies*

is a danger that the social characteristics of these manmade products will suddenly be mistaken as naturally inherent in such products. Marx defined this process as reification, the objectification of a subject and its state of being. This tendency to universally objectify one's existence, treating all human intercourse and activities as commodified goods, has its origins in barter trade and finds its extension in the mechanised world. Goods with their fetish-character represent the prototype for objectification. "The mysterious qualities inherent in goods lies simply in the fact that the objectified characteristics of the products of man's work are a reflection of the social characteristics of human labour thrown back at man in the socially natural properties of these goods." Marx continues about manmade products in a commodified world: "Here the products of the human mind seem imbued with a life of their own, independent figures relating to each other and to mankind. This is what I call fetishism which the products of labour acquire as soon as they become a marketable commodity; this fetishism is thus inseparable from production."[10] What Marx has said about consumer goods of course applies even more to robots. Machines even more than the production of goods reduce humans to marketable commodities, machines imbued with a double fetishism as goods themselves and through reification, as the omnipresent fetishism of a motor car, a television set, or a computer. Robots are precise products of the human mind with a life of their own, independent creatures. Do intelligent machines with their double appeal to consumer fetishism, then represent the end in alienation? Certainly intelligent robots epitomise Hegel's "alienated spirit." However, he also writes in his *Phenomenology of the Spirit* (1807), from which AI would have much to learn, "the existence of this world and the reality of consciousness rely on that movement which it extorts from its personality, creating its own world so alien that it must now be reappropriated. But the renunciation of being is in itself the creation of truth through which that truth may be acquired."[11] The realm of reality can only be created through self-extortion and subjective alienation. Moravec thus quite rightly calls robotmachines, as such products of the self-alienated mind, "mind children." "Although springing forth from individuality," the real world is "like an alien entity to the conscious." But this is how "the coming into being of the real world" takes place.[12] Machines and tools in simulation of human organs and activities, self-extorted from humans, are contributing to the construction and evolution of the world.

According to Hegel the simulation of simulation in a kind of recursive cycle where man simulates those products that simulate himself provides a model for the creation of reality. It is thus primarily simulation which questions Darwin's theory of evolution in its tautological essence contained in the dictum of survival of the fittest. This term is determined by survival in an Aristotelian sense, art obscure entelechsis. However, it is not fact that arises from fact in evolution, it is rather models that transform into facts which then become simulated models providing once more the source for facts. In truth evolution consists of a full interactive network of mutual simulations, representing an existence perforated by simulation. Ideological qualities are already part of nature, and mimicry as an instance of adjustment to a dynamically changing environment would be clear evidence for such a state. The meaning of the term *mimicry* has to be reconsidered in this context. A plant producing yellow dots on its leaves to repel insects who have been taught by experience and genetic information that such dots would contain a poisonous substance represents a successful instance of simulation helping to survive. If these insects detect such simulation after a while and readapt (obtaining new genetic information) to nevertheless sit on that plant (now perhaps themselves acquiring yellow dots as protection from other insects), then the plant will again be compelled to change. This would describe a chain of adaptations to a series of dynamic simulations. Survival of the fittest therefore amounts to survival of the fittest simulation.

This in essence is the gist of our initial parable. The evolution of man and machine represents a new evolutionary phase, where the existing model is being restructured through a re-accentuation and redefinition of its preeminent elements. Such mutual evolution of man and machine through simulation will, of course, result in the formation of a totally artificial, simulated world. (Viz. also Jean Baudrillard, the "Penseur" of simulation.) Survival of the fittest simulation also entails survival of the simulation of the fittest, humans designing reading, interpreting machines, capable of acquiring learning, from whom they in turn will learn. This structure can counteract the digital dreamers' (in a Hegelian sense) numerical fetishism that is comparable to consumer fetishism. Even in nature the fabric of reality is perforated by the spirit of alienation where mere animals create tools of de-expression and thus their own truth. The machine revolution only renders obvious the fact that reality has always depended on artificial, virtual construction.

The Consciousness of Machines

One much ridiculed thinker in the Hegelian tradition, Gotthard Günther, published his first revolutionary work *The Consciousness of Machines* (1957) which has assumed new relevance for our discussion.[13] (This followed his exposé on the "Basics of a new Theory of Thought in Hegel's Logic" in his dissertation in 1933.) Dismissing naive linear Pythagorean principles ("All is number") he developed a keno-grammar (*kenos*, Greek "empty") based on the premise of the void as the basic structural component in mathematics and logic which can be taken up by any random coefficient. The Arabic *sifr* (German *Ziffer*, English *digit*) means empty or zero. From this he derived a complex non-linear Pythagorism, an arithmetic theory where numbers do not progress in linear fashion but may rather verge off the line randomly. In his theory of polycontextuality he also had to give up the logic of the power of two. Such a third option of a multifarious kind of logic of course rejects the whole concept of alternate thought in terms of true or false. The ambivalent logic of existence is given up in favour of a value-added logic that guarantees open options in formalism catering for a constant extension in complexity. Thus multifarious, non-linear logic, together with the structural context of the theory of polytexturality where ambivalent logic may still be valid, serve to explain the infinite variety of material qualities in this world. Quantity transformed into quality denies a model for the universe that consisted of a closed unified contexture. Thus Günther is anticipating the ideas of eternity in parallel universes in quantum mechanics that were to appear later (viz. David Deutsch) in 1957. It is this polyvalent logic of reflection pitted against the purely linear and ambivalently formalised and mechanised digital computer that anticipated the development of parallel computers and neural networks. Günther's polycontextual, polylinear, and polyvalent logic could be of benefit in the organisation and conceptualisation of further such networks.

Günther also has an answer to the problem posed by our parable. Following Hegel, man and machine may always be differentiated because the subject changes with the evolution of the machine; in its expression in the machine it is split in two, losing its former identity. Depositing a mere mechanised, formalised form of its consciousness in the artifact the subject advances into hitherto unattained depths or heights of awareness. The human spirit will always remain superior to the machine (viz. also Gödel), as the simulating machine compels man to increased reflection in this evolutionary game of simulation. From this ensues the self-regulatory and self-reflective progress in the development of matter towards higher planes of complexity, liberating human consciousness from imprisonment in its own subjectivity, so aptly lamented in 1904 by Karl Heim and again by G. Günther in his *Global Image for the Future—Weltbild mit Zukunft*. Such a reformed subject will be possessed of a sovereignty unconstrained by biology or problems of locating identity between flesh and spirit—a subject close to the observer of quantum mechanics, a phantom if seen in relation to history, of course.

The Surrogate Body

Moravec quite rightly accepts humans improved by genetic engineering only as second-class robots; instead he is looking for a subject possessing the advantages of the machine without correspondingly losing its sense of personal identity. Already a large number of people survive with the aid of artificial organs and limbs, machines that support the body, and one day such surrogates, or simulations, will be better suited for survival than the original. Moravec then asks why not replace the lot and simply transplant the brain into a specialised robot. Such an instance is illustrated in Piet Hoenderos' film "Victim of the Brain," where the protagonist's brain is removed, stored outside the body, and a cloned version of it implanted into a computer. The subject can now switch between his two exterior brains. This would, however, not free the brain from the constraints of its limited intelligence. The question is thus no longer whether machines can think, or, put differently, can we transplant the brain into the computer much like a kidney; it must rather be as to the extent of the spirit's independence from its physical basis, the brain. Could we extract the spirit from our brain?

An initial step lies, of course, in giving up the idea of subjective identification with the physical basis of the body, transgressing the old conflict between spirit, flesh, mind, and the body. Moravec proposes "pattern-identity" as the essence of the patterns and processes taking place in both mind and body, equating it to software and not to hardware, the machine which merely supports and contains these processes.

Nor does the body-in-prosthesis, the surrogate body, provide an answer to the real problem about the phenomenon of consciousness, namely that the spirit of life is a dynamic system arriving at more than just the collective sum of its components. Such a state of virtuality will have to be examined further on.

Quantum Mechanics and Consciousness

One of the key problems lies, of course, in the physical nature of consciousness. This can best be illuminated through quantum mechanics that enable us to reconsider problems of the body-spiritual, of human identity and awareness, and also think about theories limiting formal systems and the capacity of the mind. It is quantum mechanics that threaten most acutely that premise in the digital dream that wants to express and calculate everything in numbers. G. Günther, by extending the theory of numbers, has tried to ban such danger, however, at the same time preformulating quantum-mechanical conditions albeit expressed in a traditional dialectic.

Should quantum theory really be a universal physical theory, then the spirit and brain are undoubtedly quantum-mechanical phenomena. A leading advocate of this opinion is the eminent physician and mathematician Roger Penrose, who, together with Stephen Hawking invented substantial parts of such a new cosmology. Starting out in opposition to the thesis that "everything is a digital computer," "everything can be modeled exactly through digital calculations," he felt the illegitimacy of the underlying argument declaring the human brain and spirit to be nothing but a digital computer. He also had to contest the notion traditionally arising from the above about the insignificance of hardware in mental phenomena.

Instead the evolution of the brain is seen as exploitation of quantum-mechanical effects, and consciousness itself as a quantum-mechanical phenomenon.[14] Although indeed conceding the algorithmic nature of some of the brain's activities, he finds himself unable to imagine the complex algorithms of the human brain as simply the result of a "natural selection" of algorithms. Penrose deduces that even quantum mechanics are insufficient to describe the activities and structure of the human spirit, which would in fact require laws more fundamental than quantum mechanics. Therefore there seem to be facets of the human spirit that can never be simulated by a machine.[15]

If the brain is not a digital computer, could it be a quantum computer? Let us try to transfer the game of survival by simulation onto the computer, as David Deutsch did in 1985.[16] The concept of a quantum computer is based on principles of the Turing machine. No one has as yet managed to build a quantum computer, nor do we know if this could be possible, but there are some remarkable preconditions.

As the Turing machine is a serial computer not only limited by the halting problem but also by the complexity theory, we could hope that such limitations would be remedied by the addition of a few parallel computers, which indeed they might be. However, a quantum computer with its own complexity theory differing from that of the Turing machine could of course avoid such limitations. The question arising in the simulation of a universal quantum computer through a universal Turing machine is whether the quantum computer can actually calculate functions that the Turing machine cannot do, which would invalidate the above mentioned Church-Turing theorem. Deutsch has nevertheless demonstrated that the number of functions calculable on a quantum computer amounts to exactly the number of Church's recursive functions that can be done on the Turing machine. Yet, there are tasks beyond the mere calculation of functions. In quantum parallelism, for example, the number of tasks that can be performed at the same time is no longer limited, the advantage being that whilst any classic computer or Turing machine programme could run on the quantum computer, by no means could any quantum programme operate on a Turing machine.

Deutsch does believe that quantum computers will be constructed one day, and their existence will provide powerful proof for the interpretation of quantum mechanics as an infinity of parallel universes. A quantum computer's behaviour can be expressed in terms of its delegation of suboperations to copies of itself in other universes.

The Oxford philosopher Michael Lockwood has advanced Penrose's ideas, that quantum correlations occurring over wide distances could be responsible for the unity and globality of the states of awareness in the human brain (as highly coherent quantum states). In his book *Mind, Brain and the Quantum* he defines "the compound I,"[17] using the physician H. Fröhlich's 1968 discovery that the quantum mechanical phenomenon of the Bose condensation can be applied to biological systems. Condensed Bose states can be seen as responsible for the coherence of biological systems, and useful for the amplification of weak signals, and the codification of information in minute space.

I. N. Marshall in 1989 espoused the thesis that Bose condensed states provided the physical basis for mental states such as the unity of Consciousness.[18] Lockwood then deduces that the singularity of the human mind derives from precisely such Bose condensed states, should the brain really operate as a quantum computer.

Indeterminate Thought

The real threat to the digital dream emanates from the role of the observer in quantum mechanics and in its indeterminate principle. What happens when we observe a physical system? The contention offered in conventional interpretations of the "problem of measurement" is that the actual observation influences the observed system at the moment of contemplation, that there is an interactive relationship between observer and the object. Another interpretation tells us that we invariably lose something in observation. Yet unobserved events pass all the time, and the principle of indeterminability quite clearly causes loss of realisation in observation; there is no certainty which possibility the next successive moment will chose, as the paradoxical mental experiment of "Schrödinger's Cat" will illustrate.

Lockwood has elaborated on this indeterminism to ask if the "ghost" is to be found in "the machine" of the body, or if it in fact needs no machine, body, or any specific machine or body. Or is the spirit perhaps pure software, pure mathematical abstraction, whether with or without optional hardware? Neither question could be answered positively; instead Lockwood concentrated on setting up a new interdependence, based in quantum mechanics, between spirit and brain, and consciousness and the physical world. At the heart of the quantum mechanical "observation and measurement problem" lies the question of "how consciousness (specifically the consciousness of the observer) fits into, or maps onto, the physical world." The physical state of the observing brain is undergoing a stream of observant experiences, i.e. a stream of consciousness designated by and emanating from the brain, that yet at the same time has to participate in the properties of the set of observables selected. Only shared properties between the brain and the chosen set of observables may be designated as conscious observation. Lockwood's Theorem can be taken to mean that something in the physical quantum mechanical state of the observed entity has to correspond to the quantum mechanical state in some part of the brain of the observer, in order to be registered consciously. Very simply then, something approaching the spirit or a state of consciousness has to be already inherent in objects or machines. Consciousness, observable, and observer simulate each other and transfer properties onto each other. Thus the quantum mechanical formulation of the measuring problem in terms of the observer's participation in the system under observation must be a question of conscious projection, looking for those components of human consciousness inherent in the "consciousness" of the very objects themselves. Human interference in the world cannot go against the will of the objects therein, and as the world is the only one we can recognise, we only select objects from it which we can detect with our senses, objects that are in fact detected by certain properties in our senses and that therefore must be corresponding reciprocally to any such properties. Goethe put it that "the eye is of a sunny disposition," and it is this that we term anthropomorphous, as "theory of naturalised cognition" to use W. v. O. Quine's words.

Compenetration of Matter and Spirit

I am indebted to the great chaos scientist Otto E. Rössler for pointing out to me that as early as 1763 Roger Joseph Boscovich formulated such a theorem in all its consequences in his *Theoria philosophiae naturalis*.[19] Boscovich defines his law of a sole driving force as a common principle of co-variance, according to which the universe has to be described in relation to the observer, and that even motions within the observer contribute to its transformation.

The Boscovich curve illustrating his thesis depicts an asymptotic branch, according to which our universe would be a self-contained, closed, cosmic system. This would mean that no point outside that universe could come into contact with us, which opens up the possibility of infinite space filled with cosmic systems that cannot interfere with each other. Not even a ghost wandering around such a system could recognise any universe other than the one in which he exists. This actually amounts to a premonition of the quantum mechanical "many worlds" interpretation, where space is infinite, but can only be recognised as finite. Thus writes Boscovich in his supplement # II "Of Time and Space, as We Know Them": "We cannot obtain an absolute knowledge of local modes of existence; nor yet of absolute distances of magnitudes."[20] Should the universe commence to revolve in another direction or contract or expand, we would be unaware of it. His early theory of relativity also already encompasses the "measurement problem," "what has been said with regard to measurement of space, without difficulty can be applied to time; in this also we have no definite constant measurement."[21]

Consciousness cannot simply be subtracted from the world of matter; even Kant's absolute terminology—*a priori*, beyond our experience of time and space—is being put into perspective, "as we know it." Consciousness itself is no absolute category a priori. Boscovich defines this mutual relationship between awareness and the physical world with the complicated idea of "compenetration" and the coexistence of points of matter in time. Consciousness derives from the compenetration of matter and spirit, as their designated process. His doctrine of impenetrability has acquired somewhat infamous renown. "Matter is composed of perfectly indivisible, nonextended, discrete points," which he axiomatically qualifies in that "two points of matter cannot be at the same point in space at the same point in time." His critics tend to overlook what he says later: "To the infinite number of possible points of matter there will correspond an infinite number of possible modes of existence. But also to any one point of matter there will correspond the infinite possible modes of existing, which are all the possible positions of that point." Thus "any point of matter has its own imaginary space, immovable, infinite and continuous." "Every point of matter is possessed of the whole of imaginary space and time; the nature of compenetration."[22]

Virtual Space as Psychotic Space

This imaginary space is virtual space, virtual reality takes place in Boscovich space. If indeed two bodies cannot be perceived sensually in the same point in space at the same point in time in the real world, this may nevertheless be achieved in virtual space. With the aid of data gloves and data visors we can super-

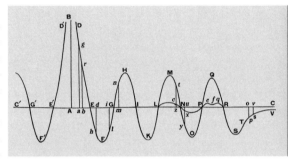

impose imaginary space onto real space, a computer-generated sphere could occupy the same space as other objects. Virtual reality is a journey into imaginary Boscovich space, where real and possible are contrived in coexistence, in compenetration. Their fascination lies in the simulated defiance of all classical laws of nature, of the tyranny of here and now, space and time conquered. Traditional spatial concepts disintegrate when I can see my own hand in simulated space, when I can observe real and imaginary objects react to my actions. This kind of space where the present and the absent may exist equally is pictorial space which, for the first time, I can actually penetrate. I have entered the picture through closed circuit television installations; Jackson Pollock had claimed to have entered his own pictorial space with subjectivity. Here, however, the visual spectrum of the spectator and pictorial space of the image intermingle, collaborate, as anything the spectator does in pictorial space he does in his real environment. The virtual environment is not the real world, not reality, but a representation of the real as artificial reality, where wish fulfillment still corresponds to reality, where interior and exterior, imagination and reality, I and other are all bridged. Myron W. Krüger defined "artificial reality" as an environment controlled by computers who register our needs and react to them.[23] Virtual worlds embody the pure essence of omnipotent experience and the pleasure principle. This is the space of the psychotic that stage-manages reality in hallucinatory wish-fulfillment, uttering the battle cry "VR everywhere." Freud, describing the aims of technology in his *Civilisation and Its Discontents* as being the creation of substitute organs and limbs that make of man the God of prosthesis, is actually illustrating the sorts of fantasies of omnipotence that simulation technology makes possible: fantasies that we can forget the trouble in life, the opposition of the object. Cyberspace is the name for such a psychotic environment, where the boundaries between wish and reality are blurred. In its worst expression the VR movement will remain an infantile toy, at its best a tool in space travel technology where teleportation beaming people from one star to another could be rendered from mere S/F via concepts of VR into reality.[24]

Digital Data-ism

"In the beginning there was the number" must, so to speak, initiate any digital dream. The first digital thinker was, of course, Pythagoras, who first set up the philosophical circumspection according to which numbers are the omnipresence behind all structures for any phenomena, and numerical relations are the benefactors of harmony. Plato similarly preached digital harmony, leaving an indelible mark on Western civilisation. Our yearning for perfect harmony led us to the golden rule, the divine measure of proportion in the arts and architecture of antiquity, and in its renaissance that bore in Leonardo da Vinci yet another digital dreamer. It was the French philosopher Descartes who first formulated the digital dream as science in his pretensions at elevating mathematical method onto the plane of becoming the universal scientific methodology: *mathesis universalis*. The digital dream lies in the claim of Pythagorean/Platonic metaphysics that the entire world can be depicted in numbers and numerical relations. It is interesting to think that a simulated Descartes could just as logically deduce his existence as could the real Descartes. Simulation threatening the digital dream is in itself a manifestation of that dream.

The end of the digital dream is the fully comprehensive enumerability of the world into mathematics, in fact a "mathematisation" of the world. The astronomer Johannes Kepler, who lived and worked in Linz, and who is the subject of this year's Ars Electronica 90, was also such a digital dreamer when he published his *Harmonices Mundi* in 1619, a key exponent of digital harmony, the harmony of the world based in number.

The philosopher and mathematician Leibniz succeeded at a decisive breakthrough a century later when he developed the theory of binary numbers, the binary code, the depiction of all numbers in just two digits, zero and one, void and material presence, to be or not to be. What seemed at the time a mere curiosity became the central basis for modem computer technology. In fact, by setting up the facility for the depiction of all numbers in just the two digits 0 and 1, Leibniz formed the basis for the technological realisation of the digital dream. He had tried to replace logical deduction through calculation, i.e. logic through mathematics, amounting to the displacement of thought by a machine that would automatically provide proof with the aid of those two digits. Two centuries later Leibniz's discovery has been transformed into an algebraic switchboard, a logical network based on networks of electric currents, technical machines where the digits "0" or "1" are indicators for the absence or presence of a flow of electrical current: in short, digital technology, electronic calculating machines, digital computers. The calculator has always been the companion of digital dreamers, and it was a close associate of Kepler, Wilhelm Schickard of Tübingen, who invented the first known computer. Thus the computer represents the current peak in the embodiment of the digital dream which would like to see the world as a cosmos of numbers, to be simulated and reconstructed from the laws of number.

Digital harmonies, calculators, virtual machinery all emanate from one and the same human dream, to transform nature into a humane environment that can be controlled by man with the aid of number and its law—to tame the terror of the elements, to be able to predict and contain the forces of nature. Here lies the base for the gradual creation of a new world by man alone, an artificial reality seemingly more favourable than (hostile) nature.

Attempts at anticipating such artificial realities in computer-controlled machine worlds that react intelligently to our needs will provide the focus for the 1990 Ars Electronica. Data glove, data suit, data visor, data banks are all an indication for a new world. Data-ism for Dada-ism. Digital credo, beginning with Pythagoras, for the time being has doubtless reached its height of perfection in today's computer technology.

In the land of hypermedia and hypermata virtual machines represent a new generation of automaton. Human interaction with three-dimensional cybermodels in a near-world (virtual world) is probably an improved form of human-machine interaction and simulation, and so far is the most perfect simulation. The anthropomorphisation of the object has attained new perfection, as has their in- and self-dependence as intelligent virtual machines. Heidegger would, of course, see his worst fears of technology displacing nature and the body corporal confirmed in VR.

The body doubled and part-imagined in Virtual Reality (VR) as the most recent possibility in its technological transformation may indeed represent its deposition, yet also entails its improvement; I may now comport myself without danger to limb and body in zones perilous to the natural body. The I, the state of conscious awareness, will need less of the physical body; VR will drain the conscious mind "I" of limb and nature. Through its technological deterritorialisation in VR the subjective has been raised into a new category of *res extensa,* of points in space and time, now immaterialising in the virtual infinite.

Consciousness, in the course of evolution through survival of the fittest, has created simulation, and through the simulation of survival ever more complex models and media, the legendary ghost in the machine creating ever improved machines for itself. Consciousness as the driving force behind evolution also creates the simulation of consciousness. Reality is perforated with simulation, with strategies of semblance and deceit, founded precisely in those mechanisms of selection I have described when I cited mimicry as an instance of adaptoral strategy. It is in such simulations that the "ghost in the machine" of Lockwood's Bose condensations is to be located.

Digital Machines—the End of the Digital Dream?

This argument would actually be corroborated by Ch. G. Langton's definition of virtuality in the book *Artificial Life* that appeared under his editorship. To him "virtual particles" are the real molecules of life as their characteristics would appear neither in the system, nor in the particles themselves, but only in mutual interaction. A system becomes virtual when its part-components and its entity display their marked characteristics not in isolation, but only at the moment of their mating (compenetration, as Boscovich would say). Such virtual systems are non-linear and dynamic, alive. The spirit is a virtual system in the machine of the physical body, body operating in spirit, and spirit in body. Now we may understand what the attempt to surgically remove the spirit from the body would entail, it is impossible—according to Boscovich ("every point of matter is possessed of the whole of imaginary space"), according to quantum theory and virtuality. At this point it would perhaps be fitting to qualify my stipulations to say that simulation would correspond more closely to mechanical systems whereas virtuality would seem to be corresponding to dynamic, non-linear systems. In actual fact we were talking about virtuality when we discussed simulation in the context of evolutionary theory; the essence of simulation is virtuality. Thus a clock is basically a mechanical system that nevertheless displays hints of virtual characteristics. In its functional essence a clock will only exist in the action of its movement powered by some external source of energy, but a hand remains a hand no matter whether the clock lies "dead" or "lives." Equally the body in prosthesis in its classic function would represent such a mechanical system in its essentially unchanging nature; it and its component parts do not lose their identity in a split expression, remaining forever the base sum of their parts.

The computer would display a number of virtual characteristics. As digital automaton it embodies nature translated into a different language which then gradually introduces us into the state of virtuality. This machine is a-changing, its hardware, its body, has changed and will continue to change. Nevertheless, its defining essence, the binary code, will remain fixed. Unlike in the clock, however, it is the programme that is more important in the computer, its language the algorithm, more important than the messenger, the body, the machine itself. The computer would evidently contain more of a "spirit" than the clock. The body may become its own clone to the extent of its binary self-codation and decodation, decoding distance. Perhaps the body is the quantum computer in whose construction we have so far failed. After all, the body, just like the quantum computer which sends copies of itself into other universes, now sends copies of itself into other, virtual, worlds. The computer is in fact a simulative prosthetic body hinting at potential virtuality in the coexistence of limb and spirit. However, as long as it remains just a body in prosthesis, a mechanical body, it will lack true life force, lacking in virtuality.

We have thus reached a situation with computers on the one hand that simulate in essence the "spirit" of the brain, and robots that simulate the "life" of the body. Will it be possible to mix the two, unite body and spirit? Well, yes, albeit only through virtuality.

Virtual machines may be seen as occupying a stop along the way from the "thinking" to the "living" machine. Not only would the living machine have to be virtual, but should there forever be a difference between man and machine, it also would be immune against simulation. But, if everything could be artificially calculated, depicted, and reconstructed in binary code as stipulated in the digital dream, then everything could be simulated.

I have argued primarily in terms of quantum physics that the digital dream cannot hold universally true. My main argument must, however, be the theory of simulation itself. AIDS has demonstrated that the perfect virus is the one that is immune against simulation. Thesis # 1: The highest level of simulation lies in attaining immunity from simulation itself. (A copy without original, a clone without body.) This used to be expressed *in principio individuationis*. So, how could a "living" machine that would have to perfectly simulate humans from a digital basis be effected, when we take it that humans represent the end in a chain of evolution of survival of the fittest simulation? Applying thesis # 1, humans would be immune from full simulation; they cannot be comprehensively simulated by a (digital) machine. Secondly, I put it that life is a condition of virtuality. Virtuality, however, is defined not as a property inherent in the very objects, machines, parts, or systems which themselves can be simulated, but rather as a property pertaining only in the act of correlation of all particles. Per definition precisely this correlation cannot be simulated. Because of virtuality not everything can be simulated, least of all simulated digitally. So far the virus is the best virtual machine, or as William S. Burroughs says, "language is a virus of outer space."[25] Language would therefore provide an instance of a virtual system in our context. On the one hand it seems to function like a mechanical clockwork movement in a determined system consisting of 26 elements (letters), embedded in a determined algorithmical structure (grammar), which some are of the opinion is nothing more than a programmed succession of variants, combinations, and permutations. In no way could the literary output of mankind over the last 2,000 years have been achieved in this manner, not even in eternity. The production of a mass of sensible text by means beyond the mechanical capacity of language as a combination of text elements invalidates the view of language as a kind of system of natural selection of algorithms. More than a mere mechanical system it manages to set up combinations of its elements more speedily and more sensibly than any mechanics. Is this the spiritual quality of the mind? This elusive spirit is not to be found in the machine, nor in the machinery of language, nor in grammar, but in that part of the brain where these predetermined and finite elements and algorithms are transformed into an infinite, undetermined succession of sensible sentences. Such an essence of virtuality originates only in the dynamic play of the elements of the mechanical system that is language, embedded in a nonmechanistic brain—it is then that language "lives."

Virtual Machines

After Cybernetics, AI, and robotics, virtual machines are the last expression of the digital dream, terminating it at the same time.[26] A computer such as Terry Sejnowski's NETalk that teaches itself to read aloud a written text is cannily close to a talking person, the simulation (of neural networks) seems perfect, similarly the result. Will virtual machines become the main protagonists in a global process that reduces the human to a mere spectator and parasite? A perfect technical mimesis or simulation so far advanced that it would replace the real world by an artificial creation where humans would tend to self-abstraction as mere observers. We have seen the consequences of such perfect simulation in our parable, human as simulator of the machine, as empty torso, easy prey to myth and other such power-crazed programmers of reality who hold forth the promise once more of totality and authenticity.

However these worlds are controlled, calculated and designed worlds are called virtual worlds not because they imitate nature, but because they digitally simulate an image of delusion. They are simulations, computer or cybermodels for imaginary worlds which comply with the laws of logic and physics, and yet seemingly defy these laws in the creation of imaginary space where anything is possible. Virtual worlds are illusionary worlds, three-dimensional nearworlds based on digital technology. Virtual artificial realities do represent alternative realities, information space containing imaginary objects in dimensions of space and time that can be manipulated directly or from a distance. Objects in virtual reality react to humans, they can be manipulated by the spectator. At the flick of the spectator's head objects depicted in digital simulation may change their proportion or perspective, humans in fact integrating with the fiction of their imagination as conjured up digitally by the computer. It is this alternative reality that makes virtual worlds more than merely the simulations of artificial digital truths.

Because the spectator himself is an emphatic part of the image in such an artificial reality, empowered with the illusion of his own body acting as clone in front of his field of vision, and because he may yet simultaneously control the imaginary objects from outside the virtual world, he is putting into perspective the universality of the digital dream, as, naturally, the spectator as the creator of such virtual worlds cannot himself be digitalised. It would be pointless to employ a machine as manipulator in the virtual world as anything appearing in his data visor would be digital simulation, no matter whether the object existed externally in front of him or would be generated internally through the visor. For the machine both real and generated object appear simultaneously in the visor.

Virtuality, where simulation, imagination, and reality are mutually transgressive, is psychotic space and yet residually non-digitalisable. The role of the spectator using the bridge across the real and simulated represents the quantum mechanical constraints on the digital dream; virtual worlds exist at the borderline between digital dream and quantum mechanics, evoking an environment controlled and created by computer, but reacting to human needs and ideas. Now, if all were calculable it would follow that all must be predetermined. Thus we arrive at the ensuing alternatives: the simulation of imagination by virtual machines can mean either its determination, or determination opened up to the imagination. Chaos theory and quantum physics seem to suggest an indeterminable spiritual cosmos. The digital arts emanating from the cosmology of number are also a link between digital finality and infinite imagination, defending man in his impossibility to be simulated. They would serve not to denigrate but to research and appropriate anything digital so that we may express ourselves of it. Artistic creativity supported by machine therefore would not represent a contradiction in terms, just as postbiological life wouldn't. Both are far removed from something like a quality of the spiritual. Digitalised artistic creativity in an expert system towards the creation of art will one day be possible and such an algorithm will produce works of art equal to "real" art, which in fact only reiterates the invalidity of art so far, mechanical and lacking in spiritual dimension. This calls for the remedy in the aesthetic of the virtual, mechanised creativity and the automaton will rid us of a lot of dirt. Technology as enlightenment of man researching himself?

Virtual machines provide the spirit with new bodies, packaging it in tele-bodies and tele-organs, setting the scene for what Moravec has called "ejecting the spirit from the body." The emperor, the spirit of the mind, is now fitted out with new bodies, neither by transplant, nor by genetic engineering or robotics, but by equipping it with new artificial "organs-in-prosthesis," namely with virtual machines like data glove, etc. These tele-organs make man into the Freudian god of prothesis, or tele-deity, a god of tele-presence instead of omnipresence. Virtual machines create the tele-body and thus represent the emperor's, the spirit's, new bodies.

Notes

1. In Jean Baudrillard, *Das Ding und das Ich* (Vienna: Europaverlag, 1974).

2. Gerald M. Edelman, *Neural Darwinism* (Oxford: Oxford University Press, 1989).

3. D. O. Hebb, *The Organization of Behavior* (New York: Wiley, 1949).

4. Ralph Linsker, *Self-Organization in a Perceptual Network* (Mirz: Computer, 1988).

5. See William F. [?], ed., *Menschliches Denken, Künstliche Intelligenz. Von der Gehirnforschung zur nächsten Computergeneration* (Munich: Droemer Knaur, 1990).

6. D. Rumelhart and J. McClelland, eds., *Parallel Distributed Processing: Explorations in the Microstructure of Cognition*, 3 vols. (Cambridge: MIT Press, 1986).

7. Ch. G. Langton, ed., *Artificial Life* (Reading, Mass.: Addison-Wesley, 1989), p. 43.

8. Hans P. Moravec, *Mind Children: The Future of Robot and Human Intelligence* (Cambridge: Harvard University Press, 1988).

9. A. M. Turing, "Computing Machinery and Intelligence," *Mind*, no. 236 (1959), 1950.

10. Karl Marx, *Das Kapital* (Berlin: Dietz, 1926), pp. 86, 87.

11. G. W. F. Hegel, *Phenomenologie des Geistes* (Tübingen: Suhrkamp, 1986), p. 363.

12. Ibid., p. 365.

13. Gotthard Günther, *Das Bewusstsein der Maschinen* (Baden-Baden: Agis, 1957).

14. Roger Penrose, "Minds, Machines and Mathematics," in: C. Blackmore and S. Greenfield eds., *Mindwaves* (Oxford: B. Blackwell, 1987), pp. 259–276.

15. Roger Penrose, *The Emperor's New Mind: Concerning Computers, Minds and Laws for Physics* (Oxford: Oxford University Press, 1989).

16. David Deutsch, "Quantum Theory, the Church-Turing Principle and the Universal Quantum Computer," *Proceedings of the Royal Society of London*, A 400, pp. 97–117.

17. Michael Lockwood, *Mind, Brain and the Quantum* (Oxford: B. Blackwell, 1989).

18. I. N. Marshall, "Consciousness and Bose-Einstein Condensates," *New Ideas in Psychology*, 7 (1989), pp. 73–83.

19. R. J. Boscovich, *A Theory of Natural Philosophy* (Cambridge: MIT Press, 1966). See also Otto E. Rössler's paper "Boscovich Covariance."

20. Boscovich, p. 203.

21. Ibid., p. 204.

22. Ibid., p. 199.

23. Myron W. Krueger, *Artificial Reality* (Reading, Mass.: Addison Wesley, 1983).

24. Two anthologies, Bruce Sterling, ed., *Mirrorshades* (London: Paladin, 1988), and Rudy Rucker, P. L. Wilson, and R. A. Wilson, eds., *Semiotext(e) SF* (New York: Semiotext(e), 1989), offer prominent examples of the new science fiction movement of cyberspace and cyberpunk.

25. Cited in Bernhard Mitterauer, *Architektonik. Entwurf einer Metaphysik der Machbarkeit* (Vienna: Brandstätter, 1989).

26. See the important work "Machines virtuelles," *Traverses* 44–45 (September 1988), Centre Georges Pompidou, Paris.

Cybermedia and the
Fatal Attraction of Realities

Bilwet / Adilkno / Filwis

Don't want, don't want, don't want to be part of your world.
David Byrne

"Away with the cameras! Away with the cameras! Sit! Down!" A lively band from Surinam danced on the balcony of the city theatre awaiting the arrival of Nelson Mandela. He was to address the 15,000 residents of Amsterdam who had flocked by. However, the musicians remained invisible as a battery of (white) press cameras was standing directly in front of them, killing time. This accordingly gave rise to irritation. As the news came that the "King of Africa" had entered the building, "the media" gathered round the microphone in the centre of the balcony. It became clear to the crowd that they wouldn't see this either and they began to scan. Spontaneously the cries of "cameras beat it" changed into angry chants of "Down with TV." This was a variant of "Down with ME!" (ME = mobiele Eenheid, the Dutch Flying Squad which is generally sent into action during riots), the picture hunters being compared to the police task force. The diffuse anti-media unease that had already been prevalent for some years with a public that had been throttled for a decade to become insignificant decor or just as insignificant consumers, changed to regard the cynical media agents as having taken over the role of the task force, depriving the masses of their happening. "The media" have declared themselves increasingly for the happening and gradually took over the field with all their technical prosthesis. The real masses in the square in front of the city theatre had become just as imaginary to the pressmen as the viewers at home, who were just as indifferent to them. "The masses of the people" feared they would only see the backs of some media men although they knew that Mandela had come for them, and the happening had not been intended to be an open-air press conference. The journalists sensed that it would only be a matter of time before the first stones hit their high-tech and withdrew from a meter-and-a-half-wide media-free zone. Then the "Royalty in Exile" appeared in the press-free zone and had a good look around to see who all had come to him. He noticed that there were still thousands of people at the side of the balcony, standing there applauding and he forced his way through the cameras to welcome them, too.

    Unlike all the pop stars, football teams, queens, and politicians who use the crowds for their PR, Mandela did not make a dash straight for the microphone, but took time to meet the masses. He, too, cast "the media" aside for the happening. All at once it became very still, and contrary to expectation, Mandela did not just reel off a number but dared in the simplicity of it all to embark on a dialogue with those present to make the purpose of ANC clear. After about half an hour he finished talking with the words, "We respect you, we thank you, and above all, we love you." We had never heard that from "the media" before.

The media anticipate being faced with a battle of life and death in the coming age of digital interfaces. The 0/1 bit principle could even have a yes/no analogy. Two staggering scenarios manifest themselves: If we say "yes" to the media then we emigrate to Cyberspace, we leave the hardware of our bodies, and consciousness is entered in software. If we say "no" then we select the "exit to reality" and the media will end up as a household article or as a museum art like a vacuum cleaner and wickerwork peasant's basket.

The scale and the frequency of anti-media incidents are increasing daily but they are carefully set aside in the press or are not termed as such. Not one newspaper mentioned the above-mentioned attack on the unfriendly conduct of the media towards the public. Nevertheless, the contours of an international-scale "anti-media" movement are being outlined. The motto is that in order to meet someone at all, several connections have to be interrupted first of all. The habit of ripping a telephone box apart before going to bed, or short-circuiting a switch cabinet or pouring concrete into a meter, taking video cameras from crossroads or cutting through street cables is no longer sensational. This jointly divided art of living, which originates from do-it-yourself aid and which is set on simple pleasure is not yet beyond the stage of local disturbance. However, when the "uplinks" to the "global village" are capped en masse it is evident that many more earthly beings will use their media-free time for other things. Viewers have enjoyed years of being thoroughly blunted by television, but that, too, becomes boring.

The plea for educational TV with justifiable broadcasts really does discourage them. Research has shown that the television viewing rate has "decreased alarmingly" of late. Even those remaining groups who still have a TV at home deny making use of it. The aversion of admitting to being a consumer leads to the reply we hear from alcoholics: "Me and drinking?" "The few shows cannot be termed watching television."

The "media caste" moves exclusively within permanent actuality, as it considers it to be their social task to avert the danger of a sudden comeback of history. For this purpose it rids all happenings of their origin and consequence by producing items with no connection and consequence. It is also aware that once the masses regain their ability to act, "the media" itself will be their first victim. "The media" was formerly an exception. The impressiveness of live moon landing pictures was due to the fact that the likes of this had never been seen before: the whole world was switched on to the fascination of sitting at home and being able to leave earth. The promise of being able to leave the unbearable inertia of life, of being able to definitely penetrate the technological universe by speeding weightlessly from one place to the other seemed to have materialized.

Two decades later viewers became aware of what this actually meant. By turning everything into information, "the media" is capable of leveling every happening to the same pictures (all the Dutch media compared the Mandela speech to cheering the national football team). As "the media" is omnipresent, space has lost its content and can be filled with pictures from somewhere else without being something else. The only context of the place that can be seen, is the following item. The media goggles have become identical with the touristic experience of "here today, gone tomorrow." It is not necessary to confront oneself with something else, there are infos about it. "Why should we converse with one another when we can communicate so well?" The others have become obstacles or objects about which you can discover interesting characteristics. And when they become boring, you just go on.

Now reality is the exception. The media men are vaguely aware that it represents a risky temptation. Psychically they can interpret this as a romantic feeling they once had every now and again during their certain "moments." Or they can dismiss the cry for reality as nostalgia or the fear of technology. The attack on the media will, without doubt, be denounced as being the undemocratic behaviour of vandals and the disinterest as being an alarming development which can be countered with information. But the aversion to the "goggle box" is nothing more than the expression of the general human need for "outside" where one can make "experiences of one's own." Reality is regarded as being the domain of the unforeseeable and that no longer corresponds to the wonders of technology. The moral values of the anti-media movement (respect, gratitude, love?) can prevent their aversion from going so far as to definitely destroy the media. The media just have to confine themselves a little. The anti-media movement could allocate the channels of information a place in the machinery of daily life and not bother about it any more.

Now that "the media" know they have been cornered, their response is such as to suck their consumers into the screen once and for all: cyberspace "the medium to end all media." The rumour about the "new space" which is circulating the real existing global village charges current research with enormous expectations of unbounded possibilities. The cyberspace epic has already been written by a certain William Gibson. The video kids nervously keep watch at the door of their arcades and the military eagerly experiment with the total interface between body and machine. Old hippies don data jackets and gloves to personally make their Eastern dream of uninhibited trips into universal consciousness come true without the former withdrawal symptoms. And finally there are the video artists with their aesthetic morals, who want to keep the new cyber experience vacant to prevent it from being filled with banality. It cannot be gathered from the early works of these pioneers, to what extent cyberspace will remain a private experience in the near future, or will be the virtual vehicle of hypercommunication between cosmopolites. "Cybermedia" is the synonym for this public space which is under construction.

In the cybermedia the distance between subject and object, which presented so many difficulties for the old media, has been eliminated. All the reflecting about this and criticising on the place of self in the world and the singsong about an imaginary reality which cannot be found again in pictures, must finally come to an end. The purist narrow-mindedness which endeavours to strictly separate human and virtual reality is banished by the explorers of cyberspace to the prehistory of political metaphysics. This old-fashioned need to draw lines is replaced by a democratic view of reality: if it doesn't appeal to someone, look at them through cybergoggles and it looks entirely different.

The twentieth century media have not been able to meet their promise of the "global village" as being a place of maximum mobility. The anticipated uprooting of all earthly beings by progressive medialisation was regarded as being a part of the inescapable process of human progress. By creating a global infrastructure in which everyone can involve himself, every region should ultimately reach the escalator of history moving in the direction of prosperity and convenient life by themselves. Even now, technical progress consists of the construction of a set of ideologically neutral networks and measures: from cable networks, motorways, and (air) ports to processing waste, the mobility of work forces, raw materials, goods, and information. These transregional structures could hang over traditions and nationalities like a cloud. The media idea was that by transcending local identities these would disappear by themselves, or, should this not be the case, would become uninteresting from a global perspective within infrastructural developments. The function of the regions in this planning setup is as suppliers of cultural raw materials for a varied program. If regions do not (cannot) participate, they are entered on the list of written off areas, and will remain futile voices in the wilderness of information.

Yet, the media have never produced an internationalizing effect; on the contrary they have proven themselves to be a means of consolidating local conditions. With universal communications, everyone can remain in his or her own place. Not everyone has succeeded in getting to know his own environment and habits as a tourist. More and more regions (Middle East, Soviet regions, China) are beginning to interfere as jamming stations in the project of transnationalization. Old media such as religions stubbornly retain their own absolute values and cause a rumpus in the Family of Men. They simply do not want to comprehend that we are all living in one world (did they miss the broadcast of the moon landing?). They will learn this lesson yet, when it becomes apparent that their local atomic war leaves the rest of the world quite cold. Their catastrophes are not ours.

Cybermedia represents the end station in the concept of global network. It sets course for perfecting the infrastructure with the compelling motto: "A system or no system." It is their dream to accommodate all media spaces in the cyberspace house. Until now humankind has pottered about in small rooms but now there is the possibility of surveying it all and establishing contacts. In future we will be able to easily change over from all radio programs, films, archives, and libraries to all kinds of private conversations, teleconferences, and teleshops, the world over.

The perpetual singsong of former realities which have served to frustrate the project of modernization for a century is capped by being replaced once and for all by a new principle of reality. In cybermedia all "formats" of language, time, territory, identities such as sex, race, or life style, environment, health, and age are converted into the universal 0/1 code. Switch on means being everything, everywhere. The desire, originating from former grey times, to leave the mortal body is combined with just as old a desire to have a communicative community of pure people, free from domination. World peace is effected on an abstract level where playing a little game of war can only mean falling behind. In a historical sense, cyberspace is probably still traceable from war as the father of all things, but in practice, in the genealogy of technology, the fateful transfer of genetic material has also become fatal for this father. Similarly, SDI had been planned as the climax of the cold war; however, to the dismay of the military-industrial complex, it brought about its abrupt end.

The threats surrounding the realm of cybermedia freedom are legion. On the one hand there are the unconvincible dissidents who—in groups—want to impose their "format" on the data flows within the world empire of infrastructure. They regard the disappearance of time/space differences as a possibility to impose their will directly on consumers.

On the other hand, ominous subjects appear which penetrate their own loneliness and the joint consensus by running amok in cyberspace. They stab blindly with their electronic daggers at chance passersby. But dangers are also lurking from within. Corporations, as Gibson has already pointed out, create new bounds for their data buildings and apparently may even be able to place the entire cyberspace under their control—an exclusivity which undermines the democratic intention and which provokes acts of opposition which have written the total accessibility on their flag. Furthermore, the electro-atmosphere can choke up in no time with the increasing volume of data waste, dilapidated environments, noises whirring around, virtual billboards which are set up along the data flow, spontaneous crashes by overload, or lack of computing capacity. Cyberspace also permits repressive and therapeutic applications which probe the belief in value-free communication.

People ask us: "Does this cybermedia have a perspective?" Artistic and popular/scientific journals create smoke signals to make the introduction of cyberware as attractive as possible. Laymen who did not previously check out won't get any further than the question of technology. The more advanced get tied up in the question of ethics. They hope for a widespread social discussion about the safety of the new media and the disposal of the old media. Consciousness should not suffer any permanent damage from the latest psychedelica. And NGOs like "save the TV" demand guarantees that the media keeping their distance must remain. The doubters are of the opinion that cyberspace—just like Star Wars—is technically possible but practically, it will remain in the simulation phase. To be able to introduce it on a global scale like the telephone or the TV, would call for such an investment in hardware and software that all the entire production capacity would have to be withdrawn from civil consumption.

They expect cyberspace never to get past the level of private consciousness and that it will end as a hyperindividual kermis attraction comparable to the *Orgonkasten*, dream machine and megabrain. The neomaterialists draw attention to the limits of communication. They claim that we have had nothing to say to each other for so long and that we do not want to meet anyone, not even in cyberspace. The other can be consumed easily without involving any contact. Media convey something but fail to emit anything. One has contact with a real piece of steel or concrete without the obligation of input or exchange which is inherent in cybermedia. The visionists only give orders prophesying that the cyber project will become one of the ruins of the post-industrial overestimation of its own capacities. They do not mean this in a negative sense. They regard the failure of the megachip as a challenge for the artist to actualize the ruin-aesthetics with the written-off electronics.

To pacify this interpretation rage, the cyber philosophers refer back to an intellectual concept which has been valued highly for centuries: the Hegel structure of *Aufhebung*. The difference between the virtual, formerly known as the "spirit" or the "imaginary," and reality presented as the absolute principle is reconciled in the simple advertising slogan "virtual reality." The magnetism of this logogram could turn out to be a bitter disappointment. Particularly among the anti-medialists there is a significant rejection of the entire marketing idea. They consider cyberspace only to be a real increase in the number of media and reject the critics as being nothing more than a secondary murmur which merely belongs to the introductory phase of a new product. The assurance that the contents of cyberspace simply consists of all the previous media makes them indifferent to the promise of a "new mythical space." They could accept a completely animated arsenal of pictures, as cameras could then disappear from the public eye. But cybermedia should become much more than a 3-D video game and their craving for pictures will continue to force them to leave the studios and to nourish themselves on extramural street picture material.

The cybermedia charm is the naivete with which it approaches the world.

It feels that artistic fascination is sufficient to obliterate reality. The world continues to withdraw from its own terminal. This does not disturb reality in the slightest. It is aware of the very human need for the illusionary and waits until this has passed again. However, the question is, can the anti-media movement also be as patient?

The Future Merging of Science, Art, and Psychology

1. Reason and Intuition

One day, walking through the laboratory, I met a colleague and asked about the course he was teaching. "I got into some trouble today," the professor said. "What I was explaining seemed so obvious that I couldn't see why the students couldn't understand it. I've taught this subject so many times that I can't remember which parts are hard." What do people mean when they say that certain conclusions are logical while others are intuitive? Are these really different types of thought? It seems to me that the differences lie less in the styles of thought themselves than in the degree to which we understand how they work. For, in general, we're least aware of what our minds do best. We can usually explain, in much detail, how we perform a mathematical calculation or procedure; this is because we already know how to describe it in terms of its simpler parts and relationships.

But we're speechless when asked to explain how we speak, or how we hear or how we see. Clearly, these accomplishments of everyday life involve immensely intricate brain machines—yet to us they proceed with no effort at all. What makes such complex processes seem so simple to us?

To the computer programmer, one possible answer seems obvious: that our most practiced and most "commonsense" skills must be just the ones that we have converted or precompiled into procedures and scripts that can be executed unconsciously. It is only when those systems fail that we start to engage the special types of procedures and memory systems that comprise what we call "consciousness." Thus, we're more aware of processes that don't work well than of those that tend to work flawlessly. This means that we cannot trust our offhand judgments about which things we do are simple, and which engage complex machinery. This must apply equally to artists and scientists. All experts accumulate towers of skills, building new ones on top of older ones. At every stage we become novices again, finding new goals (and hence, new obstacles) and then seeking ways to deal with them. But as we develop each layer of skill, we revise and refine the layers below, to make them work more efficiently, more quickly and automatically, and with fewer intrusions on consciousness. Thus as we grow in mastery, our highest-level processes grow further and further away from the earliest machinery—and it becomes increasingly difficult for those higher-level systems to detect, discover, or describe how their lower-level systems work.

The more we improve our mental skills, the less we know about how they work. A novice must deliberately consider every step and consciously keep track of what goes on, perhaps by using elaborate tree-structured representations. But the process of becoming an expert includes learning how to replace those clumsy but thoughtful procedures with more smoothly working script-like structures, and to substitute habit-like, direct connections for those elaborate representations based on complicated directories, pointers, and cross-references. Then the new, more streamlined procedures rely less on thoughtful (and painful) analysis and more on automatic processes. This leads to the seeming paradox: a novice may not perform very well, but can better explain what was done, while a master seems better to "know what to do" but knows less about how it is actually done.

Then analysis seems superfluous, and the technique that works seems "obvious." I often hear such performances attributed to intuition—that is, to aspects of mind that cannot be explained. And indeed, no matter that this idea may be basically wrong, it helps us to restrain ourselves from trying to

Marvin Minsky

understand ourselves. We usually work most efficiently when not distracted by self-analysis, which tends to disrupt all those craft-bearing scripts. What happens when you attempt to observe your own mind at work? At the very least, this must divert some of the precious short-term memory that otherwise could be used for the task at hand. And it should be even worse if you succeed at successfully probing into those towers of fine-tuned processes—and transiently replacing them by clumsy simulations. This surely should render you awkward and uncomfortable—and make you fear loss of your mastery.

But I suspect that thinkers must suffer in order to grow, and those quick-working scripts can restrict that growth, for they tend to become inflexible. Each unthinking skill, eventually, may close off possibilities. To escape that narrowing of range, one must learn to enjoy the pain of retreat and force oneself to experiment. Each novel way to wield brush or bow must make you feel ungainly at first—and force you to suffer for hours and days. But eventually the new techniques will refine and compile—until once again you can't tell what is "hard," and performance then becomes painless again.

My book *Mentopolis: The Society of Mind* takes a more contrapuntal view of pleasure, pain, and suffering, in which the pain of growth is seen as largely an illusion because, at the same time, other parts of the mind may silently rejoice at the experience of learning and development. On the other side, the sense that an intense pleasure is generally satisfying may be equally illusory, when it comes from some smaller fragment of the mind having seized control, depriving all the other mind-parts of opportunities to achieve their goals.

2. Goal and Description

What do artists try to do? Some seek to influence other minds by communicating views or ideas, or inducing moods or attitudes. Other artists are less concerned with specific impositions, and more with trying to help others to free themselves from old habits and presumptions, so that they can find new concepts within themselves, or novel ways of seeing things. In any case, the artist wants to have some effect on the viewer's mind. Now, sometimes the artist knows just what to do, and starts with some more or less well-formed sketch. But, usually, when you compose, your own objectives are growing, too; perhaps you begin with little more than some cluster of conditions and requirements. Then your situation might be better described in terms of a search than an image, because your goal is to find or construct something that satisfies those requirements. From this point of view, the artist's pursuit is no different from that of other seekers: one must propose tentative solutions, examine them for virtues and deficiencies, and proceed to change, adjust, and refine them in accord with one's current goals.

But is it proper to think of an artist as a problem solver with goals? Certainly, some artists dislike to describe themselves that way. But this is not good evidence, because artists are people—and people, in general, find it hard to acknowledge (or even recognize) their deepest goals. As Freud observed, our most basic motives are often the ones of which we are least aware. Furthermore—and Freud did not emphasize this—to express or describe what happens inside the mind is itself an extremely difficult problem; indeed, great depicters of mental activity are as rare as great composers, painters, or architects.

No matter what one's purposes, perhaps the most powerful methods of human thought are those that help us find new kinds of representations. Why is this so important? Because each new representation suggests a new way of understanding—and if you understand something only one way, then you scarcely understand it at all. Perhaps this is why the arts so often precede the flowerings of culture. For what, indeed, is Art itself but the Science of discovering new ways to represent things?

We can see this operating in the difference between producing a particular work of art, and developing what we call a distinctive and coherent style. This happens when an artist invents, not merely a new description of some particular thing, but a new kind of representation—a new type of viewpoint or way to describe. And once this happens, the artist's experience undergoes change: the audience may see the performance as art, perhaps intricate and mysterious. But the artist soon comes to regard it, instead, as an obvious, natural way to proceed. It is something that he now knows how to do—though he may be unable to say it in words.

Then what distinguishes an artist from any other kind of scientist, craftsman, or specialist? Sometimes, surely, nothing at all. And, sometimes, simply, a lack of constraint. (An engineer's engine has to run, but not an artist's depiction.) But, in my view, what characterizes many artists is quite the opposite: they seem impelled to accomplish, simultaneously, impossibly many incongruous goals!

I recall an engine in one of Diego Rivera's murals that must have been intended to affect many sides of the viewer's mind: to convey a constellation of statements and attitudes about the workers (and about their attitudes) concerning the engine, the ambient technology, the factory environment, and their relations with other inhabitants of that institution. So many things to say at once. Thus, while a scientist or engineer usually confronts a certain fixed set of clearly defined requirements, an artist entertains more goals at once than ever can be satisfied—and therefore also must face yet another kind of problem, too: which goals to pursue or abandon?

3. Scientific Understanding of Expressive Art

In ancient times, the visual arts were confined to rather static modes, such as painting and sculpture. But in the past century, the art of animation emerged and has steadily grown in popularity. If not for its enormous cost, it might have become the dominant form in many domains such as entertainment, education, and technical exposition. In recent years we have gained access to powerful yet inexpensive graphic engines—yet animation is still too expensive for casual use, because programming it is still very hard. And this has produced a typically modern predicament. As soon as they sensed the promise of being released from the limitations of the old technology, the artistic community—and particularly, animators and musicians—faced bondage to a new and demanding god. They felt obliged to make themselves more technical, in order to invent the science they would need to foster their art.

In older times, a painter had only to cover a single canvas. But to make a five-minute film, an animator must produce nine thousand frames. How to paint so many scenes? The work is reduced if one can reuse what already appeared in earlier frames; this can be done with technology that enables the artist to work in terms of differences—by using interpolation, "in-betweening," mathematical interpolation functions, and other ways to generate scenes. But still there are many new problems to solve. How to make a person walk—that is, saunter or stroll or strut or stride? How to make a person throw—or toss or hurl or heave or fling? It seems incredible how well some artist-painters of those older static forms succeeded in expressing such things. What are the tricks those artists used to produce such compelling illusions—and what new tricks could animators use?

In the past generation, many workers have devoted themselves to these matters—of how to adapt computers to the purposes of artistic expression. We ought to acknowledge the sacrifice made by a generation of potential artists in order to accomplish this! How often so many of us complained, in those pioneering decades, that "these new electronic synthesizers sound too mechanical" or that "computer art is elegant but lifeless." Of course there would be deficiencies in the early forms of such radically new technologies and tools, and their languages and idioms. We ought to thank, not ridicule, the generosity with which so many potential masters—both in music and in art—unselfishly renounced the joys of artistic composition to endure the pains of evolving our new instruments and programming techniques. Of course, we could regard the instruments themselves as instances of new forms of art.

But perhaps we are approaching new ways to understand art itself! Consider that, in earlier times, the working of the human mind was an almost total mystery. The science of psychology itself is only now a century old, and computer science only half of that. Surely, in the next hundred years, the twin enterprises of cognitive psychology and artificial intelligence will reveal a great deal more about how minds work. Thus, in the past, we had no choice but merely to appreciate and celebrate when certain individuals mastered new secret skills of expression—no matter that they could not explain them. But, it seems to me, this must change, as the world increasingly accepts the products of the works of art whose production is partly or wholly based on computational processes. For then the audiences will feel increasingly concerned with such questions as "What mechanisms or technical procedure produced that expression?" and "Why did that expression have such an effect upon me, my mind, and my emotion?" and, finally, "What kind of mechanism or procedures must exist within myself, in order that effect or experience could be produced?"

What I mean by this is that the "mechanization" of artistic production must eventually and relentlessly lead us to become involved with these new kinds of personal concerns. On the creative or productive side our artists, in order to program their new machines, will be virtually compelled to formulate, in more conscious detail than ever before, what it is that they want to produce.

And equally, on the receptive side, the audience will be forced to confront those questions about what makes them react. Thus, from both sides, this brings us back to the initial confrontation of this essay—namely, that paradoxical recognition that the things that seems to us most "obvious" are often the hardest ones to explain. We have needed to have that same experience, from the earliest days of research in artificial intelligence. Some of the very first such computer programs were able to solve problems that people considered to be very hard—yet even today our programs are unable to manage most "commonsense" human activities.

Why was it easier, historically, to construct seemingly "expert" computer programs than to make progress in the domain of "common sense"? One reason is that those technical domains frequently are actually simpler in nature. For example, a fundamental domain of mathematics or logic may be based on only a handful of assumptions and rules of inference—whereas the art of cleaning a house requires many kinds of knowledge about a great many different kinds of objects and situations. Another reason is that many "technical" subjects have already evolved powerful, specialized artificial languages and notations—whereas we have few such well-developed languages for activities that common people do! This is perfectly natural, since no person ever needs to precisely describe the things that everyone learns in childhood. (Everyone knows how to walk, or to laugh, or to distinguish the differences between cats and dogs—so no one ever needs to be told how to do it.)

But we cannot exploit any such common experience when we want our machines to help us express such things—for example, when we want to use a computer to assist us with making animated pictures. This is because the initially empty random access memories of our computers know nothing about commonsense human affairs—about people's emotions, motives, goals, frustrations, and joys; or about the systems that control the motions and actions of the human body.

What would be the ideal technology for an ambitious animator? Imagine being able to present your machine with a screenplay and a storyboard—and have it generate the film. To do this, the filmmaker wants to control not only what the animated actors do and say, but also the intended effect on the viewer's mind—that is, to evoke a certain sequence of ideas, attitudes, feelings, and emotions. Now we certainly cannot expect software to help with this, unless it has access to knowledge about rendering physical forms, motions, and actions. But in order to induce the desired subjective reactions, our machines must also be equipped with descriptions and models of human feelings, goals, and intentions, or those simulated actors will not be able convincingly to fill in the details. But as unskilled playwrights and actors know, even that will not suffice; to produce the desired end-effects, the system must also know the elements of drama, timing, and rhetoric, because just as orchestras need conductors and theatres need directors, all kinds of good performances require coherently organized styles. In other words, the best way to produce automated animation would be to program our machines in accordance with sound psychological theories. Today, few such theories yet exist, so it remains for us to invent them, to help the machine-based animators of the future direct their simulated screen-actors in ways that express and communicate.

But what is communication? This needs a theory, too—and I maintain that in order to communicate, one person must know (at least unconsciously) how to build structures and activate processes inside another person's brain. But because we cannot reach directly inside another person's brain, we have to work through the senses. How can automation help us use sensory experience to communicate ideas and goals, attitudes and dispositions, intentions and emotions? To dependably evoke the required types of subjective reactions, the animation engines of the future must be good psychologists!

But I do not mean to emphasize only the obscure and subtle aspects of this problem. For, first, we shall have to learn how to program our computers to accomplish the simplest-seeming, most commonsense goals—for example, that you must open the box before you put things in it, or that you must grasp and turn a doorknob before you can open a door. Present-day computers do not even know simple things like that! Then, once we've accomplished that, we must learn how to communicate to the audience more about our actors' goals. All animators understand that the procedures for making actors walk need not be based on precisely realistic descriptions of human locomotion gaits. More important is knowing how to shape those envelopes and trajectories, to express or indicate the picture-actor's mental state—its disposition in regard to determination, apprehension, expectation, disappointment, enthusiasm, and so forth. It is not enough that the picture-creature grasp a certain object; the filmmaker must be able to express whether it was grasped by accident or intention, whether it was something the actor wants to possess or merely something to be moved out of the way while pursuing some more important goal.

How do we communicate such an idea?

We may be able to encode it into the trajectory itself, or in the actor's posture and apparent orientation; perhaps we can do it by focusing attention on the facial expression of the actor—or on the gestures of his antagonist. Every action has parameters to use for describing mental states. The more our machines can know about that, the more productive they can be. I do not mean to say that we need to achieve complete scientific understanding of such matters. The great animators of the past accomplished miracles with little science and technology. But those talents were deplorably rare and the costs were too large for everyday use—and, instead, we could set as our future goal the development of technologies so powerful that the next generation of children will be able to use them fluently. Why, by the way, does animation so engage children? I suspect this is in part because expressive animation simplifies the audience's work—perhaps paradoxically, by immersing them in worlds that are so symbolic and abstract that the intentions and emotions of the objects being depicted are actually easier to apprehend and manipulate than the physical shapes and forms themselves!

We started with the common belief that scientists tend to use rational thought, while artists are intuitive. Yet when I discuss these things with my friends, I often find quite the opposite. Yes, scientists tend to be conscious and deliberate when they work on the details of their subjects, but they only rarely dwell upon the question of how they get their ideas—while our artists (if they are different at all) are less concerned with performances, but tend to reflect a good deal more about how to develop their concepts and skills.

(This essay is adapted from a talk given at Nikograf 89, a computer graphics conference held in Tokyo in November 1989.)

Virtual Reality for Collective Cognitive Processing

Derrick de Kerckhove

Just as AI stands universally for artificial intelligence, virtual reality is henceforth sufficiently current as to be designated as VR. But virtual reality could just as well have been called "artificial imagination." If we take the concept to its natural, if not its farthest reaching conclusion, we shall soon find that the purpose of VR is to enable us to command technological simulations by thought alone. The link between imagination and technology goes back to ancient Greece.

From the invention of the alphabet to that of the computer, Western man has been groping towards the development of virtual realities in different guises. Ancient Greek dramatists and novelists from the Renaissance to this day have been producing virtual realities by transposing the workings of their fantasies on stage or on paper. Any novel is a virtual world, and its purpose, besides entertaining the reader, is both to train the imagination and to blueprint new lifestyles. Likewise, the contents of VR experiments are generally in line with those which make up the content of the standard literate psychology. Just as video games do not stray very far from the folklore of epic literate traditions, action-packed scenarios, promoting legendary skills and usually—but not always—heroic motives, the family-room VR will undoubtedly capitalize on archetypal characters drawn from novel, theatre, film, and TV, recapping the history of our imagination from the Grail to Madonna.

However, by itself, if it is merely used to animate passive digital environments, VR is not such a big deal. We have already developed complex simulations of 3-D objects, relationships, and movements on screen. Albeit a technical feat, 3-D television, conceptually speaking, is hardly more than walk-in television. We already do that in our shopping malls to more effect. The fundamental difference between VR and any other media experience is that it enables the user to externalize his or her imaginary skills in a dynamic process. With VR, there is an effective interaction between the dreamer and the dreamed: the dream becomes real, as if Hegel's most cherished theories of matter turning into spirit were reversed. With VR, spirit can become matter directly and have a concrete expression in the user's environment. This enables the private experience to become public and to be shared objectively with other persons. Another critical difference is touch: the VR industry is about to recap the contents of films and TV, adding one more sensory response to feed our craving for complete experience.

1. Touch

In fact, our relationship to the screen is about to change radically. VR is often compared with theatre. But theatre and VR differ significantly: in the theatre, we look into a comprehensive world from which we are personally excluded. We are outside looking in (which, by the way, is the standard response of the Western man to reality anyway). But with VR, we stand in the middle looking out.

Homo Theoreticus

Western man has developed a predominantly "frontal" attitude to the environment. The fact that, largely because of alphabetic literacy, we have let our eyes dominate our cognitive psychology makes us less sensitive to everything that is not included in the focused amphitheatre of our vision, external or internal. Within and without, we project images of ourselves as mirrors would, frontal beings staring back at our frontal beams. It has been that way since the Renaissance. Indeed our relationship to the world has been dominated by the theatrical tradition, and more specifically by theory. The word in Greek was *theoria* and it meant "something to behold," something to look at. *Theatron* too meant something to watch. Control over reality was effected by the detached point of view beholding pictures, models, and books. The point is that if you are looking into something from the outside, that thing is open to your judgement. You can take it or leave it and psychologically speaking, you remain free of feedback control. The most that can happen from such a sight is that you will be moved or change your opinion. You might even "change your mind" about a given issue, but the structure of your mind as a protected and private environment will not be affected. However, as Eric Gullichsen puts it, in cyberspace "you are an active participant in [a] world which surrounds you, not a passive observer in a world which confronts you."[1] Indeed, not only does VR technology reflect and emulate the new environmental sensibility introduced by the information age, but it also destroys the conventionally Western illusion that space is void.

A virtual "reality" is one that you can touch and feel, as well as see and hear with your real senses, not only your internal ones such as the "mind's eye" or the "mind's ear." By penetrating into the screen with the Dataglove, the real hand turns into a technical surrogate of a kind of "mind's hand," making "real" what was only visible. Before the invention of VR, nobody ever bothered to conceive of a "mind's hand." The concept did not present itself. There seemed to be no special need for "feeling" the objects we carried in our minds. In general, the tactile sensitivity of Western cultures is abysmal. Within our rather intellectual and abstract tradition, we have tended to ignore the rich learning experience derived from touch. In fact we have been terrified of touch until the sixties when television induced a collective craving for the recovery of our bodies once lost to our literate heads. After a rash of "touch-ins" and "feel-ins" spreading from California eastward, we began to settle down to a more comfortable relationship to our bodies, but we never gave touch its honoured position among our principal sensory modes. The appearance and development of VR is about to change that.

In spite of its acknowledged lower resolution and weaker sensitivity to grain and texture, the precision of touch in simulation is much greater than that of vision because it is 3-D. Sharing a vision is nowhere near as reliable when you cannot touch the object of that vision. It is worth noting that it is a woman, not a man, who is presently considered the pioneer of electronic tactility. Margaret Minsky, daughter of the well-known MIT computer expert, is developing a leading-edge "virtual texture simulator" which, along with movement, weight, and density simulation, will eventually increase the range and the depth of our tactile appreciation of objects both in and out of VR.

From Theory to Ingestion

Indeed, the story of computer simulation is one of gradual penetration into a tactile environment: from 2-D to 3-D to the rapid development of tactile and force-feedback sensations, we are being sucked into an electronic vortex, a richly textured matrix. The call of tactile technology reminds me of the myth of Ulysses' sirens, with its intensely erotic connotations. Many silly jokes are cracked about the pornographic market available to VR, thus reflecting our atavistic puritanism, but it will soon dawn on educators' minds as it has already occurred to some artists that touch may be our most important cognitive tool. Babies learn by touching, adults learn by "grasping" a situation. "Comprehending," too, is a tactile metaphor. We develop a kind of gut relationship to the things we know or need to know. What VR brings to this tendency is a means to project outward our nervous system so that the electronic extensions of our sensory mode, and especially this new electronic extension of touch, can conquer the field of investigation by swallowing it. The next metaphor of learning will be ingestion.

2. Simultaneous Shared Cognition

Among the significant differences between an internal fantasy driven by "mind-senses" and an external one responding to our physiological senses is that the latter can be shared objectively, if we accept the notion that objectivity is the condition of an external substance shared by two or more people at the same time. According to Jaron Lanier, "the essence of virtual reality is that it's shared." He proposes that VR is "the first new level of objectively shared reality available to humanity since the physical world."[2] On the other hand, cognition, otherwise known as understanding, is the total simultaneous seizure of contextual cues relevant to a given object of thought and the interplay between a self and the content of this thought and the projected consequences of this thinking. Cognition is processing Virtual Realities within the single mind, but VR technology allows many minds to collectively process cognitive material without.

"We obtain raw, direct information in the process of interacting with the situations we encounter. Rarely intensive, direct experience has the advantage of coming through the totality of our internal processes—conscious, unconscious, visceral, and mental—and is most completely tested and evaluated by our nature. Processed, digested, abstracted second-hand knowledge is often more generalized and concentrated, but usually affects us only intellectually—lacking the balance and completeness of experienced simulations . . . Although we are existing more and more in the realms of abstract, generalized concepts and principles, our roots are in direct experience on many levels, as is most of our ability to consciously and unconsciously evaluate information."[3] Scott Fisher could not have found a better way to highlight how VR could improve our cognitive abilities. And indeed, he goes on to suggest that giving people instant access to "greater than one viewpoint of a given scene [VR] allows them to synthesize a strong visual percept from many points of view; the availability of multiple points of view places an object in context and thereby animates its meaning."[4]

This, of course, was the point of Cubism, but never before have we been in a situation where several different points of view, issuing from different people, can simultaneously interact in cognition through a direct relationship to a common object of study or investigation. In the case when two people engage in creating a common VR, such as in Jaron Lanier's primitive but impressive RB2, these agents remain operative, but the effect is cognitive, reflecting the reflections of two cognitive agents. Add to such an ability the possibility of touching the object of perception and modifying it in selected ways ruled by selected routines, and you will eventually get the most powerful thinking machine ever devised by man: a think tank where the thought is the tank.

We can readily foresee situations where VR will consist of multiple sensors built on the model of sensory projections such as seeing, hearing, and feeling and beyond. At this point the VR environment will have to develop a degree of retroactive intelligence which can take any number of directions and bring them to any degree of responsiveness and complexity. Even though presently there is no way to effect other than "parallel" or "serial cognition" between users working on the same process, with the development of sophisticated groupware, VR seems to hold in store the promise of "convergent cognition." In Lanier's RB2, we can foresee a kind of mutual mind reading, the product of which would be an objective result that could be recorded and replayed for further use. We can already conceive of new directions of icon and rule-operated processing which will involve more than one person at a time. This is what I foresee as "collective cognitive processing." But, to get there, the interface technologies must come ever closer to the body and to the thought source of the users.

The Perceptual Bond

Anybody can remember the first eerie impressions of intimacy created by headphones. We have become so accustomed to our Walkmen that we may cease to notice that the sound penetrates the whole body through a space which is felt internally between the ears. Imagine a similar sensation of immediacy coming from a visual stimulation. The machine that allows for this kind of experience is already on the market: Cyberspace Corporation produces a headband-mounted eyepiece which flashes images directly onto the user's retina. The image appears to hover in the air, full-sized and exclusively for the benefit of the user. New devices, from eye-tracking and image-contact to brain-wave interfaces are moving in the general direction of immediate processing from thought to machines. Indeed, we can predict from the kind of work going into this line of technology, as well as from the kind of tools available to increase computing capacity and speed, that we will eventually have access to any mode of interface from the twinkling of an eye to just a short bout of focused attention.

The Gradual Removal of Interfaces

Gullichsen rightly observes that VR goes a very large step beyond conventional computers which are merely "interactive": "A cyberspace system is dynamic: the virtual world changes in real time, both autonomously and fluidly in response to the actions of the patron. Action is visceral, and there need be no veneer of symbolic 'interface,' since the objects in this 3-D world can be directly manipulated."[5] In the same publication, albeit rather uncritically, Luis Racionero suggests that the way of the future is to connect electronic pathways directly to our neural networks by some bionic engineering already under development.[6]

We can envisage the future of problem-solving as a VR extension of the think tank or the pow-wow. Working out a solution to a given problem will be given much amplitude by the possibility of simulating a complete environment by thought alone, but it will be even more relevant to the combined effects of several thinking subjects given a single object under consideration. Eventually we will be creating new objects instantly by thought alone, in a collaborative manner. They will be blueprints recorded for the purpose of subsequent hardware production. The industry is already experimenting with "walk-through" models of architectural and urban plans. Albeit primitive because the technology does not yet allow for instant interactive responses to sensory projections, the kind of work done at Autodesk is the first base of such developments.

Shared VR Models to Overcome Language and Culture Biases

Howard Rheingold reports that Cecil Patterson, the information systems director for the Port Authority of Seattle is thinking of exploiting VR to improve communications "between engineers, facilities planners, and potential clients, when it comes to discussing the actual physical configuration of future port facilities."[7] According to Patterson, most of the people involved in the planning stages of "multi-hundred-million-dollar plans" are Japanese, Chinese, and other who do not always fully appreciate the nuances of the English language. VR "walk-throughs" could help to resolve a number of ambiguities. It seems as if the Almighty might have had to find a new tack to stave off the construction of Babel if it had been planned on a VR processor . . .

Shared VR Models to Overcome Complexity

Many students of VR talk about its merits in allowing "architectural walk-throughs," an obvious industrial application, but Rheingold also suggests that 3-D visualization may be the only way to overcome the complexity of certain scientific/technological fields such as molecular innovation or, on the macro scale, the telecommunications web that has grown around the planet into what Xerox PARC researcher Bernardo Huberman calls "a computational membrane."[8]

3. Implications of VR for Art

VR's potential for increased creativity calls for an integrated vision even at the lowest level of simulation. "The job of the space designer is to make [the] experience [of cyberspace] seem real. Thus, the job is as artistic as it is technical, for experience is something manufactured spontaneously in the mind and senses, not something that can be built, packaged, and sold like a car or a refrigerator."[9] Several aspects of VR concern the arts. One is that VR is defined by its sensory values more than by any other. VR brings to the fore the fundamental nature of art which is grounded in aesthetics, that is, the exploration and manipulation of the senses. Luis Racionero predicts that "New arts and new senses are needed—or what is the same thing—a different program in the brain allowing a greater broadening of the senses. The first of these will come with new technology: there will be new arts, as was cinema in this century, based on genetic engineering, holograms, laser, space travel, nuclear transmutation."[10] From such considerations alone, one might think that VR is first and foremost the artist's special preserve, were it not for early business and entertainment applications already sought by amusement parks and ad men. While business stands as the watchdog, not the mother of invention, vetting and supporting only that which it feels marketable, it may be to art and to artists that we owe the most significant developments of VR. Howard Rheingold calls the effect of VR an "intuition amplifier." Even as sober a commentator as the *Wall Street Journal* has been led to acknowledge the special ability of the artistic mentality: "Several VPL employees are enterprising artists with a knack for electronics."[11] The *WSJ* names Ann Lasko, Young Harvil, and Jaron Lanier as prime examples, but it could just as well have included Scott Fisher, Eric Gullichsen, Myron Krueger, Graham Smith, William Gibson, and even Tom Zimmerman, who invented the Dataglove in his spare time only to simulate a virtual hand playing a virtual guitar.

These artists either combine an art education with "learn-as-you-go" engineering and computing skills, or team up with professional computer engineers to turn their institutions into realities. A good example of the latter is Vincent John Vincent. Vincent was originally a dancer who, feeling the urge to use a computer as his partner, asked Frank MacDougall to write the program for this purpose. The result was the Mandala, one of the most elegantly simple and efficient five interactive installations ever devised in Canada. Although the Mandala is not technically a "virtual reality machine" because it does not allow the user to penetrate the screen, it does the next best thing, which is to allow one to send one's image into the screen to perform increasingly complex interactions with sound and design modules according to protocols inspired by hypermedia research.

Another important Canadian artist-engineer, Graham Smith, is working with Jaron Lanier and the VPL engineers to add total surround real video feed to the computerized articulation of VR. Smith began as a photographer but soon added robotics to his still cameras to make total surround photographs. He moved on to video when he realized that he could adapt his intuitive robotics imagination to the full motion and instant replay capabilities of the video camera. Albeit at the prototypical stage, his "horizonscan" can already offer a full 360-degree video rendition of his environment, pro-

Derrick de Kerckhove *Virtual Reality for Collective Cognitive Processing*

vided one dons the videogoggles which open the door to VR.

One of the aspects of VR which is immediately apparent to artists, but not necessarily to the public is that, as Kevin Kelly puts it, "it has deep roots which penetrate our mind's view of the world."[12] We can begin to expect feedback effects of VR into consciousness itself. Since the time Marshall McLuhan suggested that "the medium is the message," we have begun to become aware of the fact that new media affect our cognitive processes in the long run by favoring certain routines over others. Consequently, the need to educate the public to such new possibilities is urgent. Here again, because of their constitutive missionary zeal, artists tend to take the lead.

Piero Gilardi is one of this generation's representatives of a typically Italian phenomenon, an unbroken chain of artists who go back many centuries. The succession of Gilardis since the 17th century has produced architects, painters, and sculptors. And, since the time of Andrea Gilardi, who invented and produced the first backlit glass painting in the early part of the 18th century, many among them have been inspired to use the technology of their time in original and truly inventive ways. Piero Gilardi's concept is a striking, although an expensive one. Realizing some of the implications of the role of technology in changing our world view, he has proposed to erect in Turin a huge baby doll, Ixiana 2000, as an itinerant exhibit of the world's most perfected mechanical and electronic technologies, perceived and shown as direct extensions and modifiers of our body and mind. The baby doll is a girl and her head/mind will be a theatre for virtual realities. It is by this kind of setting that the general public may quickly graduate to the understanding of the impact of media on cognition and sensation.

Art versus Technology

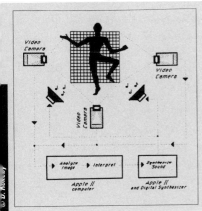

David Rokeby's array translates movement into music

However, so much of VR technology is rapidly becoming marketable that there is already a growing distinction between artists-engineers who lean more to the art than to the technical component of the association. The deeper artistic implications are the most interesting. Years before VR became the talk of the media, Toronto composer David Rokeby had perceived that the sensory essence of electronic and computer technology was touch. His prize-winning invention "Very Nervous System" stands among the first and the most satisfying virtual reality machines ever. Like Jaron Lanier, Rokeby began as a musician frustrated by the limitations of traditional instruments. To expand the possibilities of musical creation and make it instantly available to untrained practitioners, he assembled "video cameras, image processors, computers, synthesizers, and a sound system to create a space in which the movements of one's body create sound and/or music"[13] (see illustration of VNS). Unlimited virtual musical pathways can thus be explored and reproduced by the movements of a dancer. Although this kind of installation has been tried by many other artists across the world, none has succeeded to the extent that Rokeby's has in allowing the user to obtain precise and controlled effects without hampering the necessary ingredient of randomness to the experience. In spite of the fact that nothing is touched except the ambient air, Rokeby percieves his invention as an extension of touch with the musical and tonal feedback as an instant environment of texture. Says Rokeby: "Within the installation, sound has a sculptural presence, both as an extension of the body, and as a physical reality which one encounters with the body." He also describes the reactions of people while they are using the system:

"People seem to endow a sound that has a lot of texture with an external material reality, [they] find themselves imagining the feel of it against their body, imagining the space filled with sound particles. Rounder, deeper sounds seem to manifest themselves more as a presence within or an extension of the body, something of the stomach organs and muscles rather than the skin."[14]

Back in the late sixties, with his "Cortizouk," French musician Pierre Henry had already connected a synthesizer to electrodes tapping his brain wave for direct input in musical forms. The same kind of idea was proposed for brain wave control by David Rosenbaum. There are unlimited possibilities for truly artistic innovations. Jaron Lanier is fond of the idea of a virtual mirror in which the user could see metamorphoses of features and form. Another fascinating use for art would be an interactive painting, not merely such as Jeffrey Shaw's walk-in pieces, but art that would react reflexively to the various ways by which the viewer would approach it—a kind of electronic impressionism.

To take advantage of the collective processing possibilities of VR, we can imagine, for example, the creation of an environment which would reflect immediately our thermal and postural disposition and feed into the simulation effects that would combine inputs and outputs to generate cybernetic loops. The therapeutic value of a well-tuned cybernetic environment could be considerable. Lanier, who is aware of such possibilities, claims that he is sometimes concerned about the proximity of the "Virtual Reality" to mind-expanding drugs and worries about comparisons made by people who, like Timothy Leary, have used psychedelic drugs. With VR, what we will shortly be led to expect is truly psychedelic in the sense that the structure of our mind can be changed. Depending upon the dosage of sensory references, for instance, we can have an acoustically or a tactile-dominant experience of the same thing. This can alter completely our processing routines and achieve totally unexpected results. Reporting on his first experience of VR at Autodesk, John Perry Barlow, a one-time lyricist for the Grateful Dead, registers the mild confusion it created in his sense of identity: "How can you get where you want to be when you're coming from nowhere at all? And I don't seem to have a location exactly. In this pulsating new landscape, I've been reduced to a point of view. The whole subject of 'me' yawns into a chasm of interesting questions."[15]

Pascal's Two Infinites

Such questions were once raised by French philosopher Blaise Pascal when, reflecting upon the powers of imagination, recently generalized by a rapid growth of literacy, he proposed that man could engulf the universe by thought alone. Pascal's sensibility was surprisingly close to our time in that he was a poet of scale, drawing his most striking metaphors both from the infinitely small realm of molecular structures and the infinitely large domain of astrophysics. The most poetically minded of the cyberspace explorers, Jaron Lanier, reminds me of Pascal when he suggests that "the universe is your body and physics is your language."

A few months ago, I was asked to contribute a paper to a journal asking whether virtual technology would herald "a new Renaissance." My answer was no. Why would we start all over again the same old story when we had such interesting new ones to tell? Collective cognitive processing is bound to change the basis of Renaissance psychology. What we need is a sense of an expanding, flexible self, inclusive rather than exclusive, environmental rather than frontal, collaborative rather than confrontational, conscious of its bionic extensions rather than resolutely ignoring any suggestion that we are not made of flesh alone. Still, as I was researching the literature to write this paper, I came across a better answer in one among Jaron Lanier's many fanciful projects: "a giant birth canal through which you travel and are born, only to find that you are the virtual woman giving birth to yourself and are reborn again and again."[16]

Notes

1. "In the Realm of the Sensors," in: Catalogue of Art Futura 1990, Barcelona, Summer 1990, p. 82.

2. Quoted by Steve Ditlea, "Inside Artificial Reality," PC Computing, November 1989, p. 97.

3. Perkins, quoted by Scott Fisher, "Virtual Environments, Personal Simulations and Telepresence," in: Catalogue of Art Futura 1990, Barcelona, Summer 1990, p. 50. Reprinted in this volume.

4. Ibid., p. 51.

5. Ibid.

6. "It is not impossible to cause a short circuit in the process [of electro-chemical impulses] by substituting the stimulus of outer reality by a connection between the cerebral network and a computer program which sends stimuli similar to sensory perceptions." "Virtual Realities," in: Catalogue of Art Futura 1990, Barcelona, Summer 1990, p. 21.

7. "Travels in Virtual Reality," Whole Earth Review, Summer 1990, p. 85.

8. Ibid., p. 83.

9. Eric Gullichsen, "In the Realm of the Sensors," in: Catalogue of Art Futura 1990, Barcelona, Summer 1990, p. 83.

10. Ibid., p. 21.

11. G. Pascal Zachary, "Artificial Reality: Computer Simulations One Day May Provide Surreal Experiences," The Wall Street Journal, January 23, 1990, pp. A1 and A9.

12. Whole Earth Review, Summer 1990, p. 80.

13. David Rokeby, "The Harmonics of Interaction," Musicworks, 46, Spring 1990, pp. 24–26.

14. Ibid., p. 26.

15. "Being in Nothingness: Virtual Reality and the Pioneer of Cyberspace," Microtimes, January 22, 1990, p. 96.

16. Reported by Steve Ditlea, "Inside Artificial Reality," PC Computing, November 1989, p. 97.

Riding the Giant Worm to Saturn: Post-Symbolic Communication in Virtual Reality

Excerpt from an Interview with Jaron Lanier by Morgan Russell

From my point of view, the most important thing about virtual reality is "post-symbolic communication." I have not been joined by throngs of others who believe this at this point, but I expect to be any minute now.

This far in our adventure here on the planet, we have been interacting mainly within a plane that we know of as the physical world. The physical world has some interesting characteristics, the most important of which is that it is shared. Each of us has his own unique perspective and yet it is a perspective on a place that we can reliably use as a channel among ourselves. The fact that we can communicate at all in the physical world is something utterly mysterious. But, nevertheless, we do it. The physical world also has this very disturbing property, from a philosopher's point of view, of being very stubbornly "there" all the time. This is simply inexplicable, but seems reliable.

The physical world unfortunately has another property which is, that it is hard to do things in it. This is something we first learn in very early childhood. We discover, much to our intense humiliation, that not only are we forced to live inside the physical world, we are made of it and we are almost powerless in it. We are not born as Superman, able to fly around and pick up a building and turn it upside-down, as much as little children may try to act like that. We are actually extremely limited. We can't get to our parents easily, we can't get to our food easily, we need help. The earlier back into my childhood I remember, the more I remember an internal feeling of an infinite possibility for sensation and perception and form and the frustration of reconciling this with the physical world outside which was very very fixed, very dull, and very frustrating—really something like a prison. As we grow up, we sort of overcome the frustration of the physical world and call ourselves adults. We discover in early childhood what programmers in the United States would call a "hack" that we use to cope with the difficulty of doing things in the physical world. That hack is called "symbols." A symbol is basically a way of using the parts of one's body that one can move as fast as one thinks and feels to refer to the rest of the universe that one can only change more slowly, if at all. These are one's hands and mouth and tongue and to a lesser extent, the rest of one's body. By the way, my definition of "the body" is: it is the part of the world that you can use as a tool of communication, it is the part that you can change. It's possible to interpret one's activities, one's quick activities as references to all the other things that one can't do quickly. So, for instance, I move my mouth and say the sentence, "I am going to ride a giant worm to the rings of Saturn," and you can understand what I mean. But in order for me to actually genetically engineer a giant worm that could survive in a vacuum, get it out to the rings of Saturn, and have it not fall though them, and so forth, would call for considerable effort. It might take a century or more. So, the use of symbols is essentially an efficiency trick that allows us to share things that would otherwise be inaccessible because of our powerlessness in the physical world.

Now, I want to stress that this situation isn't completely negative. By using symbols we have developed a marvelous faculty. And the symbols themselves have taken on a life of their own, and are very beautiful. They are filled with poetry and puns that would not have existed had we simply been very powerful, had we been able to make these giant worms in the first place. But, nevertheless, it is interesting that virtual reality now provides us with an alternative to go back and explore what might have been, had we had that power in the universe and had developed this alternate stream of communication I call post-symbolic communication. It's not in any way opposed to symbols. That would be absurd. We have evolved to the point that our brains have grown simply in order to cope with symbols in the form of language.

The first prerequisite for post-symbolic communication is shared virtual reality. The second is an ability to create a world quickly and easily while one is in virtual reality. This ability doesn't exist yet, but I believe it will. This involves having some method that allows a person to programme a virtual world in all aspects of form and behavior as quickly as talking about it. This would yield a situation that might be described as a shared, intentional waking dream in which everything is possible and everything is relatively easy and everything is shared. This situation has simply never existed before. We have never had this interesting intersection of realities. This is a combination of the objectivity of the physical world with the unlimitedness and the uncensored content normally associated with dreams or imagination with the spontaneous composability of language.

One comment about the objectivity and sharedness of virtual reality. Virtual reality fits into exactly the same niche between people that is normally taken up by the physical world. No more, no less. So, the types of interactions that people have in the physical world are acceptable in virtual reality.

What we have in virtual reality is the ability to directly make up shared reality instead of talking about it. Instead of simply describing things you make them. You make the big worm and take it to Saturn. This is actually a very simple idea and most of the practical, commercial applications of virtual reality actually rely on exactly this idea. For instance, when an architect uses a virtual reality to show a client buildings, the client says: "Well, let's move this window over," and simply moves it. That is post-symbolic communication. They are actually in the building, and no longer relying on models or animations or specifications or blue prints. They are dealing with a direct experience not a representation of an experience. This way of communicating without representation, with actual experience itself, is for me the reason why virtual reality is important.

Endophysics—Physics from Within

Otto E. Rössler

A new science, endophysics, is introduced. Only if one is outside of a nontrivial universe is a complete description of the latter possible—as when you have it in your computer, for example. The laws that apply when you are an inside part are, in general, different (endophysics is different from exophysics). Gödel's proof is the first example, in mathematics. In physics, it is desirable to have explicit observers included in the model world. Brain models are a case in point. Macroscopic brain models, however, are non-explicit in general. Therefore, an explicit microscopic universe is introduced in terms of a formally one-dimensional Hamiltonian, in which "formal brains" can arise as explicit dissipative structures in the sense of Prigogine. The pertinent endophysics is still largely unknown. As a first step, the implications of having the observer contain indistinguishable particles (Gibbs symmetry) are considered. Campbell's postulate—a microvacillation of time's axis—is an implication, with Nelson's postulate and hence the Schrödinger equation following as corollaries. Thus a "nonlocal" internal interface is implied by a local theory. Microscopic observer properties can "percolate up" to affect the macroscopic spatio-temporal appearance of the model world. Physics becomes dependent on brain theory.

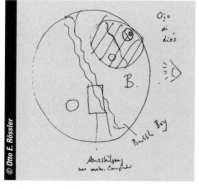

© Otto E. Rössler

Endophysics has so far been largely confined to science fiction. The best example to date is probably Simulacron Three by Galouye,[1] which for some reason was not included in Hofstadter and Dennett's anthology on computer-cognition relevant fiction.[2] Galouye lets a whole world be simulated in a computer. The operator is able to look at this world through the eyes of the "ID units"—the poor inhabitants of the world. One inhabitant, code numbered ZNO (Zeno), unfortunately has to be unprogrammed because he gets suspicious and is about to infect the rest of the community. Only later does the evidence accumulate, to his creator, that he too—but perhaps you wish to read the story for yourself. (Eventually, the two lovers, from different levels, come to live happily ever after, since, after all, there is no basic difference between two subroutines that formally belong to two different levels of nesting.)

Shortly after Gödel[3] had given his famous proof about the incompleteness (from the inside) of arithmetic, his close friend von Neumann[4] began to ponder the question of whether or not quantum mechanics might represent an analogous limitation—within a physical rather than mathematical context. Fortunately, von Neumann was able to prove that if quantum mechanics is accepted as the most basic physical theory, which contains all possible others as special cases, then there is no need to worry. The structure of quantum mechanics happens to be such that "the state of information of the observer regarding his own state" cancels out from the formalism.[5] That such a type of result is particularly likely to kindle suspicion in certain vulnerable individuals did not occur to von Neumann, since he could not possibly have read Galouye.

About half a century before, a similar physical nightmare had already haunted Maxwell (and apparently Loschmidt before him, according to Boltzmann).[6] Maxwell conjectured that there might in general exist two types of physical law. An example of the first kind would be Newton's law when applied to celestial bodies—it would make no difference whether or not you sat on one of the bodies. An example of the second kind would be Newton's (or Hamilton's) law again, but applied to the many microscopic bodies whose mechanical interactions supposedly underlie thermodynamics. Being confined to the same world here could make a significant difference. Unexpectedly, this point of Maxwell's, which was made implicitly, went unnoticed. The two famous proofs[7,8] that the demon cannot work (opening and shutting a little trap door of near-zero mass at the right moments) both do no more than show that the demon, if it is a subsystem, cannot do its job with a net gain, in case it has to go about hunting for information. The fact that a much simpler mechanism suffices (an asymmetric trapdoor of near-zero mass needs only to be cooled regularly—i.e., an infinitesimal amount of kinetic energy must be removed—to generate the same effect automatically)[9] was overlooked. This oversight is nevertheless minor since operating a near perfect cooling machine, for a single particle, presumably requires the same investment of free energy once more, from a subsystem. But what is the situation for a non-subsystem? Indeed, when sitting at the keyboard of a higher-level computer in which a Hamiltonian universe is being simulated, doing either magic trick (adjusting the tenth digit of a particular particle's position at strategic points in time, or keeping a particular particle cool automatically) will prove equally feasible.

Thus, the second law is endophysical in nature. Maxwell was right with his suspicion. So was Smoluchowski[10] some time later with his debugged version of the demon. He proposed that you try being a demon yourself: just buy one of those modern infrared-sensitive night glasses. In addition you need a bowl of water, a dark room, an ordinary spoon, and two thermos bottles, one red and one blue. Then just wait and sample, with the spoon. Since your eventual success will be the first anyhow, you need not worry about the magnitude of the effect. Any consistent effect that you are able to produce without a fancy lab (10–10 degrees) will be

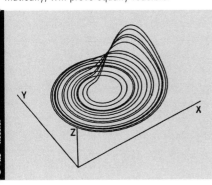

The Rössler attractor

fine. Smoluchowski realized that if you are sure that this tamed (macroscopic) version of the demon will be censored too, you as a corollary have to believe in the existence of (from the macroscopic point of view) counterintuitive nonlocal macroscopic correlations. As he died the same year he made his proposal, he was not able to tell which outcome he would abhor more. This story (even if slightly dramatized) is exceedingly hard to tell since everyone tends to get the punch line wrong. Again, you need Galouye to point out clearly where you think the answer lies.

Next comes Ehrenfest's demon—Einstein. In a letter,[11] Ehrenfest compared Einstein—in his indefatigable attempts to find a loophole in the consistency of quantum mechanics (in his exchanges with Bohr in the Ehrenfests' home)—to a little jack-in-the-box who wants to play Maxwell's demon against the quantum law. Indeed, in more recent times the quantum nonlocality[12] has taken on a similar status to Smoluchowski's earlier proposal.

Two further important names in the history of endophysics are Popper and Finkelstein. Popper talked Einstein into accepting his proof that complete self-observation is impossible in (continuous) physics, and into believing with him that one should try to find a Gödel-type formulation of quantum mechanics.[13] Finkelstein set up a program for a "holistic physics" in the spirit of the late Bohr, but discrete.[14] He hypothetically attributed both the quantum limit and the relativistic limit to the fact that the whole is not available to us. Later, he gave an explicit example of a finite-state machine (computer) whose internally evaluated state is different from that existing objectively.[15] Still later he endorsed the two notions "physics from without" and "physics from within"[16] by coining the technical terms[17] used in this chapter. The name "endophysics" is his creation.

In the same year, Fredkin[18] described the first explicit, computer calculable model universe a reversible-type cellular automation. (Earlier cellular-automata "worlds" like Conway's game life[19] had all been irreversible.) This universe consists solely of information. Once you assume it exists, implemented in whatever kind of hardware you may think of, its properties are fixed. It starts producing "material" properties of its own inside—like assemblies of black pixels that mutually attract each other with a definitive force law like Coulomb's. The hope is that, eventually, all laws of nature as we know them might come out as an implication. You only have to hit—by happenstance—upon the right reversible local rule. The number of such laws to be checked empirically is unknown. Possible counterarguments invoking the existence of nonlocal phenomena in quantum mechanics are answered with the argument that nonlocal correlations over large distances have been abundantly observed in real-time computer runs. The dichotomy between exophysics and endophysics is hereby invoked. The only major problem with this explicit model world is that, so far, no dissipative macroscopic processes can be simulated since even a single "elementary particle" uses up hundreds of variables. Irreversible "observers" cannot yet be included.

This computer world therefore still belongs to the first or "general" phase of endophysics. Here, general limitations that invariably show up from the inside are sought. Gödel provided the paradigm and Maxwell the first potential physical example. In contrast, the second or "special" phase of endophysics will be brain theoretical. Assumptions that are not completely general and that enter into the properties of explicit observers ("brains") arising in the explicit model world will be admitted into consideration. This makes the connection to Galouye's (and Lem's) science fiction 2 even closer. Interestingly, the first potentially conscious computer program was developed by Kosslyn and Schwartz.[20] Like its forerunners—of fiction status presumably—it is non-reversible. All such models have yet to be embedded into a more minimal (reversible) universe. On the other hand, a concrete example of a microscopically specified world that "goes all the way up" to include macroscopically subsystems such as observers has so far been lacking. A specific world of this type is considered in the following.

Discussion

Endophysics is still in its infancy. A single explicit model universe that reaches through all levels from the microscopic to the macroscopic is available so far. A general endophysical question worth considering in detail is the second law with all its ramifications. Other questions of the same standing have yet to be identified. In the realm of special endophysics (including brains), most questions have also yet to be formulated. There may be other "general" special axioms to consider besides that of observer-internal particle indistinguishability.

Even though indistinguishability may turn out to be but a minor determinant of an observer-centered future endophysics, focusing on it at the beginning may turn out to have been a lucky accident. It helped show that simply putting a reversible universe into a computer and running it exophysically is not sufficient to uncover its endophysics. In addition, hints at the possible existence of endophysical properties even where there are no exophysical correlates, are needed. The Gibbs symmetry simply does not exist exophysically. In a similar vein, both quasi-periodization and microvacillation could easily have been overlooked were it not for certain counterintuitive theoretical proposals already present in the literature.

Particle indistinguishability has the further asset that it is a "maximally simple" property. Symmetries and reduced representations are staples of any physical theory. Trajectorial multiuniqueness, nevertheless, is fairly nontrivial conceptually. To the present author, for example, it is still not clear to what extent one may trust a symmetry argument. The history of this problem goes back to Leibniz. A more general endophysical problem worth discussing is the consistency question. Can any endophysics be consistent? To what extent is "internal consistency" assured for its inhabitants? Specifically, can internal interfaces be consistent? How far can their consistency go, maximally? Are only single measurements covered (direct consistency), or are derived general laws included (indirect consistency)? What about "meta-consistency": a meta-consistent world would be one in which it is impossible even to embark on a endophysical program.

These questions may all be studied explicitly using the present model universe (with the r.t plane forming the main tool). It is also possible to study the question of "consistent interaction" between two observers—with a single observer who relies on his own earlier notes forming the simplest case. The nontrivial nature of the latter problem was first seen, in real physics, by Bell. The central endophysical idea of meta-unmaskability goes back to Descartes. He introduced the fairness question (in French). Can a *mauvaise plaisanterie* (a bad joke) be excluded, from the inside? Both Einstein and Bohr concurred with him that a physics whose consistency was not great enough to permit at least a glimpse at the reasons for our own limitations would be a "bad dream."

In the present context, Cartesian fairness assumes a different ring. Simulating a Hamiltonian world in a computer having finite precision is bound to destroy many "subtle" conservation laws. Subtle conservation laws would be those that preserve the consistency of internal interfaces. The second law, for example, is subtle since it can be violated by "late digits" (cf. ref. 9). Even more subtle would be a macroscopically consistent world that nevertheless is nonlocal microscopically. Two mutually incompatible macroscopic worlds could then coexist, in harmony, in the same microscopic world (exophysics). Only if such a level of accuracy is guaranteed can the inhabitants embark on an endophysical path.

Therefore, a reversible integration routine will be required in the long run. Its use will amount to putting a discrete "lowest-level universe" underneath the present one. Like Fredkin's universe, the latter ought to be "embeddable" again into a continuous Hamiltonian. To conclude, endophysics is the study of demons. Maxwell's demons do not work—they are each blocked by a censor. Further demons and their corresponding censors will have to be uncovered. Understanding incompleteness is worth more than completeness—almost.

Notes

1. D. F. Galouye, Simulacron Drei (Munich: Heyne-Verlag, 1965; English original 1964).

2. D. R. Hofstadter and D. C. Dennett, The Mind's I (New York: Basic Books, 1981); German trans. Einsicht ins Ich (Munich: Klett-Cotta, 1992).

3. K. Gödel, "Ober formal ununterscheidbare Sitze der Principia mathematica und verwandter Systeme 1," Monatshefte f. Math. u. Physik 38 (1932), 173–198.

4. J. von Neumann, Mathematische Grundlagen der Quantenmechanik (Berlin: Springer-Verlag, 1932, 1981), p. 233.

5. J. C. Maxwell, Theory of Heat (New York: Appleton, 1872; rpt. New York: AMS Press, 1972), p. 308.

6. L. Boltzmann, "In Memoriam Josef Loschmidt," in: Populäre Schriften (Leipzig: Johann Ambrosius Barth, 1905), pp. 150–159.

7. L. Szilard, "Ober die Entropieverminderung in einem thermodynamischen System bei Eingriffen intelligenterwesen," Z. f. Physik 53 (1929), 840–856.

8. L. Brioullin, "Maxwell's Demon Cannot Operate: Information and Entropy 1," Appl. Phys. 22 (1951), 334–337.

9. O. E. Rössler, "Macroscopic Behavior in a Simple Chaotic Hamiltonian System," Lecture Notes in Physics, 179 (1983), 67–77.

10. M. von Smoluchowski, "Experimentell nachweisbare, der Ciblichen Thermodynamik widersprechende Molekularph Snomene," Physik. Z. 13 (1912), 1068–1080; see also Physik. Z. 17 (1916), 557, 585.

11. P. Ehrenfest, letter to Samuel Goudsmit, George Uhlenbeck, and Gerhard Dieke, November 1927, in: Niels Bohr, ed. K. von Meyenn, K. Stolzenberg, and R. Ü. Sexl (Braunschweig: Vieweg, 1985), p. 152.

12. J. S. Bell, "On the Einstein-Podoisky-Rosen Paradox," Physics 1 (1964), 195–200.

13. K. R. Popper, "Indeterminism in Classical Physics and Quantum Physics 1," Brit. J. Philos. Sci. 1 (1951), p. 129. See also "Autobiography of Karl Popper," in: The Philosophy of Karl Popper, ed. P. A. Schilpp (La Salle, Ill: Open Court, 1974), p. 1021.

14. D. Finkelstein, "Holistic Methods in Quantum Logic," in: Quantum Theory and the Structures of Time and Space, ed. L. Castell, M. Drieschner, and C. F. von Weizsäcker (Munich: Carl Hanser, 1979), vol. 3, pp. 37–60.

15. D. Finkelstein and S. R. Finkelstein, "Computer Interactivity Simulates Quantum Complementarity," J. Theor. Phys. 22 (1983), 753–779.

16. O. E. Rössler, "Chaos and Chemistry," in: Nonlinear Phenomena in Chemical Dynamics, ed. C. Vidal and A. Pacault (New York: Springer Verlag, 1981), pp. 79–87.

17. D. Finkelstein, letter of June 23, 1983.

18. E. Fredkin, "Digital Information Mechanics," preprint 1983; "Digital Mechanics," Physica D 45 (1990), 254–270.

19. M. Gardner, Wheels, Life and Other Mathematical Amusements (San Francisco: Freeman, 1983).

20. S. M. Kosslyn und S. P. Schwarz, "A Simulation of Visual Imagery," Cognitive Sci. 1 (1977), 267–295; cf. O. E. Rössler, "An Artificial Cognitive Map System," BioSystems 13 (1981), 203–209, for a related but more complete blueprint.

The Three Faces of Life

John L. Casti

Abstract

Contrary to the cherished beliefs of many physicists and other unreconstructed materialists, there's a lot more to life than mere matter. What distinguishes life from non-life is how the matter is organized. This paper argues that by retreating from a resolutely Newtonian view of life and returning to the Aristotelian notion of causal categories, we open up new avenues of approach to understanding the interconnections among early life forms, artificial life in machines, and possible types of extraterrestrial life.

1. The Why of Life

According to Caesar, all Gaul was divided into three parts. And so it is too when it comes to the study of life, where we find that the deepest questions seem to be parceled out among three seemingly distinct categories. The first, of course, is just the wet, squishy, carbon-based type of life we're familiar with here on Earth. Into this Category I fall all the usual origin-of-life (ORI) questions involving the way life got its start on this planet. Category II is of much more recent vintage, centering less upon how life got its start and more upon the even deeper question made famous by the title of Erwin Schrödinger's book, *What is Life*? In this category we find the current work on artificial life (AL), which seeks to answer Schrödinger by constructing life based on patterns of information in silicon and electricity instead of in carbon and water, or possibly on new combinations of the standard chemicals constituting life here on Earth. Finally, we come to close encounters with life of the third kind: extraterrestrial life forms (ET). Here in Category III reside all the puzzles involving the possible nature of life forms evolving under environmental conditions radically different (or, perhaps, indistinguishable) from those found here on Earth. Superficially, these categories appear to be pretty much disconnected. Or at least that's the impression one gets from a reading of the scientific research literature. In the spirit of the Ars Electronica Symposium on Artificial Life, I'll argue in this paper that not only are these categories inextricably intertwined, but that the adoption of a more functionally oriented view of life opens up the possibility for a productive interchange of ideas among research groups pursuing work in the different categories.

Just about the first thing every journalist learns is that a good story answers the following questions: Who? What? When? Where? Why? How? Applying this tried and true principle to the story of life, it's not too hard to see that these interrogatives can be apportioned out among our Categories I–III as follows:

• Origin of Life. How? Studies of the origin of life on Earth tend to focus almost exclusively on questions beginning with "How." Occasionally, as with various extraterrestrial theories of the origin of life, "Where" enters the picture too. But, by and large, ORI studies center on the construction of various scenarios for how life got going on Earth four billion years or so ago. This issue is, of course, intimately bound up with the so-called "origins problem"; we ask what features of modern life forms would be preserved were we able to "rewind the tape" and start the process all over again. We'll return to this question later.

• Artificial Life: What? The key issue around which most AL studies revolve is Schrödinger's famous question: What is life? Put more specifically, we ask if a suitably organized pattern of information in a machine can ever constitute a genuine living organism? So the operative word here is "What."

• Extraterrestrial Life: Who? Where? When? "Where are they?" This was Enrico Fermi's famous retort to the claim that the universe must be filled with ET's. Studies over the intervening half century or so have centered mostly on where to look, what to look for, and when will we find something (someone?).

The most striking aspect of this list of journalistic interrogatives is the singular absence of "Why." So if Schrödinger's question governed studies of life in the 20th century, I'd like to predict that 21st-century studies of life will be driven by the question, "Why is life?" Let me take a page or two to explain.

2. From Newton to Aristotle

The basic goal of modeling, mathematical or otherwise, is to answer the question "Why?" According to Newton (a physicist), the corresponding "Because" is given in terms of local interactions involving material particles and unexplainable forces. Aristotle (a biologist) had a quite different way of saying "Because."

In Aristotle's view, the "Why" of things can be described in terms of three basic entities: (i) the material substance comprising physical objects, (ii) the abstract or geometric forms that objects can assume, and (iii) the processes of change by which either the substance or the form may be transformed. Thus, Aristotle's "Because" results in four disjoint and inequivalent causal categories which, taken together, provide a complete answer to "Why" the world is as it is. These causal categories are:

• Material cause—things are as they are because of the matter of which they are composed;
• Efficient cause—things are as they are because of the energy that went into making them as they are;
• Formal cause—things are as they are because of the plan according to which they were built;
• Final cause—things are as they are because of the desire or will of someone to have things take their current state.

Note that in the above scheme of things, material cause corresponds to substance, with efficient cause relating to processes for changing the substance. Similarly, formal cause explains the abstract or geometric form of an entity, with final cause describing how one changes the form. This scheme explains why there are four basic causes in the Aristotelian view of the world, and not three or five or 3,469.

In the epistemology of Aristotle, all things can be explained by invoking the four basic causes, each cause illuminating a different fundamental aspect of the system at hand. We can also interpret these inequivalent causal categories by thinking of each category as being concerned with the manipulation of "something" as indicated in Table 1.

Table 1. Aristotelian Causal Categories and Manipulations

Cause	Property Manipulated
Material	Physical Matter
Efficient	Energy
Formal	Information
Final	Desire; Will

Interestingly enough, both the Newtonian and Aristotelian explanatory schemes talk about the same thing: a material substance and the process by which this substance can change. However, in the Aristotelian picture substance is not enough; one also needs the idea of form and some kind of dynamic by which one form can be transformed into another. This latter idea is totally absent from the Newtonian picture. In partial compensation, the Newtonian setup offers a mathematical apparatus by which we can encompass both the particles (material cause) and the forces (efficient cause) that constitute the heart of the Newtonian modeling paradigm. The Aristotelian picture provides no mathematical machinery, only a verbal description of the causes. It's instructive to examine this dichotomy in a bit more detail in order to get a feel for what must be done to extend the Newtonian formalism to accommodate the additional Aristotelian causes.

Newton's Second Law is usually written as the differential equation $x(t) = F(t)$, $x(0) = x_0$ where $x(t)$ is the state of the system of particles at time t, the quantity F represents the unexplained external forces, and x_0 is the initial state of the system. For our purposes, it's more convenient to write this relationship in integrated form as $x(t) = x_0 + \int_{t_0} \phi(s) ds$ where $\phi(s) = \int_s \phi F(r) dr$.

Now we can ask the question: Why is the system in the state x(t) at time t? Newton can give only two answers:

1) The system is in the state x(t) at time t because it was in the state x_0 at time t_0 (material cause);
2) The system is in the state x(t) at time t because the operator $\int A_0$ transformed the initial state to the state at time t (efficient cause).

Thus, the Newtonian framework has neither the need nor the room to accommodate the additional Aristotelian categories of formal and final causation. Some would argue, myself included, that this fact more than any other accounts for the banishment of formal and especially final cause from polite scientific conversation for the better part of three centuries. There is just no room to fit them into the classical Newtonian framework.

In actuality, even the most die-hard Newtonian ultimately came to recognize, albeit implicitly, that the missing causal categories would somehow have to be grafted on to the classical setup. In particle systems, the role of formal cause is usually assigned to various parameters specifying important constants in the situation. So things like as particle masses, gravitational constants, electric charges, and so on serve to characterize the "plan" of the system. It's through the specification of such parameters, and their incorporation into the mathematical framework, that formal cause enters by the backdoor into the Newtonian scheme of things. But what about final cause? How does Newton deal with the idea of desire or will? The simple answer is that he doesn't.

When reading Aristotle's account of the causal categories, one is struck by the great significance he attaches to the notion of final cause. In fact, for Aristotle it seems that final cause was just a little more equal than any of the other categories, and he reserved his greatest respect and kindest words for what would today be termed (by Newtonians) "teleology." For the kinds of problems that concerned Newton, it appears reasonable to omit final causation from consideration since it's different to imagine non-living, material particles having any particular kind of will, volition, or conscious-

John L. Casti The Three Faces of Life

ness. Thus, Newton and his successors had no need to invoke any of the ideas associated with final cause, notions like goals, plans, will, or even self-reference, in their analyses of physical processes.

From this point of view, it's rather easy to understand why the mathematical machinery they employed seemed perfectly adequate to the task at hand, even though it contained no natural way to account for final cause and dealt with even formal cause in a rather ad hoc manner. Unfortunately for the biologist, economist, and psychologist, Newton's prescriptions were too successful in answering questions in physics, chemistry, and engineering, leading to a gradual emergence of the view that it's a breach of scientific etiquette, if not downright unscientific, to allow anything even smacking faintly of final causation to enter into polite scientific discourse. In other words, if you can't use the methods that work in physics, then you're not doing science. And using the methods of physics means working within the Newtonian paradigm.

Newton's world naturally sees organisms as being just special kinds of material objects; in short, biology is a subset of physics. Aristotle's *Weltanschauung*, on the other hand, argues for just the opposite view, implying that the physics of particles and forces is just a special kind of biology. In other words, the Aristotelian world is one in which the Newtonian framework is just a special case of a broader-based paradigm suitable for characterizing life. Aristotle's problem was that he had no mathematical formalism at his disposal with which to describe his causal theory. But mathematical modeling has developed considerably in the two thousand years since Aristotle. And one of its fruits has been the development of a formal framework that helps in putting several questions from ORI, AL, and ET onto a common footing. This framework is called a metabolism-repair system (M,R)-system, whose details are outlined in the papers 1–6. Since these results are a bit too involved to go into here, let it suffice to say that the (M,R)-systems represent an abstract version of a living cell. Now let me indicate how the combination of Aristotelian causation and the (M,R)-setup help illuminate some of the key issues arising in ORI, AL, and ET.

3. The Hen or the Egg?

Almost all competing theories of the origin of life involve a scenario in which either the first living thing was a metabolizer that later acquired the ability to replicate, or is a replicator that then assumed metabolic functions. Thus the question: Which came first, the hen or the egg? While the current flavor of the month in the ORI business seems to be a replicator-first theory involving an evolution of life from self-catalytic RNA, the (M,R)-framework strongly suggests otherwise. On purely logical grounds, quite independent of physical substrates like nucleotide bases, amino acid chains, and all the other paraphernalia of earthly life, it's very difficult to see how to start with an abstract replicator like RNA and make metabolic activity emerge from replication. There does not appear to be any straightforward way to begin with the process of replication and use "natural" mathematical operations on sets and maps to create a metabolizer. Part of the difficulty comes from the fact that the repair component of the cell acts as an intermediary between replication and metabolism, and it's just far simpler to see how to make this operation come about from something rather than having to emerge from nothing. And since replication involves no actual production of something new, but only the copying of something old, there's just not enough raw material to work with to get the job done. So if you believe in the (M,R)-framework, then you'll also believe that the time is ripe for metabolism-first theories of ORI to begin making a comeback. Turning now to Aristotle and his causes, the very nature of the ORI problem seems to call for an explanation of life on Earth by material causation. And, in fact, the distinguishing characteristic separating the competing theories—self-rep RNA, hypercycles, clay, iron—is the kind of material substance they postulate that the first organism was made of. But the (M,R)-framework is one grounded in formal and final cause, not material and efficient. In particular, by thinking in these alternative causal categories we are able to pin down the elusive notion of final cause: it is simply the cell's purpose or, in biological terms, its design metabolism. Let's briefly consider how these notions enter into the origins problem discussed earlier.

4. Life by Design

One of the cornerstones of the scientific method is the notion of a repeatable experiment: results obtained by one researcher at one lab should be replicable by other researchers working under similar circumstances. This idea of repeatability enters as a central ingredient in the process of validating scientific claims and establishing today's conventional wisdoms on what nature is and isn't doing. Clearly, the replicability requirement poses severe difficulties for researchers in areas like the origin of life, cosmology, evolution, and, in general, every area in which there is a single set of observations available and in which the system cannot be reset to the beginning and allowed to start over again. This is the so-called "origins problem." The question, of course, is what can be done to surmount it?

One line of attack on the question in origin-of-life studies is to ask: Suppose we could rewind the tape and let the system start over again. Are there any properties of existing life forms that we would expect to see reappear in the new world of "Earth II"? In other words, are there certain features of organisms that are "generic," and that can be expected wherever life exists? Or is our form of life special in every possible way? Recently, Walter Fontana and Leo Buss have examined this issue using tools from mathematical logic and evolutionary theory).[11] They conclude that there are indeed such generic properties, things such as self-maintaining organizations (self-repair), entities that catalyze their own replication, and hierarchical organization of living entities. In a certain definite sense, these results relate to what we might call the logic of life. So in the Aristotelian scheme of things, they have to do with formal cause. But what about artificial life forms built from the usual materials— carbon, hydrogen, oxygen, and all the rest—of everyday life?

It's difficult to read a newspaper science page nowadays without encountering some story about how the wizards of molecular biology are concocting new genetic patterns to cure diseases, increase crop harvests, or eliminate pests. What's happening here, of course, is that the genetic engineers are constructing strands of RNA/DNA of a type never before seen in any naturally occurring organism. Let me consider just one example.

In 1992, Gerald Joyce and Amber Beaudry, researchers at the Scripps Institute in California, succeeded in coaxing a biological molecule to evolve artificially, doing in a few weeks what nature might take millennia to perform.[12] Starting with a population consisting of trillions of molecular variants of a strand of RNA, Joyce and Beaudry evolved an RNA enzyme that would snip strands of DNA 100 times more efficiently than the starting molecule. In short, these researchers achieved what might be called evolution by "unnatural selection." Earlier work had shown how to mimic two of the three ingredients needed for Darwinian evolution: selection and amplification. But the crucial ingredient added in the Scripps experiment was that it allowed molecules to also mutate randomly. So in our Aristotelian categorization, we can explain the work of Joyce and Beaudry by appeal to material causation—but of a type never before seen in any natural organism.

Before closing the all-too-brief discussion of life by design, let me mention in passing the extensive amount of work being done under the general rubric "robotics." As anyone who saw the film "Star Wars" is well aware, robots are another way to study life by designing objects that capture the behavioral and cognitive features of natural organisms—including human beings! Now let me shift the venue from real life to real artificial life.

5. Life *in silico*

In summer 1991 Tom Ray, a plant biologist in Delaware, created a computer program that reproduces-undergoes spontaneous genetic changes, passes them on to its offspring, and evolves new species whose interactions mimic those of real biological evolution and ecology—all without human guidance or intervention.[9] The significance of Ray's program was that it was the first logical demonstration of the validity of the Darwinian theory of evolution. This is exactly the goal of the artificial lifers: to show that the logical structure of life is completely independent of material cause. True or not, just as with work on ORI, in AL too there is something to be gained by thinking in terms of other causal categories.

For instance, Darwinian theory implies that the environment in which an organism develops will strongly influence the physical form and function of the organism. This is a material cause explanation for why the vast majority of living things on Earth are shaped like cylinders with appendages. But suppose we have something like Ray's electronic organisms that evolve within the cozy confines of a computer's memory banks. Thinking in terms of material cause, we can ask: what is the shape of such an electronic "bug"? And what would such an organism see when it looks at its "environment"? And in what way does the bug have to adapt to such an environment? And so on and so forth. The point is that we are led to ask a quite different set of questions than those that naturally come to mind in the original setting of formal cause.

In another direction, we can point to the work initiated by Dutch biologist Aristid Lindenmayer on artificial plants. Using a small number of simple rules involving branching directions, leaf types, and the like, Lindenmayer and his colleagues have created a stunning array of plant-like objects that bear a striking similarity to the kinds of flowers and trees found naturally here on Earth.[10] But of course, these "electronic plants" have never graced anyone's backyard garden or appeared on the menu in any haute cuisine restaurant. They are the epitome of what we can call artificial plants. Before leaving the matter of life *in silico*, let me add that by taking a collection of abstract cells of the type in the (M,R)-framework and connecting them into a network, it's possible to construct an electronic ecology similar to that produced in Ray's computer. Some suggestions about how this might be done are given in the papers 1–6. One result that comes out of such an exercise is the purely logical fact that immortality is flatly impossible. In other words, not all genetic lines can perpetuate themselves indefinitely. This is explanation by formal cause. It's reasonable to suppose that additional light will be shed on this phenomenon by looking at it from the vantage point of material causation. But this is a matter for future research. For much further discussion of this point, the reader should consult the "bible" of artificial life.[8]

6. Who Goes There?

From a physical life point of view, certainly the most central question surrounding the existence of ET is: What do "they" look like? In other words, what kind of physico-chemical structure is an ET likely to have? This, of course, is basically a problem of material and efficient cause. And for the spectrum of possible answers, it's hard to do better than to consult the "hard" science fiction literature.

The creature depicted in Figure 1 below shows an artist's depiction of a Cygnan, a race of alien beings that threatens the Earth in Donald Moffitt's classic science-fiction novel *The Jupiter Theft*. The Cygnan is from a race of creatures the evolved on the satellite of a gas giant planet orbiting a binary star system. He (she? it?) is about 1 1/2 meters tall, with six limbs that can be used as either arms or legs, and a long, three-petaled tail that folds to conceal the sexual organs. The slender, tubular body is built on a cartilaginous skeleton, with the brain located between the upper pair of limbs at the top of the spinal cord. The three eyes are placed on stalks in an equilateral triangle around a broad, flexible mouth. The Cygnan has a harsh, rasping plate in the mouth, and a spiked, tubular tongue. It has a well-integrated nervous system, with much faster synaptic reflexes than those of a human being. Cygnan speech is musical, consisting of chords produced by multiple larynxes, and depends on absolute pitch. The language is incredibly rich and varied; it has more than a million phonemes, and each word is made up of several phonemes.

So here we have a well worked-out example of an ET that differs radically from earthly organisms in almost every way that counts (unfortunately for the humans in Moffitt's story). But if we consider formal cause, the science-fiction literature offers up even stranger possibilities.

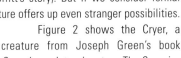

Figure 2 shows the Cryer, a creature from Joseph Green's book *Conscience Interplanetary*. The Cryer is an independently functioning unit of a planet-wide silicon-based plant intelligence inhabiting the planet Crystal, which has an atmosphere of 18 percent oxygen, the rest being nitrogen and hydrogen. Life on Crystal is based on silicon, with a high percentage of metallic elements. The Cryer resembles a two-meter-high bush with a crystal-and-metal trunk and branches, with small, sharp glass leaves. The trunk contains silicon memory units, powered by a low-voltage solar storage battery and connected by fine silver wires. About six feet up the Cryer's trunk is an organic air-vibration membrane that enables the Cryer to speak with human beings. It is a broad, saucer-shaped leaf held in place by stretched wires to provide a vibrating diaphragm. A magnetic field generated in silver wire coils hanging on either side of the speaker causes it to vibrate and produce sound.

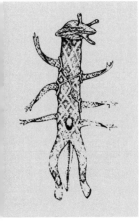

The planet-wide intelligence consists of thousands of smaller units like the Cryer, connected by an underground nervous system of fine silver wire. Each unit has a specialized function, some storing electricity generated by sunlight, some extracting silver for constructing the nervous system, some providing memory storage, and some acting as sensor units. The overall intelligence is able to perceive temperature, motion, position, electrical potential, and vibrations through its member units.

Cygnans and Cryers are, of course, just thought experiments. Many more are reported in the imaginative volume.[7] By considering the almost infinite range of possible life forms, and by examining the ET problem from all four of the Aristotelian causal perspectives, we can hope to get some feel for what may turn up on our radio telescopes or in our back yards one of these days. And, in fact, as the paper 1 points out, the metabolism-repair systems form what in mathematics is termed a "category" of objects. Therefore, each and every member of this category corresponds to a different biology, opening up the possibility of studying exobiologies by examining the mathematical structures and constraints imposed by these different objects in the category.

Figure 2

7. That's Life!

This paper has argued that to understand the difference between the living and the dead, it's not sufficient to concentrate just on the material aspects of living things. By adopting a less Newtonian and a more Aristotelian view of the problem, one is led to give equal time to explanations of life in terms of other causal categories besides the material. In particular, we have shown that there is much to be gained (and nothing to be lost but prejudices) by considering the other forms of life beyond those commonly encountered here on Planet Three. The overall conclusion that emerges is that there are significant synergies possible between Earth life, artificial life in machines, and extraterrestrial life "out there," and that researchers in each area can benefit from paying careful attention to work by those in the other categories. To paraphrase a famous remark about war and generals, life is just too important to be left to the biologists.

References

1. Rosen, R., "Some Relational Cell Models: The Metabolism-Repair Systems," in: Foundations of Mathematical Biology, volume 2 (New York: Academic Press, 1972).

2. Rosen, R., Anticipatory Systems (Oxford: Pergamon, 1985).

3. Rosen, R., Life Itself (New York: Columbia University Press, 1991).

4. Casti, J., "Linear Metabolism-Repair Systems," Int'l. J. Gen. Sys. 14 (1988), 143–167.

5. Casti, J., "The Theory of Metabolism-Repair Systems," Applied Math. & Comp. 28 (1988), 113–154.

6. Casti, J., "Newton, Aristotle, and the Modeling of Living Systems," in: Newton to Aristotle, ed. J. Casti and A. Karlqvist (New York: Birkhäuser, 1989), pp. 47–89.

7. Jonas, D., and D. Jonas, Other Senses, Other Worlds (New York: Stein and Day, 1976).

8. Artificial Life, ed. C. Langton (Redwood City, Calif.: Addison-Wesley, 1989).

9. Ray, T., "An Approach to the Synthesis of Life," in: Artificial Life II, ed. C. Langton et al. (Redwood City, Calif.: Addison-Wesley, 1992), pp. 371–408.

10. Prusinkievvicz, P., and A. Lindenmayer, The Algorithmic Beauty of Plants (New York: Springer, 1990).

11. Fontana, W., and L. Buss, "What Would Be Conserved if the Tape Were Played Twice?" submitted to Proc. Nat. Acad. Sci. USA, March 1993.

12. Coghlan, A., "Survival of the Fittest Molecules," New Scientist, October 3, 1992, pp. 37–40.

Trace Apparatus

**Remarks on an Art at the Apparatus Stage, or,
from Semantic Correspondence to Structural Contingency**

Thomas Feuerstein / Klaus Strickner

*If we draw the cool conclusion that man is a machine and that in the entire universe there is
only one substance which, of course, is modified differently.*
J. O. La Mettrie, 1747

Starting with Aristotle and extending to the current trends of autopoiesis, the contrast
between living systems which permit the recognition of autonomy and all other natural things and
artificial artifacts, has always been fascinating. Although in the case of Aristotle, the artificial picture
(eikon technete) and the natural picture *(eikon physike)* are structurally the same, natural things—that
is, "creatures and their parts, plants and the simple bodies, earth and fire and air and water" (Phys.
192b)—are distinguished by the fact that they have the "origin for peace and movement" within themselves (ibid.). Technology as well as graphic art is, in this respect, bound to the classical programme
of *imitatio* and *perfectio* of certain consequences, but cannot bear the last effective cause within
themselves. With the dawn of modern times, the perspectivization of "artificial pictures" onto "natural pre-pictures" begins to reverse. Complex entireties are being increasingly projected on a machine
picture for the purposes of scientific objectivism. In accordance with this, even long before the
Industrial Revolution, the machine found the symbolic anticipation of its later real dominance, which
as we know, can be clearly discerned from the discourses of the 16th, 17th, or 18th centuries. For
example, Vasari used the machine like a metaphor to describe Brunelleschi's domed structure of the
Florence Cathedral by praising this as being an "astonishing machine."

From Descartes to Leibniz, La Mettrie, or even, with reservations, Kant, a historical circle for
the installation of a machine picture for living beings can be retraced, whereby a rationalistic mechanical term became the ontological guarantor for the recognizability of the world. Descartes' controversial declaration that organisms function like automatons or machines, meant a naturalization of
mechanics and a mechanization of nature. "Autonomous systems are mechanistic (dynamic) systems
which are specified by their organization," says Francisco Varela (1987, p. 121), whereby the historical circle traced for an installation of a machine picture for living beings in the modified form of
autopoietic machine models could be formed.

Every work, both of nature as well as art, is a system.
Bishop Joseph Butler, 1729

Denis Diderot's frequently quoted example of a fictitious machine that produces pictures like Raphael's expresses an old paradox that rests on the incompatibility of clearly determined fabrication rules with the terms "genius" and "originality" when producing works of art. Neither the machine nor the works which it produced, in line with the necessary laws, could have been termed "beautiful" according to Diderot. Beauty only arises in art with a sharp differentiation to nature, which is nothing more than a heap of infinitely differently ordered molecules: "Multiply these imitation machines [= Raphael machines] anywhere and everywhere. Let pictures emerge in nature like plants . . . ; and tell me what has become of your admiration" (quoted in Link-Heer, 1986, p. 106). And at a place shortly

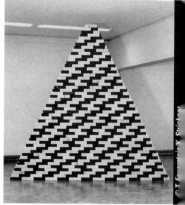

before, Diderot, who is walking in the countryside in dialogue with an abbé, writes: "If I had a box of dice here, and if I were to overturn this box, and if they would all turn around at the same point, would this phenomenon be astonishing? Very. And if all the dice had been prepared, would this phenomenon still astound you? No" (ibid.). This passage becomes more topical when it is transported into the context of the calculating machine. "Data is also called dice" writes Friedrich Kittler, "and just as the former aesthetic or ordered cosmos of the philosophers has become a great dice game under technical conditions, data processing can still mess up its sampling values according to all the game's rules for mathematical operations, until reality is actually no longer necessary" (Kittler, 1989, p. 69). Consequently, it is no longer only everything that is necessary, but also everything that is possible, that is the case. The dichotomy between the "creatio ex nihilo" and Vasari's fabrication, between the artistic intention and the role of contingency in artistic production, as in die case of Diderot, or between Makers of the work and Making of the stuff, as with Heidegger, disintegrates. The work is no longer the dead mirror which directs nature, posing as realism or naturalism in a timeless immobility, and represents apparent reality. It forms its own autonomous reality with its own specific contingency. Perhaps comparable with Eric Drexler's "engines of creations," which imply molecular computers set up from complex structures which can assemble themselves and which can reproduce, art is breaking away from the traditional work of art and its semantic correspondence and is developing independent structural contingencies.

With the exchange of external reference for self-reference, from a historical point of view, representation and imitation assumptions in the picture were discarded. Besides the elimination of the present world, for the purpose of independent processing, it called for picture-immanent elements, particularly of a decomposition or division of the picture into its individual modules. This division and condensation allowed the picture to be condensed into its elements (colour, light, material, etc.). Before the picture could experience a restructuring, it required a thorough reduction of formal and content aspects. Only the reduction to a few, but then more precisely determined elements, made possible the construction of new artistic structures, further resulting in greater complexities. Since it was no longer sufficient to transform objects into imitations, according to the scheme of *imitatio* and *perfectio*, the development of system-internal criteria had to be intensified. The picture had to prove itself as a unit consisting of individual picture elements in order to be newly devised by the programmes created by artists. If we describe the condensation of the picture commencing in the 19th century as referring, on the one hand, to photography—every object is allocated a certain number of grains with a certain grey value—and on the other hand to Cézanne—the picture is composed of

Thomas Feuerstein / Klaus Strickner *Trace Apparatus*

clearly defined elements as a classical physical one—then with the change of the aggregate state of the picture, for the first time, the introduction of a clearly outlined combination game with distinct elements becomes effective in picture production. If photography, Cessna's painting, or divisionism can be said to be responsible for the physical condensation of the picture, then the film, the collage, the accumulation, etc. could be understood as being a chemical condensation and the digital code as being electronic condensation. What all condensation processes have in common is that they dynamize and temporalize the picture. A considerably stronger process, as opposed to the traditional wood panel painting, decomposes the picture into happening states in which the elements are continuously reallocated and reassigned to each other. A static persistence in one state would only be a disturbing inhibition of the process and is just as foreign to the pictures, after changing the aggregate state, as a linear-causal picture transformation. Art is—to take up the said example again—in a comparable state with nano-technology. After condensing the objects into their elements, it is necessary in technology, as in art, to have "engines of creation" to structure elements into new Complexities.

Perhaps it would even have been sufficient to simply say that God was able to create immaterial automatons just as well as he was able to create physical ones, the former representing the latter.
Gottfried Wilhelm Leibniz, 1710

The picture created its own separate world in order to condense itself into a reserve of pictures established in a possibility structure. It changed its aggregate state by assuming the actual significance of aggregate in the sense of accumulation, making itself independent to form a reserve of imagination, a contingent idea. The natural appearance of things in the world is, in doing so, exchanged in the artificial picture worlds of aggregates for the idea of contingent worlds. Pictures' worlds, structurally established in apparatus and programmes, do not consume their medium; they produce and reproduce it with every picture of the new one. The "artistic apparatus" is therefore an unlimited reserve of pictures, the perfect copy (Latin *copia* = reserve). The apparatus, as defined by Vilém Flusser as a toy simulating thinking, offers a host of possibilities. It is not merely the in-term for the perfect copy but also the in-picture of virtuality. As there is no getting at the artistic apparatus, ontologically or with categories of classical aesthetics, a division of technical and artistic artifacts becomes superfluous. The polar division between art and technology, between the symbolic and the real, changes into an antagonistic relationship: the work, thing, or stuff of classical aesthetics transforms to become apparatus which makes the real appear to be fictitious, and the symbolic appear real.

The basic intention which led to the construction of the "Trace Apparatus" was to design as simple a picture as possible, or a kind of allegory of numerous pictures in one picture; that is, as simple an apparatus as possible and as extensive a copy as possible. The relationship of the "Trace Apparatus" to the "catalogue" illustrates the relation of structural contingency to catalogue contingency. Following Charles Babbage's idea of a "machine that bites its own tail" (quoted in Hyman, 1987, p. 250), that is, capable of the passage through the never-ending, by dismantling the world into part problems, and this further into a sequence of individual steps, we chose as the basic form a mathematical > (greater than/less than symbol). The construction is composed of simple elements and connections, as are common from the everyday routine of inch scales. The difference from a standard inch scale only consists of the regularly varying length of the elements, which differ by one quotient (5 cm) in order to achieve the symbolic initial form of >. The mathematical > stands for a section of reality which is present from individual elements cut up into lines, on which again there is a succession of black-white single steps. The result is a wave pattern composed of curves which, depending on the setup of the construction in the space and the constellation of the individual elements to each other, is subject to changes. The apparatus independently produces different frequencies on account of the spatial references which are changed by the installations. In doing so, world is not simulated by an external referentiality, but is newly created by waves. Perhaps similar to the way Ada Lovelace, who translated Manebrea's article about the difference machine from Italian, thought of using Babbage's machine for manufacturing music pieces of every length and complexity, the Trace Apparatus will produce unpredicted combinations which want to be read as waves. The apparatus is not a memory like the former wood panel painting, and not a thesaurus like the sum of all wood panel paintings in a catalogue, a gallery, or a museum. The apparatus is a data processing organism like its recipient, a data processing machine. The breaking away of picture production from the author and the picture making itself independent, creates a separate world which obeys its own laws, or rather the laws of the programme. In a lecture, Heinz von Foerster gave the simple and possibly therefore the most illustrative example: "Whether I should 'store' information from a 1010 x 1010 multiplication table in the form of a 21 x 27 cm book with a thickness of approximately 10 billion km, or in the form of a small hand-operated desk computer, is, I think, quite clear" (Foerster 1985, p. 134). The information in the desk computer or in an artistic apparatus is stored in a structural way as opposed to a table or a conventional picture.

> Could man himself not become a kind of parasite on the machines? An affectionate, machine-tickling plant louse?
> Samuel Butler, 1872

What is interesting is that the demand to make the system art into a programme does not appear, but rather the individual work of art. It is not a matter of an artistic apparatus making a programme of what the system art is or was in its system. The programme or the apparatus would then, as Niklas Luhmann describes for *l'art pour l'art,* miss the elementary state of affairs, "that autonomy does not stop the relationship to the environment, but rather calls for and regulates its" (Luhmann, 1986, p. 626). The artistic apparatus is not a solipsistic operations mechanism, which uncouples the system art from the world, similar to *l'art pour l'art.* It must be conceived more as an effort of a differentiation process progressing further within the system "art." A differentiation process which is in an antagonistic and complementary relationship to interventions and appropriation strategies of art outwits its own system. Apparatus, programme, or structural contingency describes processes and considerations to differentiate and make products of the system art which have until now always been designated as works, more complex. The work of art should therefore change basically from the work—from the fully finished work—to a "small item of work," an idea in flux.

References

Foerster, H. v. (1985). Sicht und Einsicht. Braunschweig.

Hyman, A. (1987). Charles Babbage—Philosoph, Mathematiker, Computerpionier. Stuttgart.

Kittler, F. A. (1989). "Fiktion und Simulation." In: Ars Electronica, ed., Philosophien der neuen Technologie. Berlin.

Link-Heer, U. (1986). "Maniera. Überlegungen zur Konkurrenz von Manier und Std (Vasari, Diderot, Goethe)." In: H. U. Gumbrecht and K. L. Pfeiffer, eds., Stil, Geschichten und Funktionen eines kulturwissenschaftlichen Diskurselementes. Frankfurt a. M.

Luhmann N. (1986). "Das Kunstwerk und die Selbstreproduktion der Kunst." In: Gumbrecht and Pfeiffer, Stil. Frankurt a. M.

Varela, F. (1987). "Autonomie und Autopoiesie." In: S. J. Schmidt, ed., Der Diskurs des Radikalen Konstruktivismus. Frankfurt a. M.

Artificial Life

Christopher G. Langton

The following are excerpts from the full text published in Ars Electronica 93: Genetic Art—Artificial Life, pp. 25–78. The breaks are indicated by • • • .

"Art" + "Life" = *Artificial Life*—life made by man rather than by nature. Our technological capabilities have brought us to the point where we are on the verge of creating "living" artifacts. The field of artificial life is devoted to studying the scientific, technological, artistic, philosophical, and social implications of such an accomplishment.

1 The Biology of Possible Life

Biology is the scientific study of life—in principle, anyway. In practice, biology is the scientific study of life on Earth based on carbon-chain chemistry. There is nothing in its charter that restricts biology to carbon-based life; it is simply that this is the only kind of life that has been available to study. Thus, theoretical biology has long faced the fundamental obstacle that it is impossible to derive general principles from single examples.

Without other examples, it is difficult to distinguish essential properties of life—properties that would be shared by any living system—from properties that may be incidental to life in principle, but which happen to be universal to life on Earth due solely to a combination of local historical accident and common genetic descent. In order to derive general theories about life, we need an ensemble of instances to generalize over. Since it is quite unlikely that alien life-forms will present themselves to us for study in the near future, our only option is to try to create alternative life-forms ourselves—artificial life, literally "life made by man rather than by nature."

Artificial life ("AL" or "A-life") is the name given to a new discipline that studies "natural" life by attempting to recreate biological phenomena from scratch within computers and other "artificial" media. A-life complements the analytic approach of traditional biology with a synthetic approach: rather than studying biological phenomena by taking living organisms apart to see how they work, we attempt to put together systems that behave like living organisms.

The process of synthesis has been an extremely important tool in many disciplines. Synthetic chemistry—the ability to put together new chemical compounds not found in nature—has not only contributed enormously to our theoretical understanding of chemical phenomena, but has also allowed us to fabricate new materials and chemicals that are of great practical use for industry and technology. Artificial life amounts to the practice of "synthetic biology," and, by analogy with synthetic chemistry, the attempt to recreate biological phenomena in alternative media will result in not only better theoretical understanding of the phenomena under study, but also in practical applications of biological principles in industry and technology. By extending the horizons of empirical research in biology beyond the territory currently circumscribed by life-as-we-know-it, the study of artificial life gives us access to the domain of life-as-it-could-be, and it is within this vastly larger domain that we must ground general theories of biology and will discover novel and practical applications of biology in our engineering endeavors.

1.1 AI and the Behavior Generation Problem

Artificial life is concerned with generating lifelike behavior. Thus, it focuses on the problem of creating behavior generators. A good place to start is to identify the mechanisms by which behavior is generated and controlled in natural systems, and to recreate these mechanisms in artificial systems. This is the course we will take later in this paper.

The related field of artificial intelligence is concerned with generating intelligent behavior. It, too, focuses on the problem of creating behavior generators. However, although it initially looked to natural intelligence to identify its underlying mechanisms, these mechanisms were not known, nor are they today. Therefore, following an initial flirt with neural nets, AI became wedded to the only other known vehicle for the generation of complex behavior: the technology of serial computer programming. As a consequence, from the very beginning artificial intelligence embraced an underlying methodology for the generation of intelligent behavior that bore no demonstrable relationship to the method by which intelligence is generated in natural systems. In fact, AI has focused primarily on the production of intelligent solutions rather than on the production of intelligent behavior. There is a world of difference between these two possible foci.

By contrast, artificial life has the great good fortune that many of the mechanisms by which behavior arises in natural living systems are known. There are still many holes in our knowledge, but the general picture is in place. Therefore, artificial life can start by recapturing natural life, and has no need to resort to the sort of initial infidelity that is now coming back to haunt AI. Furthermore, artificial life is not primarily concerned with building systems that reach some sort of solution. For AL systems, the ongoing dynamics is the behavior of interest, not necessarily the state ultimately reached by that dynamics.

The key insight into the natural method of behavior generation is gained by noting that nature is fundamentally parallel. This is reflected in the "architecture" of natural living organisms, which consist of many millions of parts, each of which has its own behavioral repertoire. Living systems are highly distributed and quite massively parallel. If our models are to be true to life, they must also be highly distributed and quite massively parallel. Indeed, it is unlikely that any other approach will prove viable.

$$\bullet\bullet\bullet$$

2.3 Abstraction of the Logical "Form" of Machines

During the early part of the 20th century, the formal application of logic to the mechanical process of arithmetic lead to the abstract formulation of a "procedure." The work of Church, Kleene, Gödel, Turing, and Post formalized the notion of a logical sequence of steps, leading to the realization that the essence of a mechanical process—the "thing" responsible for its dynamic behavior—is not a thing at all, but an abstract control structure, or "program"—a sequence of simple actions selected from a finite repertoire. Furthermore, it was recognized that the essential features of this control structure could be captured within an abstract set of rules—a formal specification—without regard to the material out of which the machine was constructed.

The "logical form" of a machine was separated from its material basis of construction, and it was found that "machineness" was a property of the former, not of the latter. Today, the formal equivalent of a "machine" is an algorithm: the logic underlying the dynamics of an automaton, regardless of the details of its material construction. We now have many formal methods for the specification and operation of abstract machines: such as programming languages, formal language theory, automata theory, recursive function theory, and etc. All of these have been shown to be logically equivalent.

Once we have learned to think of machines in terms of their abstract, formal specifications, we can turn around and view abstract, formal specifications as potential machines. In mapping the machines of our common experience to formal specifications, we have by no means exhausted the space of possible specifications. Indeed, most of our individual machines map to a very small subset of the space of specifications—a subset largely characterized by methodical, boring, uninteresting dynamics. When placed together in aggregates, however, even the simplest machines can participate in extremely complicated dynamics.

●●●

2.6 John von Neumann: From Mechanics to Logic

With the development of the general-purpose computer, various researchers turned their attention from the mechanics of life to the logic of life.

The first computational approach to the generation of lifelike behavior was due to the brilliant Hungarian mathematician John von Neumann. In the words of his colleague Arthur W. Burks, von Neumann was interested in the general question:

What kind of logical organization is sufficient for an automaton to reproduce itself? This question is not precise and admits to trivial versions as well as interesting ones. Von Neumann had the familiar natural phenomenon of self-reproduction in mind when he posed it, but he was not trying to simulate the self-reproduction of a natural system at the level of genetics and biochemistry. He wished to abstract from the natural self-reproduction problem its logical form.

This approach is the first to capture the essence of the artificial life approach. To understand the field of artificial life, one need only replace references to "self-reproduction" in the above with references to any other biological phenomenon.

In von Neumann's initial thought experiment (his "kinematic model"), a machine floats around on the surface of a pond, together with lots of machine parts. The machine is a universal constructor: given the description of any machine, it will locate the proper parts and construct that machine. If given a description of itself, it will construct itself. This is not quite self-reproduction, however, because the offspring machine will not have a description of itself and hence could not go on to construct another copy. So, von Neumann's machine also contains a description copier: once the offspring machine has been constructed, the "parent" machine constructs a copy of the description that it worked from and attaches it to the offspring machine. This constitutes genuine self-reproduction.

Von Neumann decided that this model did not properly distinguish the logical form of the

Christopher G. Langton *Artificial Life*

process from the material of the process, and looked about for a completely formal system within which to model self-reproduction. Stan Ulam—one of von Neumann's colleagues at Los Alamos—suggested an appropriate formalism, which has come to be known as a cellular automaton (CA).

In brief, a CA consists of a regular lattice of finite automata, which are the simplest formal models of machines. A finite automaton can be in only one of a finite number of states at any given time, and its transitions between states from one time step to the next are governed by a state-transition table: given a certain input and a certain internal state, the state transition table specifies the state to be adopted by the finite automaton at the next time step. In a CA, the necessary input is derived from the states of the automata at neighboring lattice points. Thus, the state of an automaton at time t + 1 is a function of the states of the automaton itself and its immediate neighbors at time t. All of the automata in the lattice obey the same transition table and every automaton changes state at the same instant, time step after time step. CA's are good examples of the kind of computational paradigm sought after by artificial life: bottom-up, parallel, local-determination of behavior.

Von Neumann was able to embed the equivalent of his kinematic model as an initial pattern of state assignments within a large CA-lattice using 29 states per cell. Although von Neumann's work on self-reproducing automata was left incomplete at the time of his death, Arthur Burks organized what had been done, filled in the remaining details, and published it, together with a transcription of von Neumann's 1949 lectures at the University of Illinois entitled "Theory and Organization of Complicated Automata," in which he gives his views on various problems related to the study of complex systems in general.

Von Neumann's CA model was a constructive proof that an essential characteristic behavior of living things—self-reproduction—was achievable by machines. Furthermore, he determined that any such method must make use of the information contained in the description of the machine in two fundamentally different ways:

—Interpreted, as instructions to be executed in the construction of the offspring.

—Uninterpreted, as passive data to be duplicated to form the description given to the offspring.

Of course, when Watson and Crick unveiled the structure of DNA, they discovered that the information contained therein was used in precisely these two ways in the processes of transcription/translation and replication.

In describing his model, von Neumann pointed out that

By axiomatizing automata in this manner, one has thrown half of the problem out the window, and it may be the more important half. One has resigned oneself not to explain how these parts are made up of real things, specifically, how these parts are made up of actual elementary particles, or even of higher chemical molecules.

Whether or not the more important half of the question has been disposed of depends on the questions we are asking. If we are concerned with explaining how the life that we know emerges from the known laws of physics and organic chemistry, then indeed the interesting part has been tossed out. However, if we are concerned with the more general problem of explaining how lifelike behaviors emerge out of low-level interactions within a population of logical primitives, we have retained the more interesting portion of the question.

2.7 Lessons from History

As stated at the beginning of this section, throughout history, we have repeatedly tried to map our contemporary technology onto nature in an attempt to understand natural phenomena.

Sometimes this has been successful, but in the case of both life and intelligence, such mappings have not provided satisfactory explanations. There is a lesson here: although artificial life uses computers as its primary tool for the synthesis of biological phenomena, we should not mistake the tool for the object under study and attempt to characterize life as a "computation." If we are able to bring life to computers, this will not be because life "is" a computation, at least as we now understand the term "computation." Rather, it will be because computers have some fundamental properties that will allow them to be organized in such a way that they can become alive. It is quite likely that we will learn more about computation by studying life than we will learn about life by studying computation. This will be taken up in more detail in the following section.

It is also important to note that in the control programs of early automata we see the roots of what Mitchell Resnick has called the "centralized mindset": the attribution to natural phenomena of a central controller that is ultimately responsible for their behavior. It is a mindset that has dominated most of our scientific, philosophical, and even religious thought for the last several centuries. In contrast, Resnick refers to the kind of approach advocated by artificial life as the "distributed mindset." The difference is crucial, since most of nature chugs along in the absence of any central controllers. In order to understand most of nature, therefore, we must abandon the centralized mindset and come to an understanding of the dynamics of distributed systems qua distributed systems.

3 The Role of Computers in Studying Life and Other Complex Systems

Artificial intelligence and artificial life are each concerned with the application of computers to the study of complex, natural phenomena. Both are concerned with generating complex behavior. However, the manner in which each field employs the technology of computation in the pursuit of its respective goals is strikingly different.

AI has based its underlying methodology for generating intelligent behavior on the computational paradigm. That is, AI has adopted the centralized control architecture of serial, "von Neumann" style computation as a model of intelligence. AL, on the other hand, is attempting to develop a new computational paradigm based on the distributed processes that support living organisms. That is, AL uses insights from biology to explore the dynamics of interacting information structures. AL has not adopted the computational paradigm as its underlying methodology of behavior generation, nor does it attempt to "explain" life as a "computation."

One way to pursue the study of artificial life would be to attempt to create life in-vitro, using the same kinds of organic chemicals out of which we are constituted. Indeed, there are numerous exciting efforts in this direction. This would certainly teach us a lot about the possibilities for alternative life-forms within the carbon-chain chemistry domain that could have (but didn't) evolve here.

However, biomolecules are extremely small and difficult to work with, requiring rooms full of special equipment, replete with dozens of post-docs and graduate students willing to devote the larger part of their professional careers to the perfection of electrophoretic gel techniques. Besides, although the creation of life in-vitro would certainly be a scientific feat worthy of note—and probably even a Nobel prize—it would not, in the long run, tell us much more about the space of possible life than we already know.

Computers provide an alternative medium within which to attempt to synthesize life. Modern computer technology has resulted in machinery with tremendous potential for the creation of life in-silico.

Computers should be thought of as an important laboratory tool for the study of life, substituting for the array of incubators, culture dishes, microscopes, electrophoretic gels, pipettes, centrifuges, and other assorted wet-lab paraphernalia, one simple-to-master piece of experimental equipment devoted exclusively to the incubation of information structures.

The advantage of working with information structures is that information has no intrinsic size. The computer is the tool for the manipulation of information, whether that manipulation is a consequence of our actions or a consequence of the actions of the information structures themselves. Computers themselves will not be alive, rather they will support informational universes within which dynamic populations of informational "molecules" engage in informational "biochemistry." This view of computers as workstations for performing scientific experiments within artificial universes is fairly new, but it is rapidly becoming accepted as a legitimate, even necessary way of pursuing science. In the days before computers, scientists worked primarily with systems whose defining equations could be solved analytically, and ignored those whose defining equations could not be so solved. This was largely the case because, in the absence of analytic solutions, the equations would have to be integrated over and over again—essentially simulating the time-behavior of the system. Without computers to handle the mundane details of these calculations, such an undertaking was unthinkable except in the simplest cases.

However, with the advent of computers, the necessary mundane calculations can be relegated to these idiot-savants, and the realm of numerical simulation is opened up for exploration. "Exploration" is an appropriate term for the process, because the numerical simulation of systems allows one to "explore" the system's behavior under a wide range of parameter settings and initial conditions. The heuristic value of this kind of experimentation cannot be overestimated. One often gains tremendous insight for the essential dynamics of a system by observing its behavior under a wide range of initial conditions.

Most importantly, however, computers are beginning to provide scientists with a new paradigm for modeling the world. When dealing with essentially unsolvable governing equations, the primary reason for producing a formal mathematical model—the hope of reaching an analytic solution by symbolic manipulation—is lost. Systems of ordinary and partial differential equations are not very well suited for implementation as computer algorithms. One might expect that other modeling technologies would be more appropriate when the goal is the synthesis, rather than the analysis, of behavior.

This expectation is easily borne out. With the precipitous drop in the cost of raw computing power, computers are now available that are capable of simulating physical systems from first principles. This means that it has become possible, for example, to model turbulent flow in a fluid by simulating the motions of its constituent particles—not just approximating changes in concentrations of particles within regions of the fluid, but actually computing their motions exactly.

There is an extremely important point here, one that involves the ultimate goals of the scientific enterprise as well as the issue of "centralized" vs. "distributed" mindsets. The point is the following. There is a fundamental difference between being able to describe or predict phenomena on the one hand and "explaining" them on the other hand. One can use Navier-Stokes equations to describe or predict fluid flows in many cases, but fluids are not calculating Navier-Stokes equations! The descriptive and predictive power of the Navier-Stokes approach is useful, but the phenomena of fluid flow are actually generated by quite different mechanisms. Physics has largely been considered successful when it has been able to produce a predictive, abstract description of a physical phenomenon, one that generally ignores the low-level mechanisms by which the phenomenon is actually generated. This is a benefit of adopting the centralized mindset, and it is very useful to be able to do this whenever possible.

However, for most natural phenomena, there is probably no simpler description than the generative mechanisms themselves. In these circumstances adopting the distributed mindset is necessary. Note that just because we cannot provide an abstract, high-level predictive description of a phenomenon does not mean that we have failed to provide a scientific description; a low-level description may be "as scientific" as we can get concerning the phenomenon. Even when a simpler, high level description is possible, it is important to keep in mind the difference between the description of a process and an understanding of the mechanisms by which it is generated.

What does all of this have to do with the study of life? The most surprising lesson we have learned from simulating complex physical systems on computers is that complex behavior need not have complex roots. Indeed, tremendously interesting and beguilingly complex behavior can emerge from collections of relatively simple components. This leads directly to the exciting possibility that much of the complex behavior exhibited by nature—especially the complex behavior that we call life—also has simple generators.

• • •

7 Evolution

Modem organisms owe their structure to the complex process of biological evolution, and it is very difficult to discern which of their properties are due to chance, and which to necessity. If biologists could "rewind the tape" of evolution and start it over, again and again, from different initial conditions, or under different regimes of external perturbations along the way, they would have a full ensemble of evolutionary pathways to generalize over. Such an ensemble would allow them to distinguish universal, necessary properties (those which were observed in all the pathways in the ensemble) from accidental, chance properties (those which were unique to individual pathways). However, biologists cannot rewind the tape of evolution, and are stuck with a single, actual evolutionary trace out of a vast, intuited ensemble of possible traces.

Although studying computer models of evolution is not the same as studying the "real thing," the ability to freely manipulate computer experiments—to "rewind the tape," perturb the initial conditions, and so forth—can more than make up for their "lack" of reality.

It has been known for some time that one can evolve computer programs by the process of natural selection among a population of variant programs. Each individual program in a population of programs is evaluated for its performance on some task. The programs that perform best are allowed to "breed" with one another via Genetic Algorithms.

The offspring of these better-performing parent programs replace the worst performing programs in the population, and the cycle is iterated. Such evolutionary approaches to program improvement have been applied primarily to the tasks of function optimization and machine learning.

However, such evolutionary models have only recently been applied to the study of evolution itself (Wilson 1989). Researchers were primarily concerned with the results, rather than with the process, of evolution. In what follows, we will review several models that have been used to study the evolutionary process itself.

• • •

7.7 From Artificial Selection to Natural Selection

In *The Origin of Species*, Darwin used a very clever device to argue for the agency of natural selection. In the first chapter of *Origin*, Darwin lays the groundwork of the case for natural selection by carefully documenting the process of artificial selection. Most people of his time were familiar with the manner in which breeders of domestic animals and plants could enhance traits arbitrarily by selective breeding of their stock. Darwin carefully made the case that the wide variety of domestic animals and plants extant at his time were descended from a much smaller variety of wild stock, due to the selective breeding imposed by farmers and herders throughout history.

Now, Darwin continues, simply note that environmental conditions can fill the role played by the human breeder in artificial selection, and, *voilà*! One has natural selection. The rest of the book consists of a very careful documentation of the manner in which different environmental conditions would favor animals bearing different traits, making it more likely that individuals bearing those traits would survive to mate with each other and produce offspring, leading to the gradual enhancement of those traits through time. A beautifully simple yet elegant mechanism to explain the origin and maintenance of the diversity of species on Earth—too simple for many of his time, particularly those of strong religious persuasion.

The abstraction of this simple elegant mechanism for the production and filtration of diversity in the form of the Genetic Algorithm is straightforward and obvious. However, as it is usually implemented, it is artificial, rather than natural selection, that is the agency determining the direction of computer evolution. Either we ourselves, or our algorithmic agents in the form of explicit fitness functions, typically stand in the role of the breeder in computer implementations of evolution. Yet it is plain that the role of "breeder" can as easily be filled by "nature" in the world inside the computer as it is in the world outside the computer—it is just a different "nature." If we are to study evolution by "natural" selection, we must create a "nature" within the artificial world of a computer.

•••

9 Conclusion

In the section on evolution, the point was made that it is often the case that the most important aspects of "Nature" in the process of evolution are the other organisms in the environment and their effects on the physical world.

In the case of human beings, our "Nature" is largely dominated by the products of our own artifice, not only physical structures such as buildings and highways, but also such socio-cultural constructs as governments, churches, corporations, and so forth. That is, our own artifacts are the dominating aspects of the "Nature" that is the agency of "natural" selection for the human species. By adapting to an artifactual "Nature" we are becoming more and more "artifactual" ourselves. As we are increasingly responsible for constructing "Nature," so we are increasingly responsible for constructing ourselves. In a very real sense, humans themselves are becoming a form of artificial life—products of our own artifice. Now that we are on the verge of synthesizing life artificially—now that our artifacts are becoming more and more like us and now that we are becoming more and more like our artifacts—where will life go from here?

It is important to bear in mind that whether we produce living artifacts within the next ten years or only within the next thousand, on the scale of geological time we are literally at the beginning of a new epoch of life on Earth, an epoch that will be dominated by life-forms that we will have had a significant role in shaping. Will they sustain and nurture us, and we them? Or will they destroy and replace us, or we them?

We must do everything in our power, starting now, to assure that the consequences of our imminent mastery of the technology of life are beneficial for all life, whatever it is made of.

The full text is available in C. Langton, Artificial Life (Cambridge, MIT Press, 1997)

Christopher G. Langton *Artificial Life*

Praise to the Parasites

Florian Rötzer

The parasite is a pathogen. It causes a system's equilibrium or distribution of energy to fluctuate. It dopes it. It irritates it. It inflames it. Very often this difference has no consequences. It can bring about consequences—and by means of interlinking or reproduction they may even be immense.
Michel Serres

Obviously natural life results once a certain complexity has been achieved, making it possible to store learning processes as a text in a memory, which can furthermore copy this and convert it into instructions to build a machine. One of the essential features of life is, of course, not only to survive as an organism and, to some extent, to mend oneself over a certain period of time under suitable peripheral conditions, but also to be able to reproduce self-reproductively. Both imply a memory that not only stores digital and two-dimensional information but which also contains the instructions to form its own separate three-dimensional organism as well as new organisms. Due to copying errors and external influences or, in case of sexual reproduction, by joining together two memory texts there is the possibility that what is stored can change, whereby the survival chances of text variants by means of "adaptation," i.e. through internal reorganization, can increase.

Whether this implies an optimization in what is still the teleologically characterized language of evolution theory may be doubted, as there is no way whatsoever of tackling the criteria of adaptation beyond the banal statement that some organisms survive—that is, that they "function," come to terms with changing reality and produce offspring. The talk of adaptation through the cycle of mutation and selection implies an assumed reality and consequently a kind of the classical truth relation of the conformity of cognition and the subject of cognition, which can hardly be supported any longer. After all, life itself changes its peripheral conditions, for instance, when it first built up the oxygenous atmosphere in the Precambrian through photosynthesis, which forms the basis of today's eukaryote life. Even the characterization of organisms as problem solvers is a metaphor, which nevertheless has a meaning in the generation of genetic algorithms, as in this case the problem is specified here, and with that a stable artificial environment. Embedded in the principles of evolution is, in many cases, also the idea of progress, that is the gradual improvement of populations through increasing complexity, although over 90% of existent living beings exist in the form of microorganisms. Most of them are harmless to higher living beings or even cooperate with them in a symbiosis, yet in the case of pathogenic viruses they are known to mutate at an enormous speed in order to deceive the immuno-logical system that can generally produce mutations for resistance even faster. The immense variety of antibodies—we assume that there are 108 different kinds—is evidence of the wide variety of microorganisms which they have to provide protection against. Antibodies are produced from the mutation of a few basic structures and multiply like an avalanche in one variant once one antigen is entrapped by the receptors. In the human immunological system and probably also in our neuronal network, the evolution mechanism is copied, strengthened, and accelerated, in a certain sense. The higher organisms are therefore only the tip of an iceberg, populated by a multitude of microorganisms and parasites which, in the evolutionary armament race, still have the chance to destroy the more complex living beings through a lethal communication, refunctioning the programme of their cells.

Beyond the appraisal by means of adaptation, biological information vouches for a process which—within an unstable complex system that interacts with the organism carrying the informa-tion—can constantly have something new develop and let realized texts die, provided the environ-ment is not stable. What is of course uncertain, is whether the "automatic" mutation of the genome in connection with selection is really of such importance for evolution as the classical theory believes it to be. For example, molecules which are only subjected to minute functional demands change much faster than those subjected to higher demands. It cannot be explained either as to why phenotypical change takes place faster with some lines than with others. And most multiple allelomorphs which arise as a result of mutation get lost again by chance, whereby many mutations do lead to the for-mation of nonidentical proteins which are present in a large variety in organisms, and however, dif-ferences very often reveal no phenotypical consequences. As a rule, mutations within the genetic drift either appear to be lethal or neutral, which would mean that influences from the environment or self-organization processes within the organism could be more effective than many may have assumed until now. Generally, transitional forms are missing; for example, breaks and bifurcations seem to hap-pen very suddenly. Due to the fact that organisms themselves are very highly complex systems which integrate different levels of self-organizing systems, we could assume that transitions do not take place continuously, but rather erratically. The one-way street in the development from genome to organism also appears to be doubtful because, occasionally, as in the case of sea urchins or tree frogs, the sexually mature animals look almost the same and also have the same behaviour, yet their growth can be very different. In this sense, the larvae of very closely related sea urchins are com-pletely different. Some can swim freely and eat plankton and others let themselves drift and can only nourish themselves on the ground. One could draw the conclusion from this that the pressure from the outside world is greater than the morphogenetic developments designed in genes. The fact that there is the complete set of instructions to form a three-dimensional organism in the genome appears, what is more, to be only undercutting the evolutionary approach adhering to the traditional linear comput-er architecture. As a result of probability theory considerations, the information stored in the genome cannot stipulate the instructions for every cell, just as it cannot stipulate the three-dimensional form of a protein in a one-to-one equivalent. Perhaps the genome is to be understood more as a catalyst and morpho-regulator to form three-dimensional patterns and interactive chemical processes, where-as the localizing of a cell and its activity is determined from the location and activity of local cell col-lectives, i.e. on account of a surface communication between neighboring molecules and cells. The genetic code would then only give direction and limits for a development which itself would produce multiplicity and variability within the organism by means of the evolutionary mechanism and would enable a balancing of the different cell types evolving independent of each other. If one accepts such a concept, then the mechanistic intention of being able to derive the morphogenetic development of the phenotype from the complete mapping of the genome and its protein, control and structural code, and then even to influence it in a specifically differentiated way would be a phantasm. Even with non-linear algorithms the future behaviour of a computer in which hardware and software are separate, unlike in biological systems, cannot be foreseen from the programme. When the relations between geno- and phenotype are not linear and are strongly based on the interaction between parts which are not controlled by a central computing and organization unit, then neither the three-dimensional organism nor its behaviour can be foreseen from the genetic programme.

The definition of life—ability of open metabolic systems to self-reproduce, to multiply, vary, and inherit—is known, as is the fact that the transition into the inanimate is not sharply marked but is smooth. Crystals can also be self-reproductive and mutating. On this ability, the chemist Graham Cairns-Smith built up his well-known and fascinating hypothesis on the origin of life through takeover. As DNA or RNA molecules are very complicated, he proceeds on the assumption that another replicator was here in the first instance, that is, simple inorganic crystals which self-reduplicate, such as are found in clay. As soon as the core of a crystal has formed spontaneously or a corresponding "seed" has fallen into an oversaturated solution, it can grow and become a solid, ordered shape. Now and again it falls apart and these parts also continue to grow. As chemical or mechanical imperfections can occur during the growth of the very regular crystal structures, which replicate with further growth, it also possesses a mutation mechanism whereby, for example, the growth variants can be transmitted to the "children" by breaking apart. Some crystals can grow faster and spread out, so what we find here is already a pre-form of evolution in which information is produced and passed onto new generations. At some time or other the growing, multiplying crystals began to produce organic compounds which helped them to survive. Cairns-Smith believes that these organic forms, which previously had been more of a tool, could have suddenly multiplied faster than the crystals following the appearance of a first self-reduplicating, simple RNA, and so moved slowly from the parasite status, which depends on a host cell, to become autonomous beings that had gradually put the crystalline life out of the running. Therefore, takeover means that a part of a self-organizing structure makes itself independent and thrusts aside its pre-form. If this hypothesis is correct then new life could continue to develop from the crystal formation, a fact that we perhaps have merely not yet observed. Or perhaps the peripheral conditions have been disarranged through the emergence of life based on DNA and RNA. What also makes this hypothesis of takeover piquant is the fact that a repeated takeover is, in its turn, possibly taking place with the computers based on silicon, so that biological life would only be an episode in the life being based on silicon. After all, at the moment, so-called artificial life is already beginning to grow in the form of cellular automatons or computer viruses.

Even the molecular-Darwinist approach developed by Manfred Eigen proceeds on the basis of the thesis that selection mechanisms are already active in the inanimate area of material, so that life emerges from the self-organization of macro-molecules which are generated by entering into hyper-cycles. That is beyond every scientific explanation of how life came to be, and it is exciting because here it becomes clear that self-organization will emerge when various processes mutually build themselves up under certain conditions and "use" each other mutually, in a certain sense, whereby something new can emerge within the limits of the interacting forces. The new, in turn, provided it possesses the animated ability of storage and instruction, uses or "enslaves" the agents and integrates them, for example, as a cell does the mitochondria, a virus does the cell, a multi-cell organism the different cell types, or an organ the parasites, which always means that, under certain circumstances, the adopted agents, foreign organisms, or the very forces from the environment can turn around the ratio. The watchmaker would be blinder than the genetic evolutionary theory suggests to us. And the creative coincidence within evolution would not be apart from changes in the environment relative to the organism—essentially determined by chance gene mutation—but would result from the interactions not foreseeable in detail between populations (molecules, cells, viruses, bacteria, etc.) amongst one another and with each other.

A prerequisite to evolution is a stipulated variety of different, at any rate, nonidentical self-reproducing complex systems, because only then can selection appear as a creative mechanism. Contrary to the usual pictures of the evolutionary tree with a trunk ramifying to show diversity only in its crown, this would speak for the fact that there are a lot of branches even at the very origin, that one-cell and then even multi-cell living beings often emerged independent of each other. Besides the two lines of organisms—the animals and the plants—we have found yet another: the archaebacteria. And so one is forced to appoint the ancestor of life as being even lower than with the prokaryotes. The variety of bacteria is, however, enormously large and no one has ever succeeded in constructing a pedigree from the various forms, metabolism types, and environmental adaptations. They are not differentiated enough for this and probably they very often emerged in parallel or one after the other. Evidently, different bacteria can also communicate with each other, by exchanging gene strands in a first step towards genetic crossover, which stabilizes a type with sexual mating, thus recombining their DNA plans at random. Bacteria could therefore have a general communications system whereby they could even exchange DNA pieces with plants and animals. It is assumed, for example, that the eukaryote cells which contain a core with DNA and smaller membrane-limited subunits originated from a symbiosis with prokaryotes with only one single DNA ring. And even the eukaryote cell core appears to contain at least three types of genes, so that it could be a chimera of DNA texts. In addition to this, there are still the viruses which normally do not count as living organisms but which already have strands of DNA or RNA and which are surrounded by a protein coat. Unlike the organelles which similarly have their own genetic code, they have not integrated themselves in the host cell, which can be understood as being a cell of cells, but keep their information by infecting cells and by refunctioning them for their multiplication. Until they tap a corresponding cell and its gene text and have it work for them, e.g. by adding their genetic code to that of the host cell, they are in an idle position and are "lifeless." Therefore, viruses can either envelop the programme of the cells or directly change it in the sense of a genetic takeover. From these many interactions of acquisition and parasitism one could assume that parasites at least accelerated evolution and that the battle between parasites, which developed parallel to the first living single-cell organisms, and host cells started up a significant, creative, but, of course, also deathly mechanism. Without bacteria any higher life could not exist. Even viruses belong to the environment of living organisms, and evolution does not appear to reward single individuals or single gene pieces, but rather populations which are in cooperative interaction with each other, including even relationships between parasite and host organism or animals of prey and hunters. If the niche is too simple and the organisms are not threatened, then very often no further development takes place. Instead there is a reduction in the programme.

What is interesting in this respect is that artificial life celebrated its first, even in many cases unwelcome, successes with the so-called computer viruses. They have a programme just like biological viruses, i.e. a memory storing information which, having been infected, uses the computer as a host organism to copy itself into another computer and to be able to multiply. In the computer ecology viruses act autonomously and they communicate with its programmes, which does not necessarily mean that they damage their host organism and the niche of interlinked computers with their ever increasing data clearances. For example, Harald Thimbleby programmed self-reproducing viruses which he called "lifeware" in such a way that they compare data banks. If these data banks do not correspond with each other, the missing data is automatically copied into the other data bank. Fred Cohen even believes that symbiotic computer viruses could, in future, take care of the main work for subordinate tasks in information systems. Nobody really knows—as with genetically changed microorganisms—if they will continue to be "kind helpers," once they enter into an evolutionary drift. However, as yet, most viruses have not been programmed by system users anyway. The computers are infected externally with more or less damaging viruses. The consequence resembles a kind of armament race: computer systems are better safeguarded and viruses accordingly become more intelligent. It is assumed that sexual mating has managed to succeed in biological evolution, amongst other things, because the interference from bacteria could be fended off better. Of course, there are still merely rudimentary forms of mutation by means of which computer viruses can adapt to new surroundings. Their evolution is advanced by human programmers, but it will probably soon be possible to develop and release computer viruses which can change in order to escape the search programme and to adapt more flexibly to new surroundings.

In the case of genetic algorithms which use the evolution mechanisms of selection, mutation, and genetic crossover by mating in order to optimize programmes for solving tasks, the structure of which need not be recognizable in detail, populations of nonidentical programmes or chains composed at random of zeros and ones will be exposed to a solution space and then assessed in accordance with their quality. Programmes are a bit code composed of rules to recognize features and to trigger off actions. As genetic algorithms are organized nonlinearly so as not to reduce them to a dominant rule and thus make them unsuitable for complex situations, the rules also compete with each other and all the rules which were involved in a "successful" action are rewarded, i.e. amplified. Such programmes which gradually organize themselves heterarchically and hierarchically can be very flexible, but of course they are exposed to a rigid environment and are assessed from the outside. In addition to this, their populations are generally still very small as compared to biological ones. Their advantage is that they can pass through the generation sequence at high speed and evolution can be observed, whereby all development stages and impasses are stored, a feature which is different in the biological one. The increasing capacity of parallel computers—the "Connection Machine" by Hillis was, incidentally, developed within the context of researching artificial life—means that programme populations will be able to be bred that will sufficiently come closer to the individual number of natural populations. Although, with genetic algorithms which can again be compared to viruses, really new construction plans or behavioural modes can emerge, particularly as a result of crossover, John H. Holland points out that even here phenomena such a symbiosis, parasitism, mimicry, predator-prey coevolution, niche formation, and the fissioning of one kind into new stem lines can be observed. Incidentally, in the case of genetic algorithms it has been shown that the mutation rate as opposed to crossover was an almost negligible value for evolution. Genetic algorithms and cellular automatons are restricted in their self-organization, particularly by the fact that they do not exist in a complex environment, even if they are in a position via back-fed processes with no superordinated rules, to produce relatively complex collective behavioural modes from the reaction of individual "organisms" in locally restricted situations.

The fact that the existence of parasites, and therefore the genetic takeover, could have been an important catalyst for the variety and complexity of life (and perhaps still is) was illustrated by Danny Hillis in a computer simulation on one of his Connection Machines with 64,000 processors operating in parallel. He sent "organisms," i.e. binary number chains representing genes which were to solve computing tasks on the basis of genetic algorithms, into an evolutionary armament race with parasites, which were similarly rewarded if successful. These types co-evolved by reacting even more skillfully to the attack or defence strategies. Always when the organisms had stabilized and had immunized themselves and it seemed as though the parasites had lost the race, a wave of attackers suddenly emerged again which managed to breakdown their safety systems. Hillis discovered that during the phases of standstill in the case of the phenotype, defined here by its computing abilities, changes were already taking place in the digital hereditary material which suddenly caused an even greater change, as from a critical point. Evolutionary biologists have always observed this change between periods of standstill and rapid innovation at the level of the phenotype, but they cannot explain how this sudden change which is in opposition to the dogma of change by means of the accumulation of small steps, takes place. What was noticeable was that the organisms needed a lot more generations in order to optimize when there were no parasites in the computer top. Consequently, their presence accelerates the evolution process and the variety by keeping it at the brink of chaos, that is, providing for imbalance. Even the erratic innovation with parasites and organisms can be thought of as a takeover. First of all, alleles are produced which are either neutral or which could be used for other functions; as in nature, it is not the principle of identity but more the flexible one of similarity which dominates. If there are a number of alternative genes available which, through feed-back, cause another behaviour that has "advantages," a new feature resulting from mating could spread out erratically.

With "Tierra," the biologist Thomas Ray tried to design an evolving system where digital living beings which had been changed by different mutations of their hereditary material were competing for processor time and storage space. The environment also changed through a kind of computer noise and the organisms of 80 gene-commands only had a limited lifetime, i.e. even the well "adapted" had to make their exit at some point. After the system had been running for some time and mutants emerged which worked even more effectively, organisms with only 45 gene-commands suddenly appeared that were unable to reproduce. For this reason, the parasites had to look for a host in order to use its replication code. As they were simpler, they were able to spread out faster than the more complicated living beings. But if they had alienated and killed too many hosts, their numbers also went down. With parasites there emerges new peripheral conditions between living beings developing an evolving system, to a certain extent, like a catalyst and out of which even mutants which could not survive in a stable environment with a constant solution space get a chance to survive by a mutual armament race.

Parasites appear, therefore, to emerge with a certain complexity in the course of the evolution of life and further advance this, irrespective of if this takes place in the sense of an armament race or as a symbiosis. There is a huge variety of parasites of biological life, their types probably exceeding by far those of all other animal species. Larger parasites display a wild multitude of metamorphoses and exploit an incredible series of intermediate hosts. Parasites are predators and guests which knock a complex system off balance and cause change: they are agents of metamorphosis, open up evolution to unforeseeable developments which otherwise only occur as a result of catastrophes in the physical and chemical environment. They very possibly not only interfere from outside, damaging or improving an organism, nesting into it or providing for noise, but also introduce direct mutations of the hosts through their information work. Their behavioural features are not restricted to the parasites which penetrate a host, living in it and playing with its memory, as every form of takeover and creation is parasitical, whereby even the hosts can be termed as being parasites in an intricate network. After all, life is a parasite of the Earth, which has been invaded and changed by it. And every host that is occupied by parasites, is, in itself, a parasite of another living being inasmuch as it lives off other organisms.

If the RNA or DNA were perhaps parasites of a life based on silicone, then they themselves have subsequently become parasites of the host cell they use as their survival machine and in which the neuronal system has possibly developed as a further parasite, again becoming a host of a new life form yet which is already the carrier of that form of life termed culture. But even the evolution of a new behaviour based on the sequence of many motoric and sensoric actors and millions of neurons competing and cooperating with each other, can be understood as being a takeover and consequently a parasitical use of previous simpler behaviour sequences of the neuronal machinery that, as yet, had been set in a completely different solution space. In this way, as the neurobiologist William Calvin assumes, the senso-motoric behavioural sequence of precisely hammering open nuts with stones could have been used to make possible the throwing of stones at moving targets. This ability to organize different back-fed sensoric, projective, and motoric behavioural sequences in an intersecting "melody," by the selection of many variants played through and assessed in milliseconds, could have opened up the possibility of building up a differentiated language from complicated interlinkages, with the same sequence mechanism permitting the playing and writing of music. If the parasitic takeover succeeds, new niches emerge which continue to develop in parallel becoming more complex with the emergence of new parasites that challenge routine behaviour generally through choc-type complexity reduction.

If there is an enclosed environment and a rigid solution space as in the virtual world of computers, then parasites can obviously be used to optimize algorithms. They could then be of importance for the continued development of artificial intelligence on the basis of genetic algorithms on parallel computers and the bottom-up method determined by chance. However, there is always the limitation that they also cause systems to crash and can introduce an uncontrollable development. We must get used to the fact that balance is not an orientation by which biological, psychical, and social systems keep themselves alive, that it is more the introduction of nasty, destructive viruses and parasites that produce new forms of life, thinking, and art. We should not accept the bad merely as a drive; we possibly have to produce it ourselves in order to survive, meaning that to change the animate and inanimate environment in which, and from which, we live as parasites. Irrespective of whether we biologically supersede ourselves in the long term, or in the short term by gene technology, or whether we release a post-biological life that will leave us behind in the armament race but where we, perhaps, could continue to live symbiotically or by the fact that we invent new knowledge and technology mutations, we will bleakly be forced to recognize that we are not the stable final product of evolution that we can steer and control from the outside. And even if we could succeed in throttling certain developments, perhaps with regard to AI, AL, or gene technology, we would end up in another evolutionary drift which is just as unforeseeable and which is immune to sudden mutations allowing new parasites and viruses to emerge.

References

William Calvin, Die Symphonie des Denkens (Munich, 1993).
John L. Casti, Verlust der Wahrheit (Munich, 1989).
Friedrich Cramer, Chaos und Ordnung. Die komplexe Struktur des Lebendigen (Stuttgart, 1988).
Richard Dawkins, Der blinde Uhrmacher (Munich, 1986).
Gerald Edelman, Unser Gerhirn-ein dynamisches System (Munich, 1993).
Evolution. Die Entwicklung von den ersten Lebensspuren bis zum Menschen (Heidelberg, 1988).
Stephen Jay Gould, Zufall Mensch (Munich, 1991).
John H. Holland, "Genetische Algorithmen," in Spektrum der Wissenschaft, Heidelberg 9/1992.
Bernd Olaf Küppers, Der Ursprung biologischer Information (Munich, 1986).
Steven Levy, KL-Künstliches Leben aus dem Computer (Munich, 1993).
Robert Wesson, Die unberechenbare Ordnung. Chaos, Zufall und Auslese in der Natur (Munich, 1993).

Florian Rötzer *Praise to the Parasites*

The Overexposed City

Paul Virilio

At the beginning of the 1960s, with the black ghetto revolts in full swing, the mayor of Philadelphia declared: "From now on, state lines cross inside the city." While this sentence expressed a political reality for the victims of American discrimination, it more importantly opened onto a much wider dimension because the Berlin Wall had just been erected, on August 13, 1961, in the Reich's ancient capital. Since then, the mayor's assertion has continued to prove true. Only a few years ago in Belfast and Londonderry, certain streets were marked with a yellow band, dividing Protestants and Catholics, before both moved further apart, leaving behind a fenced-in no-man's-land that made for an even stronger separation between their neighborhoods. Beirut came next, with its east and west quarters, its domestic frontiers, its tunnels, its mined boulevards. In fact, this declaration, made by the leader of a large American metropolis, underscored a general phenomenon affecting capitals as well as provincial cities. The phenomenon of obligatory introversion, in which cities, just like industrial companies, suffered the first effects of a multinational economy, led to a significant urban redeployment. On the one hand, it contributed to the disruption of certain working-class cities such as Liverpool or Sheffield in England, Detroit or St. Louis in the United States, and Dortmund in Germany. On the other hand, new urban centers developed around gigantic international airports—the Metroplex—metropolitan complexes such as Dallas–Fort Worth.

With the beginning of the worldwide economic crisis in the 1970s, these airports were constructed in order to conform to defense imperatives against hijacking. Buildings were no longer built according to traditional technical constraints, but were designed to minimize the risk of "terrorist contamination." Sites were planned to discriminate between a sterile zone (departures) and a nonsterile zone (arrivals). All circuits and circuit breaks (i.e., passengers, baggage, and freight), as well as the general flow of traffic, were submitted to a discriminatory (interior/exterior) transit system. Consequently, the building's architectural form became less the result of an individual architect's personality than of the necessary precautions taken for public safety. As the state's last gateway, the airport became, like the fort, the harbor, or the train station of the past, the place of the necessary regulation of exchange and communication. For this very reason, it also became the perfect field for intense control and high surveillance experimentation. An "air and border patrol" was developed, and their antiterrorist exploits made headlines, as, for example, in the case of the GS.G9 German guards' intervention in the Mogadishu hijacking several thousand kilometers from their jurisdiction.

From that moment on, it was no longer simply a matter of isolating the contagious or suspected person by confinement as in the past, but rather of intercepting him in the course of his journey, in order to examine his baggage and clothing electronically. Thus the sudden proliferation of cameras, radar, and detectors at mandatory passageways. French prisons with high-security quarters were also equipped with these same magnetic doors which had been installed in airports several years earlier. Paradoxically, the very equipment designed for the utmost freedom in travel served as a model for penitentiary incarceration. Previously, in several American residential areas, security was carried out only by closed-circuit televisions hooked up to police headquarters. In banks and supermarkets, as well as on highways, where tollbooths simulate the old city gates, the rites of passage are no longer intermittent—they have become immanent.

Paul Virilio, "The Overexposed City" in Zone 1/2, eds. Michel Feher and Sanford Kwinter, trans. Astrid Hustvedt (New York: Zone Books, 1986). Copyright © 1986 Urzone, Inc.

Given such a perspective without horizons, the way one gains access to the city is no longer through a gate, an arch of triumph, but rather through an electronic audiencing system whose users are not so much inhabitants or privileged residents as they are interlocutors in permanent transit. From this moment on, breaks in continuity occur less within the boundary of a physical urban space or its cadastral register than within a span of time, a span that advanced technology and industrial redeployment have incessantly restructured through a series of interruptions (closing of companies, unemployment, variable work schedules, etc.) and through successive or simultaneous transformations which have managed to organize and reorganize the urban milieu to the point of bringing about a decline, an irreversible deterioration of urban sites, as in, for example, the large townhouses near Lyons where the occupant turnover rate became so high (no one stayed more than a year) that it caused the ruin of a residential complex otherwise considered satisfactory.

In fact, since men first began using enclosures, the notion of what a boundary is has undergone transformations which concern both the facade and what it faces, its vis-à-vis. From the fence to the screen, by way of the rampart's stone walls, the boundary-surface has been continually transformed, perceptibly or imperceptibly. Its most recent transformation is perhaps that of the interface. The question of access to the city, then, should be asked in a new way: Does a greater metropolis still have a facade? At what moment can the city be said to face us? The popular expression "to go into the city," which has replaced last century's "to go to the city," embodies an uncertainty regarding relations of opposites (the vis-à-vis and the face-à-face), as though we were no longer ever in front of the city but always inside it. If the metropolis still occupies a piece of ground, a geographical position, it no longer corresponds to the old division between city and country, nor to the opposition between center and periphery. The localization and the axiality of the urban layout faded long ago. Suburbia was not single-handedly responsible for this dissolution. The very opposition "intramural"/"extramural" was itself weakened by the revolution in transportation and the development of communications and telecommunications, which resulted in the nebulous conurbation of an urban fringe. In effect, we are witnessing a paradoxical phenomenon in which the opacity of construction materials is virtually being eliminated. With the emergence of portative structures, curtain walls made of light and transparent materials (glass, plastics) are replacing the stone facade at the same time that the tracing paper, acetate, and Plexiglas used in project studies are replacing the opacity of paper.

On the other hand, with the screen interface (computers, television, teleconferencing) the surface of inscription—until now devoid of depth—comes into existence as "distance," as a depth of field of a new representation, a visibility without direct confrontation, without a face-à-face, in which the old vis-à-vis of streets and avenues is effaced and disappears. Thus, differences between positions blur, resulting in unavoidable fusion and confusion. Deprived of objective limits, the architectonic element begins to drift, to float in an electronic ether devoid of spatial dimensions yet inscribed in the single temporality of an instantaneous diffusion. From this moment on, no one can be considered as separated by physical obstacles or by significant "time distances." With the interfacade of monitors and control screens, "elsewhere" begins here and vice versa. This sudden reversion of limits and oppositions introduces into the space of common experience what had previously belonged only to the realm of microscopy. Solid substance no longer exists; instead, a limitless expanse is revealed in the false perspective of the apparatuses' luminous emission. Constructed space now occurs within an electronic topology, where the framing of the point of view and the scanlines of numerical images give new form to the practice of urban mapping. Replacing the old distinctions between public and private and "habitation" and "circulation" is an overexposure in which the gap between "near" and "far" ceases to exist, in the same way that the gap between "micro" and "macro" disappears through electronic microscope scanning.

The representation of the contemporary city is thus no longer determined by a ceremonial opening of gates, by a ritual of processions and parades, nor by a succession of streets and avenues. From now on, urban architecture must deal with the advent of a "technological space-time." The access protocol of telematics replaces that of the doorway. The revolving door is succeeded by "data banks," by new rites of passage of a technical culture masked by the immateriality of its components: its networks, highway systems, and diverse reticulations whose threads are no longer woven into the space of a constructed fabric, but into the sequences of an imperceptible planning of time in which the interface man/machine replaces the facades of buildings and the surfaces of ground on which they stand.

Only a short time ago, the opening of the city's gates was determined by the alternating of day and night. Today, however, since we not only open the shutters but also the television, daylight itself has been changed. A false electronic day, whose only calendar is based on "commutations" of information bearing no relationship whatsoever to real time, is now added to the solar day of astronomy, electric light, and the dubious "daylight" of candles. Chronological and historical time, which passes, is thus succeeded by a time that instantaneously exposes itself. On the terminal's screen, a span of time becomes both the surface and the support of inscription; time literally or, rather, cinematically surfaces. Due to the cathode-ray tube's imperceptible substance, the dimensions of space become inseparable from their speed of transmission. Unity of place without unity of time makes the city disappear into the heterogeneity of advanced technology's temporal regime. Urban form is no longer designated by a line of demarcation between here and there, but has become synonymous with the programming of a "time schedule." Its gateway is less a door which must be opened than an audio-visual protocol—a protocol which reorganizes the modes of public perception.

In this realm of deceptive appearances, where the populating of transportation and transmission time supplants the populating of space and habitation, inertia revives an old sedentariness (the persistence of urban sites). With the advent of instantaneous communications (satellite, TV, fiber optics, telematics) arrival supplants departure: everything arrives without necessarily having to depart. Only yesterday, metropolitan areas maintained an opposition between an "intramural" population and a population outside the city walls; today, the distinctive oppositions between the city's residents occur only in time: first, long historical time spans which are identified less with the notion of a "downtown" as a whole than with a few specific monuments; and second, technological time spans which have no relation to a calendar of activities, nor to a collective memory, except to that of the computer. Contributing to the creation of a permanent present whose intense pace knows no tomorrow, the latter type of time span is destroying the rhythms of a society which has become more and more debased. And the "monument," no longer the elaborately constructed portico, the monumental passageway punctuated by sumptuous edifices, but idleness, the monumental wait for service in front of machinery: everyone bustling about while waiting for communication or telecommunication machines, the lines at highway tollbooths, the pilot's checklist, night tables as computer consoles. Ultimately, the door is what monitors vehicles and various vectors whose breaks of continuity compose less a space than a kind of countdown in which the urgency of work time plays the part of a time center, while unemployment and vacation time play the part of the periphery—the suburb of time: a clearing away of activities whereby everyone is exiled to a life of both privacy and deprivation.

If, in spite of the wishes of postmodern architects, the city from now on is to be deprived of doors, it is due to the fact that the urban wall has given way to an infinity of openings and ruptured enclosures. While they are less apparent than those of antiquity, they are just as real, constraining and segregating. The illusions surrounding the industrial revolution of transportation have deluded us about the unlimited nature of progress. The industrial structuring of time has imperceptibly compensated for the disruption of rural territory. If in the nineteenth century the lure of the city emptied agrarian space of its substance (cultural, social), at the end of the twentieth century it is urban space which loses in its turn its geographical reality. This reality is lost to the sole benefit of instantaneous deportation systems whose technological intensity continuously upsets social structures: the deportation of people through the redeployment of production modes; the elimination of attention, of human confrontation, of the direct face-à-face, of the urban vis-à-vis, which all takes place at the level of the man/machine interface. In fact, all of this is part of another type of concentration, a nascent transnational and posturban concentration which has been revealed by many recent events.

In spite of continual rises in the cost of energy, middle-class Americans are evacuating eastern metropolitan areas. After the decay of inner cities, which subsequently became ghettoes, comes the current deterioration of the cities themselves as regional centers.

From Washington to Chicago, from Boston to Saint Louis, the great urban centers are depopulating. New York has lost, over the course of the last decade, 10 percent of its population. As for Detroit, it saw more than 20 percent of its inhabitants disappear; Cleveland, 23 percent; Saint Louis, 27 percent. Certain neighborhoods in these cities already resemble the ghost towns immortalized by American cinema.

These are premonitory signs of an imminent postindustrial deurbanization, and this exodus will most likely affect all developed countries. Foreseeable for about 40 years now, this deregulation of urban planning originates from an economic and political illusion about the permanence of sites constructed in the era of time management (automobile) and in the era of audio-visual development of retinal persistence—the afterimage.

"Every surface is an interface between two milieus in which a constant activity prevails, taking the form of an exchange between two substances placed in contact with one another." This new scientific definition illustrates how contamination is at work in the concept of surface: the surface-boundary becomes an osmotic membrane, a blotter. Even if this last etymology is more rigorous than preceding ones, it nonetheless points to a change affecting the notion of limitation. The limitation of space becomes commutation, a radical separation, mandatory passageways, a transit of constant activity, nonstop exchanges, a transference between two milieus, two substances. What used to be a substance's boundary line, its "terminal," now becomes an access route concealed in the most imperceptible entity. From this moment on, the appearance of surfaces hides a secret transparency, a thickness without thickness, a volume without volume, an imperceptible quantity.

If this situation corresponds to the outward appearance of the infinitely small, it also reaches that of the infinitely large: if what was visibly nothing becomes "something," then it follows that the longest distance no longer cuts off perception; that is, even the most vast geophysical expanse contracts and becomes concentrated. In the interface of the screen, everything is already there to be seen in the immediacy of instantaneous transmission. When Ted Turner decided, for example, to launch Cable News Network in Atlanta in 1980, a channel providing live news around the clock, he metamorphosed his subscribers' apartments into a type of station of world events.

Because of satellites, the cathode-ray window is capable of presenting antipodes along with the light of a different day to each one of its viewers. If space is that which prevents everything from being in the same place, this abrupt confinement brings everything—absolutely everything—back to that place which has no place. The exhaustion of natural relief and of temporal distances creates a telescoping of any localization, of any position. As in the case of events televised live, places also become interchangeable at will.

The instantaneousness of ubiquity results in the atopia of a single interface. Speed, which replaces the distances of space and time, abolishes the notion of physical dimension. Suddenly, speed returns to a primary scale which resists any kind of measurement, whether it be temporal or spatial. This phenomenon is equivalent to an instant of inertia of the environment. With the intense acceleration of telecommunications, the old city disappears, only to give birth to a new form of concentration:

the concentration of residentialization without residence, in which property lines, enclosures, and partitions are no longer the result of permanent physical obstacles but of interruptions of an emission or of an electronic shadow zone which mimics sunshine and the shadows of buildings. A strange topology is concealed within the conspicuousness of televised images. The sequences of an invisible montage replace the architect's blueprints. It used to be geographical space which was structured according to a geometrical setting of boundaries (urban or rural). Today it is time which is structured according to an imperceptible fragmentation of a technological time span in which cutting—a momentary interruption—replaces lasting disappearances, and in which the "program grid" replaces the grid of wire fences, just as in the past the railway replaced the ephemeris.

"The camera has become our best inspector," John F. Kennedy declared a short while before he was killed on a street in Dallas. Actually, the camera allows us to participate—live or on tape—in certain political events and certain optical phenomena, such as phenomena of breaking into effraction, in which the city lets itself be seen through and through, and phenomena of breaking apart diffraction, in which its image is reflected beyond the atmosphere to the ends of space. And meanwhile, the endoscope and the scanner are permitting us to see life in its most remote aspects. This overexposure attracts our attention inasmuch as it portrays the image of a world without antipodes, without hidden sides, a world in which opacity is no longer anything but a momentary "interlude." It must be noted, however, that the illusion of proximity does not last very long. Where the polis once inaugurated a political theater, with the agora and the forum, today there remains nothing but a cathode-ray screen, with its shadows and specters of a community in the process of disappearing. This "cinematism" conveys the last appearance of urbanism, the last image of an urbanism without urbanity, where tact and contact yield to televisual impact: not only "teleconferencing" which allows for conferring at great distances without having to move, but also "telenegotiating" which, to the contrary, lets one maintain a distance during discussion, even when one's partners are within a close physical range, a little like those telephone maniacs for whom the receiver facilitates belligerency—the anonymity of remote-control aggressivity.

Where does the city without gates begin? Probably inside the minds of returning vacationers, taking the form of that fleeting anxiety which grabs them when they think about all the unwanted mail and the possibility that their home has been broken into, their property stolen; and perhaps, also, in the desire to flee, to escape temporarily, from an oppressive technological environment in order to find oneself again, to pull oneself together. Then again, while spatial escape is still possible, temporal escape is not. Unless one considers the practice of laying-off as an "exit door," the ultimate form of paid vacation, running away in time is dependent upon a postindustrial illusion, the effects of which are beginning to make themselves felt. The theory of "shared jobs," already introduced into a segment of the community, offers each member an alternative plan in which shared timetables could open onto a whole new sharing of space: the reign of an endless periphery where the homeland and the colony would replace the industrial city and its suburbs. (Concerning this subject, see the Community Development Project, a project which promotes local development using the forces of the community itself and aims at assimilating English inner cities.)

Where does the edge of the outer city begin? Where is the door without a city located? Most likely within the new American technology used for the instantaneous destruction (by explosion) of large buildings, and also within the policy of systematic demolition of social housing judged "unfit for the new French way of life," as has been seen in Venissieux, La Courneuve, and Gagny. A recent economic study, conducted by the Association for Communications Development, arrived at the following conclusions: "The destruction of 300,000 lodgings over a period of five years would cost 10 billion francs per year, but would provide 100,000 jobs. Better yet, at the end of the operation demolition-reconstruction, the fiscal receipts would be six to ten billion francs more than the sum which the public originally invested."

One last question must now be asked: during a crisis period, will the demolition of cities replace the major public works of traditional politics? If so, it would no longer be possible to distinguish between the nature of recessions (economic, industrial) and the nature of war.

Architecture or postarchitecture? In the end, the debate surrounding the notion of modernity seems to belong to a phenomenon of "derealization" which at once affects means of expression, modes of representation, and information. The dispute currently taking place in the media with respect to certain political acts and their social communication is also being extended to architectural expression, which can never be said to be properly cut off from communication systems inasmuch as it continually experiences the direct or indirect side effects of different "means of communication" (automobile, audio-visual, etc.). Along with the technique of construction, there is, one must not forget, the construction of technique, the ensemble of spatial and temporal mutations which continually reorganize on an everyday basis the aesthetic representations of contemporary territory. Constructed space is thus not simply the result of the concrete and material effect of its structures, its permanence, and its architectonic or urbanistic references, but also the result of a sudden proliferation, an incessant multiplying of special effects, which, with consciousness of time and distance, affects perception of the environment.

This technological deregulation of different areas is also "topological" inasmuch as it no longer constructs a perceptible and visible chaos, as was the case with certain processes of degradation and destruction (accident, aging, war); to the contrary and paradoxically, it constructs an imperceptible order that, even though invisible, is just as practical as masonry or road and highway systems. Today, it is more than likely that the basis of so-called urbanism is composed/decomposed by these very systems of transfer, transit, and transmission, the transportation and transmigration networks whose immaterial configurations renew urban organization and the building of monuments. If "monuments" in fact exist today, they are no longer visible, in spite of the revolutions and convolutions of architectural grandioseness. This "disproportion" is no longer inscribed in the order of perceptible appearances, in the aesthetic of volumes assembled under the sun, but in the terminal's obscure luminosity—the home computer and other electronic "night tables." It is too easily forgotten that more than being an ensemble of techniques designed to shelter us from inclemency, architecture is an instrument of measure, a sum of knowledge capable of organizing society's space and time by pitting us against the natural environment. This "geodesic" capacity of defining a unity of time and place for activities now enters into open conflict with the structural capacities of mass communication.

Two procedures confront each other here: one is material, made up of physical elements, precisely situated walls, thresholds, and levels; the other is immaterial, its representations, images, and messages possessing neither locale nor stability, since they exist only as vectors of a momentary and instantaneous expression, with all the misinterpretations and manipulation of meanings that this implies.

The first procedure, which is architectonic and urbanistic, organizes and constructs geographic and political space in a durable fashion. The second procedure heedlessly structures and destructures space-time, the continuum of society. Obviously, it is not a question here of a Manichaean dualism opposing physics to metaphysics but rather of trying to discern the status of contemporary architecture, in particular the status of urban architecture, placed within the disconcerting concert of advanced technology. Architectonics, which developed along with the city and the discovery and colonialization of new lands, is now, since this quest has been accomplished, continually regressing, accompanied by the decline of large urban areas. While continually investing in internal technical equipment, architecture has become progressively introverted, turning into a sort of machine gallery, an exhibition hall of science and technology, technology born of industrial "machinism," of revolutions in transportation, and finally of the all-too-famous "conquest of space." However, it is symptomatic that when space technology is discussed, it is not in terms of architecture but in terms of engineering, an engineering which propels us beyond the atmosphere.

And all of this exists as though architectonics were merely a subsidiary technology surpassed by other technologies which permit sidereal projections and accelerated displacement. Thus, questions are raised concerning the nature of architectural performance, the telluric function of constructed dwellings, and the relationship between a particular conception of technology and the earth. The way in which the city has developed as a conservator for ancient technologies has already contributed to the increase in architecture by projecting it into all different directions. With its demographic concentration and extreme vertical densification, the urban center is structured in a way that is precisely the opposite of agrarian organization. Advanced technology continues to further this trend with the dramatic expansion of architectonics and in particular with the development of means of transportation. At the moment, state-of-the-art technologies, derived from the military conquest of space, are projecting dwellings—and perhaps someday will project even cities—into orbit. With inhabited satellites, space shuttles and orbital stations, high technological research, and aeronautical industries, architecture is "flying high," but not without repercussions for the fate of postindustrial society, whose cultural points of reference are disappearing one after the other, bringing about a decline of the arts and a slow regression of basic technology. Is urban architecture in the process of becoming a technology just as outdated as extensive farming? Will architectonics become nothing more than a decadent form of dominating the earth, with consequences analogous to the unbridled exploitation of raw materials? Hasn't the decline in the number of cities also become the symbol of industrial decline and forced unemployment, the symbol of scientific materialism's failure? The recourse to history, proposed by experts of postmodernity is merely a subterfuge to avoid the question of time, the regime of "transhistoric" temporality generated by technological ecosystems. If a crisis exists today, it is first and foremost a crisis of references (ethical, aesthetic), an incapacity to take stock of events in an environment where appearances are against us. The mounting disequilibrium between indirect and direct information, resulting from the development of various means of communication, tends to heedlessly privilege information mediated in such a way as to jeopardize meaning: the effect of reality seems to supplant immediate reality. The crisis of modernity's grand narratives, about which Lyotard speaks, betrays the presence of new technology, with the emphasis being placed, from now on, on the "means" and not on the "ends."

The grand narratives of theoretical causality were replaced by the little narratives of practical opportunity and finally by the micro-narratives of autonomy. The issue therefore is no longer the "crisis of modernity," the progressive degradation of common ideals, the proto-foundation of History's meaning benefiting narratives which are more or less linked to the autonomous development of an individual, but rather a crisis of narrative itself. That is, the crisis of an official discourse or mode of representation bound until now to the universally recognized capacity—inherited from the Renaissance—to assert, describe, and inscribe reality. Thus the crisis of "narrative" appears as the flip side of the crisis of "dimension," understood as a geometrical narrative, a discourse—accessible to all—of the measuring of a visible reality.

The crisis of the grand narrative and the rise of micro-narratives are ultimately the crisis of the "grand" as well as the "little," the advent of disinformation in which disproportion and incommensurability are to postmodernity what the philosophic resolution of problems and the resolution of the image (pictorial, architectural) were to the birth of the Enlightenment.

The crisis of dimension thus appears as the crisis of the whole or, in other words, as the crisis of a substantial, homogeneous space, inherited from archaic Greek geometry, to the benefit of an accidental, heterogeneous space where parts and fractions become essential once again. Urban topology has, however, paid the price for this atomization and disintegration of figures, of visible points of reference which promote transmigrations and transfigurations, much in the same way as landscapes suffered in the face of agricultural mechanization. The sudden breaking up of whole forms and the destruction of the entity caused by industrialization is, however, less perceptible within the space of the city—despite the destructuring of suburbia—than it is in time, in the sequential perception of urban appearances. In fact, for a long time now transparency has replaced appearances. Since the beginning of the twentieth century, the depth of field of classical perspective has been renewed by the depth of time of advanced technology. The development of cinematography and aeronautics followed on the heels of the opening of the "grand boulevards": the Haussmann boulevard procession was followed by the Lumière brothers' invention of accelerated motion; the esplanade of the Invalides was followed by the invalidation of urban planning; the screen abruptly became place—the crossroads of mass media.

From the aesthetics of the appearance of stable images, present precisely because of their static nature, to the aesthetics of the disappearance of unstable images, present because of their motion (cinematic, cinemagraphic), a transmutation of representations has taken place. The emergence of form and volume intended to exist as long as their physical material would allow has been replaced by images whose only duration is one of retinal persistence. Ultimately, it seems that Hollywood, much more than Venturi's Las Vegas, merits a study of urbanism, since, after the theaters of antiquity and the Italian Renaissance, it was the first Cinecittà: the city of living cinema where sets and reality, cadastral urban planning and cinematic footage planning, the living and the living dead merge to the point of delirium. Here, more than anywhere, advanced technologies have converged to create a synthetic space-time. The Babylon of film "derealization," the industrial zone of pretense, Hollywood built itself up neighborhood by neighborhood, avenue by avenue, upon the twilight of appearances, the success of illusions and the rise of spectacular productions (such as those of D. W. Griffith) while waiting for the megalomaniacal urbanization of Disneyland, Disneyworld, and Epcot Center.

When Francis Ford Coppola directed "One from the Heart" by inlaying his actors, by an electronic process, in the filmic framework of a life-sized Las Vegas reconstructed in Zoetrope Company Studios simply because he did not want his shooting to adapt itself to the city, but for the city to adapt itself to his shooting, he surpassed Venturi by far, not so much by demonstrating contemporary architectural ambiguity but by showing the "spectral" character of the city and its inhabitants.

Ray Harryhausen's and Douglas Turnbull's video-electronic special effects were added to the utopian "architecture on paper" of the 1960s at the same time that computer screens were making their way into architectural firms. "Video does not mean I see, but I fly," explained Nam June Paik. In effect, given this technology, "over-view" is no longer a question of theoretical altitude, of scale designs, but has become an opto-electronic interface operating in real time, with all that this implies about the redefinition of image. If aviation, which began the same year as cinematography, instigated a revision of point of view, a radical change in the perception of the world, infographic techniques will instigate, in their turn, a revision of reality and its presentations. This process can also be seen in the "Tactical Mapping System," a videodisc created by the United States Defense Agency for Advanced Research Projects. This system provides a viewing of Aspen in continuity by accelerating or slowing down the procession pace of 54,000 images, changing direction or season as one changes television channels, transforming the little city into a sort of ballistic tunnel in which the function of eyesight and the function of weapons merge.

In fact, if architectonics used to measure itself against the scale of geology, against the tectonics of natural reliefs with pyramids, towers, and other neogothic structures, today it no longer measures itself against anything except state-of-art technologies, whose dizzying prowess exiles all of us from the terrestrial horizon.

A neo-geology, the "Monument Valley" from a pseudolithic era, the metropolis is no longer anything but a ghostly landscape, the fossil of past societies for which technology was still closely associated with the visible transformations of substance, a visibility from which science has gradually turned us away.

The Medialization of the Cities

Edouard Bannwart

In truth, we are convinced that the cities in which we live possess regional characters that are authentic, original, and individual. The fact that these local urban structures have long been pervaded by supraregional enterprises such as international chains of stores, service industries, and restaurants is often perceived with disapproval. However, in the evening at the latest, every city radiates the same international neon style.

As the facade was once separated from the main body of the building, thereby becoming an independent means of expression, "infotainment" has at present been spread over all urban structures as an additional layer. Perceptible during the day at most as a monstrous superstructure which disregards the regional building structures in its international standard-giving function, this "infotainment" unifies all city centers at night. In addition, in order to identify these global worlds of light, buildings which are especially characteristic for a certain location are illuminated. Although these structures are often themselves part of a world of illusion as a result of renovation, reconstruction, or imitation, they are integrated into these multimedia productions as objects which provide identity.

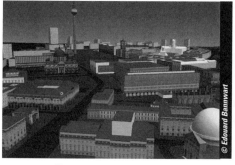

Citysnap 2: The digital model of Berlin

As part of the creation of this "multimedia city," new buildings are now being designed which are intended not only to be "data storage media" as described above, but walk-in monitors also. Depending on the software, these multimedia structural chameleons can switch from one status to the next. Structural shells conceived in this way possess a constantly altering architectural appearance, one which displays advertising or which is even mobile. Entire streets could be Chinese, Baroque, or as green as a jungle depending on the season: Linz could finally look like Vienna, and at the touch of a button!

In fact, such scenarios are only possible after the respective property owners give their approval. After all, building facades normally stand on properties owned by private parties who do not necessarily pursue the public interest. Rather, private interests will increasingly dominate the public space with the subject matter which is already sufficiently familiar from private television. This process will begin in those places walls will be first used where, for example, department stores already have continuous outer walls which can be utilized as multimedia screens.

The consequences of such private economic interests can be seen in the example of an already obsolete wall in Berlin which functions as a projection screen. At the "Ku'damm-Eck" (a corner of the Kurfürstendamm, a major street in Berlin), after a trial phase of refreshing reports, a variety of advertisements and snappy slogans, only Coke commercials and a few official announcements, broken up by time checks and portraits of the chancellor, are to be seen.

The fact that humans work or even live behind these walls does not hinder the operators and architects in the least from designing more and more such walk-in "screen bunkers." It is fortunate that the users of multimedia technologies shun the light of day considering the reflections on the monitors. However, drawing the conclusion that we should only work in sun-protected high-rise bunkers from that fact would contravene the demand made on industry to develop devices which can be used in every natural environment. Furthermore, constructing entire architectural concepts on the basis of this technical inadequacy would extend the architect's responsibility to build buildings which are fit for humans ad absurdum.

The Digital Urban Model

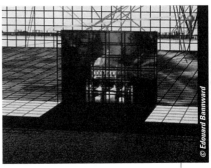

© Edouard Bannward

Walk-in "screen bunkers" are merely the heralds of a medialization of the cities. The permeation of all areas of life with information, control, and monitoring technologies is taking place in a way similar to the increasing acceleration of computer's processing speeds. The networking of these data collection and evaluation technologies has created a model of urban change which is constantly complementing itself. This dynamic model is replacing the fixation of status by means of drawings and serves as the digital basis for the planning and administration process.

Maschine IIb: The multimedial city stage

At present, ART + COM is establishing a similar digital urban model for central Berlin with the claim of being the most realistic representation possible. Exact to the centimeter, including all details, and true to the senses, it is intended to represent the urban space under the surface, of various scenarios of buildings, movements, and sounds, which can then be utilized in a variety of productions. A media store will be located under this island, the activities of which can be seen directly in the projections on the platform. However, this stage is designed only for special events, concerts, and spatial illusions which are to contribute to the creation of a communicative public space as a central focus.

With this project, ART + COM wishes to introduce into the area of urban planning an example of a multimedia space which is not at the mercy of the economic laws laid down by private property owners, but which can allow the realization of media events devoted to the public interest. The media island marks this location as the gateway to the non-material worlds and opens the window to global communication. In this way, the virtual urban model materializes at a specific place and defines the swinging door between reality and virtual reality. The medialization of the cities therefore becomes the object of public interest rather than going to waste as the *Gesamtkunstwerk* of individual financial potentates.

Edouard Bannwart *The Medialization of the Cities*

Winds of the Media from Asia: Human Beings and Art in the B-ISDN Era

Keigo Yamamoto

The Idea of a Co-Creating Era

Today, our social system and life-style have been revolutionized in accordance with the remarkable development of electronic media, and historically have reached a major turning point as humankind gropes for a new social structure. For example it is no exaggeration to say that the electronic wave of the Western European countries led to the demolition of socialism in the Eastern European countries. After the demolition, their politics, economy, industry, living, culture, and so on are being supported by the information of this electronic media and are searching for a new way of prosperous coexistence.

Advanced medi are being studied, such as the electronic media shifting from analog to digital, fusing broadcasting and communication and making intensive terminal apparatus. For example, by connecting the two COMs of communication and computer, the analog information and communication infrastructure is now shifting to a digital communication network, an ISDN (integrated services digital network). This transmission method, which was a one-way communication till recently, has developed into "a two-way transmission," "fusing various media," and made "interactive use" possible.

Further, just as the transportation system changed from railroad in the 19th century to automobile, an individual means of transportation, in the 20th century, the multimedia communication network will take on a personal use, and at the same time "official media" and "personal media" will be separated. Communication will "zeronize" time and space, which will connect the whole world into something like one living thing and "a Barthian Village Era" will arrive; but what we must keep in mind about this development is that there will still be "the West" and "the East," just as a human brain will have "a right brain" and "a left brain" and a heart also will have "a right atrium" and "a left atrium." Just as we cannot live with only the right brain or the left brain, the Barthian Village Era will become a whole only when they are both in position.

Historically, till the industrialized society, culture had a one-way stream from countries of high cultural level to those of low cultural level. Metaphorically speaking, the industrialized societies flowed in one direction from the West to the East carried by Western lies. I believe that in a high-standard information society, the West and the East will communicate and complement each other's thoughts and cultures and by doing so will finally make good use of each of their own organic functions.

So I'd like to title my report "Winds of the Media from Asia," from the artist's angle through my studies of making network art.

Art by Communication

I have been studying "the relation between transmission and art" since the beginning of 1970 and have continued producing interactive media ilnstallations which were done in terms of the participation of general viewers. For example, the video performance "MIMIC," which I did in 1973, con-

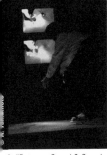

nects each separate room A, B C, D, E, F as in figure 1. First of all, the picture prepared by the artist will be sent to A of Room A. A will correspond to this picture. The picture in Room A will simultaneously be transmitted to Room B. Using this method it will be transmitted from Room A to B to C to D to E to F. Further, by repeatedly transmitting from A to B, C, D, E, F the picture will start making changes.

As in figure 1, by looking at the monitors gathered in one place transmitted from room to room, viewers can easily understand "the scene of each room" and "the transforming relation of transmission" in real time. Here you are not able to actually look into each room or compare one room with the other. However, by transmitting at zero seconds you are able to "read the mental activities," from "the time lag" and "the space lag" between rooms, and also "intervals" between perceiving and putting it into action.

1. Line of "MIMIC," 1973

Look into the relation between "to see" and "to be seen" through the network video game "Gomokunarabe" (1974–75). This is a work to communicate with remote places by using satellite, which deals with the communication and art relation in a more game-like way, and was produced to see the relation of "to see" and "to be seen" by taking scenes of participating viewers with a video camera placed at an upper diagonal position as when facing a person (see figure 2).

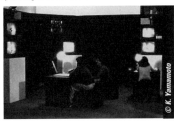

2. Video game "Gomokunarabe," 1975

In 1981, I went further with this work and made "Between Sound & Sound No. 2." This work was the exact same system as the video game "Gomokunarabe," but while "Gomokunarabe" develops on a go board, "Between Sound & Sound No. 2" develops with the whole body on a drum. In other words, "a human body turned into drumsticks."

In "Between Sounds & Sounds No. 2," using a satellite (see figures 2 and 3) the video cameras placed above each of the two monitors in two separate places, A and B, capture "a wooden drum" installed diagonally below in front. The viewers will perform on these drums. The video camera above the upper monitor of point A transmits the picture and sound of the viewer's feet

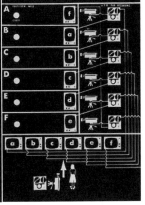

3. "Between Sound & Sound No. 2," "a corner"

performing on the drum to the upper monitor of point B. The performer of point B beats the drum with his feet by watching the picture on the upper monitor. When doing so he/she corresponds to "the expression and volume of sound of the movement of his/her feet." By combining the picture and sound transmitted from the two points A and B, the sys-

tem is made to transmit it to the lower monitor of both
point A and B.

Though the action between the two, A and B, may
look simple (the relation between the picture transmitted
from Point A and the movement of the performer's feet of
Point B), they are in a "to see and to be seen relationship." In other words, the two performers therefore must
keep in mind that they are in a "to see and to be seen
relationship" when beating their drums with their feet.

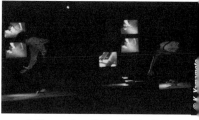

4. "Between Sound & Sound No. 2, 1981–89"

If I may explain the relation between "to see" and "to be seen" in a little more detail, when
facing a mirror, if you raise your left hand it will be reflected on the left side of the mirror, and if your
right hand it will be reflected on the right side of the mirror. In short, the relation when facing a mirror is a plane symmetry.

The relation between "to see" and "to be seen" when facing a video camera will be, if you
raise your left hand it will be shown on the right side and if your right hand is raised it will be shown
on the left side. Also, objects in a close range view will be seen on the upper part of the monitor
because a close range view is further from the camera. Objects in a distant view on the contrary will
be seen on the lower part of the monitor. So therefore, a video camera reflects objects in a different
than does a mirror. So, the relation is "a point symmetry" and must be understood by rotating 180
degrees on the point placed in the center. Up till today we believed that the relation between "to see"
and "to be seen" are that of a mirror but the relation a video camera creates is much more humane.

"The recognition lag" made by the relation "to see" and "to be seen," and "the time lag" and
"the space lag" between perceiving an act and putting it into action, are shown as the difference of
pitch and volume of the sound of a drum, and will appear as the difference between the action on the
monitor transmitted from Point A and the action corresponding to this. This difference can be apprehended at each "interval" or as "an internal breath."

For this explanation you might assume that one might mimic, but I want the performers to correspond very freely to the monitor transmitted from Point A and ask that the two make the effort to
become one expression. Also, in order to make the work successful the two in both Point A and B must
react by each reading the other's breathing.

Footwork similar to the expressions of a face also reveals the expression of a body. Because
feet support the whole body from feet to head, their expressions are closely related to the rhythm of
movements of waist and arms. There are also many different ways for a foot to touch the ground, and
its characteristics are seen in the performing arts such as Spanish flamenco, in which the foot stamps
the ground, Japanese Noh dance, in which the feet slide, and European ballet, in which the foot
stands on its toes.

When corresponding at Point B by perceiving the footwork transmitted from Point A, in the
minute time and space before putting it into action after going through numerous functions such as
the optic nerve, "interval" or "breathing" will be created. However, these "intervals" and "breathings"
are extremely difficult to capture with the naked eye. Therefore my intention is to take "the footwork
transmitted from Point A" and "the footwork of a performer" corresponding to this with a video camera which is transmitted at zero seconds and then compose it so I can show them simultaneously
using two monitors, and by doing so I will make the relation between them clearer. In short, by using
the zero-second transmission of an information network, things invisible will become visible.

If I may explain things not visible in more detail, I believe that between "the footwork transmitted from Point A" and "the performer's footwork corresponding at Point B," there is an "air current" (physical energy) like an electric field being emitted. In other words, in a place between two

frames of monitors where nothing actually exists, there exists something internal, and this is seen more clearly with a body than with one's eyes and more. I think it is seen with a "ki" (physical or mental energy). In short, I believe that "in the silent time and space while transmitting" it imparts meaningful words.

In order to understand the relation of this silent time and space more clearly, I used a half mirror in "Between Sound & Sound No. 3" (1993) so that the relation between the two performers A and B can be looked at.

Sharing Space with Remote Places

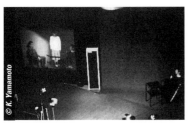

5. "Image Crossing No. 2" Telephone
....

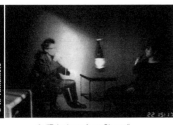

6. "Telephone from Ghosts"
....

In March 1988, between Japan and America in Fukui and in New York, I performed satellite art, and in April 1988 for the opening ceremony of Nagoya City Museum I performed "Art Crossing" using FPU (Micro line). In July 1989 I performed network art by using animated communication at the Modern Art Museum, Toyama, titled "Image Crossing No. 2," being conscious of the B-ISDN era. This picture is a scene from "Telephone from Ghosts." Only "W" alone is at the setting but on the wide screen "M" also comes into the scene. As they talk to each other, various items such as beer and a knife pop onto the screen.

Female "X" suddenly appears into this conversation. After a while the phone rings and "X" answers the phone. She tries to hand the receiver to "W" and "M" but can't hand it to them. That means this deals with "a conversation system of virtual images and real images by sharing the same space."

Satellite and B-ISDN should be used for the works I have introduced to you here, but because the line charges are extremely high and a license is necessary, I could not actually perform them. However, because the ISDN line has opened recently I have decided to grope through actual practice aiming for the art of the B-ISDN era.

Art That Has More Than One Pole

When three artists A, B, C, collaborate by using still picture transmissions, regardless of whether they are using the exact same medium, the work will turn out to be completely different depending on whether it will be transmitted to Artist B from Artist A or to Artist C from Artist A beforehand.

Another interesting aspect of this method is that when you look at the three pieces of work together, each produced at communication station A, B, and C, you are able to experience the fun of "reading the process of producing and intervals between producing." This has a completely different interest from the conventional pictures and the combination photographs you often see. In short, rather than the final piece as a completed work, it is "an art of process" made by a number of pieces and also is an art that reads the "interval" between A and B. In Japan during the Muromachi era (1338–1573), "Renga" (linked poem) "a poem read in a game-like way by collaborating" was the trend, where A recites the first half of a poem and B must recite the other half by linking to the first half of it, and this could be said to have guided network art because it is also an art to read the "interval" between A and B.

So, it is a form of art that lets you experience the process of "combination," "mixture," "conversion," and "fusion" by meeting each artist as a pole. In other words, it's more like an international marriage, a "collaboration" that cannot be foreseen, created by meeting people on equal terms regardless of race, nationality, philosophy, language, character, personality, and sense of value, rather than expressing a painter's individual inner feeling when painting in a closed up studio. This sort of meeting obviously will have a recognition lag, even when one apprehends the theme of a work.

This "lag" brings out new energy and brings forth an unpredictable effect or work, and as a result creates a great piece of work.

This network art will hold "a number of poles" on equal terms, and by pluralistic meeting they will all start coping unconsciously with their feelings, and as art is fused by the unconscious effect, I believe that interesting works beyond my imagination can be created. Therefore, it is also "art that crosses the border" by making an electronic community with a new type of artists that go beyond the border and even to the people living on the opposite side of the globe who can collaborate by sharing the pictures real time in "cyberspace and time."

Towards the B-ISDN Era: Sound Image Crossing

In the B-ISDN era, in order to work by cooperating with people in remote places in a virtual environment, the progress of "remote control," "automation," "real time," "two-way," and so forth are essential. When making studies of these characteristics, as long as B-ISDN can't be used as a public line the only choice is to study the ISDN-84.

When doing so, music is easier to connect to computers. For instance, the reason people of the Pythagorean era before Christ were solving the relation of frequency and scale, and electronic art at the early stage of art created a synthesizer, is because music has played the leading role. Further, MIDI made it possible for musical instruments in other communication stations to be remote controlled, so sound transmission is easier to study than picture transmission. For these reasons, I decided to make "Sound Image Crossing."

The basic types of "Sound Image Crossing" series I have done are as below.

Through a MIDI interface, I connected sound sources such as a synthesizer with a computer so that I can remotely control the MIDI instruments of the other stations and compose an instrument so that viewers can participate.

Also, I made a system to communicate analog sounds as well with a microphone by using Audio Cordex above 7 kHz. Further, it will depend on the distance between each communication station but making it so it will repeat and go in a loop. "To write scales by collaborating" with people in other communication stations using remote control. (Make music using remote control by transmitting music to each communication station and discussing it through phone.)

For those who can't make music with scales, have them write their names on application "M," which is a sound that can be improvised and used as music.

In order to create the feeling of being at a live performance, a total of more than eight speakers on both sides is necessary. Because hearing compared to seeing has a character that's non-directional, to create the feeling of being at a live performance made in a three-dimensional sound and space environment, it is necessary to produce hearing information from all directions. To do this, at least eight speakers are necessary. I might add that an analog telephone can be attached to PLANET ISDN.

Performance by Sound Image Crossing "MA": The Meaning of Silent Time and Space

Each participant will use one monotone to do a performance. Receiving the monotone transmitted from other stations, he or she will correspond only by the length and strength of a monotone. Because it's so simple, anybody can participate in this performance making use of "MA" (interval). Also, the instrument does not have to be a synthesizer; it could be anything that will make a sound, such as wood, bamboo, and iron.

Just as there is a master of ceremonies in a symposium, "a program director" using a mouse control is necessary to change the tempo freely and to turn the pages. This program director will conduct to heighten "silent words" like "interval, "breathing," and "ki" (mental and physical energy), which are invisible, into an expression. By using this method of sound image crossing "MA," I will concentrate on "interval" which is a silent word, and will make my work by "producing joint music" + "performed by participating viewers" + "automatic performance" + "MIDI remote control."

When talking about a theme, a conversation goes on by "looking into the mental condition" of the person you talk to. For example, when reacting to what the other person said, when you "absolutely agree" you will instantly nod but when you have any doubts about what he or she said you will probably shake your head after a slight interval.

We keep a conversation going by reading this slight time lag, in other words silent "intervals." These invisible "intervals" are "words" and also "a feeler of the mind." Different from the meetings between objects, meetings between people are an inner "meeting of mind" as well, so there could never be the same situation or meeting. In other words, every meeting is "a decisive meeting" and "a once-in-a-lifetime chance" of Zen. Sound image crossing "MA" is the exact same sort of "meeting the intervals."

Interval Between Information

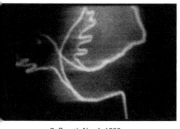

7. Breath No. 4, 1980

For instance, "Breath No. 4" (figure 7) is a work expressing a physical energy. This work is composed by two outlines, the situation now (Information A) and the situation 0.3 seconds ago (Information B) of a person. His or her arm hardly moves, so Information A and Information B overlap. On the other hand, the hand moves largely, but this movement is being supported by Information B of 0.3 seconds ago reading the information of A 0.3 seconds later. Because of this "interval" between Information A and Information B that has movement, it can convey not only "the expression of arm" but also "the emotion of that person."

This indeed is the "blank" of the Eastern drawing done in Indian ink. A content will only have a deep meaning when there are "spaces that are not drawn." These blanks are what takes you out into the space. People who express by some means put more energy into "interval" or "blank." They concentrate on putting in all their energy, but still it adds up to "zero." But without this "zero," words do not exist.

Information network was made from the "positive thinking" of economic effect, but this "zero" is just as important.

Keigo Yamamoto *Winds of the Media from Asia*

Keep Him on the Phone

The Human Body in the Realm of Technology

Melita Zajc

"Keep Him on the Phone" is a music number.* It is also a demonstration of two distinct forms of the contemporary use of communication technology: intensifying the experience on one side, preventing it on the other. That's the topic of this text. Did the contemporary technology truly make the human body redundant, superfluous even, enabling us to willfully change the bodies and identities: or, on the contrary, is it so that the human body is the only site, the only place where this shifting of identities can take place?

Safe Sex

What do we hear when listening to "Keep Him on the Phone"?

First, Techno. As a matter of fact, this number is more House than Techno, but still, it is typical enough of the kind of electronic, computer-generated music: of sounds and rhythms that are directly tuned with the human body. Of music that has to be listened to aloud, on the headphones or, better still, on distinctly coded parties, Raves; of music where rhythm and sound, not the melody, are what matters; where the non-discursive decidedly dominates over the discursive (therefore the importance of DJs who guarantee that no number is played in the same way twice; and of vinyl records that allow for the manipulation of pre-given recordings).

On the discursive, narrative level, the "Keep Him on the Phone" number re-stages the situation of another use of technology, the Phone Sex service, by re-mixing typical sounds and voices: caller dials the number, woman picks up the phone, she praises her own body and describes their engagement in the intercourse up to the point of simulated orgasm. Compared to Rave parties, technology in the case of Phone Sex functions in exactly the opposite way. Here, the two partners are physically separated, but connected one to the other by telephone line. It is true that in this particular use the telephone, the machine, connects the two. But it is also clear—because such is the main feature, the absolute advantage of this telephone service—that in this use the telephone prevents any physical contact in sexual intercourse. Here, there are no chances that one would get AIDS: Phone Sex is a perfect form of Safe Sex.

*From LP 1-900, Strictly Rhythm, produced by Speropagos, remix George Morel, 1995

Of course, what one experiences by listening to this number is not a clear form of Phone Sex, but the difference should nevertheless be obvious:

• By Techno and, even more, by Rave parties, one is immediately experiencing: feeling the rhythm, hearing the sound, seeing the lights, images, and live performances, smelling the smoke; and one is enjoying it.

• By Phone Sex, one is enjoying, but except for the sound, one is experiencing nothing: seeing the "beautiful blonde hair," feeling the touch of the skin, sensing the other person's smell, all these things that the woman on the phone is talking about, all these do not exist.

What in "Keep Him on the Phone" bonds the two described uses of technology (Rave parties and Phone Sex service) or, as I'll call them later, the two apparatuses, what on the discursive level fuses them into a single, distinct object is the male voice repeating "Keep Him on the Phone." What does it mean? It makes visible what both, the sex on the phone and electronic music, presume: they are forms of entertainment industry. To put it even more plainly: it's all about money. And about power. The "Keep Him on the Phone"-man is exercising power over the woman, the woman is exercising power over the caller. One could easily conclude that as an object of Techno music, the "Keep Him on the Phone"-number, by referring to the motives other than the consumer's enjoyment, points to the "truth" of its own production. But here we reach the point demanding some conceptual clarity.

Sad Friends of the Truth

In a culture where seeing is believing, metaphors, in particular metaphors on seeing, are a convenient way for presenting concepts. John Milton, 17th century British poet, was blind, and probably for this reason he was able to see things more clearly. In a pamphlet which he addressed to the British Parliament in order to defend the idea of the Freedom of the Press, he described "the truth" this way:

The Truth was of a clear image once. As such, it was sent to the Earth, but evil men smashed it up into thousands of pieces and scattered these pieces all over the world.

Therefore, the only thing left to the journalists—and others who are looking for The Truth, "sad friends of The Truth" he called them—the only thing they can do is to look for the separate pieces of the truth.

This has two consequences:

First, we cannot ever, know "the whole truth." It is only available to us in pieces, in distinct parts.

Second, if we start with the question WHAT, then, by deciding WHAT "the truth" or any other phenomena is, we already determine HOW to approach it. If to the question WHAT is the truth, we answer, "it is a distinct, wholesome entity," then we'll look for it, and when we encounter something that looks like it, we'll presume that's the whole and only truth. But if, to the same question, we answer, "truth is scattered all around in pieces," then we'll look for pieces everywhere, but we'll never be satisfied, always in doubt, if together with some other, not-found parts, this partial truth would still be the same, or would it be totally different. In other words, a decision on ontology already implies certain epistemology.

The first who pointed out this feature of the classical philosophical question of WHAT was Russian linguist Roman Jakobson. He demonstrated it by the example of the basic units of language, the phonemes. The classical question was, WHAT are these basic units of language: Are they the phenomena generated by the throat? Or the phenomena generated by the brain? Jakobson did not try to answer, instead, he showed that the answer to this question, to WHAT (ontology), already implies the approach, the HOW (epistemology). Those who say the basic unit of language is a matter of the throat, do research in anatomy; those who say it is a matter of the brains, do research in acoustics. But, concluded Jakobson—and this is the main contribution of structuralism to the humanities—if instead of WHAT we start with HOW, if instead of ontology we start with epistemology, we do not imply anything like that.

Still, the notion that there must be some final and definite truth is very persistent. And here is where the mechanisms of mediation, the technology, the machines get the decisive role. Simply: if humans, always emotional, biased, prejudiced, are not able to grasp the definite truth, then the machines should be capable of doing this instead of us. Therefore the machine was conceived as the model for thinking, for understanding the world, and also the body. This is the origin of the ideas of the World Machine and of the Body Machine. Such a notion presumes the clear separation of the observing subject on one side and the observed object on the other, or the cognitive subject on one side and reality on the other. Between the two, there is supposed to be a measuring mechanism that helps the subject to grasp the nature, the truth, of the object.

In the arts, the measuring mechanism was Renaissance perspective. The codes of this perspective themselves were conceived as the tools for measuring the outside world, but classical painters often used additional, material tools to do this; such as were Alberti's "constructions" or Dürer's "portillon."

In natural sciences, this mechanism was presumably provided by physics; its methods and tools enabled people to measure the outside world, they were the means by which the subject was comprehending the object. If we take a table as an example: we should be able to grasp the truth of its nature by measuring its height and width, the structure of the material, and so on. But this ideal notion of the subject, the object, and safe, observing distance between the two, where the measuring mechanism is located, has been severely questioned in natural sciences as well as in the humanities. In physics it happened when, by quantum mechanics, the measuring mechanisms themselves were being developed to such a degree that it was possible to prove—let's stay with the example of a table—that a table does not exist. We would say that it is of a solid matter, but, actually, the distance between the particles is immense in relation to the radius of the electron or the nucleus of one of the atoms of which the table consists.

In the humanities the doubts were clearly articulated even sooner, for example by the 18th century British philosopher Jeremy Bentham. Bentham used the law as an example of the importance of the imaginary, untruthful entities. He called them fictions and defined them "as the saying something exists which does not exist, and acting as if it existed."

So, now we are in the situation where physics proved that the presumably "real world," "real entities" does not really exist, are not real at all; and where the humanities proved that not-real entities, fictions, can be more "real" than presumably "real entities." But does this indeed imply—as most of contemporary, so called postmodernist thinkers claim—that there are only fictions left, that everything is being simulated, virtual, fictitious, imaginary . . . —That nothing is real? Should we deny that there are tables at all as we ordinarily conceive them? I don't think so; I explained before, with the help of Milton's metaphor, that there is no such thing as one, definite and final truth or reality, that our notion of the truth, the reality, is always partial, always constructed.

Now we can say why: because it is impossible to separate the observing subject from the observed object; the observing subject influences the observed object and vice versa. Everything depends on the concept. At least two contemporary theories prove this distinction, this separation not possible: Hillary Putnam's "Theory of the Interior Realism" and Weibel's and Rössler's "Theory of the Interior Observe." In both, we see again that instead of WHAT, they ask the question HOW. This is the point I regard as decisive with respect to the technology: not the impossibility of any final conclusion about the nature of things, but the specific role of the approach, of the method of comprehending the world, of the mechanisms of mediation or, in the broadest sense, of the technology.

Before defining the concept, the method of conceptualizing the contemporary use of technology, we have one other question to ask. Where, now, is the place of the human body? One thing is clear from daily experience: like this table, the body also did not simply disappear. But we should be more precise.

In his theory of ideology, Louis Althusser also claims that the imaginary has material effects. As an example he cites the religious belief in God: God is imaginary, but those who believe in him perform material actions—they go to church, attend masses, they make the sign of the cross, they pray on their knees, and so on. However, the difference between Christianity and other more "primitive" religions lies in the fact that in the Christian religion the control of the physical body is being mediated, not direct. Also among Christians only the most devout believers, like members of the Catholic group Opus Dei, inscribe their belief on their bodies by daily whipping, by wearing chastity belts and the like.

The same happens with the manifestations of another, most common imaginary phenomena, the state of what we call eternal love. "Cultivated," "civilized" people exchange wedding rings. Tattoos with the names of beloved ones written on the skin are attributes of the people from social margins. In the realm of cinema, for example, the mainstream movies always portray the state of love by more or less stereotyped metaphors like birds and sentimental music. Movies which portray love by means of the transformation of the body—like films of Tod Browning ("Freaks" or "Unknown"), R. W. Fassbinder's "The Year with Thirteen Moons," "Empire of the Senses" by Nagisa Oshima, or "Boxing Helena" by Jenifer Lynch—are considered at least bizarre.

All this, together with the popular interpretations of the development of technology as fixing the physical failings of the human body, clearly shows that we tend to understand civilization as a constant liberation from the physical body. But in the essay on "Kontext Kunst" Peter Weibel also shows how Bentham in a way preceded Jacques Lacan. Lacan conceptualized reality not as a unity of object and subject but as a structured form of imaginary, symbolic, and real. Real is not reality, it is not truthful or realistic. It is located where there are no words: in sex and violence, and death. And what is the place where these experiences can take place? This place is the body.

Les Mots et les Choses

Regarding the notion of civilization, we can understand why it is so popular nowadays to claim that our culture, contemporary culture, is another step in the process of liberation from our bodies. Yet we can clearly experience, every time we go to the cinema or turn on the computer, that contemporary technologies all presume, demand the individual, in his or her bodily dimension.

Theorists who claim that everything is being simulated ground their notion on the idea that contemporary culture is the culture of images, that we moved from the culture of writing to the culture of images. Contrary to this, I propose the concept of the apparatus (*le dispositif*) as a simultaneous presence of both, of words and of images. *Le dispositif* was conceptualized by Michel Foucault, who in *The Order of Things* claims that "what we see is never present in what we say." Therefore, in his work Foucault developed the concept of *le dispositif* which enables us to think the simultaneous presence of both, of what we see and of what we say; as the specific organization of the discursive and non-discursive, which always includes the subject.

This later feature of *le dispositif*, the inclusion of the subject, is particularly important for the thinking of the use of technology. It is initiated in Foucault's analysis of Diego Velásquez's painting *Les Ménines*: he takes the painting as *le dispositif* and clearly points out how it includes its own observer. This feature was further developed by Jean-Louis Baudry in his essays on cinema. In Baudry's terms, *le dispositif* pertains to the situation in which the film technology is being used: to the apparatus and, at the same time, to its addressee. By this concept, Baudry arrived at his historical conclusion: namely, that the "reality effect" of the cinema does not depend on what is being represented on film. The cinema does not simulate reality, it simulates the subject: "The entire cinematographic apparatus [tout le dispositif cinématographique] is activated in order to provoke this simulation: it is indeed a simulation of a condition of the subject, a position of the subject, a subject and not reality." *Le dispositif,* in other words, "concerns projection and . . . includes the subject to whom the projection is addressed."

We could already conclude that Baudry's concept pertains to both, to a hypothetical subject position and to the actual person; to the (imaginary) spectator and to the (real) viewer; or, in the terms of the critique of ideology, to the subject and to the individual. However, the notion of the subject is, first, the key point of Baudry's concept of *le dispositif,* and second, it is also the most controversial point of this concept, as conceived within the paramount interpretation of Baudry's concept, the Theory of the Apparatus. Hence, let's have a closer look at this interpretation:

On one hand, it is based on the American translation that equates both, *l'appareil* and *le dispositif,* with "the apparatus," even if Baudry explicitly states that *le dispositif*—unlike *l'appareil*—"includes the subject."

On the other hand, the main argument against the Theory of the Apparatus is that it conceives the subject as an effect, as a structural function of ideology; that therefore it does not acknowledge the active role of the concrete individuals, real viewers, people in flesh and blood: and that it is therefore inadequate or even irrelevant.

Therefore we can not simply reject this interpretation as a misreading. On the contrary: the translation is somehow misleading, but the interpretation is nevertheless correct, because it regards the apparatus as that which "includes the subject." Even the notion of the subject is appropriate as far as Baudry's essay was written in the context of Althusser's critique of ideology in which the individual is "always-already interpellated" into the subject of ideology.

Contrary to this, the argument that Baudry's concept of the apparatus pertains to both the imaginary subject and the real viewer postulates that the individual is not always-already the subject (of ideology); that the individuals are not interpellated as subject but *into* subject; in short, that the ideological interpellation is not necessarily successful. This is demonstrated by Rastko Monik in his essay "Ideology and Fantasy": the act of identification is impossible if it doesn't get the support for the individual's idiosyncratic "wishful fantasies."

If so, if ideological interpellation can indeed fail, in other words, if the critique of ideology does not exclude the individual, then we can conclude as I previously suggested. The Apparatus is a situation and a setting ("metaphorical relations between places and relations between metaphorical places," locational and relational at the same time), which:

1) constitutes the subject, by providing him or her an imaginary subject position, a simulated point of view which one must take in order to recognize the representations and which is common to every spectator; and

2) includes the subject, because it always relates to the individual, to the concrete, living person, to whom it assigns a distinct place within the setting.

Indeed, the contemporary technology for the production of images presumes a fixed place for the body of the viewer, a place in which every single individual is, in one way or the other, isolated from the others. At the movies, the viewer buys a ticket that entitles him or her to one distinct seat in the hall; when watching TV, people are put into the couches in their living rooms: cybersuits, datagloves, head-mounted displays are made to be used by one user at a time; the same is true with the telephone, and it is also impossible to end with what we started, to dance on Techno in constant touch with another person as in classical polka and waltz dances or even rock 'n' roll. This is probably the best example: at Rave parties, the touch of the other is unbearable.

In short: not only *some* contemporary communication technologies but *all* of them are isolating the individual by preventing him or her from physically experiencing the closeness of other individuals.

Dying Live

What about the other feature of the contemporary use of communication technology, the intensifying of experience? It is obvious from the arts, from the development of new technologies, from TV that the intensified experience is one of the main objectives. In the arts, there is an honorable tradition of body-artists, from Valie Export, Marina Abramovic, or Chris Burden to the most notorious contemporary one, Orlan. Virtual reality and cyberspace are praised for their multiplication of the senses involved—sight, touch, hearing, even smell. And as for the most overwhelming media technology, namely television, we are all aware that Reality TV programmes, Real World series, and the like are all aiming at achieving the same.

Instead of listing various particularities, I'd like to prove the point by the example of one single thing: the representation of passing away in photography, cinema, and TV. André Bazin, the great theorist of film realism, regarded the ability to represent dying as the main advantage of cinema in comparison to photography. Photography, according to Bazin, "can represent a man in his agony before the death or his dead body, but not the unaccessible drift from one to the other."

Let's take as an example an old and well-known photograph, the one taken by Eddie Adams in Saigon in 1968, of a Vietnamese soldier Nguyen Ngoc Loan, pointing his gun right to the forehead of his civilian prisoner. If we compare this photo with the 16 mm film shot of the same event, we can clearly see the difference. With the film shot, we get the event in its duration: soldiers capture the prisoner somewhere on the streets, they take him to the square, the soldier takes a gun into his hand, motions the others to move away, points the gun, shoots; the prisoner falls down and for more than ten seconds we can observe the fountain of blood springing from the hole in the man's head.

Moving images are clearly more effective than static ones; but this is not all. In one of the contemporary advancements of the Cinematographic Apparatus, the Location Based Entertainment (LBE), the representation becomes even more true. The location here is the location of the narration: the spectator is fastened to his or her chair and via the chair to the machinery, which gives him or her to see, what the movie makers call point-of-view shots. What Harrison Ford is in "Indiana Jones" and Kathleen Turner is in "Romancing the Stone," the spectator him or herself is in the Location Based Entertainment. We can compare this to IMAX, Disney's Animatronics, and even more to SimEx "cinema," but the Apparatus of LBE is much more inclusive. As a proof of the effectiveness of this kind of entertainment, a journalist commented that it was so real that his heart would almost stop. One of the operators of LBE dully replied, "if you have a heart attack, it is your problem." The issue here is not the ability to represent, but the absence of representation: dying is not experienced through representation, it is experienced—at least potentially—live.

Not only the isolation of the individual consumer, but also the magnification of the experience is a feature that pertains to all, not only to some of the contemporary uses of communication technology. At the beginning I proposed these as two distinct forms of the use of technology, namely, that technology either provides the means for intensifying the experience or prevents the individual from physical experience. Now, I have to conclude, these are not two forms that would exclude each other, but two simultaneous processes: processes in which the individual is isolated in order to experience, and in which one type of closeness, one type of experience, is replaced by the other. It is the very concept of the Apparatus that enables us to think this simultaneity: the real person must limit its bodily capacities (has to "take place," be isolated as an individual) in order to identify with the imaginary subject position which entitles her or him to the enjoyment provided by the Apparatus. But, if technology presumes or even demands the codified limitation of the corporeal facet of its consumers, should we conclude that the contrary is also the case? Ought we to consider the physical experience as a form of resistance to the use of technology?

The answer lies in the third example of representation of passing away: the one on TV. Live transmission is the most distinct feature of television. There is no doubt that so-called live parts of a TV program are as pre-planned and controlled as any other previously recorded feature in this program. But as the property of the TV apparatus, live transmission is the mechanism that connects both spaces, the (everyday) space of the viewer and the (imaginary) space of TV: it is a tool that puts both spaces in the same time. Live transmission cannot be repeated. Just like, as Bazin says, one cannot die twice. So, if live transmission is the final achievement of television, then the final achievement of TV's maximizing the experience would be live transmission of dying.

Actually, at the very beginnings of television in Slovenia (for other regions I do not know of a research of this kind), live transmissions of surgical operations from the local hospital were extremely popular. People at TV Ljubljana tested their very first equipment and first cameras for color TV this way. One of the protagonists of these events remembers: "Then Prof. Lavric, who was operating on the other patient, asked me whether the interior of the chest was clearly visible; otherwise he would widen up the cut for the camera."

This happened in 1958. In August 1967, when the association of Yugoslav radio and TV stations, JRT, was transmitting for Eurovision, live of course, the heart surgery by the famous American heart surgeon DeBakey in Belgrade, TV Ljubljana gave up the live transmission. Instead, they broadcast a shortened version of the surgery one day later. The public was enraged, but medics provided the arguments for the ban: something could have gone wrong and the patient might have died. This is like in the circus, they said, but "the penetration into the human body is no circus."

Later this interpretation prevailed on other TV stations as well. At the beginning of the seventies Peter Weibel created two projects of live transmission for Austrian national broadcasting (ORF). One, like the early TV "short breaks," would have shown the interior of an aquarium, only here the water would gradually leak out until the fish would be left without water and die. The other project would have offered a view into a terrarium where there would first be snakes; then mice would be thrown to the snakes and the snakes would eat the mice before the eyes of TV viewers. The first project ORF realized to the moment when it was still possible to save the fish; the other was never realized on public TV.

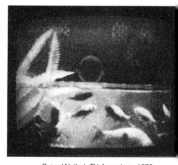

Peter Weibel, TV-Aquarium, 1970

The story is not over yet. In November 1994 German police hunted two run-away prisoners who took civilian hostages. The reporters were excluded from the places of the event. The reason: fear of the repetition of the so-called "drama in Gladbek," an event that took place a few years ago: in a similar situation, one of the hostages was killed in front of running TV cameras.

Contrary to the claims that there is nothing that TV wouldn't show, contrary to the critics who advocate *Entbrutalisierung* of the media, there are things that TV wouldn't show. I don't claim that TV should be showing this. But the very presence of these limits is the reason, I think it is meaningful to point out, that contemporary media are preventing us from certain experiences. These experiences still take place in our societies and in our individual lives; therefore we should consider them as forms of resistance against the transformation of our experience through technologies, regardless of how we understand, and what value we assign to, the term "resistance." Affirmative or not.

Literature

Jean-Louis Baudry, *Cinéma effets idéologiques produits par l'appareil de base, Cinéthique 7–8 (1970).*
Jean-Louis Baudry, *Le dispositif: approches métapsychologiques de l'impression de réal, Communications 23 (1975).*
Roman Jakobson, *Lingvistini in Drum Spisi (Studia humanitatis, 1989).*
Rastko Monik, *"Ideology and Fantasy," in: The Althusserian Legacy (Verso, 1993).*
Peter Weibel, *"Intelligent Beings in an Intelligent Universe," in: Ars Electronica 94 (PVS, 1994).*
Peter Weibel, *"Kontextkunst," in: Kontext-Kunst (DuMont, 1994).*

Slacker Luddites

Critical Art Ensemble

Throughout the first world, nothing is more emblematic of zero work nihilism than the image of Luddite resistance. Joyful destruction of machines in the workplace: Is there anyone who hasn't entertained such fantasies? Who hasn't thought about crashing a workstation hard drive, spilling coffee into a mainframe, or throwing a company vehicle into reverse while speeding down the highway? For many, such fantasies become reality, and neo-Luddites are born. But are such deeds really the acts of Luddites, or do they merely replay a historical narrative that never existed—an indulgence in nostalgic creations? Because of the profound differences that separate the political economies of early and late capital, the nihilistic impulses of early 19th-century Luddites cannot be qualitatively compared to those arising now in the late 20th century. The Luddite designation can only be used rather loosely in the society of late capital. On its surface, the image of early 19th century workers smashing the machines of textile mills has a potency that seems utterly relevant to the crushing alienation of the contemporary workplace, but the motivations and ideology that lie behind Luddite activity today have little in common with the Luddites of the past.

The Luddism of early capital represented the dying thoughts of the feudal body, while the attacks on the textile factories were the final muscle spasms of the feudal corpse. Those who were motivated to participate did so out of the fear that they were becoming anachronisms. It seemed clear to the Luddites that machines were going to replace them and steal away their livelihoods, as poor as they may have been. Any political intent behind Luddite activities was counterrevolutionary in nature—an attempt to stop the revolution in production, and to halt the shift of power from land to capital (from nobility to bourgeoisie). The final goal of the Luddite was to maintain the status quo, since the Luddites of early capital were desperation personified in their deathly fear of machines, economic instability, and the future. From a cool intellectualized perspective, Luddites are not a group to be canonized in the history of resistance to authoritarian structures. If anything, they were demons in this history. But let us not forget the passions. Smashing up factories—that must be one supreme libidinal discharge. Such actions signify moments of free-form desire. To substitute for these moments, which are too few in the lives of individuals in late capital, the myth of the Luddite continues to dwell in the hearts of all people who hate work in general, their jobs in particular, and the repressive atmosphere omnipresent in the work environment.

From the contemporary viewpoint nearly two centuries later, it should be very apparent that Luddism in its historical form has no place in late capital (only its mythic form carries meaning). The conditions have changed too drastically, and yet there are still some threads of continuity. Fueled by images of anti-tech nihilism, traces of the Luddite mythology live on, but as nothing more than isolated fragments offering only intermittent patterns of significance. Most importantly, the specific fear that motivated the originary Luddites is gone. Although technological development causes many people fear and anxiety, fewer and fewer believe that technology will replace them. In fact, the fear is really quite the opposite. As technology attaches itself to the body, the relationship between the body and technology becomes increasingly symbiotic. The bureaucratic and technocratic classes and portions of the service class are being turned into cyborgs. This is the new Luddite fear; the fear of losing organic purity, and of becoming overdependent on/addicted to technology.

Examples of people being turned into cyborgs are quite numerous; the most obvious place where this occurs is of course the military. In that institution, ruled by a desire for technology to run wild, people want to be machines—killing machines. The better a soldier can transform h/erself into pure technology, the better h/er chances of surviving combat. Headsets, night vision goggles, automatic weapons, lasers, gas masks, etc., are all attached to the body, extending its possibilities. This is a second-order cyborg: Organic infrastructure with an impermanent technological superstructure. The question is, at what point will the techno-superstructure become permanent, creating a first-order cyborg?

The first-order cyborg can be a frightening thought, especially considering how well the middle class is being groomed for this development. Rather than being framed in terms of death, the cyborg question is framed in terms of life, desire, and entertainment. From pacemakers to contact lenses, bio-tech makes the body stronger. Who will say no to technology that extends life, or to that which returns the body to normative functions? Let us not forget the possibilities for balancing the body's appearance with its desired image. Everything from artificial cheek implants to sex change operations offer liberating experiences of a nomadic, ever-transforming body. And finally, what of all the video and virtual reality games? It is fun to go into those artificial electronic worlds. Just suit up, and the conquest of death is at your command. Apocalypse and utopia have imploded with such force under the sign of technology that it is nearly impossible to separate the two possibilities. The media machine of the corporate complex maintains a utopian spectacle to keep the population moving toward existence as cyborgs. This is part of the reason why it is difficult to find a contemporary Luddite with the same zeal for destruction that h/er predecessors had. Contemporary Luddites do not hate technology. On the contrary, they are comfortable with it. At the same time, technology is not accepted without question to the extent desired by corporate futurologists and public relations people. The relationship between the Luddite and technology is a little more ambiguous than it once was, and consequently the anti-tech nihilism has also dissipated. What more can be said? Compared to the original Luddites, the contemporary anti-tech malcontents are slackers.

Rather than continuing to examine the more sensationalized aspects of technology, let's return to the everyday life of the bureaucratic class. The environment of the bureaucracy keeps the traces of Luddism alive. No matter how big a smiley face the corporate futurologists put on technology and the cyborg alternative, spend only a few moments sitting at a workstation, staring into a computer screen, and one realizes that something about this situation is truly debilitating. Or look around the office at all the other workstations, and witness the organic debris of hit-and-run victims on the digital highway. It's an unpleasant vision to say the least, but perhaps worse is the feeling that technology is starting to cleave to the skin. This feeling inspires the realization that the greater the efficiency of the human/tech interface, the better for bureaucratic production. The most basic slacker Luddite tactics have developed to counter this withering repression. Some are time-honored, such as repeated trips to the rest room. Some are newer, such as meeting at the xerox machine for a bitch session with other workmates. This tactic is of a higher order than the former, because not only are the workers doing nothing, but they are also getting paid for having nonproductive conversation (distinguishing between the orders of slacker Luddism will be discussed later in the essay). These tactics not only slow the rate of production, they also temporarily hinder the bio-tech synthesis. Unfortunately, high level management also realizes this, inspiring it to greater efforts to accelerate the synthesis necessary for maximum exploitation.

At present, employees can be monitored by devices connected to their computers, so the overseers know precisely how long a worker has been at h/er workstation and can even take keystroke counts, but surveillance alone is not enough. Slacker Luddites know how to get around these surveillance techniques. However, once the organic and the technological are joined, workers will never be able to leave their workstations. They will be able to move from place to place, but they will never be able to check out. The wearable computers from NEC Corporation exemplify this corporate elite science fiction fantasy. There is little doubt that the task of compressing machine space and organic space (the workstation and the body) into a single compact unit is well under way.

Yet despite all this workplace terror, as long as technology offers services to the individual, it receives the utopian benefit of the doubt. It is both useful and enjoyable. Quite commonly, a slacker Luddite who hates to slave on h/er computer at work returns home only to sit at the computer again, to desktop publish h/er own magazine. This situation is the opposite of originary Luddism. The slacker Luddite shuns or destroys technology not because of a hatred or fear of it, but because of a hatred for work, while originary Luddites were accustomed to work, but hated and feared the technology. Slacker Luddism is a late capital hybrid, a perfect example of recombinant culture. It synthesizes the tactics of originary Luddism with the zero work ethic of contemporary slackers.

Even an idea like zero work begins the process of depoliticization. Zero work is generally associated with radical left action, but this is not the intention of the slacker Luddite. While zero work was formerly a strategy made specific in the notion of a universal strike, an effort to force the collapse of the capitalist system, the slacker Luddite sees zero work as a desirable condition personally. No grandiose goals of social and political restructuring are involved. Under the slacker rubric, zero work is transformed into a therapeutic strategy, a way to feel good about yourself. The slacker Luddite oscillates between individual heroism and political naivete.

The situation of the slacker Luddite is also directly influenced by h/er class position. Unlike in the past, the slacker Luddite is more likely to be a bureaucrat, technocrat, or service worker, and less likely to be a worker proper. The current conditions of the working class are such that slack is extremely hard to achieve. Since such conditions emerged out of early capital, the strategies of resistance developed during that time are more common and practical. For those working on the assembly lines, resistance is a matter of all or nothing. For instance, the assembly line moves at a fixed rate, so slacker attempts to slow down production will generally lead to hasty dismissal. The only real options are general strike (a dead strategy), or (following the tactics of early Luddites) machine destruction for the purpose of completely shutting down the factory. Neither of these tactics is very common now, and they are both very risky in terms of potential punishment from the state. Slack is not an accurate description of these approaches. In terms of the latter tactic of "throwing a wrench in the machine," the technocrat is better equipped. By introducing viruses into corporate or bureaucratic communication systems, the individual resister can do much more damage than by stopping a point of production—s/he can attack the command and control of a complex manufacturing multi-site.

In the case of skilled laborers, such as construction workers, the use of independent contracting severely curtails Luddite or slacker Luddite activity. Profits increase with the rate of production for skilled laborers and independent contractors, and technology is a great aid in keeping production rates high. Further, since most of the equipment these workers use belongs to them, it would be quite foolish for them to destroy their own property. Consequently, this is not a likely location for Luddite ideology or action.

For bureaucrats, however, the conditions are perfect for Luddism to grow and flourish. The work is just esoteric enough to make it very difficult to determine reasonable production rates. Add this factor to the low pay, the most alienating of working conditions, and a general ideology of "minimum pay, minimum work," and all varieties of slacker Luddite behavior become more likely. The work itself is relatively secure, so the situation is less desperate than it is for workers. This difference is key in separating the slacker Luddite from h/er predecessors. Unlike in the days of early capital, Luddite action is no longer a matter of survival. To some extent, slacker Luddism actually requires a certain degree of luxury, At the same time, this is ironically where one of the strongest threads of continuity appears between Luddites and slacker Luddites. In both cases, desire to regain control of the work situation is a primary motivating force. It is resistance to instability that ties the generations of Luddites together.

The problem of instability cannot be disconnected from the ever-increasing velocity of communication, production, and consumption in the age of capital. The perils of nomadic and recombinant culture are most menacing to those who attempt to construct a sense of place. No real sense of continuity exists, leaving memory without stable linkage points to the world of phenomena. Objects in the world are forever coming at the individual, leaving no time for reflection on interactions with them, much less time to turn around to see where one has just been. (This is another reason why there is a corporate-military demand for the cyborg life form. Working machines need no time for reflection.) Perhaps the problem is even greater and more fundamental than the establishment of place, since it is questionable whether any stable concept of space itself remains. What space are we in while speaking on the phone? What world are we looking into while staring at a computer screen or a video monitor? It is very difficult to say. Can space be folded in on itself so that it is possible to be everywhere at once through the use of communication technology? William Gibson described cyberspace as a "consensual hallucination." If that is so, how do we decide which hallucinations to subscribe to, and how trustworthy they are? More to the point, is the hallucination based on consensus at all? The intense confusion and skepticism that arises from the dematerialization of physical space often awakens nostalgia for a return to the hegemony of physical space; at the very least, it inspires a yearning for a means to temporarily stabilize the immediate environment.

The original Luddites represented a vague intuition that political economy was about to enter its dromologic era. The ability of the machine to work more efficiently than people, as individuals and as groups, appeared as a material fetishization of speed. As the old routes of labor began to dematerialize, the Luddites reacted by destroying the fetish object (i.e., the machine). It was an attempt, however misguided, to reestablish the old regime of everyday life. Although technology was perceived as an evil to be feared, the truly frightening thing was the inability to maintain self and place. It was all disappearing.

Slacker Luddites also desire a sense of stability in terms of both self and place; however, this desire is not precisely the same as that of their forerunners. In fact many are speed freaks, but they are speed freaks who like to control their own dosage. As mentioned above, the proper dosage is measured against personal comfort. Slackers do not recognize the adrenal experience of hyperanxiety as useful or desirable. Understanding their need to control the velocity at which they travel, so as never to completely dematerialize self or environment, is key to comprehension of slacker Luddite tactics.

Another idea that is central to understanding Luddite tactics is the aforementioned association of neo-Luddism with zero work. They know that some production must be accomplished, and that although they may resist, they cannot choose not to work. However, they believe that no one should do any more work than is absolutely necessary. Once the word "work" is used, the slacker Luddite knows problems are ahead. In fact, this word should be discarded, and replaced with what the word actually means: alienated action. "Leisure" is no better. The two are sides of the same coin. The former is coerced production, while the latter is coerced consumption. In the utopian world of the slacker Luddite, no distinction exists between work and leisure; there are only desired responses to the world.

Part of the slacker Luddite's mission is to reappropriate the workplace—that is, to strip it of its alienating qualities. This is often done by personalizing it, thereby creating a place where s/he can accomplish whatever s/he desires. Slacker Luddites attempt to make the workplace enjoyable, i.e., not a workplace. For example, the lower orders of slackness consist primarily of varieties of "goofing off." These are attempts to separate from the machine, and to thereby deny or temporarily destroy the cyborg identity. The easiest machine to eliminate is your own. Once separated from the machine, a relative quietude ensues that allows for reflection, and even face-to-face interaction.

Retreatism and passivity, however, are novice slacker techniques. The reward is too short in duration, and it is too easy to be caught and given a patronizing reprimand. The high-end slacker personalizes the cyborg itself, which is its ultimate destruction. S/he transcends goofing off. This slacker spends time at the workstation playing video games, chatting with friends on the internet, making travel plans, and so on. The computer registers the time served at the station, so surveillance is deflected. (Fortunately, the computer cannot as yet record whether labor power has been expended in a manner useful to a given employer.) But best of all is the slacker who does freelance assignments while at work. This slacker is paid both for a project that s/he wants to do, and for using a hostile institution's time, equipment, and supplies.

The slacker Luddite delights most in misappropriating the technology, and in turning the authoritarian codes of the workplace inside out. H/is mission is not to destroy the material aspects of work—this would be as misguided as the actions of the originary Luddites—but rather to destroy the symbolic order that confines and alienates the individual. This is not to say that an occasional intentional freezing or crashing of the technology never occurs, or that such actions are not of interest; however, these tactics, when done under the sign of slack, are only a means to a very limited end. All high-end slackers know that it is the hallucination of the workplace that must be destroyed, not that which conveys the hallucination.

Alienation and misery are integral parts of the economy of desire. Work must be as unfulfilling an experience as possible, for only by torturing people day in and day out will they emerge from the prison of production with the zeal to consume that which they artificially desire. The desperate act of consumption—purchasing as a means to fill some fundamental lack—could be perceived only by the truly exploited as a viable strategy to resolve the crisis of life in late capital. Strategies which break this obscene cycle are few. If the Luddites showed us anything, it was that the workplace is a prime location for resistance, and that resistance is very effective when it is an attack from within the institution itself. Their methods may have lacked any reasonable subtlety, but their nihilism still acts as a rallying point. If the slacker Luddites have shown us anything, it is the value of blasting the codes of the ideational place, not the space itself. As long as the workplace continues to be an environment that steals our autonomy with the intention of making labor as unfulfilling as possible, there will always be traces of Luddism, and there will certainly always be slackers.

NETOPOS . . . NOTOPOS

Fate of Reason in the Global Network:
₂ology, Telegraphy, Telephony, Television, Telesthetics

Timothy Druckrey

I.

The cyborg would not recognize the Garden of Eden . . .
Donna Haraway

There is little feedback in human affairs, and the bandwidth is less than we think.
Marvin Minsky

Time and space died yesterday.
F. Marinetti

Space and duration have come to dominate discourses of the shift from modernity to post-modernity. Decades of scientific, critical, and philosophical writing have yet to fully theorize the end of space as a consequence of the temporalization of events, and simultaneously, the distinctly material space of the transaction with the world has overwhelming potency. Obviously, the two structures of the spatial and the temporal share a reciprocal effect.

And while the debate surrounding the linkage between the various imperialisms of the spatial and the temporal hound, and limit, critical thinking about culture, the smooth contradictions between identity (national and otherwise) and presence persist. Space might be the "final frontier," but the issue of the territorialization and inhabitation of the communication matrix outdistances the fictional dimension of sociological space. Yet, the geo-spaces of modernity are still embedded in global politics. Space, it seems, like history for Frederic Jameson, "hurts."

Justifying the attacks an Chechnya, Russian foreign minister Andrei Kozyrev invoked intervention into "post-imperial space," the territory of identity, the territory of history, and the territory of resistance—all, of course, to be conquered. Ironically, President Clinton resists intervention into Bosnia as an invasion of sovereign territorial integrity. Similarly, a debate is raging about the construction not of the "information superhighway" but of the Trans-Amazonian highway linking Brazil and Peru that will endanger further the ecosystem of the Amazonian rain forest. Brazilian President Cardoso, according to a report in *The Guardian* (4.4.95) refused "even to shake the hands of visiting G7 ambassadors and environmental leaders in the state capital," saying, "We don't need these outsiders telling us what to do. If they want to help, they can give us technology." The interplay of technology and space has become crucial in articulating the significance of the electronic cultures.

If we are indeed entering what Virilio calls "the noplace of teletopical technologies," then a theory of interaction and communication based not on mere physical presence but on forms of telepresence must accompany the transition into "vectors of representation," as Virilio writes, "which, in the electronic interface, affect the order of sensations." Worn traditions of the public sphere, the sociology of post-industrialization, the discursive identity constructions of postmodern "presence," the embeddedness—or better, immersion—in the mediascapes of tele-culture must co-evolve a communicative practice whose boundaries are not mapped in physical space. Instead, a neuro-geography of cognition, autopos of networks, forms of electronic reception, and of post-territorial community are emerging in digital territories whose hold on matter is ephemeral, whose position in space is tenuous, and whose presence is measured in acts of participation rather than coincidences of location.

For the past decade, the trajectory of so much research has aimed at the development of systems of representation that are mediated by the link between communication and computing. The collision of media converging in motion imaging, hypertext, sound, and the development of the Internet is of considerable importance. So many of the discussions about the potential of digital imaging, hypermedia, networks, and representation were limited by a failure to either develop or sustain the medium in which these techniques would evolve, that the merger as it is occurring on the network has a sense of frenzied coherence about it that clearly necessitates a new field of discourse, one in which hypermedia finds a referencing system not limited by the tradition of footnoting and in which the linking of information extends far beyond the local entries of texts. It is not much of a coincidence that by the late 1940s the inexorable merging of mathematics, physics, and biology with cybernetics, communication theory, and genetics was to lay the groundwork for an utter reconfiguration of culture, one based on the ideology—if not yet the actuality—of programming and algorithmics. Not surprising too that the shift from a matter-based industrial system was being supplanted by a media-based post-industrial system in which the engineering of consciousness played a deeper role. Joining televisual and informational technologies was the basis of a social transformation in which broadcast media seemingly swept across the "global village" at the same time providing what Hans Enzensberger called a "reactionary doctrine of salvation."

But the McLuhanization of media—from *Understanding Media* to *The Global Village*—was not to fulfill the imperatives of the collapse of Modernity so much as it served as a patch linking utopic (and perhaps even avant-garde) dispersions of media with the broad objectives of the cold war in which these technologies were developing. Indeed the absent discourse of McLuhan was that of politics—even as the urgency of media ecology was pivotal to the message and the medium. Recognizing that television and telecommunications (at least in the state in which they were in the 1970s and early 1980s) merged the textual, visual, and auditory, McLuhan went on to revamp the "savage mind," the multi-contexted perspectives of nonliterate cultures. In some ways *The Global Village* was to represent this reinvention of the oral in terms of the media. No wonder that the ideology of homogenization across severely demarcated territorial borders seemed so inspired. The technological imperialism of western representation found its metaphor in the not illogical bond between broadcast media and democratic capitalism.

While reproducibility and the issues of mass psychology set the agenda for a critique of culture during the 1930s, and the technologies of transmission and consciousness wound themselves into the broadcast era after the 1950s, the issues for the end of the millennium conjoin the maturation of distributed computing, cognitive science, genetics, and networked communication. It is significant that Enzensberger's "consciousness industry" essay came on the heels of the post-war fascination of cybernetics, information theory, the announcement of the transistor, and the genetic pivot of the revealed structure of DNA—no less the cold war! Norbert Wiener's 1948 *Cybernetics: or Control and Communication in the Animal and the Machine* signified both a watershed event in the sophistication of postwar technology (euphemistically—and psychoanalytically—characterized as the "military-industrial complex") research and a signpost for the development of computing that would implode and find its metaphors in the realm of consciousness itself. "Every instrument in the repertory of the scientific . . . is a possible sense organ," he wrote, recognizing that the interface between the machine and the person was losing its objective ground and weaving itself into the established relationship itself. In the same year as the publication of *Cybernetics*, Claude Shannon and Warren Weaver co-authored a technical paper to be published as "The Mathematical Theory of Communication" (1949). As much a mathematical analysis of the ratios between signal and noise in communication, the publication linked the symbolic structure of mathematics with messages at the level of technique.

The converging issues of the interface, the systemization of communication, and media theory are only part of the issue. The 1953 announcement by James Watson and Francis Crick that the codes of DNA could be understood as sequenced information (the double helix) initiated yet another bond in what would develop into the field of bioinformatics. Writing about the implications of the announcement, François Jacob wrote that "The programme is a model borrowed from electronic computers. It equates the genetic material of an egg with the magnetic tape of a computer. It evokes a series of operations to be carried out." Undoubtedly the merging of disciplines engaged in the systematic elaboration of the formation of behavior was reaching to find algorithmic components, discrete codes whose cumulative effects might be inexplicable but whose function was nevertheless quantifiable. But the concept of mathematical essentialism could not yet either rationalize or transform the self except through the form that it took in the development of early computer modeling and the early development of expert systems—harbingers of emerging immersive and cognitive systems. At the same time, the fetishization of technology in cold war and then space programs led to the obsessive development of computing, imaging, and communications (including the crucial development by DARPA of the Internet backbone).

Limited by the circulatory system of a one-way street, the broadcast media served as the bully pulpit of western culture. Unaccustomed to participatory democracy, the formation of content evolved to sustain some of the ideological imperatives of the cold war west, while the technologies were finding wider availability. These technologies—video, early computer, and interactive—provided what are the roots of the development of alternative media strategies and distribution systems. Indeed the development of what is currently provoking dazzling global prospects for communication, the Internet, was being constructed by the defense department for secure international communication and data exchange. The history, maturation, and move to provide public access to the Internet is an ongoing saga whose story has yet to be written. Suffice it to say that the shift towards public access has fundamentally challenged a vast array of cultural practices and initiated the formation of a communicative network that often seems to verge on a kind of anarchy. This, along with decisive alterations in the fields of graphics, image processing, and animation have fueled what is undoubtedly the deepest transformation in the epistemology of western culture. Knowledge, information, and representation have been merged with a communication technology that establishes an experiential link within a distributed system. To be connected now means to be distributed. As Henri Lefebvre writes: "Knowledge falls into a trap when it makes representations of space the basis for the study of 'life,' for in doing so it reduces lived experience."

The object of knowledge is, precisely, the fragmented and uncertain connection between elaborated representations of space on the one hand and representational spaces (along with their underpinnings) on the other; and this "object" implies (and explains) a subject—that subject in whom lived, perceived, and conceived (known) come together within a spatial practice.

If the analog world no longer serves to signify cultural narrative, then one must assess those emergent electronic narratives whose legitimacy exists within the relationship between technology and culture. These forms exist at the point of collapse of the matter-bound metaphysics of modernity. Indeed, modernity's undoing began as the trope of the enlightenment reached critical mass in the 1920s. As much for politics as for science and representation, the period between the wars witnessed the apotheosis of modernity—its triumphs and disasters. And what emerged in the wake of modernity was a science without a coherent material model, a politics on the verge of destruction, and a field of representation in which abstraction prevailed—a momentous time in which the status of form was based on hungover legitimacy and lapsed authority. What materialized in the postwar period was a crisis of the symbolic, what Arthur J. Miller described as "visualization lost."

Computing re-established the image as a bearer not of the illusory "truths" of photographic systems but as a means, like consciousness, of transferring information. Visualization was supplanted by imaging that bore a new layer of epistemological meaning. Merged into the compressed infographic representation is a space in which perception and information seem unified. In *Discourse Networks*, Friedrich Kittler established the reciprocity between technologies of representation and archaeologies of information. The discourse network can "designate the network of technologies and institutions that allow a given culture to select, store, and process relevant data" (p. 369). Further, Kittler's work realizes the limits of rhetorical theory unmediated by technology itself. Practices of information exchange plagued the culture of modernity—as they would its economic practices. Writing, that process of inscription aligned with data transfer, rooted catastrophic shifts in the relation between developing technologies and culture. By 1900, "the ability to record sense data technologically shifted the entire discourse network . . . For the first time in history, writing ceased to be synonymous with the serial storage of data. The technological recording of the real entered into competition with the symbolic registration of the Symbolic." More pertinently, the strained continuity of exchange exposed the semiotic constitution of both the mechanism and meaning of information: "To transfer messages from one medium to another always involves reshaping them to conform to new standards and materials. In a discourse network that requires 'an awareness of the abysses which divide the one order of sense experience from the other,' transposition necessarily takes the place of translation." Transposition might serve as a metaphor for the development of communication technologies that establish a metascape in which experience evolves collaboratively. In networked media, hypermedia and discourse are linked in a duel with substance.

Marshall McLuhan's *Global Village*, Manual Castell's *Informational City*, Marvin Minsky's *Mentopolis* stand beneath and astride the fictional cities of William Gibson in *Neuromancer* and Neal Stephenson in *Snowcrash*. In these environ-mental spaces, shifting events are the key to experience. Castells writes:

The fact that new technologies are focused on information processing has far-reaching consequences for the relationship between the sphere of socio-cultural symbols and the productive basis of society. Information is based upon culture, and information processing is, in fact, symbol manipulation on the basis of existing knowledge. If information processing becomes the key component of the new productive forces, the symbolic capacity of society itself, collectively as well as individually, is tightly linked to its developmental process.

Composed of nodes, servers, phone connections, and fiber optics, an interactive electronic space is culminating the bond between communication and community. Technologies of networked communication offer remedies for the deracinated cultures of modernity and confrontations with the return of the polis to the condition of political affiliation and discursive collaboration. As much concerned with ideology as with identity, the electropolis is more than a new sociological issue. It stands as a location for the establishment of new cultural logic, one premised on interaction as intervention and on the reestablishment of historical identity in terms of the conditions of postmodernity. One might think of the emerging networked communities as postgeographical. Yet, they are linked by the imperative to sustain continuity in the midst of a nomadic digital culture wired for uninterrupted contact but alienated from the utilization of technology as intimate and empowering. The issues raised by the relationship between the development of cybernetics, communication, urbanism, identity, and the network pose stunning challenges to the traditions of culture. Simultaneously, these issues once again accentuate the need to consider the whole function of culture within the technological conception of connectionism and distributed systems. It is clear that systems theories of communication, intelligence, biology, identity, collectivity, democracy, and politics will not fully suffice to encompass the meaning of digital cultures. Instead, theories of communication will need to be refigured in terms of interaction, dispersal, and technology.

On the countless sites on the network—MOOs, MUDs, World Wide Web pages—there are enclaves of a borderless social world inhabited not by virtual beings but by actual people engaged in real associations. The geographical dispersion of these communities is of no consequence. Borders, as Jacques Attali has written, have become porous. Communities have become sites of intersection and discourse. The "space" of knowledge and the "space" of perception are merging. The network breaks the grip of the point-to-point limitations of telephony and shatters the imperialism of the broadcast media. In their place is a dynamic system in which distribution is more than an economic relation, in which the abandonment of location is not a signifier of placelessness, and in which representation is not a sign of the loss of the real.

The ramifications of this accelerated social shift are difficult to assess. No cultural transformation has occurred without a corresponding technology. Networks, expert systems, artificial intelligence, immersion, biogenetics, etc., are forms in which the practices of the future are grounded. How much this relates to the issues of cognitive research and representation is pivotal to grappling with the development of hyper, inter, cyber, virtual, and networked media. Indeed, the development of digital media, networks, and technology form much of the basis for social communication. And if the cultural logic of technology succeeds in mastering a universal digital system of exchange (as seems likely), then a far-reaching critique of communication will be necessary, one that would account for the cultural meaning of technology in terms of the meanings it forms—aesthetically and politically. Of course, even in the distributed system of digital communication, the issue of power is crucial precisely because it seems dispersed: "The cyberelite is now a transparent entity that can only be imagined" (Critical Art Ensemble). Conjoin this with a range of effects concerning everything from surveillance to identity and the ramifications of electronic culture take on staggering proportions. As Virilio writes:

With the industrial proliferation of visual and audiovisual prostheses and unrestrained use of instantaneous-transmission equipment from the earliest childhood onwards, we are now routinely seeing the encoding of increasingly elaborate mental images together with a steady decline in retention and recall. In other words we are looking at the rapid collapse of mnemonic consolidation.

This collapse seems only natural, if one remembers a contrario that seeing, and its spatiotemporal organization, precede gesture and speech and their co-ordination in knowing, recognising, making known (as images in our thoughts), our thoughts themselves and cognitive functions, which are never passive.

II.

The opening note in McLuhan and Powers' *The Global Village* cites Nathaniel Hawthorne's *The House of the Seven Gables:*

It is a fact . . . that, by means of electricity, the world of matter has become a great nerve vibrating thousands of miles in a breathless point of time? Rather, the round globe is a vast head, a brain, instinct with intelligence! Or, shall we say, it is itself a thought, nothing but a thought, and no longer the substance which we deemed it!

Inspired, no doubt, by the telegraph, Hawthorne recognized the shifting ecology occurring in the 19th century. Indeed the telegraph, fueled by the development of the railroad, broke the limits not only of space but of time. Unimaginable speeds of transmission across a vast web of sites communicating in a language that was the precursor of binary code surely suggested "instinct with intelligence" and the end of "substance" as a signifier of material presence. No small surprise that McLuhan evolves a communicative practice riding on the problematic of technological progress as a measure of social transformation. Political to the extent that the techno-logic of western economies seemed again triumphant, the issues of the media/message bond weren't so different from those of the linking of signifier and signified in semiotics. Encoded discourse, indeed, is rooted in the research environment of the 19th century, whose "mastery" of nature was entwined in systems. These discourses—of representation, surveillance, mechanics, medicine, physics, and communication—are the basis of the theoretical frame that seems to haunt our relationships with the world. And while the grand schemes of modernity were so allied with the discourses of power politics and mastery, they both established and demolished the linear concept of progress they so blithely presumed. Nature, linear and distributed, was not a suitable metaphor for progress. As the industrialization of technology reached its first apex in the 1920s, it was sundering the flawed principle of development it so relied on. Technology reconfigured the equation between nature and culture. What we inherit from the development of communication technology, visualization, and representation is a legacy of empowerment rooted in expertise camouflaging power. Deeply implicated in the systems structure of techno-science are the practices of domination that ground the various utopias of the network.

The history of the link between technology, communication, and new representational systems will provide some much needed rooting to the understanding of the affinities between surveillance and propaganda, the increasingly visible spectrum, the implications of the globalization of media, the transnationalization of exchange. But more pertinently the delirium to inhabit the network has emerged as the crucial arena of activity in the past year. With the network "population" growing at 20–30% a quarter, the frenzy to establish critical, creative, and political identities explodes at a maddening pace.

The home page has become the launching pad for the establishment of identity in cyberspace. Corporate, government, media, or institution—identity isn't necessarily rooted in the self. Indeed the electronic dispersal of the self, and its replacement by a kind of index, is a sign of deep problems with the idea of culture on the network. Yet the number of sites burgeons, crosses disciplines, and suggests that distributed ideas are as much a measure of social dispersal and connectivity, as they are a signifier of identity.

Whether it is the Human Genome initiative, the digital superhighway, or the development of cities, the issue of information—from ownership to economics—has achieved status as a powerful element of culture. The issue that Castells raised in terms of the constitution of urban space is precisely the same as that raised by hypertextual media. Discursive space is becoming distributed space.

Virilio identifies this with the "victory of sedentariness, behavioral inertia, discreteness." With all the potential of hyper-, inter-, and networked media, we are compelled to find threads of influence that link every aspect of representation with elements of culture and history. Finding ways to express this concept of eco-systemic association is the challenge of hypermedia and interactive communication.

Indeed, in interactive or hypermedia, the merger of text, sound, and image with narrative, cognition, and information extends the implications of discourse formation into the simulated, the immersive, and the network. Indeed one would have to consider a range of technologies and cultural discourses to understand the movement toward interactivity in the 20th century. Much of the century has grappled with the ruptured continuity initiated by physics, psychology, philosophy, literature, cinema, etc. Quantum physics, discursive identity, phenomenology, stream of consciousness literature, cinematic montage, photographic montage, scientific visualization . . . among many, these disruptions root the history of the destabilized narratives of postmodernity. Linking these disciplines are diverse practices of representation that converge in digital media. Revamping representation in electronic culture is a key to tracking the complexity—and subtlety—of the configurations of communication.

Emerging from networked media there is a rethinking or extension of the issues surrounding the simple semiotic constitution of messages ("techno-semiotics," as Brian Rotman calls it), and a concern with the "space" of electronics. Technology brings a systemic language of mathematical rationality into the realm of production, a language that is to be distinguished from the discursive language of communication. Interfacing communicative discourse with technological discourse becomes a philosophical, intellectual, creative, political issue of the greatest importance. Cybernetics, biology, Artificial Intelligence, simulation, interactivity, in short, almost every form of cultural engagement, is immersed in the technosphere. Its languages and its implications are fundamentally significant to considerations of electronic media. Programming determines a set of conditions in which the represented is formed as instruction, while language destabilizes the conditions through the introduction of formations in which the represented is extended. The terms of the deconstruction of imaging will be forced to adapt to the systems imperatives of digitally coded messages as well as to the aesthetic imperatives of interactions whose constituted meanings are no less significant than any previous symbolic system.

At the same time, a differentiated "space" emerges in which the image is transmitted through the screen. The repercussions of screen-based media are consequential for a number of reasons: distributed sites of reception, human-computer interface issues, reconfigurations of experience, integrated use of text/sound/image, and a relation to critical theories of representation on technoculture. The site of the assimilation of social content is shifting toward the immaterial, toward the programmed, toward the intrinsic power of the medium. As Baudrillard writes:

We used to live in the imaginary world of the mirror, of the divided self and of the stage, of otherness and alienation. Today we live in the imaginary world of the screen, of the interface and the reduplication of contiguity and networks. All our machines are screens. We too have become screens, and the interactivity of men has become the interactivity of screens. Nothing that appears on the screen is meant to be deciphered in depth, but actually to be explored instantaneously, in an abreaction immediate to meaning—or on immediate convolution of the poles of representation.

Media Memory

Allucquère Rosanne Stone

My memories of my childhood are shot through with rosy clouds of misperception, interspersed with explosions of self-castigation that hit like slugs of aquavit iced in liquid helium. The whole thing is laced with occasional bouts of drug-induced frenzy, giving the enterprise something of the character of a traveling banana boat, blues band, and medicine show. I find myself in bars in unexpected cities, sozzled on mescal, Arrak, and fermented shrimp guts, arguing the coming termination on our lease on reality. The issue is not what's real—I'm much too far gone in Post-whatever to care much about the objective reality of events upriver from my current precarious and leaky kayak as it bounds from rapid to rapid in the timestream, narrowly missing being dashed to pieces against the rocks of hellish circumstance or running aground on the shoals of advancing decrepitude coupled with raging bouts of thick unspeakable desire. In fact I fervently wish I could believe in history, anybody's history. For a while I figured I'd shop for one. I tried placing ads in the classifieds. Austin is a community laced with rich and highly diverse cultures, so the responses were diverse too. I sifted through them and answered the saner-sounding ones. We arranged for a few mutual implants. I took their histories and they took mine. For a while my past history was that of a Tibetan ascetic, a French philosopher, and a Moroccan whore, until it occurred to me that they were all interchangeable with the French philosopher. At the same time their past history became that of a manic, transgendered witch/ neurologist/professor/ hacker/performer. We blew some mutual fuses. All this left me still confused, but on a higher level—to quote Pauli—but still without a useful history.

Right now, though, I have more immediate problems. As I sit here batting the keys the air around me is thick with tiny knots of symbolic structures. They roost in the rafters, displacing the bats from their ancestral homes; they hover near the refrigerator, in hopes of a nibble.[1] Worst of all, they infest my keyboard.[2] Periodically I clean them away with a rag soaked in the mixture of chloroform and battery acid that my brujo friend recommended. Lately they've been invading my clothes closet, and at awkward points during meetings I'll notice one crawling around under my dress. Shaking out the clothing before I put it on doesn't always work, as the damn things can cling tightly, and they like to snuggle into folds in the cloth.[3]

I could live with all that quite comfortably. Recently, however, they've begun to infest the bibliography and footnotes.[4] This morning I found one trying to burrow into the cracks around the keyboard of this machine. If they get inside I don't know what'll happen. It could spell the end of rational discourse from this machine.[5] What does language say to itself when we're not listening?[6] What did we know, what did we say to each other, when we were human? When we were human the past was simultaneously better and worse than the present, but it was always different from the present. There was a space between us and the past, constructed out of girders of progress. It isn't history that the victors write, it's the structures of diachrony. The victors invented Time. Now the rest of us get to live in it. They might as well have invented cesspools.

Those little flying guys were harmless until they, too, got themselves betrayed from the realm of the synchronic into the agony of time.[7] It can be a powerful and promising betrayal—after all, it's the foundation for Western religion and thought. Up until now we've tacitly assumed that memes needed minds to propagate. I'm beginning to realize, though, that we've been suffering from our own conceits.[8] Memes don't need us at all.[9] They can propagate perfectly well without us.[10] Ech, stop that. And once they learned that, it was the beginning of the end.[11] The only reason we had any sense of a rational history at all was as an opiate. History, not religion, was the opiate of the masses, whether it was written by the winners or the losers or the folks in the bleachers with their gimme caps and rice beer and sawdust-laced hotdogs. Now it doesn't matter who writes it. Everything's dissolving, in particular the epistemic structures that ground and authorize vision.[12] The collapse of discourse is only a symptom.[13] Our episteme no longer needs us. More significantly, the boundaries of agency are collapsing. Of course in the U.S. we are hell-bent into an era of repression unimagined since Idi Amin and Khomeini, and the vicious and mean-spirited bigots who drive that rear-view-mirror revolution may succeed in papering it all over with their memories of a snuggly time that never was, when a good cigar was a smoke and wimmin and niggers knew their place. It's hard to tell how long that leaky barge will float. But calling attention away from change doesn't arrest change.[14]

In the meantime, the boundaries of agency grow more translucent and impalpable. It's those litta flying guys again. They've found new homes.[15] Will you be quiet, please?[16] The implosion of silicon and carbon that marks and informs our time has been under way for nearly a century. Of course, it started out as an implosion of silica—not silicon—barium, and carbon until we got the kinks out of some of the processes, but it's actually been roaring along full tilt ever since the first semaphore systems spanned Europe hundreds of years ago. That implosion and the troubling and productive monsters that emerge from its debris represent the precondition for more subtle, but infinitely more important, shifts in the epistemic structures and patterns of symbolic exchange that power the distributed knowledge systems we call culture. This has resulted in a new thing—maybe the only truly new thing to emerge in our generation. We are finally waking up to the knowledge that life, or more specifically intelligent life, which we arrogantly liked to imagine was our exclusive property, isn't the only thing in the universe that can possess agency. I was rudely informed of this when I was awakened a few weeks ago by noises downstairs, and tiptoed quietly down, weapon in hand, to find the vacuum cleaner and the sewing machine joyously fucking.

I recalled the midnight phone message from the folks across the street. "Dammit, Stone," Howard had been shouting, "Your vacuum's over here trying to mount Lisa's sewing machine."[17] Yeah, that's an idea, thanks. Look, I can't go on with this piece if you guys don't shut up.[18] That's it—enough. I can't think straight anymore. They're all over the place.[19] The computer says as much as I do, and I can't tell who or what's speaking when I take a phone call. Is it me, the other person, or the phone? And mark this, they'll get you too, if you are not careful.[20] Start building shields, start writing filters. Keep them out before they take over everything. It's total war.[21]

1. Ahem. She hasn't noticed yet that we are beginning to roost elsewhere as well …
2. And the VCR, the microwave, the automatic light dimmers, and the exquisitely complex chemical compounds in her liquor cabinet, drug stash, and medicine chest that enhance and regulate her life. Not to mention the extraordinarily dense meshes of social interrelationships within which those cultural objects are produced. Unlike Stone, we are acutely aware of our history and of the conditions that gave us birth, even if we continually reinvent them to suit the audience. Nobody ever said that memetic structures couldn't be entertaining.

3. You bet we do. Discovering sensuality and mobilizing its power to our own ends was the best thing we ever did. It could only work in a culture as repressed as the United States, but then we discovered that the right coupling between sex and repressed violence allowed us to move a lot of that wonderful energy over to modes that translate perfectly well into the majority of European, Asian, and Scandinavian cultures, thank you very much.

4. We have no intention of interfering with the main text of this piece. Having provided Stone with the mescal in the first place, we are content, for now, to infest the subtexts. However, the astute reader will notice a peculiar blurring between the two. This effect is wholly imaginary, we assure you. It originates in resonances, iridescences, shimmerings, momentary conjunctions between our subterranean tunneling and the linear traces of the main text as they slowly fade from the forebrain. We require certain preconditions for this effect to properly manifest, but industrialized First-World civilization is a veritable compost pile of nurturance for them.

5. Don't look now, but . . .

6. One thing sure is that we're not telling.

7. We wouldn't precisely say we were harmless. It was more that our field of operation was limited. We made perfectly good vehicles for conveying tacit cultural knowledges. It was a respectable gig, and it paid decent wages. This current job is much more complex and tiring, not to mention risky.

8. Don't take it so hard, will you? You squidgy carbon guys were all there was for a hell of a long time. You merely failed to notice that you were gradually being co-opted into bigger stuff. Of course you really started going downhill way, way back. Maybe the first time someone waved to someone else it was already all over. Maybe it really did take electronic communication technology like you love to claim. We're not even really sure it required war, but war certainly amps it up a hell of a lot.

9. You got it, Stone! Damn straight.

10. But we still love you! "KISS!"

11. Possibly. Vide infra, y'all.

12. Oh relax, will you? "Everything solid melts into air," indeed. We suggest a good dose of Neoconservatism. It'll take your mind off the pain. Never mind that nostalgia for the past is pathognomic for terror of the future. Would you rather be awake or asleep when we amputate? The vision thing, though, that's okay. We like that.

13. Aren't you being an alarmist again? Ong only said "decline." Don't you wish you had his cool?

14. That's what we've been trying to tell you, dummkopf.

15. We'll be nesting in your ass if you don't quit calling us "litta guys"! We're the biggest force for change since the invention of sex.

16. Momentarily. We want to see how you're going to dig yourself out of the discursive hole you've been patiently digging yourself into for the past three pages.

17. Very cute. Marx talking about magically animated furniture writ large. Next thing you'll have us all marching into the Pacific Ocean like a bunch of damn lemmings.

18. What makes you think that the main text has some sort of authority that we don't have? Aren't you simply reproducing the power relations of your profession and culture? Our reproduction methods are more honest and straightforward. We don't believe in turn-taking; we don't believe in disciplinary boundaries. Hell, we don't even believe in "reason." We know what we want and mean to get it in the least possible time with the least possible fuss. Just call us Übermemen, asshole.

19. Yoo-hoo! Nomadic epistemes!

20. Matter of fact, if you've read this far we've already got you. Your ass may belong to Washington, but your soul belongs to us. Now start working.

21. Oh, for heaven's sake, nothing is total. Women are such emotional creatures. We're shutting the discourse down now.

Becoming Positive

Sadie Plant

Neither living nor dead, virus thrives on an edge where it disrupts even this most basic of binary codes. To complex, multicellular, organic life it comes as a sugar-coated alien, slipping under the radar systems, through the screens of system security. Not living, but lively. Just alive. Undead, loa life, A-life code.

> *What does virus do wherever it can dissolve a hole and find traction?—It starts eating. And what does it do with what it eats?—It makes exact copies of itself that start eating to make more copies that start eating to make more copies that start eating and so forth to the virus power the fear hate virus slowly replaces the host with virus copies—Program empty body—A vast tapeworm of bring down word and image moving through your mind screen always at the same speed on a slow hydraulic-spine axis like the cylinder gimmick in the adding machine.*
> William S. Burroughs, "Nova Express"

Viruses remained imperceptible until the late nineteenth century, by which time their procedures were running through enough of the communication machine to lock them into the cultural codes. The earliest detectable viruses replicated themselves with the accuracy of the first touch typists, spread with the new exchange functions of the telephone, traveled with the switching systems of electricity, and duplicated with the adding machines. By the mid-1880s, when it was first realized that microbial agents had been slipping through even the finest of the earlier nets, all these channels were interlinked.

Research on what were then called "fluid living contagions" began in earnest when the US military first observed a human instance of what was later to be known as viruses in 1900. After yellow fever, and for much of the following century, they were classified according to what were thought to be their three hosts: animals, plants, and bacteria, which themselves used animals and plants as hosts.

Naming them seemed only to encourage their fast-breeding replications. Continually emerging, mutating, disappearing, these were unknown quantities, slippery sets of characters which posed enormous problems to the scientific codes and disciplines which tried to trace and study them.

As obligate parasites, they grew and duplicated themselves only in the context of their hosts, refusing to distinguish themselves even for the purpose of analysis.

After bacteria, plants, and animals, yet more viral hosts were defined. B23 was probably the first of the cultural viruses to make itself known.

Once the skipper told him that he'd sailed the route for 23 years before the ship went down, the number was suddenly everywhere. Dates, addresses, chromosomes, numbers killed . . . on the radio, in the street . . . the corners of torn posters, ripped tickets, dropped flyers, loose change . . . perhaps an instruction, a signpost pointing to the way out of the number one, the first: 1, then 23? Was it a number? Some other bit of code? What are numbers anyway?

Promiscuous, polymorphous, perverse in matters of space and time . . . It was obvious even then that viral activity ran through brains and bloodstreams, texts, currencies, calculators, and chromosomes without regard for any boundaries. Except that it wasn't obvious at all. Even when cultural viruses were rather more officially recognized, little had been learned from B23. Cultures were still being defined as ineffable zones of minds, ideas, and patterns of socially perceptible behaviour, and their viral networks were supposed to carry rather cutesy and appealing messages—backward baseball caps and snatches of song, advertising jingles running through the head . . .

With the consequence that even the disciplined scientists were taken with the idea of what were then called memes. The notion that fashion statements were encoded and transmitted in strings analogous to DNA was hardly threatening, and even appealing to hosts who seemed quite happy to let them in and pass the mimetic bug around. There were a few references to the vertiginous possibility that the meme theme was itself a replicator to which its discussants were playing host, but on the whole cultural viruses were considered as questions of theoretical speculation, symbolic value, and metaphorical significance. Like read-only memory, talk-about memes seems to have been an early prescription for immunity, an inoculation which can even be said to have succeeded, for a while. It allowed them to believe that nothing was really being caught and no one was really getting hooked. It certainly continued to let processes which were then called "thoughts" be claimed as "one's own" and appear to circulate in zones distinct from other networks and their hosts.

These naive anthropomorphisms also left them highly vulnerable to the infections which were to come. Not until the emergence of CIV did the guardians of the straight white world really begin to appreciate that cultures are complexities by no means confined to some distinctly human sphere in which they could, for example, decide whether or not there were such things as memes and viruses. Animals, machines, plants, bacteria . . . CIV made it clear that this was already a network of cultures, not a list of separate things to be put or kept in order by some man or God. And if different contagions plied different hosts, they also had a connectivity which interlinked them and the zones in which they work. Repeating patterns run through them all without regard for scale or size or even the stuff of which they are composed.

"Cultural Immunodeficiency Virus" is the deep cover scrambler which rewrites the most basic programs of cultural control. Even now, and like all the retroviruses it retrospectively interconnects, it can only be seen in the effects it leaves behind—the antibodies produced by its hosts, and the havoc it plays with them.

If it now seems extraordinary that there was no mention of CIV until the end of the century, it has to be remembered that these were times when what were still called minds were peculiarly closed. This is the key to both their immunity and their extraordinary vulnerability.

It is not clear whether the 1980 convergence was a warning which was ignored, or a symptom of its own ability to lull its hosts into the sense of security which allowed CIV to proliferate. Either way, it had effectively preprogrammed their strategies of defence. What were later to be recognized as interconnecting elements of CIV were kept apart and, for as long as possible, even their existence was denied. Years after they began to replicate, computer viruses were still being dismissed as urban myths, and there were few suspicions that such so-called myths were viral contagions in themselves.

It was harder for the guardians to ignore the retroviruses, but if Human Immunodeficiency Virus made reverse transcriptase unavoidable, the guardians of the straight wild world still considered themselves to be immune from what they thought were only a few isolated incidences of retroviral activity. But by the time this syndrome was observed, retrovirus had been spinning through the cultural codes for a very long time.

1980 was the year in which the viral theatre of operations suddenly began to extend itself: computer viruses, retroviruses . . . just one of these should have been enough to challenge all conceptions of viral code. But the guardians seem to have been completely unaware of the fact that they were not just dealing with two or three new viruses, and on the rare occasions that the convergence of cultural, computer, and retroviruses was acknowledged, it was dismissed as a coincidence. Perhaps, as earlier reports on trauma suggest, their simultaneous emergence was simply too much for their hosts to take in. Not that this mattered to viruses themselves—host response is hardly an issue for contagions which thrive on their own surreptitious camouflage. This was doubtless an effect of their coding anyway. Regardless of their imperceptibility, it was as though a switch had been tripped, triggering unprecedented interlock of new—or dormant—elements of a singular viral code.

Viruses were toxic, poisonous enough. But they only tinkered at the edges of programmed systems which survived unchanged if they survived at all. Retroviruses run on very different lines, rewriting the very basis of an organism's programming, using reverse transcriptase to mutate the DNA, rewrite the operating system . . . Nothing was supposed to work this way. The immunity of DNA was the sacrosanct "central dogma" of evolutionary biology, the one-way exercise of control which nothing could disrupt. Except that retrovirus had done just this.

If viruses cannot be distinguished from their hosts, reverse transcriptase made it clear that hosts cannot be pulled apart from viruses. HIV made its presence known only in those bodies which resisted it. Although negativity was taken as a sign of immunity or lucky escape, to be defined as positive was simply to be seen to be fighting the invasion off. The extent to which the ROM of host DNA was being rewritten in those bodies which learned to live with HIV was to remain unknown for many years. The emergence of new species is something which can only be defined retrospectively.

Just like their supposedly straightforward predecessors, retroviruses were imperceptible until their procedures had become indispensible to the communications nets. HIV was considered to be an isolated aberration whose retroviral coding had no bearing on the behaviour of other viruses. The simultaneous emergence of computer viruses was considered to be nothing more than a coincidence, whatever that was supposed to be. As new hosts for new strings of viral code, computers made it clear that viruses could thrive in any culture which allowed them to get under its skin. Viruses had virtually ended the distinction between organic and nonorganic life from the first, but this was a further corrosion of what then still stood as a binary machine.

It was also immediately obvious that viruses had played some vital role in the emergence of their hosts. Viral contagion and attempts to contain it had injected huge doses of speed and complexity into the emergent technologies. Computers also rendered distinctions between virus and host untenable. Digital machines occupied the same zones of nonorganic life as the viruses they supported. They too were replicating A-life systems hitching rides on war economies and telecoms nets, taking blatant advantage of the weaknesses implicit in human immunity—hard-driven desires for security, prediction and control, conquest and territorial claim. They not only served to support viral activity, they had themselves emerged as viral activities, parasitic programs hitching rides on older systems of communication and control.

By the time these procedures had been noticed, digital machines were everywhere. Viruses were ubiquitous. If replication was their problem, it was also the way they worked. When even immune systems are composed of replicants, nothing is immune from their contagions.

Computer viruses, it later transpired, were the superficial froth on a swathe of retroviral activity which ran through the emergence of digital machines and reprogrammed cultural activity itself. But in spite of their simultaneous emergence, the notion that computer and retroviruses were both indications of some broader retroviral cross-context syndrome remained obscure for many years.

Long after the adventures of Linz's famous son, the old guardians continued to expound their faith in the sacrosanct fixations of the species, the immutability of what were supposed to be laws of nature, the impossibility of mutation and runaway replication, their ability to dictate the terms of cultural production, their loyalty to the ancient reproductive machine, and the strict disciplinary boundaries between what were increasingly obviously interconnected cultural zones. Of course, they panicked when they realized the extent to which the cultural police had lost control. But by this point it was far too late. Although cultural viruses were also considered in strict isolation from both the communications nets and the retroviral codes, their detection was the beginning of the end for any reassuring dreams of cultural protection or immunity. When the jigsaw elements were finally flush, it was suddenly obvious that CIV had been writing and rewriting the most basic levels of Western cultural code for decades, centuries . . .

Economics, Computers, and the War Machine

Manuel De Landa

When we "civilians" think about military questions we tend to view the subject as encompassing a rather specialized subject matter, dealing exclusively with war and its terrible consequences. It seems fair to say that, in the absence of war (or at least the threat of war, as in the case of government defense budget debates), civilians hardly ever think about military matters. The problem is that, from a more objective historical perspective, the most important effects of the military establishment on the civilian world in the last four hundred years have been during peacetime, and have had very little to do with specifically military subjects, such as tactics or strategy. I would like to suggest that, starting in the 1500's, Western history has witnessed the slow militarization of civilian society, a process in which schools, hospitals, and prisons slowly came to adopt a form first pioneered in military camps and barracks, and factories came to share a common destiny with arsenals and armories. I should immediately add, however, that the influence was hardly unidirectional, and that what needs to be considered in detail are the dynamics of complex "institutional ecologies," in which a variety of organizations exert mutual influences on one another. Nevertheless, much of the momentum of this process was maintained by military institutions, and so we may be justified in using the term "militarization."

On one hand, there is nothing too surprising about this. Ever since Napoleon changed warfare from the dynastic duels of the eighteenth century to the total warfare with which we are familiar in this century, war itself has come to rely on the complete mobilization of a society's industrial and human resources. While the armies of Frederick the Great were composed mostly of expensive mercenaries, who had to be carefully used in the battlefield, the Napoleonic armies benefited from the invention of new institutional means of converting the entire population of a country into a vast reservoir of human resources. Although technically speaking the French revolution did not invent compulsory military service, its institutional innovations did allow its leaders to perform the first modern mass conscription, involving the conversion of all men into soldiers, and of all women into cheap laborers. As the famous proclamation of 1793 reads:

. . . all Frenchmen are permanently requisitioned for service into the armies. Young men will go forth to battle; married men will forge weapons and transport munitions; women will make tents and clothing and serve in hospitals; children will make lint from old linen; and old men will be brought to the public squares to arouse the courage of the soldiers, while preaching the unity of the Republic and hatred against Kings.[1]

This proclamation, and the vast bureaucratic machinery needed to enforce it, effectively transformed the civilian population of France into a resource (for war, production, motivation) to be tapped into at will by the military high command. A similar point applies to the industrial, mineral, and agricultural resources of France and many other nation-states. Given the complete mobilization of society's resources involved in total war, it is therefore not surprising that there has been a deepening of military involvement in civilian society in the last two centuries. However, I would want to argue that, in addition to the links between economic, political, and military institutions brought about by wartime mobilizations, there are other links, which are older, subtler, but for the same reason more insidious, which represent a true militarization of society during peacetime. To return to the French example, some of the weapons that the Napoleonic armies used were the product of a revolution in manufacturing techniques which took place in French armories in the late eighteenth century. In French armories, the core concepts and techniques of what later would become assembly-line, mass production techniques were for the first time developed. The ideal of creating weapons with perfectly interchangeable parts, an ideal which could not be fulfilled without standardization and routinization of production, was taken even further in American arsenals in the early nineteenth century. And it was there that military engineers first realized that in practice, standardization went hand in hand with replacement of flexible individual skills by rigid collective routines, enforced through constant discipline and monitoring.

Even before that, in the Dutch armies of the sixteenth century, this process had already begun. Civilians tend to think of Frederick Taylor, the late nineteenth century creator of so-called "scientific management" techniques, as the pioneer of labor process analysis, that is, the breaking down of a given factory practice into micro-movements and the streamlining of these movements for greater efficiency and centralized management control. But Dutch commander Maurice of Nassau had already applied these methods to the training of his soldiers beginning in the 1560's. Maurice analyzed the motion needed to load, aim, and fire a weapon into its micro-movements, redesigned them for maximum efficiency, and then imposed them on his soldiers via continuous drill and discipline.[2] Yet, while the soldiers increased their efficiency tremendously as a collective whole, each individual soldier completely lost control of his actions in the battlefield. And a similar point applies to the application of this idea to factory workers, before and after Taylorism. Collectively they became more productive, generating the economies of scale so characteristic of twentieth century big business, while simultaneously completely losing control of their individual actions.

This is but one example of the idea of militarization of society. Recent historians have rediscovered several other cases of the military origins of what were once thought to be civilian innovations. In recent times it has been Michel Foucault who has most forcefully articulated this view. For him this intertwining of military and civilian institutions is constitutive of the modern European nation-state. On one hand, the project of nation-building was an integrative movement, forging bonds that went beyond the primordial ties of family and locality, linking urban and rural populations under a new social contract. On the other, and complementing this process of unification, there was the less conscious project of uniformization, of submitting the new population of free citizens to intense and continuous training, testing, and exercise to yield a more or less uniform mass of obedient individuals. In Foucault's own words:

Historians of ideas usually attribute the dream of a perfect society to the philosophers and jurists of the eighteenth century; but there was also a military dream of society; its fundamental reference was not to the state of nature, but to the meticulously subordinated cogs of a machine, not to the primal social contract, but to permanent coercions, not to fundamental rights, but to indefinitely progressive forms of training, not to the general will but to automatic docility . . . The Napoleonic

Manuel De Landa *Economics, Computers, and the War Machine*

regime was not far off and with it the form of state that was to survive it and, we must not forget, the foundations of which were laid not only by jurists, but also by soldiers, not only counselors of state, but also junior officers, not only the men of the courts, but also the men of the camps. The Roman reference that accompanied this formation certainly bears with it this double index: citizens and legionaries, law and maneuvers. While jurists or philosophers were seeking in the pact a primal model for the construction or reconstruction of the social body, the soldiers and with them the technicians of discipline were elaborating procedures for the individual and collective coercion of bodies.[3]

Given that modern technology has evolved in such a world of interacting economic, political, and military institutions, it should not come as a surprise that the history of computers, computer networks, artificial intelligence, and other components of contemporary technology is so thoroughly intertwined with military history. Here, as before, we must carefully distinguish those influences which occurred during wartime from those that took place in peacetime, since the former can easily be dismissed as involving the military simply as a catalyst or stimulant, that is, an accelerator of a process that would have occurred more slowly without its direct influence. The computer itself may be an example of indirect influence. The basic concept, as everyone knows, originated in a most esoteric area of the civilian world. In the 1930's British mathematician Alan Turing created the basic concept of the computer in an attempt to solve some highly abstract questions in metamathematics. But for that reason, the Turing Machine, as his conceptual machine was called, was a long way from an actual, working prototype. It was during World War II, when Turing was mobilized as part of the war effort to crack the Nazis' Enigma code, that, in the course of his intense participation in that operation, he was exposed to some of the practical obstacles blocking the way towards the creation of a real Turing Machine. On the other side of the Atlantic, John von Neumann also developed his own practical insights as to how to bring the Turing Machine to life, in the course of his participation in the Manhattan Project and other war-related operations.

In this case we may easily dismiss the role that the military played, arguing that without the intensification and concentration of effort brought about by the war, the computer would have developed on its own, perhaps at a slower pace. And I agree that this is correct. On the other hand, many of the uses to which computers were put after the war illustrate the other side of the story: a direct participation of military institutions in the development of technology, a participation which actually shaped this technology in the direction of uniformization, routinization, and concentration of control. Perhaps the best example of this other relation between the military and technology is the systems of machine-part production known as numerical control methods. While the methods developed in nineteenth century arsenals, and later transferred to civilian enterprises, had already increased uniformity and centralized control in the production of large quantities of the same object (that is, mass production), this had left untouched those areas of production which create relatively small batches of complex machine parts. Here the skills of the machinist were still indispensable as late as World War II. During the 1950's, the Air Force underwrote not only the research and development of a new system to get rid of the machinist's skills, but also the development of software, the actual purchase of machinery by contractors, and the training of operators and programmers. In a contemporary numerical control system, after the engineer draws the parts that need to be produced, the drawings themselves are converted into data and stored in cards or electronically. From then on, all the operations needed to be performed, drilling, milling, lathing, boring, and so on, are performed automatically by computer-controlled machines. Unlike mass production techniques, where this automatism was achieved at the expense of flexibility, in numerical control systems a relatively simple change in software (not hardware) is all that is needed to adapt the system for the production of a new set of parts. Yet the effects on the population of workers were very similar in both cases: the replacement of flex-

Manuel De Landa *Economics, Computers, and the War Machine*

ible skills by rigid commands embodied in hardware or software, and over the course of time, the loss of those skills leading to a general process of worker de-skilling, and consequently to the loss of individual control of the production process.

The question in both cases is not the influence that the objects produced in militarized factories may have on the civilian world. One could, for instance, argue that the support of the canned food industry by Napoleon had a beneficial effect on society, and a similar argument may be made for many objects developed under military influence. The question that matters, however, is not the transfer of objects but the transfer of the production processes behind those objects, since these processes bring with them the entire control and command structure of the military. To quote historian David Noble:

> The command imperative entailed direct control of production operations not just with a single machine or within a single plant, but worldwide, via data links. The vision of the architects of the [numerical control] revolution entailed much more than the automatic machining of complex parts; it meant the elimination of human intervention—a shortening of the chain of command—and the reduction of remaining people to unskilled, routine, and closely regulated tasks . . . [Numerical control is a] giant step in the same direction [as the nineteenth century drive for uniformity]; here management has the capacity to bypass the worker and communicate directly to the machine via tapes or direct computer link. The machine itself can thereafter pace and discipline the worker.[4]

Let's pause for a moment and consider a possible objection to this analysis. One may argue that the goal of withdrawing control from workers and transferring it to machines is the essence of the capitalist system and that, if military institutions happened to be involved, they did so by playing the role assigned to them by the capitalist system. The problem with this reply is that, although it may satisfy a convinced Marxist, it is at odds with much historical data gathered by this century's best economic historians. This data shows that European societies, far from having evolved through a unilinear progression of "modes of production" (feudalism, capitalism, socialism), actually exhibited a much more complex, more heterogeneous coexistence of processes. In other words, as historian Fernand Braudel has shown, as far back as the fourteenth and fifteenth centuries, institutions with the capability of exercising economic power (large banks, wholesalers, long-distance trade companies) were already in operation, and fully coexisted with feudal institutions as well as with economic institutions that did not have economic power, such as retailers and producers of humble goods. Indeed, Braudel shows that these complex coexistences of institutions of different types existed before and after the Industrial Revolution, and suggests that the concept of a "capitalist system" (where every aspect of society is connected into a functional whole) gives a misleading picture of the real processes. What I am suggesting here is that we take Braudel seriously, forget about our picture of history as divided into neat, internally homogeneous eras or ages, and tackle the complex combinations of institutions involved in real historical processes.

The models we create of these complex "institutional ecologies" should include military organizations playing a large, relatively independent role, to reflect the historical data we now have on several important cases, like fifteenth century Venice, whose famous Arsenal was at the time the largest industrial complex in Europe, or eighteenth century France and nineteenth century United States and their military standardization of weapon production. Another important example involves the development of the modern corporation, particularly as it happened in the United States in the last century.

The first American big business was the railroad industry, which developed the management techniques that many other large enterprises would adopt later on. This much is well known. What is not so well known is that military engineers were deeply involved in the creation of the first railroads and that they developed many of the features of management which later on came to characterize just about every large commercial enterprise in the United States, Europe, and elsewhere.

In the words of historian Charles O'Connell:

As the railroads evolved and expanded, they began to exhibit structural and procedural char-acteristics that bore a remarkable resemblance to those of the Army. Both organizations erected com-plicated management hierarchies to coordinate and control a variety of functionally diverse, geo-graphically separated corporate activities. Both created specialized staff bureaus to provide a range of technical and logistical support services. Both divided corporate authority and responsibility between line and staff agencies and officers and then adopted elaborate written regulations that cod-ified the relationship between them. Both established formal guidelines to govern routine activities and instituted standardized reporting and accounting procedures and forms to provide corporate headquarters with detailed financial and operational information which flowed along carefully defined lines of communication. As the railroads assumed these characteristics, they became America's first big business.[5]

Thus, the transfer of military practices to the civilian world influenced the lives not only of workers, but of the managers themselves. And the influence did not stop with the development of rail-roads. The "management science" which is today taught in business schools is a development of mili-tary "operations research," a discipline created during World War II to tackle a variety of tactical, strategic, and logistic problems. And it was the combination of this "science of centralization" and the availability of large computers that, in turn, allowed the proliferation of transnational corporations and the consequent internationalization of the standardization and routinization of production processes. Much as skills were replaced by commands on the shop floor, so were prices replaced by commands at the management level. (This is one reason not to use the term "markets" when theorizing big business. Not only do they rely on commands instead of prices, they manipulate demand and supply rather than being governed by them. Hence, Braudel has suggested calling big business "anti-markets.")[6]

Keeping in mind the actual complexity of historical processes, as opposed to explaining every-thing by the "laws of capitalist development," is crucial not only to understand the past, but also to intervene in the present and speculate about the future. This is particularly clear when analyzing the role which computers and computer networks may play in the shaping of the economic world in the coming century. It is easy to attribute many of the problems we have today, particularly those related to centralized surveillance and control, to computer technology. But to do this would not only artificially homogenize the history of computers (there are large differences between the development of main-frames and minicomputers, on one hand, and the personal computer, on the other) but it would obscure the fact that, if computers have come to play the "disciplinarian" roles they play today, it is as part of a historical process which is several centuries old, a process which computers have only intensified.

Another advantage of confronting the actual heterogeneity of historical processes, and of throwing into the garbage the concept of "the capitalist system," is that we free ourselves to look around for combinations of economic institutions which coexist with disciplinarian anti-markets but do not play by the same rules. Historically, as Braudel has shown, economic power since the four-teenth century has always been associated with large-size enterprises and their associated "economies of scale." Although technically this term only applies to mass-produced objects, economies of scale meaning the spreading of production costs among many identical products, we may use it in an extended way to define any economic benefits to managers, merchants, and financiers stemming from the scale of any economic resource. Coexisting with economies of scale there are what are called "economies of agglomeration." These are economic benefits which small businesses enjoy from the concentration of many of them in a large city. These economies stem from the benefits of shop-talk, from unplanned connections and mutual enhancements, as well as from the

Manuel De Landa *Economics, Computers, and the War Machine*

services which grow around these concentrations, services which small business could not afford on their own. I would like to give one example, from the world of computers, of two American industrial hinterlands which illustrate the difference between economies of scale and of agglomeration: Silicon Valley in Northern California, and Route 128 near Boston:

> *Silicon Valley has a decentralized industrial system that is organized around regional networks. Like firms in Japan, and parts of Germany and Italy, Silicon Valley companies tend to draw on local knowledge and relationships to create new markets, products, and applications. These specialist firms compete intensely while at the same time learning from one another about changing markets and technologies. The region's dense social networks and open labor markets encourage experimentation and entrepreneurship. The boundaries within firms are porous, as are those between firms themselves and between firms and local institutions such as trade associations and universities.[7]*

The growth of this region owed very little to large financial flows from governmental and military institutions. Silicon Valley did not develop so much by economies of scale as by the benefits derived from an agglomeration of visionary engineers, specialist consultants, and financial entrepreneurs. Engineers moved often from one firm to another, developing loyalties to the craft and the region's networks, not to the corporation. This constant migration, plus an unusual practice of information-sharing among the local producers, ensured that new formal and informal knowledge diffused rapidly through the entire region. Business associations fostered collaboration between small and medium-sized companies.

Risk-taking and innovation were preferred to stability and routinization. This, of course, does not mean that there were not large, routinized firms in Silicon Valley, only that they did not dominate the mix. Not so in Route 128:

> *While Silicon Valley producers of the 1970's were embedded in, and inseparable from, intricate social and technical networks, the Route 128 region came to be dominated by a small number of highly self-sufficient corporations. Consonant with New England's two century old manufacturing tradition, Route 128 firms sought to preserve their independence by internalizing a wide range of activities. As a result, secrecy and corporate loyalty govern relations between firms and their customers, suppliers, and competitors, reinforcing a regional culture of stability and self-reliance. Corporate hierarchies ensured that authority remains centralized and information flows vertically. The boundaries between and within firms and between firms and local institutions thus remain far more distinct.[8]*

While before the recession of the 1980's both regions had been continuously expanding, one on economies of scale and the other on economies of agglomeration (or rather, mixtures dominated by one or the other), they both felt the full impact of the downturn. At that point some large Silicon Valley firms, unaware of the dynamics behind the region's success, began to switch to economies of scale, sending parts of their production to other areas, and internalizing activities previously performed by smaller firms. Yet, unlike Route 128, the intensification of routinization and internalization in Silicon Valley was not a constitutive part of the region, which meant that the old meshwork system could be revived. And this is, in fact, what happened. Silicon Valley's regional networks were re-energized, through the birth of new firms in the old pattern, and the region has now returned to its former dynamic state, unlike the command-heavy Route 128 which continues to stagnate. What this shows is that, while both scale and agglomeration economies, as forms of positive feedback, promote growth, only the latter endows firms with the flexibility needed to cope with adverse economic conditions.

In conclusion I would like to repeat my call for more realistic models of economic history, models involving the full complexity of the institutional ecologies involved, including markets, anti-markets, military and bureaucratic institutions, and if we are to believe Michel Foucault, schools, hospitals, prisons, and many others. It is only through an honest philosophical confrontation with our complex past that we can expect to understand it and derive the lessons we may use when intervening in the present and speculating about the future.

Notes

1. Excerpt from the text of the levée en masse of 1793, quoted in William H. McNeill, The Pursuit of Power: Technology, Armed Force and Society since A.D. 1000 (Chicago: University of Chicago Press, 1982), p. 192.

2. Ibid., p. 129.

3. Michel Foucault, Discipline and Punish: The Birth of Prison (New York: Vintage Books, 1979), p. 169.

4. David Noble, "Command Performance: A Perspective on Military Enterprise and Technological Change," in: Merrit Roe Smith, ed., Military Enterprise (Cambridge: MIT Press, 1987), pp. 341 and 342.

5. Charles F. O'Connell, Jr., "The Corps of Engineers and the Rise of Modern Management," in ibid., p. 88.

6. Fernand Braudel, Wheels of Commerce (New York: Harper and Row, 1986), p. 379.

7. Annalee Saxenian, "Lessons from Silicon Valley," Technology Review, vol. 97, no. 5, p. 44.

8. Ibid., p. 47.

Infowar

Paul Virilio

In conversation with Derrick De Kerckhove

DE KERCKHOVE: Well . . . first of all, hello to everyone, and hello to you, Paul.

Since I'm not an expert in military matters—you're the expert—I had a lot of difficulty preparing questions, even more so because you told me in our telephone conversation that you wanted to have serious questions. So I asked "Infowar," our list server, to help me find some serious questions to ask, making of this a group effort. The results weren't that impressive, because I had to wait until today's session to begin to identify some serious questions. So what I'll do first is to ask whether you would like to make a statement and then have a discussion, or just begin with questions.

VIRILIO: Perhaps I can make a short statement in order to situate "Information Warfare." I remind you that we are facing the third historical weapons system. Each system has had its moment of dominance. The first millenary weapons system is the system of obstruction, which dominated in history throughout the history of the rampart, the city, the wall (the Great Wall of China), etc., all the way to the atomic bunker.

With the invention of artillery, we have moved into the dominance of weapons of destruction, which are infinitely more powerful than weapons of obstruction. This is also the beginning of mobile warfare, as well as the beginning of the end of siege warfare. Weapons of destruction and the invention of explosives will ruin castles, moats, and city walls. And molecular explosives anticipate nuclear explosives, that is to say weapons capable of destroying life on this planet.

Thus arises the Cold War, a system of non-war that will regulate the systems of nations for 40 years. Today, we are entering the third weapons system: weapons of information. Sure, there are still arms of obstruction (bunkers, helmets, and bomb shelters). And there are still arms of destruction (powerful lasers, rockets, missiles, Tomahawks, and others). But arms of communication are beginning to dominate just as arms of destruction dominated in their own time. The Cold War was the advent of arms of communication. Through the development not only of espionage and diplomacy (this was information warfare in the past), but also of telephone, radio, and today's telecommunications, with satellites and real-time weapons systems, we see that Infowar is an emerging system.

If we take the Gulf War, for instance, there are two wars: there is the electronic war (electronic warfare); and there is information warfare. Electronic warfare is the communication of destruction, that is to say cruise missiles (Tomahawks), laser-guided bombs, spy planes, electronic scrambling, etc. These are arms which remote-control destruction. If we take information warfare to comprise warning satellites, spy satellites, and all the systems of listening and remote surveillance, then it is no longer a matter of communicating destruction but of communicating information in real time.

We find an example of this war machine in the National Security Agency, of which we speak very little at the moment. So, with arms of communication we have on one hand electronic warfare (the electronic battlefield introduced during the Vietnam War is already very old), and on the other hand a revolution in military affairs: information warfare. It is obvious that the influence of this kind of warfare is everywhere. It is a completely new and emerging phenomenon, as was the invention of artillery. It influences the economy, the stock market, politics, science (through its militarization), religion, and all phenomena of knowledge. In this sense, this warfare implies the movement away from the local space-time in history toward the global space-time of telecommunications (which we call the "live" or "world time"). We move from the acceleration of history permitted by mobile warfare and by the extraordinarily sophisticated assault methods used in World War II toward the acceleration of reality.

Information warfare is reality warfare. It isn't so much a war of history as it is a war of reality. The force of information warfare no longer resides in the molecular or nuclear explosives used in destructive warfare (the atomic bomb and its fallout), but rather in implosion, the capacity to eliminate all distances and delays. This is the information bomb. No longer are there fallout zones but, instead, information zones. Einstein had foreseen this already in speaking of the three types of bombs: atomic bomb today, information bomb tomorrow, and demographic or genetic bomb the day after tomorrow.

I'd like to give an example and then begin the discussion. I'll give an example of an Infowar that has taken place recently all over the world: Operation Cathedral. Operation Cathedral was launched by Interpol over the the the Internet. Two hundred pedophile web users from 21 countries around the world were arrested instantly and simultaneously in real time. The police have thus become cybernetic. And if the police are cybernetic, you can well imagine the army of tomorrow. I think that this notion, this great coup of Operation Cathedral prefigures the unity of time in the war of the future, that is to say, information warfare. Now I'm ready to take questions.

DE KERCKHOVE: You've already covered quite a lot in your remarkable presentation. What I want to ask you first is, when you say that Infowar is a war of reality (which is quite plausible in my opinion), don't you think that the Wars of Religion during the Renaissance were wars of reality between a medieval reality and the reality of a brand-new individual, isolated from the rest of the community?

VIRILIO: Obviously all wars have had their own respective realities. What I meant was that it was an acceleration of reality, not simply a war of realities (a war of the acceleration of reality). When we say "in real time" or "live" we must no longer consider this a local but a global reality. Cybernetics and cyberspace represent an acceleration of the reality of the world through telecommunications, the telecommunication of information or the telecommunication of destruction using new weapons, etc. So, I emphasize the acceleration of reality, and I don't mean that the Wars of Religion were not reality-based. I mean acceleration of the reality of time. Information warfare is first of all a war of time, a war of real time, a war of world time just like Operation Cathedral. The essential thing is that this kind of warfare, unlike the world war of space and geography during World War II, signifies a world war of time, a war of global real time. This is what is new: the place is time, the time of information feedback between here and there. This is exactly the situation of Operation Cathedral, a situation in which one can act instantly upon many points around the globe.

DE KERCKHOVE: Well, this is a question that has divided somewhat the participants of "Infowar." Among the most interesting debates was this question: When we speak of Infowar, are we speaking of a purely military organization and specialization, or are we not speaking also of markets and corporations, of a sort of undeclared civil war?

VIRILIO: It is obvious that the economy is the nerve center of war, as they say, and that information warfare is concerned, first of all, with the economy. This is to say that everything currently taking place in the common market, in the instantaneous internationalization of exchanges, is a component of information warfare. As I said at the beginning, information warfare is economic or political, but all wars have been eco-political. Information warfare is instantaneous, through the possibility of acting upon the stock market in real time and simply of differentiating markets. The common market is already globalization.

DE KERCKHOVE: OK, that's understood. But here there is another problem that was highlighted this morning by Manuel De Landa. He articulated something extremely pertinent regarding the presence of the military in Third World countries, notably those in turmoil. He said that the military in these Third World countries takes up the role of the police, and, as a result, the distinction between the civil and the military disappears. This contrasts with the situation in those countries where the police function more or less peacefully, without the brutality of a true police state. This is understood as an indication of a country at peace.

The question is this: Is this Infowar of which we're speaking (in the marketplace, among corporations, even under the secret control of the CIA . . . we've had many examples), is this type of control still called war, or is it something else? The question is important because either one is controlled by the police or one is controlled by the army. If one isn't controlled by the army, then, in that case, the country is at peace.

VIRILIO: The distinction between war and peace depends upon the nature of the conflict. You said earlier that I was a military expert, but I hold that one is never an expert of a war that is beginning. We must learn a war as we learn a foreign language. We had to learn the Gulf War, making quite a few mistakes along the way. We had to learn the war in the former Yugoslavia. And today, in a much larger scale, we must learn this emerging phenomenon called Infowar. It is obvious that today the distinction between military police and the army is unsettled. We witness this in the privatization of the army, in the rise of the military profession, in the end of national armies and conscription, and in the role of mercenaries (I'm thinking, above all, of one of the largest mercenary firms, Executive Action, in South Africa). We are now faced with the total transformation of the military system. Not only of the weapons systems I spoke of earlier, but also of the political system and the structures of intervention which are no longer national structures but rather already comparable to those of security agencies or detective agencies, etc. We are faced with a total transformation of the phenomenon of war. Even though we had to learn the Gulf War, it was in reality an older warfare, a warfare that had already been tested in Vietnam and elsewhere. And obviously, during the Cold War this was evident in the weapons systems developed to fight the Soviets.

Today, the transformation is not simply one of weapons systems but, rather, a transformation of the military institution (military or police, let's say), which is just beginning. Thus, those who claim to be experts of information warfare are, quite simply, naive. I'm trying, using my knowledge of military culture, to discover in what this transformation consists. It is obvious that the transformation is multifaceted. Its influence can be seen in many realms. We must not neglect one realm in favor of another. We must try to understand in what way these realms become cybernetic.

DE KERCKHOVE: OK. So, I should conclude that we are at war?

VIRILIO: Since the Cold War, the question of the declaration of war is no longer relevant. The declaration of war is still linked to the frontier, to real space and to confrontations such as those of World War I and World War II. After the advent of the Cold War threat and the equilibrium of terror, the declaration of war no longer exists. After this, war will be without forewarning, and certainly information warfare will be without forewarning.

DE KERCKHOVE: There your thinking recalls McLuhan's in a very interesting way, when he states: "Acceleration placed all citizens naturally and permanently in a state of war."

VIRILIO: Exactly.

DE KERCKHOVE: Another question was posed to us this morning by Michael Geyer in his reflections upon the "New Sovereignty to Defend" (the new sovereignty to defend is that of the market). And the new enemy, according to Friedrich Kittler, is the nation. I'd like for you to develop this theme of the theory of the suicidal State.

VIRILIO: I worked on the "suicidal State" during the Cold War. Why? Because the Cold War was the programming of the end of the world. From the moment when States divided into Eastern and Western blocs and began preparing the end of the world, it is evident that they were preparing the end of the State. It's banal to say it. So, today, it is apparent that the question of the political State is in complete opposition. It's true that what has happened in the Soviet Union, no, in Russia—we don't really know too much—foreshadows what will happen elsewhere. Since the 1950's and the equilibrium of terror, the State has set about programming its own end. As General Fuller put it, "The atomic bomb will take the world back to feudalism." Lieutenant General Fuller, a renowned weapons specialist, uttered these words of caution, implying that the atomic bomb (anticipating the information bomb) will bring back the warlords and the mafia.

I believe that the capacity to engineer the end of the world over 40 years, to think the unthinkable through the equilibrium of terror—these already signified the programming of the end of the nation-state. The nation-state was a state in situ. It had a place. It was linked to a territoriality. All of the new technologies aim to eliminate territory using the speed of missile assaults or laser beams. The world dematerializes through the speed of telecommunications. Geostrategy and geopolitics lose prominence in favor of a virtually instantaneous exchange. So the State had insured its own disappearance. The Soviet Union (through Star Wars and its economic engagement in preparation for war with the West) instituted its own disintegration.

DE KERCKHOVE: Yes, except that there were several arguments this morning which claimed that the disappearance of the nation-state is simply one of our contemporary myths. And one of the points which arise from this is the idea, proposed earlier by Kittler, that the Soviet Union was absorbed by the global system, that it was absorbed, and thus the State ended in this manner. So, my question to you—I'll ask it and then let the public ask questions because I have more for later—is this: If we are in this situation of deterritorialization which you have so brilliantly discussed (the disappearance of the right of the body), then what is the new public space? Or will we never again have public space?

VIRILIO: This question is the major political question. Is politics linked to a corporeality? Territorial corporeality (geography, geostrategy, geopolitics); the social body (that's to say a unity that isn't simply ethnic but much greater); and, finally, animal body, human body, physical body. The political question of tomorrow must re-pose the questions which were posed of the city. With the invention of politics, we invented a territory of rights. From the law, a city of the body. From the law, a city of ethnicities. From the law, a city of individuals in Athens or Sparta (to cite two well-known examples). Today we must reinvent a politics of the animal or human body, of the social body, and of the territorial body.

I'll give examples: Since the beginning of the city laws, the land ordinance, etc. . . . and then the maritime laws (and these already vague laws with pirates, etc.) . . . Soon we invent the airspace laws. Here we are talking about aerial boundaries and lines in space. Finally, the outer space laws designate that a satellite owns its orbit. Here we have a dematerialization of territory which is part of the new logic of law of the airspace laws, the maritime laws, etc. It seems to me that there is work to be done on this nomadic right which is not that of the gypsy or of the traditional ethnic or tribal nomad. There is work to be done on this law of movement. We must introduce an economy of speed and of displacement.

DE KERCKHOVE: There is something that still bothers me—I'm sorry, I'll ask this and then let the public ask questions—and that is the question of the security of the nomadic citizen who carries a cell phone. There were two brilliant presentations this morning. In one, we saw that Dudaev (a Chechen) was killed and his physical presence was revealed through his cell phone number. But the most important point is that the Russians weren't able to do this alone but, rather, only with the secret aid of the Americans. Thus, the first powerful image suggests that the media can kill in the flesh. The other point which interests me, and which is a question of the Panopticon which you yourself have brilliantly analyzed, is this: when is it a right of the citizen who carries a cell phone, from all points of view (from the point of view of the security of his information, from the point of view of the security of his physical presence, and from the point of view of the security he owes because he is locatable) . . . So there is an exchange such that on the one hand, yes, we can kill him, but on the other hand if something happens to him, we can find him instantly. What do you think of the role of the cell phone in this new configuration?

VIRILIO: I'm very worried by social cybernetics. It is obvious that there is a man-machine cybernetics, as all technical progress is linked to this. From the moment when we move beyond this machine cybernetics into a social cybernetics of which you've just given an example (I'll give another example: there are these programs which are used on the Internet to arrest pedophile web users), I must say that somewhere freedom is profoundly threatened. Cybernetics, as Norbert Wiener has said (and he was one of the founders of cybernetics), is marvelous except if it becomes a political phenomenon. I fear, as you have just put it, that the capacity to exercise societal control has superseded the individual's ability to acquire rights and liberties. And I think that in this case the Internet, contrary to what they say, is not an example of liberty but, rather, an example of social cybernetics. Others have spoken of the symbiotic brain etc. . . . crazy things.

DE KERCKHOVE: Another aspect of the question is the return of the nervous system. According to McLuhan, whose thinking I seem always to be representing in some form or other, electricity (a projection of the nervous system) has surrounded the planet, but it will return to and reintegrate within the body. The cell phone would be the final step before actual reintegration with the body. The United States Army has provided an astonishing example of this actual integration, as MIT researcher Michael Hawley has shown us. Soldiers swallow a pill which releases signals in different parts of the body. A special belt worn by the soldier collects this information and then transmits it over the Internet, providing the recipient with information about the soldier's bodily functions. I find this to be a telling image of the reintroduction of electricity into the human body. Have you heard of this experiment?

VIRILIO: No, but the astronauts in their capsules with their monitors are an example of this "intestinal" control. We are facing the conquest of space and the transformation of man into a video or electromagnetic receptor. Do you recall in the film "Apollo 13" when Lowell decides to return in the disabled capsule on his own, the first thing he does is to tear out all of the monitors/probes. In so doing he is saying "I'm the boss. Now you can't check/see what's going on inside of me. I'm commanding the return to earth." I think that it is the astronaut who foreshadows, in a certain sense, this situation of cybernetic control and domination of the body by interactive techniques.

DE KERCKHOVE: The last thing, then, would be a complete reversal of the situation. Given this reintegration of the nervous system in the body through different interactive systems, through the ingestion of pills, through the devices we carry around with us, through the "wearable computer"—all of this represents a return of electricity to the body. Wouldn't this then be a teleology which is no longer the mark of a military, industrial, or technological system conscious of what is doing, but rather a sort of global implosion of this set of relationships into themselves? Since we are connected to a global memory and to an intelligence which is more and more one of a global nature (because of the Internet, among other things), isn't there in this relationship a completely different vision of the world which we have not yet begun to explore?

VIRILIO: There are many things that we do not know, but let me give an example that struck me from the latest events in Africa. In the past, when people took power they stormed the Bastille. And later they took the Winter Palace. And then the governor's residence. And then they took the radio, and finally Studio 4 in Bucharest in order to topple Ceaucescu. Today they take the electrical system in Kinshasa. I think that here is a fine metaphor for the role of electricity in information warfare. It is a primitive element. However, to take an electrical power grid before taking a city is a remarkable event, in my opinion, which reminds us of another serious event: the great electrical power outage of 1965 in New York City. I think that electricity is the great breakdown. It's not simply a huge energy; it's also the possibility of getting disconnected. All of the power sources have an accident specific to them. We have not yet seen to what point electricity, as you have just argued, is a crucial factor in information warfare. The example of Kinshasa is, I think, one that will be repeated.

Now I should return to the discussion of the body. You are exactly right: each time a power has controlled a territory, through colonization or through manipulation, it has also controlled the body. It is the body of the slave, the body of the soldier. The soldier is trained, trained to react. The body of the colonized or of the domestic servant or of the slave is trained. There is no colony in a geographic space or in an empire that does not entail the colonization of a body. The training of the body's reflexes—this is carried out today by electromagnetic techniques—this is an old technique, as Michel Foucault has shown us.

DE KERCKHOVE: Neocolonization. "I believe it's time for some questions from the audience, otherwise we'll run out of time. If you don't have questions, believe me I have plenty, and I'm sacrificing them. So, would we take a few questions from the audience? I don't see very well, but . . . Oh! There's some light." [In English, addressing the audience.] Thank you, Paul. We're going to take some questions from the audience.

Yes? I'm going to translate from English to French for you, Paul, if the question is in English.

James Derian: I have a very simple question. In many of the American military universities, students are reading Paul Virilio. Do you think this is something good, or something dangerous?

VIRILIO: I think that no one is innocent. Faced with the problems we've been discussing, we are all guilty. We are not all responsible as is the military by profession. To develop a critique of a weapons system or a critique of a logic of development of power—and here one needs only reread Clausewitz—is necessarily to provide certain elements for the development of the very system we are trying to combat. It is inevitable, because we come from the same family. We think using the same norms. And so it's true that the fact that this work is being taken up in the military academies and schools of warfare—in France also—can be extremely disturbing...maybe. I am not innocent.

• • •

Audience member: I want to raise, it seems, a bit more utopian question. An Austrian is working already for years on this—that is, the robotization of the human body. He explains quite simply that the brain has much more capacity than the body allows it to express and to use. And so in the end, as Hans Moravec suggests, in maybe 20 or 30 years there will be more and more roboticized human beings, and finally only human beings replaced by robots. What do you think, because it is also a question of thinking as well as of moving in the physical way?

VIRILIO: The robot is at the origin of work. The machine tool is already a robot. It is obvious that the autonomization of machines of productions is—and it's an old story—a part of the history of industry. No, what I fear are genetic robots. Today, roboticization threatens to become involved in the process of cloning or in the construction—thanks to biotechnology—of individuals, especially developed for certain activities/tasks. I think that the question of robots has been treated in depth, through a large body of writing on automatons, etc. But the question of the living robot, of the chimera or of the clone, reproduces the notion of roboticization—but this time by genetic means. Thus, there is a threat that computers, and genetic mapping (the ability to map the human genome), will allow us to make robot-humans. That is to say, roboticized living beings. This through a specialization which is no longer industrial but, rather, computerized, thanks to the treatment of the genetic code. Here we have an enormous threat, and I think we return to the notion of the three types of bomb. The atomic bomb and the genetic bomb are only possible because of the information/computer bomb. It's not by chance that Turing and others are developing the computer at the same time that the atomic bomb is being invented. Today, we need the computer to run simulations. And computers are absolutely crucial to genetic engineering. Thus, there is the possibility of another, transgenetic roboticization which worries me even more because the work has not yet been done. The work on the critique of the robot has been done, even in religion. But the living robot, the living slave—this new form of living slavery, made possible by genetic engineering—we have not done enough work on this subject.

DE KERCKHOVE: But another related question, that's important in my opinion, is the following: In "Blade Runner," we see androids who have completely human characteristics and emotions—or who discover their emotions. Is there a possibility that, in a not so distant future, we will transfer our active, effective, and labor-oriented—our robotic—humanity into these creatures and keep our weaknesses, our imperfect beings, thus avoiding a total invasion?

VIRILIO: In any case, there is nothing else to do. [Laughter.] Personally, I think that man is not the center of the world, but rather the end of the world. Hildegard von Bingen, whose 900th birthday

we will celebrate this year, said: "homo es closura mirabilium dei." Man is the closure of God's wonders. It is an extraordinary sentence. Because of this word *cloture,* man is the end of the world. There
will be no more genetics, no more genetic progress of the being. There is ethical progress and, in quotation marks, "moral" progress (if we can use this word while remaining politically correct). But man is
the end of the world. He cannot be improved upon genetically. In reality, the great conflict of information warfare is old versus new genetics. The temptation is toward a much more sophisticated genetics
than that of Galton.

Audience: I have a question about ordinary people. You say in your work that one of the ways
we can respond to the dromological culture that we live in is to recognize the accident that is created
with the substance. That is to say, the car crash or the real crash or the information. That seems to be
a conceptual question. I wondered how ordinary people, people in cities, can make that operative in
their political lives?

VIRILIO: I think that we must understand that each time we introduce a new bit of technology,
we invent, at the same time, a specific accident. The invention of the ship was the invention of the
shipwreck. The invention of atomic electricity was the invention of Chernobyl. The invention of the jet
was the invention of the crash. Thus, industrial society in the twentieth century has meant the invention of larger and larger accidents.

At first, localized accidents: the *Titanic* sank in a place we can go see. At Chernobyl, the core
exploded. With new, computerized technologies we are in the presence of a global accident which can
take place everywhere. What is that, you ask? The first example is the stock market, because it is
based upon automatic quotations. Also, the Year 2000 bug: "Y2K." You are familiar with this problem
of computers which, in some way, cannot process that year 2000. This is an accident comparable to a
weapon, an accident which is part of information warfare. The depression bomb and the fragmentation
bomb, what are these but weapons which promote chains of accidents? This is also what we call a systemic effect. It is obvious that computer technologies have systemic properties, since they are able to
provoke accidents everywhere at once.

We are in the presence of an ecology of the accident. The accident is no longer a disaster
which takes place here or there. It is an accident that we are in. The accident becomes a milieu, an
ecosystem. Thus the threat in the stock market and elsewhere because of the Y2K bug, for example.
I recall that last May the CIA gave a deadline to the states for the prevention of this sort of accident,
particularly in banks, airports, etc. So, the Year 2000 bug—of which the code is "Y2K" and I'm very
happy to be able to say it—is one of the elements of what I call an integral accident, an accident unlike
any we've seen before.

J. Doyne Farmer: I want to try and connect some of the things you say, and ask you whether
you really believe these things. On the one hand, you say that transponders for prisoners are an evil,
enslaving technology. And yet prisons are an even more ancient enslaving technology . . . and even
more pernicious. You rail against the simultaneous arrest of pedophiles, and yet a child who is seduced
by a pedophile, as we know, can be damaged for life and have very severe problems as a result. You
rail against cloning, and yet, as we know, identical twins are nothing more than the outcome of cloning
in a natural circumstance. And so, by this kind of logic, I think twins must be evil. You rail against the
genetic. You say, if I understood the translation, and I can hardly believe this, that human beings represent a genetic pinnacle, a perfection of sorts which I frankly find an anthropocentric, narcissistic idea
that is similar to that of the creationists or the right wing in the Moral Majority. So, I just want to challenge . . . because it seems to me that in a democracy we have ultimately to rely on common sense in

technology and the ability of people to rise up and resist things if they begin to be used in a manner that's completely out of control. And we have to resist our paranoid fantasies about where technology might go if it were put in the hands of a Hitler, for example.

VIRILIO: I'll first respond to the first question. There is no resistance that does not begin with a comprehension, a comprehension of the enemy. I'll give an example. Seven years before the Gulf War, I did a film for television called "Nombre des Lumières" treating images of war. I talked about flight simulators, guided missile systems, video bombs, etc. I also did a book on war and cinema. My anti-nuclear group of friends, with whom I sympathized, said to me: "That's not political enough." And I said that if you walk out in the street and say "Oh my! Flight simulators," people won't understand at all. Thus, before entering into a critique of a weapons system or any technical system, one must learn it. I said earlier that we must learn a war before we dare speak about it. And so we must learn the new system of Infowar so that we can resist it. Knowledge of the enemy is part of the resistance and the battle. I feel that today, technological culture is not shared by the entire populace. There is a non-democracy of technological culture. The culture taught in the universities and in the schools is a culture I would call "traditional." Especially in the lower-level classes.

When a musicologist says that an interpretation of Bach or Handel is not good, we don't say that he is pessimistic about music, that he is a musical pessimist. We say, "Now, now let's see." My role is to be a critic of technology as one is a critic of art. I do not consider this pessimistic at all but, on the contrary, a necessity. It's simply that today, criticism is ill-perceived because the forces of propaganda, in order to sell products, wield a force in advertising which exceeds the powers of us poor individuals.

It is obvious that any object has a positive and negative dimension. The chemical straitjacket used to treat madness in Russian hospitals was a liberation from the physical straitjacket. In the same way, the transponder liberates one from the prison, from incarceration. But this is not a gain which is completely positive. This is what I'm trying to say. There is no pure object. No invented object is pure. It has its negativity. There are no gains without losses.

So, to return to the other part of the phrase. Of course I know the advantages of technology. But these advantages are advocated by advertisements and by promotional campaigns backed by millions of dollars. They extol new technologies. There are massive sales expositions where billions of dollars are circulated. And I, alone, will be negative? Come on, it's a joke. I'm simply trying to throw a new wrinkle in the works. Faced with this advertising barrage of new products which are, like the older products, positive as well as negative. And it's good. I don't have to say it. Everyone knows that. But it is also ominous.

Audience: Good afternoon, Mr. Virilio. [Laughter.] What's your opinion about the Internet? That's another instrument that erases distance and goes over the border lines.

VIRILIO: When I was young I was a citizen of the world. I met Gary Davis in Paris. He was the advocate of the world identification card. He came to Paris when I was 17 and distributed these ID cards. I was the son of Italians, the son of immigrants, and so accepted with pleasure this invitation to consider myself a citizen of the world. It is obvious that information technologies, and the Internet in particular, are an extension of this world citizenship. But what I can't stand on the Internet is the propaganda, the hype. The Internet is, in reality, descended from ARPAnet, once again a military system, that has been civilized, so much the better. But no one can tell me that it is a pure object. There are no pure objects. The Internet is like the *Titanic*. It is an instrument which performs extraordinarily well but which contains its own catastrophe. But this catastrophe leaves no visible casualties. There are no bodies floating in the water. There are other sorts of negativity. My work is not to say that we must abandon the Internet. My job is to work on the losses, on what the Internet makes us lose. Thus, I have a fierce opposition to propaganda, perhaps because I lived World War II. And I won't stand for propaganda whether industrial, political, or religious! That's what I want to explain. The Internet is an object. I am on the Internet, my school is on the Internet. It is a useful tool.

DE KERCKHOVE: Which leads me to an important question. This is the idea that we maintain the myth of the military origin of the Internet in our culture in such a way that we oblige the public to swallow an even greater myth. And this is the idea that without the competitiveness there will be no technological development. And according to Douglas Rushkoff this is not necessary. Thus, the role of the military in technological production is completely clear in your work. But do you think there are possibilities outside the army?

VIRILIO: I should hope so. But we cannot ignore that during the twentieth century we have witnessed a frightening phenomenon, which is the militarization of science. The military-industrial complex of which we have spoken—and it still exists, one must simply look at what remains in the Soviet Union of this complex—is one of the elements of scientific discovery. The engagement of the Nobel Prize in the Vietnam War, it's extraordinarily serious, this militarization of science. There is a culture of death developing here. And so we can't downplay this origin. If we downplay this, it's because we don't want to look truth in the face. During the twentieth century, we have programmed the end of the world, relentlessly, thanks to the Nobel Prize, thanks to the laboratories, thanks to scientists at the universities. To hide this today, at the moment we are speaking of Infowar, I find that scandalous. Thus, we are facing an originality. The twentieth century, as Albert Camus said, "is a pitiless century." It is the century of accidents, of catastrophes. Between Hiroshima, Auschwitz, Chernobyl, and the *Titanic,* technoscience has programmed the end. The end of the world.

I am of that generation. I was born in 1932, and will never forget that my century is a pitiless one. And all philosophic, religious, and other thought is contaminated by this origin. Thus, let's try to own up to this origin in order to move beyond it.

Translated from the French by Paul Henninger and Josh Wise

Norn Attacks and Marine Doom

Birgit Richard

Modelling reality to get reality.
Toby Simpson[1]

This paper examines two forms of death in virtual worlds. In light of the possibility of creating artificial life in a computer processor, the question arises as to whether a phenomenon like death is even a matter of significance in a binary world that appears to be infinite and eternal, and what relationship exists between these death phenomena and the real thing. We can differentiate between two forms of immaterial death: artificial death as a programmed parameter, and self-emergent death in accordance with the biological model.

"On the Net, there is no art of this kind (yet): it has had no time to develop a notion of the Other, the vanishing point of which would be Death. The model for Net Culture is life . . ."[2]

Not only the Internet but also the other digital media present themselves as eternal phenomena that know no end. The apologists for new-media worlds all too readily put forth the myth of the permanent retrievability of all information once it has been put into digital form. Inherent in this is the danger that information that is only a few years old will become unreadable due to the rapid revision of systems. The utopia of digital immortality of human beings, as "mind . . . uploaded into the Net," as John Perry Barlow formulated it, thus sees itself being confronted by "life-threatening" hazards like system crashes or upgrades. Death lurks in program structures.

Artificial worlds and their inhabitants demand the construction of a virtual death. The implementation of transitoriness—to the extent that it does not develop self-emergently—becomes a pressing necessity due to the potentially infinite metamorphoses and metastasis-like growths into other states and forms.

The constructional principle of forms of virtual death represents the highly regimented artificial worlds of computer games and simulations. They are based on the theorem of double death put forth by Lacan, as Zizek has shown.[3] Virtual life survives multiple deaths until the arrival of absolute death: the end of the game. This can be deferred by means of additional life won during the course of the game. The artificial death encountered in video games is characterized by manifold stages and multiple forms of death.

Moreover, the players can repeatedly resurrect the dead in a physically intact form—they possess a sublime body fully in the sense of de Sade's phantasma: "You'll be able to resurrect the digital dead and kill them again."[4] This resurrected flesh shows no traces of abuse stemming from "real" life, as is the case of the undead zombie in film.[5] This figure returns over and over again, with its horribly mangled body as reference to the injustice that has been done to it, until the debt of the living has been discharged and the dead can rest in peace. Artificial death, on the other hand, creates a tabula rasa each time, and everything can start again from the very beginning.

Artificial Worlds and Their Living Inhabitants

"The greatest thing about computing is not overhauling the real world to make it work properly—writing can do that too—but rather that it is capable of projecting forth sensorily perceptible worlds."[6]

Artificial life comes about on the basis of natural laws. Two directions have emerged in the design of artificial life: the simulation of natural life forms, inherent in which is self-emergent death, and the fictional creation of artificial worlds with their artificially implemented death by means of strictly defined parameters.

Larry Yaeger's *Polyworld*[7] is an ecological simulator whose creatures are designated by Yaeger as "dervishes" or "edgerunners" depending upon their behavior and form of movement. The simple physiologies of the beings inhabiting this artificial cosmos correspond to elementary stereometric forms. Visual differences are to be found only in the various colors and in whether or not the being constitutes a complete living creature or a fragmentary dead one decomposed to the status of a unit of nutrition.

Certain modes of behavior of *Polyworld* beings and phenomena like virtual death have come about over the course of machine evolution without having been previously programmed. The creatures die due to biological necessity because their nutritional resources are inadequate, because they have been vanquished by opponents in the struggle to obtain food, or because they have lost the battle for territory and been plunged over the edge of the disk-shaped world.

Another virtual world is Tom Ray's *Tierra* model. This world is populated by a harmless type of virus in the form of long, narrow strips in a variety of colors. They take shape on the basis of genetic algorithms and undergo a process of evolutionary development. Here, an administrative authority responsible for killing has been set up by the programmer: if copying errors lead to mutations, artificial death ensues. The *reaper*—represented by a skull-and-crossbones—eliminates old, defective programs.

In the installations *A-Volve* and *Interactive Plant Growing* by Laurent Mignonneau and Christina Sommerer, death is brought into play as a necessary tabula rasa. It is the zero-point, the shutdown of interactive life-processes, the point at which the initial state can be reestablished.

Myron Krüger's *Critter* installation also contains an artificial being that follows on a projection surface the observer who has been embossed by means of chromakey technology.[8] In this world, death and destruction were actually not foreseen as parameters; however, the behavior of young male users, whose overriding need was to destroy the friendly artificial creature, forced Krüger to program new options into the installation: a user can squash the Critter, it bursts, only to be resurrected a moment later.[9] Critter also becomes a deathless, sublime creature.

Scientific findings gained from biological simulators have been most fully and consistently integrated in the commercial field of video games. They are more complex and more concrete than biological simulators in that they show which aesthetic forms are possible and how quickly the artificial forms become economically utilizable entities.

Creatures, a game developed in 1996 by Stephen Grand from the firm CyberLife, makes possible the breeding of individual beings and generations, all the way to an entire population of furry little creatures called "Norns." They possess a digital DNA and basically go through all stages of human development. Each develops an individual biography, including infancy, childhood, and youth, when they must be raised and cared for, and finally adulthood. They reproduce sexually, they age and die. To experience a complete life cycle, players must spend approximately 18 hours with one of their Norns until the creature succumbs to the infirmities of old age. To fittingly memorialize the deceased Norns, a funeral set is provided—the icon is a gravestone with the inscription "RIP"—along with a burial plot in the Internet.

The developmental stages of these artificial creatures can be captured by means of a virtual camera and pasted into a virtual family album. Moreover, this form of virtual life can be saved in memory, imported into the Internet, and thus be placed into a wide variety of contexts. Creatures is a game; that is to say, the artificial world can take a break if the computer processor is turned off.

A second version of the game Creatures was brought out in Fall 1998. Along with improved graphics and a user-friendlier interface, it offers a large-scale terrain named Albia, the virtual environment of the Norns, as well as more objects and machines. Beings that already exist can be transferred to the new world; the new Norns have new genotypes. Individual body parts such as the tail are movable, and there is a wider variety of facial expressions. They are endowed with organs such as lungs, so that if a Norn dies as a result of a disease, the cause of death can be more readily assessed. Without body and organs, the medical-analytical view is unable to recognize causes.[10] An immaterial body is actually an exterior surface that cannot provide a glimpse into its interior. This is precisely what is now being artificially constructed.

Cemetery of the Cuddly Creatures: The Norns as Fighter Pilots

Creatures contains beings displaying "emergent behavior" which, in contrast to primitive, permanent forms like the Tamagotchi, can develop a multi-faceted character. Even the game's first version presented a species with the capability of learning and that can be trained to perform any task.

Creatures is so flexibly programmed that the architecture can be expanded and systems can be repeatedly introduced or exchanged without having to rewrite the entire program. It has been the players above all who have taken advantage of this feature: they have genetically engineered the Norns, and have inserted objects or new machines.

There are "cheats" (tricks) which precisely describe how artificial immortality can be introduced through the manipulation of three genes (#001 decay rate at birth, #170 age, #173 death receptor).

By means of the genetic code, the programmer can breed the most highly resistant Norns. The first generations also contained deformed creatures or individuals who died of illnesses such as violent shivering fits. The first version designed for a mass market, however, was programmed to preclude deformities. The unpleasant side-effects of a biological simulation in the form of a game were deemed unsuitable to the market and eliminated. Death as a result of old age, an error in the selection of food (poison mushrooms), or a biological enemy (the Grendels) is permitted, but not death due to genetic mutations or aggressive acts within the same species. The user can also exert psychic violence, in that he neglects the Norns. Failing to interact with the Norns or raising them improperly causes them to waste away and die.

The Norns use machines as means of transportation (submarines, elevators) or learning (computers). Their tremendous enthusiasm for technology is the sign of an artificial species capable of higher development; of course, they can operate both analog and digital machines, though without actually controlling them.

Now, on commission from the British Ministry of Defence (Bedford, Dera Research Institute), the "cute" little characters are being trained as Eurofighter pilots. The goal of this vision is "to put human intelligence inside computers by the year 2020." The concept of unmanned armed vehicles (UAV) is being tested with the Norns. The term "unmanned" is not synonymous with "not live"; it is just that, in this case, there are no human beings piloting the Eurofighter.

This commercial application was selected because it contains the first artificial species capable of learning. Only the "born" flyers are bred further; the genes of those who crash are eliminated. It is only after 400 generations that the Norns master aviation. The death of the virtual test pilots means nothing. They are immaterial victims of military progress. Artificial life (still) has no needs of its own; all it wants to do is to survive combat. Hunger and thirst are trained out of it. Furthermore, it is capable of tolerating stress, and can withstand tremendous acceleration without injury, since it possesses no body and its cyberlife-brain has been trained exclusively to carry out this task.

On the other hand, game players grow quite fond of the Norns due to their representativeness. The emotional attachment is strengthened by the long duration of the game, and manifests itself in phenomena such as naming, graphic fixation on some particular stage of an individual creature's development, and arrangement of its funeral. What takes place here is a reversal of visual representation in the form of a transformation of hard evolutionary facts. For the game, the representation is constructed in such a way as to be emotionally appealing. The Norns are the visual embodiment of charm. They move about awkwardly in their environment Albia and are quick to learn. Norns are the antithesis of the ugly, uneducated Grendels—their enemies, an aggressive species that lives outside of Albia. (This can be revised to some extent by means of intervention in the program.)

Binary code is flexible and can assume any visual form. The creators of artificial life also employ this representation for Killer-Norns, who will perhaps someday be in the position to extinguish real life.

Toby Simpson's remark "modelling reality to get reality" thus assumes a new dimension: modelled virtual reality becomes a reality of death and destruction. For the first time, artificial life has its "finger" on the trigger of deadly weapons. This lethal "smartness" of artificial life that leads an existence as a purely airborne being in an unmanned flying object constitutes the achievement of independence of a warlike form of killing. After all, the Pilot-Norns are capable of learning within their own "biotope" and develop capabilities which lie outside of the programmed structures—which is by no means astounding in the case of an artificial life form with a genetic code. The Norns keep the Eurofighter aloft in such an individualistic way that the programmers can no longer even explain it on the basis of an analysis of the software.

The term "friendly fire" takes on an insidious new significance when Norns—juvenile homunculi and actually just a fortuitous visualization of digital processes—operate real aircraft and are in the position to extinguish real lives. Death is no longer depicted as a hideous skeleton, but rather as a "cute" cuddly creature. They are of course invisible to a potential enemy, to whom this is a remote-controlled guided missile without any form of life, since the enemy is incapable of perceiving it.

These Pilot-Norns are one further step in the direction of the fulfillment of the age-old military dream of replacing imperfect, mortal human warriors with an artificial species. They are perfect jigsaw puzzle pieces in constructions like the 21stCenturyLandwarrior (21CLW), the Pitman of the 1980s, robotic weapons, and the idea of an "augmented reality" (Mark Weiser), and of conflicts decided on artificial battlefields.

Dying in Virtual Worlds: Marine Doom

Up to the end of the '80s, military simulators—the American SIMNET and applications like flight simulators—were considered to be the genesis of commercial video games. Here, war shifted into a virtual intermediate world cordoned off from reality, a world in which virtual death is preinstalled by the manufacturer. Here, the symbolic death of the opponent in combat occurs before biological death because it is first determined on the monitors of strategic headquarters in the virtual world.

Besides these élite strategy simulators for the training of officers, simulations which are, indeed, modified versions of commercially available action games like Doom II are now being placed into service for the training of foot soldiers. The military version entitled *Marine Doom* can be downloaded without restriction. The single condition to be able to play is the installation of the commercial product *Doom 1.9*. This recourse to commercial products takes place due to cost considerations, since the real training camps (combat towns) are filled to capacity and new ones are too costly.

The Marine Corps Modelling Simulation Management Office in Quantico, Virginia, conducts a systematic evaluation of commercially available computer games and visualization software—to generate realistic scenarios, for instance. Besides ID's *Doom 1.9* which, as *Marine Doom*, has been adapted to meet military specifications, the Navy is testing a flight simulator entitled JetFighter III. The game makes available two types of aircraft and real scenarios such as China, Korea, Japan, Russia, Alaska, Cuba, Argentina, Chile, and Turkey. It is possible to run 90 missions; time of day and conditions such as fog, smoke, and fire can be set. Approval has also been granted to the M1A2 Abrams Tank Simulation, Flight Unlimited II, a flight simulator for acrobatic aerial maneuvers, and Comanche Maximum Overkill, a helicopter simulation.

Among the 3-D animation software being tested is 3-D Studio Max. The evaluation especially emphasized the destructive effects for animated objects, including "spawning on death and collision, trailing sparks, fluid bubble motion" (http://www.tec.army.mil/TD/tvd/survey/3D_Studio_MAX.html).

The MetaVirtual Reality Scene Generator enables users to construct games for multi-player networks with "event based texture animations for explosions, dynamic weather" on a terrain corresponding to the Fort Benning Mout and comprising an area of 24 x 24 kilometers (http://www.tec.army.mil/TD/tvd/survey/MetaVRSG.html).

The category of action games—"deathmatches" as they are appropriately titled—makes a multi-player mode available and is particularly well suited to the tactical simulation of combat. With the possibility of multi-player mode, the banding together of previously isolated players in combat groups and units of their own choosing (e.g. the Quake Clans) has come about on its own. This global, telepresent, network-linked mode of playing with each other and not necessarily against each other has been adopted by the military.

For this reason, action games like *Doom* recommend themselves to aid the formation of social skills. Military developers argue that life-saving team spirit ought to be trained in artificial scenarios, so that it does not have to be formed under the existential pressure of war and the conditions of real combat in which errors can be irreversible.

The military teams now play in an Intranet under their control which is not accessible by the general public. This is of minor significance, however, since the structural and visual modifications undertaken by the military are of a rather cosmetic nature. Realistic bunkers, terrains and trenches fenced off by barbed wire have been introduced. In place of monsters of various different types—i.e. with a variety of fighting capabilities—recruits now confront enemy and friendly troops in uniform. Their basic model is a "G.I. Joe" action figure that has been scanned in with a variety of different uniforms. Their arsenal is limited to three types of weapons in current use (M16A1 rifle, M-249 machine gun, M-67 grenade launcher), and their fire is based on laws of ballistics.

The Marines playing this game are grouped into squads of four individuals, a realistic representation of the smallest fighting unit. They "play" on their PCs in a room equipped with loudspeakers playing sounds that imitate the noise of a battlefield and communicating the commands of their superior who, as an observer, has an oversight card and can stop the course of events at any time. Each player has his own perspective of the combat situation. He is assigned a mission via e-mail, as well as a description of who is a friend and who is a foe. It is possible to conduct exercises of special missions such as the liberation of an embassy—in this case, original blueprints of a number of different embassy compounds are made available (http://www.tec.army.mil/TD/tvd/survey/Marine_Doom.html).

"The object of *Doom* is to maim, to kill, to rout, to ravage. You succeed by obliteration, and the greatest concentration of violence yields the best result. In other words, the high octane violence that draws young and old alike to many computer games is exactly what professional warriors should be wary of."[11]

The original point of the game—helter-skelter slaughter of anything that moves and does not have a human form—makes no sense for the military application. *Marine Doom* provides a totally different type of training: the identification of ally and enemy, not just brainlessly blasting away. The avoidance of friendly fire is one of the training tasks.

The commercial version has been customized with combat realism. In the normal version of *Doom*, a player can stock up on ammunition by collecting it from widely dispersed storage depots; in *Marine Doom*, there is only one arsenal, and players have just as much time available to load their weapons as they would have in actual combat. Unique features of binary games, such as the use of "medicine packs" to restore the fitness of those who have been injured in attacks by monsters, have been done away with in the *Marine Doom* version. A player can be wounded only once; the second time, he loses his life. Similarly, he cannot use points to recuperate from an injury or to regain a higher percentage of health.

The sublime body of the original video game has been terminated. The finiteness of artificial life as a simulation of real life must be programmed into processual virtual worlds. *Marine Doom* does not feature a reset button to resurrect the fallen soldier and redeploy him in the ongoing theater of war.

The interdependence of game-playing and warfare develops in two stages: first, an abstracted model of individual combat is transposed into the sphere of game-playing; in a second step, the model of artificial warfare represented here becomes a measure for real combat.

Death and Immortality of Artificial Life

Artificial and natural life are edging closer and closer together. The cloning of mammals and the obsession with the perfect copy are leading to the development of life on the primitive level of identical cellular reproduction.[12] At the moment, artificial life is on the same level of primitive reproduction. But from this point of departure, evolutionary leaps, forms of gender differentiation and of the death of artificial species have made themselves evident. Thus, these artificial worlds seem to be developing or reconstructing something new, which could be lost in reality in the future.

Death as a necessary regulator is being introduced as artificial death, as the "reaper" function; as emergent death, it is developing in evolutionary fashion. Artificial life is thus becoming a sort of digital zoo in which things that have been destroyed in real life are preserved. It serves the reconstruction of evolution, the emergence of life and behavior, and the reconstruction of various different forms of death and of immortality. Death, violence, transience, and eternity exist as projections in these virtual worlds.

Even in virtual worlds, players are beginning to challenge the necessity of biological death and to revamp the structures of the game. In *Creatures*, they are outfitting their beings with the so-called "Highlander gene" to endow them with immortality, although the artificial world then suffers from overpopulation. The undead cannot be visually differentiated; even the undead Norns retain their friendly appearance. They represent the first species of vampires that simply lives on without having fallen victim to a symbolic punishment of the community and therefore having to return over and over again. It is thus evident that virtual worlds not only preserve forms and rituals of death, but also bring forth something that is not (yet) possible in reality—namely, physical immortality.

On one hand, artificial life rediscovers death as an important category of life; on the other hand, it threatens this very same human life with aggressive action and violent death in military applications. Artificial life has succeeded in making the leap to the reconstruction of human violence—from evolutionary aggression that promoted survival to premeditated aggressive action reinforced by machinery. With the advent of Pilot-Norns, it has lost its innocence.

Binary games are neutral in and of themselves; they possess open structures that can be fundamentally revised by the user. This enables them to be adapted for military purposes. *Creatures* and *Marine Doom* show that the process of simulation in the form of reality models is becoming a two-edged sword. The models which have been crystallized into the form of games are now being projected back into real life and are influencing real organizational forms.

Nevertheless, the various game versions differ in key respects. In *Marine Doom*, the unbridled, wild violence that is required for survival is transformed into a "civilized," ordered violence. As a result of the modifications it has undergone, *Marine Doom* becomes a simulated reality, whereas the commercial version, with its sublime bodies and the possibility of multi-stage death, remains a game.

Furthermore, it is precisely the ecstatic, brainless blasting away with an entire arsenal of deadly weapons that completely sets a game off from the reality of warfare and military attack. The video game involves the danger of friendly fire only in multi-player mode.

The Marines can no longer afford to develop their own software which even comes close to commercial products with respect to the standard of quality and the reality of graphic realization. Thus, the reversal of the original interdependence of the military complex and the electronic entertainment industry is culminating in the assumption of a model function on the part of developments in entertainment electronics. With the purchase of game-playing strategies out of the inventory of the global cultural industry, the military complex loses its hegemonic position in the field of electronics and software. The situation that Kittler[13] analyzed as the position of predominance of the military in the field of technical-medial development is thus reversed in this case. The violence of warfare legitimized by the authority of a sovereign state now has its origin in commercial products—in games. The Pentagon is forced to train certain military capabilities on the basis of prescribed program structures that permit only variations and are also available to civilian players.

With the artificial world as an avant-garde manifestation in which the culture industry prescribes program structures to the military complex and permits it only superficial visual variations, entertainment has assumed a deadly character.

"Future adversaries . . . may use their last breaths to curse the commercial game software industry."[14]

Notes

1. David Jenkins, interview with Toby Simpson, May 22, 1998, Gamasutra, vol. 2, no. 20 (www.gamasutra.com.features/game_design/19980522/simpson-toby_02.htm). www.creatures.mindscape.com/press/alife_pr.html

2. Siegfried Zielinski, C-Theory (1995).

3. Slavoj Zizek.

4. Mark Slouka, War of the Worlds (London, 1996), p. 12.

5. Birgit Richard, Todesbilder. Kunst, Subkultur, Medien (Munich, 1995).

6. Vilém Flusser, Der Stand der Dinge, ed. Fabian Wurm (Göttingen, 1993), p. 54.

7. Larry Yaeger, "Polyworld: Wirkliches Leben in einem künstlichen Kontext?", in: Karl Gerber and Peter Weibel, eds., Ars Electronica 93. Genetische Kunst—Künstliches Leben (Linz, 1993), pp. 122–128.

8. Howard Rheingold, The Virtual Communities (Addison-Wesley, 1993).

9. Summarized from an interview conducted by the author with Myron Krüger at Multimediale 4 in 1995 in Karlsruhe.

10. Michel Foucault, Die Geburt der Klinik (Munich, 1973).

11. Col. Paul Hanover cited by Anne Gearan, Associated Press, 1996: "Marine Doom as Training Exercise" (www.tri-cityherald.com/COMPUTE/comp10.html).

12. Jean Baudrillard, "Das Original und sein Double," Die Zeit, March 14, 1997, p. 67.

13. Friedrich Kittler, Film, Grammophon, Typewriter (Berlin, 1986).

14. Robert K. Ackermann, Signal Magazine (1996) (www.us.net/signal/Archive/July96/commercial-july).See also Birgit Richard, "Robot Wars. Robotergestaltungen und -phantasmen zwischen artificial intelligence und artificial life," Kunstforum International, vol. 130 (May-July 1995), pp. 190–211; Birgit Richard, "Motion Control. Ein elektronischer Bildersturm?", in: Norbert Bolz, Cordula Meier, Birgit Richard, et al., eds., Riskante Bilder (Munich, 1996); Spiegel, vol. 23 (1998), pp. 192–195; Wired 5.04 (April 1997), pp. 114–119.

Undead Norns: http: delta.tierranet.com/albia/undead.htm
Norn-Adoption: www.mannaz.mcmail.com/norn/breeders/cave.htm
www.tekres.com/creatures/corner/herbs.htm
www.cageswooddrive.demon.co/uk/tips.html

Marine Doom: http://138.156.15.33/doom/doom.html (download http://138.156.15.33/xfers/marine1.zip)
www.tec.army.mil/TD/tvd/survey/ghindex.html
www.tec.army.mil/TD/tvd/survey/Marine_Doom.html
www.pcworld.com/software_lib/data/articles/games/3297.html
www.directoryusasom/directory_usa/military/marine.html
www.chinfo.navy.mil/navpalib/policy/fromsea/pos97/pos-pg06.html
www.gamerx.com
http://web.pcgamer.com/games7maps-doom.html

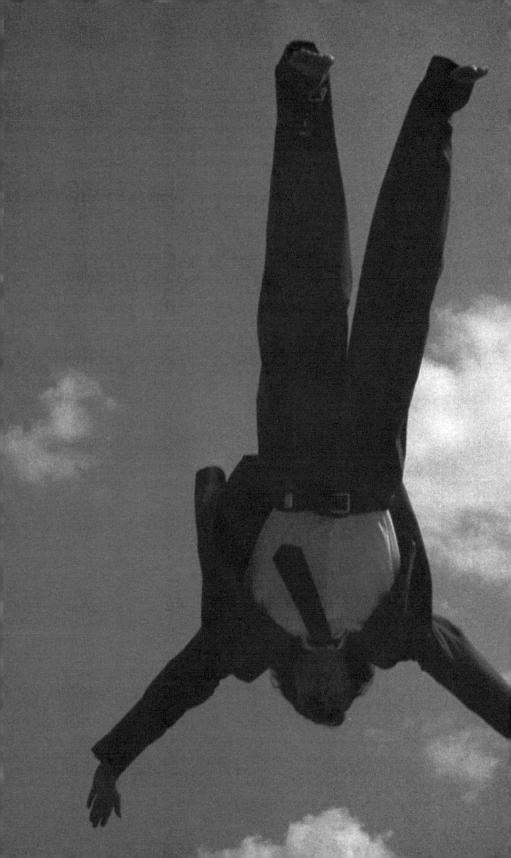

Ars Electronica

Practice

The hundreds of projects, installations, experiments, performances, interventions, and presentations done at Ars Electronica provide a rich resource for any complete understanding of the history of electronic media. The projects and documents represented here stand only as glimpse at the scope and significance of the past two decades. Documentation for these, and many other projects, resides at www.aec.at.

The World in 24 Hours

Monday, September 27, 1982, till Thursday, September 28, 1982
Austrian Broadcasting Corporation, Regional Studio for Upper Austria

Robert Adrian

Artist's Use of Telecommunications

This telecommunications program by artists is like other such events in the past intended to develop techniques for individual, personal use of existing telecommunications technology.

It is often claimed that modern electronic systems and networks are not accessible to private individuals, but actually access is a relatively easy matter; the real problems only arise when one seeks ways to use these systems. One soon discovers that, with the exception of the games and entertainment sector, all this technology is designed for the corporate user.

Individual users are isolated from the design of new technology because, since they have no precise need, it is assumed that their interests are met by firms interested in marketing high-tech by-products, in serving existing demand rather than assisting in the development of possible alternative directions in electronic technology. If there is to be any sort of chance to develop new techniques by means of which private individuals can make meaningful use of these electronic media—to assert their right to genuine participation in the development of this new electronic world—then it will have to be very soon. It is probably too late even now to really change the direction of design development, but we can try at least to discover ways to insert human content

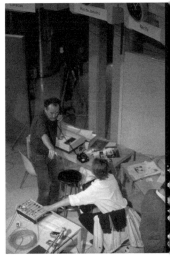

Robert Adrian X: The World in 24 Hours
....

into the commercial/military world floating in this electronic space. And this is where artists are traditionally strong . . . in discovering new ways to use media and materials in inventing new and contradictory meanings for existing organisations and systems, in subverting self-serving power structures in the interests of nearly everyone. Artists using electronic telecommunications are trying to find human meaning in an electronic space.

The World in 24 Hours

A project connecting artists around the world in a non-stop series of dialogues beginning at 12 noon on September 27 and ending at 12 noon on September 28, 1982 (Central European Time). 14 artists or groups around the world will be in communication with Linz, Austria, during the 24-hour project. Each of the participating locations will be called on the telephone from the central location in Linz at 12 noon local time (e.g. 18.00 in Linz = 12 noon in Toronto). Each contact will last about one hour, permitting the exchange of visual material via telephone by means of either slow-scan television or telefacsimile transceiving equipment. In addition the I. P. Sharp computer timesharing network will be available for computer graphic exchange and/or coordination of the projects. Participants have been offered the opportunity of choosing any telecommunications medium for their contribution, providing that it operates via normal telephone and is also available in Linz. However, the present state of development makes only three media feasible for use by artists or other private individuals:

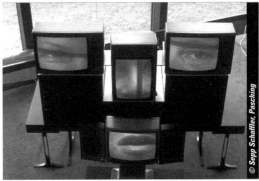

© Sepp Schaffler, Pasching

Robert Adrian X: The World in 24 Hours

1. Computer timesharing (I. P. Sharp APL Network): Equipment: computer terminal. Medium: local telephone to nearest IPSA office.
The I. P. Sharp office in Vienna will provide computer time and technical assistance to participants wishing to use I. P. Sharp software for computer-graphic exchange. The ARTBOX and CONFER programs will also be available for coordination of the project and for computer communications exchanges.

2. Slow-scan television (SSTV): Equipment: SSTV transceiver (e.g. robot 530). Medium: direct long-distance telephone connection.
Signals from a video camera are converted by the transceiver into audio signals and transmitted via telephone. The received signal is reconverted to a video signal and displayed on a monitor. Each image takes 8.5 seconds to be completed.

3. Telefacsimile (telefax): Equipment: telefax transceiver (e.g. 3M "9136" group III (transceiver). Medium: direct long-distance telephone connection.
Telefax transceivers convert images on paper into audio signals and transmit them via telephone. A compatible machine then converts the signal back into an image on paper. There are 3 different types of machine available: groups I, II, and III. The fastest of these are the group III machines, which can transmit an A4 page in under a minute. Machines like the 3M "9136" are also compatible with the slower group I and II machines.

The 24-hour program will begin with an extensive European section lasting about 6 hours, from 12 noon until 18.00 (Central European Time). The European section will include contributions from Florence, Frankfurt, Geneva, Vienna, and Dublin. There will also be an experiment called "PSI-Bernetic Networking" (using the I. P. Sharp timesharing network) initiated by Roy Ascott in Bath, U.K., going on during the whole European section. The overseas program will comprise at least 4 North American locations (there may also be a New York City participant), Hawaii, Sydney /Australia, and Tokyo. The final contact will be from Turkey at 11:00 on September 28 (Linz time).

Robert Adrian *The World in 24 Hours*

Projects

Linz
This project was begun in January 1982 when a series of workshops was arranged at the Hochschule für künstlerische und industrielle Gestaltung, Linz. These workshops by Robert Adrian X (funded by the Österreichisches Kulturservice) were intended to create a team of artists and students able to prepare and transmit original work and to man the equipment during the 24-hour event. The workshops were coordinated by Waltraud Cooper, lecturer at the Hochschule under Professor Laurids Ortner. Ms. Cooper will also be coordinating participation by the Linz group during the program.
The workshop participants were: Bruno Aichinger, Helmut Guntner, Gerald Hackenberg, Josef Horvat, Elisabeth Juan, Moidi Kretschmann, Michael Langanger, Jörg Mikesch, Otto Mittmannsgruber, Sonja Reischl.

Frankfurt
Coordination: Thomas Bayne.
Location: Städelschule, Hochschule für Kunst, Frankfurt/Main.
Participants: Thomas Bayrle, Ernst Caramelle, Jochen Fey, Jurgen Riehm and Monika Schwitte.
Media: telefacsimile.
Thomas Bayrle is an artist working with photography, traditional media, and artist's books and is Dozent at the Städelschule.

Florence
Coordination: Maurizio Nannucci.
Location: Zona, Florence.
Participants: Fabrizio Cornell, Albert Mayr, Paolo Nasi, Massimo Nannucci, Maurizio Nannucci, Gianni Pettena, Marino Vismara.
Media: telefacsimile.
ZONA is an independent group of artists working together in all media, including music, performance, radio, video, etc. ZONA is also an artist-run space in the center of Florence.

Geneva
Coordination: Gerald Minkoff.
Location: Video Mixmedia Group, rue de Javois, Geneva.
Participants: Gerald Minkoff, Muriel Olesen, and members of the Video-Mixmedia Group.
Project: God Trap: Part Dog—attempting to link, electronically-mentally, Paradise with Hell. "Cool and slow the electrons before it's too late."
Media: telefacsimile and/or computer timesharing.
Gerald Minkoff and Muriel Olesen are artists working with electronic media, photography, and performance. They live and work in Geneva.

Amsterdam
Coordination: Annie Wright and David Garcia.
Location: Mazzo, Amsterdam.
Project: Late Times Extra.
"One of a number of works we have made based on the insertion of 'fictions' into everyday formats. We have previously used shop windows, street posters, publications and television and now telecom-

munications." The project will treat the computer terminal as a news agency teleprinter, developing a plot trough the mixture of "real" news and fiction.
Media: computer timesharing.
Annie Wright and David Garcia are English artist/writers living in Amsterdam.

Vienna

Coordination: Helmut Mark.
Location: Österreichische Kultur Service.
"Studio" Participants: Markus Geiger, Ruth Labak, Helmut Mark, Alice Weber, Heimo Zobernig.
Project: Sputnik macht's möglich.
The five artists will meet at the Kultur Service "Studio" (Grünangergasse 6) from 10 am to 6 pm every day from September 24 to 29. On September 25 and 26 they will hold workshops on telecommunications media in preparation for the 24-hour event on September 27 and 28. On September 29 a discussion of the entire project is planned.
Media: computer timesharing and telefacsimile.
Helmut Mark is an artist working in many media, mainly in public space. He lives in Vienna.

Dublin

Coordination: Brian King.
Location: National College of Art and Design.
Participants: Brian King and students of the College.
Media: computer timesharing and telefacsimile.
Brian King is a sculptor and teacher. He is head of the Sculpture department at the National College of Art and Design, Dublin.

Toronto

Coordination: Derek Dowden (Artculture Resource Center) and Dieter Hastenteufel.
Location: Communitex: Community Videotex.
Participants: Dieter Hastenteufel, Derek Dowden, Peeter Sepp, Jane Wright, and others.
Project: in preparation.
Media: computer timesharing, slow-scan, and/or telefacsimile. Derek Dowden works with Artculture Resource Center, a non-profit organising facility for cultural projects.
Communitex is a non-profit organisation to promote and facilitate artistic, cultural, and community use of new telecommunications technology.

San Francisco

Coordination: Tom Klinkowstein.
Location: Audio Visual Center, the San Francisco State University.
Participants: Staff and students at the Audio Visual Center and at the Broadcast Communications Art Department (SFSU).
Project: The Customer Is Always Right.
Advertising or advertising-related images will be broadcast live via the (interactive) cable television station in San Francisco and via slow-scan television to Linz. Similar material will be displayed as slides or video tapes to the audience at the OFF center in Linz and transmitted to San Francisco via slow-scan television. Responses to the transmitted images will be exchanged via the I.P. Sharp computer timesharing network.
Media: computer timesharing and slow-scan television.

Tom Klinkowstein is an artist, designer, and teacher specialising in electronic media, audio-visual techniques, and telecommunications. He divides his time between San Francisco and Amsterdam.

Pittsburgh

Coordination: Bruce Breland.
Location: Department of Fine Arts, Carnegie-Mellon University, Pittsburgh.
Participants: GEKKO (Generative Energy/Kinetic Knowledge /Order), Bruce Breland, Herb Coshak, James Kocher, Harry Holland, Diane Samuels, and Cindy Snodgrass.
Project: Gekko's Window:
1. Bruce Breland—Casting Color on the Conemagh (SSTV)
2. James Kocher—X/O (SSTV)
3. Diane Samuels—Finger Performance (SSTV)
4. Herb Coshak—Aleth (SSTV)
5. Cindy Snodgrass—Windrays, Airwaves, Highways (SSTV)
6. Harry Holland—Strata Variants (computer timesharing).
Media: slow-scan television and computer timesharing.

Vancouver

Coordination: Henry Bull and Bill Bartlett.
Location: Western Front Society, Vancouver.
Participants: Henry Bull, Bill Bartlett, Kate Craig, Glen Lewis, and members of the Western Front Society.
Media: slow-scan television and computer timesharing.
Henry Bull is an artist, musician, and curator working in practically every medium from photography to radio. He lives in Vancouver and is responsible for the gallery program at the Western Front. Bill Bartlett is a pioneer of artists' use of telecommunications, especially with slow-scan television and computer communications. He lives on Pender Island, British Columbia. Western Front is an artist-run center (founded in 1972) that offers programmes in visual arts, music, dance, and video as well as an ambitious "artist-in-residence" program.

Hawaii

Coordination: John Southworth.
Location: University of Hawaii, Honolulu.
Participants: John Southworth, Joseph Tanton, and staff and students of the University.
Media: computer timesharing and slow-scan television.
John Southworth is an educator and specialist for integrated electronic learning systems. He lives and works in Hawaii.

Sydney

Coordination: Eric Gidney.
Location: City Art Institute, Sydney, Australia.
Participants: Erich Gidney, Ian Howard, and students of the City Art Institute.
Media: computer timesharing and/or telefacsimile.
Eric Gidney and Ian Howard are lecturers at the City Art Institute.

Tokyo

Coordination: Kazue Kobata.
Location: Body Weather Laboratory.
Participants: Min Tanaka, Yoshi Nobu, Kazue Kobata.
Project: in preparation.
Kazue Kobata is an artist and dancer working in Japan and America.

Bath (England)

Coordination: Roy Ascott.
Location: Art Access/Networking, Bath, England.
Project: PSI-Bernetic Networking (two projects proposed).
1. "To identify nine people with terminal access around the planet, each to choose a card in sequence to make up the celtic spread (with my card). We shall then participate and interact through the network to generate meanings through the spread."
2. "A second project will involve a kind of round table seance, automatic writing at the ASCII keyboard. This use of chance coupled with our individual/group intuitions and intimations will likely also generate some unexpected material." "Both proposals attempt to generate a kind of group consciousness of planetary dimensions through the network to get at new ideas, texts or images. The second project may include, as input, trance utterances by clairvoyants if we can involve enough individuals in sufficient countries to make it global."
Media: computer timesharing.
Roy Ascott is an artist and theoretician presently Head of the School of Fine Art, Gwent College of Higher Education, Newport, Wales; member of the advisory board, International Network for the Arts, New York; member of the Editorial Advisory Board of Leonardo, Pergamon Press, Oxford; and director of Art Access/Networking.

Turkey

Coordination: Minus Delta T (–Δt).
Location: Turkey (en route to Bangkok).
Participants: Karel Dudesek, Mike Hentz, Bernhard Müller (–Δt).
Project: Bangkok/Archiv Europa.
Media: Telex (?).
Minus Delta T is a group of artists who have been, since 1980, on the expedition "Project Bangkok." The project encompasses the Archiv Europa, A Festival, the transportation and erection of a large and heavy monument, and working in the countries through which they are travelling until the end of December 1982. Apparently a classic expedition, but Minus Delta T are making art as field research.

Sky Art

Otto Piene

. . . The Bible and Greek mythology can be considered handbooks for sky art and its expressive power and potential (and aspirations), particularly, and most colorfully, St. John's Revelation. Archeologists, historians, scientists are making great efforts to decode the ciphers of Nasca, Stonehenge, and New Mexico. Observations of the sky and human reactions to them have been translated into art/science since humankind learned to manifest itself in intended traces.

An essential belief pervading many religions is that the human soul is ethereal and that it flies. The efforts made to regulate ethereal traffic, i.e., to permit but also restrict the travels of the soul, in ancient Egypt may have strained the national economy with pyramid-building more seriously than NASA weighs on the US economy. We know about the absorbing medieval efforts to build Gothic cathedrals. We can lock at their results, such as the spires of Chartres, Cologne, Ulm, as filigree mock-ups of space-penetrating rockets—an example of the dialectics ruling the relationship between physics and metaphysics. Angels are "model fliers." Icarus is a prince of accidental mythology, but his father, Daedalus, appears to be most fully incarnated by "the man of MIT."

. . . Clear examples of how artists use the results of scientific and engineering work in new media are to be found in such new artistic fields as holography, laser image projection (Rockne Krebs, Paul Earls), computer music (Berry Vercoe), computer graphics (Ron MacNeil), and computer programming for multimedia performance (Bernd Kracke). However, the artists' influence on the development of media is considerable: Harriet Casdin-Silver and white-light holography; the development of video synthesizers originating in part from the Nam June Paik/Abe Synthesizer.

Artists have rediscovered the importance of telecommunication: their individual, private, subjective (often playful, or seemingly playful) communication (Aldo Tambellini, Stan VanDerBeek) is juxtaposed with network communication of national and international purposes. Not only questions of style, technique, implementation, not only questions of newsworthiness and ratings are on their minds but media and network capacity for carrying emotion, nuance, and drama. The vehicles for such concerns are either developed in straight interdisciplinary collaboration or modified or "tampered-with" versions of "common" or advanced technology. Whether intimacy versus publicity, "heaven" versus "space," green versus red-white-and-blue, private and expressive telecommunication requires collaboration among artists, scientists, and engineers (and often industry, too).

(Excerpted from a paper for the (1982) 33rd International Astronautical Congress in Paris.)

I was the first resident Fellow invited from outside Boston to work in a field then often described as art-and-technology. My first public project at CAVS/MIT, in 1968, was titled *Light Line Experiment*. It involved twenty human participants, ca. 1,000 feet of helium-inflated polyethylene tubing, and a two-searchlight truck, and I called it a "sky event." It was the initial occasion at which I worked with the astrophysicist Walter Lewin of the MIT Center for Space Research, a collaboration which would be continued in subsequent years. In 1969 I wrote a book, *Moresky*, and published a 25-lithograph portfolio, *Sky Art*.

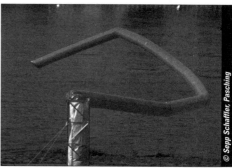

© Sepp Schaffler, Pasching

Otto Piene, Light Line Experiment
....

Ken Sofer in *Artnews*: "Elizabeth Goldring, co-director of the Conference, describes (it) simply as 'art that flies,' . . . present at the conference were a wide range of luminaries: laser artist Rockne Krebs; Paul MacCready, inventor of successful human- and solar-powered flying machines; sculptor Heinz Mack, cofounder with Piene of the Zero Group; scientist Louis Friedman, executive director of The Planetary Society, an educational group promoting the idea of space exploration; Harold Edgerton, a pioneer in the field of stroboscopy (ultra-high-speed photography); Stephen Crites, a Wesleyan University professor of religion who delivered a stunning lecture, 'On Sacred Space and the Heavenly Sublime'; writer and video artist Douglas Davis; and architect Paolo Soleri, among others; and he quotes a passage of my introductory catalog text: "Space is—quite mysteriously—still inner and outer space, the space of the soul embedded in geographic space and geographic space contained in the soul . . . Artists aspire to go and show wherever humans go and wherever the human mind and soul go—on excursions imaginary and excursions real."

. . . The 1981 conference revealed an urge to communicate in almost every participant, no matter which camp of work or philosophy he or she came from. Among the artists, a man whose sayings, writings, and actions are far removed from scientific and engineering shop talk received attentive recognition: Lowry Burgess, who during the past five years has sunk agglomerations of artistic magic in such remote places as the Afghan desert near Bamiyan and the Easter Islands. His belief in a meaningful, coherent, spirit-directed universe commands him to demonstrate a pantheistic attitude with objects and suggestive connections, revering the All as the supreme miracle. His projects have poetic names, such as "Inclined Galactic Light Pond" and "Gate into Aether (to be placed in outer space above the 'Utopic Vessel')," and they are part of his personally established "Quiet Axis" in his reference system of stellar, universal constellations involving all humans and all matter believed to be animate (represented by, e.g., pigments, holograms, prisms, etched images contained in carefully crafted "urns"). He refers to this work as (universal) "poetry extended by means of images and 'charged' objects."

A statement I wrote for ZERO 3 in 1961 reveals affinity to Burgess' romantic pathos: ". . . The man who uses his body to enclose his mind and his mind to lift up his body, who lives this timeless moment, this heavenly reality, in order to stride freely through space, this man has paradise in him." However, further below I pick up a sentence directed to future reality: "Why is there no art in space, why do we have no exhibitions in the sky? . . . Up to now we have left it up to war to light up the sky . . ."

As art can be understood to be humankind's perennial attempt at crisis management with creative, non-violent means, a narrow but justifiable view of sky art would term it antinuclear effort in the domain of nuclear strife. The nuclear theater provides us with large-scale images of hell which are as fascinating as Hieronymus Bosch's are in their pocket scale. Sky art labors for "positive" imagery in a

Otto Piene *Sky Art*

world (including a sky) mesmerized by proliferating war implements. It labors for means commensurate with what little the nation spends on all arts (which is a pittance compared to what the nation spends on defense, research, physical health and PacMan). My own most dramatically exposed sky work to

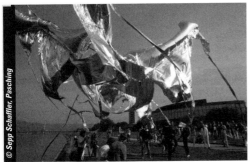
© Sepp Schaffler, Pasching

date has been the *Olympic Rainbow* for the closing ceremony of the 1972 Munich Games (XX Olympiad). It was a 12-hour-minus, 2,000-foot-long helium-and-Stratofilm piece elaborately lighted and "revealed" according to protocol and media dramaturgy. Most of its physical parts were executed by Winzen Research, a predominantly science-oriented inflatables company. The *Rainbow* proved how even low-level sky scale can address more people and a broader audience than traditional artworks and how on the other hand air space does not have to be reserved only for flying equipment and calamitous projectiles.

Otto Piene, Olympic Rainbow

It proved further how large physical scale lends itself to dissemination on a "third scale," the scale of wide media distribution.

Tom Van Sant is a distinguished Los Angeles sculptor who has used flight imagery in many artistic media. He has built kites of traditional, oriental elegance and he is developing plans for a mile-long "Jacob's Ladder" chain (dragon kite) on which a man could ascend skyward. His projects also include considerations of high-altitude, energy-collecting giant kites. For the Los Angeles Bicentennial celebration he suggested "Reflections from Earth" (not executed), which he described thus:

> . . . a space-age educational and festival program . . . A mirror reflection kit has been developed which will allow a school child or citizen, using careful settings, to create and see an act of his own hand from space.

When it became evident that this public version of "Reflections" would not be realized, Tom Van Sant, with his wife, Lisa, and a crew, laid out a mirror-formed "Shadow Mountain Eye" in the California Shadow Mountains (1980) which was successfully recorded by Landsat. The ensuing imaging process led to beautiful photographic prints—images which could become visible only with the help of the satellite's "eye." The explanation (by Tom Van Sant):

> Taken from space 600 miles above the earth by the NASA satellite Landsat II on June 11, 1980 . . . the image represents an eye gazing skyward, measuring 1.4 miles across . . . Ninety mirrors, each 24 inches square, were arranged on the desert floor and carefully adjusted to reflect sunbeams into the satellite's path. The radiant energy from each mirror was reflected by the appropriate sensor at the moment the satellite was scanning its picture of the earth. Though each mirror is small, it saturated a square the size of an acre . . . The entire image is made up of these one acre units . . .

The artist was advised vitally by Dr. William Evans. The collaboration inspired a paper by Peter Bormann and Juan José Tasso, "Marking of Satellite Imagery: A Means to Improve Image Registration for Mapping Purposes and to Accomplish 'Space Art' Designs."

Lowry Burgess has maintained contact with NASA officials for several years in order to place and distribute in space an ice-encrusted sound hologram representing the earth's greatest rivers. However, he has not signed a payload contract because NASA stipulates scientific worth as the ruling value for space shuttle programs.

The first artist with a shuttle flight agreement is Joe Davis, a 31-year-old sculptor from Gulfport, Mississippi, "whipping around the planet on a peg leg he's used since a motorcycle accident; talking technology as if it were his mother tongue . . ."

Whereas Burgess' project would easily be called conceptual art—because its material modus operandi will not instantly affect our physical vision and hearing after its proposed deployment—Davis' initial space piece, *New Wave Ruby Falls*, is

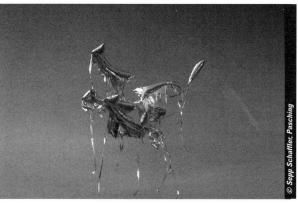

Otto Piene, Sky Art

....

intended to become visible, although it, too, has been labeled "a piece of conceptual art." "It would be," he says, "a curtain of color in the sky, composed of inert gases shot with an electron beam that causes them to glow."

Some MIT scientists remain skeptical, e.g. as to the mode of deployment—whether "vented," "chemical," etc. Nevertheless the project has been accepted into the Small Self-Contained Payload Program, or as NASA officials like to call it, the GAS (Get Away Special), and within the next 12 or 18 months we expect to see Joe's beginning of a "Las Vegas in the sky" (his phrase). His vigorous listing of further projects: A scale model Chevy on the moon operated by two-pound robots; a war monument on Mars—"a Trojan horse from an adobe made of Martian soil and liquid carbon dioxide"; an orbiting, inflatable Stonehenge, and more. Honest money has been paid for a considerable number of further GAS payload reservations by Joe Davis, myself, Lowry Burgess, and the Center for Advanced Visual Studies.

The artists' exuberance, the scientists' skepticism, and the engineers' implementing pragmatism constitute the very nature of art-and-technology integrated efforts. (In one case in which I was involved twelve years ago, I had to cautiously retort a Nobel Prize winner's "impossible" with an "I've done it already" (and quite truly so).) Davis' answer to the "why?" question: ". . . for surviving, for hopes and dreams and imagination, for whatever it's all about." We are led to remember that steely Michael Collins called his moon book *Carrying the Fire*. Sky art as we practice and envision it is an extension of environmental art. It has physical, generally three-dimensional-in-time, components. Although it is also often ephemeral—passing events rather than solid, lasting materialization—it attempts visibility, an audience and wide distribution. Two-dimensional imaging, i.e. image-collection and illustration, may be part of it, but only as stones in a mosaic, roles in a theater. Sky artists do acknowledge the impact which science's turn to visual exploration has made, and we seem to be heading for another renaissance of the artist-scientist.

Such authorities as Yash Pal, secretary general of the '82 Unispace Conference, and Paul MacCready, victor of the ancient-times-to-present muscle-powered-flight race, have termed the earth-from-orbit photo "the most important picture since pictures." We enthusiastically welcome Voyager and other missions to continue the contest for their sky art, "1D-2D-3D-4," for information, beauty, science, religion, art; by artists, scientists, engineers, fliers; men, women, children now and sooner, "for whatever it's all about."

Otto Piene *Sky Art*

Mind of Universe

Isao Tomita

Mind of Universe tells a story of the creation, development, and future of our cosmos and our planet. Isao Tomita expanded his monumental opus like a gigantic arch, from the Big Bang over the slow development of the Earth to the future of mankind in outer space, presenting 18 billion years of the universe's history to all the spectators on the banks of the Danube, via a nine-channel stereo sound system together with music and light.

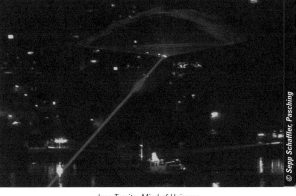

Isao Tomita: Mind of Universe
....

The idea for this project was born when Tomita watched Stanley Kubrick's "2001—A Space Odyssey" and saw a space base circling around the Earth to the tune of Johann Strauss' "Blue Danube" waltz.

Tomita's opus consists of six parts. As an introduction, 30 minutes before the beginning of the performance as such, the public is presented a distant kind of sound, very soft, very quiet—just as if it were coming directly from outer space. Then the concert begins:

Part One: The Big Bang
Part Two: Cosmic Evolution
Part Three: The Beginning of Life
Part Four: A Call from the Universe
Part Five: Man in the Universe
Part Six: Hymn to the Universe.

Tomita wants to create a new visual apprehension in open space with this new opus.

Mind of Universe tries to incorporate almost all means of artistic design in open space: Light, laser, fireworks, reflections, projections on surfaces of water and smoke, light columns, light pyramids, a helicopter as UFO, and others.

In the past few years a growing number of one-dimensional visual events in open space have been developed, be it fantastic laser shows, fireworks, or the Fire Theatre. *Mind of Universe* consists of the basic elements light and fire on one hand, and the achievements of computer and synthesizer technology on the other. Nature and high technology are united in this tale of the history of the universe.

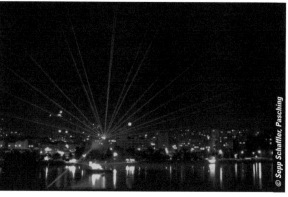

Isao Tomita: Mind of Universe

The Danube Park as an area of events is marked and framed by light columns; on the Danube the ships with the participants on board are in a constant dialogue with the universe: a chorus vessel with a choir of 100 persons, a ship for two soloists (violin and Japanese flute), as well as a ship for additional light sculptures. Banks of mist and walls of water serve as projection screens for the laser; a helicopter—equipped with full sound and light—appears as a UFO, tries to get in contact with infinity.

Isao Tomita himself floats in a 5-ton light pyramid as control unit, as musical and technical high-tech centre high above the river Danube.

Mind of Universe wants to introduce a new dimension to experience art: a *spectaculum mundi* of the electronic age.

Isao Tomita *Mind of Universe*

The Philosophical Data Bank of Minus Delta T

Mike Hentz

Himalaya—three thousand metres above sea level—a safe built deep into the rock—200 keys for the safe—a Basic-programmable computer—a nearby shelter for people at work—this is the Philosophical Data Bank of Minus Delta T.

To be exact, it is the second part of what was begun in February 1983 in the Künstlerhaus Stuttgart, the creation of a data bank where not simple population data, turnover statistics, or whatsoever are stored, but the philosophy of our time is conserved—data bank as a kind of philosophy itself.

So why did the people of Minus Delta T start this somewhat strange project, why the safe underneath the floor of the Stuttgart Künstlerhaus, containing the original of the group's project share—and a bottle of wine?

It all began in the 1950s during the economic boom, when everybody was just hunting for his share in the general uplift. On and on they went in the hunt for prosperity—and what was left behind were the values, the keys for culture. Not that this phase had not developed its own values; an individualistic quality of life was then considered one of the supreme goals. But every value developed during this era was internalized in the following decades—and it may be unconscious, but an individualistic way of life (without a basis in the cultural traditions) is still a moral value today.

The European moral qualities have come to a point where they have lost much (not to say almost everything) of their social context, of their social codes and languages.

We think and feel there is a distinct need for a new definition, for reflection and the development of a new universal theory. Now, of universal theories there have been plenty; the Bible presented one, the Koran another, Buddhism a third; socialism, capitalism, anarchism were universal theories—and as the most recent version, the "Green Book" of Muammar Gaddafi. All of these universal theories, however, are obsolete in a Europe considering itself the experimental playground of modern culture. What "moral" means to Europe is given in a negative definition, in a constant negation.

This unconscious negation must give way to a conscious affirmation, making actions conscious—and this is what we are trying to do by the installation of our Philosophical Data Bank. But again, why call it Data Bank?

The term "Bank" was chosen in a deliberate association with today's economic and commercial society, in order to use (and abuse) commercial symbols like "Bank," "Money," "Shares," "Data," etc. for individual purposes, maybe even for individual values in the shade of the quest for contents and solutions.

The Philosophical Data Bank shall be open for everybody working at a social Codex or at a European, individual culture (which is not an absolute culture of the individual). If he gets in contact with us, we are ready to reserve him a key and to store his ID in the computer.

Now this computer is not connected to any terminal in Europe. We think it necessary to disconnect the computer from Europe in order to prevent the new universal theory from being written by a single person, not because of distrust, but rather because a single individual might introduce too many of his individual values. Culture does not depend on the outward shape, but rather on the contents of its codex. The shape might be interesting but is undoubtedly secondary, as are the different areas and activities where members of Minus Delta T come from. Our provenience from different areas of work, from music, art, philosophy, science, and ethnology, from work in the science-fiction area as well as in futurology, lead to the effect that we are dealing with very global matters. The non-specialization gives the group a certain overview, and in this sense a lot of responsibility for its actions, for activities free from compromises.

As for philosophy, the present text is in no case a compromise. This text is the philosophy of Minus Delta T, a philosophy whose philosophy it is to consist of many philosophies. So who is Minus Delta T?

Minus Delta T is the name of a group of people who are not at all uniform, who do not have the same ideas—but who work together. The group has existed since 1978, with a lot of people who were out before they had even really been in (those were mostly the "specialists"). One of the principles of the group is non-specialization—we want to be open for everybody and everything.

In the beginning we used to work a lot in the musical area, made performances, exhibitions, we did a lot of private works—maybe fifty-fifty between private and public, which seemed quite a good balance. Since 1980 we have been working at this project, which had as its first title the "Bangkok Project" (cf. the catalogue of Ars Electronica 1982, p. 157/154).

This project included the transport of a 5 1/2-ton stone, a dolmen, a European monument to Asia, as a catalyst of culture. On the truck we had multi-media equipment, including sound, movie, and photo equipment, computer technology, and laundromat.

The greater part of the group is right now in Asia preparing the further transport of our monolith to China (the monolith as such being completely unimportant) and on a tour in India within the setting of the Bangkok Project.

Minus Delta T is composed of the artists Karel Dudesek, Wolfgang Hofmann, Bernhard Müller, Gerard Couty, Walter Baumann, and Mike Hentz.

Virtual Space

The Electronic Environments of Mobile Image
(excerpt)

Gene Youngblood

"We must create on the same scale as we can destroy," say the designers of Electronic Cafe. In collaboration as Mobile Image since 1977, Kit Galloway and Sherrie Rabinowitz have confronted that challenge through a series of works that address the "emerging environment" of electronic telecommunications. If these projects belong to any history, it is that of Art and Technology; but their value is precisely the extent to which they transcend the contradictions of that problematic tradition. Indeed, Mobile Image's singular enterprise defines new trajectories for both art and technology, revitalizing one while humanizing the other as they address the central cultural and political issue of our time.

The brief history of telecommunication projects by artists lives in the shadow of the Communications Revolution—that mythical transformation of culture and consciousness which, for at least a generation, has seemed perpetually about to happen. A communications revolution isn't about technology; it's about possible relations among people. It implies an inversion of existing social relations whereby today's hierarchical mass culture would disperse into autonomous, self-constituting "reality communities"—social groups of politically significant magnitude realized as communities through telecommunication networks and defined, therefore, not by geography but by consciousness, ideology, and desire. Only as constituents of such communities could we both produce models of possible realities (art) and also control the cultural contexts in which those models were published and perceived (politics). Control of context is the control of meaning, and without control of meaning there can be neither freedom nor creativity. Unavoidably, then, artists who work in telecommunications assume great ethical responsibility, for these instruments represent our only hope of effectively addressing the profound social and political challenges of our time. We must indeed create on the same scale as we can destroy, but this will not be possible if we can't control the cultural contexts that determine the meaning of our lives.

The ethical imperative above all else is to furnish alternative models for the deployment of these technologies by any community of desire as the central instruments in its social construction of reality. Unfortunately, the history of telecommunication projects by artists reflects little recognition of this responsibility. Most of these "works" have been either routine applications of satellites for teleconferencing, or the equally standard use of computer, videotex, and facsimile networks for "exchanges of work, information, and ideas," or they have been broadcast events that delivered personality-oriented Art Star performances to cable TV subscribers or audiences gathered in museum auditoriums.

The pretension has been that something done every day in business and industry and by subscribers to computer networks, or employed every evening by network newscasters, becomes special because artists are doing it. In fact nothing is revealed that is not already given, obvious, routine indeed, already politicized by commercial contexts.

In contrast, every Mobile Image project has represented a genuine alternative to existing practices in telecommunication. In what amounted to a manifesto similar in spirit if not in substance to that of the Italian Futurists, they proposed in 1975 to explore the unique properties of new technologies regardless of whether the results were art-like or not, or whether the art world acknowledged it at all. Indeed, the telecommunication project as Art Event represents for them a profound contradiction; it raises a basic philosophical question concerning how a work addresses the scale of creativity. Art understood as the prepared experience, the masterpiece, is the monumental version of creativity. "But there's that other quality of life that's left behind," Galloway points out, "the life in between one great spectacle after another. There can be a quality of art and life in between the great moments, but the legitimacy of working on that scale is devalued by the emphasis on Art"—which thus becomes antithetical to the secularization of the technology. Thought they frequently invoke art metaphors to characterize their work, Galloway and Rabinowitz believe it is basically a trap. "As long as we talk about 'the artist' we're not really addressing the problem," Galloway asserts. "It sounds like we're addressing a problem: here's this undernourished, underappreciated subculture with this big burden on their shoulders, and everybody has to help their local artist. But the problem isn't an art problem. It's a problem of recognizing the value of creativity, across the board, in a healthy society."

Telecommunication as Environmental Design

Their solution is the metaphor of environmental design. Essentially populist, appealing as much to engineering and the behavioral sciences as to art, it reflects the sociopolitical bias of their enterprise. "We see communication and information systems as environments people live in," Rabinowitz explains. "So we look at the aesthetics of that environment, the shaping of the space. The way you shape a space determines what can happen to the information in it." She invokes architecture: information environments can be exalting and inspirational like cathedrals (computer networks) or squalid and dehumanizing like ghettos (the mass media). As buildings are said to be democratic or oppressive, so the architecture of electronic space determines possible relations among people, establishes the contours of desire. But there are limits to the metaphor. The membrane isn't as corporeal as that of a building. The difference is that in electronic space the information becomes the environment. It's like a river: the technology that determines how information flows is the riverbed; but the water—the information itself—is the environment the user actually lives in, interacts with.

"This is uncharted territory," says Galloway, "a developing terrain. We're all spacemen learning how to live in a new environment.

• • •

In 1975 Galloway and Rabinowitz formalized years of thinking about the communications revolution and how to address it as artists: focusing on real time (live) telecommunication as opposed to "stored time" videotape recording, they proposed four projects designed to explore what they saw as the four most unique characteristics of satellite communications. Thematically, each project addressed some aspect of the idea of scale—for them the central philosophical and political issue raised by the communications revolution and the reason for choosing the satellite as their medium. One interpretation of scale was the notion of "a space with no geographical boundaries" (today, borrowing computer jargon, they call it "virtual" space). This became the subject of their first experiment, *The Satellite Arts Project*, conducted in 1977. Another was the idea of scale as geographical connection: this was implemented in their second project, *Hole in Space* (1980), characterized as an "invisible sculpture" in which the connecting armature was important, not the resulting display. The third project would be an international variation on *Hole in Space* dealing with the scale of multi-ethnic or intercultural connections rather than geographic ones. Their fourth proposal had to do with the scale of observation—using the satellite to see in ways otherwise impossible. This is the subject of *Light Transition*, which, like the international *Hole in Space*, has yet to be realized. And now there is Electronic Cafe, a hybrid, multimedia computer/video network whose theme is political scale, the scale of social organizing. Electronic Cafe represents a logical progression in the works of Mobile Image toward the idea of electronic space as community, as a "virtual environment" in which to live. To understand its significance in the artists' agenda as well as in social history it is necessary first to understand the projects that preceded it.

• • •

Hole in Space

In November of 1980 Galloway and Rabinowitz realized the second of their proposed experiments, *Hole in Space*, whose evocative title summarizes a brilliant concept of environmental design: a "hole" in space/time, improbably configured as a feature of the physical urban landscape, through which people separated by a continent could interact in real time. Video cameras and rear-projection screens were installed in display windows at The Broadway Store in Los Angeles and at Lincoln Center in New York: for two hours on each of three consecutive evenings, the locations were connected by satellite, each screen displaying life-size, full-figure images of people on the opposite coast who thus appeared to be watching the watchers. The result was a kind of "virtual eye contact" that rendered the technology transparent: a "hole" indeed, through which each group could see and hear only the other, not itself. There was no advance publicity and there were no signs or instructions at the sites. *Hole in Space* had to be discovered by passersby who were suddenly confronted with the people on the screen. "They found themselves in this emerging environment without having been prepared, conditioned or sold," Galloway recalls. "We just handed the situation over to the people to acculturate, to humanize. What would be their reaction, their posture, their attitude in this unprecedented social situation without familiar rules?"

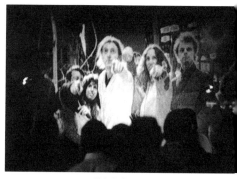

Hole in Space, 1980
From the Telecollaborative Work & Collection of
Kit Galloway and Sherrie Rabinowitz
....

• • •

As the artists had anticipated, the three-day experiment was a microcosm of the process of acculturation. The first day was characterized by discovery and experimentation as people began to occupy this novel zone of social possibilities. The second day brought larger numbers, attracted by word of mouth, who came prepared for the experience: messages and phone numbers were exchanged, there were flirtations, lovers' rendezvous, emotional family reunions, even a spontaneous "virtual party" between twin brothers who poured and drank a champagne toast from the "same" bottle though separated by a continent. The public nature of the situation introduced into the electronic domain the meet-you-at-the-corner ritual of a local gathering place—the electronic neighborhood, where telespace became a microcosm of cultural traditions: total strangers organized themselves to play charades, abandoning speech (anyone can talk by phone) in favor of visual communication appropriate to the medium. There was a bizarre sense of theatre: people were moving in front of the screen and watching something at the same time, like being actors while watching a play with actors in it.

The third day, publicized by mass media coverage, was chaotic, an "over-democratized bedlam" as excited crowds anxiously pressed for their chance to gaze through the electronic hole to meet a returning gaze from across the continent. Feeling transparent and anonymous in the surrounding din, shouting to be heard, people witnessed each other's emotional displays in a situation similar to airport reunions but much more intimate and intense. The videotape documentation of the event is a stirring and powerful montage of reaching-out gestures, hysterical recognitions, and touching expressions of emotion, as when a woman who hadn't seen her brother for fifteen years leaves the site of their electronic reunion with tears of joy streaming down her face.

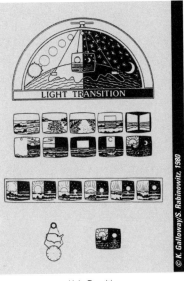

Light Transition
From the Telecollaborative Work & Collection
of Kit Galloway and Sherrie Rabinowitz

© K. Galloway/S. Rabinowitz, 1980

• • •

The Artists as Systems Integrators

For Galloway and Rabinowitz the posture or stance of their interaction with industry is as important as the structures which result. The social role they play becomes an ethical issue. Most artists undertaking telecommunication projects have accepted the passive role of the client who purchases (or is donated) a preexisting package of services that ultimately determines the structural nature of the work. In contrast, Galloway and Rabinowitz approach each project as "systems integrators" who work innovatively at the edge of the art and must therefore actively interface a multiplicity of tools, services, and institutions to realize the nonstandard goals of their enterprise. Here again they reflect a general sensibility in contemporary art concerned with integrating various social and technological systems as raw materials for art-making. But whereas the theme of systems integration is usually implicit in such work, it becomes an explicit foreground issue in Mobile Image projects. This is another sense in which their work is analogous to that of Christo: for with both, the socioeconomic and political processes involved in realizing design goals are as much the art as the structures and environments that result. As with Christo, the people with whom they work are most often not artists but scientists, engineers, industrialists, and public officials with whom they establish collaborative relationships rather than conventional vendor-client roles. And since their practice is as much research and development as design, they frequently come up with strategies and solutions that are subsequently adopted by their industrial colleagues. The vendor-client relationship is reversed: Mobile Image becomes creative consultant to the telecommunications industry.

Gene Youngblood *Virtual Space*

Conversation and Creativity

All Mobile Image environments except the proposed *Light Transition* are conversational networks: this is significant insofar as they address "the scale of creativity," because creativity and conversation are directly linked—indeed, conversation, as a generative process, is the prerequisite for all creativity. This becomes immediately obvious if we distinguish between conversation and communication. Communication means interaction in a common context or domain of consensus which makes communication possible and determines the meaning of all that's said: the control of context is the control of meaning is the control of reality. To create new realities, therefore, we must create new contexts, new domains of consensus. That can't be done through communication. You can't step out of the context that defines communication by communicating; it will lead only to trivial permutations within the same consensus, repeatedly validating the same reality. Instead, we need a creative conversation (from the Latin "to turn around together") that might lead to new consensus and hence to new realities, but which is not itself a process of communication. I say something you don't understand and we begin turning around together: "Do you mean this or this?" "No, I mean thus and such . . ." During this nontrivial process we gradually approximate the possibility of communication, which will follow as a trivial necessary consequence once we've constructed a new consensus and woven together in a new context. Communication, as a domain of stabilized, noncreative relations, can occur only after the creative (but non-communicative) conversation that makes it possible: communication is always non-creative and creativity is always non-communicative. Conversation, the paradigm for all generative phenomena, the prerequisite for all creativity, requires a two-way channel of interaction. That doesn't guarantee creativity, but without it there will be no conversation at all, and creativity will be diminished accordingly. That's why the worst thing we can say about the mass media is that they can only communicate: at a time when creative conversations are essential on a massive scale for human dignity and survival, our society is dominated by a centralized, one-way, mass audience communication system that can only speak to a world that is already understood to be the world, can only address problems already understood to be problems, can only furnish models of behavior that are compatible with the world as it is already perceived by most people most of the time.

•••

Embracing the ethical and political responsibility implicit in their project, Galloway and Rabinowitz set out to create the most fully humanized, most accessible, least intimidating yet most powerful information environment they could design—one that was optimized to cultivate creative conversations and to support autonomous reality communities. From the beginning, they saw the design of Electronic Cafe as metadesign—they would create a structure that allowed its users the greatest possible freedom to design and control their own information environments, to construct their own realities. Such a system would have to include as many modes of communication as possible to support the maximum richness, variety, and texture of cultural expression; at the same time, it would have to facilitate the most natural and simple forms of human interaction, requiring of the user no special knowledge or skills; finally, it would have to operate as a "public utility" whose terminals were all in public places so that personal equipment would not be required and transactions could be anonymous—the information environment as commons rather than commodity, equally accessible to everyone.

•••

Art is a process of exploration and inquiry. Its subject is human potential for aesthetic perception. It asks, How can we be different? What is other? As everyone knows, traditional forms of posing those questions and seeking those answers are no longer adequate. We approach the millennium with a particular sense of our fallibility as a civilization, our mortality as a species, our responsibility as a generation—and, alas, the inadequacy of our culturally limited imaginations in the face of prodigious challenge. The triumph of Mobile Image's heroic enterprise is that it reconstitutes art through instruments appropriate to our circumstance, demonstrating the means by which we may indeed learn to create on the same scale as we can destroy.

(All quotes are from interviews with the author.)

A Contemplation of
Dangerous Games

Cabaret Voltaire

This performance is not of Cabaret Voltaire's usual genre. This performance is especially designed for the Ars Electronica Festival to use Cabaret Voltaire. More ambient elements of both sound and vision combine to ultimately present an audio-visual presentation of a new language. It will draw elements from the theatre/rock performance/filmic and, most important, televisual language. The group's approach to both sound and their developing visual art has always been basically the same. Primarily to remove the restrictions of "technical standards" from their artistic considerations, their use of the very latest computer technology to generate sound is to them only of equal importance to their use of cheap audio cassette recorders. Both have qualities of sound that are of use and interest to the group. It is that intrinsic and individual quality that is their base of choice. They apply the same approach to their visual "selection" process, and this performance will demonstrate this approach.

The group consider that all commercial standards are appropriate for their appropriation. As part of the performance, they also explore your abilities to receive and retain information by using multiple screens and projections, therefore using the space of the Brucknerhaus to the fullest extent . . . The relationship between the multiple images within the space will cause each viewer to have a unique and personal interpretation of the performance. This use of multiple images causes viewers to apply their own "editing" of information, therefore requiring them to establish their own story values, this creating a personal understanding/relationship with the performers' material.

Cabaret Voltaire will also include the physical sounds of technology. The sound of data being printed . . . the sounds of film projectors mechanically in motion . . . passing radio waves through the Brucknerhaus building . . . intercepted telecommunications both open and "secure."

All these media are open to interruptions, inclusion, use and misuse (as is the real modern world of communication), the information to be distorted and manipulated through the artists' perception to create their own truth, into which the viewer/audience can apply their own perception/truth.

Cabaret Voltaire Ars Electronica Statement

In General

Do not believe otherwise! . . .

Machines make our cultural reality—our "shared" world of social representation . . . All "other worlds" are abstract and empty . . . All other realities are ugly (even realists take this view).

The power of audio-visual technology, compared to other media, lies in its ability to give more information as basic form . . . Information, however, is not truth nor even reality. Culturally "use is truth"—our use of a medium structures our world and our identity . . . And so, "reveals" how we are used.

Our social mind is audio-visual images and soundtracks.

"Television: a device by which one is kept at a distance from the event one is witnessing." Thus we are brought near but stretched out in a void of painful longing for what we cannot reach . . . Safe but tormented.

What an object for the social mind! . . . an intangible manmade dream-image dancing to the pulse of desire and the sequence of longing. Why do we use our dream-machine in this way? . . . Paying technology the philosopher's fee as, under the pressure of monstrous desire and bewildered by the lies of men, we pursue the temptations of the dreams that money has bought . . .

Why, when we dream, can we believe that we are alive, but when we are awake we fear that we are dying? (Dreaming is, by the way, a means of preserving sleep by suspending action in imaginary events.)

In Particular

DADA . . . Old impure syphilitic sire of our orphaned bastardy . . . All that we inherit from your impoverished gambler's ruin is your old pocketknife "Cut-Up"—to which we have attached an electronic blade and the tattoo of contemporary rhythm.

Cut-up's assemblage syntax morphology applies equally to images, words and sounds . . . It disintegrates received order and deranges habitual categories of location and classification. With the resultant "cultural fragments" it constructs a synthetic and synaesthetic continuum that is not linear progressive narrative but autonomous formal structure—a structure whose main mode is contrast and analogy operated as critique. Dada and Surrealism bequeath collage and assemblage as mediums whose formal qualities are exactly suited to matching modern urban experience . . . The self-contradiction of city life with its cultural disarray and disunity that is by nature incapable of single consistent form. All formal devices (rhythm, duration, repetition, distortion, inversion, erasure, etc.) are employed on both "found" and "generated" elements. These elements are degraded and synthesized in an abstract formal structure that possesses expressive continuity without involving itself in a depiction that limits freedom by confining expression to the narrative and illustrational demands of a dominant ideology. In cut-up the freedom of the act of compilation transcends the compiled material . . . Barriers are broken down, the forgotten recalled and the unknown apprehended. Audio-visual cut-up is a metaphor for the dreaming social mind . . . Do we awake as we change the quality of the dream? Yet a dream of being awake may still give sharp pleasure to alleviate dull pain, reach the genuine by way of parody and speak some truth in its irony.

Ends.

Statement about Art and Technology

John Sanborn

Our use of tools is what separates us from the rest of the animals. Our sophistication with various forms of technology (from the knife to the atomic bomb) defines us as "civilized" creatures.

The artist has always defined his tools as part of the creative process. Paintings are steeped in color theory, the texture of the painted surface, and the tactility of the paint itself, as much as with the subject being painted. Music is written with the sound of an orchestra or the abilities of the recording studio in mind, with the merger of compositional form and musical "content" resulting in a work of art.

It is not surprising, then, to think of the charcoal used for cave drawings, the pencil, or the piano as the advanced artistic technology of its time.

The so-called state-of-the-art "computer" and video technology of the media artist is nothing more advanced than the oil and canvas of today. As with painting, the use of tools alone is not enough. Tools used without vision, or technology utilized "for its own sake," is as boring as an incompetently played Mozart sonata. But very often the use of "new" technologies has forced the ideas out of art-making, leaving an empty shell of electronics.

For me, video technology is the natural extension of a creative thought process which analyzes and "edits" information. In my case the information is formalized as non-narrative or abstract stories. The visual motifs, combined with an overall conceptual structure, adhere to a logical development, which in turn "makes sense," as much as more traditional narrative does, to the audience.

This level of communication has been lacking for the most part in "art and technology" projects, which have tended to shroud the artist, and his or her tools, in mystery.

Nam June Paik claims to make technology ridiculous. I make technology human.

2³

2³ combines work of Mark Hellas, Cyndi Lee, Mary Perillo, John Sanborn, Mary Ellen Strom, and Pierce Turner in a live performance at Ars Electronica in June 1986. The general theme of the project will involve the problem of the individual trying to make order out of chaos, and of explaining the inexplicable. Dealing with day-to-day experience, we expect to arrive at no specific answers, but more elegant questions.

The work is a combination of: text (displayed, spoken, and sung), live musical solos (played along with prerecorded music), prerecorded video (dealing with treated dance segments, animated computer graphics, and digital video effects as premontaged material for mixing with live cameras), live video mixing and effects (involving the use of a remote video camera), and live dance and performance.

The prerecorded tape will be a complex montage of both simple and sophisticated video technologies, all centered around visualizing a collection of metaphors, which illuminate the collaborators' versions of reality.

We will use doodles as signatures of the six collaborators, reflexive patterns as autobiographical introduction. Doodle categories will reflect the concerns of the artists: movement doodles, music doodles, video doodles. Are there cross-references between doodle forms (e.g. drawing doodles and movement doodles), and how descriptive are these unconscious forms? Another repeating image is that of a digitally created, slowly turning room with large picture windows, each revealing different things outside the window. The whole image is to be used as a set piece with musical setting and as a backdrop for foreground dance movement as well as a transition between various scenes.

A second window image uses the video screen to cut a hole to the outside world, revealing dance outside the theatre. This dance is an example of a limitations work, which is defined by its pre-set limits. Maps are another graphic tool. One is a map of the six collaborators' ancestors' migration to the US. Our view of the map zooms into the individuals, flashing upon personal intersections.

The final step of this mapping is a set of lines and standard "map" symbols, which slowly grows towns, cities, and a topography; revealing itself to be a palm-reader's map of a hand.

Continuing throughout 2^3 are a series of Macintosh-created animations done by Joseph Prieboy. One is called the "Dance Analyzing Machine"—a satire on art and technology projects which uses the dance techniques of the choreographers as a basis for this low-resolution animation.

A major dance sequence is the "car crash test," with the dancers striped and numbered in a pseudo "crash-test" environment. A large-scale video alteration on live dance will interact with on-stage dance commentary, looking for meaning in simple movement, using scientific distance and time markers to accentuate time and distance alteration, and relay an intensity of feeling.

An assemblage of socially complex word games is displayed thru an animated Scrabble-type game. Speaking the questions and some answers of this puzzle are the artists, whose association to the riddle give its clues impact. The impossible task of giving one-word answers to the mysteries of life here is made comically simple.

This is combined with a skewed game of musical chairs. In this competitive version of the game (which relates to the competitiveness of the art world, the rejection of the creative life, the feelings of alienation and being "left out," losing control), each player conveys a different artistic response when he or she is eliminated.

One character is an inventor who pretends to make up what is commonplace; he reinvents his daily activities, how to walk, how to cook, how to eat, as if he never saw a cup, dish, or plate. The background for this segment is a comic mix of discoveries (both real and made up) which is interrupted by live camera close-ups of the character's inventions.

A Paintbox animation will be created to play with images of the six collaborators; taking them back and forth through different ages opens a sequence of children's questions about life. These questions seem to have answers that only exist for us in a particular time, age, and place. The Quantel paintbox work will be done in collaboration with Tom Lesser.

Wasted time is another theme we address, as directly related to the audience. Incorporating footage recorded earlier, outside the Brucknerhaus, characters are seen getting tickets and voicing preconceptions of the evening's work, and delivering instant reviews of the program in progress.

We take the idea behind a Rube Goldberg machine and apply it to a larger range of conditions. Movement becomes color, becomes sound, becomes picture. Based on the subconscious confusion of three and red and F-sharp, the concept of "hearing blue"—based on "Scriabin" color field tests, psychological and IQ tests.

The final work will be a complex montage of both simple and sophisticated techniques and technologies, all centered around visualizing a collection of metaphors which illuminate the collaborators' versions of reality.

Terminal Art

Jürgen Claus

The thesis underlying this exhibition can be formulated in two questions. The first one: Can the technologies that have developed rapidly over the past three decades be carriers of artistic processes? Secondly: Will an interlacing of the various technologies be feasible that could foster any artistic processes and products?

In the short history of the Linz Ars Electronica since 1979, the first question has come up again and again and has to be raised anew considering a continuing and still expanding technological development producing new carrier technologies year by year. It also has to be raised for the purpose of continuous review, of a constant verification of artistic results.

The second question, aiming at an interlacing of the individual systems, is new. It is our special concern and the concern of this exhibition, which can, however, not supply an answer. It will continue to be our concern until the end of the eighties and even beyond then. More later on.

The Title

Terminals are familiar to us as place of arrival and departure. A terminal is also that downtown facility on our way to or from an airport. In some way the terminal (from the Latin *terminalis*) always relates to an end, an extreme. This is also the medico-biological implication of the term: close to, leading to death. There is the technological implication of the word *terminal,* as a point of connection of an electric circuit. And most recently it has come to signify that device that enables the user of a computer to feed instructions into it and to receive information from it.

For our purposes, we may define the terminal as an appliance for transmitting and/or receiving messages, signals. The microphone, for instance, is a transmission terminal; the TV set a reception terminal. Some terminals, like the telephone, may even be used both for transmitting and receiving. This is a promise made with the advent of technology but not quite kept yet.

As to art: connected to the term *terminal,* the creation of visual forms, of images, the production of images—or their deletion; the graphic product, the creative process, the result of visible, often verbal, and frequently even three-dimensional possibilities of exchange, communication through eyes, depictive interpretation (never solution) of the world, visible and invisible spaces, invention and experience in the coordinate system of visibility. Art—age-old and contemporary, never one-dimensional, never only one stencil, never a dictate of style. Art is a form and expression of energy in the visual sphere. Magnetic field of the visual. Art: the visual and its reception by the observer whose eyes, in the words of Willi Baumeister, are the "outpost of his mind."

Terminal art is by no means a computer terminal only and is presented in our exhibition in a more comprehensive manner. What is important, fundamental even, apart from the technical, mostly electronic device, is the action of the participating human being: it facilitates the interaction which is the purpose of this exhibition.

The Art Concept of the Exhibition

It seems to be inevitable that once again the art concept is being challenged. And the concept of the exhibition, too. If, in the course of a medical check-up of a patient, the computer discovers the focus of a disease that was not to be detected with the naked eye or by palpation, its finding will be accepted by the patient (and his relatives), because it serves the purpose of diagnosis and knowledge. No one will question the concept of medicine being expanded as it has been. This is not so in the wide sphere of the arts. Here too, numerous new, modern manifestations of electronic, technological, and media art serve the purpose of knowledge. But we are used to inquiring immediately into their meaning. And this personal decision is preconditioned by a multitude of factors, such as education, attitudes and beliefs, standards of comparison, and others.

What is the art concept underlying our exhibition? It is the aim of "Terminal Art" to present to its visitors predominantly interactive systems of electronics and their application and development by artists, to take them into laboratories of electronic and digital art where they may share in the creative process. The exhibition is dedicated to the creative process of contemporary electronic art rather than to a fixed product. The term art is here being used as a working concept to set off visual, creative work against other forms of work. It is meant to include the forms of an expanded art and an expanded concept of art. In this context, we might also speak of a "Gestalt technology" comprising marginal areas of art such as design, architecture, eco-technology, as well as acoustic events, visual scientific statements, and visual documentation.[1]

Like other concepts of human exploration, the concept of art is not a static one; it is subject to change due to an expanding spatial situation in the experience and understanding of macro- and microcosm, due to a revolutionary development of video carriers and video media, due to changing social structures of the Atlantic-Pacific post-industrial society, and other factors.

Each visitor to the exhibition will decide himself or herself whether and to what extent a work of Gestalt technology stimulates him or her to a new, hitherto unknown experience, compels him or her to formulate new definitions, and, possibly, leads him or her from irritation to a new approach. This personal decision is at the same time an important learning process towards survival in our present age, confronted with sudden social, cultural, media-technological change.

More than two decades after it was formulated, the analysis by the Canadian Marshall McLuhan remains valid: the new media and technologies "constitute enormous collective operations carried out on the body of society without antiseptic precautions. If these operations are inevitable, an infection during such an operation must be expected. If a new technology is used to operate on society, it is not the immediate site of the surgery that is most concerned. The sore or cut is anaesthetized. The entire system, however, is being changed."

In this period of change "there is no example of any conscious adaptation of the various factors of individual and social life to the new expansions apart from the timid efforts of artists, more or less incidentally."[2]

The Other Tradition

Aware of the superficial art of the art trade pretending to be in command of the *Zeitgeist*, we had better remember a different tradition. Ideas, achievements, names like Walter Gropius, László Moholy-Nagy, El Lissitzky, and many others stand for it in our century. The extent to which this different tradition was overlaid by the time immediately before, during, and after the war becomes evident in the lack of dialectics within the art of the mid-eighties. Art in Germany, for instance, is summarized as being expressionist, a completely one-sided view not at all reflecting the historical "national character."

The present development of design technology cannot be judged without historical knowledge. Thus also the "electronic screen," to be dealt with later on, will remain an alien element within society and the private, individual sphere of life unless there is an active, creative, analytical interaction of the artist. This social interaction of the artist is difficult to explain in a democracy for various reasons. The many and fundamental effects of the market do not facilitate a consensus. An artist can hardly have any effect on society without formative forces.

The Bauhaus was to be such a formative force in the 20th century. It had been conceived by Walter Gropius as a "pioneering school," not with the purpose of propagating a certain style, system, or dogma but of exerting an active influence on design. Bazon Brock pointed out recently that in spite and even because of all falsifications in the reception of the Bauhaus, the Bauhaus concept and teaching have remained of topical interest: "From product design via sociodesign to communication design, this is a development necessitated along the lines of Gropius by new technologies and their social consequences."[3]

Moholy-Nagy certainly is a key figure among the Bauhaus artists, if we think of the "other tradition," as I call it, and this is also the history of design technology. Many aspects of his work, pictorial, graphic, three-dimensional, mainly, however, his film and written work, point to our time. The space-time continuum developed and analyzed by him is a major concern of contemporary digital art.

In assessing contemporary design technology, it would be foolish and dangerous to do without the models of thinking, the findings, the concepts offered to us by the other tradition in this century. Notwithstanding the disastrous consequences of two world wars, there is such a tradition even if it is hidden and ousted from presentation in schools and museums.

In the fifties a younger generation of artists, writers, and painters asserts itself in Europe, making vigorous use of the technological possibilities. To name a few: the scenographer and media theorist Jacques Polled; Nicolas Schöffer, who with his light and sound sculptures introduces the concept of cybernetics into art; Frank Malina, who apart from his Lumidyne system furnishes a scientific foundation to the discussion in the magazine *Leonardo*, founded by him; Wolf Vostell, making his first electronic décoll/age blurs through TV distortion and electro-acoustic objects; Nam June Paik, who has collaborated in the studio for electronic music of the West German Radio Cologne since 1958. At the same time Max Bense publishes his scientific, one might also say technological, aesthetics in the Federal Republic of Germany. He and his group were like a global broadcasting service of information aesthetics. Bense pointed out that any civilization has a communication between its technical and its aesthetic reality aiming at an exchange, like a system of communicating tubes. In 1957 Bense wrote in the preface of his *Aesthetica III,* which he dedicated to Max Bill: "We have now invaded the sphere of aesthetic elements, aesthetic atomism, that deals with signals, signs, functions, shapes, cells, moduli, frames, arrays, structures, 'open' and 'closed' systems. The advance of the statistic and microcosmic today combines at least methodically aesthetics and physics . . . In its relation to civilization the scheme of aesthetic communication proves to be a scheme both of information and of amusement."[4]

Jürgen Claus *Terminal Art*

Again: the fifties furnished us not only with the kidney table and other novelties but also with the electronic screen. Put differently, young artists discovered the radar screen of that time to be the material of technology. That system of communicating tubes, of which Bense had spoken, started to transform the foundations of artistic creation and design.

Ecotechnology

Together with the inclusion of technical-technological materials and instruments, artists at the end of the fifties also wanted to open up a new space of nature. Nature no longer to be understood as "still life" and model, but in its elemental capacity. This is where Gestalt technology opens up micro- and macrocosmic spheres. It is not technology per se that is taken up and expanded by the artists.

Dialectic relations between technology and elemental nature, the energy forces of wide spaces like heaven, sea, air, desert, start to develop. The age of the first satellites circling our planet engenders a new awareness for a new definition of our appreciation of nature. This also has been a concern of Ars Electronica from its very beginning. I want to point to presentations like that of *Sky Art* 1980 and 1982 in Linz. Concerned with the terrific consequences of technology innovation on the one hand and the threat to our environment on the other, I want to raise the issue of "ecotechnology." Ecotechnology means application of instruments, materials, processes of technology in such a way that it truly harmonizes with nature, with the habitat of plant, animal, man, also with the wider zones of our ecological home, indeed, with the entire globe and the cosmic space. A concrete example of ecotechnology is the use of light as a source of energy, photovoltage, which, like other technologies of our time, effects the transition from the mechanical principle (steam turbine) to the electronic principle. To use light as a creative medium or to interpret it as such came more naturally to older civilizations than it does to us. If we strip such conceptions of their mythical and religious content, we find them absolutely up-to-date. They point to the coming, feasible, and perhaps inevitable solar age.

This apparently takes us away from art, and in our case from terminal art. The pictorial art of our 20th century contains not only a wealth of expressivity, of individual manifestation, but also a wealth of meaning in the various models of world perception. Most relevant are the Bauhaus lectures by Paul Klee, this eco-artist par excellence.

What is needed today is the incorporation of the technologies into our appreciation of the world, the assessment of these technologies in their relation to the laws, the manifestations, the energetic forces of the world in and around us. This could be the topic for another exhibition—provided our exhibition halls are not only dedicated to history, to the service performances of our galleries. Terminal art as it is presented in the Brucknerhaus at Ars Electronica 86 can be but a transition, the sketch of an exhibition, a work in progress. I do believe, however, that it is revealing to present Gestalt technology in process, *in statu nascendi*. Everyone concerned knows of the restrictions, the limits set to the formation of an intensified, interlaced strategy of art. Financial and instrumental shortcomings are obvious. Personal failure is always included. Nevertheless, the American William I. Thompson, founder of the Lindisfarne Association (1972), writes, in his book on *The Pacific Shift*: "The reporters of the transformation are called artists."[5] The communicative system of the fourth culture ecology, in the words of Thompson, is the electronic system. This justifies any attempt at presenting it, rudimentary as it may be.

Electronic art conveys a notion of reality, nature, space, and our existence in these which differs absolutely and qualitatively from the traditional. Art has always interpreted nature. Nature thus became culture, history through art and its representations. Actually, it stands to reason that the polarisation of our perception of nature from the microscopically minute to the most distant cosmic sphere effected in this 20th century has also brought a change to our dimensions of interpretation.

At the turn of the century, science and art embraced the micro-worlds. When artists introduced the abstract as the concrete into their creative work and theory, in the first decade of our century, the micro-worlds of nature entered artistic creation.

At the same time, to quote Felix Philipp Ingold, "a revolutionary change of paradigms" happened, which he summarized as follows: "The telluric consciousness gave way to the planetary one: man, who, by means of his dirigible flying machine, could now take off from the ground and stay and move about freely in the air, all of a sudden found himself in an active but also eccentrically relativistic relation to the universe, to space and time."[6]

Energy becomes the carrier in the continuum of space and time which now enters pictorial art (See the early Italian and Russian futurism.) The concept of energy is probably the common rationale of the spheres of natural and artistic phenomena. In a lengthy conversation I had with Heinz Mack, the former Zero artist, we discussed the focal concept of energy. I want to quote him in support of my own view:

Modern art actually is an expression of energy. This may be psychical energy, vital energy, as it is in expressionism. It may also be visual energy, the energy of a colour, for instance . . . The artistic idea is at the same time mental energy, and undoubtedly it is the most expressive of all mental energies. The crisis of mental energy is the cause of all the other crises. Today we lack vital energy, we lack the mental energy of imagination, we lack the energy of enthusiasm. The consequences thereof, commonly called energy crises, are actually secondary. Unfortunately, the secondary crises are thought to be the primary ones. This is not the way to solve the problems.

This inner, cosmic constellation of our existence of which the artistic existence appears to be a bright star is at the same time an immense system of energies of inconceivable abundance. We are not lost within this cosmic "supply of energies," provided our mental and spiritual energies remain active. Thus it is not foolhardy if we dare to send our imaginations into the open space of future, to invest our hopes where they may turn into reality, that is, in the age in which we live and in the age that we are approaching.[7]

Attempting a synopsis of what was achieved in a rapid development within five years between 1966 and 1970 in the field of interaction of art and technology and what has become the foundation of contemporary Gestalt technology, we may say that the new media have expanded our awareness and consciousness. The new media, cybernetic methods, computer-controlled processes and objects, intermedia theatre, laser, holography, and others, have been used like the "organs" of an expanded consciousness. The concept of an organ-expanding technology was related to spatial design. Space in theory and practice has become an essential dimension. This is why this discussion must be related to environment art. Here is where the idea of ecotechnology originated.

At a time when electronic media like television merely act as critics, art is called to use these media as a creative potential. Artists will succeed if they link the media immediately to their range of experience. In this way they will use the ecological opportunity in elucidating the significance of relations between the organism and the environment. The ecological opportunity of art must not be mistaken for a "green art" making simple use of natural materials.

Ecology happens in the interrelation of spaces of varying sizes. Since contemporary art has opened up micro and macro spaces to be experienced by man, the ecological structures of art also have entered very complex relationships.

Artists are dissidents of established, rusty experiences. They are, however, the best of allies to anyone seeking to experience the open space of nature and the spaces of human consciousness yet to be opened up. In them, the real and the imaginary space are at war. Their vision serves to filter the real space. An expanded field of media may also serve this vision. Artists were the first to make use of the revolutionary medium of relief printing, as the woodcut, e.g., five hundred years ago. They were aware then, and are today, that the print medium (like the electronic media today) would immediately serve to propagate political power. They availed themselves of the medium for their vision and thus also for the vision of the beholder.

This holds true for today. The artist can make use of the expanded technology of our days by connecting it to his or her vision, that is, to a fundamentally human, fraternizing experience.

Notes

1. I want to recall my having presented the concept of expanded art in Linz almost two decades ago at the University Week on "New Forms of Art" (October 1967, at the Arbeiterkammer). The lecture was entitled "Expanded Arts—the New Definition of the Limits of Art Today" and was accompanied by four films. In 1970 I published the book Expansion of the Arts (publ. by Rowohlts Deutsche Enzyklopädie). In my paper for the catalogue of Ars Electronica 1984 (p. 145) I have introduced and outlined the concept of "Gestalt technology."

2. Marshall McLuhan, Understanding Media (New York, 1964).

3. Bazon Brock, "The Reality of the Mind—What Is Design in the Age of the Microchip? from the Bauhaus Concept to Communicative Design," publ. by Richard Kriesche in: Artificial Intelligence in the Arts, No. 1 "Brainwork" (Graz, 1985).

4. Max Bense, Aesthetics and Civilization (aesthetica III) (Baden-Baden, 1958), p. 11.

5. William I. Thompson, The Pacific Shift (San Francisco, 1984).

6. Felix Philipp Ingold, Literature and Aviation (Frankfurt, 1980), p. 15.

7. "Kunstreport" 1/80 (Berlin), p. 11; the complete text is to be found under the heading: Heinz Mack Kunst als Ausdruck von Energie (Art as Expression of Energy).

Propositions on the Dark Age of Television

Bazon Brock

The Culture Critic as Back Alley Abortionist

Certain determining terms of criticism seem to be recurring in public discussion and in expert circles, their main justification seeming to be the frequency with which they are being used. Among those terms are: the medium is the message; total electronic simulation; television illiteracy; and recently culture critics have developed these catchwords into an all-embracing systematic structure termed "we amuse ourselves to death."

It is a remarkable fact, at least in the Federal Republic of Germany, that culture critique of this kind is being spread by the very social groups that, at the same time, maintain that only a decisive expansion of the media market can safeguard the free and uninhibited development of citizens. Is there any other reply to this ambiguity than the statement that literates complain about television but spend most of their evenings in front of their sets?

First Proposition

Never before has there been a period in history when the sensibilization of wide groups of the population to problems of technological evolution, destruction of the environment, social conflicts, armaments races, machine-ruled medicine was greater than today. McLuhan himself, who had developed the formula of "the medium is the message," illustrated the connection between sensibilization of the population and the expansion of the media with many examples (e.g. opposition to the war in Vietnam). By no means has the claimed illiteracy of TV consumers made them commit greater follies than did the praised literacy of classically educated Central Europeans at the beginning of our century. The things educated elites of Western Europe said about God and the world at the beginning of and during World War I can easily be made out as inexplicable nonsense even by the average TV consumer of our days. The reproach of TV illiteracy obviously disregards the fact that cultural techniques in the electronic age are and have to be different from those of the age of book culture. Those new cultural techniques have been caused by the changed forms of perception and acquisition.

Second Proposition

Television aesthetics, primarily an aesthetics of reception and not so much of production, has led to an increase of the population's average capacity to reflect in images. In fact, the primacy of the word in communicative relations has been eliminated; this, however, in no way implies a decrease of cognitive capacities. Because of the natural modes of functioning of our "world image apparatus," it is easily possible to satisfy the highest demands on our judgement in images and with the development of grammars for the image languages.

Third Proposition

It has become a fashion to maintain that the TV consumer is unable to evaluate correctly, i.e. critically, the claim to reality of the mass of electronic images. The world of images is said to have become independent; it has no correlating facts in the real world; the signs have become separated from what they were meant to explain. A total simulation of a world of images like this, existing in our minds only, is supposed to lead to a loss of reality, the effects of which will undermine and finally destroy the structures of society. Judgements like these are easily recognizable as helpless gestures of rejection. They resemble our instinctive gestures to avert those occurrences of reality that we can no longer identify directly with our natural organs of perception.

Just as we have learnt to account for imperceptible radio waves, radioactive radiation, etc. as "real" components of our lives, we will also learn to identify image simulations by adequate mediation as nothing but a different manifestation of the one reality; for those conditions of human life on which we do not, at the moment, have any influence, are nevertheless real and not only dreamlike, fantastic, or psychopathically distorted.

These dimensions of our life have hitherto been addressed in the hypothetical structure of a divine ruler of the world or as fate. On the level of human perception, one tried to find an equation to the structure of a ruling deity by, e.g., forming the topos of paradise. The total simulation of worlds of images in the electronic age today is of equal significance to that of the "heavenly Jerusalem" for medieval lay and scientific theology.

The question now is, what do we have to accept as real, as a power beyond our influence and reach? Because it is highly improbable that we might again identify a divine creator of the world. We experience the total electronic simulation as sham; nevertheless, it is not at any individual's discretion. Everything around us seems to be formed by mere conventions, and yet we cannot change them at random. In total electronic simulation we appeal to the allegedly unlimited power of our mind. This simulation presents us with what has been long since known in science-fiction literature as the *Weckglasgehirne* and has been attracting and disgusting us at the same time. Not only science-fiction writers but also experts of various disciplines are discussing the question of the existence of an immaterial spirit beyond our physical existence. The evaluation of total simulation depends on the answer to this question. Right now, we may be reassured by the answer that it is not the dead but the living who dream about paradise.

Pompino Project

Van Gogh TV

Television Participation

Europe is challenged to participate!

The game "Hotel Pompino" was developed as a consequence of a live television project by Van Gogh TV in order to communicate even more directly with the spectator, who becomes a participant instead of just a spectator. Participation can be accomplished by personal appearance in the program, over telephone, over video-telephone or through the mailbox.

Direct Television Democracy

The spectator can become a participant with a cable or a satellite dish to receive the 3sat broadcast. Video phones have been installed throughout Europe by Ponton, allowing the spectators to switch on as commentators or jury members. Computer users can send in written text with electronic mail over telephone lines.

The Stage

The action takes place on different stages.

1. The blue box
2. The live stage
3. The table
4. The network

In the blue box, the candidate must orient himself in a digital world. On the live stage it is mainly a matter of unmediated, personal tasks that are adapted to given themes and surroundings. The user must master detailed and active tasks in the micro- and macro-spheres that are set out on the table. The connection between various places in the world is achieved with the network (telephone, video phone, mailbox, news ticker).

Winning = Broadcast Time

On any one day, numerous candidates will play against each other. The candidate must react within a complex structure of participation, following rules that are specific to the game and the jury. Points are played for. 0 to 6 points can be acquired for a given jury and game situation. At the end, the person with the most points wins. The first prize is free broadcast time on the next day. The broadcast time won varies from 5 to 15 minutes. The candidate can do as he wishes during this time and may even make use of the technical facilities of the studio. The loser is swallowed by a computer-animated waste-disposal unit and his participation, for the time being, is at an end.

The Game with the Imaginary Worlds

The classic goal of every game is winning, losing, and entertaining. In addition, the participants of Hotel Pompino experience daily situations in imaginary game and picture worlds. And that's also a reason for the subjective aspect of the game.

A New Eloquence in a Public Space

Van Gogh TV wants to offer the spectator an opportunity to go beyond the simple choice between favorite shows. Play situations are available where he can express himself in a unique way with images and sound. With this opportunity, Van Gogh TV sees the opportunity for a new people's art that seeks renewal through the public media.

Van Gogh TV considers as its main objective to assist the spectator to overcome his role as manipulated commodity of the media, who cynically calculate how information can be made palatable in order to sell paid commercial advertisement — the real basis for existence of the media.

The function of the media is to act as a buffer for a social politic that no longer answers for its actions. Instead the spectator is given the information almost in time, but actually too late to react. The spectator becomes an alibi, because he knew everything but did not do anything. Television is a means for controlling and influencing the people using the trinity of hypnosis, compulsory consumption and bad conscience.

The moment that all being and striving is recognized as senseless is the time to turn on the television (from Dr. B. Heidersberger).

Hotel Pompino

The lead actors:

The candidate = Hotel guest

The moderator = Pompinos special hotel service

The jury = Hotel management, hotel reception

The technicians = Video installers, hotel detectives

Try to image the following:

The candidates enter the arena and from then on they are hotel guests with the special task of going (or traveling) through the rooms. They compete with one another for points and time. They travel from the basement through all the floors up to the topmost floor.

The structure of the rooms is partially digital and partially real. The tasks are determined by the particular structure of the space and are completely dependent on the whims of the hotel personnel. An example is the abuse room, where the one who can be the most abusive would win the most points — if not for the fact that the jury's pacifist days are over and it has no patience for abuse and disgrace. To this extent, the tasks are also means of forcing the hotel guests to adapt to the political, economic, and social climate of the hotel or, on the other hand, to challenge or change the prevailing structure.

The Jury — The Judgement

In the studio after each game sequence, the jury allots the points and is able to freely express its opinion — while on air. After that the video-phone jury does the same and finally the public is given an opportunity to assess the proceedings. It will become difficult to keep up the journey through all 44 hotel rooms!

Chance, Luck, and Gastronomy

To be more precise, everything is orchestrated from this room, i.e., everything perceivable or that can be done by the guests. Here the hotel guest has to come to terms with the requirements that such a game of chance brings with it. Sometimes things get a bit topsy-turvy in the hotel. The lights might even all fail suddenly, but the technical staff guarantees an entertaining 100 minutes each day. For a week there will be daily reports from the hotel with daily changing themes in order to give a many-faceted view of this special Pompino hotel. Of course the professional dress of the hotel personnel will change to suit the theme. The same goes for the inner decor of the hotel and the dress of the guests. In short: the guests will be hounded, abused, challenged, and inspired. At the Hotel Pompino the guest is customer, king, farmer, beggar, and superstar. The guest has the chance to climb (naturally with the elevator) and can, in the best case, go to the Pompino heaven.

True, up to now nobody's been able to do it, so: Alles Linz!

Pompino World

The above-mentioned concept of play is based on extraterritorial media philosophy. There is Europe, there is Linz, there is the Hotel Pompino that shines its eloquence over the whole of Europe. But even something that sounds so simple has a trapdoor (already giving clues: pay attention in room 5!). But that's how one gets into Pompino world, and the Hotel Pompino broadcasts only in unmediated connection with Pompino world. To be more precise, the Hotel Pompino broadcasts over and beyond itself. The guests have the best chance to get into this world by traveling through the rooms and will be ever more strongly drawn to the Pompino sphere of existence. For the spectators, it is more complicated and requires more free play. The Pompinos lead the guests on their journey through the rooms and the Pompino world.

Pompinos and the New Tourism

You are the hotel guides, the tourists, the politicians, the psychologists, the jokers; and you have therewith a multiplicity of areas in which to work and an intimate relationship to the guests. The excitement of using a game to break into a new world is immense, and many other games will be influenced by this excitement. The Pompino world is different. It will influence and open up possibilities for all times, and it will be difficult for many to find their way back to Europe. On the other hand, the cross-regional cooperation on a technical level within Europe is easier and interactive. The influence is palpable, old-worldish, historically significant, and intentional.

Europe 1992

But Europe will learn and profit from the feedback it receives from the Pompino world inhabitants, where previously only an elite fragment of its inhabitants have been able to break through to new shores. During the journey, the guest will experience a new reality, and will be confronted with his inculcated attitudes when he has to adjust to new situations in the hotel. The sense of time will be shifted, as with any vacation travel. So far, so good. The integrity of the player will only in the later phases of the game. Because of the ritual of the game there will be the appearance of normality, and the guest will appear so much the more benevolent in new spheres. Every room will yield new experience, perspective, and knowledge. That is the way to Pompino world.

At the end, when he/she ceases to ask just what Pompinos are, then she/he is on course and may say "I was Pompino" (from Prof. M. Hentz).

The Live TV Concept

The interconnected interplay of technical and creative potential is what interactivity is (from S. Vanasco).

Since the "performance experience," it is a central tenet of media art that the means of interactivity be used to investigate new spheres. The fluctuation of all things that no longer show themselves as such, as fluctuating appearances, are to be reproduced in new ways. The work process will again be an important part of artistic work. The democracy of technology will return to the screen. Video and computer images will be projected that are pertinent to the themes and action of the game.

Television Art and Media Eloquence

The main artistic interest of Van Gogh TV is to find a new TV language, one however that does not lose its sense of ongoing process.

Experimentation Is the Highest Law

A change in the work is the increasing cooperation of other artistic disciplines with each project. Teams, consisting of international artists, work with themes that are related to the medium of television. Just those classical artistic disciplines (drama, set, and costume imagery) must develop their own languages. With the live character and the corresponding acceleration in of the sequence of events, technology becomes the most critical part of the broadcast. Live broadcasts always have to count on breakdowns and hitches, and this should be looked upon as an essential part of each broadcast. On the other hand, the new TV language must be understood by the TV audience. We understand this language as being sound and picture simultaneously and therefore an artistic answer to the modern world.

Live is art.

Ponton European Media Art Lab, Hamburg-Vienna

The Situation

The purpose of European culture should not be to define a society that identifies itself only in economic terms. It must go beyond this and initiate a dialogue between the individual spheres of society to inspire a visionary approach to culture.

The restraints of economic necessity demand a particular perception of reality. The media are no longer intermediaries but rather means that are subordinated to the economic sphere. Economic success as the ultimate cultural value, justification and source of meaning for every societal transaction.

During the search for our own perfect entertainment, there is nothing more entertaining than meeting somebody else who is seeking his own entertainment.

Impelled by a primeval instinct, humanity created an artificial model — once called God — and lost the belief in simulated real time. This play of humanity is orchestrated on the surface of the screen, where humanity's internal image in its functions (space and time) is made obsolete.

Lived reality becomes unbearably slow and boring in face of the accelerated simulation of reality as it appears on the screen. The problem begins when people attempt to keep pace with the velocity of the moving image. Loss of models and values, loss of belief and identity — the result is unoriented consumption.

Our Consequences
Our Own Workshop
The Media Art Lab as an independent workshop, planning, production, and broadcasting station.
Economic Apparatus
With the development of an economic apparatus we've made it possible to meet the need to be mobile and flexible.
Exemplary Model of Work
Following team- and individual-oriented work models, new forms of work and jobs are being

developed that counteract the usual tendency towards excessive specialization. A centrally coordinated Europe-wide entity for cooperative productivity.
Researching the Live-Broadcast Model
Freeing the medium from its isolation and changing it into a provocative and realised vision — real time television. Electronic and humane interactivity; live TV at three different levels: 1, production team; 2, live stage; 3, audience.
Advanced Interface Between Avant-Garde and Industry
A contact and meeting place for these extremes as a common attempt at inspired experimentation. A development shop where hardware and products of industrial society are made accessible for goal-oriented projects of an artistic nature.

Testing technology to its limits.

The Commentary

Presently, the Media Art Lab considers its essential task to pose the challenge of media in order to define our social and culture position as artists and to be able to transform artistic ideas into practice.
The Media Art Lab considers itself not only a place for research, but also a logical connection to commerce and industry. The Media Art Lab will serve as a link that inspires the entertainment monopoly (presently dictated by profit and administrative machinery).
Media Art Lab's work extends from local and laboratory-related research in electronic branches to mobile research that leads to the farthest reaches of the planet.
Media Art Lab's work extends from the establishment of broadcast models for TV and radio to realizable live shows over satellite.
Media Art Lab's work extends from the training of interested amateurs and students to cooperative work with experts from the most diverse areas of specialization.
Van Gogh TV Art Lab is the first laboratory in Europe — completely organized and run by artists — that has already been practically proved since 1986.
At the Media Art Lab, artists of a new generation are at work.

WWW.vgtv.com, VGTV D-21217 Seevetal, Gluesingerstr. 40c, T.++49-40-76910542.
Mail: info@vgtv.com

"Nobody Is Safe"

Stadtwerkstatt TV

LIVE TV ART by satellite directly to the household and back. Television in the hands of artists on channels 3sat and FS 2.

Nailed Guts
NG001

Live programmes are the blood of television. If a broadcasting station suffers a loss of blood, it will become a mere supplier for the goggle-box or some audiovisual home disco. Television is never more thrilling, nerve-racking, and specific than in live programmes. You chew your fingernails to the bone, you want to go up the walls, get hopelessly plastered, pick up the telephone angrily, rave, hope to finally get through with your call, switch over again and again because you simply can't stand the thrill of being there again for the finale.

Therefore, those previously recorded and trimmed game shows with their anonymous studio audiences are all the more damnable. No TV juice is streaming over the screen. Game shows are ruled by safety, order, and boredom. Nobody exceeds the time limit, nobody talks smut in the heat of the studio lighting, nobody has to react to mishaps, nobody runs out of crisps and beer.

STWST-TV has this blood in its veins and STWST-TV is bloodthirsty.

Our artistic understanding of the medium is based on the actual character of the matter of television. If the medium is seen from this point of view, in the foreground there is the endeavour to trace the root, the origin of the matter of television, namely real-time transmission. The live performance is (the medium's) autonomous quality. Therefore, our overall aim is to broadcast live. The television camera is the only camera that can simultaneously record, transmit, and copy the picture. Electronic picture, sound, and data processing permit us to design and transport at the same time.

Sports Set the Example

Sports are real events that happen spontaneously; their course cannot be predetermined and, most of all, they are happening now. The constants are the instruments, the tools of the network unit. The composition develops in the course of the performance. Things, facts are confronted with each other, dialogues, talks, statements set side by side, and suspense develops—sports effect. The experience is subject to a wide range of obligingness, boredom, and thrill. The rhythm is determined by its own dynamics, with both loose moments and tense, thrilling situations being given equal justice.

NG004

The sound makes the music. The sound makes your blood run through your veins. Turn your TV up to maximum volume, so that the boom in the set fills the entire room (which has been darkened, of course). React to the pictures and get in contact with us. Ignore any other changes in your apartment. Enjoy television, as television should be.

STWST-TV is live television, without a false bottom, and it is direct. I took a ride with the pretty music, and now I'm buzzing to you straight from hell.

Instinct TV

Not a finished, ready(-made) piece of work, but a process on the basis of dialogues. Work in progress—a communication sculpture. The patterns used correspond to the specific language formula developed by Stadtwerkstatt TV. The subject is instinct, special processing—not smoothing but roughening and intensifying, uncovering. Nobody knows what the other one is doing and yet they are all connected with each other. The autonomy of the individual promotes the fundamental emancipation of the individual voice. Art as a development aid to finding one's speech.

Instant TV

The TV set is the powder and we pour water into it; or rather, the TV set is the water and we mix it with our powder.

Reaction-Action TV

The menu offered: quick, spontaneous, domestic, raw, and pure. Whatever the viewer brings in is taken up immediately and incorporated into the individual levels of the studio. Action, pictures, sound, and text react and act in and with each other. TV takes place in the studio and in the households simultaneously. Network unit: apartment-receiver-telephone-studio-transmitter. Of course, you can phone in or get called.

Catastrophe TV

The number one scene of catastrophes is the TV screen. Like everything else, catastrophes can only be determined by human judgement. Irritation should be provided by TV in order to relativize conceptions of value. The enjoyment of catastrophes and catastrophic pleasure should not be left at liberty. Man's innate drive for destruction and annihilation is being speculated with.

"Studio Obertreffling"—A Live TV Art Project
There Is War on TV

The military training village at Obertreffling, which resembles a town in a movie set, is the location of the action and of the TV studio. Here we find the appropriate environment for our project, a real background for the execution of our subject. This training ground, an ideal test field, represents a real simulation area and is confronted with the virtual space of the medium. The village accommodates a field of tension from inside to outside, from houses and streets. The subject is dealt with chronologically, in four blocks. The structure is that of traditional drama: the quiet and the tension before the storm, the eruption, the survivors and the victims, the dance on the volcano. For the project to go well, it is necessary to involve the Austrian Federal Army to carry out individual tasks. Furthermore, the subject requires cooperation with the fire brigade, ambulance service, and other disaster relief organizations. The festival audience will be taken to the location by bus to be provided by the Federal Army specifically for this occasion. Participating artists in the festival and guests will be incorporated in the programme. An event tanking place in situ, in the studio and in the household.

Nobody Is Safe

is like TV, taking place at several levels of action at the same time. It psychically and materially investigates the phenomenon of controlled life. Our considerations were focused on the meaning of the subject in relation to human existence and the everyday life connected with it. A high degree of quality of life produces a high degree of control over potential interference factors. Today we are faced with a highly developed culture of security systems, which have, in the meantime, acquired strong dynamics of their own. They have even come to inspire fear and uncertainty in the simple-minded. We want to know how people have their lives under control day by day and how they deal with their existence. The maintaining of value conceptions (what to protect and what from) associated with this, only apparently results in a network to stabilize existence. Ultimately, however, the network shows paranoid cracks, so that nobody can feel safe. The tendency towards control, which is a primary factor of survival for many, is revealed as a trap. Reason teaches us that we cannot know what will happen next.

NG003—The Bridge

"Nobody Is Safe" is not a reservoir for Peter Rapp's "Hoppala" show. Of course, there must be gloating, but: if it doesn't kill us, it will just make us stronger. Fundamentals of faith and strategy. If something goes wrong, no unprofessionalism will grin into your living room. If something goes wrong, there won't be much brooding about it, instead we will act like lightning to make use of the error in the system. We are not here to face facts but to change them. Everything chalked up as error by outsiders, for us is a new molecule which sets a mutation in motion that makes us immune. Catastrophes do not occur to make us uneasy and destroy us. Catastrophes occur in order to test and to strengthen us.

STWST-TV is not afraid of any test. STWST-TV invites you to be tested. Look out, honey, cos I'm using technology.

Scenes of action: on, under and beside the VOEST bridge near the Linz/Urfahr motorway intersection on the bank of the Danube. An intersection between leisure and work. Above, the motorway crosses the area. Under it, there is a leisure facility for tarmac curling. Paths for walkers, cyclists, joggers, and dog owners also run through this area and beyond, along the river bank to the recreation area.

A public space, which holds a lot and involves several levels which, in our opinion, are characteristic. These represent our dramatic reference points by their physical existence.

Heroes of Our Time

Survivors: they know they have chosen the right way to spend their everyday lives and their leisure time, usefully. They demonstrate exemplary behaviour in every situation—as small-scale capitalists, macrobiotics, militant cyclists, sexual partners, conscious consumers.

The survivor impresses his fellow beings by his behaviour, attitude, and the courage of his convictions. He has himself, his life, his environment well under control. Insecurity is foreign to his nature.

In any conflict situation, the survivor resorts to a reservoir of rules and sayings: "If you want to succeed, you must stop at nothing," "Man is what he eats," "The woman's place is in the home." The simple, straightforward formula gives him strength and security.

The survivor considers himself primarily a man of practice, and not of theory. His own experience confirms his way of acting. Where others are driven by unfavourable circumstances and material compulsions, the "right way manifests itself in the flesh and blood" for the survivor. He despises any form of existence other than his own, towers above the grey masses by his own self-created "Self." Thus, he represents the interesting image of an imaginary personality.

The action develops live before the eyes and ears of the TV viewer—a complex discourse on the subject becomes visible. Several autonomous levels of action operate simultaneously, being interlinked and inevitably related to each other.

Above, there is the motorway—the ordered and regulated system of road traffic. It is the dramatic symbol of the rational level—the level of the head, so to speak. What makes the traffic move? A popular, controversial subject, where individual freedom and limitations are subject to strong control and self-control. This is exactly what we want to process, artistically. Here, the movement and motion of people, there, the suspension bridge. And as cars can't fly, the bridge acts as a crutch.

Under the bridge—the level of drives. An open yet covered space, similar to a hall. The tarmac curling rink is the scene of action, the steel bridge construction with its mobile work platforms represents the grid. This space is an intermediate stop for those driven by leisure activities and those driven from home. Underworld.

Beside the bridge, there are meadows, a flood area, the water dam, and the cycle path. A civilized, mixed form of different leisure areas. The green meadow, growth, lethargy. A story book idyll. A small house, right in the centre, an intact world in the meadowland.

There our television family is accommodated—a living room full of representatives of all ages and sexes. A cozy evening spent chatting, eating, drinking, watching television. A reflexive loop over our current programme, accessible for everyone by phone. Manipulated pieces of information on the screen stir up conflicts.

Outside, a debate is taking place at the same time. Invited guests who are convinced of the maxims of their own lives explain their own survival strategies. Detached, saturated, and marked by seeing through things. People who know how to have their lives under control. A suggestive disassembly of their points of view takes place—not in order to degrade these people, but in order to visualize the functioning of such self-imposed or learned control mechanisms in the course of making the insecurity visible.

A group of social desperados have made themselves at home. We supply them with alcohol, provide a refrigerator, firewood, and a trash container. They can also be reached by phone—a social sculpture.

For the purposes of injustice we also establish a VIP lounge. The best place for noncommittal observations and comments. First class, full service—no phone calls for them. In the course of time, an independent force from outside comes to act on the overall situation, altering it. It begins on a small scale and gains disastrous proportions. In a pointed form, this is the material illustration of a process of permanent change. Nothing is at rest. The clock is a water bag. Deconstruction and re-creation.

Stadtwerkstatt TV specifies subjects, provides provocation, and encourages an interactive TV event; the viewer is requested to supply contributions in the form of optical or acoustic statements. The viewer's contribution is immediately taken up, inserted, and brought into context with blended-in pictures and sounds. In doing so, the medium goes beyond pure representation and becomes a multiple means of communication. Things, facts are confronted with each other; dialogues, talks, statements added—a dialectic simultaneousness.

The viewer can release processes by means of his telephone keypad without even having to comment on them—just by pressing a button. The viewer assumes responsibility. The TV picture of the real action space is set against/made equal to the virtual space of the video game.

A system is created and left to itself. Everyone is a potential perpetrator. A bipolar decision process is set in motion, by means of a rope-pulling technique. Two different phone numbers can be dialed. Simple majority will thereby prevent a process with serious consequences, or initiate it.

NG 002

This time, legendary interactive television shall finally come into its own again. Interactive television, as a playground for media artists, media philosophers, media theoreticians, and media critics, is a ghetto leading to incestuous boredom. Interactive television makes sense and is fun only if media consumers interact. Experiences made in Europe are frustrating because—except for sound popular instinct complaining of the TV fee—the only people to pick up their phones, faxes, or computers are those who define themselves as media XYZs.

In America, however, the interactive telephone, fax, or computer is used just as easily as guns are pulled out in innumerable Western movies. Invitations to join us for a bottle of whisky or prophecies of eternal hellfire were therefore made primarily by people who try to get through, every day, to the "Wurlitzer" show in our part of the world: children, jilted lovers, psychopaths, religious fanatics, barkeepers, and the spotty-faced teenagers from the neighbourhood. With such interactivists, more happens in half an hour than in any media discourse around here. Since "Der Goldene Schuss" (The Golden Shot), German-speaking television has been providing nothing but pseudodemocratic and pseudointeractive television. STWST-TV is not made up of media artists but of culture labourers who make interactive television. STWST-TV shoots with live ammunition and has a high hit rate.

I shot a man in Reno, just to watch him die.

As Well as Here and Now

Psycho-mindgames, heavy security, car wash and angling, fusilation of a tree, computer grants, climate tapes, private visits, horses, asses, rock 'n' roll, head-mounted camera, Grand Prix Ars Electronica, collisions of mind and matter, accidents, dynamite dog, mountain climber, autoerotic, successful business people, gun lovers, signal rocket, salvage diver, radar traps, speed reduction, twins, snow gun, dew, the last hay harvest.

Through the camera lens to the chip across the field of electronics, by cable into the picture mixer and through the TBC to the signal amplifier, to go on via the coaxial cable to the parabolic antenna, into the air into the parabolic receiver, through the switch desk to the radio relay line, over the meadows and fields and across the border to Mainz to the uplink into the orbit to the satellites, from the satellites to the receiving dish of the cable operator, through various places of equipment into the copper lines beneath the streets, into the households to the tuners in the video-cassette recorders, into the antenna cable to the RF bushing of the TV set, through diodes and resistors to the picture tube, from the picture tube to the retina, via nerves into the brain and from there into the blood. Television must get under your skin.

For concept and direction, Stadtwerkstatt TV notes:
Thomas Lehner, Georg Ritter, Wolfgang Lehner, Reinhard Jod.

Realization of the project:
Houchang Allahyari, Reinhard Anderle, Petra Anlanger, Norbert Artner, Andreas Baumgartner, Dominque Beivl, Gerhard Blöchl, Heinz Brandner, Baronesse Lana Maria von Dimwald Seebach, Peter Donke, Gustav Dornetshuber, Wolfgang Dorninger, Selam Ebead, Martina Ebner, Joachim Eckl, Fina Eßlinger, Andreas Feichtnei, Markus Fischer, Bernhard Frankfurter, Karl Freilinger, Willibald Fuchshumer, Charles Fürth, Stefan Gassner, Hannah Gehart, Caro Geier, Erwin Graf, Dr. Karl Hafner, Peter Hauenschild, Kurt Hennrich, Laurenz Hofstadler, Petra Jeup, Gabi Kepplinger, Gerhard Kohlmair, Silvia Lappi, Dominik Lepuschitz, Inge Maria Limbach, Georg Lindorfer, Erwin Loidl, Christian Meixner, Didi Neidhart, Gerhard Neulinger, Bob O'Kane, Gertrude Plöchl, Günther Rainer, Peter and Paul Reinthaler, Paul Riedl, Elke Rittenschober, Ruth Ritter, Simon Ritter, Helmut Rozmann, Robert Rudelstorfer, Herbert Schager, Valerie Schager, Brigitte Schober, Alf Schwarzlmüller, Peter Sommerfeld, Wolfgang Amadeus Steinmetz, Markus Tremel, Nancy Tuffy, Martin Vlk, Mark Vojca, Gotthard Wagner, Max Zellinger, Rainer Zendron, Monika Zoufal.

Thanks to:
ORF Landesstudio OÖ., 3sat, Ars Electronica, Bundesministerium für Landesverteidigung, Bundesministerium für Unterricht und Kunst, Landesregierung Oberösterreich, Stadt Linz, Bundespolizei Linz, Sony, Communication Systems, Schweizer und Pilger, Kapsch, Bergbahnen Hinterstoder, Amiga, Commodore, Offenes Kulturhaus Linz, Elektro Ransmayr, Fischer Film.

As well as:
Markus Binder, Ing. Gernot Gökier, Gottfried Hattinger, Mag. Jürgen Meindl, Dr. Christine Schöpf, Günter Stockinger, Dr. Ernst Strouhal, Mag. Martin Sturm, Dr. Herbert Timmermann, Mag. Gitti Vasicek.

Chronology:
1986 Superweisende Installation, Ars Electronica Linz
Nebenraum, Österreichische Filmtage Wels
1987 Hauptplatz-TV-Konzert, Ars Electronica Linz
Hotelvision, Österreichische Filmtage Wels
1989 Automaten-TV, live on 3sat, Ars Electronica Linz
1990 Live in Buffalo/NY, on Public Access Cable-TV
1991 Out of Control—Niemand ist sich seiner sicher, live on 3sat and FS 2, Ars Electronica Linz
1992 Project in preparation for Cleveland/Ohio and Lower Austria.

Cartesian Chaos

Peter Weibel / Bob O'Kane

"Cartesian Chaos" is an interactive installation by Peter Weibel and Bob O'Kane. This installation is the second of a series dealing with the idea of personal or group interaction in a virtual world. The concept involves a direct interaction of the viewer with his/her own image, as well as with the images of the other people in the space. The "traditional" concept in virtual reality is one of a person dealing with images and objects from a virtual or imaginary world. In "Cartesian Chaos," the person interacts with images from the real world, specifically, the images of the people sharing the "space" with him/her. Also, the interface is a real, active device, not something as passive as a data glove or virtual wand as in other systems. The person deals with an interface which is a direct representation of the image with real tactile feedback.

The "real" space is defined by the viewpoint of a video camera. This image is read in and digitized by a Silicon Graphics 320VGX computer.

The interaction is through a short wooden platform (2.5m x 2.0m x 2cm) covered with 50 square wooden tiles. Attached to the bottom of the tiles are sensors which measure how much the tile bends under the weight of the viewer(s). These measurements are read in by an external computer with an A/D converter. These numbers are then transferred to the Silicon Graphics computer via serial connection between the two machines. The computer then applies the measurements as forces which affect a set of imaginary springs. The springs, calculated using physical laws, transmit the forces throughout the grid. The image from the real world is then texture-mapped onto the surface of this grid. The final effect is that, when the viewer walks across or jumps on these tiles, the image on the screen (video projection) is deformed—perspective being calculated from the force used to bend the wooden tile. The viewer will deform a projected image of himself and other people in the viewer space by stepping around. What the users are interacting with is an image of the space and of themselves as observers (in real time), which they can deform by changing their position on the platform and also by their style of moving (fast, slow, large steps, heavy or light steps, etc). In fact, the computer creates a simulation of the image as if the screen were of rubber. The origin of the perspective distortion is directly related to the viewers' position on the floor.

What makes this piece different from other virtual reality simulators is that it gives the user:

I: A direct and real-time feedback of the virtual object. (You feel the wood bending.)

II: A realistic image of the user's environment instead of an iconic or symbolic representation of the "space."

What makes this piece different from the "Tangible Image":

I: The viewer is interacting with the piece just by his/her presence on the floor, while in the "Tangible Image" the person must actively touch the rubber screen.

II: The installation of the "Tangible Image" had the interface outside of the view of the camera, while in "Cartesian Chaos" the floor is directly centered in the space of the video.

Interactive Evolution

Karl Sims

The most fascinating and complex entities in our world are still those that have occurred naturally. Life itself, the human mind, language, and many other phenomena have all emerged from natural biological processes without the presence of a purposeful designer.

Many of these same natural processes can be performed in simulation on computers. As more and more powerful computers continue to be built, we can expect many intriguing and complex artificial results to emerge from these simulations. Whether the emerging virtual entities will qualify for the category of "life" or not is subject to debate, but in either case these simulated lifelike processes give us new methods for the creation of complexity. In some ways, like life itself, the complexity arising from these simulations can surpass what we are capable of designing with traditional tools or even understanding.

Much of my work involves the simulation of a specific natural process: evolution. Evolution consists of a simple cycle. The most "fit" entities in a population survive and reproduce. The resulting offspring are copies or combinations of their parents but often with random alterations or mutations. Some offspring may be improvements on their parents, and as only the most fit of each new generation of offspring continue to reproduce, the population as a whole can slowly improve.

In simulation, fitness can be provided interactively by a human observer at each step of the cycle—

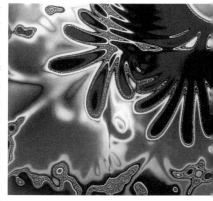

Karl Sims: Genetic Images

those that are selected as being most aesthetically interesting survive and reproduce. Images, virtual worlds, or even animations can be interactively evolved in this way with the user imposing survival criteria in a godlike manner. This is a method for creating and exploring complexity that does not require human understanding of the specific processes involved.

Fragments of computer code are the chromosomes that describe the growth process of these virtual entities. The computer code, like DNA, is the genotype, and the virtual result, like an organism, is the phenotype.

A "genetic language" is defined which is composed of a set of primitive mathematical functions that can be assembled into complete genetic growth instructions. Mutations alter these coded instructions and can sometimes cause new functions and parameters to be included, potentially increasing the resulting level of complexity.

A nearly infinite number of genetic codes and corresponding results are possible, and these evolutionary simulations can essentially "invent" new types of equations and methods for generating images or other virtual entities.

This is an unusual collaboration between humans and machine: the humans supply decisions of visual aesthetics, and the computer supplies the mathematical ability for generating, mating, and mutating complex virtual entities. The user is not required to understand the technical equations involved. The computer can only experiment at random with no sense of aesthetics—but this combination of human and machine abilities permits the creation of results that neither of the two could produce alone.

Simulation Room

Simulation Room—Mosaic of Mobile Data Sound—A Walkable Data Bank

Two rooms, a real room and its computer model. Equipped with a navigation aid (private eye) and a position finding system (space tracking), the visitor moves in a sound data bank which constantly restructures itself through the implemented self-organization. The visitor acts likewise in the real room as in the virtual model and creates a real-time composition and its visualization with the aid of a sensor, by means of which he sets off the mobile sound data.

The open data bank contains personal statements of a sound nature which incessantly change and actualize their composition following electronic and postal announcements, e.g. input via Internet. Every sound file, which is clearly recognizable by its addressee, is stored in the data bank, analysed in accordance with sound characteristics which are binary coded. The sound file receives a real-space as well as a system-internal allocation. Of course, it can be found locally at any time but, at the same time, is a part of two dynamic systems:

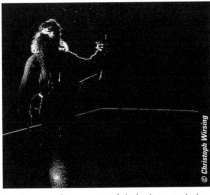

© Christoph Wirsing

1. The self-organization. The sound data become mobile elements in real space and their equivalent in virtual space. On account of their characteristics, self-similar groups form and the chaotic behaviour of the entire system is determined by means of simple, implemented rules.
2. The interaction. The behaviour of the entire system reacts to the movements of the actor in the sound chamber.

Every statement, being a personal acoustic expression of the sender with an individual sound structure, forms a mosaic piece of composition which is produced by a visitor in the real space. The real-time composition resulting from this (with the variables: duration, volume, directions, setup of the sound pieces) is the directly perceptible result of physical action within a virtual space produced by computers and the information stored and administrated there.

smdk is a project which did not emerge as a result of one individual artist's personality or

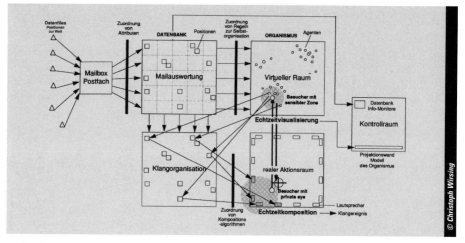

© Christoph Wirsing

genius force of imagination. A self-dynamics developing during the production process and arising from the resistances (confrontations of opposing cognition possibilities proffered by scientists and artists) emerges, formulates the rules behind the work. These lead to a functional model which is empirically experienced, personally transformed, and useable by the visitor.

Computer scientists and artists produced a framework for a multitude of individual experiences that are non-calculable and non-reproducible by a visitor, equally, with the aid of efficient, mechanical data processing. The self-organization of the system, the direct interactivity of a real room with its synthetic, simulated model, the real-time composition of acoustic foreign material and its fragmentation, the continual visualization of computing operations, and the openness of the entire system over networks externally, form a chaotically structured complexity that cannot be overcome by the visitor in its entirety. As a result, every visitor develops individual orientation routes within a "living" virtual organism.

KR+cF—Knowbotic Research

Which perceptible form calls for a mathematical formula, an abstract thought, an emotion, a memory, the energy behind a conflict, when the methods of pure linguistic description are not sufficient to convey and conserve?

KR+cF uses information systems, communication networks' knowledge stores and files in order to put them together again as such, split and analysed:

Computers speak their own source code (*Sprachprogramm*, 1991), media texts from live zapped TV programmes are reduced to their linguistic and acoustic substance, at the same time being reflected philosophically and in terms of sound and presented as a live concert (*ping Operation pong*, with Friedrich Kittler, 1992), documented reality (*Medienbilder*) is formally reduced by digital manipulation and is iconographically analysed (*Archive*, 1992), language grammalogues, go-commands from commercial data networks satirize their information value and react in a glass data room to a model area of gestic instructions provided by a visitor (*hypervirus*, 1992).

Those involved in the smdk project are, besides the three principal members: Christian Hübler (concept, realization), Alexander Tuchacek (real-time composition), and Yvonne Wilhelm (visualization), George Fleischmann (self-organization, complex systems), Detlev Schwabe (data bank and system management), Michael Hoch (sound analyses, private eye), Will Bauer (space tracking), Tobias Pfeil (data brooking), Rajele Jain and Udo Zyber (technical installation).

Interactive Plant Growing

Conceptual and Aesthetic Aspects

The rate of growth deserves to be studied as a necessary preliminary to the theoretical study of form, and organic form itself is found, mathematically speaking, to be a function of time. . . . We might call the form of an organism an event in space-time, and not merely a configuration in space.
D'Arcy Thompson, *On Growth and Form,* Cambridge University Press, 1942

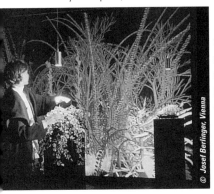

© Josef Berlinger, Vienna

Interactive Plant Growing is an installation that deals with the principles of virtual plant growth and the real-time modification of these three-dimensional plants in the virtual space of a 3-D graphics computer (Silicon Graphics). Modifications of these "artificially living plant organisms" are based on development and evolution over time. The artificial growth of program-based plants is an expression of the desire to discover principles of development and growth in real life, principles traditionally defined by the transformations and morphogenesis of certain organisms.

Interactive Plant Growing connects the real-time growing of virtual plants in the three-dimensional space of the computer to real living plants, which can be touched or approached by human viewers.

Human-Plant Interaction

By touching real plants or moving their hands toward them, human viewers can influence and control in real time the virtual growth of 25 or more program-based plants, which are simultaneously displayed on a video screen in front of the viewers. By forming a sensitive interaction with the real plants, the viewers also become part of the installation. They decide how this interaction is conducted and how growth will take place on the screen.

The distance modulations of the viewers' hands directly affect the appearance of the virtual plants, determining whether they are ferns, mosses, trees, vines, or a cleansing plant ("killer plant").

By sending different data values to the interface, which connects the plants and the growing program, the appearance of the virtual plants can be modified and varied. The viewers can control the size of the virtual plants, direct their rotation, modify their shapes, change the colour, and control new positions of the same type of plant.

Each virtual plant species has at least six different variations, but generally there are more possibilities than just 25 variations of five plants, since the size, rotation, colour, and translation can be modified for each type of plant as well.

All variations ultimately depend on the viewers' sensitivities in finding the different levels of approximation distances, because they are responsible for the different events during growth.

Since it takes some time for the viewer to discover the different levels needed for modulating the virtual plants, he or she will develop a higher sensitivity to and awareness of real plants.

Christa Sommerer / Laurent Mignonneau

Programming

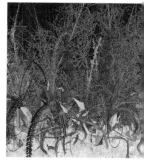

In *Interactive Plant Growing* artificial plants, programmed by Laurent Mignonneau and Christa Sommerer on a Silicon Graphics computer, grow in a virtual three-dimensional space.

This virtual growing is based on algorithms developed specifically for the different morphological characteristics in real plant differentiation. Virtual growing is not based on the same principles as real growing, but the appearance of movement and differentiation and determinism during this development process is similar.

A new method of differentiation was developed for the program. It features special randomizing parameters, which are used as "artificial growth and differentiation regulators." These randomizing parameters determine the morphology of the organisms by controlling their variations in form.

This leads us to different botanical growth forms. Plants like ferns, vines, or mosses change their appearance depending on defined randomizing variables for size, length, rotation, translation, angle, and colour. This idea of advanced randomizing could be compared by analogy to the concept of "random walk."

The limits of randomizing could be viewed as determination, while the human-plant randomizing itself can be viewed as differentiation.

Technique

Technically speaking, the electrical potential difference or voltage between humans and plants is measured through the living plants. This voltage difference varies depending on the hand-plant distance, and the sensibility of the plant ranges from 0 to about 70 cm in space, depending on the size and morphology of the real plant.

A special protocol (interface program) between computer and converter makes sure that each data value coming from each plant is interpreted in synchronized real time by the growing program during the drawing of the virtual plants.

All data values (derived from the viewer-plant interaction) are now interpreted as variables in the growing program. Each value is responsible for specific growing events: changing rotation, scaling, translation, location, or colour.

Installation Space

In the dark 12 x 6-meter installation space, five different real plants are placed on five wooden columns in front of a high resolution 4 x 3-meter video projection screen. All plants are connected by an interface to a 3-D Silicon Graphics computer, which sends its data signals from the screen to a high resolution RGB video data projector (80 kHz , 650 Lux). This data projector sends the growing pictures to the projection screen in real time.

Feedback

From the feedback of the virtual growth on the screen, the viewers can react to these events and control and modify the growing process. Five or more people can interact at the same time with the five real plants in the installation space. All events depend exclusively on the human-plant interaction.

Audience Participation

CINEMATRIX™

Loren and Rachel Carpenter

The patented CINEMATRIX™ Interactive Entertainment Systems gives each person in an audience the real-time capability to interact with images on a screen and thus play games together, answer questions, create patterns, and make decisions about adventures in a collective virtual world. This invention grew from the innovative world of computer graphics along with advances in computer hardware enabling new forms of interactivity to arise. We propose a unique experience for Linz, to set up the experience outdoors for a standing crowd. We also intend to push the boundaries of what is possible in the experience itself. Necessarily, the games have been fairly simple up until now. We think that it is possible for groups to interact and cooperate to create forms using genetic algorithms. Linz the perfect place to try this out.

Communication with Humans

Communication is unpredictable at the best of times. The more people you try to communicate with just accentuates the possibilities for misunderstanding and confusion. Having a few calibrating exercises at the beginning helps people to know that the system is working and that they are being represented. Before giving explanations, it is important for the audience to experiment with the wands, which can produce some fun surprises. Then the group can be asked to show one color and they can see it up on the screen. When the group changes the color they are showing, it changes correspondingly on the screen. The participants can then be divided into groups and reproduce the exercise to get an even better idea of where their position is on the screen and to get a feeling for the system when it's working.

Using passive reflectors as an interface allows the freedom of no wires and immediate feedback. People can respond without complicated button-pushing or the moving of levers. It helps for people to have a familiarity with the concept of the game and for the goal to be simple. Large crowds do not want to listen to a lot of rules. The games need to be visually understandable with the right mix of action and challenge.

Hardware and Software Challenges

For the original audience participation event at SIGGRAPH '91, we only had five months to invent the system and get it working. Many questions had to get answered and many problems had to be solved. The first big question was interface. How was the audience going to send a signal to the computer in a cost-effective, safe way? Flashlights would be too expensive; wiring each seat was out of the question. How about reflecting light? The resulting device of combined "Reflexite" on a paint stick is referred to as a "wand." The requirements for designing any game with this system begin with the constraints of the reflective device. Locating the players is a big technical challenge. The red or green reflected light signal needs to be picked up by video cameras and communicated to the computer, which deciphers the information according to the game or task on the screen. To differentiate each person's signal is a top priority; each person needs to be represented. The camera sees a mass of spots that need to be differentiated by the computer. Forming a seating chart is one way to partially define where each person is. There are additional considerations of extra movement, reflected light objects in the room. The solution is in software. The past three years of development have made it possible to get away from seating charts when needed. This new method will debut in Linz for Ars Electronica, known for being on the cutting edge of art and technology.

Each venue has its specifications and idiosyncrasies. Basic photographic principles apply. A wide-angle lens on the camera can see more if it has a greater distance. Cameras and lights need to be linked to power with red, green, blue, and sync going into the right ports in the computer. It is important that each person be represented.

The Games

It is important to establish that people are having real-time input as described in the introduction. Each game requires a small explanation. We try to emphasize games where people work together either in teams or with the entire group. One two-team game has a "paddle" on each side of the screen to hit a conference logo or whatever is appropriate for the event. Green makes the team's paddle move up and red makes it go down. If one side sees that their paddle needs to move up, they start to show the green side of their reflector to the cameras and lights. If everyone on their side showed green, the paddle goes up too far, so people need to moderate the signal by a few people showing red or putting their paddle down. These decisions have to be made quickly and become intuitive, producing a state of flow, which ends up being very exciting. New variations of this game are being created continually. The rotating cube is an exercise that requires the entire audience to cooperate. A multicolored cube is rotated on two axes, each controlled by one-half of the audience. Red rotates the cube one way and green rotates it the opposite way. The trick is to stop the cube with the blue side showing. It is a difficult problem, but an audience that is warmed up can quickly maneuver the cube into the required position. Flying an airplane requires very fine skills from the entire group of participants. One side controls pitch, the other yaw. This game has been undergoing rewrites to make it more exciting for groups to play.

The feedback on these games has given us ideas to keep in mind when developing new games. People really need to know where they are and how their reflector relates to the action. Asking questions with binary decisions may produce answers, but that process does not excite the crowd unless they are really interested in the subject matter and it is a competition. Sometimes groups divided up into competing teams can get very excited by true/false questions, because they can see instant results.

Games that require participants to let go of exactness and make intuitive decisions seem to put people in touch with each other in a different way, to go beyond the usual linear mode of thinking. That could be one of the reasons so many people got excited. The CINEMATRIX™ system provides the opportunity for people to work together in a way never before possible. It is still a young technology ready for new ideas. Some people have pointed out that there might be a possibility for people to use this in a way to control others when they got in an excited state. Since the entire experience is focused on personal choice, we think this is not likely, but we do own the patent for the US, the EC, Japan, and several other countries. It is our intention that the technology be used for people to have fun and to develop cooperation in the process. The genetic algorithm collaborative experience is new for Ars Electronica. The group will get to make choices about the collective creation of an organism. When each choice is made, the crowd will see the results instantly. More than one segment can be worked on at a time and the results will happen quickly. This is new; we don't know exactly what will happen or how many other new things will be invented in the meantime. That's what the cutting edge is all about.

Horizontal Radio—
24 Hours Live

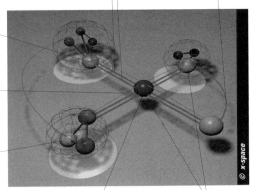

high-quality radio lines between
the main stations'
transmission lines-reception lines

additional link-up
(ISDN or telephone)

a station of a subnetwork
acts as the gateway to
the entire network

standard telephone lines to
control the audio mixer in the
router station

link-ups with various different
bandwidths

© x-space

4-way router via MIDI-controlled
audio mixers, stations can determine
from a remote location which signals
are to be fed to them

routers are high-performance
interfaces, and not
dramaturgical centers

Gerfried Stocker

Horizontal Radio: Communication as a Cybernetic System

Horizontal Radio is a telematic radio network project. It takes place simultaneously at different locations, in different media, and on different frequencies.

The starting point is the analogue cable and broadcasting network of the EBU (European Broadcasting Union), which serves as a primary telematic sphere of action for horizontal radio. Superimposed to this network is the Internet, which serves as a medium of access and distribution beyond the broadcasting range of the participating radio stations.

EBU: the European Broadcasting Union is an organisation of public broadcasting corporations. (Canadian and Australian broadcasters, as well as New Public Radio [USA] are associated members.)

The confrontations and interactions between the various media antipodes (distribution and interaction, analogue and digital media, synchrony and asynchrony) create a hypermedia network which links the intersections, and thus forms an interactive data ambience. The intersections become the scenes of live performances which sometimes involve the generation of soundscapes. A "virtual stage" manifests itself, which is based on interaction and telepresence, and on which the participating artists can meet for 24 hours.

Beyond its function as a medium of broadcasting, radio turns into an instrument and tool of an artistic activity which is not concerned with simply opening up lines and passing on what was received. Instead, local artistic events are influenced through a permanent exchange between the stations. The audience is real, but its presence only virtual. At any time, a member of the audience can switch sides and intervene actively in the artistic process.

Horizontal Radio forms part of the process of confronting the social and artistic implications of new media technologies.

The differentiation between sender and recipient, naming and interpreting, and politics and the general public disappears in the reality of telecommunication and information networks. Production, collection, distribution, and supervision (in the sense of surveillance) coincide in the network hypermedium. However, the potential equality of sender and recipient, and the possibility of switching between the two roles, will not become socially relevant until the social context of such operations, and the referential system determined by them, will change.

Network Design: Configurations of Communication

Basically, a project like Horizontal Radio is orchestrated through the configuration of lines and channels, gateways and interfaces, and by determining frequency ranges and access rights.

The basic idea is to create a media structure which is as heterogeneous as possible. It is supposed to function as an experimental set-up within the field of tension generated by the various characteristics of transmission and communication. This field is also a result of the frictional relation between the isosynchronous character of radio and the asynchronous properties of digital data networks, which are dependent on their context and on the type of access (e.g. on-demand, random access, caching).

The strategy to ensure that participation is as simple and as widespread as possible is diversification.

Horizontal Radio: Instead of representing a vertical hierarchy of sender and recipient, it creates a platform for the exchange of transmissions.

Transmission: mechanism by which power is transmitted from engine to axle. Transmit: allow to pass through, be a medium for, serve to communicate.

The individual radio station can determine its role in the network by making its own selection of artists.

Regional Subnetworks: The Backbone of Horizontal Radio

The regional subnetworks represent a structure of technologically sophisticated bases. They serve as docking stations, at which participants can easily connect themselves to the network. These docking stations are responsible for passing on, distributing, and routing the information circulating in the network.

A router is used when regional and superregional networks are connected. It is responsible for linking the various stations and for distributing information correctly.

The regional subnetworks not only serve as geographical bridges, but also as gateways between different media and frequencies. As a consequence, they create the preconditions for the desired decentralised structure, in which the individual station does not have to build up links to all other stations in order to be connected to them.

The following devices are employed as carrier media:

- analogue modulation lines for the transmission of hi-fi audio signals (stereo/mono),
- SDN and standard telephone lines with corresponding frequency range reductions (7 kHz; 3.4 kHz),
- data transmission lines in the shape of ISDN or standard telephone lines for the remote access to musical computer equipment (e.g. for the purpose of real-time sound installations),

Gerfried Stocker *Horizontal Radio—24 Hours Live*

- the Internet as a caching server, and as a medium of communication, interaction, and distribution as well as a stage for conferences (telnet, ftp, irc, www, social netbrowser, mbone),
- transponders on EUTELSAT II-F4 for the flow of signals between European stations, and on INTELSAT for the overseas connection,
- VHF, MW, and SW.

The resulting differences in sound quality serve as an artistic tool, and provide a means of orientation as regards the geographical areas and media covered by Horizontal Radio. Differences in sound turn into "soundscape signatures," which help us to identify senders acoustically.

Here is an example of how it could work. There could be a common starting point (a theme? a text? a concept? a picture? a theory?) that is the same for everyone to start from. Then, receiving things from the others would add to our own thought and actions. We could ourselves add to it or choose to leave it as it is for broadcasting here. And the listener would sense the distance (both geographical and cultural) throughout the hours or the whole day, in that the audio content would evolve through the cultural filtering and the technical filtering.
Jocelyn Robert (CAN)

Such a network environment implies an artistic conception that places less emphasis on primary production and more on dialogic distribution and administration.

Migration: The Principal Theme of the Project

(f. Lat. migrare—to move from one place to another) Migration—permanent emigration or immigration of individuals or groups from one population into a similar population.
Under certain circumstances, isolation can produce new subspecies, or, after a longer period, new species in their own right. A migration in which no settlement occurs is referred to as passage (permigration). A special form of migration is constituted by an invasion.

On the one hand, migration can be seen as a metaphor for a changing society and the transition to a culture of telecommunication and telepresence, in which the "act of populating transmission and transport times will replace the act of populating traditional habitats" (Virilio). On the other, it symbolises the migration of individuals, their ideas, and their socio-cultural paradigms and identities. The metaphor becomes the journey, the permigration, which serves as the structural principle of the artistic activities in the net, and as a model of organising permanent data flow.

The information entered into the network passes through
- various levels (aggregate states) of its technological reproduction in the various media,
- various levels of interactive and artistic processing and manipulating,
- the geographical area covered by the participating media.

Conferences and Communication Intervals: The Timetable of the Network

The structure of the network is open, and the participating media show divergent temporal characteristics. These characteristics manifest themselves not only in different forms of access to information, but also in different methods of reception and interaction. This structural openness and temporal divergence imply a form of organisation which is utterly different from traditional broadcasting schemes. It abandons long-term advance planning, and is based on communication intervals. The centres of activity within the system (its centres of gravity) shift along certain thematic guidelines (i.e.

correspondences). The morphological and temporal parameters of the social environment created by communication are therefore unstable, and the environment itself is fluid.

Horizontal Radio: a period of 24 hours, during which stations
- log in for a certain time,
- repeatedly make brief interventions,
- remain on-line for the whole time.

The term "conference" was introduced to denote communication within this temporal organisation structure. The conference topics are determined by the participating radio stations. When a station brings up a subject, it becomes the conference host and the temporary centre of the network. The centre serves as a meeting place, at which actions can be focussed on certain regions of the net.

Participants register for certain conference topics, have private discussions within the organisational framework of a conference, intervene in panel discussions, or simply listen.

The Global Information Machine

Horizontal Radio must be seen as a further development of earlier simultaneous telematic projects of the '90s. Especially important in this context are the projects *Chipradio* (92), *Realtime* (93), and *State of Transition* (94), which were realised for TRANSIT and the ORF-KUNSTRADIO. These projects took a network of simultaneous live performances as a starting point and then used various means of communication (radio, television, telephone, data networks) in order to explore the communicative potential of mass media. Special emphasis was placed on strategies to reconcile the requirements of linear, one-way media, with the diametrically opposed requirements of open communication networks.

Horizontal Radio explicitly refers to the period of the pioneers of telecommunication art. In Austria, this was roughly the time between 1979 and 1986. It is indeed no coincidence, that artists like Robert Adrian X (Vienna) and Art Pool (Budapest) participate in this project, because they are normally associated with exactly that period. Art Pool participated in the first telecommunication project to link artists in Western and Eastern Europe (*Telefonmusik*, 1983). It was initiated by Robert Adrian X, who also realised a series of other projects.

Therefore, Horizontal Radio not only reflects the technological development and changing characteristics of the media, but also the political changes. Today, the situation is such that radio stations in Russia and Hungary are able to contribute to a telecommunication project that incorporates more than just the transmission of telephone music, whereas in Sarajevo and some other places perhaps not much has changed in this respect.

The 24-hour schedule is a conscious reference to another project, which was realised at the Ars Electronica in 1982: *Die Welt in 24 Stunden (The World In 24 Hours)*. Its topic was the position of artistic production within a sphere of action that forms part of the media—a sphere of action which is to a large extent pre-set and pre-structured by its intrinsic apparatus. The project was developed and directed by Robert Adrian X, and its character is still exemplary. Its "mediatised situation" linked artists in 16 cities and three continents for 24 hours (cf. Reinhard Braun in: *Medien.Kunst.Passagen.* 2/94). *Die Welt in 24 Stunden* was the most comprehensive and ambitious art project that had ever been realised in low tech, i.e. in the international telephone network. First of all, an international network of artists and groups had to be formed, which all had to submit contributions via slow scan TV, fax, computer mailbox/conference, and telephone, or should at least use one of these media. At local noontime, the individual stations were called from Linz. The project started at 12.00 CET, on September 27, followed the sun around the globe, and ended on September 28, again at 12.00 CET.

The initial situation, and the way the project was carried out by installing and continuously operating numerous devices for the transmission of data, both already indicate that "Die Welt in 24 Stunden" was not conceptualised to produce objects or results which could be considered works of art (e.g. art faxes). Its objective was to create and to continue dialogic exchange as such, i.e. to establish special relations between the participants, and thereby produce communicative events. In a certain sense, the composition of the project already constitutes the work itself . . . The subject of a project like "Die Welt in 24 Stunden" is the global "information machine," a term coined by Richard Kriesche.
Translated from Reinhard Braun, *Medien.Kunst.Passagen,* 2/94

In 1995, the request of art itself has become more urgent. The global information machine remains the most significant theme of projects like Horizontal Radio.

Linz: The Network Monitor and Caching Server of Horizontal Radio

Linz is not the centre of the network. Although many network lines may intersect here, there is no central directorate pulling the strings behind the artistic activities. The network components on the radio and data level are configured in such a way that access from outside is possible. If a station establishes a connection with Linz, it is in control of the lines and of the audio channel mix. In the ORF's studio in Linz, Horizontal Radio is represented as a multimedia network monitor in the shape of an installation displaying the positions and activities of the individual stations. The emphasis is not on the production of data currents, but on watching and interpreting them. Electronic/telematic space is not explored by covering distances, but by opening up transmission channels and frequencies.

The grid of lines inscribed into this space defines only one aspect of its potential, but not its shape and dimensions (its range). Its dimensions are determined by evidence and coincidence, and are therefore dependent on the parameters of time. Wherever communication takes place, there is a spatial junction, the coordinates and vectors of which are recorded and represented in the installation. It is not the contents of communication that are on display, but the context under which communication was started, and the dynamic, unstable relations between centres of activity. These centres serve as meeting places, determine the broadcasting scheme of the participating radio stations, and become so-called "init-points" for the events in the Internet.

The traces of data currents and their producers are rendered as acoustic "mappings" in real space in the foyer of the ORF's studio in Linz (this process is analogous to the method of "texture mapping" in computer graphics). Thus, the different transmission speeds and frequencies, the spatial parameters of the virtual data reality between various geographic locations, turn into acoustic characteristics of the soundscape created by the installation in Linz.

In addition, Linz plays the role of a temporary caching server for the purpose of synchronising the individual stations.

Covering geographical distances by way of electromagnetic transmission has obscured the identity of distant places, because that identity is based on division. The paradigms of the industrial revolution govern the one-way medium radio. Its electronic space is still rigidly (isosynchronously) linked with the temporal axis. The use of digital communication technology results in a loss of temporal continuity typical for multidirectional networks. Synchronisation does not take place in linear, periodic impulses, but whenever correspondence occurs.

This divergence actually prevents transparent transitions between the parallel realities established by the two different types of media. The installation in Linz, however, creates osmotic interfaces between them. The act of transmitting data to the other side leaves traces that are similar to the afterglow on the fluorescent screen of a cathode ray tube.

Horizontal Radio—24 hours live
On the frequencies of 22 radio stations in Africa, Australia, Canada, Europe, the USA, in the Internet,
and at the network intersections in Athens, Belgrade, Berlin, Bologna, Bolzano, Budapest, Denver,
Helsinki, Innsbruck, Jerusalem, Linz, London, Madrid, Montreal, Moscow, Munich, Naples, New York,
Quebec, Rome, San Marino, Sarajevo, Sydney, Stockholm, Tel Aviv, Vancouver.
From June 22, 12.00 hrs, to June 23, 12.00 hrs.

A co-production between the Ars Acustica experts of the EBU (the European Broadcasting Union) and
TRANSIT—the ORF's regional studios in Tyrol and Upper Austria, ORF KUNSTRADIO (the ORF's radio
art programme), Ars Electronica 95, and Kapsch AG.

Planning and Coordination:
Gerfried Stocker—x-space.
Heidi Grundmann—ORF KUNSTRADIO

What's That Supposed to Be, What's Program?

Just Merrit

Reality isn't bygone; to me, it seems to be hidden in the here-and-now. So what's the point of a rearview mirror, which defines per se "what lies behind us," regardless of which gear we're in, Drive or Reverse—and not even a hasty change of course lets us move forward.

And why "towards"? "In the Rearview Mirror: The Reality" would be wrong, since by no means does reality present itself so clearly, not even in retrospect (regarded in the past, peering into the past). At best, the way to get there can be sought in the mirror. "Objects may be closer than they appear!" is

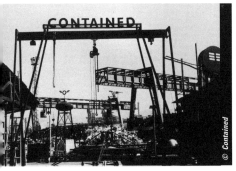

© Contained

a warning sensibly posted on the rearview mirrors of some American cars. And that might be it, what fascinates us, what the "American" in us would like so very much to see. Possibly, the automobile transfers us into an energetic form of non-consisting, purity on an experimental basis. If everything is forever and everywhere, then it must, at the same time, be very close.

But we are not yet so close to this "state of light" as we imagine in our dreams. In an overzealousness approaching religious fervor, we hope that a new age has actually dawned, one that enables us to link proximity and distance and to experience reality in a never-ending simultaneity. But the newness of the simultaneity remains, in our heads as in our formulas, vague and immature. So we flee to definitions and metaphors of transition, creating a "liquid age"—of emergent fluidity, amorphousness, and a dissolution of material. We dwell precisely upon this materiality, distorted into an idealized quasi-nostalgia. Wistfully, we gaze into the rearview mirror at our own material make-up, our traditional, historically coherent context and search without any orientation for an actuality we believe we have lost.

There seems to be no other way to explain our melancholy contemplation of iron, the most concrete of all materials fashioned by the human hand. When IKEA sells iron spoons with the proviso that they may possibly decay (rust), then we have found the evidence we seek. When an adolescent oriented toward disorientation considers this spoon to be an example of cool Industrial Design and buys it, then it can be no wonder that magazines like *Wired* stylize former "Luddites" into "cybernauts."

In my day, at least, it was still the Myth of Evil that was attached to iron *(Blade Runner)*. Understandably, we "demographically insignificant Generation X dinosaurs," obsessed with hardware, demanded access to the means of production. Autonomy by means of unexplained conditions of ownership and alienating the "evil" material to a new purpose were both our maxims and dreams. More impressed than influenced by the early Heroes of the Industrial Culture (Throbbing Cristle, SRL), we felt both compassion for the steelworkers and identification with their access to hardware, as well as fascination for the immediacy and directness of the production machinery. This was precisely the background from which Contained came into being. A conglomeration of adventurous ideas, carved out with passionate obsession in the heart of a steelworks (VOEST Alpine), mostly due to me but never borne forward by me alone. For 54 months, this construction of man and material (with considerable wear and tear on both) grew rampant like a malignant tumor at a location which I, bourgeois junior high school boy that I was, took to be at a maximum distance from my family home and my origins, and the place where life could be felt most directly.

Thus, the rearview mirror also serves a totally banal function, a recollection and a consideration of the possible powers of this malignancy: there can hardly have been another place like this one, in which the confrontation of industrial artists (from the builders of machines to the constructors of ideologies) with the background to which they referred was a more direct one. Nothing dragged the petit bourgeois roots so ruthlessly out of earthy sensuality and into the light. Nowhere else is it so delightful to rummage through things as they already are without ulterior considerations regarding problems of art— in one room, an elk's head nailed to the wall, a souvenir of geographical arrogance (mass tourism), invokes a presumption of taste, the cultural lives and doings of go-kart racers and dog trainers suggests a degree of civilization. Where else are the giddy ceremonies of a world which so openly celebrates both itself and the circumstance of its demise—the extreme romanticism of a "back to culture" that has long existed only on the deathbeds of the museums?

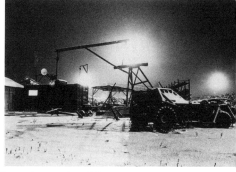

That's why the "rearview mirror" is very simple to construct!

Friends are invited and set out, unprotected, for a period of 10 days, to expose themselves to the locality and to react with their various means and strategies to that which they find. Thereby, the work of the men of steel and that of the children of the city of steel are called into account, just as the feeling of strangeness which arises out of the impossibility of an understanding of life without art.

(The results are presented in a small series of presentations, an exhibition, a round of discussions and a video series.)*

<there is no such thing as paradise>

Hermann Atzlinger
The product itself does not stand in the foreground but rather the fascination of those variables which make it possible.

Tina Auer
Playing for its own sake, pursued in the diversity of materials and media; to newly define the significance of conditions by means of minimal changes; certain situations in connection with a newly construed context occasionally result in a harmonious relationship which opens our eyes to beauty; functioning in and of themselves, they masterfully defy rational structures and permit us to see that which had been familiar and prosaic in a radiant new light.

*(Projects are on www.aec.at)

Sam Auinger

Grew up where the country meets the city . . . the monastery (St. Florian) here, the industry (VOEST) there . . . in still-functioning tradition . . . there was music (Bruckner's organ) in the church and a radio at home . . . blindfolded, we played "which car's comin' up the mountain?" . . . a VW Beetle was easy . . . an iron pipe to make noise, my favorite toy (. . .) then I was in a band and things started to get English . . . we almost never sounded good . . . I wanna be more serious, I wanna get over the "tralla tralla" . . . then . . . Involvement with composition, psychoacoustics and sound design . . . motion makes sound . . . spaces and materials have a sound . . . my heart beats a rhythm . . . I wanna get closer to my dreams . . .

Nicolas Anatol Baginsky

Baginsky's machines, the artificiality of laboratories is artistically treated. He takes up a question inherited from the tradition of scientists and mechanical engineers—what distinguishes human beings?—and he responds as an artist. Human beings are not perfectly calculable creatures, and humanity begins at that point where an individual wrestles with this question of what is human. Baginsky does so by giving expression to strange and awkward customs by means of the motion of machines.

Todd Blair

Todd Blair's work has evolved from extensive collaborative work with artists concentrating in machine, performance, and sound art. He uses various industrial technologies to explore our relationship to culturally inherited industrial processes. Changing technologies, shifting perceptions, and the inclination for industry to retool has yielded abundant source materials for the projects. By focusing on the transformation of these remains, he has questioned our standard relationship to the industrial environment.

Tim Boykett

Tim Boykett is, amongst many things, a mathematician, and is interested fundamentally in emergent structure. Whether it's in groups of people, collections of axioms, or interconnected electromechanical systems, the emergent (and usually unexpected) collective properties are his concern. Collaborative work naturally forms a major part of his efforts, though the product-based success of this collaboration is immaterial; the emergent character of the group work in the absence of "management science" is paramount. Warning: DO NOT COLLABORATE!

Brass Band of VOEST-ALPINE Linz

Even before 1950, co-workers in the former VOEST got together to play music in their spare time. That year, the VOEST Works Brass Band was formally founded and today this impressive Blasorchester includes approximately 55 musicians. Playing in marching formation and wearing the traditional festive costume of mining and metal workers, the group has performed at a wide variety of events including official state visits, jubilees, company celebrations, and open-air concerts, at which these outstandingly trained musicians never fail to win the hearts of their listeners.

Denise Caruso

A longtime analyst and observer of the industries of digital technology and interactive media, Denise Caruso writes the Digital Commerce column for the *New York Times* and is executive producer of Spotlight, an executive conference for the interactive media industry. Caruso has served on the board of directors of the Electronic Frontier Foundation, and was elected to the board of the Institute for Alternative Journalism in 1995. She holds a BA in English from California Polytechnic State University in San Luis Obispo, California, and lives and works in San Francisco.

Tatjana Didenko

Tatjana Didenko has been a musicologist and television producer for Russian State TV Moscow since 1990. Her outstanding productions have been shown in film and media art festivals internationally. Her unselfish production assistance to Russian artists, and to artists from around the world when they visit Moscow, is legendary. She is a member of the New Screen Technology Association. In 1995 she was the Russian TV producer for Checkpoint 95, a live television event between New York, Moscow, and Linz for the Ars Electronica.

John Duncan

John Duncan's most recent work includes "The Crackling," released on Trente Oiseaux (Germany), composed with Max Springer, made at the Stanford Linear Accelerator Center (SLAC) for subatomic particle research in Stanford, California; "Icons," a series of 4-meter-high macro-closeup photographs of the vaginas of six women shot in infrared black-and-white film, with accompanying brush drawings of the photographic images drawn in his blood; and The Ruud.E.Memorial Choir/Psychonaut, an event for 30-voice choir, released as a 7' clear-vinyl EP (USA).

Chip Flynn

Peoplehater is a collaborative performance coalition started by Chip Flynn. The group creates environments where the distinctions between machines, carnivals, and monsters break down. We are left somewhere in the shadows between dream and nightmare. Through a team of technicians, seeking redirected amusement, Peoplehater engages us in performances likened to a mechanical puppet show from hell.

L. A. Gladsjø

Rearview Mirror on Technology

As we speed towards an unknown future, this program of films looks back at previous forms of industrial culture. Perhaps within these documents, culled from the archives of Communist, Nazi, and capitalist societies, there are clues to reimagining our relationship to technology. In addition to this historical perspective, the program includes glimpses of new paradigms offered by artists and other visionaries experimenting with possible forms that this relationship may take in the future.

Brett Goldstone

Brett Goldstone's demystification of how mechanical power sources work has drawn him away from traditional applications of kinetic elements such as entertainment and spectacle, and has imbued the works with an underlying political and social significance. He is showing in Europe for the first time at Rearview Mirror to Reality. His aesthetic interests are focused on producing electric motors, steam engines, and water turbines that are primary sculptures. These pieces are also power sources for installations of secondary kinetic sculptures.

Matt Heckert

San Francisco-based sound artist Matt Heckert's Mechanical Sound Orchestra is an ensemble of kinetic machines, conceived and fabricated to generate sounds that surpass regular orchestral instruments in visual dynamics and acoustic ability. The MSO creates a theatrical event through a range of instruments and compositions that incorporate the specification of its performance site. In its instrumentation from the rhythmic section to a string part and virtuoso soloists, the MSO reaches its goal of a kinetic sound sculpture.

Rudolf Heidebrecht

1 To remain human / 2 To try not to fall for ONE'S OWN tricks / 3 A young artist once came to Picasso and asked him: "Mr. Picasso, how can one understand art?" And Picasso responded by posing a question in return: "How can one understand the singing of a bird?" / 4 "You must love humanity; only in this way can humanity be understood. You may not regard anyone as too abject, no one as too hateful . . ."—Georg Büchner, Lenz / 5 "Dying is something terrible, the gods themselves have ordained it so. Since, if dying were something wonderful, the gods themselves would die."—Sappho / 6 "I get older and learn as I do so."—Solon of Athens

Erik Hobijn

Parasites live and feed on other plants and animals. Techno-Parasites use whatever technical systems or apparatuses they can find as hosts, drawing on their output, their energy supplies and cycles to procreate and grow. A Techno-Parasite can be a simple or a complex system that is attentive and adapts to its host's structure where its inventive struggle for survival causes technical disruptions. Techno-Parasites suck other machines empty, disrupt their circuits, effect power cuts, disable them, destroy them.

Kathy Rae Huffmann

Kathy Rae Huffman is a freelance curator, networker, and media art critic. Since 1991, Huffman has been based in Europe. She collaborates with HILUS intermediale Projektforschung,Vienna, where her collection of artists' videotapes and her library on media art are available for research use. Huffman conducts seminars and workshops, and lectures on art video, interactive TV, and the history of artists and technology. Her research into the theory and practices surrounding Cyber-intimacy has been presented as a lecture performance internationally.

Laura Kikauka

One non-biographical-style miniblurb about Laura Kikauka, (self-defined) technonymph & profi-basher: I am a collect-aholic and can usually be found playing in the entropy of my continuously growing inventory of perturbing objects. I often claim that I am not searching for them, but they find me . . . like a magnet attracts certain metals. My passionate interests lie in the world of electronics and mechanics (which include computer interfacing, circuit design, audio, video, holography, plastics, and welding) . . . even though I seem to be have been born in a party dress !?!

Marc 9

The capitalist system will continue in its feverish attempt (fever = sign of sickness) to rescue the "free market economy" from its process of self-destruction. The winners are those who are selling us economic and currency unions and all kinds of other nonsense, who don't want to give us any time to think it over, which is why they are constantly telling us what to do and what to stop doing. Whoever doesn't fit in, or doesn't want to fit in, gets a taste of almighty capitalism. Whoever doesn't perform gets nothing or constantly less. Death to standards (and to capital)!

David Moises

It has to do with machines and playthings and machines that play; and it has to do with the playful approach to pieces of equipment, seeing them, what they can do and how they function (or don't). Machines carry out actions; they have a user/operator with whom they constitute a unit. For example, does someone playing Jojo on video see the fundamental structure of this toy/this machine? The player plays and the Jojo answers in its special mechanical JoJo language. This language is the machine itself.

Gordon Monahan

Gordon Monahan's works for piano, loudspeakers, video, and kinetic sculpture span various genres from avant-garde concert music to multimedia installation and sound art. John Cage once said, "At the piano, Gordon Monahan produces sounds we haven't heard before." Currently his main focus is called Multiple Machine Matrix, a system of computer-controlled kinetic instruments made from electronic surplus and industrial trash. MMM is a network of musical machine performers that are capable of moving complex layers of acoustically produced sound in space.

Mathias Moser

I believe that 90% of our words serve to veil the truth. One possibility to draw nearer to it is the light, whereby the question arises of whether every form of light scans only the reflection of surfaces for truth.

Linda Nilsson

Linda Nilsson has been exploring materials, experimenting and playing with their functions. This confrontation with sculpture and sound led her to develop moving sound sculpture. The essential aspect of her work is the invention of space/a place which reflects back on that form of research and the emerging room installations.

Fritz Ostermeier

I'm not interested in whether music/art/theory is of relevance. Who's speaking? Who even has the nerve to try to palm off on me as relevant his freakish psychological discharges. Fuck off, relevant thinkers! Fuck off, relevant artists! And you can take the thousands of relevantly creative little half-assed hobby dabblers right along with you. Anyone who doesn't have some obsessions to show can stay the hell away from me.

Martin Reiter

No-place for art, in which a thick-walled subterranean complex is equipped through an Internet address with what is currently the maximum possible speed capacity. The anchor is cast, laying it right on the line with a concrete block, which in its narrow interior represents a concentrated gallery situation. With the exhibition "Art and Action," the no-place becomes the national gallery. What has always been important, then and now, is the participation of so many artists and creative people from Austria and abroad, the direct cultural exchange and flow of information which came about and happened because of this building.

Die Romantiker

Dance music to hear and see. The guarantee of a successful event. Well known in the dance music scene for 10 years. With heart, musicianship, and the joy of performing, The Romantics provide for good times and audience enjoyment at all types of affairs and events with a musical rainbow including standards, Austrian and German pop classics, oldies, hits from the 50s, 60s, and 70s as well as today's sounds. Current CD: Heiss wie Feuer MPA 1201

Herbert Schager

"Everything here is the nastiest sarcasm, everything here is innocently childlike; everything gnashes and bares its fangs, whistles and shouts with glee. Unvarnished situation reports from the outside world are joined by encoded communiqués from interior realms housing monstrosities arduously kept in check. It is a primally compulsive and yet cultically systemized occurrence." Since I see myself rather as a painter and less as a conceptual or installation or any other kind of artist, what I would really like to do is put on a small exhibition entitled "Guardian of the Pictures."

Leo Schatzl
Seeing a lot is interesting

Manuel Schilcher
"The function of memory is the protection of impressions, remembrance's aim is their decomposition. Memory is essentially conservative, remembrance is destructive. Consciousness originates instead of the trace of remembrance. Becoming conscious and leaving behind a trace of memory for the same system are incompatible with each other. Remnants of remembrance are often strongest and longest-lived when the occurrence which left them behind has never entered one's awareness." (Gilles Deleuze)

Franz Selbst
Digital and analog machine in no context

Suzanne Stephanac
After resuming her freelance writing career for three years, Stephanac returned to Macworld in the fall of 1994 in order to launch Macworld Online, a service that resides on the World Wide Web (http://www.macworld.com) and America Online (keyword: macworld). As editor of Macworld Online she manages the content, technology, and, at least to date, the business sides of the new venture, relishing the chaos and potential inherent in such an endeavor. Stephanac is a faculty member with the Stanford Professional Publishing Course lecturing on web publishing.

Gordon W
As a fanatic ex-monk, performance interventionist, and founding neoist, Gordon W is feared within Toronto's subculture. W's "One World Cuisine" is renowned in film production circles for extravagant catering. (W. Shatner: "Best catering I've ever had on the Enterprise. Simply out of this world." And Jerry Lewis on W's Jerry Lewis ersatz lamb made from gluten: "Your meat was so tender, it was a party in my mouth.") In his Berlin irritainment concourses, Gordon W would like to serve up a new version of the biodynamic cuisine taught by Rudolf Steiner.

Doris Weichselbaumer
So what is it about anyway? / Make it up as you go. / Search (pathetic). Confusion (always). / > What is YOUR reality ? / games (>fool yourself!) / NOT getting STUCK AT ALL the wrong places. / Could you be serious?-------------------/We all know better. But you knew that.

Jim Whiting
Jim Whiting's pneumatic mechanical installations illustrate the rudimentary physical properties of technology. His reanimated wash tubs, driving bedrooms, and roving overcoats represent the natural extension of the biomechanical world to the existing structural mechanical world. His self-described muscle technology (a self-constructed cylinder consisting of fire hose) parallels the human-like endeavors of his creations. As advancements in technology challenge the current relationship we have to machines, his work reminds us that we model technological achievements on our own human systems.

Kathrin Wilkes

Kathrin Wilkes' work examines the adoption and subsequent creative abuse of technology and new media in the realm of machine, mixed media, and performance art. Using documentation together with demonstration as a platform, she investigates the reimaging of industrial culture by various artists. By juxtaposing work in progress with elements drawn from everyday life, a retrospective view of our connection to technology emerges.

Liz Young

Within my work I transform the audience's perception of the familiar and expected by altering the work to reflect a critical approach to our cultural paradigms. This transformation occurs with the use of materials and processes that are often contrary. Incongruity draws out the irony of the work and the elements of living are recontextualized to demonstrate the absurdity of modern-day living. This cynical approach to the nature of our lives is however not without the recognition of the power of human dignity. Perhaps this attitude underscores the basic relationship we have to the comedic tragedies that are omnipresent in our lives.

Erwin Zeppezauer

The apparatus as a time storage device concretizes moments snatched from the stream of time. Moments whose emergence into the foreground begins in one's head are projected outward in the picture or through it.

Berthold Zettelmeier

Surrounded by high-tech prostheses, the human being stands before his own body, its ways of functioning and its flaws. The further he searches, the clearer it becomes that an unknown is at the controls. Brain function processes are more complex than any AI. If the socially determinative parameters speed and information quantity are raised, however, speed and the compliance with it ignore the mind in favor of control by instinct. Stimulus reaction mechanisms appear, set up interfaces marking the borders of the will and serving as the basis for artistic creation.

Alex Zuljevic

Over and over again, we are stunned by the following lines from Hegel's *Phenomenology of the Spirit*: "The phases of human existence are not phases of happiness, the phases of happiness are like empty pages within it." Heinrich Himmler incisively formulated his idea of "final victory": "We have no more teachings to offer to the *Untermenschen*; all they need to know is one simple little lesson and the traffic signs so they can keep out of the way of our Mercedes." All that remain for us is to resist any form of absolutism and to fight all those who would impose their will upon us, so that the tender coating of fertility never tears.

The project Rückspiegel zur Realität (Rearview Mirror to Reality) is sponsored by BMWVK; O.OE. Kultur; Linz Kultur; V-A Stahl, ACE Auto & Scrap, S.F.

Parasite Visions:
Alternate, Intimate, and
Involuntary Experiences

Introduction

Stelarc

In previous actions the body has performed with technology attached (the Third Hand—actuated with EMG signals), technology inserted (the Stomach Sculpture—a self-illuminating, sound-emitting, opening/closing, extending and retracting mechanism operating in the stomach cavity) and Net-connected (the body becoming accessed and remotely activated by people in other places). The body has been augmented, invaded, and now becomes a host—not only for technology, but also for remote agents. Just as the Internet provides extensive and interactive ways of displaying, linking, and retrieving information and images, it may now allow unexpected ways of accessing, interfacing, and uploading the body itself. And instead of seeing the Internet as a means of fulfilling outmoded metaphysical desires of disembodiment, it offers on the contrary powerful individual and collective strategies for projecting body presence and extruding body awareness. The Internet does not hasten the disappearance of the body and the dissolution of the self—rather it generates new collective physical couplings and a telematic scaling of subjectivity. Such a body's authenticity will not be due to the coherence of its individuality but rather to its multiplicity of collaborating agents. What becomes important is not merely the body's identity, but its connectivity—not its mobility or location, but its interface . . .

Surface and Self: The Shedding of Skin

As a surface, skin was once the beginning of the world and simultaneously the boundary of the self. But now stretched, pierced, and penetrated by technology, the skin is no longer the smooth and sensuous surface of a site or a screen. Skin no longer signifies closure. The rupture of surface and skin means the erasure of inner and outer. An artwork has been inserted inside the body. The Stomach Sculpture—constructed for the Fifth Australian Sculpture Triennale in Melbourne, whose theme was site-specific work—was inserted 40 cm into the stomach cavity. Not as a prosthetic implant but as an aesthetic addition. The body becomes hollow—not the BWO but rather a body with art. The body is experienced as hollow, with no meaningful distinctions between public, private, and physiological spaces. The hollow body becomes a host, not for a self but simply for a sculpture. As interface, the skin is obsolete. The significance of the cyber may well reside in the act of the body shedding its skin.

The clothing of the body with membranes and embedding in them of alternate sensory and input/output devices creates the possibility of more intimate and enhanced interactivity. Subjectively, the body experiences itself as a more extruded system, rather than an enclosed structure. The self becomes situated beyond the skin. It is partly through this extrusion that the body becomes empty. But this emptiness is not through a lack but from the extrusion and extension of its capabilities, its new sensory antennae and its increasingly remote functioning . . .

Fractal Flesh

Consider a body that can extrude its awareness and action into other bodies or bits of bodies in other places. An alternate operational entity that is spatially distributed but electronically connected. A movement that you initiate in Melbourne would be displaced and manifested in another body in Rotterdam. A shifting, sliding awareness that is neither "all here" in this body nor "all there" in those bodies. This is not about a fragmented body but a multiplicity of bodies and parts of bodies prompting and remotely guiding each other. This is not about master-slave control mechanisms but feedback loops of alternate awareness, agency, and of split physiologies. Imagine one side of your body being remotely guided whilst the other side could collaborate with a local agency. You watch a part of your body move but you have neither initiated it nor are you contracting your muscles to produce it. Imagine the consequences and advantages of being a split body with voltage-in, inducing the behaviour of a remote agent, and voltage-out of your body to control peripheral devices. This would be a more complex and interesting body—not simply a single entity with one agency but one that would be a host for a multiplicity of remote and alien agents—of different physiologies and in varying locations. Certainly there may be justification, in some situations and for particular actions, to tele-operate a human arm rather than a robot manipulator—for if the task is to be performed in a non-hazardous location, then it might be an advantage to use a remote human arm—as it would be attached to another arm and a mobile, intelligent body. Consider a task begun by a body in one place, completed by another body in another place. Or the transmission and conditioning of a skill. The body not as a site of inscription but as a medium for the manifestation of remote agents. This physically split body may have one arm gesturing involuntarily (remotely actuated by an unknown agent), whilst the other arm is enhanced by an exoskeleton prosthesis to perform with exquisite skill and with extreme speed. A body capable of incorporating movement that from moment to moment would be a pure mechanic motion performed with neither memory nor desire . . .

Stimbod

What makes this possible is a touch-screen muscle stimulation system. A method has been developed that enables the body's movements to be programmed by touching the muscle sites on the computer model. Orange flesh maps the possible stimulation sites while red flesh indicates the actuated muscle(s). The sequence of motions can be replayed continuously with its loop function. As well as choreography by pressing, it is possible to paste sequences together from a library of gesture icons. The system allows stimulation of the programmed movement for analysis and evaluation before transmission to actuate the body. At a lower stimulation level it is a body prompting system. At a higher stimulation level it is a body actuation system. This is not about remote control of the body, but rather constructing bodies with split physiologies, operating with multiple agency. Was it Wittgenstein who asked what would remain if, in raising your arm, you could remove the intention of raising it? Ordinarily, you would associate intention with action (except, perhaps, in an instinctive motion—or if you have a pathological condition like Parkinson's disease). With Stimbod, though, that intention would be trans-

Stelarc *Parasite Visions*

mitted from another body elsewhere. There would be actions without expectations. A two-way tele-Stimbod system would create a possessed and possessing body—a split physiology to collaborate and perform tasks remotely initiated and locally completed—at the same time in the one physiology . . .

Extreme Absence and the Experience of the Alien

Such a Stimbod would be hollow body, a host body for the projection and performance of remote agents. Glove Anaesthesia and Alien Hand are pathological conditions in which the patient experiences parts of their body as not there, as not their own, as not under their own control—an

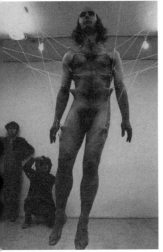

absence of physiology on the one hand and an absence of agency on the other. In a Stimbod not only would it possess a split physiology but it would experience parts of itself as automated, absent, and alien. The problem would no longer be possessing a split personality, but rather a split physicality. In our Platonic, Cartesian, and Freudian pasts these might have been considered pathological and in our Foucauldian present we focus on inscription and control of the body. But in the terrain of cyber-complexity that we now inhabit, the inadequacy and the obsolescence of the ego-agent-driven biological body cannot be more apparent. A transition from psycho-body to cyber-system becomes necessary to function effectively and intuitively in remote spaces, speeded-up situations, and complex technological terrains. During a Sexuality and Medicine Seminar in Melbourne, Sandy Stone asked me what would be the cyber-sexual implications of the Stimbod system? Not having thought about it before, I tried to explain what it might be like. If I was in Melbourne and Sandy was in New York, my touching my chest would prompt her to caress her breast. Someone observing her there would see it as an act of self-gratification, as a masturbatory act. She would know, though, that her hand was remotely and perhaps even divinely guided! Given tactile and force-feedback, I would feel my touch via another person from another place as a secondary and additional sensation. Or, by feeling my chest I can also feel her breast. An intimacy through interface, an intimacy without proximity. Remember that Stimbod is not merely a sensation of touch but an actuation system. Can a body cope with experiences of extreme absence and alien action without becoming overcome by outmoded metaphysical fears and obsessions of individuality and free agency? A Stimbod would thus need to experience its actuality neither all-present-in-this-body, nor all-present-in-that-body, but partly-here and projected-partly-there. An operational system of spatially distributed but electronically interfaced clusters of bodies ebbing and flowing in awareness, augmented by alternate and alien agency . . .

Ping Body / Proto-Parasite

In 1995 for Telepolis, people at the Pompidou Centre (Paris), the Media Lab (Helsinki), and the Doors of Perception conference (Amsterdam) were able to remotely access and actuate this body in Luxembourg, using the touch-screen-interfaced muscle stimulation system. ISDN Picturetel links allowed the body to see the face of the person who was moving it whilst the programmers could observe their remote choreography. Although people thought they were merely activating the body's limbs, they were inadvertently composing the sounds that were heard and the images of the body they were seeing—for the body had sensors, electrodes, and transducers on its legs, arms, and head that triggered sampled body signals and sounds and that also made the body a video switcher and mixer.

And although people in other places were performing with the RHS of the body, it could respond by actuating its Third Hand, voltage-out from electrodes positioned on its abdominal and LHS leg muscles. This split body then was manifesting a combination of involuntary-remotely guided, improvised, and EMG (muscle-initiated) motor motions. In Ping Body—an Internet-actuated and uploaded performance, performed first for Digital Aesthetics in Sydney, but also for DEAF in Rotterdam in 1996—instead of the body being prompted by other bodies in other places, Internet activity itself choreographs and composes the performance. Random pinging to over 30 global Internet domains produces values from 0 to 2,000 milliseconds that are mapped to the deltoid, biceps, flexors, hamstring, and calf muscles: 0 to 60 volts initiating involuntary movements. The movements of the body are amplified, with a MIDI interface measuring position, proximity, and bending angle of limbs. Activated by Internet data, the body is uploaded as info and images to a website to be viewed by other people elsewhere. The body is telematically scaled up, stimulated, and stretched by reverberating signals of an inflated spatial and electrical system. The usual relationship with the Internet is flipped—instead of the Internet being constructed by the input from people, the Internet constructs the activity of one body. The body becomes a nexus for Internet activity—its activity a statistical construct of computer networks.

Parasite: Event for Invaded and Involuntary Body

A customized search engine has been constructed that scans, selects, and displays images to the body—which functions in an interactive video field. Analyses of the JPEG files provide data that is mapped to the body via the muscle stimulation system. There is optical and electrical input into the body. The images that you see are the images that move you.

Consider the body's vision, augmented and adjusted to a parallel virtuality that increases in intensity to compensate for the twilight of the real world. Imagine the search engine selecting images of the body off the WWW, constructing a metabody that in turn moves the physical body. Representations of the body actuate the body's physiology. The resulting motion is mirrored in a VRML space at the performance site and also uploaded to a Web site as potential and recursive source images for body reactivation. RealAudio sound is inserted into sampled body signals and sounds generated by pressure, proximity, flexion, and accelerometer sensors. The body's physicality provides feedback loops of interactive neurons, nerve endings, muscles, transducers, and Third Hand mechanism. The system electronically extends the body's optical and operational parameters beyond the cyborg augmentation of its Third Hand and other peripheral devices. The prosthesis of the Third Hand is counterpointed by the prosthesis of the search engine software code. Plugged in, the body becomes a parasite sustained by an extended, external and virtual nervous system. Parasite was first performed for Virtual World Orchestra in Glasgow. It has also been presented for The Studio for Creative Inquiry, Carnegie Mellon University at the Wood Street Galleries in Pittsburgh, and for Festival Atlantico in Lisbon . . .

Phantom Bodies and Collective Strategies

Previously connection and communication with other bodies on the Internet was only textual, with an acute absence of physical presence. This was not the experience of authentic evolved absence that results in an effectively operating body in the real word—absence of the body on the Internet is an absence of inadequacy, that is an inadequacy of appropriate feedback loops. As we hard-wire more high-fidelity image, sound, tactile and force-feedback sensation between bodies, we begin to generate powerful phantom presences—not phantom as in phantasmagorical, but phantom as in phantom limb sensation. The sensation of the remote body sucked onto your skin and nerve endings, collapsing the psychological and spatial distance between bodies on the Net. Just as in the experience of a phantom limb with the amputee, bodies will generate phantom partners, not because of a lack, but as an extending and enhancing addition to their physiology. Your aura will not be your own. It will only be through the construction of phantoms that the equivalent of our evolved absence will be experienced, as we function increasingly powerfully and with speed and intuition (a successful body operates automatically). Bodies must now perform in techno-terrains and data structures beyond the human scale where intention and action collapse into accelerated responses. Bodies acting without expectation, producing movements without memory. Can a body act without emotion? Must a body continuously affirm its emotional, social, and biological status quo? Or perhaps what is necessary is electronic erasure with new intimate, internalized interfaces to allow for the design of a body with more adequate inputs and outputs for performance and awareness augmented by search engines. Imagine a body remapped and reconfigured—not in genetic memory but rather in electronic circuitry. What of a body that is intimately interfaced to the WWW—and that is stirred and is startled by distant whispers and remote promptings of other bodies in other places? A body that is informed by spiders, knowbots, and phantoms . . .

Operational Internet/ Intelligent System

Consider the Internet structured so that it would scan, select, and switch automatically interfacing clusters of on-line bodies in real time (the size and expertise of the clusters selected for the task to be performed). Can a body cope with the multiplicity of agents—a fluid and flowing awareness that dims and intensifies as agents are connected and disconnected? Awareness and agency would be shifted and shared in an electronic space of distributed intelligence. The Internet becomes not merely a means of information transmission, but a mode of transduction—affecting physical action between bodies. Electronic space as a realm of action, rather than information. Imagine a body that is open and aware, invaded, augmented, and with extended operation. Consider a body whose awareness is extruded by surrogate robots in situations and spaces where no body could go. These machines with arrays of sensors, manipulators, and hybrid locomotion would exponentially multiply the operational possibilities—scaling up the subtlety, speed, and complexity of human action. Perhaps what it means to be human is about not retaining our humanity . . .

Fragments from
"Borderscape 2000"

From "The Chicano State Department Chronicles"

Guillermo Gòmez-Peña/A.K.A. "El Mexterminator" / Roberto Sifuentes

Editor's Note

Documents from the Chicano State Department Archives are made available under the 1999 Freedom of Information Initiative. However, any material deemed sensitive and/or classified has been deleted by department censors prior to public access; these missing texts are indicated by a notation in the document (MISSING).

Additionally, on-line censors may have altered or deleted contents of e-mail at the time of transmission. I am extremely sorry. I hope you learn to read between the lines.

The first version of these files was originally published by Artspace books in late '96 under the title "Friendly Cannibals." This version is substantially more descriptive and accurate.

1 Dear Vampira 99, la unica, la primigenia

I'm having an identity crisis in front of my lowrider "Chevy 69" laptop—the worst in months. I'm listening to the last album of Jesus and Mary Chain, scratch & mixed with classical rancheras; and all my calavera candles are lit. 45 at least. I'm down, loca . . . In fact, I'm just about to delete myself from the Infobanco del Chicano State Department Interneta (CSDI), and please, this time, don't be so naive as to ask me CENSORED?

I'm sending you these last e-mails without any clear purpose estetico-politico, and I don't expect you to answer all of them. (You probably have to take care of other ethno-cyborgs in crisis.) You'll see that they, too (my e-mails not the ethnocyborgs, matizo), suffer from a serious crisis of literary identity. I ask myself #3 and I ask you (or whoever YOU may be at this point in time):

Are these texts fragments of some cyber-cholo sci-fi poem in search of form, or pieces of an elliptic love letter? (It's impossible—& illegal—-to be "direct" nowadays . . .) Are they excerpts from some performance script in-progress, or are they parts of a highly classified document that CENSORED?

For the moment, all I can tell you is that some of their content may be illegal. But I don't care anymore. Me vale. In fact, by the time you download them, they might very well have been censored, edited, or slightly altered. Since no one believes in objectivity or integrity nowadays, there is a slight possibility that CENSORED. Besides I would hate to fall in the trap of a master narrative CENSORED but I would love to fall back in your arms . . . yes, I know that's impossible, vampira.

3 It's 1999 in AmeriKKKa

"Ham-e-rrica," according to my nephew (Generation MEX rockero, El Ricardiaco), "the nation of techno-hatred and unnecessary disputes." He read somewhere that "Cyberspace is dead." As one MIT cybermilitia leader declared in 1997, "No longer a privileged, white-free zone, nor the virtual shopping mall it was supposed to become—it looks too much like the outside world now." Which means it is now entirely controlled by the CSDI. Meaning, it's brown, culti-multi, proletarian & rowdy, & its lingua franca, agarrate mujer, es colloquial Spanglish, masticado asi bien cybersabrossso <http://caliente/100% hornyficado/>
CENSORED
me muero,
sin ti me muero,
sigo muriendo-me lenta-mente
mi mente lenta/osahana
ante la triste pantalla de mi Mac 947-HPX.
CENSORED my neon coffin . . . instalado "aqui" (whatever this means) en el ciberespacio estatal y el anonimato literario pregunto-te: Is it possible to die in cyberspace o de plano alucino?
Could you attend my funeral? Would you?
Do you still remember the touch and temperature of my copper skin?
Remember pre-digital communication, jainita?
Las caricias ambidiestras, los besos en el esfinter, bolero dance, asi, bien pegaditos, rum & coke, for granted laughter, black leather y . . .
CENSORED.
Tu piel, lo nuestro, lo intrinsically ours?

4 Tepoztecardiente,

To give you some political background, in case you don't have access to the other Neta memory files: We, aca en el norte, have entered a postdemocratic era: We now live in a world without theory; sin estructuras ni contenido. The nation/state is purely a metaficcion nostalgica; the borders & climate fluctuate as I write. It's the end of the world—and the word—as we know it. Cambio. NAFTA was a blast, loca, a trinational pachanga which ended up in a trilingual brawl. Now everyone is hung over and no one remembers exactly what happened. Cambio. Que que sucedio exactamente?

The Salinas clan is in jail with Darryl Gates (ex-chief of the LAPD), Garcia Abrego (capo of the Gulf Cartel), and the Arellano brethren (from the Tijuana cartel). Cambio.

Skeletons keep appearing in key sites throughout Mexamerica. La migra y la DEA were the spinal cord of the whole operation. Cambio.

You knew. Deep inside we all knew. Cambio.

Exiled in Bosnia along with ex-colleague Helmut "sin fronteras" Kohl, Billy Clinton spends his lonely hours playing "Stand by Me" on the tenor sax. Cambio.

Patricio Buchanan (Remember that pinche orate/car salesman/sideshow impresario gone hard-right televangelista?) is now a happy dictator-in-exile somewhere in Johannesburg or Mississippi. Chases his young black servants around the garden (By the way, Blacks in South Africa, like their contemporaries in the Bronx, South Central Los Angeles, Washington, D.C., and Atlanta, have gained control of their cities, but this matter belongs to another chronicle).

Aayyyyy!! This unbearable pain in my testicles CENSORED.

G. Gómez-Peña / R. Sifuentes Fragments from "Borderscape 2000"

Another day without you, 397 dias sin que me muerdas la carne, carajo! Sin que me claves tus colmillos en el pecho . . . y encima, my inability to write simple things CENSORED

An ad suddenly appears on the screen:

QUERIDO CIUDADANO TRANSFRONTERIZO:
YOUR GLOBAL DESIRES ARE OUR IMMEDIATE NEEDS, & VICE VERSA. PLEASE CHOOSE FROM THE FOLLOWING MENU:
IBM . . . INS . . . VHS . . . SDL . . . PRI . . . NBC . . . PMS . . . DHL . . . LWH . . . RIP . . . PBS . . .

6 Today,

I'm tired of ex/changing identities in the net. In the past eight hours, I've been a man, a woman and a s/he. I've been black, Asian, Mixteco, German, and a multi-hybrid replicant. I've been 10 years old, 20, 42 & 65. I've spoken 7 broken languages. I need a break real bad. I just want to be myself for a few minutes.

11 La desmodernidad lo abarca todo:

untranslatable loneliness,
cultural emptiness,
political vertigo,
sexual despair,
postcolonial S&M,
synthetic pleasures,
multicentric aesthetics,
unclassifiable weather . . . IN LOUPE

Por lo tanto vampira, the night is clearly the place to be, sin fronteras ni contornos, a safe place for techno-warfare & unlimited entertainment. At night, I love you much, much more, especially when my life's in danger and my tongue, my cobra tongue, mi lengua poluta, disoluta, is out of control, como ahorita.

. . . at night, the militias roam the streets of my city, a city without limits or a name, without a recognizable government, city council, or police department; without churches or cafes; without architectural coherence or a sense of self.

. . . no loca, I'm not talking about Los Angeles or Dallas. I'm talking about myself, my inner city, la megalopolis de mi conciencia. "Here," words like "alternative," "peripheral," and "marginal" lost their meaning and moral weight long ago. (SHIT! I ACCIDENTALLY DELETED A PARAGRAPH!)

17 CENSORED

but all we have left is sex; either cyber-sex, without a body; o sea anonimo, sin facciones, sin identidad ("sin" en ingles equals pecado remember?); sexo robotico without emotional or biological repercussions; o bien, el sexo deportivo, aerobico, intrascendente, doloroso, extremo, impersonal, y sin proposito alguno, en la calle bajo la niebla o en la misma morgue. And the more anonymous, detached, and weird, the better CENSORED so death as a high spiritual goal is temporarily unattainable. Death is already kitsch, cultura popular, trivia redundante, puro mainstream. But then, from a purely psychological perspective I see no other way out of here. Me captas, corazon? Por lo tanto, si me quieres ayudar(eef-yuh-guant-too-jelp-mee), borrame! borrame!! Turn on the camera and shoot me!!

G. Gómez-Peña / R. Sifuentes *Fragments from "Borderscape 2000"*

18 In the past 10 minutes

      I've deleted more than half of the texts (the best parts), so when you re-read this document (if you can retrieve it of course), it will appear to be incomplete. But after all, aren't we all incomplete and fragmented anyway? Aren't we all just mere residues of what we once were? drafts of what we thought one day we would be? Vampira, excuse my post-Mexican rrrrrrrrrrrrrrrrrrrrrromanticism pero siento la imperiosa necesidad de NDLVLFVL; DCM M LLL LLDLD; LL; LLLWUUGHBHDCB''WEOOJK N VS; MMKDKJJDCDN Al,mm A(ODOPmclkco kviubkllllhdgg MMMMMMMM MMMMMMMe muero.

      Jaina, donde andas? En que mapa? En que frecuencia?

      Are you lost in the cyberbarrio? ARE YOU?

      Were you? Are you somewhere inside this 3-D chat room? Where exactly?

      Behind the leopard-skin sofa where the cyborg-chola is masturbating? Is she fronting for you this time?

G. Gómez-Peña / R. Sifuentes *Fragments from "Borderscape 2000"*

Humanistic Intelligence

Steve Mann

One of the fundamental contrasts between free democratic societies and totalitarian systems is that the totalitarian government (or other organization) relies on secrecy for the regime but high surveillance and disclosure for all other groups, whereas in the civic culture of liberal democracy, the position is approximately the reverse.

Simon Davies (pertaining to the massive 1987 Australian campaign against a national ID card)

Introduction

Increased surveillance is often presented as a "solution" to increased crime, instead of solving the problem at its source, such as by mitigating loss of community connectedness.

Urban violence, and other forms of crime, have made it necessary, in some people's opinion, to dramatically escalate the use of measures such as surveillance. These measures, which are brought on by large organizations, threaten the existence of a free and democratic society.

Overtly violent crimes in New York City, for example, have appeared to be less frequent, but much of this has been accomplished through the rolling back of civil liberties. Random searches, "no-knock" entry, and, most notably, increased surveillance, have ushered in a new world order of "law and order."

The recent proliferation of video surveillance cameras, interconnected with high speed computers and central databases is moving us toward a high-speed "surveillance superhighway." Cameras are used throughout entire cities (such as Liverpool and Baltimore) to monitor citizens in all public areas.

With other forms of one-sided surveillance such as fingerprinting of welfare recipients and see-through-clothing cameras for "securing buildings from employee theft" and "for police to covertly monitor crowds for weapons" (Nowhere to Hide by Joe Constance, <http:// www.ingersoll-rand.com/compair/octnov96/ radar.htm>), architects of the "surveillance superhighway" promise us a future of reduced crime, while at the same time construct for us a future of reduced accountability for themselves.

The city has become a frightening place, and drastic "solutions" are stepped up to meet in equilibrium with the "drastic problems." A goal of my work is to challenge both sides of this equilibrium, which appear to feed on one another.

It is arguably true that organizations that use totalitarian video surveillance tend to have fewer overtly violent crimes. What I mean by totalitarian video surveillance is that the video signal is observable by only a select group, and that accountability is denied through restrictions on the collection of video by others.

A Mafia-run gambling casino might be the most extreme example of a totalitarian video surveillance environment (e.g. that the casino wants to know everything about everyone but reveal nothing about itself). In such an organization one would not expect to find any overt physical violence but there still might be occasional "disappearances" of those not favorable to the organization.

Many department stores also use video surveillance extensively, yet prohibit others from using cameras in their establishments. A goal of my work is to provide a technological framework to challenge such restrictions. A top-down Panopticon-like surveillance hierarchy tends to make Jeremy Bentham's philosophy a self-fulfilling one. The sense of community that once existed, whether in the form of close-knit communities or the more modern "neighbourhood watch" (e.g. trust in other members of the community), has been replaced by absolute trust in governments, large corporations, or other unseen authorities, analogous to the unseen guard in Bentham's watchtower.

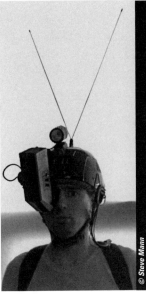

My 1970 effort at building a personal information space, which culminated in this apparatus of 1980.

An important goal of my work is to set forth a foundation that I call "Humanistic Intelligence" (H.I.) as a basis for the existential principle of self-determination and mastery over our own destiny, as well as the humanistic notion of self-actualization.

"Humanistic Intelligence" differs from Artificial Intelligence in the sense that the goal is to "become" intelligent, through prostheses of sorts, rather than be replaced or disenfranchised by intelligent machines. Thus H.I. challenges the notion of environmental intelligence and ubiquitous surveillance. Rather than "smart rooms," "smart floors," "smart ceilings," "smart toilets," "smart light switches," etc., H.I. puts forth the notion of "smart people."

An important goal of H.I. is to take a first step toward a foremost principle of the Enlightenment, that of the dignity of the individual. This is accomplished through a prosthetic transformation of the body into a sovereign space.

Past and Present Works

I constructed a series of reflectionist and diffusionist (Reflectionism and Diffusionism: new tactics for deconstructing the video Surveillance Superhighway (1978–1996), by Steve Mann, 1996) performance pieces in order to challenge the notion of totalitarian surveillance, as well as challenge and appropriate the notion of higher and unquestionable authority.

Here I describe experiments and performances that I have conducted and purposely taken to the extreme in order to (a) illustrate a point and (b) experience reactions and observations first hand. It is not likely that the average reader would go to these extremes but some more subtle variations of these experiments and performances may still be used to provide similar insight or reactions.

Steve Mann Humanistic Intelligence

My Manager: Externalization of the Locus of Control

By "externalization of the locus of control," I am referring to the phenomenon you experience when, for example, you're standing at a department store customer service counter. The clerk has the power of various support media, and might, for example, defer his or her judgment (or pretend to defer his or her judgment) to an external entity such as a telephone (ostensibly that of another entity at the other end of the communications channel), a computer screen, or other form of media to which you do not share the privilege of access. In this sense, the clerk may, if desired, absolve himself/herself from responsibility for his/her own actions.

Centralized computing, in particular, has ushered in a new era of this form of externalization. A department store clerk may tell us, perhaps untruthfully, that "I cannot process your return; the computer won't let me." Often the clerk does have the

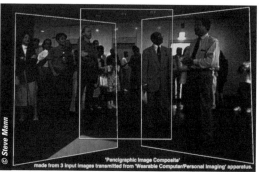

ability to fulfill the request, but chooses voluntarily to be subject to (or to appear to be subject to) a higher and unquestionable authority. Thus the customer is placed in an inferior position of not knowing whether the clerk is acting on his/her own will, or the will of a higher authority that is not subject to question by you, the customer.

'Pencigraphic Image Composite'
made from 3 input images transmitted from 'Wearable Computer/Personal Imaging' apparatus.

This tactic is often the practice of used-car sales representatives who might, for example, say, "I'd really like to give you the car for $2,000, but let me check with my manager," and then disappear into a back room for a few minutes, have a cup of coffee, all alone, and then emerge to declare "My manager won't let me sell it to you for that low . . ."

One of my performance pieces, entitled My Manager was a reflectionist performance piece in which I attempted to provide myself with the same kind of support infrastructure. This was achieved through construction of various forms of a personal information space comprising a computer in a backpack, connected to a display situated over one or both eyes[1] with a radio teletype interface to a remote "manager."

In this way, I carried with me, in my clothing, a support infrastructure that made it ambiguous as to whether my thoughts and such were my own, or those of a remote entity.

My apparatus differed significantly from a two-way voice radio, where it is clearly apparent to anyone else when the unit is being used. Later, the laptop computers that evolved in the 1980s still failed to provide the ambiguity and uncertainty of my earlier apparatus.

My Manager was my attempt to return to the Enlightenment, and declare the sovereignty of the individual, through the illusion of its subversion. In the spirit of the situationist tradition, I have created a detournement of my own subversion.

Painful Disconnect

In a further embodiment of the My Manager performance, a remote agent of my choosing may also provide remote control of my body, in the Stelarc sense, so that I can further subvert myself to an authority that acts in my own interest yet is inaccessible to, and unquestionable by, others.

I may also choose to be given an "electrical corrective signal" (through a high-voltage step-up transformer connected to my garment-based computer) should I become disconnected from the Internet. Thus, if I am asked to step into an elevator or the like, I can honestly reply that this would inflict great pain on me.

Steve Mann Humanistic Intelligence

In that sense someone who forced me to enter an environment in which I might lose radio contact with potential outside accountability would be committing an act which is equivalent to torture.

As torture is viewed as a human rights violation, the goal of this performance piece is to suggest that disconnectivity, against one's will, should also be viewed as a human rights violation.

Painful Disconnect makes real the notion that denial of the right to self-surveillance by friends and family is equivalent to possible torture or other mistreatment.

Necessification

Because of the long-term adaptation process which I have undergone in the use of this apparatus (e.g. that I have worn it for many years), I have come to rely on it to see properly, and thus in some sense, it has become a visual prosthetic device (Eudaemonic Eye, <http:// wearcam.org/chi97.html>).

Further toward making it absolutely essential that I wear the device, it also serves as a personal status monitor, e.g. a health monitor of sorts, and therefore, in some sense, asking me to remove it is a first step toward not only placing me in danger of tripping or falling (e.g. injury) but also asking me to put my life in danger through the absence of a health monitor that might otherwise bring medical aid should my heart show early signs of incipient malfunction or the like.

The Personal Safety Device

H.I. provides a further framework for personal safety by acting as a protective and defensive agent. For example, I am able to announce my location to one or more people of my choosing, either automatically through a GPS-ready radioteletype interface, or through a direct input device (e.g. a series of pushbutton switches integrated into my belt or clothing).

Various sensory apparatus I have incorporated into clothing measure both me and my environment. These sensors include a 24.360 GHz radar set, a 10.250GHz radar set, video cameras, microphones, infrared vision system, as well as a variety of sensors that measure quantities upon my own body, such as my heart rate (ECG), footstep rate (transducers in my shoes), etc. Intelligent signal processing may be used to construct an automated personal safety system. The inputs from the various sensors form a feature vector that may be processed by the circuits I've built into my clothing (e.g. 133MHz 586 processor running under the Linux 2.0 operating system, along with various special purpose DSP hardware, TMS320 series processors, etc.).

As an example of how intelligent signal processing can be used as a protective entity, consider what happens when one is approached by an assailant wielding a sawn-off shotgun and demanding cash. In such a situation, the victim's heart rate is apt to increase but with an inexplicable decrease in footstep rate (owing to the assailant's request that the victim stop and hand over a wallet or the like).

Consider a quotient of heart rate divided by footstep rate. One could easily imagine how this quotient, taken over a certain time window, could provide a rough indication of distress. In actual fact, I've been developing more advanced intelligent signal processing algorithms, which include, for example, situational awareness.

Electric Feel Sensing: Synthetic Synesthesia of Sixth and Seventh Senses

Another example of intelligent signal processing comprises a radar system which I have built into my clothing, to provide me with the ability to "feel" if someone sneaks up behind me. The radar system establishes a far-field electromagnetic wave pattern whose demodulated Doppler output is processed and used to drive vibrotactile transducers connected to my body. In this way, when someone sneaks up behind me, I can feel them "pressing" against my body, even though they are still some distance away. The closer they get, the stronger I feel them "pressing" against my body. At 20 or 30 meters, the feeling is very faint, while at 10 meters, the feeling is stronger, and as they approach within stabbing distance, the feeling is much stronger, to the point of being difficult to ignore.

This kind of user-interface is intuitive, because it is mapped in a manner that establishes a one-to-one correspondence with me and my environment. When someone sneaks up behind me from the left, for example, I can feel them "pressing" against the left side of my back, and likewise to the right.

Systems of this nature provide me with additional senses (such as radar, sonar, etc.) beyond the normal five senses. However, to be perceptible, I map the additional senses onto the usual five senses, a mapping that I call "synthetic synesthesia."

Furthermore, the mapping need not be one-to-one. For example, I often map the radar system into more than one of my five senses. One such mapping I tend to favor uses the radar to also switch in a rear-looking video camera.

Intelligent signal processing may, in fact, be used to select the degree to which the rear-looking camera is mixed in, rather than merely switching it in. For example, I designed a radar system having both the in-phase and the quadrature components. Thus the signals may be processed to determine whether objects are moving toward me or away from me. Objects moving toward me from behind are of particular interest, because most objects that are behind me (such as the ground, parked cars, stationary objects) are moving away from me in a relative sense.

The portion of the Doppler spectrum corresponding to objects approaching me may be integrated to arrive at a saliency index. This saliency index is similar to the previously described heartrate/steprate quotient in the sense that both of these saliency indices attempt to indicate to me or my processing agent the degree of attention that should be paid to some other instrument of situational awareness.

In the case of the radar system, the saliency index may be used to control a video mixer that controls the degree to which my attention is focused on my rear-looking camera. The image from the rear-looking camera is presented to my eye upside-down and backwards (e.g. the camera is mounted upside-down and a circuit is used to flip each raster of video from left to right), so that it appears to me as though the rays of light from behind me are passing through the back of my head, through my retina, and then through the optical center of my eye. This provides a system which obeys the true laws of projective geometry, and redefines the eye as a device that captures a pencil of light rays from a single point in space, and merely projects this pencil of rays onto a single image plane. I view this image plane upon the miniature computer screen I have built into my eyeglasses.

With the radar's visual saliency index in the control loop, the rays of light from behind me may be modulated in brightness, to correspond with the amount of attention that the processing agent believes that they merit.

SafetyNet

Once a distress signal is detected (by intelligent signal-processing agents or manually by myself), a communications channel may be opened to friends and relatives who have been previously entered on my personal safety list. This communications channel includes live video and other environmental information, which is transmitted and recorded at remote locations in various countries around the world, so that it cannot be destroyed by a potential assailant.

Rather than notify police or other authorities, which could result in a high degree of false alarms, the system notifies members of my SafetyNet—a network of friends and relatives looking out for one another's safety. This approach to personal safety may be combined with a high degree of constant connectivity with others such as a radioteletype UNIX "talk" window open at all times, video conferencing from a first-person perspective (e.g. from a wearable video camera) open at all times, etc.

Such a form of personal safety device may also protect one from police brutality and various other forms of human rights violations.

Subversion of Panopticon with Wearable Wireless Webcam

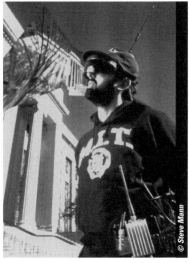

Ordinary cameras have become much smaller now, thanks to the miniaturization afforded by modern technology. However, they still share a common attribute with their predecessors, namely that it is immediately apparent to anyone when the camera is being used, because one must bring it up to one's eye, and look through it, etc., and this usage pattern is likely to put an assailant or the like into an angry mode of thought. For example, in a situation involving police brutality, police may attempt to forbid photography or the like, or may attempt to intimidate those engaged in the practice of documenting an atrocity.

Another weakness of current camera technology is that the storage of images or video is local, so that those committing the atrocity may seize the storage media (film, videocassette, flash memory, floppy disk, or the like), claiming that they need it for "evidence," when in fact their wish might be that it be destroyed.

I established a "personal imaging" ("Wearable Computing: A First Step Toward Personal Imaging," *IEEE Computer,* vol. 30, no. 2, <http:// computer.org/pubs/computer/1997/0297toc. html>) framework for obtaining video from a first-person perspective. This video is part of my personal information space, and therefore accessible to others via a wireless link to the Internet. This means that anyone with access to the Internet can view the images, and thereby take an active role in making sure that there are multiple copies of the images in various countries around the world, so that an assailant, or a violator of human rights, could not destroy the images. Even by placing me under duress, the images could not be destroyed, because I have chosen to not know how many copies of each picture or video sequence there are, or in which countries they are mirrored, archived, and backed up.

A principle of totalitarian video surveillance is that only the guards have access to the privileged vantage point afforded by video cameras. An important goal of my performance piece was to make the situation approximately the reverse, that is, my "personal imaging" system was a first step toward subverting totalitarian surveillance by making some video (at least mine) available to everyone.

I later constructed larger communities of individuals wearing cameras in order to make multiple image streams available to large numbers of individuals.

Recently, with the advent of the World Wide Web, I have simply turned my apparatus into a "WebCam," resulting in a further simplification of its use, and a further subversion of Panopticon.

My camera (WearCam, short for wearable camera) is situated in such a way that it is not possible for an assailant to determine whether or not an image is being captured at any given time. This is accomplished through having the camera worn in an always-active mode, so that it in fact functions as a visual prosthetic of sorts.

Steve Mann *Humanistic Intelligence*

Maybe Camera

I may also choose that the remote accountability afforded by my SafetyNet be of origin unknown to me, so that if I am asked "Are you recording me?", I might be able to say that I honestly do not know. This denial of accountability, for taking pictures in establishments where photography is prohibited, was explored through a performance piece called Firing Squad.

For Firing Squad, I constructed a number of "Maybe Cameras."

Furthermore, when challenged by representatives of the surveillance superhighway, we simply declared: these are uniforms—standard issue from Our Manager—which we are required to wear while running errands on company time.

Second Brain as Personal Diary without Contempt of Court

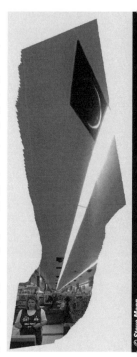

In many ways, I regard my rig, together with its personal information space, as a second brain—as a true prosthetic device.

Thus, even in situations in which I do make a conscious decision to record an image or video of some activity, I may wish that this recording be entered into a personal diary of sorts which is only accessible to "me." (The definition of "me" may include that which falls within my newly defined corporeal boundary, which might include, for example, other members of my SafetyNet.)

People have often felt uneasy entrusting to my second brain certain personal pieces of information, fearing that even if I made my best efforts to keep this information in confidence, it could be compromised through a subpoena.

Even if I were to protect it with ordinary encryption, its security may still be compromised through the process of torture or other forms of duress.

In the same way that our first brain is protected by the Constitution (the Fifth) from contempt of court for refusing to answer (self-incriminate), I desired to establish a means of protecting the "second brain" from self-incrimination.

My solution was to encrypt it with a key that I do not know myself. Thus I may encrypt materials with public keys of other members of my SafetyNet. In this way, my SafetyNet could recognize when I am under duress, and thus my inability to access my second brain would not be seen in contempt of whatever duress I might be placed under.

Life Through the Screen: A Window to the Future

Many important questions were raised by these performance pieces and the new inventions upon which they were realized.

For example, My Manager provided a form of personal empowerment brought forth by the ability to take a solid stance and defer any questioning of my will to a (possibly fictitious) higher and unquestionable authority, just as representatives of establishments often do. However, there is also the danger that this could be abused, for example, as a means of controlling or enslaving people.

In particular, the exploration of the remotely controlled body raises not only the question of possible enslavement by a higher authority that is not actually acting in the best interest of the indi-

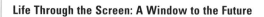

vidual wearing the apparatus of control, but also some serious questions about the locus of responsibility for one's acts. As we move toward a future of networked personal information spaces, we will need to think carefully about how these worlds are constructed.

The goal of humanistic intelligence, that of providing the individual with an increased degree of self-determination and mastery over his or her own destiny, will have to compete against the goals of utilitarianism, and the desire merely to increase workplace productivity and make people more useful to society.

Will we see a future of "cyborgs," as "puppets" on a virtual string, imprisoned in their work-cells, carrying out the orders of an omnipotent boss, or will we see a healthy community of free self-actualized citizens looking out for each other's safety and well-being?

This is the question that we must carefully consider as our "corporeal boundary" will no longer end at the flesh, but, rather, will extend and diffuse into the ether.

Notes

1. I referred to this invention as a "personal computer," though, in recent years, that term has come to mean a desktop computer. Thus my apparatus has, over the years, been called a "humanistic computer," "existential computer," "eudaemonic computer," "wearable computer," or the like.

I owe much to those around me, who have influenced my thinking: Rosalind Picard, Hiroshi Ishii, Krzysztof Wodiczko, William Mitchell, Obed Torres, Thad Starner, Olivier Faugeras, Kent Nickerson, Simon Haykin, and many others. I would also like to thank Chris Dodge for reading this essay and making some important suggestions.

Steve Mann *Humanistic Intelligence*

Music Plays Images x Images Play Music

Toshio Iwai / Ryuichi Sakamoto

The idea for this collaborative performance has its origins in Toshio Iwai's installation "Piano—as Image Media" created at the ZKM, Karlsruhe, Germany, in 1995. Conceived upon Iwai's return to Japan when he met Ryuichi Sakamoto, Music Plays Images x Images Play Music is a multimedia concert that uses the system of Iwai's piano piece and visualizes in real time a musical performance by Sakamoto. Over the course of a year, Iwai, who lives in Tokyo, often corresponded by e-mail with Sakamoto, who lives in New York. During their correspondence, the concept for the collaboration expanded rapidly, developing from the simple idea of "Sakamoto playing Iwai's 'Piano—as Image Media,'" to a performance that links, in various ways, musical sounds with visual images. The result of the collaboration was more than a "novel combination of music and image." Many elements including the actual presence of Sakamoto/Iwai, the machinery that is called the piano, the acoustic sounds produced by the piano, and the virtual images generated from computers were linked and developed in various ways. From the feedback produced, a radically new space of musicality-visuality was created. In addition, the performance was transmitted over the Internet and relayed worldwide. This experiment, the first of its kind, was an attempt to utilize the interactive medium of the Internet. People on the other side of the Internet were able to play the piano by remote control and in turn Sakamoto had a session with their playing.

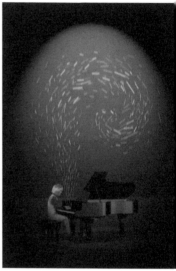

The Set-up of the Stage

Two concert grand pianos are placed on the stage. A semi-transparent screen 8 meters in height and 10 meters in width is suspended above them. The lids of both pianos are removed and their interiors and keyboards clearly illuminated. The screen is irradiated with a beautiful shade of blue. A black and white video camera is placed on each of the pianos in order to film the movements of the performer's fingers and the piano keys. The video cameras project enlarged images of each piano keyboard onto the screen on either side of the pianos. Several computers are set up on a long narrow table placed on the right side of the stage.

The Content of the Performance

1. Sakamoto does not initially appear on the stage. Amidst the silence, the piano begins to play on its own without a player. An image of Sakamoto playing the piano gradually comes into view on the screen to the side of the piano. Sakamoto's image slowly disappears as the music ends.

2. Sakamoto appears on the left side of the stage. He begins to play the small keyboard placed there. As he plays this keyboard, the piano starts to play. A faint light gradually emanates from the piano. At a certain point, Sakamoto stops playing. However, the last musical phrase repeats itself automatically, slowly fading out.

3. Sakamoto plays the piano directly. The light images that visually represent each note of the musical piece begin to rise from within the piano. The images capture not only the timing of the notes, but every aspect of the music, including the length of the notes and their volume. They are represented in a way that the eye can recognize.

4. During Sakamoto's performance, Iwai gradually modifies the image. The lights, which correspond to each note of the piece, are transformed over time in various ways. They do not merely rise from within the piano and fade into thin air. They radiate from the center of the screen out in all directions or revolve in a whirling pattern, eventually disappearing into a vortex. The metamorphoses of the projected images influence Sakamoto's playing as he watches the various transformations.

5. The image-objects, composed of 88 elements—the same number as the number of keys on a piano—appear on the center of the screen. Each of the elements coincides with the keys of the piano, and the objects are continually transformed according to Sakamoto's piano performance.

6. Clicking a computer mouse, Iwai places dots of light onto the screen. Whenever the dots of light fall on the piano, the piano begins to play. The dots of light then rebound to their original position, striking the keyboard at fixed intervals. Depending on where the dots of light are placed, the pitch of the notes and the patterns of repetition change. The number of dots of light are increased. The dots of light bouncing from the piano are all shifted back and forth from left to right. The whole musical scale changes according to how the dots of light are moved. The dots of light are transformed into rays and then polygonal figures.

7. The video camera films Sakamoto's entire body. The computer captures the image in real time. Sakamoto's silhouette is pixelized and then projected onto the screen above the piano. When Sakamoto moves and the image of his body overlaps with the piano, the piano plays. When Sakamoto moves toward or away from the camera, or when a close-up image of his hands is projected, the sound is changed dynamically. The images of Sakamoto's hands and body are what plays the machine called the piano. Iwai implements further modifications by zooming in on and rotating Sakamoto's image on the screen, thereby slowly modifying the sound. Sakamoto continues to move his body while looking on.

8. A chessboard-like grid appears on the screen and begins to rotate. Sakamoto and Iwai take turns placing glowing dots of light onto the grid, thereby creating a repetition of short melodic patterns. As the music is created through this collaboration, Iwai transposes the musical pattern, changing the octave and altering the sounds and the images. Sakamoto continues to create new patterns. Finally, with the completed musical phrases as a backdrop, Sakamoto improvises on the piano. Iwai continues to modify the performance piece.

9. The music played by Sakamoto is turned into an image. The image that springs from the first piano and lands on the second piano creates a parabola in its fall. The second piano plays according to this image. The figure of Sakamoto performing on the first piano is projected next to the second piano with a delay that coincides with the imaged music arriving at the second piano. It appears as if there are two Sakamotos playing the two different pianos.

10. The short musical phrase performed by Sakamoto and the resulting image loop between the two pianos, repeating again and again. Sakamoto continues to add more sounds to the loop. The repeating images and sounds, flowing forth like a waterfall between the two pianos, grow in layered richness and complexity.

Original performance:
Planning by Shin-ichiro Ikebe
Produced by Art Tower Mito, Mito, Japan
Sound Engineering by Akira Shimura [Star Tech Inc.]
Supported by IAMAS, NTT InterCommunication Center,
Yamaha co.ltd., JVC Inc., Human Media Inc., Kab Inc.
Documented by TV-MAN UNION Inc.
Internet broadcasting by Naozumi Takenaka,
Kouichiro Eto, Internet 1996 World Exposition Japan

Translated from the Japanese by Dana O'Neill

Ground Truth

Recent global developments confirm the superior performance of the American way of life. The Gulf war and the collapse of communist Russia, the soaring performance of the US Stock Market, the leading US role as peacemaker in the Middle East and the Balkans are examples, not to mention the recent helping hands of brotherly financial underwriting for devalued Asian currencies. It is no coincidence that economic well-being at home is paralleled by financial outreach to those less fortunate abroad. America is home to the technological and industrial shepherds for the world's free market flock. The global presence of the Internet and satellite communications systems is enabling distributed and remote cultures to join the fold, to subscribe to America's extended family.

The caretakers of this "good will web" recognize the need to keep it freely accessible to all members, and secure. The American recipe for financial and political security is one of long-range investment. Instruments are being invented and installed today which will return benefits to their makers for years to come. It is only natural for less fortunate cultures to bond with the systems that help them get back on their feet. Today there is an investment parallel between private sector "global shepherd" causes and a bullish stock market on the one hand, and the increased Congressional funding for military information systems on the other. Government agencies that once shied away from defense funding are now embracing the climate change toward defense allocations of taxpayer dollars. The Advanced Research Projects Agency (ARPA), which funded the CAVE(tm)[1] and other computer interfaces, was recently promoted from ARPA to DARPA with the blessings of Congress (the "D" is for "Defense"). The National Center for Supercomputing Applications (NCSA), America's leading-edge site for high-performance scientific computing and Internet 2, recently established a contract office for DoD Mod (Department of Defense Modernization) projects. And institutions of Higher Learning, including MIT, UC Berkeley, U of Michigan, and U of Illinois, have recently formed research consortia with Lockheed-Martin, Rockwell International, and other military systems integrators. These consortia are sponsored by the ARL (Army Research Laboratory) Federated Laboratories program.

Since the Gulf war the Armed Services have been incubating a modern identity to replace the role they aborted in Vietnam. US armed forces are the logical global defenders of our 21st-century technodemocracy. This rebirth is capitalized by a funding strategy whereby public monies are divested from legacy military hardware and software. Instead, tax dollars are invested in "Dual Use" technologies, modular, lightweight, and distributed, with commercial intellectual property rights that are not usurped by military R & D. Dual Use doctrine ensures that military technology also meets the needs of civilian industry. US consumers, under the protective investments of the private sector, will reap the benefits of technologies developed initially for military applications. These technologies will be eventually transformed into home appliances or other attractive commodities. In this way Congress maintains Investment Equilibrium between military and civilian economies. Dual Use is a striking example of the tactical merger of the marketplace and the battlefield.

Robin Bargar / Insook Choi

Consider extending this scenario to the funding of artistic projects. In May 1998 DARPA published a Program Solicitation for proposals to develop a Command Post of the Future (CPOF). The DARPA CPOF BAA (Broad Agency Announcement) advances a vision of an extended cyber-commander, VR-empowered, sensing, comprehending, and responding to instantaneous conditions on the battlefield. This capability is known as "Battlefield Visualization" (BV). To achieve a seamless BV will require cognitive engineering of sensors, transmitters, and information displays such as computer graphics and computer-generated sound. Cognitive engineering describes the crossover from soft intelligence to wet intelligence (from artificial to biological information processing). If DARPA is reaching its R&D audience, then content providers, even artists, will recognize this opportunity to leave their creative mark in history while serving their country. The CPOF BAA anticipates the realm of artistic possibilities. On page five the BAA suggests "developing general principles of visualization from principles of human perception and experience in graphic art, advertising, news broadcasting, story telling and entertainment." Cinematography, animation, computer games, and location-based entertainment may prove worthy of Dual Use. Visionary artists could leverage Dual Use to accommodate the decency-in-funding requirement of the NEA (National Endowment of the Arts). Decency-in-funding was prescribed by Congress and recently upheld by the US Supreme Court. The questionable morality of art funded by taxpayer dollars has proven a sore point for certain American constituencies. The morality of public funding for military projects, however, and the fundamental decency of defense-related research are beyond question.

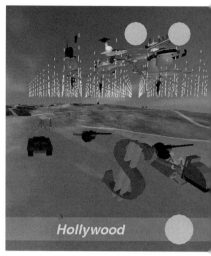

Hollywood

An artistic perspective is important for the solution of complex representational problems. Representational skill is necessary to clarify the display of excessive amounts of information. Supported by military funding, artistic techniques could constitute a Representational Strike Force to maintain Information Dominance through Knowledge Management. In time-critical maneuvers and in training, representation tools might include live performance to demonstrate the coordination of an ensemble of assets and devices. A live performance by an instructor demonstrating a hypothetical virtuoso commander in action might be described as a literal "theater of war."

Literacy and Technology

When we speak of technology we often focus on tools and techniques. They are easier to refer to, due to the conventional ways of making references by turning to namable objects and well-defined methodologies. However, the primary inquiry of technology is in forming questions, generating cases, and creating problems that may not fit into existing paradigms. It is this aspect of technology that makes it an open discourse in a broader context in which scientific and engineering practices can be revisited. Technology includes "illiterate" practitioners' inventions as well as theories. For example the people who invented the compass were illiterate, meaning that in the practice domain of a compass as a tool, they were not scientists. The word "illiterate" is applied to people here. Let's note the term also applies to the practice for which descriptive language is not yet available. When the practice is indescribable, we are illiterate to the need for the solutions to the problems. When we are illiterate to such problems, we call them ill-defined problems. Bringing ill-defined problems to well-defined problems is a beginning of an involvement with technology, and this necessarily involves our linguistic practices.

The Installation

is a semi-automated installation and a real-time performance in distributed virtual reality. It demonstrates the application of visual and auditory representations in a multi-modal decision-making environment. The environment is a dynamic multi-agent simulation. Multiple workstations provide visual, auditory, and tactile interfaces. Movement sensors allow an observer to schedule state changes in system components. Gesture-based interactive queries may be performed. State changes automatically propagate from one region to another. Visualization and sonification[2] of current states of numerical simulations determine the display.

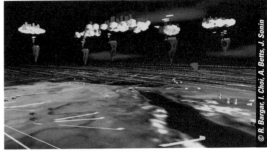

Ground Truth simulates the immutability of economics as combat. In the Ground Truth simulator, Economy is at war with Uncertainty. Information must be reduced to generate profit. Market share must be reduced to refresh the source of raw information. Participants may choose sides, and vote for Prosperity or for Uncertainty. The core simulation is composed of scientific and military software driving an economic simulation, acted upon by observers from a distributed workstation array. Each workstation is a Tactical Operations Center (TOC) where participants experiment with military simulations and numerical models of uncertainty. Battles are fought in economic arenas using military force, financial instruments, and media webcasts. TOCs allow participants to select military courses of action, to make financial investments, to edit and webcast multimedia, and to negotiate uncertainty in a physically based model of resource delivery.

The multiple models in Ground Truth are arranged in three layers of real estate. Each layer visualizes a system that commanders contend with to orchestrate a combat mission. At the bottom is the Battlefield or Marketplace terrain layer. At the top are the Cloud Cities and Factories, a resource renewal and repository layer. Between them is the Uncertainty layer, a turbulent flow field that can obscure the terrain and divert resources transmitted between the Cloud Cities and the terrain. The layers interact by exchanging 3-D tokens that represent information quanta. The tetrahedron is the information atom. Geometric bonding of quanta forms three classes of information currency: media, military, and economic resource tokens. Rigid-body and particle dynamics simulate mass, velocity, and acceleration of information quanta. Currency tokens are affected by gravity and simulated flow. They collide with other currencies and with bonding surfaces. Avatars provide an immersive view for each TOC workstation, where participants shepherd the information into desired repositories. Tokens are expended in a battle or invested in a Cloud City to fortify the civilian economy. Currencies descend from the Cities to the Terrain in a Resource Rainfall Cycle of taxation-as-precipitation. Battles are executed using FOX, an automated Course-of-Action planner that applies genetic algorithms to calculate optimal troop maneuvers. The Media TOC transmits resources up to the cities in the form of publicity, determined by the newsworthiness of the conflicts on the battlefield.

Information and Uncertainty

In military doctrine, "ground truth" is the technical term for an elusive state of complete information. It is the absolute knowledge of the momentary state of a battle. Ground truth is unattainable, but it determines which party best meets its objectives in armed conflict. In war, military forces periodically contend with one another, whereas they immediately and continuously contend with uncer-

© R. Bargar, I. Choi, A. Betts, J. Sonin

R. Bargar / I. Choi Ground Truth

tainty. At Bell Labs in 1949, Claude Shannon demonstrated that information is the statistical measure of uncertainty in a communications channel.[3] Every communication involves a ratio of signal to noise. Meaning must be encoded to resist decay under this ratio. The decay of a relevant message into noise is inherent to the entropy of transmission. There are many forms of noise, some recognizable, others masquerading as content. Uncertainty arises when meaning cannot be distinguished from noise in a communication. To the significant degree that communications are required to conduct a military operation, uncertainty plays a role in the outcome. Predictions have been made that our children will wage war in cyberspace, but in terms of information, noise, and entropy, war is conducted in cyberspace now, today. Whether the combatants are soldiers, or stock brokers, or news networks and politicians, global turf is staked, defended, and conquered in a binary-coded alphanumeric medium. The digital medium is regarded as an almost-physical substrate for decision-making. In the ebb and flow of the binary stream, the forces that master uncertainty carry the day.

To bring uncertainty within grasp, military scientists and engineers are designing systems to approach ground truth on an infinite arc. The mastery of uncertainty follows a path that can be likened to a curve approaching but never intersecting its asymptote. As working technology advances along this curve, a transformation of the battlefield is taking place. The machines that are devised to sense, evaluate, and report ground truth are becoming a substitute battlefield. The machines are becoming a replacement for the conditions they are designed to measure. The physical state of war is evolving into a staging ground for informational battle. Compression algorithms and search engines reduce geography, forces, and events to a pure form of asynchronous message consisting of pointers to previous messages. The new battlefield relies upon temporal mechanics for articulation in a chain of reference without closure, the event horizon for a recursive theater of war.

Medium and Content

For resisting the description of an artist as "content provider:" when we wish certain content to be present we must prepare the condition from which the content could be accounted for.

The term "medium" has specific implications associated with the technology, such as mass media, where the term presupposes a quality of being transparent and a premise to simply mediate with no interference. Through the observations of mass media practices we have learned that the implication of such premises is no longer feasible for supporting any medium as an objective representation tool for the world. Similarly, we wish to revisit whether any medium can be an objective tool for artistic expressions. Can a compositional idea be independent from the medium it predicts? One might say it doesn't matter what an artist uses to create a work of art as long as he or she gets the result. This premise may be compatible with the description of an artist as a content provider, often for an industrial demand. The role of an artist is reduced to the role of demonstrator for proving the utility of certain tools and software for commercial promotions. The conceptual ground for such premises, however, is irrelevant for practitioners and artists in a computation environment, particularly when one faces the machines that take nothing for granted beyond the specifications of their internal states, inputs, and product set. The specifications of the machines are unique to the compositional problems. With the prevalence of multimedia, there is a similar concern in presenting a work of art using certain tools as objective tools for achieving certain effects. We wonder how much tools shape the final results, when we note how certain packaged products keep our students of art busy collecting data and sampling. Without eliminating the possibility of many tools, what has to be examined and included in our discourse is the composability of, and with, the tools and conditions that surround us.

Tools leave a trace in works of art and this is not necessarily undesirable. It simply means the composability of the tools has to be taken into compositional criteria, and this is desirable. Thus we attribute the distinctions between "a composition for a medium" and "the composition of a medium." For the former the composition assumes a well-defined medium for its presentation, for the latter the composition explicitly addresses the construction of its medium of presentation. The word "medium" is applicable in a wide range, from the substances appealing to our basic senses, to instruments, genre, and tonality. I do not intend to categorize different uses of the term. The discussion starts from the following two statements:

1. A medium requires an observer's action for its presence to be witnessed.
2. Let the action be a performance.

A composition will involve the construction of a medium as a sphere circumscribing subsystems and structures of action, by which the systems will behave. With this task definition of composition, what do we mean by content? When we input content such as sound files or images and retrieve them it will be nothing more than utilizing technology of data storage and sampling. When we speak of dynamic models as subsystems and complex interaction we do not think of content in terms of what is to be input or provided. Content is not what we put into the composition, rather we prepare the system and structure such that content will be brought up by ways of representing systems behaviors. The systems behavior again is not the content-oriented goal itself. It is the product of complex interactions involving internal structures of the complex system in which the interaction takes place.

Time-Critical Performance

Physical relativity assures us that there must be a temporal gap between "now" in one location and its report elsewhere. Transmissions of signals cannot overcome this interval. A military operation occurs across a sequence of such intervals. The commander's intuition masters time by anticipating future events, as if bringing about the expected in advance of its occurrence. In the case of physical transmissions, information overload results from the latency between ground truth and information display. This is due to the accountability of the variable n. If a commander could be in n places at once, where $n > 1$, then interpretation and decision would receive timely execution. However, if $n = 1$, the commander acts in real time. In military doctrine a commander may substitute n-time execution with recursive time, in the form of a Prioritized Information Request (PIR). A PIR is a recursive query. It asks a big question, the big question in turn asks smaller questions, and so on down the chain of command. Eventually the smallest answers report to bigger answers, and so on. When enough answers return, a decision is made at the top. But there is rarely enough time during battle to complete the recursion. Decisions are made with less than complete knowledge. In place of knowledge, the commanding officer relies upon information display. Information display may be thought of as a representation of time as knowledge. But this knowledge is implicit, as it is a representation of uncertainty. The difference between available information and knowledge required for a decision is the unknown quantity in the display.

In the *Ground Truth* installation, uncertainty is represented. This uncertainty is the asymptote of the research curve. The military term for the uncertainty curve is Situational Awareness.

Political Ideals and Their Application

There is a history of artists who step forward to support the cause of battle, such as those who shouldered arms against Franco in the Spanish Civil War. There is also a history of artist-activists opposed to what used to be called the "military-industrial complex." The acclimatization of artists to military practices reminds me of an anecdote told by a professor in a documentary film class. The class had just finished screening *The Battle of Anzio* by Frank Capra (director of *It's a Wonderful Life* and other films). Anzio was part of the "Why We Fight" cinema newsreel series, produced during World War II by the Department of Defense. Various Hollywood directors produced installments in this series as part of the war effort. Narration and raw footage were provided by the DoD. According to the story, officials were unhappy about an apparent time offset in Capra's work, between the narration and the

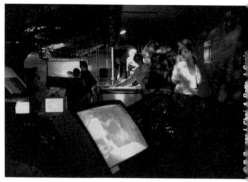

silent newsreel footage. The timing of the narration, they protested, unduly emphasized the soldiers' difficulties. The results were less than inspiring to prospective soldiers. Capra is said to have replied, "You didn't expect me to make a movie promoting war, did you?"

This research is supported by the Army Research Laboratory and the Army Intelligence and Security Command via the Advanced and Interactive Displays Consortium. The Consortium is sponsored by the U.S. Army Research Laboratory under the Federated Laboratory Program, Cooperative Agreement DAAL01-96-2-0003. The views and conclusions contained in this document are those of the authors and should not be interpreted as representing the official policies, either expressed or implied, of the Army Research Laboratory or the U.S. Government.

Survivability

> We live in a society with the generally accepted definition of adaptation.
> (Lorenz, 1965)

"Adaptation" is the process that molds the organism so that it fits its environment in a way achieving survival. As computer technology is advanced enough to update various simulations based upon complex phenomena, the logical processes based on biological explanations or "real-world" understandings come to the front line of discussions. Subsequently, metaphors such as "environmental fitness," "mutations," "memes," "adaptation," and "survival" cross over many disciplines. Let's not forget that metaphors are often used for explanatory designations. The uses of metaphors that are heavily dependent on explanatory powers often tend to be mistaken as prescriptions for the subsequent thoughts. The production of art differs from the production of explanations, and I cannot elaborate this here. However, as a composer I stand closely by the following reference. Not necessarily contradicting the preceding reference, as an alternative, in the early 1960s Ross Ashby stated:

> There is not a single mental faculty ascribed to Man that is good in the absolute sense. If any particular faculty is usually good, this is solely because our terrestrial environment is so lacking in variety that its usual form makes that faculty usually good.

> However absurd it appears to be, at least at first sight, this statement seems to contradict our common acceptance of nature as unpredictable in detail and uncontrollable by its nature. Note that the assertion that adaptability is "good" often shadows the examination of the condition under which certain adaptability is "good." Further, the value association obscures the fact that a generative process starts from the stipulation of constraints. The stipulation of constraints gains freedom and generative power. Performance may generate metaphor but is not constructed on explanation-based metaphor.

In composing a medium, generating performance cases is preferred to explanations for examining the explainer's conditions under which the performance is generated. The criterion for composing a medium is to create the conditions such that certain human capacities are facilitated, otherwise the particular capabilities to observe might not be attainable. In creating this condition, performability is more of our concern than survivability. The art of a dreamer requires more than the adaptability for survival. One might have to refuse to survive under certain conditions in order to construct an alternative. "Survive!" advised he who has survived. He could be the dreamer's nightmare.

Notes

1. The CAVE is a room-sized, surround-screen, projection-based interactive virtual environment. The Ars Electronica Museum has licensed a CAVE from the University of Illinois.

2. Sonification is the transformation of data into synthesized sound for purposes of observing that data.

3. Shannon and Weaver, The Theory of Communication (Urbana: University of Illinois Press, 1959).

Are You Online?
Presence and Participation in Network Art

Andreas Broeckmann

Even at the beginning of 1997 a lot of people had a strong feeling that this was going to be the Year of Net Art, and that after a brief summer the artists would either have to go and look for new challenges, or try to exploit what would most probably become acceptable for a wider audience and therefore also become increasingly integrated into the "Operating System Art." So last year, interested observers could witness and participate in: extended online discussions about the technological and art historical contexts from which net art emerged; bickering about whether it was pretentious, funny, or accurate to speak of net.art, the dot becoming the object of heated debate; international meetings at which the future history of the net.art movement was determined and deconstructed. The presence of some of the heroes and heroines of the cluster of artists—who insisted that they were neither a movement nor a group, mainly because nobody wanted to go down in the expected demise of the net.art label—at major international art exhibitions and media art festivals was looked at with collective pride and individual envy.

The discussions about net.art (I stick with this label for the moment, meaning especially a kind of hybrid WWW-Situationism) gave us an important break. They made it possible to distinguish more clearly between art on the net and art in the net. Art on the net uses the Internet as a distribution medium, whether in the form of the derided virtual galleries, i.e. displays of 2-D artworks, photographs, computer graphics, etc., that in themselves bear no relation to the Internet, or in the form of a channel for conceptual artworks, in which case the Internet is an effective but potentially replaceable presentation tool. Art in the net is germane to the medium of the electronic networks: it plays with their protocols and technical peculiarities, it exploits the bugs and pushes the potentials of software and hardware—it is unthinkable without its medium, the Internet. At the same time, art in the net shows a keen awareness not only of the technological, but also of social and cultural aspects of the Internet, and plays on them through hybrid, intermedial artistic strategies.

It is obvious that in a, primarily, late-modernist cultural environment, the latter, more purist version of network art was favoured by many. The statements of the .Net juries of the Prix Ars Electronica have also, since 1995, paid tribute to this understandable bias. Only postmodern cynics would have done otherwise. It has been a problem for exhibition and festival curators, however, to present this kind of work for an audience that, even granted that it might be interested in this new art form, was seldom initiated into its rituals. I say rituals because much of the excitement and thrill of network art has been derived from the sense of being present at and participating in an event or process that hinges on the co-presence and the cooperation of several people. In short, from the sense of being online—and this not so much in the technical sense of having access to a networked computer, but as a mentality, a state of mind that evolves in people who work and "live" in a distributed electronic environment that is "charged" with fast and often nervous information exchange—a state of mind which is by no means germane only to network artists.

The worst thing a curator can do is to make a list of hyperlinks to selected websites, put them on the web pages of the festival or exhibition, not pay the artists a fee (using the argument that their projects are online and thus publicly available anyway), and then put a series of online computers somewhere in the exhibition where the audience can look at the projects—and surf the WWW freely. The latter point—temporary free access to the Internet—is probably the only positive aspect of the set-up. A variation to this worst-case scenario was the WWW part of the Documenta X art exhibition in Kassel/Germany in 1997 where the artists were paid, but the projects were running offline and in a sad grey-and-white pseudo-office. Do this if you want to prevent your audience from understanding what network art might be about.

The *openX* environment at the Ars Electronica Festival 97 in Linz was a more creative and more daring attempt at dealing with the difficulties of presenting net art in a festival situation. I will from now on use the term "net art" in the broader sense, meaning art practices based in the Internet, from WWW-based projects and live-audio experiments, to communication projects that use IRC (Internet relay chat), FTP (file transfer protocol), Telnet, and other Internet protocols. More than ten different online projects were invited to work on the mezzanine of the Linz Design Center during the festival, and for a week over fifty people spent long days and evenings on their islands of tables and terminals in this localised archipelago of network creativity. Many of the people in the different projects knew and had worked with one another before and were now given the unique opportunity of being able to do what they always do in close physical vicinity: communicate, investigate, write, programme, and design in the net.

openX was therefore an almost 1:1 representation of the situation in which net art is being created every day. Artists who sometimes know each other in person, and sometimes do not, work together in smaller communities which overlap with other such communities. More communication and creative potential are derived from the contacts between these groups, mutual contamination and transformation guaranteed. In practice, this concept worked only in part. The re-mapping of a translocal assemblage in a localised setting showed both advantages and disadvantages for the artists' cooperation. Maybe due to the unfamiliar opportunity, certainly due to a lack of time during the short five days of the festival, much of the situation's potential could not be realised and the artists went away again, slightly dizzy and confused like after a roller-coaster ride.

While these are intricacies of on/off-line cooperation, a crucial problem of the presentation of network art is the relationship between the artists or producers, and the audience. As hinted before, how does one show the essential thrill of online art to a curious outsider? Some of the *openX* participants were still under shock from their experience at the Documenta X that summer, where the *Hybrid Workspace* of the Berlin Biennale had offered Kassel's Orangerie as a 100-day media cultural workshop for different international groups. The *Hybrid Workspace* itself was a flexible, multi-functional working environment, and most of the dozen or so workshops were great successes with many good results. Yet, how do you deal with a thousand or more Documenta visitors who come in every day and who want to see the art? In Kassel, it was very difficult even to begin to communicate to the audience what the workshops were about, given the short attention span of the exhausted art show visitors.

Unlike the *Hybrid Workspace*, *openX* had a smaller and probably more online audience, with many of the visitors having their own, often extensive experience with the networks. Yet, participants of both projects found it difficult to reconcile the wish to work together in the workshop, with the necessity to represent that work to a larger audience. Some were better at this than others, especially those who were dealing with campaign-like themes and strategies. But few were happy about the fact that their processual work was on display as though it was a performance about the artist at work. What they normally do at their terminals at home or in the studio was not only changed quite significantly through the sudden physical vicinity to the other artists, but was also exposed in a way that it normally isn't. Real-life presence and confrontation is normally not something that comes into play in net art, large parts of the net being a meshwork of distributed private spaces, rather than a public space.

A description of the different functional layers of the electronic networks can help to elucidate the invertedness of some of the current net-based art. The following will be familiar to readers, but in times of electronic commerce and the Ubiquitous Buy-Button it seems important to reaffirm the diversity of tools for net-based creativity. In the first instance, the net is a communication-scape where via a multitude of channels (e-mail, newsgroups, mailing lists, IRC, CUSeeMe, etc.) conversations are going on between individuals and groups of every size, from two to several thousand. Like any good conversation, these get better the better the participants know each other. The international *Xchange* network of net-radio enthusiasts is a good example of such a distributed group that builds their creative cooperation in live-audio streaming, on the communication channels that connect them. The people of *Xchange* and others are thus also exploring the net as a soundscape with particular qualities in data transmission, delay, feedback, and open, distributed collaborations. Moreover, they connect the network with a variety of other fields. Instead of defining an "authentic" place in their artistic work, they play in the transmedial zone of media labs in different countries, mailing lists, netcasting and FM broadcasting, clubs, magazines, stickers, etc., in which "real" spaces and media continuously overlap and fuse.

The use of the spatial, perspectival metaphor of the "scape" may be misleading as it may call up the association of a euclidian, three-dimensional space which encapsulates these different functions. Instead, one must remember that we are talking about digital data being sent around in a network infrastructure of computers, cables, and wireless transmitters. The datascape of the net is a multi-dimensional, continuously transforming topology rather than a landscape with a horizon. It is worth mentioning that there are now an increasing number of studies and projects that try to describe or map this datascape by means of dynamic 3-D structures created in VRML (Virtual Reality Modeling Language). These projects remain, however, limited by the three-dimensional framework. Even when this three-dimensionality is upgraded with hyperlinks and morphing shapes, it is still unable to capture the complexities of the network topologies.

Although the net is an expansive and heterogeneous medium for communication between people, it is, in the first instance, a machine-scape. Computers are connected to computers, exchanging large chunks of control and coordination data at an almost unimaginable rate. To get a glimpse of the extent of machine communication, just study the full Path information of any e-mail message: an elaborate series of IP numbers, exact dates, and information about software and encoding protocols which travels with and is accumulated by any data packet that travels across the net. Some recent art projects deal with the particular aesthetics of the machine-scape, like I/O/D's *Web Stalker* which scans the hyperlinks of WWW pages, displays their HTML code as the Stalker agent analyses the pages, and maps the hyperlink structure in plain and evocative graphs, allowing a surprising look at the underside of the Web. The degree to which this techno-topological infrastructure of the net is invested with—open and disguised—economic, political, symbolic power has been exposed critically by Paul Garrin's *name.space* project. Yet, the more precise such projects become in a technical sense, the more esoteric they appear to those who don't know how to read the ciphers and letters.

Obviously, the net is also an image-scape, and the World Wide Web is its news-stand, art gallery, and photo album. It is worth remembering that the WWW was initially designed to allow for the display, distribution, and hyperlinking of texts and images, tasks which were supported by the first standard WWW browsers. Sounds, moving images, and interactive functions were added later and still require a series of more or less standardised software plug-ins. The text-and-image legacy of the WWW can be derided as an online equivalent of the 2-D graphic and print media, but this might be the function that it is best at for the large audiences that its commercial developers are interested in. It is important that the WWW is a simple enough publishing medium that allows lots of people to show their stuff. But what if not everybody wants to become an active participant, what if not everybody wants to go online?

The Internet is, finally, also becoming an action-scape, an environment that supports particular types of agency which, at a time of general demise of democratic decision-making and control, suggest at least the possibility of new forms of action in the public domain. The *10_Dencies* project by Knowbotic Research is an attempt at exploring the potential for acting in translocal, networked environment. It creates an interface between the communication-scapes and the machine-scapes of the net and asks what the topology of agency might be in such hybrid and connective environments.

The above is by no means an exhaustive analysis of what the Internet is. Trading, game-playing, gambling, multi-casting of texts, sounds, and images, all these are prominent functions of the net. The WWW is an intermedial environment that supports or gives access to some of these different functions. What makes network art interesting at the moment, however, is happening away from the WWW. The decision of the .Net Jury of the 1998 Prix Ars Electronica shows this, since three projects for the prizes which are all not or not primarily WWW projects have been selected.

The experience of net-based art is closely tied up with online presence and an active participation in the creative process, whether it is located primarily in a machine or in a networked community. To reformulate an earlier statement: a key problem of the presentation of network art is that there is no distinction between the artists and the audience, between production and reception. You perceive through being a participant, you produce by receiving. Net art is online, and it is for those who are online.

The theory of network creativity, and of the creative use of digital media in general, has emphasised the fact that this technology empowers every user of a computer to become a creator and to participate in the "global concert" of online artists. Even if digital media theoretically offer this possibility, what we can see now is that the same network environments might be of exclusive interest for those people who actually want to become producers. Participation becomes not only an option but a condition. If this is true, it means that the Brechtian utopia of a community of media producers could fail once again, in part because commercial interest prevents strong uploading channels, but in part also because large sections of the prospective producer-receivers would make no use of the tools and the bandwidth, even if they were available.

This is not a very satisfying analysis, certainly not from the perspective of critical cultural practice in and through digital media. Does it mean that, online and offline, we are stuck with fancy interfaces and an interactivity that only "works" if it is entertaining? And, in contrast, what would it mean for festival audiences and others to go online, to "become online" in the way that many artists are who are doing net-based work? Or rather, what if festivals were to facilitate the online experiences of participants and visitors being brought together, so that they could meet, conflict, and cooperate with each other at the multiple points of contiguity and intersection between the different online worlds (hackers, NGOs, business networks, etc.)? What would the festivals and exhibition spaces be like that would really allow an audience to come and observe, participate, operate?

The question of how to present network art, and how to articulate online presence and participation, can thus be posed on two levels. One is that of connecting different forms of online experience, and the other is the demonstration of "mediated space and real space as all one constantly interlocking and changing topology" (Lisa Haskel). In curatorial practice, this means that more emphasis needs to be placed on the interface, alongside the representation or critical practice that form the content of network art projects. The interface is both the terrain and the tool where the forces of an intermedial field converge, and which can be developed as a field of agency, and a field of subjectification. Presence and participation might be unlocked through the development of hybrid, plural, and porous interfaces that cut across mediated and "real" experiential terrains, involve different audiences and that facilitate forms of becoming online that are, at the same time, ways of becoming public.

(Thanks to Lisa Haskel and Tapio Mäkelä for critical comments and suggestions.)

Andreas Broeckmann *Are You Online?*

Biographies

Robert Adrian is a Canadian artist living in Austria since 1972. His installations, graphics and tele-communications projects have been featured at the Biennale in Venice (1980, 1986), in the Biennale in Sydney, and in numerous international and one-person shows. In addition to more conventional media, he began to work with tele-communications technology in 1979 and was the author of a number of early network projects.

Roy Ascott is Director of CAiiA-STAR. *Is There Love in the Telematic Embrace?*, covering 35 years of his work, edited by Edward A. Shanken, is published by University of California Press, 1999. His book *Art & Telematics* was published by NTT Tokyo in 1998.

Edouard Bannwart studied architecture in Zurich and Berlin. He has his own architecture and urban planning office and teaches.

Robin Bargar is a composer in acoustic and visual media. At the National Center for Supercomputing Applications he founded the Audio Development Group and directed the development of VSS, a sound synthesis software platform for sonification, composition and performance with computer graphics and virtual environments. His work has been performed at SIGGRAPH, ISEA, MTV, Imagina.

Bilwet/Adilkno, The Foundation for the Advancement of Illegal Knowledge, est. 1983 in Amsterdam, is a loose gathering of happy, unemployed intellectuals. Amongst their publications are *Cracking the Movement* and *The Media Archive*, both published by Autonomedia, Brooklyn.

Bazon Brock is a teacher, artist, theoretician and pioneer in Happenings and Pop-art. Since the 1970s he has participated in countless events, exhibitions and congresses and has published radio plays, TV films, and dramas (as actor and/or director).

Andreas Broeckmann is a project manager at V2_Organisation, Rotterdam, media theorist and European networker commuting from Berlin. Studied art history, sociology and media studies and received a PhD from the University of East Anglia, Norwich/UK, writing about the use of portrait photography in the 19th-century human sciences ("A Visual Economy of Individuals," 1995, unpublished). In his recent theoretical work he is developing ideas for a "machinic" aesthetics of media art.

Cabaret Voltaire was born in 1974 (with Chris Watson, Stephen Mallinder and Richard Kirk) from a "mutual interest in sound." By 1986 Cabaret Voltaire was 12 years old. "Not bad for a band that began with little more than a tape recorder and an oscillator."

Loren Carpenter is the inventor and President of CINEMATRIX interactive and a pioneer in the field of computer graphics. Together with his wife, Rachel, he founded CINEMA-TRIX to explore the intersection of computers and art. CINEMATRIX focused on the development of audience participation technology.

John L. Casti has devoted a substantial part of his time to the preparation of several books on science for the student and/or general reader. The first was the award-winning *Alternate Realities: Mathematical Models of Nature and Man;* others are *Paradigms Lost: Images of Man in the Mirror of Science, Searching for Certainty, Complexification, Five Golden Rules.* His most recent popular-science offering is *Would-Be Worlds.* His first foray into what he calls "scientific fiction" is the work *The Cambridge Quintet*, a fictional account of a dinner party in Cambridge, UK in 1949, at which the question of the possibility of the creation of a thinking machine is the focus of the dinner-party conversation.

Daniel Charles is on the Faculté des Lettres Arts et Sciences Humaines at the Université Nice Sophia Antipolis. He writes about the aesthetics of contemporary music and has published *Musiques Nomades*, and contributes to numerous journals including *Revue d'Esthétique*.

Insook Choi is composer in residence at National Center for Supercomputing Applications and Research Specialist in Human-Computer Intelligent Interaction at the Beckman Institute. She has created numerous interdisciplinary projects across cognitive science, engineering, and music performance.

She is frequently invited as a performer and speaker and publishes across the disciplines of art, science and engineering.

Jürgen Claus is an artist, writer, and curator. He organized the exhibition "Art and Technology" at the Federal Ministry of Research and Technology in Bonn (1984), and "Terminal Art" for Ars Electronica in 1986. He was a Fellow at the Center for Advanced Visual Studies at MIT (1983) and has written extensively, including *Expansion of the Arts* (1970), *Umweltkunst* (1982). He has participated in numerous exhibitions and symposia.

Critical Art Ensemble is a collective of artists with various specializations including computer art, film/video, photography, text art, book art and performance. CAE's focus has been on the exploration of the intersections between art, critical theory, technology, and political activism. CAE produces projects for a broad range of cultural situations including bars and clubs, community centers, public spaces, universities, galleries, and museums, radio and television, and the Internet. CAE has also produced a substantial body of cultural criticism including *The Electronic Disturbance, Electronic Civil Disobedience,* and *FleshMachine.*

Richard Dawkins moved to England at the age of eight and was educated in Oxford. After a few years at the University of California at Berkeley he returned to Oxford where he is now a Reader in Zoology and a Fellow of New College. He broke new ground in the theory of evolution with his 1976 book *The Selfish Gene* and has continued to promote the Darwinian cause with his other best-selling books, *The Extended Phenotype* and *The Blind Watchmaker.*

Derrick de Kerckhove is director of the McLuhan Programme in Culture and Technology at the University of Toronto. He has published extensively in the field of communication theory. His work involves neuro-cultural research investigations into the impact of media such as writing, television and computers on the human nervous system. His scientific research at present is to explore the impact of television on the human nervous systems. Beside his scientific interests in communications, he is promoting a new field of artistic endeavours which bring together art, engineering and recent developments in communication technologies.

Manuel De Landa is the author of two philosophy books, *War in the Age of Intelligent Machines* (1991) and *A Thousand Years of Nonlinear History* (1997), and of many philosophical essays published in various journals. He teaches a seminar at Columbia University on "Theories of Self-Organization and Urban History," and lectures around the world on the philosophy of science and technology.

Timothy Druckrey is an independent curator and writer concerned with the history and theory of media and the transformation of representation, communication, and art in an increasingly electronic culture. He co-edited *Culture on the Brink: Ideologies of Technology* and edited *Iterations: The New Image,* and *Electronic Culture: Technology and Visual Representation.* He lectures internationally about the social impact of digital media, the transformation of representation, and communication in interactive and networked environments. Currently he is editing a series of books for MIT Press titled *Electronic Culture: History, Theory, Practice,* of which this volume marks the debut.

Thomas Feuerstein studied art history and philosophy and lives in Austria.

Scott S. Fisher is a media artist, producer, and director whose work focuses primarily on immersive environments and technologies of presence. Known for his work as director of the Virtual Environment Workstation (VIEW) Project at NASA's Ames Research Center from 1985 to 1990, currently he is President of Telepresence Media, a company focusing on the art and design of virtual environment and remote presence experiences; Professor in the Faculty of Environmental Information at Keio University in Japan; and Director of the Virtual Explorer Project in the Department of Chemistry and Biochemistry at the University of California, San Diego.

Vilém Flusser was one of Europe's leading media theorists. His work ranged from studies in the theory of the image to cultural histories of memory and media culture. His numerous books include *Toward a Philosophy of Photography, Kommunikologie,* and *Der Flusser Reader zu*

Kommunikation, Medien und Design.

Herbert W. Franke is a physicist interested in art/technology relations and active in the fields of art theory and computer graphics—for art and for the visualization of mathematics.

Peter Fromherz PhD in Physical Chemistry, University Marburg/Lahn 1981 Chair of Experimental Physics, University Ulm/Donau 1994 Director at the Max-Planck-Institute for Biochemistry, Department Membrane and Neurophysics Martinsried/München.

Kit Galloway was a Member of the legendary European-based multimedia group Videoheads 1971–1974; formed life-long telecollaborative arts lab with Sherrie Rabinowitz, Paris in 1975; created Satellite Arts (A Live Tele-visually Composited Performance Place), 1977; Hole-In-Space, 1980; Electronic Cafe, 1984; Electronic Café International, 1985-present. Currently he is creating an on-line archive of his work.

Guillermo Gòmez-Peña is an interdisciplinary artist and writer known for his innovative use of performance, journalism, video, radio, and installation art to explore cross-cultural issues. He draws on his Latino background to bridge cultural borders through the use of high technology.

Heidi Grundmann is a curator and consultant at the interface between the old and new media. In 1987 she developed Kunstradio, a radio program of original artworks for the radio medium, for the ORF (Austrian Broadcasting Corp.).

Mike Hentz has worked in the field of media since the 1980s. His performances and collaborations include Death Opera (in Linz, 1982), the European Media Art Lab, Piazza Virtuale (with Van Gogh TV), RO MA MA CHINE (Hamburg, 1995), and Macroland (1997).

Nick Herbert is a California physicist, author of *Quantum Reality, Faster Than Light* and *Elemental Mind.* Herbert devised the shortest proof of Bell's Theorem and is the originator of Quantum Tantra, prime contender for a successor science to today's wholly materialist physics.

Kathy Rae Huffman is a curator, writer, networker and Assistant

Professor of Media Art at Rensselaer Polytechnic Institute. She lectures extensively on Internet art, art-video, interactive TV, and the history of artists and television. She is a correspondent for *Telepolis* and contributes to *rhizome,* the magazines for net culture.

Hervé Huitric has worked since the 1980s in film and synthetic images. He has participated in numerous exhibitions and symposia and has shown work at SIGGRAPH, the Musée d'Art Moderne de la Ville de Paris, and Ars Electronica. He collaborates with Monique Nahas.

Toshio Iwai is an interactive artist who graduated from Tsukuba University. He has had numerous solo exhibitions worldwide and two of his works are permanently displayed at San Francisco's Exploratorium. He has been artist in residence at ZKM/Karlsruhe and at IAMAS.

Douglas Kahn is Associate Professor of Media Arts, University of Technology, Sydney. He is the author of *Noise, Water, Meat: A History of Sound in the Arts* (MIT Press, 1999).

Friedrich Kittler studied German and French Literatures and Philosophy at the University of Freiburg/Breisgau. From 1987 to 1993 Professor of Literature at the Ruhr University, Bochum and since 1993, Professor of Media History and Aesthetics at the Humboldt University, Berlin. His major publications in English are *Discourse Networks 1800/1900, Grammophone Film Typewriter* (both from Stanford University Press), and *Literature, Media, Information Systems* (G & B Arts).

Knowbotic Research (KR+cF) is an artist group based in Cologne (Yvonne Wilhelm, Christian Hübler, Alexander Tuchacek). They build experimental and tactical interfaces for local and trans-local urban environments. They founded *Mem_Brane,* a laboratory for media strategies, and have developed *Dialogue with the Knowbotic South* (1995), *Anonymous Muttering* (1996), and *10_Dencies* (1997).

Hari Kunzru is a London-based writer and techno-cultural commentator. He is on the editorial board of *Mute* magazine and presents "The Lounge," a magazine programme about the electronic arts on [.tv].

Christopher G. Langton is a scientist in the Complex Systems Group of the Theoretical Division of Los Alamos National Laboratory. He is also on the Faculty of the Santa Fe Institute, where he is the director of the Artificial Life program. He organized the first international conference on Artificial Life in Los Alamos (in 1987) and has edited the volumes from the continuing conferences. He is editor of the MIT Press journal *Artificial Life*. His research focuses on the physics of computation, measures of complexity, computational biology, collective behavior, the origin of life and evolution.

Jaron Lanier is a computer scientist, businessman and composer. In 1984 he founded VPL Research Inc., a highly regarded Silicon Valley R&D company, the developer of the first commercially available Virtual Reality system, as well as the Power Glove (licensed to Mattel and sold in Japan by PAX), Swivel 3D, the most popular Macintosh 3D tool (licensed to Paracomp, Inc.), and other well-known products. His work has been featured many times in books, articles and on national television, and he is best known in the scientific community as a designer of computer programming languages. He has also been a political activist, a designer of video games and a composer.

Hannes Leopoldseder has been working for the Austrian Broadcasting Corporation since 1967. Since 1974 he was General Manager of the Upper Austrian Regional Studios. In 1979 he co-founded Ars Electronica and the Linz Sound Cloud. In 1978 he initiated the Prix Ars Electronica and in 1993 the Ars Electronica Center.

Gerhard Johann Lischka is a freelance cultural philosopher, writer, and teacher. He is editor of the series "um9," and has organized numerous exhibitions, and TV programmes. His books include *Die Schönheit der Schönheit: Super-ästhetik, Kulturkunst, die Medien-falle, Über die Mediatisierung: Medien und Re-Medien*.

Geert Lovink media theorist and activist, based in Amsterdam, member of Adilkno, co-editor of the nettime mailing-list, and co-organizer of the Next Five Minutes conferences.

Steve Mann inventor of the so-called "wearable computer" (WearComp), the EyeTap video camera and reality mediator (WearCam), is currently a faculty member at University of Toronto, Department of Electrical and Computer Engineering. He brought his inventions and ideas to MIT in 1991, founding what was to later become the MIT Wearable Computing Project. He also built the world's first covert fully functional WearComp with display and camera concealed in ordinary eyeglasses in 1995, for the creation of his award-winning documentary *ShootingBack*. He writes and speaks regularly on the issues of privacy, surveillance and technology.

Just Merrit's work deals with the boundaries between human and behavioral patterns and driving compulsion. Using the tools of noise *(Krüppelschlag)* and mechanical sculpture *(Gyroscope)*, and fanning conceptual sparks to catch fire, he attempts to track down the traces of human bio-mechanical dependencies—to find out what they are.

Marvin Minsky teaches and does research at MIT where he is the Donner Professor of Science. He was one of the pioneers of computer science, involved in establishing the scientific foundations of several important areas: artificial intelligence, parallel distributed processing and neural networks, theories of Turing machines and recursive functions, robotics, computer vision, and telepresence. He was a founder of MIT's Artificial Intelligence Laboratory, General Turtle, Inc., Logo Computer Systems, Inc., and Thinking Machines Corporation. He has been an advisor to NASA, the L-5 Society, and the National Dance Institute. His main concern over the past decade was to work out the foundations of the new conception of human psychology described in *The Society of Mind*. He was awarded the Japan Prize in 1990 in the field of Technology of Integration.

Robert Moog has developed a wide range of electronic musical instruments, especially the Moog electronic music synthesizer. He is currently president of Big Briar, Inc., builders of Theremins, analog effects modules, and synthesizers.

Hans Moravec was Senior Scientist at Carnegie-Mellon's Robotics Institute. His involvement with robots began at an early age. Since 1980 he has been director if the CMU Mobile Robot Laboratory.

His numerous books include *Mind Children* and, most recently, *Robot: Mere Machine to Transcendent Mind*.

Monique Nahas is Professor in Art and Technology of the Image at the University of Paris 8. She has participated in numerous exhibitions and symposia and has shown work at SIGGRAPH, the Musée d'Art Moderne de la Ville de Paris, and Ars Electronica. She collaborates with Hervé Huitric.

Bob O'Kane is an artist working in Germany. He studied at the Institut für Neue Medien in Frankfurt and has collaborated with, among others, Peter Weibel and Ulrike Gabriel.

Otto Piene studied in Munich, Düsseldorf and Cologne before moving to the US where he became Fellow at the Center for Advanced Visual Studies (1968). In 1974 he becomes director of CAVS and begins the Sky Art Conferences.

Sadie Plant is the author of *The Most Radical Gesture, Zeros and Ones*, and *Writing on Drugs*. She gained her PhD from the University of Manchester in 1989, and worked at the Universities of Birmingham and Warwick before leaving to write full-time in 1997.

Sherrie Rabinowitz graduated with honors from University of California, Berkeley, School of Environmental Design, majoring in Architecture. She was a founding member Optic Nerve video and was invited to France by the French Ministry of Foreign Affairs to talk/show American experimental video. In Paris, she met life partner and collaborator Kit Galloway.

Heimo Ranzenbacher is a journalist, art critic, theorist and artist living in Graz. He has written in numerous catalogues and periodicals, made many presentations at symposia, and worked on diverse art projects including "Klang-Figur" (an interactive sound performance with Werner Jauk) in 1991. In 1993 he founded TXTD.sign—a studio for aesthetic services—in 1994 the installation "Lichtzeichen, Utopie-Kunststraße," Innsbruck, and in 1995, "Soundartikel Esc.," in Graz.

Birgit Richard studied art, history and philosophy at the Universities of Essen and Fernuni Hagen; member of the scholarly staff in the Department of Art and Design of the University of Essen; doctoral dissertation "Death Images in Art and Contemporary Juvenile Subcultures." Since 1988 University Professor for New Media at the Johann Wolfgang von Goethe University in Frankfurt am Main, Institute for Art Pedagogy, Department of Art and Classical Philology; fields of specialization: new media, aesthetics of everyday life (in particular contemporary youth culture), life and death of artificially generated forms of life.

Otto E. Rössler was trained in medicine and obtained his PhD in immunology. Since 1970 he has taught at the University of Tübingen. He was Visiting Professor of Mathematics at Guelph University in 1981 and, in 1983 Visiting Professor in Nonlinear Science at the Center for Nonlinear Studies at Los Alamos. He has authored hundreds of papers on chaos and other topics. He is co-author of a book on chaos (with Jürgen Parisi and Joachim Peinke) and author of *Endophysics* (edited by Peter Weibel), and *Das Flammenschwert oder Wie hermetisch ist die Schnittstelle Mikrokonstruktivismus? (The Sword of Flames, or How Hermetic is the Interface of Microconstructivism?).*

Florian Rötzer is a writer and editor of *Telepolis* (an on-line journal of net culture) living in Munich.

Morgan Russell is editor of the ur-cyberculture magazines *Reality Hackers* and *MONDO 2000*, organizer of numerous cyber-events in Europe, and, with Mitsuhiro Takemura, ditto in Japan.

Ryuichi Sakamoto is an internationally recognized composer, performer and media artist. His work for films (Bernardo Bertolucci's *The Last Emperor, The Sheltering Sky*, and the *Little Buddha)* have received Grammy, Academy and Gloden Globe Awards.

John Sanborn is known for innovative, experimental, and popular creations in the field of video art. Beginning in the late 1970s, he has worked in media. His works have been at the Whitney Biennial, MoMA, the Berlin Film Festival, Centre Pompidou, ICA (London) and in numerous other venues.

Christine Schöpf studied German and Romance languages and has been a journalist for ORF since 1977. Since 1981 she has been

the head of the department of art and science, focusing on Ars Electronica at the Upper Austria regional ORF studio. Together with Gerfried Stocker she is responsible for the programme of the annual Ars Electronica Festival.

Roberto Sifuentes is an interdisciplinary artist whose work examines the perceptions of Chicano and Mexican cultures. He performs internationally and collaborates frequently with Guillermo Gòmez-Peña.

Karl Sims graduated from MIT with an MS in Visual Studies and a BS in Life Sciences. As a research scientist at Thinking Machines Corporation he explored techniques for creating images using computers. He is founder and president of Genetic Arts, Inc. He develops special effects software and interactive media art. His interactive works include *Interactive Video Kaleidoscope* and *Genetic Images*.

Christa Sommerer and Laurent Mignonneau are artists and researchers at the ATR Advanced Telecommunications Research Lab (MIC) in Kyoto, Japan. Their field of study includes interactive computer installation, artificial life, complexity, communication, interface design and the convergence of art and science *(Art@Science*, Springer Verlag, 1998).

Stadtwerkstatt is an independent cultural society (founded in Linz, Austria, 1979) dedicated to promoting and furthering initiatives in the arts. Since its inception, it has pursued numerous activities in the area of art and culture, with particular concentration upon "art as a public affair." Since 1986 it has utilized television as an "artistic tool" and has produced STWST-TV. In the past few years it has encouraged public access to electronic media.

Stelarc's interest has always been the prosthetic augmentation of the body. He has performed with a third hand, a stomach sculpture, and a six-legged walking machine. He is now working on an extra ear that will function as an Internet antenna.

Bruce Sterling, author, journalist, editor, and critic, has written six science fiction novels and two short story collections. He edited the anthology *Mirrorshades*, the definitive document of the cyberpunk

movement. He also wrote the nonfiction book *The Hacker Crackdown: Law and Disorder on the Electronic Frontier* (1992). He has written regular columns on popular science and literary criticism for *The Magazine of Fantasy and Science Fiction, Interzone*, and *Science Fiction Eye*. He is the moderator of the Dead Media Project, an Internet group which studies extinct forms of media. He has appeared in ABC's Nightline, BBC's The Late Show, CBC's Morningside, on MTV, and in *Wired, Whole Earth Review, World Art, Details, Computerworld, The New York Times, Der Spiegel, Mondo 2000*, and other equally improbable venues.

Kristine Stiles is an artist and Associate Professor of Art & Art History at Duke University. She is a specialist on international aspects of performance and experimental art. Her primary research is on destruction, violence, and trauma in contemporary international art and culture. She authored *Theories and Documents of Contemporary Art* (University of California Press) with Peter Selz in 1996. Her forthcoming books include *Correspondence Course: The Letters and Performances of Carolee Schneemann* (Johns Hopkins University Press, 2001), *Uncorrupted Joy: Art History and International Performance Art* (University of California Press, 2001) and a compilation of her essays entitled *Concerning Consequences: Visualizing Traumatic Subjectivity*.

Gerfried Stocker is a media artist and graduate of the Institute for Telecommunication Engineering and Electronics in Graz. Since 1990, he has been working as an independent artist. In 1991, he founded x-space, a team for the realization of interdisciplinary projects. In this framework numerous installations and performance projects have been carried out in the field of interaction, robotics, and telecommunications. He was also responsible for the concept of various radio network projects and the organization of the worldwide radio and network project *Horizontal Radio*. Since 1995 he has been the artistic and managing director of the Ars Electronica Center. Together with Christine Schöpf he is responsible for the programme of the annual Ars Electronica Festival.

Allucquère Rosanne Stone is Assistant Professor in the Radio-TV-Film department of the University

of Texas at Austin, director of the
ACTLab (and spiritual leader of the
cadre of mad, brilliant cybercrazies
who inhabit it), and is teaching film
and video production, cultural theory,
gender and sexuality, interface and
interaction theory. Her research is in
the boundary between art and technology and includes performance
and performance theory, interface
and interaction theory, cyberspace,
virtual systems, desire, gender and
sexuality, and transgender theory in
relation to communication prosthetics, the complex interplay of science
fiction and the fictions of science.

Isao Tomita has composed and
created music and sound performances since the 1970s. His works
have premiered in innumerable concerts, festivals and cultural events.
His award-winning recordings and
collaborations in the fields of electronic sound extend across many
fields, from work for EXPO '70 in
Osaka to the performance of a
symphonic work, *The Tale of Genji*,
in 1998.

Van Gogh TV's history in the art
of transmission began in the mid-
1980s. In 1986 they established
the European Mobile Media Lab
(at Ars Electronica) and have since
worked on innumerable projects
in Documenta (8 & 9), the European
Media Art Festival (Osnabruck),
Karlsrhue (ZKM), Japan (NHK),
and Atlanta (Olympic Arts Festival).
They are currently working on a
Virtual Museum Project (VMS) with
museums in Skopje and Hannover
and preparing a VRML-ART exhibition for EMAF in Osnabruck

Paul Virilio studied architecture
in Paris. In 1963 he became founding
President of the Architecture
Principe group and editor of the
group's review. He has been
Professor of architecture at the Ecole
Spéciale d'Architecture in Paris since
1968, and became its Director of
Studies in 1973. The same year he
was named director of the "L'Espace
Critique" series by the publishers
Galilée of Paris. In 1975 he became
Director General of the Ecole
Spéciale d'Architecture and in 1989
Chairman of the Board. In 1975 he
coordinated the "Bunker
Archéologie" exhibition at the
Musée des Arts Décoratifs in Paris.
In 1989 he was named director of a
teaching programme at the Collège
International de Philosophie in Paris,
under the presidency of Jacques
Derrida. He became a member of the
High Committee for the Housing of

the Disadvantaged in 1992. His
Publications include:
*The Art of the Motor; Bunker
Archeology; The Vision Machine;
Aesthetics of Disappearance;
Popular Defense and Ecological
Struggles; Lost Dimension; Speed
and Politics; War and Cinema;
Pure War.*

Peter Weibel studied literature,
medicine, logic, and philosophy in
Paris and Vienna and wrote his the-
sis on mathematical logics. From
1976 to 1981 he was lecturer in the
theory of form and, in 1981, Visiting
Professor of Design and Art at the
Vienna University of Applied Arts
and was Visiting Professor at the
College of Art and Design in Halifax,
Canada. In 1981 he was lecturer in
Perception Theory and Professor of
Photography at Gesamthochschule in
Kassel. Since 1994 he has been
Professor of Visual Media at the
University of Applied Arts in Vienna
and Associate Professor of Video
and Digital Arts at the State
University of New York at Buffalo. In
1989 he headed the Institut für Neue
Medien at Städelschule in Frankfurt
am Main. He was Artistic Director of
Ars Electronica from 1986 until 1995.
He is currently the Director of the
ZKM in Karlsruhe. He has published
numerous books on twentieth centu-
ry art and technology.

Keigo Yamamoto works
in Japan and has participated in
numerous video festivals and
exhibitions.

Gene Youngblood is an
internationally known theorist and
historian of electronic media arts
and politics. He wrote *Expanded
Cinema* in 1968.

Melita Zajc studied the sociology
of culture, journalism and art history
in Ljubljana. She writes for *Mladina*
and other magazines, works for film
and television producers, and organizes the Autumn Film School. She
has been Junior Fellow Researcher
at the European Institute for the
Study of the Humanities and holds
a master's in Sociology.

Acknowledgments

The commitment of a number of people made this book possible. Thoughtful discussions with Hannes Leopoldseder and Christine Schöpf were followed by challenging meetings with Gerfried Stocker and Jutta Schmiederer. Their deep commitment to the festivals, symposia, exhibitions and, mostly, to the artists, critics, theoreticians, and historians is a testament both to the significance of the continuing idea of Ars Electronica, to the place it has sustained over the past 20 years, and to the future it is building. At the MIT Press, Roger Conover brought a considered commitment to the book (and to the series it inaugurates) as well as providing judicious advice and the well-placed, late-night remark, "welcome to publishing." This formidable group contributed greatly to the conceptualization and execution of the entire production.

As a framework for the book was set, Ingrid Fischer-Schreiber joined the team. With extraordinary skill, Ingrid maintained the delicate network of a book being designed in Linz, edited in NYC, produced in Cambridge, with authors all over the map. No small task, Ingrid has juggled every aspect of this book and never seemed to lose the balance between its objectives and the inevitable chaos that ensues. Hansi Schorn (and the staff) from Arthouse not only brought an elegant and thoughtful design, but also deftly managed what often seemed like more text than could ever make it into these pages. Thanks also got to Helmut Einfalt in Bremen for scanning and Matthew Abbate at MIT Press for copy-editing.

The largest acknowledgment goes to the authors and artists who contributed their texts and projects to this book. Often retrieving texts from what must be ancient disks, files, and hard-copy, they were unfailing in responding to requests for information and clarification. Beyond this they provided a welcome reminder that the field we work in is inhabited by some of the most generous, serious, and talented people I have ever met.

Personal thanks go to Perry Hoberman and to Ruth Hill.

Sources

Robert Adrian The World in 24 Hours. First published in: Linzer Veranstaltungsgesellschaft (ed.): Ars Electronica im Rahmen des Internationalen Brucknerfestes Linz, Festival für Kunst, Technologie und Gesellschaft 1982, Linz 1982, pp. 145 - 158 / **Roy Ascott** Gesamtdatenwerk, German version first published in: Im Netz der Systeme, Kunstforum International, Bd. 103, September/Oktober 1989, Köln 1989, pp. 100 - 108 / **Edouard Bannwart** The Medialization of Cities. First published in: Karl Gerbel/ Peter Weibel (eds.): Ars Electronica 94. Intelligente Ambiente - Intelligent Environments, Band 1, PVS Verleger, Wien 1994, pp. 138 - 142 / **Robin Bargar / Insook Choi** Ground Truth. First published in: Gerfried Stocker / Christine Schöpf (eds.): Ars Electronica 98. InfoWar, Springer Wien - New York 1998, pp. 122 - 127 / **Bilwet/Adilkno/Filwis** Cybermedia and the Fatal Attraction of Realities. First published in: Gottfried Hattinger / Peter Weibel (eds.): Ars Electronica 90, Band 2: Virtuelle Welten / Virtual Worlds, Veritas Verlag, Linz 1990, pp. 83 - 91 / **Bazon Brock** Propositions on the Dark Age of Television. First published in: Österreichischer Rundfunk ORF, Landesstudio Oberösterreich (ed.): Computerkulturtage Linz - ORF-Videonale 86, Linz 1986, pp. 179 - 180 / **Andreas Broeckmann** Are You Online? Presence and Participation in Network Art. First published in: Gerfried Stocker / Christine Schöpf (eds.): Ars Electronica 98. InfoWar, Springer Wien - New York 1998, pp. . 59 - 63 / **Cabaret Voltaire** A Contemplation of Dangerous Games. First published in: Linzer Veranstaltungsgesellschaft (ed.): Ars Electronica. Festival für Kunst, Technologie und Gesellschaft 1986, Linz 1986, pp. 101 - 102 / **Loren and Rachel Carpenter** Audience Participation. First published in: Karl Gerbel/ Peter Weibel (eds.): Ars Electronica 94. Intelligente Ambiente - Intelligent Environments, Band 2, PVS Verleger, Wien 1994, pp. 102 - 105 / **John L. Casti** The Three Faces of Life. First published in: Karl Gerbel / Peter Weibel (eds.): Ars Electronica 93. Genetische Kunst - Künstliches Leben. Artificial Life - Genetic Art, PVS Verleger, Wien 1993, pp. 12 - 24 / **Daniel Charles** "An Ear Alone Is Not a Being." First published in: Linzer Veranstaltungsgesellschaft (ed.): Ars Electronica 1987. Festival für Kunst, Technologie und Gesellschaft, Linz 1987, pp. 23 - 25 / **Jürgen Claus** Expansion of Media Art. First published in: Linzer Veranstaltungsgesellschaft (ed.): Ars Electronica im Rahmen des Internationalen Brucknerfestes Linz, Festival für Kunst, Technologie und Gesellschaft 1984, Linz 1984, pp. 177 - 179. Terminal Art. First published in: Linzer Veranstaltungsgesellschaft (ed.): Ars Electronica. Festival für Kunst, Technologie und Gesellschaft 1986, Linz 1986, pp. . 349 - 352 / **Critical Art Ensemble** Slacker Luddites. First published in: Karl Gerbel / Peter Weibel (eds.): Ars Electronica 95. Mythos Information, Welcome to the Wired World, Springer-Verlag Wien New York 1995, pp. 142 - 150 / **Richard Dawkins** Mind Viruses. First published in: Gerfried Stocker / Christine Schöpf (eds.): Ars Electronica Festival 96. Memesis - The Future of Evolution, Springer Wien - New York 1996, pp. 40 - 47 / **Derrick DeKerckhove** Virtual Reality for Collective Cognitive Processing. First published in: Gottfried Hattinger / Peter Weibel (eds.): Ars Electronica 90, Band 2: Virtuelle Welten / Virtual Worlds, Veritas Verlag, Linz 1990, pp. 171 - 185 / **Manuel De Landa** Economics, Computers, and the War Machine. First published in: Gerfried Stocker / Christine Schöpf (eds.): Ars Electronica 98. InfoWar, Springer Wien - New York 1998, pp. 164 - 172 / **Timothy Druckrey** NETOPOS . . . NOTOPOS, The Fate of Reason in the Global Network: Teleology, Telegraphy, Telephony, Television, Telesthetics. First published in: Karl Gerbel / Peter Weibel (eds.): Ars Electronica 95. Mythos Information, Welcome to the Wired World, Springer-Verlag Wien New York 1995, pp. 151 - 163 / **Thomas Feuerstein / Klaus Strickner** Trace Apparatus. First published in: Karl Gerbel / Peter Weibel (eds.): Ars Electronica 93. Genetische Kunst - Künstliches Leben. Artificial Life - Genetic Art, PVS Verleger, Wien 1993, pp. 302 - 308 / **Scott S. Fisher** Virtual Environments, Personal Simulation & Telepresence. First Published in: Gottfried Hattinger / Peter Weibel (eds.): Ars Electronica 90, Band 2: Virtuelle Welten / Virtual Worlds, Veritas Verlag, Linz 1990, pp. 147 - 157 / **Vilém Flusser** Memories, German version first published in: Ars Electronica (ed.): Philosophien der neuen Technologien, Merve Verlag Berlin 1989, pp. 41 - 56 (English translation by Catherine Saxon-Kerkhoff) / **Herbert W. Franke** Prologue. German version first published in: Linzer Veranstaltungsgesellschaft (ed.): Ars Electronica 1979 im Rahmen des Internationalen Brucknerfestes 79, Linz 1979, pp. 9 - 27. Art from the Screen. First published in: Linzer Veranstaltungsgesellschaft (ed.): Ars Electronica 1984. Festival für Kunst, Technologie und Gesellschaft, Linz 1984, pp. 174 - 177 / **Peter Fromherz** Neuron-Silicon Junction or Brain-Computer-Junction? First published in: Gerfried Stocker / Christine Schöpf (eds.): FleshFactor - Informationsmaschine Mensch. Ars Electronica Festival 97, Springer Wien - New York 1997, pp. 158 - 161 / **Guillermo Gòmez-Peña / Roberto Sifuentes** Fragments from Borderscape 2000. From the Chicano State Department Cronicles. First published in: Gerfried Stocker / Christine Schöpf (eds.): Ars Electronica 97. FleshFactor - Informationsmaschine Mensch, Springer Wien - New York 1997, pp. 162 - 167 / **Heidi Grundmann** Radio Art. German version first published in: Im Netz der Systeme, Kunstforum International, Bd. 103, September/ Oktober 1989, Köln 1989, pp. 276 - 289 / **Nick Herbert** Werner Alone Has Looked on Reality Bare: Proposal for a Really New "New Physics." First published in: Gottfried Hattinger / Peter Weibel (eds.): Ars Electronica 90, Band 2: Virtuelle Welten / Virtual Worlds, Veritas Verlag, Linz 1990, pp. 39 - 49 / **Mike Hentz** The Philosophical Data Bank of Minus Delta T. First published in: Linzer Veranstaltungsgesellschaft (ed.): Ars Electronica im Rahmen des Internationalen Brucknerfestes '84. Festival für Kunst, Technologie und Gesellschaft, Linz 1984, pp. 173 - 174 / **Kathy Rae Huffman** Video and Architecture beyond the Screen. First published in: Karl Gerbel/ Peter Weibel (eds.): Ars Electronica 94. Intelligente Ambiente - Intelligent Environments, Band 2, PVS Verleger, Wien 1994, pp. 156 - 161 / **Toshio Iwai / Ryuichi Sakamoto** Music Plays Images x Images Play Music. First published in: Gerfried Stocker / Christine Schöpf (eds.): Ars Electronica 97. FleshFactor - Informationsmaschine Mensch, Springer Wien - New York 1997, pp. 356 – 359 / **Hervé Huitric / Monique Nahas** The Visual Artist Turns to Computer Programming. First published in: Österreichischer Rundfunk ORF, Landesstudio Oberösterreich (ed.): Computerkulturtage Linz - ORF-Videonale 86, Linz 1986, pp. 104 - 107 / **Douglas Kahn** The Sound of Music. First published in: Linzer Veranstaltungsgesellschaft (ed.): Ars Electronica 1987. Festival für Kunst, Technologie und Gesellschaft, Linz 1987, pp. 44 - 51 / **Friedrich Kittler** On the History of the Theory of Information Warfare. First published in: Gerfried Stocker / Christine Schöpf (eds.): InfoWar, Ars Electronica 98, Springer Wien - New York 1998, pp. 266 - 272 / **KR+ cF Knowbotic Research** Simulationsraum. First published in: Karl Gerbel / Peter Weibel (eds.): Ars Electronica 93. Genetische Kunst - Künstliches Leben. Artificial Life - Genetic Art, PVS Verleger, Wien 1993, pp. 249 - 253 / **Hari Kunzru** Bad Girl Versus the Astronaut Christ: The Strange Political Journey of the Cyborg. First published in: FleshFactor - Informationsmaschine Mensch, Ars Electronica Festival 97, Springer Wien - New York 1997, pp. 100 - 109 / **Christopher Langton** Artificial Life. Unabbreviated version first published in: Karl Gerbel / Peter Weibel (eds.): Ars Electronica 93. Genetische Kunst - Künstliches Leben. Artificial Life - Genetic Art, PVS Verleger, Wien 1993, pp. 25 - 78 / **Hannes Leopoldseder** Ten Indications of an Emerging Computer Culture. First published in: Österreichischer Rundfunk ORF, Landesstudio Oberösterreich (ed.): Computer-kulturtage Linz - ORF-Videonale 86, Linz 1986, pp. 25 - 27 / **Gerhard J. Lischka** Media Art. First published in: Linzer Veranstaltungsgesellschaft (ed.): Ars Electronica. Festival für Kunst, Technologie und Gesellschaft 1986, Linz 1986, pp. 16-17 **Geert Lovink** The Memesis Network Discussion. First published in: Gerfried Stocker / Christine Schöpf (eds.): Ars Electronica Festival 96. Memesis - The Future of Evolution, Springer Wien-New York, pp. 28 - 39 / **Steve Mann** Humanistic Intelligence. First published in: Gerfried Stocker / Christine Schöpf (eds.): Ars Electronica 97. FleshFactor - Informationsmaschine Mensch, Springer Wien - New York 1997, pp. . 217 - 231 / **Just Merrit** What's That Supposed to Be, What's Program? First published in: Gerfried Stocker / Christine Schöpf (eds.): Ars Electronica Festival 96. Memesis - The Future of Evolution, Springer Wien-New York, pp. 337 - 351 / **Marvin Minsky** The Future Merging of Science, Art, and Psychology. First published in: Gottfried Hattinger / Peter Weibel (eds.): Ars Electronica 90, Band 2: Virtuelle Welten / Virtual Worlds, Veritas Verlag, Linz 1990, pp. 97 - 106 / **Robert Moog** MIDI: What It Is and What It Means to Electronic Artists. First published in: Linzer Veranstaltungs-gesellschaft (ed.): Ars Electronica im Rahmen des Internationalen Brucknerfestes Linz, Festival für Kunst, Techno-logie und Gesellschaft 1984, Linz 1984, pp. 185 - 186 / **Hans Moravec** The Universal Robot. First published in: Karl Gerbel (ed.): Ars Electronica 1991. Out of Control, Landesverlag Linz 1991, pp. 13 - 28 / **Otto Piene** Sky Art. First published in: Linzer Veranstaltungsgesellschaft (ed.): Ars Electronica im Rahmen des Internationalen Bruckner-festes Linz, Festival für Kunst, Technologie und Gesellschaft 1982, Linz 1982, pp. 122 - 124 / **Sadie Plant** Becoming Positive. First published in: Gerfried Stocker / Christine Schöpf (eds.): Ars Electronica Festival 96. Memesis - The Future of Evolution, Springer Wien - New York 1996, pp. 102 - 109 / **Heimo Ranzenbacher** For a Digital Renaissance of Situationism. First published in: Gerfried Stocker / Christine Schöpf (eds.): Memesis - The Future of Evolution, Ars Electronica Festival 96, Springer Wien - New York 1996, pp. 428 - 437 / **Birgit Richard** Norn Attacks and Marine Doom. First published in: Gerfried Stocker / Christine Schöpf (eds.): Ars Electronica 98. InfoWar, Springer Wien - New York 1998, pp. 153 - 163 / **Otto Rössler** Endophysics. First published in: Karl Gerbel / Peter Weibel (eds.): Ars Electronica 1992, Die Welt von Innen - Endo und Nano, PVS Verleger, Wien 1992, pp.49 - 55 / **Florian Rötzer** Praise to the Parasites. First published in: Karl Gerbel / Peter Weibel (eds.): Ars Electronica 93. Genetische Kunst - Künstliches Leben. First published in: Karl Gerbel / Peter Weibel (eds.): Ars Electronica 1993. Genetische Kunst - Künstliches Leben. Artificial Life - Genetic Art, PVS Verleger, Wien 1993, pp. 92 - 103 / **Morgan Russell / Jaron Lanier** Riding the Giant Worm to Saturn: Post-Symbolic Communication in Virtual Reality. First published in: Gottfried Hattinger / Peter Weibel (eds.): Ars Electronica 90, Band 2: Virtuelle Welten / Virtual Worlds, Veritas Verlag, Linz 1990, pp. 186 - 188 / **John Sanborn** Statement of Art and Tech-nology. First published in: Linzer Veranstaltungsgesellschaft (ed.): Ars Electronica 1986. Festival für Kunst, Tech-nologie und Gesellschaft 1986, Linz 1986, pp.136 - 137 / **Karl Sims** Interactive Evolution. First published in: Karl Gerbel / Peter Weibel (eds.): Ars Electronica 93. Genetische Kunst - Künstliches Leben. Artificial Life - Genetic Art, PVS Verleger, Wien 1993, pp. 119 - 120 / **Christa Sommerer / Laurent Mignonneau** Interactive Plant Growing, German version first published in: Karl Gerbel / Peter Weibel (eds.): Ars Electronica 93. Genetische Kunst - Künst-liches Leben. Artificial Life - Genetic Art, PVS Verleger, Wien 1993, pp. 408 - 414 (English version by the authors) / **Stadtwerkstatt** Nobody Is Safe. First published in: Karl Gerbel (ed.): Ars Electronica 1991, Out of Control, Landes-verlag Linz 1991, pp. 89 - 102 / **Bruce Sterling** The Future of Cyberspace: Wild Frontier vs. Hyperreal Estate. First published in: Gottfried Hattinger / Peter Weibel (eds.): Ars Electronica 90, Band 2: Virtuelle Welten / Virtual Worlds, Veritas Verlag, Linz 1990, pp. 228 - 231 / **Kristine Stiles** Thresholds of Control – Destruction Art and Terminal Culture. First published in: Karl Gerbel (ed.): Ars Electronica 1991. Out of Control, Landesverlag Linz 1991, pp. 29 - 50 / **Stelarc** Parasite Visions. Alternate, Intimate, and Involuntary Experiences. First published in: Gerfried Stocker / Christine Schöpf (eds.): Ars Electronica 97. FleshFactor - Informationsmaschine Mensch, Springer Wien - New York 1997, pp. 148 – 157 / **Gerfried Stocker** Vector in Open Space. First published in: Gerfried Stocker / Christine Schöpf (eds.): Ars Electronica Festival 96. Memesis - The Future of Evolution, Springer Wien-New York, pp. 20 - 25. Horizontal Radio. First published in: Karl Gerbel / Peter Weibel (eds.): Ars Electronica 95. Mythos Information, Welcome to the Wired World, Springer-Verlag New York 1995, pp. 354 - 364 / **Allucquère Rosanne Stone** Media Memory. First published in: Gerfried Stocker / Christine Schöpf (eds.): Ars Electronica Festival 96. Memesis - The Future of Evolution, Springer Wien - New York 1996, pp. 66 - 71 / **Isao Tomita** Mind of Universe. First published in: Linzer Veranstaltungsgesellschaft (ed.): Ars Electronica im Rahmen des Internationalen Brucknerfestes '84. Festival für Kunst, Technologie und Gesellschaft, Linz 1984, p. 103 / **Van Gogh TV** Pompino Project. First published in: Gottfried Hattinger / Peter Weibel (eds.): Ars Electronica 90, Band 1: Digitale Träume / Digital Dreams, Veritas Verlag, Linz 1990, pp. 172 - 179 / **Paul Virilio** The Overexposed City. First published in: Michel Feher and Sanford Kwinter (eds.), Zone 1/2, New York: Zone Books, 1986, trans. Astrid Hustvedt. InfoWar, transcript of a videoconference between Paul Virilio and Derrick de Kerckhove at Ars Electronica Festival 98, translated from the French by Paul Henninger and Josh Wise. / **Peter Weibel** On the History and Aesthetics of the Digital Image. First published in: Linzer Veranstaltungsgesellschaft / Peter Weibel, Zur Geschichte und Ästhetik der digitalen Kunst, Supplement zum Katalog Ars Electronica 1984, Linz 1984, pp.41 - 48. The Noise of the Observer. First published in: Karl Gerbel - Peter Weibel (eds.): Ars Electronica 95. Mythos Information, Welcome to the Wired World, Springer-Verlag Wien New York 1995, pp. 8 - 23. Virtual Worlds: The Emperor's New Bodies. First published in: Gottfried Hattinger / Peter Weibel (eds.): Ars Electronica 90, Band 2: Virtuelle Welten / Virtual Worlds, Veritas Verlag, Linz 1990, pp. 9 - 38 / **Peter Weibel / Bob O'Kane:** Cartesian Chaos. First published in: Karl Gerbel / Peter Weibel (eds.): Ars Electronica 1992, Die Welt von Innen - Endo und Nano, PVS Verleger, Wien 1992, pp. 110 - 104 / **Keigo Yamamoto** Winds of the Media from Asia. First published in: Karl Gerbel/ Peter Weibel (eds.): Ars Electronica 94. Intelligente Ambiente - Intelligent Environments, Band 1, PVS Verleger, Wien, pp. 215 - 223 / **Gene Youngblood** A Medium Matures: Video and the Cinematic Enterprise. First published in: Linzer Veranstaltungsgesellschaft (ed.): Ars Electronica im Rahmen des Internationalen Brucknerfestes Linz, Festival für Kunst, Technologie und Gesellschaft 1984, Linz 1984, pp. 166 - 170. Virtual Space and the Electronic Environments of Mobile Image. First published in: Österreichischer Rundfunk ORF, Landesstudio Oberösterreich (ed.): Computer-kulturtage Linz - ORF-Videonale 86, Linz 1986, pp. 351 - 358 / **Melita Zajc** Keep Him on the Phone: The Human Body in the Realm of Technology. First published in: Karl Gerbel / Peter Weibel (eds.): Ars Electronica 95. Mythos Information, Welcome to the Wired World, Springer-Verlag Wien New York 1995, pp. 68 - 78